About the Cover Image

Plate with a Vase of Flowers

The eighteenth century saw the rapid rise and development of the export porcelain industry in East Asia for a European market fascinated by chinoiserie. The object depicted here is a wonderful example of East Asian cross-cultural influences: enameled porcelain (originating in China), crafted in the Japanese *Hizen* regional style of Imari ware by a colony of Korean potters working in secluded Japan. The European connection is notable as the piece was part of the collection of Augustus II, elector of Saxony and king of Poland, obtained through Dutch merchants in their role as the sole Europeans allowed to trade in Japan at this time.

Patterns of East Asian History

Patterns of
East Asian History

CHARLES A. DESNOYERS
La Salle University

New York   Oxford
OXFORD UNIVERSITY PRESS

Oxford University Press is a department of the University of Oxford. It furthers the University's objective of excellence in research, scholarship, and education by publishing worldwide. Oxford is a registered trade mark of Oxford University Press in the UK and certain other countries.

Published in the United States of America by Oxford University Press
198 Madison Avenue, New York, NY 10016, United States of America.

For titles covered by Section 112 of the US Higher Education Opportunity Act, please visit www.oup.com/us/he for the latest information about pricing and alternate formats.

Library of Congress Cataloging-in-Publication Data

Names: Desnoyers, Charles, 1952- author.
Title: Patterns of East Asian history / Charles A. Desnoyers.
Description: First edition. | Oxford University Press : New York, [2019] |
    Includes bibliographical references and index.
Identifiers: LCCN 2018044956 | ISBN 9780199946464 (pbk.)
Subjects: LCSH: East Asia—History.
Classification: LCC DS511 .D47 2019 | DDC 950—dc23 LC record available
    at https://lccn.loc.gov/2018044956

BRIEF CONTENTS

CONTENTS

LIST OF MAPS

PREFACE

*P*atterns of East Asian History marks the third volume in Oxford University Press's highly successful Patterns series, which currently includes *Patterns of World History* in its third edition and *Patterns of Modern Chinese History.* These offerings are college-level introductory texts whose purpose is to provide beginning students with an entree into complex fields of history with which American students have generally had little or no exposure. The approach of all the volumes revolves around the idea of using recognizable and widely accepted patterns of historical development as a loose framework around which to structure the material both as an organizational aid to the instructor and as a tool to make complex material more comprehensible to the student. As we have stressed in previous volumes in the series, this approach is *not* intended to be reductionist or deterministic, or to privilege a particular ideological perspective, but rather to enhance pedagogical flexibility while providing a subtly recursive format that allows abundant opportunities for contrast and comparison among and within the societies under consideration. As with the other volumes in the series, the overall aim is to simplify the immense complexities of history for the beginning student without making them simplistic.

All the historical fields covered in these volumes (world history, Chinese history, East Asian history) now face lively internal debates concerning various topics, and one of the goals of the series is to introduce students to these discussions in order to stress the idea that historians are not monolithic in their ideas or approaches, but more often than not disagree with each other, sometimes vigorously. Thus, all the books employ certain pedagogical features designed to enhance the sense that "the past," as William Faulkner put it so memorably, "is not dead; it isn't even past." Chapters begin with a vignette designed to crystallize a particular situation or idea emphasized within that chapter or section and include a feature, "Patterns Up-Close," designed to examine a particular concept or event at a deeper level to enhance the material in question. Because chapters 9 and 10 constitute essentially one long chapter on China from 1895 to the present, the vignette for both chapters opens chapter 9 and the Patterns Up-Close feature for both is in chapter 10.

In the case of East Asia, one problem that immediately presents itself is how to define the area as a specific region. Geography offers some clues but nothing hard and fast and instantly identifiable, such as the Indian subcontinent. China, of course, is at the heart of East Asia geographically, but how far should one define the region beyond its historical borders? Should Mongolia be considered part of East Asia? Should Southeast Asia? In many respects, the cultural connections offer more coherent boundaries, but even these are contested. Some would include what is often called the "Sinitic Frontier" that includes the states and societies on the Chinese periphery that have been touched by Chinese culture in one form or another. This is fairly safe ground for the three states most commonly included in regional histories and sourcebooks: China, Korea, and Japan. But even these are not always taken together: for example, the Association for Asian Studies organizes its regional councils on the model of "China and Inner Asia," "Northeast Asia" (including Japan and Korea), and "Southeast Asia" (including Vietnam). The United Nations Statistics Division includes Mongolia along with China, Japan, and Korea, although Mongolia shares much less culturally with these three nations than Vietnam, which is listed separately in Southeast Asia. Some regional political spokespeople from countries generally designated as "Southeast Asian" have advocated including the members of their regional Association of South East Asian Nations (ASEAN) along with China, Japan, Korea, and Taiwan, as comprising a greater "East Asia."

One can also find ready opposition to what might be called the "Chinese impact-indigenous response" model. Certainly, much of the history of Vietnam and Korea consists of attempts to break free of Chinese political influence; Mongolians and Manchus have long struggled—even when their empires included China—to not be assimilated culturally by China, and Tibetans and various Central Asian peoples today, as in the past, resist the tide of what they term "cultural genocide" emanating from the People's Republic.

Yet in the case of all these places, contact with China marked vital turning points in their societies. Korean and Vietnamese states for short periods held territory within what ultimately constituted China. More generally, however, both places underwent long periods of invasion and occupation by various Chinese dynasties that left their written language, systems of government, and cultural, philosophical, and religious traditions as their legacies. Japan actively borrowed Chinese systems to make the clan-based central kingdom of Yamato into a self-designated empire. Mongolia existed only as part of a large territorial expanse inhabited by a multitude of nomadic groups who periodically raided and clashed with the Chinese states to the south until the time of Genghis Khan. While remaining culturally distinct from China—even devising their own written language and adopting a variety of religious beliefs—the high point of their imperial ambitions came with the conquest of Song Dynasty China and the creation of their own Chinese regime: the Yuan Dynasty (1280–1368). Tibet, whose language springs from the same family (Sino-Tibetan) as the Chinese dialects, maintained its cultural distinctiveness even when incorporated into the Qing Empire by Manchu rulers—themselves struggling to maintain their own cultural distinctiveness—whose vision was a universal multicultural state.

The often fraught relationship of these states with China raises another conceptual problem in studying the area: the question of modernity. How should we define it, and when can we say it began for the region as a whole? Can we even designate a period for the majority of these states when we might say that their modern periods were under way? In the case of China, scholars have over the years suggested beginning the modern era as late as 1840 and as early as the Song Dynasty (960–1279). For Japan, key dates include the wholesale adoption of Chinese political and cultural systems during the *Taika* (Great Reform) of 645; the beginnings of imperial Heian Japan (after 794); the creation of the shogunate (1185); the Tokugawa period (1603–1867); the "opening" of Japan by Perry in 1853; and the Meiji Restoration (1868–1912). In the case of Korea, the coming of Buddhism and Chinese culture (fourth and fifth centuries); the creation of the *han'gul* writing system (fifteenth century); and the first treaty with Meiji Japan (1876) might all plausibly be used. Similar problems surface with Vietnam. The creation of the Mongol super-empire in the twelfth and thirteenth centuries seems a fairly logical and convenient place to situate the start of that country's modern period.

The Mongol interval, although brief, does provide a kind of jumping off point for the organization of this volume. Recent scholarship has suggested that in controlling such a vast area, encouraging trade, setting up a number of proto-capitalist institutions such as the widespread use of checks, paper money, even insurance, and practicing a considerable degree of religious toleration, the Mongols played a direct role in ushering in the early modern period throughout Eurasia. Moreover, their rule touched every region with which we are concerned, except for Japan—though they made two attempts to invade the island empire. Thus, this volume, like *Patterns of Modern Chinese History*, begins with chapters that provide a prologue to what we have designated as the modern period, whereas the greater part of the book covers material after the Mongol Empire acquired China in 1280.

As noted above, the central approach to this book, as with the others in the series, is that of *patterns*. Within this overall rubric, a considerable amount of attention is given to three elements: *origins*, *interactions*, and *adaptations*. For example, one noticeable pattern, given the widespread effects of the monsoon, is the dominance of rice production throughout much of the area. This is *not* to adopt a Marxian "Asiatic mode of production" approach or to point to Karl A. Wittfogel's insistence on the determinism of "hydraulic society," but to note that the techniques of wet and dry rice production were widely diffused, widely practiced, and allowed for and demanded substantial populations for production. The exact origins of wet rice cultivation are unknown, but interactions among innumerable persons and groups over the centuries spread and continually revitalized its techniques and plant strains, with local and regional adaptations over the course of millennia.

More directly traceable are the patterns of cultural diffusion and incorporation—involving origins, interactions, and adaptations from core to periphery—that have continually played out across the region. China's Shang

Dynasty, for example, diffused its culture widely across the Yellow River basin. When the former Shang client state of Zhou conquered the Shang, they spread much of the Shang culture they had adopted over most of North China. We have noted above the profound cultural exchanges that marked China's relations with Vietnam and Korea, and from Korea to Japan. Sometimes the periphery becomes the new core: Japan, transformed in the late nineteenth and early twentieth centuries into an aggressively expansive industrial power through contact with the West, became for a time a model for Chinese and other East Asian reformers to emulate. Indeed, it provided an important model for China's present economic power. Moreover, Japan's colonial occupation of Korea, Manchuria, and Taiwan for half a century left a considerable cultural and industrial legacy in those regions—although one sown with pain and bitterness. As the world's second-largest economy, China has emerged as the dominant Asian core—with Japan and India close behind—and is daily accelerating its cultural and economic influence on the world stage.

A related pattern is one rather like the relationship between ancient Greece and Rome: the latter, it was said, conquered militarily, but the former conquered the conquerors culturally. From the time of the Shang and Zhou down to the present, China's immense cultural gravity has pulled those outsiders who have militarily subdued it or sought to subdue it into a graduated process of *Sinification*. Some, like the nomadic groups of the northern tier, sensing opportunity during dynastic upheavals, have conquered regions, settled down, and intermarried with the locals. For example, the Toba of the Northern Wei kingdom ultimately begat the Sui and China's most cosmopolitan dynasty, the Tang. Although they conquered the world's largest empire, the Mongol Yuan Dynasty in China found itself forced to adapt in many ways to Chinese norms of government, and constantly strove to maintain its own culture in the face of immense pressures to assimilate. This was even more pronounced in the case of China's last imperial dynasty, the Manchu Qing. Having already adapted to Confucian norms before their conquest of China, the Manchus struggled to keep from being ethnically, physically, and culturally subsumed by their subjects until the dynasty toppled in 1912.

This book is organized into thirteen chapters plus a brief epilogue, a number that allows instructors to move at a comfortable pace within a standard semester. The chapters are relatively short, enabling instructors at institutions using a trimester or quarter system to utilize the book as well. This volume is laid out in two parts: Part I, "Creating East Asia," includes Chapters 1 through 4, from Neolithic times through the Mongol interval. Part II, "Recasting East Asia to the Present," follows the histories of individual countries from the fifteenth century onward. As in the other *Patterns* volumes, chapters generally follow a format of political history, followed by economic, social, cultural, and scientific/technological issues, as well as the opening vignette and "Patterns Up-Close" feature mentioned above. Thus, courses employing this book can also use it thematically in terms of the internal structure of the chapters and the recurrent emphasis on various historical patterns.

Charles A. Desnoyers,
November 24, 2018

ACKNOWLEDGMENTS

As was the case with the other books of the Patterns series—*Patterns of World History* and *Patterns of Modern Chinese History*—the conception and creation of this volume have been an exciting and wonderfully collegial enterprise. In all three books, I have had the singular good fortune to have benefited from the guidance, insight, and inspired eyes and hands of the talented and dedicated people at Oxford University Press. Hence, I wish to thank them all collectively for their continual enthusiasm and hard work in bringing this volume to publication. Of particular note is editorial assistant Katie Tunkavige, who took what had been all too many vague directions regarding illustrations and turned them into vibrant and often stunning embodiments of the material described in the text. I would like to thank Claudia Dukeshire, who handled the editorial production, and Patti Brecht, who copyedited the text.

I have also received considerable help and support from a number of valued colleagues. As they were with *Patterns of Chinese History*, my History Department chair, Stuart Leibiger, and the members of the Sabbatical Committee at La Salle University deserve great thanks for allowing me the time needed to work on this manuscript. Needless to say, those dear friends and colleagues who taught and traveled with me have my special thanks in making this project possible. To my students in the classroom over the years, you have given me far more than I can say in inspiring the writing of this book.

I would like to offer a special kind of thanks to my friend and editor, Charles Cavaliere. More than anyone, Charles has made these three volumes possible: in conceiving them, keeping us on task in writing them, in providing an endless stream of suggestions with regard to the design, format, and illustrations of the books, and in supervising every phase of their production. He has indeed been the prime mover of the Patterns series.

No note of thanks would be complete without acknowledging those readers and reviewers whose comments have added so much to this volume: Clayton D.

Brown of Utah State University; Desmond Cheung, Portland State University; Margaret B. Denning, Slippery Rock University; David Kenley, Elizabethtown College; Charles V. Reed, Elizabeth City State University; Walter Skyra, University of Alaska Fairbanks; John Stanley, Kutztown University; and Peter Worthing, Texas Christian University. They all have my heartfelt gratitude for their advice and criticism, and I hope I have done them justice in incorporating their suggestions. Any errors of fact or interpretation that remain are strictly my own.

Finally, I wish to thank my wife Jacki for her immense patience, fortitude, and support—to say nothing of her faith, hope, and love—throughout all these projects. None of this would have been possible without you.

NOTES ON DATES AND SPELLING

The dating system used in this book is the current standard for historians, in which Before Common Era (BCE) and Common Era (CE) have supplanted the older and more Western-centered BC and AD. Events in the remote past are sometimes given as "years ago" (YA) or "before present" (BP). The spellings of names, places, objects, etc., that have long remained standard have been retained for the convenience of the reader. In most cases, these will also include current academic romanizations. Thus, the city of Guangzhou will also be referenced as Canton, and Jiang Jieshi will be identified by the more widely recognized spelling of his name as Chiang Kai-shek.

The system used in rendering the sounds of Mandarin Chinese—the northern dialect that has become, in effect, the national spoken language in the People's Republic of China and in the Republic of China on Taiwan—into English in this book is *hanyu pinyin*, usually given as simply pinyin. Most syllables are pronounced as they would be in English, with the exception of the letter *q*, which has an aspirated "ch" sound. *Zh* carries a hard "j," while *j* itself has the familiar soft English sound. Some syllables are also pronounced (particularly in the region around Beijing) with a retroflex "r." Thus, the word *shi* in some instances sounds more like "shir." Finally, the letter *r* in the pinyin system has no direct English equivalent, but may be approximated by the combining the sounds of "r" and "j."

Japanese terms have been romanized according to a modification of the Hepburn system. The letter *g* is always hard; vowels are handled as they are in Italian—*e*, for example, carries a sound like "ay." Diacritical marks to indicate long vowel sounds, however, have been omitted.

For Korean words, this book uses a variation of the McCune–Reischauer system, which remains the standard used in English-language academic writing, again eliminating diacritical marks. Here again, the vowel sounds are pronounced more or less like those in Italian.

For Vietnamese, the standard renditions are based on the modern Quoc Ngu ("national language") system in current use in Vietnam. The system was developed in part by Jesuit missionaries and based on the Portuguese alphabet. As in the other romanizations of East Asian languages, the diacritical marks have been omitted.

Because of the several competing systems of romanizing Mongolian terms, such as Mongolian Cyrillic (BGN/PCGN), the closest Latin equivalents have been used in this book. Famous names, such as Genghis Khan (more properly transliterated as "Chinggis), have been given according to standard, widely recognized spellings.

ABOUT THE AUTHOR

Charles A. Desnoyers is professor of history and former director of Asian Studies at La Salle University in Philadelphia. He has previously taught at Temple University, Villanova University, and Pennsylvania State University. In addition to serving as History Department chair from 1999 to 2007, he was a founder and long-time director of the Greater Philadelphia Asian Studies Consortium, and president (2011–2012) of the Mid-Atlantic Region Association for Asian Studies. He is a lifetime member of the World History Association and served as co-editor of the organization's *Bulletin* from 1995 to 2001. In addition to numerous articles in peer-reviewed and general publications, his work includes *A Journey to the East: Li Gui's "A New Account of a Trip Around the Globe"* (2004, University of Michigan Press), *Patterns of World History* (with Peter Von Sivers and George B. Stow; 2011, 2013, and 2017, Oxford University Press), and *Patterns of Modern Chinese History* (2017, Oxford University Press).

Patterns of East Asian History

An Open Empire. *Music played an important role in Tang China and was enjoyed privately as well as on public occasions. This glazed earthenware sculpture, dated to 723 ce, shows three musicians riding a Bactrian (two humped) camel. Their long coats, facial hair, and hats indicate that they are from Central Asia, Indeed, the lute held by one of the riders is a type of musical instrument that was introduced to China from Central Asia in the second century ce.*

PART I

❧

Creating East Asia

Timeline

ca. 780,000 BCE	"Peking Man"
ca. 50,000–20,000 BCE	Modern *Homo sapiens* foraging groups established in eastern Eurasia
10,000–8000 BCE	First Neolithic settlements in Yellow River Valley; beginning of Jomon Period in Japan
ca. 7000 BCE	First evidence of rice cultivation in Yangzi Valley
5000–1500 BCE	Yangshao culture develops along Yellow River
4500 BCE	Dongsan cultures, Vietnam
2205–1766 BCE	Traditional dates for Xia Dynasty, China
1766–1122 BCE	Traditional dates for Shang Dynasty, China
ca. 1400 BCE	Earliest "oracle bone" caches with archaic Chinese writing
ca. 1300 BCE	Introduction of chariot to northern China
1122–771 BCE	Western Zhou Dynasty, China
770–256 BCE	Eastern Zhou Dynasty, China
403–221 BCE	Warring States Period, China
604 BCE	Traditional date for birth of Laozi
551–479 BCE	Traditional dates for life of Confucius
300 BCE–300 CE	Yayoi Period, Japan
221–206 BCE	First Chinese Empire under Qin; first iteration of Great Wall begun
202 BCE–8 CE	Former Han Dynasty, China
37 BCE–935 CE	"Three Kingdoms" of Korea: Koguryo (37 BCE–668 CE), Paekche (18 BCE–660 CE), and Silla (57 BCE–935 CE).

CHAPTER 1

≺○

The Region and People

As we noted in the preface, the geographical or topographical borders outlining a distinct "East Asia" are nebulous, even contested enough for some to argue that they are essentially nonexistent. As we also noted, even the cultural borders of the most common yardstick, the influence of Chinese culture, although easier to detect than geographical ones, are still subject to debate. The approach taken here, therefore, is necessarily subjective, though, hopefully, not without foundation.

Although several different approaches to what constitutes East Asia emerge in various texts and scholarly works, the one we utilize in this volume tends toward the expansive side. That is, many texts concentrate exclusively on China, Korea, and Japan both because of their proximity to each other and their cultural connections. We will extend our scope somewhat further by including Vietnam—more commonly studied as part of Southeast Asia—but discussed here because of the long-term Chinese presence and cultural influence. We will also include Mongolia, often placed in the category of "Inner Asia" or Central Asia. Although both places remain culturally distinct, they are included here because of their long relationship with China and many other parts of the region, with Mongolia having included China, Korea, and Tibet as part of its own empire from 1280 to 1368.

Like the influence of the Hellenistic and Roman worlds, that of imperial China became widespread throughout East, Northeast, and Southeast Asia. Chinese writing, literature, law, government, and philosophy, as well as imported systems such as Buddhism, came to overlay local social, cultural, and religious customs and practices. Because these practices were often imposed from the top down, however, they met frequent resistance at the village and clan level. Thus, tensions between elites and locals continually played out in the assorted Korean kingdoms and Vietnamese states against a backdrop of invasion and collaboration, while in Japan similar tensions arose after the Yamato government remade itself along Chinese lines. From the beginning, all these societies asserted their political independence from the Chinese. Their position on or near the Chinese border, their role as havens for refugees, and the continual pressures of possible invasion, however, provided a conduit for Chinese cultural diffusion—in the case of Korea, through the peninsula to the islands of Japan. One could generalize and say that for the peoples on the Chinese periphery, shifting relations with the Middle Kingdom provided both unity and disarray in the struggles of different states for local dominance.

VARIED GEOGRAPHIES

Taken as a whole, Eurasia encompasses virtually every kind of geographical feature and form of climate that is found on Earth: vast mountain ranges, huge deserts, polar ice, rain forests, alluvial plains, savanna and steppe land, and some of the largest rivers in the world. Within the areas we define as East Asia, nearly all these features may be found, with the exception of polar ice, though to be sure, the northern reaches of Manchuria extend considerably above 50 degrees north latitude, approximately the same as the Aleutians and extreme southern Alaska. Some of the East Asian states are marked by a predominant geographic or topographic feature: Mongolia, for example, is largely grassy steppe land with some mountains and desert and is landlocked. Vietnam is largely subtropical forest and cleared farmland. China, Korea, and Japan offer the most varied topography. All contain mountains, plains, watercourses, and coastlines, thus allowing for a wider range of subsistence, both in Paleo- and Neolithic times, and after the establishment of agriculture and (except for Mongolia and the northern Chinese borderlands) more or less sedentary living.

Although fixed borders have marked the formal boundaries of the states in modern times, not all of them have prominent geographical features that may be said to delineate "natural" dividing lines: as an island nation, Japan through much of its history has had the sea as its protective barrier, but its empire and territorial claims have at times extended far beyond the home islands, reaching their greatest point during the early years of the Pacific War (World War II). The Korean Peninsula is conveniently marked off from the rest of Northeast Asia by the Yalu (Amnokkang) River, but its kingdoms have at times extended beyond it, whereas Chinese empires have frequently pushed to the south of it. The borders of China with the northern plains and Gobi Desert that ultimately constituted Mongolia were historically porous enough to require the building and maintenance of the Great Wall, though its ability to deter invaders was rather limited. A similar fluidity marked the frontiers with Vietnam.

As for the area as a whole, although there are some spectacular geographical features along its borders, not all of them are suitable as delineations in setting the region off from the rest of Asia. Of the dramatic natural borders, the Himalayas, and their related mountain ranges—Karakoram, Pamir, and Tian Shan—that separate the Tibetan and Chinese borders from India, Bhutan, Nepal, Pakistan, Afghanistan, Tajikistan, Kyrgyztan, and Kazakhstan are the most distinct. The western deserts, the Takla Makan, Gurbantungut, also made for formidable barriers, though the region's main conduit to the outside, the Silk Route[s], passed above and below them. The Mongolian border with Russia is marked in part by the Tannu-Ola Mountains, whereas farther to the east, the Ussuri and Heilongjiang (Amur River) mark important frontiers between China's northeast (the former Manchuria) and Russia—the dispute over which resulted in a short border conflict between the former Soviet Union and People's Republic of China (PRC) in 1969.

It is the interior features, however, that show the greatest variation, although the core of the region, China, Korea, Vietnam, and Japan, also share some important features that have allowed them to pursue parallel subsistence strategies, especially those related to rice cultivation. Although this is somewhat less true in Japan, which has only a small percentage of arable flat land and no real rivers to speak of, all these regions have cultivated rolling, flat landscapes—in many cases, river bottom land; in some cases, terraced hills and mountains—all of which are well watered, to intensively cultivate wet rice and in higher, less watered regions, dry rice. The heart of this cultivation lies in the area historically part of China.

The Chinese Landscape

Unlike India, with its dramatic natural boundaries, China is only partially defined by geography. In addition to river systems such as the Amur and Ussuri in the north, the Salween in the southwest and the Red in Vietnam have also represented past borders, although not impermeable ones. The northern and western deserts—the Gobi, Ordos, and Takla Makan—have also served as historic boundaries that frequently passed in and out of the hands of successive Chinese dynasties as their emperors sought to curb the incursions of nomads, or control Central Asian trade routes (see Map 1.1).

China's population has historically been concentrated in the major river valleys and along the coast. The rivers, generally flowing west to east, and having their sources in the glaciers and lakes of the greater Himalayan system, are separated by plateaus and uplands in the western regions and by flatlands such as the North China Plain as the watercourses approach the sea. Three main river systems have remained the principal avenues of agriculture and commerce: the Pearl River in the south; the Yangzi River—at 3,988 miles, the third longest in the world; and the Yellow River, where the most influential early Chinese societies developed.

Rising in the highlands of Gansu and flowing north to the Ordos Desert, the Yellow River then turns south and east out of Inner Mongolia for 500 miles before making a final bend to the east and the sea, a total distance of 3,000 miles. The river gets its name as a result of the loess—a light, dry, mineral rich soil deposited by centuries of strong winds—it picks up as it flows, giving it a reddish-yellow tint. The rich soil carried by the river has brought abundant agriculture to northern China, but the constant buildup of silt also causes the river to overflow its banks, resulting in devastation of fields and villages in its path.

This building up and bursting of natural levees, along with earthquakes and occasional human actions—such as the dynamiting of dikes during World War II to slow Japanese invaders—have caused the Yellow River to change course 26 times during the last 3,000 years. Its mouth has shifted several times above

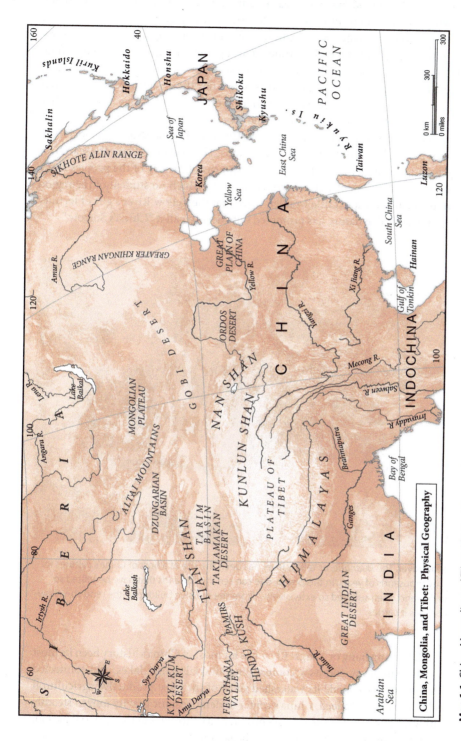

Map 1.1 China, Mongolia, and Tibet: Physical Geography

and below the Shandong Peninsula, assuming its present course to the north following massive floods in 1854–1855. Not surprisingly, efforts to control the river have occupied a prominent place in the mythology, history, and social organization of the region from earliest times. Throughout China's early period of fragmented kingdoms, the Yellow River states all had water conservancy ministries aimed at safeguarding the land and people from the river's excesses. This was intensified during the imperial era, and local officials and village headmen alike took active roles in flood prevention and relief.

The degree to which geography is destiny is still a vital issue in the social sciences, particularly for the earliest civilizations. The question of how the search for agricultural stability has influenced the patterns of history of the peoples along China's most turbulent watercourse is one from which no student of the region can ultimately escape. Little wonder, then, that the Yellow River's gift of fertility but unpredictable nature has prompted outsiders to call it "China's Sorrow."

Yellow River. The *Huanghe*, or Yellow River has been the site of a host of China's cultures for many thousands of years. In this photo, one can see the flatlands that have benefited so much—and often suffered so extensively—from the massive buildup of the reddish-yellow *loess* soils it carries.

The Chang Jiang or Yangzi River has for most of China's history been its most important highway and its accompanying alluvial plains, lakes, and connected watercourses have made its watershed some of the most productive agricultural land in the world. Indeed, China's center of demographic gravity moved steadily southward as a result of the region's productivity throughout the imperial period. As early as the sixth century CE, work began on the Grand Canal system to link the Yangzi to the Yellow River in order to carry tribute grain and other supplies to northern capitals like Chang'an (modern Xi'an), Kaifeng, and, with the canal extended north to the Beihe (Northern River), to the modern capital of Beijing. The canal is still a vital supply line today. The completion of the massive Three Gorges Dam complex in 2012 has now made the river the world's largest generator of hydroelectric power, edging out the Itaipu Dam on the Brazil–Paraguay border, the previous record holder.

The Pearl River, which flows east to the city of Guangzhou (more widely known as Canton), is fed by innumerable small streams in the uplands of Guangdong, Guangxi, and Yun'nan provinces. As it nears its delta, it also spawns numerous small channels and streams, many of which flow into the Pearl River Estuary. This network of waterways provided shelter for centuries for smugglers, pirates, and rebels, and was a prime area for the transactions of the opium trade in the early nineteenth century. Like the Yangzi basin, it is extraordinarily productive, and its position below the Tropic of Cancer allows for a virtually uninterrupted growing season and three rice crops per year.

The Great Regulator: The Monsoon

Like India, Bangladesh, and Southeast Asia, most of the region we are studying as East Asia is governed climatically by one of the most extensive—and regular—weather systems in the world: the **monsoon system**. The region's exceptions are Tibet, where the barrier of the Himalayas stops most of the moist warm air from the system and directs it toward the Ganges Plain in India and Bangladesh, and Mongolia, where the effects of the northern sweep of the system have dissipated and been largely cancelled by the continental pattern of the deep Asian interior. The effects of the monsoon are among the world's most regular and intense, and it is difficult to overstate the impact the monsoon has had on the world's agricultural patterns, crops, and techniques since Neolithic times.

The term derives from the Arabic word *mausim,* for "season," although the pattern itself was well known for millennia. As with the heat that moves in the opposite direction and spawns hurricanes in the Atlantic, the warm air comes from the vast African interior, picking up moisture over the Indian Ocean. In India and Bangladesh, it collides with the cold air and continuous mountain barrier of the Himalayas and dumps vast amounts of rain on the region. It sweeps through Indonesia and Southeast Asia, moving up through the eastern Chinese warm regions with its effects felt as far north as southern Korea, Japan, and Taiwan. The winds carry moisture from southwest to northeast from June through October and create substantial—sometimes catastrophic—rainfall amounts throughout the region. In the winter months, the winds reverse direction and pull dry air down from Central Asia. During this dry season, rainfall is scant or nonexistent over large areas. It is also an important reason for the desertification of so much of the deep Asian interior.

Because even minor variations in the timing of the cycle or the volume of rain may spell potential flood or famine, the arrival of the spring monsoon is even today greeted with nervous anticipation from India to Shanghai. China's climate, though conditioned by the monsoon like the Indian subcontinent and Southeast Asia, however, is far more varied. The area south of the Qin Ling Mountains marks the northern boundary regulated by the monsoon, with warm temperatures and abundant summer rainfall. During the summer monsoon season, rainfall amounts can range from about 40 inches per year in the eastern coastal city of Hangzhou (Hangchow) to over 70 inches in the subtropical south. North of the monsoon line, however, temperatures and rainfall amounts are influenced more by the continental weather systems of the Eurasian interior. Thus, northern China is subject to blistering summers and frigid winters with sparse and unreliable rainfall.

One of the long-term effects of this climatic split has been that although the Yellow River valley was the home of China's first recorded civilizations, the population centers, as we have seen, steadily moved south to the monsoon areas. This has posed some difficulties since, as noted above, the political center of the state has tended to remain in the north and over time became increasingly dependent on food shipments from the south, a situation that frequently tempted rebels and invaders to interdict them.

Mountains and Deserts

While China continues to be, as it has been for millennia, the world's most populous state, a quick look at its population distribution shows that the greatest percentage of its people live almost exclusively along the coast or in river valleys. Although population pressures and political crises have periodically pushed, and government incentives have sometimes pulled, people into mountainous regions and, over the last century and a half, into the arid far western regions, vast areas still remain sparsely inhabited, even uninhabited. In many cases, the people living in these regions are members of one or more of China's 55 recognized minority groups, many of whom have lived more or less in isolation until recently. Some are the descendants of groups forced to flee during times of rebellion, famine, or dynastic change, the best known of which are the **Hakkas** (*kejiaren*) of South China.

As one moves away from the river valleys of South China into the forested uplands and stark limestone *karst* formations—for centuries a source of inspiration for Chinese landscape painters—the population density dissipates rapidly. As one approaches Qinghai and the Tibetan regions, the land takes on an alpine character: foothills, plateaus, and ultimately some of the world's highest mountains. Tibet's capital, Lhasa, is the world's highest capital city at 12,087 feet above sea level, and its climate is designated as "mid-latitude semi-arid." Yearly temperatures average 45 degrees Fahrenheit, whereas average annual precipitation is only 16 inches. Tibet's remoteness served to largely isolate it from the effects of Indian and Chinese politics, although Tibetan and Chinese forces battled each other periodically from the mid-600s. As far back as the eighteenth century, Chinese regimes have claimed suzerainty and sovereignty over it. A briefly independent Tibet fought a war (Sino-Tibetan War) against the Nationalist Republic of China and its affiliated warlords from 1930 to 1933 over disputed territory in

Qinghai. Events in the mid-twentieth century further eroded that isolation when forces of the People's Republic occupied Tibet in 1950 and quashed a rebellion there in 1959, forcing the Dalai Lama to flee to India. More recently, under the rationale of speeding "development" in Tibet, Chinese migration there has been encouraged, aided by the opening of the Qinghai-Lhasa railway. Tibet's subsistence economy of herding and small farming has been steadily subsumed into the rapidly expanding Chinese GDP, and the Tibetans themselves have complained bitterly and demonstrated against being economically, demographically, and culturally swamped by the Chinese government and its migration efforts.

North of Tibet in China's extreme west lies some of the driest, lowest, and most remote territory in the world: the Tarim Basin and Takla Makan Desert. The Turpan (Turfan) Depression, near Urumqi, at 508 feet below sea level is the third lowest dry land spot on earth. The region is so hot and dry that it is often referred to as "The Furnace of China." The surrounding desert itself, part of a belt running from the Gobi along the Chinese-Mongolia border, is one of the largest shifting sand deserts in the world. Its character comes in part from its location, which is among the world's furthest from any sea or ocean, and also from the Kunlun, Pamir, and Tian Shan mountains that nearly surround it. There are some remote villages along the Hotan River that runs part of the year through it, but life of any sort is a rare sight with average rainfall amounts below .4 inches. Small wonder that the famous Silk Route divides into two branches on coming to the region, one of which winds to the north and one to the south of it.

Eurasia's Eastern Branch: Korea

The terrain of the Korean Peninsula resembles in many ways that of the adjacent region of Manchuria. The north is mountainous, marked by the Nangnim and Hamyong ranges running northeast to southwest, with the Taebaek chain running north and south along the coast facing the Sea of Japan. The Amnokkang (Yalu River) and Kangnam Mountains form the present dividing line with Manchuria, but as noted above, Korean kingdoms have at times extended far beyond them into modern China's northeast. The areas south of the modern city of Seoul are somewhat flatter, but the entire peninsula is generally hilly and agriculture has historically been concentrated in the river floodplains and coastal alluvial flats.

The climate is continental in the north but influenced by the northern reaches of the monsoon system in the south. As in northern China, summer and winter temperatures tend to be extreme with distinct rainy (summer) and dry (winter) seasons. Because of the configuration of the mountains and the peninsula's position along the northern perimeter of the monsoon, rainfall amounts differ widely: from average lows of 30 inches in the northeast to 60–70 in the southwest. Like the western side of the Japanese islands, however, it is largely blocked by Japanese mountain ranges from the moderating weather effects of the Japan Current.

The difficulties of the terrain and the ever-present possibility of drought have rendered the challenges of the region similar to those facing agriculturalists in northern China, with crops such as millet and wheat dominating, and rice farming catching on only much later in the south where rainfall and the terracing of hillsides made it feasible. Scholars have noted similarities to archaic Greece, where geography fostered the development of isolated, independent communities, although early on a degree of cultural unity appears to have prevailed.

The Island Perimeter: Japan

The four main islands that for most of its history constituted Japan, *Honshu, Hokkaido, Kyushu,* and *Shikoku,* contain a varied set of climatic conditions, although more than any other place in East Asia they are influenced by the surrounding sea. The northernmost island of Hokkaido has cold, snowy winters and relatively cool summers, a quality that made its city of Sapporo the site of the 1972 Winter Olympics (in 1998 the city of Nagano on Honshu was Japan's other Winter Games venue). The central island of Honshu, bisected roughly north to south by substantial mountain ranges, has a temperate to subtropical climate on the eastern side—where it is moderated by the Japan Current—and a colder, more continental climate to the west of the mountains on the side facing Korea and northeastern China. The small southern island of Shikoku and the southernmost island of Kyushu have an abundance of warm, moist weather and are largely governed by the monsoon system.

The formation of Japan's islands from volcanic activity means that only about one fifth of their territory has historically been arable. Moreover, unlike China, Korea, and Vietnam, Japan has no large river systems that have provided in other regions the irrigation and floodplain silt from which civilization sprang. In the narrow plains and valleys, however, the majority of which are on the temperate Pacific side of the mountains, the soil is mineral rich and the rainfall abundant. Nonetheless, the islanders from early on have also had to face the limitations of the land in supporting a steadily growing population. This was particularly true after the introduction of rice culture to the islands, which supplanted the mode of settled and migratory fishing villages that dominated the subsistence economy until the third century BCE. Like the Korean Peninsula, the ruggedness of the land tended to force its people to live in politically isolated, culturally united communities. Thus, communication by water was often the most convenient method, both among the Japanese home islands and across the hundred-mile strait to southern Korea (see map 1.2).

The Southern Branch: Vietnam

The topography of Southeast Asia as a whole is similar from the borders of Assam in India to the Mekong Delta in the south of what is now Vietnam. Divided by several major river systems—the Irawaddy, Salween, and Mekong—running roughly north to south, and by the Red River, running northwest to southeast through Hanoi and meeting the Gulf of Tonkin at Haiphong, their watersheds are separated by low to medium mountain ranges running generally parallel to them. Even today, much of the region is heavily forested with abundant rainfall supplied by the summer monsoon, which acts as the region's principal climatic regulator. The river valleys and coastal plains are believed to have supplied the wild ancestors of the first rice plants, as well as some of the world's first domesticated fowl, sometime after 8000 BCE (see map 1.3).

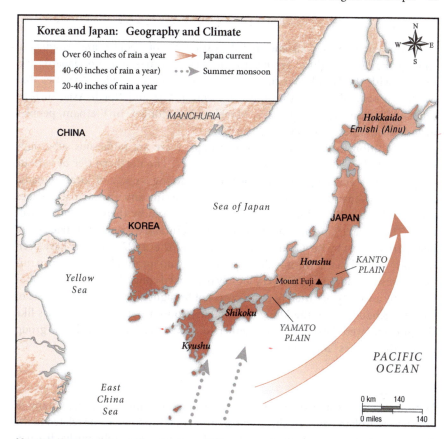

Map 1.2 Korea and Japan: Geography and Climate

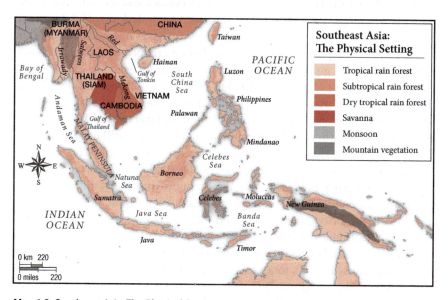

Map 1.3 Southeast Asia: The Physical Setting

EAST ASIAN ETHNICITIES AND LANGUAGES

East Asia encompasses an enormously varied set of peoples and languages. Among the largest ethnic groups are the Han (China), Yamato (Japan), and Korean, with the Han by far the largest. Other groups include ethnicities that overlap to some degree with groups in Central Asia and North Asia, such as Tibetan, Uyghur, Kazakh, Kyrgyz, Manchu, and Mongol. In Vietnam, peoples include Vietnamese, Khmers, and Lao-Mon.

In addition to these major ethnic groups, there are numerous subgroups within and along the borders of historical states. The northern tier of various Chinese states and empires contained a bewildering variety of local nomadic ethnicities, a situation complicated further by differing and unsystematic names given to them by the Chinese over the centuries, and by their constant movement. The ancient *Xiongnu*, for example, who maintained a powerful state before being driven west by the Chinese Han Dynasty (202 BCE–220 CE) may have been distantly related to the Huns—although this is by no means clear—who also migrated west. A widespread but very loosely organized congeries of nomadic tribes known by a variety of different names was not brought together until the time of Genghis Khan to form the Mongols. Similarly, loose federations of peoples like the Jurchens were later brought together to form a self-proclaimed new group calling themselves "Manchus."

China and Taiwan

Within the East Asian states, there were dozens of minority groups, many of which were isolated or nomadic, some of different ethnicities, some related to the majority populations but linguistically, and in some cases, religiously, distinct. China has by far the largest number of such minorities and officially recognizes 55 separate groups, with 19 "undistinguished" groups lacking official recognition. According to 2016 figures, the Han majority makes up 91.57 percent of the PRC's 1.375 billion people. Of the next five largest groups, the Zhuang (of South China) number 17 million; the Hui—Chinese Muslims who are mostly ethnically Han—number 11 million; Manchus come in at 10.4 million; the Muslim Turkic Uyghurs of western autonomous region of Xinjiang number 10 million; and the southern Miao people come to 9.5 million. Tibetans and Mongols come in at ninth and tenth, respectively, numbering 7.5 and 5.9 million. The smallest of the recognized groups is the Tatars, with a mere 3,556 people. The "undistinguished" number is cumulatively 640,000. The Hakkas, mentioned above, are treated as a subgroup of the Han and number approximately 34 million.

Although politically distinct, Taiwan (Republic of China, ROC) recognizes a number of minority groups as well, some also recognized by the PRC, like the Mulao, others unique to the island. Historically, Taiwan was peopled by speakers of the Austronesian language family, perhaps distantly related to the Polynesians of Oceania. Most lived as foragers, particularly on the forested, mountainous eastern side of the island. As Chinese refugees and settlers began to arrive, particularly after the Manchu Qing Dynasty overthrew the Ming in 1644, tensions and open warfare between the indigenous peoples and the outsiders remained common. Taiwan's colonization by Japan from 1895 to 1945, and the massive influx of mainlanders accompanying the Communist victory over the National-ist ROC in 1949, continued to keep tensions on a low boil. Thus, Taiwan's pres-ent government officially recognizes 12 indigenous minority groups, whereas the government of the PRC, which claims Taiwan as an unrecovered province of Greater China, lumps all such groups under the title of *Gaoshan*.

Tibet

Recent genetic research indicates that in terms of ethnicity, Tibetans are most closely related to a number of Central Asian populations as well as Han Chinese. A current theory holds that sometime between 9,000 and 15,000 years ago, the genetic group that would become the inhabitants of the Tibetan plateau and its adjacent regions in China split from the Han, shortly afterward separating themselves from the Sherpas. As a population long adapted to a mountain envi-ronment, Tibetans have developed a relatively high level of nitric oxide in their blood, allowing greater dilation of blood vessels and better utilization of oxygen at altitudes above 14,000 feet. Currently, the majority of Tibetans (7.5 million ac-cording to the PRC) live in the People's Republic of China's Tibet Autonomous Region (TAR) and in autonomous prefectures in the nearby provinces of Gansu, Sichuan, and Qinghai. The surrounding Himalayan nations of India, Nepal, Bhutan, and Sikkim also have Tibetan populations, with India's being by far the largest, at just under 190,000. Many Tibetans have fled to India since the re-pression of 1959, most of them clustering around the Himalayan Indian state of Dharamshala, the site of the Tibetan Government in Exile and where the Dalai Lama resides.

The language family from which the *Tibetic* languages—a group of related but mutually unintelligible languages—spring is *Sino-Tibetan*, within which one also finds the Chinese dialects. The subfamily in which the Tibetic languages reside is called *Tibeto-Burman* as distinct from the Sinitic or Chinese languages. It thus bears some resemblance and shares some basic vocabulary with the languages spoken to the south along the western perimeter of Southeast Asia. Related dialects are also spoken by peoples in Assam and India's northeastern provinces. Because of the isolation of so many mountain-dwelling peoples, a number of these languages developed their own writing systems distinct from Chinese. Classical Tibetan, for example, is a literary language widely used in Buddhist works since the eighth century. (See Map 1.4.)

Mongolia

The Mongols are defined today as an ethnic group inhabiting the area of the modern state of Mongolia as well as the Chinese Inner Mongolia Autonomous Region, Xinjiang, and the Russian regions of Buryatia and Kalmykia. Their origins are somewhat murky, like those of many nomadic peoples along China's northern and northeaster tier, because of the many names by which other peoples have identified them. The ancestors of some of the Mongol groups may have been

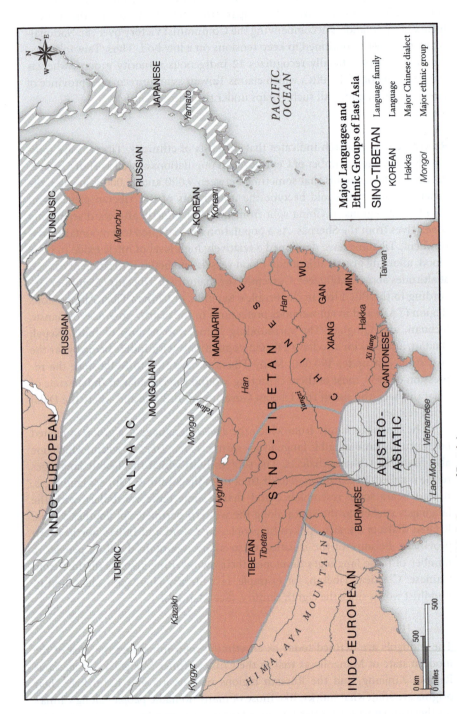

Map 1.4 Major Language and Ethnic Groups of East Asia

members of the *Zhukaigou* culture of the Ordos Desert, which lasted from perhaps 2250 to 1500 BCE. One group of their descendants, the Xianbei, ranged widely through the western part of the northern tier. In western Eurasia, they were associated with the Scythians. The Chinese **Shiji** (*Records of the Grand Historian*) mentions a people called *Donghu* (Eastern Barbarians) in their relations with the Xiongnu. Fourth-century CE histories record a border people called *Shiwei*, a term that was used to cover a number of the Tungusic-speaking peoples from modern Mongolia to Manchuria. One also finds isolated references to "Mongols" in records from the Tang Dynasty (618–907) to the time of Genghis Khan (1162–1227). It was Genghis Khan who united the various loosely-related tribes under the Mongol umbrella and established them as a distinct ethnic group. Today, the term "Mongolian" encompasses the Khalkha ("proper") Mongols, Buryats, Oirats, Kalmyks, and a number of loosely affiliated groups under the heading of "Southern Mongols." Currently, there are about 2.8 million Mongols in the independent state of Mongolia and about 5.9 million Mongols in China's Inner Mongolia Autonomous Region and other areas of the PRC.

Linguistically, as we have noted, the various Mongolic languages are from the large, although contested, Altaic language family, named for the people originally inhabiting the region around the Altai Mountains of southern Mongolia. Included in this family are the Turkic and Tungusic language groups, as well as (according to some scholars) Koreanic, Japonic, and sometimes **Ainu** groups. The debate concerning the Altaic languages revolves around the question of whether all these languages indeed have a common origin or if they are related by contact and diffusion (called *aereal interaction*) within a particular region.

Korea

The ethnic origins of the Koreans are still obscure, although the slim archeological and linguistic evidence seems to point to a Central Asian homeland with links to the Altaic-speaking peoples. In this sense, the modern Korean language may be distantly related to such languages as Mongolian and Manchu, and possibly the Turkic languages such as Uyghur. A linguistic and ethnic tie with Japan is possible as well due to the proximity of the islands. East and Northeast Asia was home to some of the world's first pottery, though the potter's wheel did not arrive in the area for millennia. In the case of the Korean Peninsula, potsherds dating from 4000 BCE have been uncovered in striated styles not unlike the **Jomon** wares of Japan.

Japan

Like the first peoples to inhabit the Korean Peninsula, the origins of the Japanese are obscure. Two distinct groups appear to have migrated to the islands from the Asian mainland via Ice Age land bridges, perhaps 10,000 to 20,000 years ago. Their descendants, the Utari, are today regarded as Japan's aboriginal peoples and referred to by the Japanese as *Ainu*, the "hairy ones," or in early imperial times as *Emishi*. Their physical features, tribal hunting society, and language mark them

Some Modern East Asian Ethnicities. East Asia encompasses an enormous area and is home to many diverse ethnic groups. Among those pictured here are a Mongolian woman dressed for life on the steppes (A); an elderly man from the Republic of Korea (South Korea) (B); a woman dressed in the traditional costume of the Miao, one of more than 50 recognized minority groups in the People's Republic of China (C); and a contemporary group of Japanese schoolboys (D).

as distinct from the later arrivals. Details of their religious practices have led some anthropologists to link them to the peoples of Central Asia and Siberia.

The later inhabitants may have originally come from the peoples who migrated to Southeast Asia, Indonesia, and eventually the Central Pacific. They may also have been descended from later Polynesian travelers and migrants from the Asian mainland. The linguistic evidence suggests a very tenuous connection to Korean and even to the Altaic language family. Japan's long linguistic isolation, however, renders its ultimate origins obscure for the present.

CONCLUSION

Although they encompass many different ethnicities, at least two major language families, and inhabit a wide diversity of environments, the region and the peoples we define in this volume as "East Asia" share some important commonalities. The region itself, though containing few "natural" borders marking it apart from other regions, is contiguous among its modern member states, as it has been historically. Biologically, the majority of the inhabitants share similar physical characteristics. In terms of culture, the region as a whole at one time or another has been influenced by China. In the case of the "Sinitic core" of Korea and Vietnam, Chinese culture was planted by invasion and diffusion; for Mongolia and Tibet, long-time contact, Mongolian empire building, and Chinese hegemony and incorporation (Tibet) have resulted in various degrees of cultural accommodation; as for Japan, its adoption of Chinese culture was voluntary. Even with insistent efforts to forge national identities of their own in all these cases, the region itself remains distinct from the surrounding Russian and Indian cultural spheres.

CHAPTER 2

The Middle Kingdom: China to 1280

Whatever else one could say about Li Si, he was ambitious. According to the not overly sympathetic Han Dynasty chronicle, *Shiji* (*The Records of the Grand Historian*), by perhaps China's most famous historian, Sima Qian, Li "knew how to elucidate his schemes":

> The king of Qin wants to swallow up the world, to call himself emperor, and rule it. This is the moment for commoners like myself, the harvest season for those with ideas to expound. . . . Therefore I plan to go west and speak to the king of Qin! (Watson, 1989, pp. 179–180)

And indeed he did. Li and his colleague Han Fei had been students of the Confucian thinker Xunzi. Unlike Confucius himself and his chief expositor, Mencius, however, Xunzi, living at the height of China's Warring States Period (403–221 BCE), could not bring himself to see human nature as inherently leaning toward good. Li and Han Fei had taken this fundamental assumption and expanded it into a nearly totalitarian vision of a political system in which the ruler was the sole arbiter of what was good, and the only good was what would benefit the state. The people must be governed by strict, impartial, universally applied laws with severe punishments for even the smallest infractions. Armed with these ideas, later known as "Legalism," Li traveled to Qin.

He had picked his benefactor well. The state of Qin for over a century had been moving in precisely the direction outlined by the Legalists. Moreover it had been quietly expanding its western borders and carefully steering its relations with the other Chinese states within the vestigial Zhou dynastic system to maximum advantage. And so Li made his pitch to the Qin king, Ying Zheng:

> Now the feudal lords are so submissive to Qin that they are like so many provinces and districts. . . . This is an opportunity that comes once in 10,000 ages. If one is lazy and fails to act quickly, the feudal lords will recover their strength and join in an alliance against Qin. (Ibid., p. 180)

The king followed Li's advice. Within a decade he had prevailed against all opponents and created China's first empire in 221 BCE. Ying Zheng now took the title

Qin Shi Huangdi: First Emperor of the Qin. As for Li, he achieved the pinnacle of his ambition and was made chancellor.

The first emperor moved swiftly in fulfilling his vision of state building. His draconian law codes were enacted. Weights, measures, even the writing system were standardized. All the feudal positions were eliminated in favor of a central bureaucracy; all the old states were eliminated in favor of a system of provinces and military districts. Work on what ultimately became China's two most popular modern tourist sites, the Great Wall and the terracotta warriors guarding the First Emperor's tomb complex, was begun. The price, however, was for too many unacceptably high in monetary and human terms. For Li, therefore, the physical transformation of the new empire was not enough; it must also exist under strict ideological control. Dissenters, particularly the Confucians, were to be ruthlessly eliminated, as were all books except for those expressly approved by the state.

The death of the first emperor, however, a few years later in 210 BCE spelled disaster for Li, although it would be another two years before he met his fate. Having concealed the First Emperor's death and now caught in a power struggle at court, with rebellion breaking out in the empire, he was condemned to a particularly brutal death with his son and relatives. After suffering tattooing and mutilation, he was cut in two.

Although neither Li Si nor the Qin Dynasty survived the First Emperor by very much, their legacy had a definitive impact on East Asia for more than 2,000 years. From this time until the second decade of the twentieth century, China would remain, with one long and several short interruptions, an empire. The long-lived Han Dynasty (202 BCE–220 CE), which succeeded the Qin, adopted its administrative structures and divisions, and softened its centralized bureaucracy by making its own version of Confucianism the state ideology. It would be this package of Chinese high culture—with the later addition of Buddhism—that would become the high culture of Korea, Vietnam, and Japan, with elements of it affecting even Mongolia and Tibet. Amidst this enormous diffusion of ideas and institutions, the writing of history on the Chinese model would have a central place—and the rise and fall of Li Si would be one of its most arresting morality tales.

In this chapter, we shall examine Chinese and, by extension, East Asian *origins*, *interactions*, and *adaptations* up to the coming of the Mongols and their incorporation of imperial China into a super-empire. We will also deal with Chinese and foreign conceptions of *patterns* of the Chinese past available through archaeological and literary records. We will explore the development and maturation of various Chinese states. Finally, we will look at China's influence on people and groups in East Asia as a result of those interactions, particularly the often debated idea of **sinification**: the making over of peoples and cultures along Chinese models.

CHINA AND THE NEOLITHIC REVOLUTION

It has often been noted that the first civilizations—people living in agriculturally supported cities—sprang up along river valleys. In this respect, China formed the eastern, and chronologically the last, of a belt of agrarian–urban cultures that included the Tigris and Euphrates-centered civilizations of Mesopotamia, the early kingdoms along the Nile in Egypt, and perhaps the largest of all, that of the Harappans, along the Indus in India. All these areas receive relatively little rain and rely on their river systems to replenish and irrigate the soil. All of them, too, were the product of a period of incubation during which people began the extensive domestication of plants and animals, developed trade, and established religious sites. All these factors allowed the first agricultural villages to ultimately grow into recognizable form as cities (see Map 2.1).

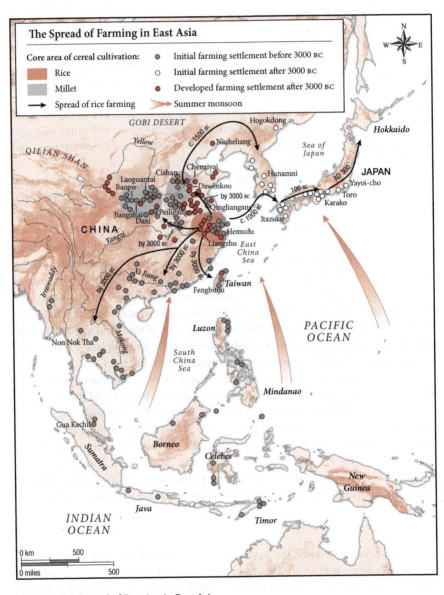

Map 2.1 The Spread of Farming in East Asia

Neolithic Origins

The last glacial retreat around 12,000–13,000 years ago brought with it perhaps the most important revolution in human history: the transition from foraging to food *production* in settled communities. Over the next 5,000–7,000 years, settlements based on agricultural surpluses began to appear throughout East Asia. This **Neolithic Revolution** of agriculture developed very quickly in a number of places in China. It appears that in both China and Southeast Asia the domestication of rice first took place, perhaps as early as 7000 BCE. *Millet*—a hardy cereal domesticated from several strains of Eurasian grasses—was already being grown in the north. Early strains of wheat and barley, perhaps originating from the Middle East, may also have been grown. Chickens, pigs, sheep, cattle, and dogs were also widely raised, although current debate questions whether they were domesticated independently or arrived as part of interactions with other areas.

The best known and most thoroughly studied of the thousands of Neolithic sites across China is Banpo Village on the outskirts of modern Xi'an. Banpo is a carefully excavated and reconstructed exemplar of *Yangshao* **culture**, which

Banpo Village. Banpo Village, near the modern city of Xi'an, remains a popular tourist stop as well as a rich Neolithic archaeological site. Photo (A) shows the entry and an interior view of a typical circular dwelling in the village. The photo (B) displays foundations, post holes, and storage pits.

flourished from 5000 to 3500 BCE. Pottery was a signal Neolithic development and Yangshao communities had kilns capable of generating temperatures high enough to fire a wide variety of brightly painted storage pots, vases, etc. decorated with animal and geometric designs. The villagers also fashioned a wide array of stone implements to support the hunting, gathering, and fishing with which they supplemented their subsistence agriculture.

Yangshao villages yielded artifacts and structures that were to have long-standing significance in the everyday lives of villagers throughout northern East Asia. Some of the dwellings at Banpo contain raised clay beds with flues laid through them—an early version of the *kang*, the fuel-efficient combination stove and heated bed still found in older farming homes. Also, silkworm cocoons and bone needles suggest the earliest occurrence of *sericulture*— silk weaving. Perhaps more exciting—and controversial— are pottery fragments bearing abstract pictures of animals and geometric figures bearing some resemblance to later Chinese characters.

Another Neolithic system of communities along the Yellow River was the *Longshan,* or "black pottery," culture. Located to the east of the Yangshao areas, although with considerable overlap, Longshan artifacts date as far back as 4500 BCE. **Longshan culture** was the last widespread Neolithic set of communities along the North China Plain, and branches of it survived until they were absorbed by the Shang state around 1500 BCE.

The most outstanding product of Longshan artisans was a distinctive, highly refined black pottery, following designs and functional forms still popular in China, Japan, Korea, and Vietnam today. Some of the pieces are so delicate

Longshan Pottery. Stem cups and goblet, dating to about 2000 BCE. The graceful, even elegant lines of Longshan, or black, pottery wares are not only distinctive but also established patterns for ceramic and bronze designs that are still imitated today.

and nearly transparent that they resemble the famous "eggshell porcelain" of later periods. This advance in ceramic sophistication came in part through introduction of the potter's wheel from western Eurasia, perhaps in the mid-third millennium BCE, which permitted unprecedented precision in molding round and curved figures. In addition, improved kilns—reaching firing temperatures in excess of 1,800 degrees Fahrenheit—and initial experimentation with kaolin clays began a long process of development that reached its high point with the matchless porcelain of the Song and Ming periods. These techniques and designs would later be diffused throughout East, Central, and Southeast Asia (see Map 2.2).

THE FOUNDATIONS OF THE DYNASTIC SYSTEM

Although the oldest fragmentary written records in East Asia are the **oracle bones** used by diviners in the Shang Dynasty (tr. 1766–1122/1040 BCE), the first real historical accounts in China arrive much later with the *Shujing* (known variously as "the Book of History" or "the Classic of Documents") in the seventh century BCE. Scholars have debated its reliability for millennia because its texts were written down centuries after the events it covers allegedly occurred. Nonetheless,

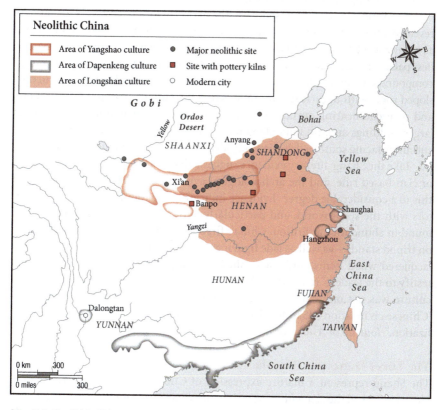

Map 2.2 Neolithic China

along with the oracle bones, it remains a vitally important source on China's first three dynasties: the Xia, Shang, and Zhou.

The *Shujing* claims that a series of mythical "culture heroes" and "sage kings" reigned from 2852 to 2205 BCE. These figures were said to have introduced many of China's basic elements and institutions: medicine, divination, writing, agriculture, fire, sericulture (silk production), the calendar, and astronomical cycles. Following the culture heroes were three celebrated sage kings: Yao, Shun, and Yu. Yao and Shun set the pattern for ethical rule and chose their successors from among the most worthy men, not their own family members. Yu was said to have labored for decades to control the rivers and watercourses of the region, so Shun chose him as his successor. Departing from precedent, however, Yu created China's first dynasty, the Xia.

The Three Dynasties: The Xia

Due at least in part to the legacy of history writing in China, East Asian countries have all developed strong historical traditions. In China, the habit of recasting history through the experiences and biases of succeeding dynasties makes it at times slippery source material for historians. The problem is especially acute with regard to the Xia. Were they simply an invention of Zhou chroniclers to establish a narrative thread to their own dynasty? Was their alleged state, in fact, a kind of Shang mythology absorbed into the Zhou tradition?

Excavations at *Erlitou* in southern Shaanxi Province from the 1950s on have revealed a city dating from roughly 2000 to 1600 BCE that at its height may have had as many as 30,000 inhabitants. The enclosure includes what is perhaps China's earliest palace. In addition, the plan of the structures within the city's various walled compounds resembles that of later official residences: post and beam construction, sloped roofs with upturned ends anticipating the famous "rising phoenix" motif, and non-load-bearing curtain walls of plastered brick or masonry. Most of the larger buildings are also built along north–south axes with their courtyards and entrances facing south, a direction considered propitious even today.

Like the Shang, literary evidence suggests that Xia leaders exercised a family- or clan-based rule, and the archaeological evidence at Erlitou seems to support this to a considerable degree. Evidence indicating the role of the elites as mediators with the spirit world, and particularly with the ancestors of rulers, is also found in abundance at Erlitou. China's first bronze ritual vessels—wine beakers on tripod stands—as well as jade figurines, turquoise jewelry, the world's earliest lacquered wood items, and cowry shells—used as a medium of exchange—all testify to the leaders' religious and social roles. For scholar Sarah Allen, "Erlitou culture was not only an ancient civilization in China, it was an early form of 'Chinese civilization'" (Sarah Allen, "Erlitou and the Formation of Chinese Civilization," *Journal of Asian Studies* 66, no. 2 (May 2007): 490).

The Three Dynasties: The Shang

The Shang represent a mature expression of Chinese Bronze Age civilization. Here, we find all the elements of agrarian–urban society: a highly original method of bronze casting, a substantial and diverse agricultural base, an increasingly centralized politico-religious system, a sophisticated class structure, an independently developed written language, and, of course, cities.

The system of dynastic rule said to have been instituted by the Xia continued under the Shang. Shang social and political organization was kinship-based, with an emphasis on military power. Members of the king's extended family controlled politics and religion, with more distant relatives acting as court officials. Unlike other Bronze Age societies, there was no distinct class of priests. Rather, spirit mediums and diviners were widely used by Shang rulers and exercised considerable influence at court. The rulers themselves, as the highest living link to the ancestors and other beings occupying a spirit realm, were the embodiment of both religious and secular power.

The Shang fielded both defensive armies and expeditionary forces aimed at expanding their territories and forcing neighboring states to pay tribute. For the most part, these forces consisted of infantry armed with spears, and pikes with axe heads, and were organized into companies of 100 men. Perhaps as early as the fourteenth century BCE, evidence begins to appear in Shang tombs of two of the great innovations of ancient warfare: the horse and the chariot. Moreover, like the potter's wheel, these were among the items that we can authoritatively say were introduced from the outside. In this case, the evidence points to Indo-European migrants who ranged far and wide across Eurasia and spoke a language that became the parent tongue of a linguistic family that includes nearly all the European languages as well as Sanskrit, the sacred language of Hinduism. It was the Tocharian speakers in this language family who played such an important role in spreading a host of ancient technologies throughout the eastern part of Eurasia. In the history museum of the modern city of Urumqi in China's far western province of Xinjiang, one can see today several extraordinarily well-preserved mummies of these migrants discovered in the Tarim Basin—as well as what may be the world's oldest pair of trousers.

The use of chariots in China seems to have been shortly preceded by the widespread introduction of the horse, an innovation that had already revolutionized transport and warfare throughout much of Eurasia. Interestingly, however, the use of horses as mounts for

Tarim Basin Mummy. Central Asia's Tarim Basin, one of the lowest points on Earth, is also one of the driest, making it a perfect environment for preservation. It was also a place where some of the earliest interchanges took place between the peoples in China and the earliest Indo-European migrants. Remains up to 4,000 years old have been recovered. Here, the remains of a much more recent figure, "Yingpan Man" complete with mask, shows remarkably little deterioration and his clothes, though nearly 2,000 years old, look almost new.

cavalry or archers did not really become important in the Chinese states until centuries later. Nonetheless, the relative scarcity of horses and suitable breeding grounds for them in China ultimately made trade with Central Asia extremely important as a source for the animals. Ultimately, it would be China that refined and popularized two inventions that are said by many scholars to have "created" the medieval Eurasian world: the stirrup and the horse collar.

Because of the system of kinship-based rule, the personal well-being of the elite and the prestige of the regime as a whole depended in large part on military power and harmony with their ancestors. Hence, Shang rulers constantly mounted campaigns for tribute and labor service from vulnerable states. Among the settled peoples to the west, the most prominent were the Zhou, based around modern Xi'an, and enlisted as allies and clients. For their part, the Shang circulated local and foreign items such as bronze vessels, weapons, and jade throughout the region and beyond.

The Three Dynasties: The Zhou

Unlike the Xia and Shang dynasties, the nearly nine centuries of Zhou rule are extensively documented. In addition to the *Shujing*, literary works like the *Chunqiu* (Spring and Autumn Chronicles), *Zuo Zhuan* (The Commentaries of Mr. Zuo),

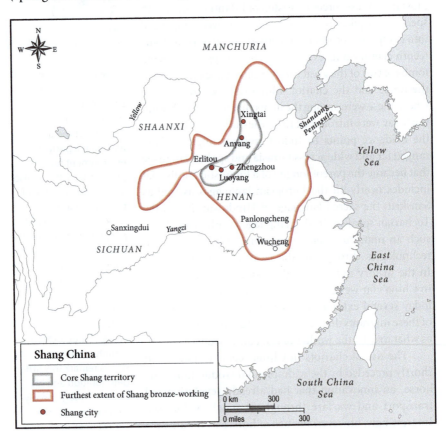

Map 2.3a Shang China

and later compilations such as the *Shiji* (Records of the Grand Historian) by the second-century BCE historian Sima Qian considerably amplify our source material. They also begin to elaborate a wholesale questioning of existing values in a society that was increasingly undergoing the stresses of growth, wealth, and political competition.

One of the revelations of the oracle bones has been to flesh out aspects of the literary record. An important example of this appears to be that by the twelfth century BCE, the Shang state had been considerably eroded by an assortment of nomadic and settled peoples to the north and west. The literary record of their successors, the Zhou, implies that Shang attempts to strengthen the control of the ruler coincided with increasing dissolution and corruption, thus letting the **Mandate of Heaven** slip from their grasp. Therefore, it appears the Zhou kings Wen , Wu, and Cheng and Cheng's regent, the duke of Zhou, pushed their holdings eastward at the expense of the Shang from 1122 BCE. Sometime around 1045 BCE, Zhou forces captured and burned the last Shang capital and stronghold near Anyang (see Map 2.3). As the *Shujing* put it:

> Heaven has rejected and ended the Mandate of this great state of Yin [the Shang]. . . . It was because they did not reverently care for their virtue that they early let their Mandate fall. . . .

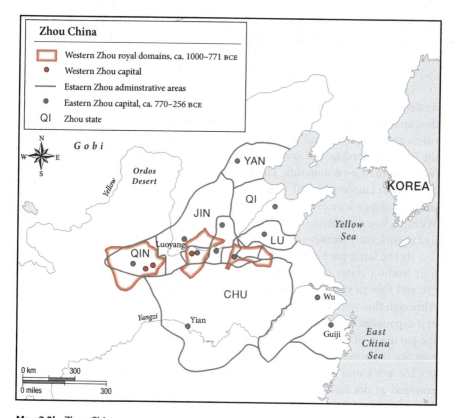

Map 2.3b Zhou China

(from William Theodore De Bary and Irene Bloom, compilers, *Sources of Chinese Tradition*,vol. 1, 2nd Edition, New York: Columbia University Press, pp. 36–37)

Thus, we have an expression, repeated throughout nearly all Chinese historical literature, of the universe, expressed as "heaven" (*tian*), acting as a moral force in human affairs. The ruler, as the mediating element in humanity's triangular relationship with Heaven and Earth, must hold all three elements together in harmony by just rule. If rulers become unjust, they lose Heaven's Mandate and rebellion is justified. It is expected as well that the patterns of history include a **dynastic cycle** in which families of rulers initially govern justly but over time stagnate. This is followed by decline, loss of mandate, and ejection by newcomers who found the next dynasty.

By the end of the eleventh century BCE, a network of over 100 smaller territories was organized under Zhou control. Zhou rulers placed family, distinguished subjects, allies, and even some defeated Shang notables in leadership positions of these territories under a graded system of hereditary ranks. By the eighth century BCE, however, the more powerful of these territories had begun to consolidate their holdings into states of their own. Although these states would continue to pledge their loyalty to the Zhou court, they increasingly worked toward promoting their own interests, which resulted in a weakening of Zhou political power. A half-century of war among court factions, border struggles with nomadic peoples, and a devastating earthquake further weakened Zhou power, resulting in the court being driven from its capital at Xi'an in 771 BCE and relocating to the east in Luoyang. This forced move marks the end of the Western Zhou period and the beginning of the Eastern Zhou era (770–256 BCE).

The Zhou system of decentralized government called ***fengjian***, usually rendered as "feudalism," gave considerable autonomy to its local rulers and was thus an important reason for the weakening of the central government. As these rulers grew in power and their economies flourished, they became less loyal to the Zhou leadership and some even went as far as naming themselves "king" (*wang*) of their own domains. The prestige of the Zhou court also suffered after its flight to Luoyang in 770. The court's new isolation was especially important since its dependencies were in a period of tremendous economic expansion. Within a few generations of the relocation to Luoyang, Zhou control and power had significantly weakened in absolute as well as relative terms.

By the latter part of the sixth century, a rough balance of power among the four leading states of Jin, Chu (the premier state of the southern periphery), Qi, and Qin (a rising force in the old Zhou homeland near Xi'an) held sway. Although this system functioned for several decades, new powers on the periphery, expansion into non-Zhou lands, and civil war in Jin ultimately precipitated the partition of that state in 403 BCE, marking the formal opening of the Warring States period. By its close, Zhou itself had been absorbed by the combatants (in 256 BCE), and as we saw in the opening vignette of this chapter, Qin had emerged as not just the dominant state but the creator of a unified empire in 221 BCE.

Economy and Society

The large size of the territory claimed by the Zhou Dynasty, and the enhanced trade that this expansion entailed, added to the wealth and power of all the rulers of its increasingly autonomous dependencies. The expansion of these dependencies to the Yangzi River basin brought much of East Asia's most productive farm- land under some form of Zhou control and stimulated increased interaction with the inhabitants of the region.

In the north, the introduction of the soybean from Manchuria, with its high protein content and ability to fix nitrogen in the soil, boosted crop yields and pushed growers to cultivate more marginal lands. The rotation of wheat and different varieties of millet allowed for more intensive farming. The use of more efficient ox-drawn plows and increasingly elaborate irrigation and water-conservancy efforts pushed yields even further. In the south, the Zhou dependencies developed rapidly as rice cultivation facilitated population growth. By the mid-sixth century BCE, the Zhou kingdoms taken together constituted the world's most populous, and perhaps richest, agriculturally based urban society.

In an attempt to untangle the more confusing aspects of *fengjian* land arrangement, the Zhou were the first among many dynasties to attempt to impose a uniform system of land tenure in China. Later writers, most notably the philosopher Mencius, would look back nostalgically on the **well-field system**—a method of land division said to have been devised by the duke of Zhou. In this arrangement, each square *li* (one *li* is about one-third of a mile), consisting of 900 *mou* (each *mou* is approximately one-sixth of an acre), was divided into a grid of nine plots. Individual families would each work one of the eight outside plots, while the middle one would be farmed in common for the taxes and rents owed the landowner or local officials. The term "well-field" comes from the Chinese character for "[water] well" (井, *jing*) that resembles a grid. Whether the system as idealized by Mencius was ever widely practiced is still a matter of debate among scholars. It did, however, remain the benchmark against which all subsequent attempts at land reform were measured, even into the twentieth century. By the late 500s BCE, the needs of individual governments to use the wealth of their states to support their militaries and developing bureaucracies prompted them to institute land taxes based on crop yields. Depending on the state and the productivity of the land, these tended to vary from 10 to 20 percent of a family holding's yield.

New Classes: Merchants and Shi

Also contributing to the decline of Zhou rural-based feudal society was the rise of new classes. For the first time, the literary record now includes references to merchants. The growing power of this new class began a long-term struggle with various governments for control of such vital commodities as salt and iron. It also marked the beginning of the perception of merchants as a parasitic class whose drive for profit from trafficking in the goods of others endangered the stability of Zhou social institutions. Accompanying the rise of a merchant class was the steady advance of a cash economy. The coining of money was becoming widespread by the late Zhou, including the round copper "cash" with the square middle hole—symbolically depicting Heaven and Earth—which remained almost unchanged for over 2,000 years.

Although often viewed with distaste by the landed aristocracy, merchants were nonetheless seen as resources to be tapped. Their independence and mobility, along with the steady growth of cities as centers of trade, helped spur political and economic centralization as the rulers of Zhou territories attempted to create more inclusive systems of administration. Direct taxation by the state, uniform law codes, and administrative restructuring were increasingly altering the old arrangement of mutual obligation between aristocratic landowners and dependent peasant farmers. Here, members of the new **shi** class—drawn from the lower aristocracy and wealthier commoners—who, like merchants, were divorced somewhat from the older structures of rural life, took on the role of bureaucrats and advisors. From the ranks of the *shi* would rise many of China's most famous thinkers, starting with Confucius.

Bronze Owl from Fu Hao Tomb. Shang Dynasty bronzes are unique in form and in their fabrication. Unlike the "lost wax" method of casting in other Eurasian cultures, the Chinese model utilized two separate molds. Shang and early Zhou bronzes are also notable for their stylized *taotie* designs and decoration of real and mythological creatures. This bronze owl is from the tomb of Fu Hao, the consort of Shang king Wu Ding, and is part of one of that dynasty's richest troves of funeral artifacts.

Family and Gender in Ancient China

In marked contrast to later Chinese court life, in which the seclusion of women was a central aspect, elite women of the Shang often participated in political—and even military—affairs. We can catch a glimpse of this reflected in the objects found at the burial site of Fu Hao, discovered in 1975. The most prominent of the 64 wives of Wu Ding, Fu Hao's burial artifacts—hundreds of bronzes, jade, and bone ornaments, as well as the sacrificial skeletons of 16 people and 6 dogs—help bring to life a woman whose existence, although well established in written records, has otherwise been elusive.

For example, inscriptions on oracle bones in Fu Hao's tomb indicate that she wielded considerable power and influence even before becoming Wu Ding's principal wife. Prior to coming to court at the Shang capital of Yin sometime in the late thirteenth century BCE, she owned and managed a family estate nearby and was apparently well educated in a number of areas that would serve her well in palace life. She both supervised and conducted religious rituals at court and during military expeditions. As Wu Ding's chief confidant, she advised him on political and military strategy and diplomacy. She even conducted her own military campaigns against Shang adversaries. The king apparently considered her so wise and beloved that after her death he frequently appealed to her for guidance through divination with oracle bones.

Although elite Shang women like Fu Hao appear to have shared a comparatively egalitarian role with male rulers, the Zhou era marks a period of transition in their status. To the extent that such literature as the *Book of History* and the *Poetry Classic* of the early Zhou era address issues of women and power, women were still depicted as occupying important positions as mentors and advisors. The wives and concubines of rulers in many instances had their own sets of records and genealogies, an important asset among the powerful in this family-conscious society.

However well-educated and capable, though, late Zhou women seldom ruled in their own right. In fact, the treaties during this period in many cases specifically barred women from involvement in state affairs. The same general trend may be glimpsed at other levels of society as well. The enormously complex web of family, clan, village, and class associations of the Zhou era reflects considerable respect for the wisdom and work of women, but these skills were increasingly seen as best exercised in the home instead of in the public sphere. The later development of state-sponsored Confucianism, with its preponderant emphasis on filial piety, ushered in a markedly secondary role for women as governing the "inner domain" of the home, whereas men ruled the "outer domain" of public life and power.

Religion, Culture, and Intellectual Life

In many respects, the evolution of Chinese religion follows a similar pattern to that of other agrarian–urban societies. The first Chinese gods were local deities that inhabited a spirit world presided over by a ruling god. Unlike other religions of remote antiquity, in China the rulers' ancestors occupied the highest rungs of the spirit world and worship largely consisted of communication with them by various means.

Two aspects that mark Shang religious, intellectual, and political life as distinctive and original are oracle bones and the writing system. The king seeking guidance would either himself or with a diviner ask a question of the ancestors. The bones, usually the shoulder blades of oxen or the undershells of tortoises, were then heated and tapped with a bronze rod, and the resulting cracks were interpreted as answers. The queries and responses were generally added later as a record of the procedure. Such matters as propitious times for battle, justifications for invasion, and the worthiness of officials are heavily represented among the oracle bones, as are matters related to royal births, deaths, marriages, and pregnancies.

Oracle Bones. Shang "oracle bones" used extensively for divination were first identified at Anyang a little more than a century ago and contain the earliest confirmed examples of Chinese writing. Kings or their diviners would ask questions of ancestors or gods, heat the bones, and interpret the cracks to find the answers to their inquiries. The questions and answers were then inscribed on the bones, usually the plastrons (undershells) or tortoises or (here) the shoulder blades of oxen.

Chinese Writing

Several thousand distinct symbols have been identified on the oracle bones, and many are clearly ancient versions of modern Chinese characters. Even in their ancient form, Chinese characters contained two basic elements: the "radical" that conveys the category of meaning to which the character belongs; and the phonetic part that usually both makes the meaning more specific and offers a guide to its pronunciation. Many radicals are stylized pictures representing concrete objects: In its earliest form, for example, the Chinese character for the sun was a circle with a dot in the center. In its modern form, it is still recognizable as 日. As a radical, it forms a component of many characters related to light. For example, the radical for sun (日) placed with the character for moon (月) means "bright," 明.

Characters combining concrete objects, such as the sun and moon here, are often used to depict abstract ideas, in this case, "brightness" or "brilliance."

Perhaps more than any other factor, the Chinese written language had a tremendous influence on the course of East Asian history. Although it requires extensive memorization compared to the phonetic languages of other cultures, it is remarkably adaptable as a writing system because the meaning of the characters is independent of their pronunciation. Thus, speakers of non-Chinese languages could attach their own pronunciations to the characters and, as long as they understood their structure and grammar, could use them to communicate. This versatility enabled Chinese to serve as the first written language not only for speakers of the Chinese family of dialects but also Vietnamese, Korean, and Japanese. Even today, despite the development of written vernacular languages in all these countries, the ability to read classical Chinese is still considered to be a mark of superior education. Moreover, the cultural heritage transmitted by Chinese characters continues to inform the worldviews of these societies.

Ritual and Religion

Although scholars are more or less agreed that China's earliest bronze artifacts were brought in through trade with Western Asia, the first bronze casting techniques in China likely arrived via Southeast Asia. Shang and early Zhou ritual bronzes, with their richly stylized *taotie* motifs—fanciful abstract reliefs of real and mythical animals incorporated into the design—are utterly unlike anything outside of East Asia.

The use of bronze vessels constituted a central part of Shang religious ceremonies among the elites. Indeed, a number of Shang and Zhou ceremonial vessels passed through the hands of subsequent dynasties and came to be seen as the tangible marks of the Mandate of Heaven. Offerings of meats and grains (wheat, millet, and occasionally rice), as well as wine, were a regular part of Shang ritual.

Scholars are still unresolved as to whether *Di*, sometimes given as *Shangdi*, was the chief Shang deity, or referred to a larger group or council in the spirit realm. In any case, Di presided over the spirit world and governed both natural and human affairs. Di was joined by the major ancestors of the dynastic line, deities believed to influence or control natural phenomena, and local gods appropriated from various Shang territories. The religious function of the Shang ruler was to act as the intermediary between the world of the spirits and that of humanity. Hence, rituals appear to have consisted largely of sacrifices to ancestors to assure their benevolence toward the living. As the Shang state grew more powerful and commanded more and more resources, the size and scope of the sacrifices also increased. The Shang also practiced human sacrifice. The evidence suggests that the death of a ruler was the occasion to slaughter hundreds of slaves, servants, and war captives, perhaps to serve the deceased in the spirit world.

The Zhou, like other conquerors after them, sought to give legitimacy to their reign by adopting many of the forms of art and ritual practiced by the defeated Shang. As before, the ruler maintained his place as mediator between the

Shang Bronze. Shang bronze-making techniques and motifs resulted in highly original designs and vessels that were often imitated by their successors. The ritual food vessel pictured here, called a *li ding*, is decorated with a distinctive *taotie* motif containing prominent eyes and scrolling horns. It was found at Anyang and dates to ca.1200–1050 BCE.

human and divine worlds. The Zhou era, however, marked a turn toward a more abstract, impersonal, and universal concept of religion. Di, the chief Shang deity or group of deities, began to give way to the more distant Zhou idea of "Heaven" (*tian*) as the animating force of the universe. By the late Zhou era, this concept had become central to nearly every major Chinese religious and philosophical tradition. It was this more abstract heaven whose mandate gave the right to rule to all subsequent Chinese dynasties.

THE HUNDRED SCHOOLS: CONFUCIANISM AND DAOISM

Of the philosophical or religious systems that have been most influential in China's history, two, Confucianism and Daoism, are indigenous. The third, Buddhism, arrived somewhat later from India via Central Asian trade routes during the first century CE. All three, especially Confucianism and Buddhism, would go far to shape the cultures of East Asia down to the present. The seedbed of the first two, however, may be found amid the increasingly turbulent Eastern Zhou era. Indeed, by the third century BCE, there were so many competing ideas in play that the era is customarily referred to as the time of the Hundred Schools of Thought.

Self-Cultivation and Ritual: Confucius

As with so many religious and philosophical figures from antiquity, the historical Confucius remains a somewhat shadowy figure. He is said to have been born in 551 BCE to a family named Kong, whose members still maintain genealogies tracing their ancestors back to him. In Confucian texts, he is referred to as "the Master" (*zi* or *fuzi*) or "the Master Kong" (**Kong fuzi**). European missionaries in the seventeenth century rendered *Kong fuzi* into Latin, where it became "Confucius." He was a man of that new class, the *shi*, and is said to have spent much of his early career seeking a position as a political advisor to the courts of several of the Zhou states in northern China, although his search for employment was largely unsuccessful. He did, however, attract a group of followers as he made the rounds as an itinerant teacher. Although the writings attributed to him and his immediate disciples do not outline a systematic philosophical scheme as such, the core ideas of his vision represent a consistent view of a universal ideal of a moral order to which the dedicated may aspire regardless of their social position.

Confucius drew heavily from his understanding of Yao and Shun, and the Zhou dynastic founders Wu, Wen, and the duke of Zhou. As presented in the *Lunyu*, or *Analects*, the Master's ideas represent a view

Kong Family Compound in Qufu. Though scholars still debate the authenticity of claims of authorship and descent from Confucius, the Kong family has insisted on their lineage and maintained this compound in Qufu in Shandong Province. Emperors have bestowed the title of "Duke Yansheng" on the eldest male of the line since 1055 CE. The most recent holder of the title Kung Te-cheng (Pinyin, Kong Dezheng) died in 2008 in Taiwan at the age of 89. He claimed to be the 77th main-line descendant of the Sage.

of human beings as inclined toward ethical behavior. One of the key concepts shared by Confucius with many other Chinese philosophical schools is the idea of a transcendent *dao* (Tao). As we will see with the Daoists below, there are certain fundamental patterns that are manifestations of the **dao** ("the Way") of the universal order. For Confucius, one of these patterns is that of human society as a kind of extended family from the ruler down to the peasant. In fact, it extends beyond human society in the sense that, through the mechanism of Heaven's Mandate, the ruler is responsible to Heaven for the state of human society. Although this view is avowedly hierarchical rather than egalitarian, the mutual obligations present at every level serve as checks for Confucius on the arbitrary exercise of power. When asked to sum up his philosophy in one word, Confucius answered "reciprocity": "Do not do unto others what you would not have them do unto you."

Confucius believed that individuals should practice the qualities of **ren** (benevolence, or humaneness toward others) and **li** (the observance of ritual, or rules of decorum) as guides to appropriate behavior. The practice of *li* throughout society—formally through ritual, informally through the behavior of role models such as parents, elders, teachers, and officials—would at a minimum allow people to police themselves and encourage individuals to aspire to *ren*. Thus, people who demonstrated these qualities would not only perfect their own character, but also set an example for the rest of society.

Living during a time of great social and political turmoil, Confucius not surprisingly directed much of his thought toward ways of improving government and society. Unlike systems that seek to do this by improving institutions, however, Confucian doctrine places great emphasis on personal transformation and responsibility. In this schema, good government begins with educated leaders and officials of strong ethical character. In this sense, those who would rule should be the **junzi**—"gentlemen" or "superior men" whose virtues include a humane temperament, courtesy, kindness, and diligence. Since the goal of society is to create a moral order among human beings to hold the cosmos in balance, rulers and officials who embody these attributes would set the correct example for their subjects to follow. Thus, the Confucian emphasis on government and society as a kind of school of moral development created an approach that aspired to go *beyond* simply obeying laws. The *Analects* sums this up succinctly: "Lead them [the people] by rules of decorum [*li*] and they will develop a sense of shame [i.e., a collective sense of proper behavior], and moreover, will become good."

By the time Confucius died, traditionally said to be in 479 BCE, he had attracted a loyal following of adherents to his teachings. Two later students of Confucian doctrine—Mencius and Xunzi—continued to spread the teachings of the Master, with their own distinctive contributions. Both men, however, ended up moving in very different directions. In the long run, it would be Mencius who would be seen as the inheritor of the "authentic" Confucian tradition. Xunzi's chief disciples, whom we met in the opening vignette, Han Fei and Li Si, would become the architects of China's unification under the short-lived and draconian philosophy of **Legalism**.

Mencius and the Politics of Human Nature

By Mencius's time, the intensity of the competition and continual warfare among the Zhou states had spawned most of the Hundred Schools of Thought as thinkers questioned fundamental assumptions about private and social good (see Map 2.4). Not surprisingly, given the chaotic times, their answers varied from the radical individualism of Yang Zhu (ca. 440–360 BCE) to the arguments for universal love and altruism of Mo Di (ca. 470–391 BCE). Some, like Sun Zi (fl. fifth century BCE), turned to what they considered to be remorselessly practical matters such as examining the nature of armed struggle in his famous *Art of War*.

For Mencius (*Mengzi* or "Master Meng") (372–289? BCE), people were fundamentally oriented toward ethical behavior, but must continually work to understand and refine their natural inclinations in order to avoid being led astray by negative influences. Mencius traveled throughout China spreading Confucian ideals, especially as a basis for government practice. The *Mengzi*, or Book of Mencius, is written in more of a narrative form than the *Analects*, and fleshed out by stories, parables, and debates with advocates of other schools, particularly those of Yang and Mo.

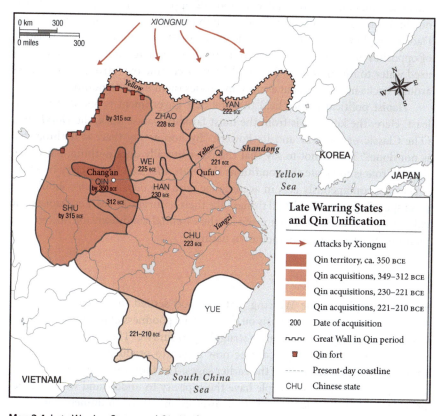

Map 2.4 Late Warring States and Qin Unification

As the center of both power and moral authority, the ruler had a primary duty to maintain *min sheng* (the people's livelihood) and uphold the social order. The ruler should not seek to pursue profit but rather set the example of "righteousness" (*yi*), appropriate behavior toward all according to social rank; and *ren* (benevolence, or humaneness) as espoused by Confucius. Mencius revived the old "well-field" system as a model of just land tenure in order to support this idea. A ruler who abused or neglected his subjects, however, upset not just the social order but the cosmic order. In such a case, the people had not only the right but the obligation to invoke the Mandate of Heaven and depose him.

Paradox and Transcendence: Laozi and Daoism

Although most Chinese philosophical schools accepted the concept of the *dao* as the governing principle of the universe, they varied as to the best means of achieving harmony with it. For Confucians, study and self-cultivation to the point of intuitive understanding put the individual in tune with the *dao*. For followers of the Daoist tradition attributed to Laozi (Lao Tzu, tr. b. 604 BCE), the Confucian path *prevented* harmony with the *dao*. Daoists rejected the Confucian emphasis on personal responsibility and ethical social behavior because it implied following a specific course of *good* behavior. The *dao*, however, encompasses the *entire* universe—including good and evil and *all* opposites and paradoxes. Hence, no single path of action would lead an individual to union with it. Instead, the Daoists taught that only through a life of quiet self-reflection and contemplation of opposites and paradoxes might an individual come to know the *dao*. Daoists used water to illustrate how the "weak" will overcome the "strong": water flows around rocks in a stream but eventually erodes them down to nothing.

Daoist political theory held that the best government is one that governs least. Here, the key idea is from the most famous Daoist work, the **Daode Jing** (The Classic of the Way and Its Power): "By non-action there is nothing that is not done." This is not to say that the ruler literally does nothing, but rather that his role is to create the conditions that *naturally* lead to a society in which everyone spontaneously acts in accordance with the *dao*. The ruler should not push specific policies but let all things take their natural courses. For Daoists, the ruler is thus like the field that provides the essential conditions for flowers and plants to grow according to their own natures.

THE STRUCTURES OF EMPIRE

As the struggles of the Warring States Period settled into their final phase, Confucianism, with its emphasis on the essential goodness of people, seemed less and less appealing to many rulers struggling to survive. The collateral branches of the Confucian philosophical tree now began to produce ideas that seemed radically at odds with those of the earlier sages. The most influential of these was Xunzi (tr. 298–219? BCE). People have the capacity to understand what is good, he asserted, but are able to regulate themselves only through immense and constant effort. Moreover, government must take an active role in regulating them.

Although the immediate development of Legalism as incorporated by the state of Qin came from Xunzi's students Han Fei (d. 233 BCE) and Li Si (d. 208), its roots may perhaps be traced back much further.

Most directly connected to the Legalist school was *The Book of Lord Shang*, detailing the ideas of Gongsun Yang (Shang Yang, d. 338 BCE) the architect of Qin's rise to prominence during the late fourth century BCE. Here, one sees most of the elements that would be refined and completed during the creation of China's first empire: strict impartial law; severe punishments for small infractions; an emphasis on only "practical" subjects in education; and the sanctioning of war as an instrument of state policy.

As we saw in the opening vignette, such policies were powerfully attractive to Han Fei and Li Si. In the system they created, all old *fengjian* privileges of rank were leveled in favor of uniform laws and practices based on the will of the ruler in a highly centralized state. Order would prevail in the state only through the institution of strict, detailed, and explicit laws diligently and impartially enforced. In keeping with the idea that obedience on small matters led to compliance on larger ones, they imposed harsh punishments—forced labor, mutilation, in some cases, death—for even the tiniest infractions.

It followed that all subjects be required to serve the state through productive activities. As the *Book of Lord Shang* had insisted, agriculture and military service were central to the well-being of the state. Individuals were encouraged to take up either or both of these as their livelihood; any other occupation was discouraged or prohibited, and work was compulsory for all. In order to suppress dissent and encourage approved thinking, only government-sanctioned history and literature were tolerated. In short, says Han Fei, the government must be like a mother lancing a boil on her infant: although the baby screams from the immediate pain, he or she is better for it in the end. The price exacted during the Qin's short duration, however, was considered by many contemporaries and nearly all succeeding generations of Chinese commentators to have been far too high. Yet its ruthless concentration of power and resources finally made possible the forced march to empire that no preceding regime had been able to effect.

The First Empire, 221 to 206 BCE

Qin's position as a small, poor, far western frontier state made it in many ways an unlikely candidate for empire. Its position and relative poverty, however, provided what at the time were unrecognized advantages over its opponents to the east. As a frontier society, encouraged by its emphasis on agriculture, it promised land to peasant cultivators as the state seized territory from nomadic peoples to the west. Qin's relative isolation also kept it out of many of the internecine fights that plagued the interior Zhou dependencies and eroded their resources; at the same time, policing its expanding territories encouraged military preparedness. By 350 BCE, Qin rulers began reorganizing the state along the lines envisioned in Lord Shang's treatise. In less than a century, they had eliminated the rump state of Zhou itself in 256 BCE and began the final subjugation of the dynasty's remaining states.

They then drove south and eliminated the opposition of the many tribal peoples below the state of Yue. From there, they drove into *yuenan* (south of Yue)—the northern part of modern Vietnam—thus beginning a long and often bitterly contested relationship with Southeast Asia. In the north and west, Qin armies fought a series of campaigns to drive nomadic peoples, especially the **Xiongnu**, from newly established borders and secure the trade routes into Central Asia.

Qin Shi Huangdi

The year 221 BCE saw the ascension of the Qin king Ying Zheng (r. 246–210 BCE), who now proclaimed himself **Qin Shi Huangdi**, the First Emperor of the Qin. With Li Si as his chancellor, he instituted the Legalist system throughout his newly won empire. With virtually unlimited resources and the ruthless drive of the First Emperor, the new regime began a series of projects during the next dozen years that are still astonishing today in their scope and ambition. The Chinese writing system was standardized, as were all weights, measures, and coinage. The people were organized into a system of mutual responsibility. Hundreds of thousands of laborers worked on roads, canals, and a multitude of irrigation and water conservancy projects. As a safeguard against attacks by northern nomadic peoples, tens of thousands of laborers were conscripted to cobble together the numerous defensive walls of the old Zhou states along the new empire's northern tier. Stretching over 1,400 miles, this massive project under the direction of Meng Tian (d. 210 BCE) would become the first iteration of the Great Wall of China.

What most people remember the First Emperor for, however, is the massive tomb complex he ordered built for himself, which, according to the *Records of the Grand Historian*, would signify "a rule that would be enjoyed by his sons and grandsons for 10,000 generations." A part of the tomb was discovered in 1974 by a peasant digging a well outside the modern city of Xi'an. Excavation of the complex unearthed an army of thousands of life-sized terracotta warriors with removable heads and individualized features marching in close-order drill to protect Qin Shi Huangdi after his death.

After a reign of a dozen years as emperor, Shi Huangdi died. Soon after his death, the empire erupted in rebellion. Ironically, the government's severe laws and punishments now worked against it as officials attempted to conceal the revolt's extent for fear of torture and execution. At the same time, Li Si provoked additional discontent by conspiring to keep the First Emperor's death a secret in order to rule as regent for the monarch's son. He was captured attempting to flee the rebellion and, as we saw in the opening vignette, executed in particularly grim fashion in 208 BCE. After a brief civil war and an attempt to revive a version of the old Zhou system of decentralized government, a general named Liu Bang put an end to the fighting and restored order to the region. He proclaimed himself emperor in 202 BCE and called his new dynasty the Han.

The Imperial Model: The Han Dynasty, 202 BCE to 220 CE

It is often said that the Qin forced the structure of empire on China, whereas the Han continued this practice behind a more benign ideology. The Han retained the centralized political system of Qin ministries and *commanderies*—districts

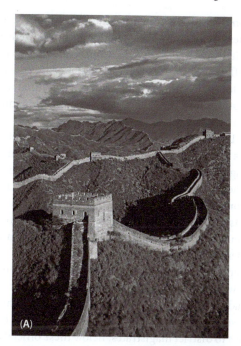

Qin Projects. (A) The Great Wall at Jinshanling Pass, northeast of Beijing. Though these sections of the wall were rebuilt in the early fifteenth century CE, this prospect shows some of the detail and intricacy of its fortification and also gives us an idea of the immensity of its structure. (B) One of the most important archaeological finds of the twentieth century was the tomb of the First Emperor on the outskirts of modern X'ian in 1974. Theories abound as to the reasons behind the individualized faces on the removable heads: One holds that they were taken from real soldiers; another is that they were symbolic of the emperor's universal rule over China's many peoples. The immense museum complex now at the site is one of China's most popular tourist attractions.

under military command—but combined these with more moderate Confucian ideals of government as a moral agent. Though its books were banned and many of its scholars buried alive under the Qin, Confucianism survived and, although there were key differences in the evolving model of its government-sponsored version from the ideas of Confucius and Mencius, it endured with some interruptions and modifications for over 2,000 years. It still retains considerable cultural power in East Asia even today.

In this sense, Liu Bang, who had taken the reign name of Gaozu (r. 202–195 BCE), represented a new kind of ruler. He had been a peasant and so had little stake or interest in bringing back the old feudal system of the Zhou. Having received from the Qin an administrative structure more or less intact, he retained it for ease of pacification and control. Within that structure, however, he enacted a number of reforms: token distributions of land were made to some members of the upper ranks; taxes and labor obligations widely reduced; and the most severe punishments under the Qin rescinded.

As the Han empire expanded—reaching a population in 2 CE comparable to that of Rome, with just under 60 million—so did its bureaucracy. Setting a pattern for the administration throughout much of the history of imperial China, officials were divided into graded ranks, ranging from the heads of imperial ministries to district magistrates. Below these officials were clan leaders and village headmen. Landowners were responsible for collecting taxes for themselves and their tenants, whereas the lower officials recorded the rates and amounts, kept track of the labor obligations of the district, and mobilized the people during emergencies (see Map 2.5).

Although Confucianism served as the foundation for the Han educational curriculum, Confucian doctrine had changed in some significant ways from the early teachings of Confucius and his disciples. Thus, the Confucianism that finally received state approval included elements reflecting the new realities of Han rule. A number of Confucian ideals—humane, righteous, filial behavior by the powerful—were linked with Daoist ideas of the ruler as divorced from day-to-day administration, and Legalist notions on centralization and the role of officials. The pre-dynastic ideal of passing rulership on to the country's most able men was again set aside: for stability and continuity's sake, it was decided that a dynasty had to be hereditary. The ideas of Heaven's Mandate and the dynastic cycle, however, were retained and strengthened.

Expanding the Empire

Like the idealized interpretation of the dynastic cycle favored by Chinese historians, the initial part of the Han era was marked by expansion and consolidation. A significant part of that expansion came during the reign of the emperor Wudi (141–87 BCE). In addition to once again driving into the Korean Peninsula and south into Vietnam, Wudi moved deep into the interior of Asia.

As had the Qin, and like many of his successors, Wudi faced the difficulty of defending the empire's long, sparsely populated northern and western boundaries from diverse groups of nomadic peoples, especially the Xiongnu. Hoping

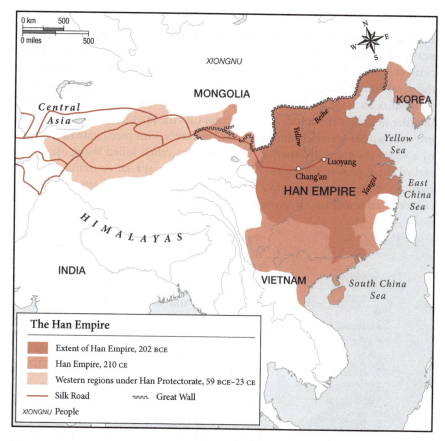

Map 2.5 The Han Empire

that a strong Chinese presence would discourage potential invasion, he encouraged the emigration of settlers to the region—a practice many of his successors, including present-day ones, would follow. He also extended and fortified the Great Wall. Because the Han had also expanded into the narrow corridor in the west adjacent to the Central Asian trade routes marking the developing Silk Road, Wudi and his successors mounted repeated expeditions into the area, built numerous guardhouses, and stationed garrisons along the way. In 89 CE after a lengthy conflict, the Han finally succeeded in destroying the Xiongnu state.

Wudi employed strategies that later became famous as the "loose rein" and "using barbarians to check barbarians": he tried diplomatic efforts, offering the Xiongu food and other necessary supplies, but when those efforts failed, he mounted military campaigns against them. As did the Romans with the Germanic peoples on their periphery, he also doled out favors to some groups as a way to cement their loyalties in order to use them to guard the frontiers against other, less pliable groups. The Han also adopted the practice of culturally assimilating nomadic peoples. Along with the imposition of Han rule came the Chinese writing system and the infusion of Confucian ideology and practices.

Downturn of the Dynastic Cycle

The Han era has traditionally been divided into the Former or Western Han (202 BCE–8 CE), and the Later or Eastern Han (24 CE–220). During a brief interval between 8 and 24 CE, the dynasty was temporarily interrupted when a relative of the royal family, Wang Mang (45 BCE–23 CE), seized power. Wang attempted to nationalize the land and redistribute it according to the old "well-field system" in order to reduce the abuses that had crept into the land tenure system and the growing gap between rich landowners and peasants. This precipitated a rebellion by a secret society called the Red Eyebrows. The rebels killed Wang Mang and sacked the capital of Chang'an. Although an imperial relative restored the dynasty, the capital was moved to a safer location in Luoyang, but the empire, now reduced in size and resources, never fully recovered.

Han Guardhouse. Han expansion into Central Asia and expanded trade along the routes of the Silk Road required garrisons and fortifications at key points beyond the Great Wall to protect travelers and settlers from attacks by nomadic peoples like the Xiongnu. The ceramic model illustrated here is typical of such outposts. The upper stories have protected balconies for archers and spearmen, whereas the lowest story provides a place for domestic animals such as the ducks depicted in the photo. Note the crossbowman barely discernible in the left rear of the upper story.

For a time, however, the general prosperity of the regime continued to mask its weaknesses and Chinese historians would label the Later Han as one of China's four great "Restorations"—periods during which dynasties in decline were able to temporarily recover their dynamism. By the late second century CE, however, the restored dynasty was showing signs of strain. In a pattern that would be repeated a number of times in future dynasties, ambitious internal improvements ordered by Han emperors were increasingly carried out by *corvée* labor. Like Rome during its "crisis of the third century," the increased costs of defense, growing labor obligations for peasant cultivators, and loss of arable land led to an accelerating decline. As if to underscore the rhythms of the dynastic cycle, internal battles within the imperial family, aggravated by the increasing regional power of Han generals, and the rise of the Daoist Yellow Turbans after 184 CE, finally brought the Han Dynasty to an end in 220 CE.

The Centuries of Fragmentation, 220 to 589 CE

The long period of turmoil and fragmentation between the end of the Han era and reunification under the Sui Dynasty (589–618) is traditionally divided into the era of the Three Kingdoms (220–280), the overlapping Six Dynasties Period (222–589), and the also overlapping period of the North and South Dynasties (317–589). As had been the pattern with the Zhou and the Qin, it would be a people on the periphery of the Chinese world that would ultimately create the next dynasty and recreate the empire (see Map 2.6).

In this case, it was the eastern Mongolian people known as the Toba, part of a larger group the Chinese called *Xianbei*, who established the state of Northern Wei (386–585) along the old northern Chinese heartland of the Yellow River basin. We noted earlier how the Han pursued policies of sinification toward outside peoples. For the Toba, the power of Chinese civilization was even greater in attracting and ultimately assimilating those moving into Chinese territory. By the beginning of the sixth century, the descendants of the Toba and nomadic groups ranging across the borders of Northern Wei and neighboring states had formed a kind of ethnically hybrid society—taking Chinese names, marrying into the leading families, reviving old imperial rites, and tackling the perennial problem of land reform. In organizing a program of land redistribution to the peasants, they helped pave the way for the return of centralized administration, military service, and tax collection. In this respect, Northern Wei provided a prototype for a renewed bid for empire. In 589, a general named Yang Jian succeeded in uniting most of the old Han territories and called the reunified dynasty the Sui.

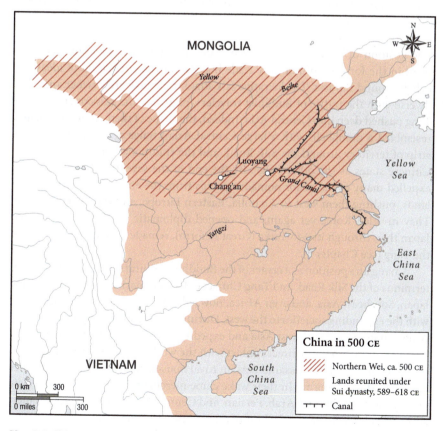

Map 2.6 China in 500 CE

Like the Qin and Han before them, the Sui pushed into Korea in their zeal to rebuild the empire, once again opening a conduit for a flow of Chinese influence that would soon spread in a thoroughgoing way to Japan. Like the Qin as well, the forcefulness with which they pursued empire building prompted unrest among the people. Moreover, their use of forced labor for monumental building projects, including huge palaces, roads, and perhaps most ambitious of all, the **Grand Canal**, created unrest as well.

Linking the Yangzi River with the Yellow River, the Grand Canal actually consists of several canals and accompanying natural water systems stretching for 1,550 miles, and is still in use today. Through the remainder of the imperial period, it facilitated the shipment of large quantities of tax rice and other food crops from the south directly to the capital at Chang'an. The canal would ultimately be extended even further to the Beihe in order to service the later capital at Beijing.

A rebellion following the death of the second Sui emperor, Yangdi, brought the precocious 16-year-old Li Shimin to power. Li encouraged his father, Li Yuan, the duke of Tang, to rebel and with him had the new Sui emperor killed. Supporting his father's bid for the throne, he cofounded the Tang Dynasty in 618. After a few years, he forced his father, who had taken the reign name of Gaozu, to abdicate, and Li assumed power in his own right in 627 as the emperor Taizong.

China's Cosmopolitan Age: The Tang Dynasty, 618 to 907

The position of Tang China, and especially its capital at Chang'an, made it a pivot in the fortunes of not only trade but also in the circulation of ideas and beliefs around Eurasia. The lucrative Silk Road trade now grew richer and more diverse with the traffic of Buddhist travelers, pilgrims, and missionaries, as the Tang pushed deep into Central Asia. Indeed, the shape of their empire ultimately resembled a dumbbell, with a large Central Asian bulge at one end, a narrow strip of territory around the Silk Road, and the traditional territories of earlier Chinese states as the other bulge. By the end of the seventh century, they had expelled many of the major nomadic groups from the empire's western borderlands, pushing them west to Anatolia, Eastern Europe, and the Mediterranean. They invaded Korea yet again, and opened diplomatic relations with Yamato Japan that, through its 645 Taika (Great Reform), remade itself along the lines of the Tang (see Chapter 3).

Chang'an's position as a center of the Buddhist cultural sphere and the eastern terminus of the Silk Road, and Tang China's enhanced maritime trade with India, Japan, Southeast Asia, and even Africa, now led to China's first direct encounters with the expanding societies to the west. During the seventh and eighth centuries, Arab conquests in Southwest Asia and expeditionary forces driving into Central Asia brought China into direct contact with the world of Islam. Even before this, in 674, members of the Sassanid Persian royal house fled advancing Arab armies and arrived in Chang'an. In their wake came merchants who established a taste among the Tang elites for Arab, Persian, and Central Asian musical forms, dance, silver and glass artwork, and a host of other items (see Map 2.7).

China's major cities now had quarters set aside for foreign traders, which by the end of the Tang era included Jews, Nestorian Christians, Zoroastrians,

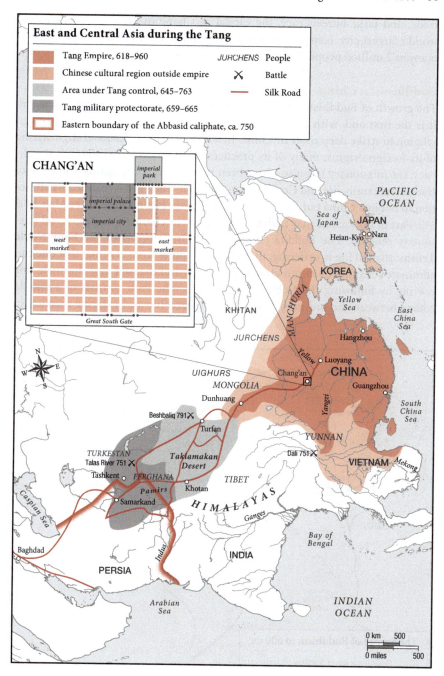

Map 2.7 East and Central Asia during the Tang

members of the major Indian traditions, and the beginnings of what would one day be a substantial Muslim minority. Arab and Indian intermediaries extended trade from China all the way to the East African coast and past the Mediterranean to the developing lands of Europe. With the expanding empire, flourishing trade, and large bureaucracy, the capital of Chang'an grew into perhaps the world's largest city, comparable in size to Baghdad and Constantinople, with as many as 2 million people living in its metropolitan area.

Buddhism in China

The growth of Buddhism in China is to some extent a surprising phenomenon. It is the first and, with the exception of Islam in some areas, the only foreign religion to strike deep roots in China. In addition to the occasional stigmatizing of its foreign origins, many of its practices—monasticism, egalitarianism, celibacy, the missionary impulse—have been regarded as going against the grain of traditional family life and Confucian virtue. Why then has it retained its attraction in not just China but East Asia as a whole over two millennia (see Map 2.8)?

Part of the answer may perhaps be found in its character as a universal missionary religion. The Buddha ("Enlightened One") preached the **Four Noble Truths**: that all life is suffering; that suffering comes from craving; that one can eliminate suffering by eliminating this craving; and that one can eliminate this craving by following the Noble Eightfold Path. The Path consists of a middle course between the ordinary pursuits of civilized life and extreme asceticism,

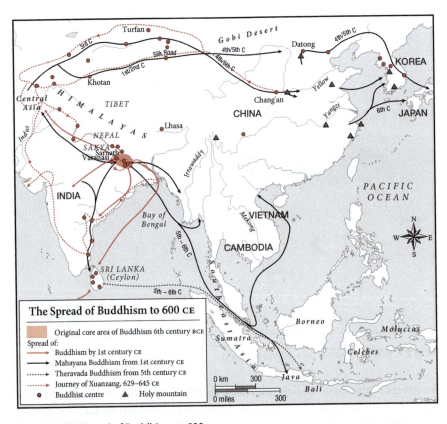

Map 2.8 The Spread of Buddhism to 600 CE

and calls for nonviolence toward sentient beings, kindness, right conduct, and "mindfulness," in order to reach a state of calm nonattachment to the things of this world. One may then transcend the state of constant death and rebirth as one apprehends universal truth and the karmic soul "blows out" like a candle—the origin of the term *nirvana*.

Though born of the Indian religious traditions that developed into Hinduism, followers of the new belief insisted from the beginning that it was applicable to all. Thus, Buddhism was actively propagated by its adherents. By the mid-first century CE, when it is initially mentioned in Chinese accounts, Buddhism had already split into the major divisions of Theravada (Hinayana), which had established itself in southern India and Sri Lanka, and was moving into Southeast Asia; and Mahayana, which would be established in China, Tibet, Mongolia, Korea, Vietnam, and Japan.

PATTERNS UP-CLOSE

Creating an East Asian Buddhist Culture

The incompatibility of the Chinese written language with the Sanskrit and Pali Buddhist scriptures meant that missionaries had to rely heavily on transliterations, borrow extensively from Daoist terminology, and invent a new and diverse vocabulary of Chinese terms. Over the next several centuries, this eclecticism resulted in a proliferation of sects and a growing need on the part of Chinese, and later, Korean, Japanese, and Vietnamese, converts to travel to India for study and guidance.

The travel account of the Chinese monk and early pilgrim Fa Xian, who journeyed throughout Central Asia and India from 399 to 414 in search of Buddhist works, contributed greatly toward understanding the growing Buddhist world. It was the more famous pilgrim Xuanzang (596–664), however, who was destined to have the larger impact. Xuanzang journeyed through Central Asia and Afghanistan to India in 623 and remained for sixteen years. His travels took him nearly 10,000 miles, and he brought back an extensive collection of scriptures written in Pali on palm leaves, many of which are still housed in the Great Wild Goose Pagoda he had built just outside Xi'an. His travels were later immortalized in the popular sixteenth-century collection of fabulous tales called *A Journey to the West*. Xuanzang founded an imperially sponsored translation bureau at the Great Wild Goose Pagoda and the *Faxiang* "Consciousness Only" school he popularized was influential not only in China but in Korea, Japan, and Vietnam as well. It arrived separately from India in Tibet, and later found adherents among the Mongols. Some of Xuanzong's translations are still used today.

(*continued*)

The four centuries between the collapse of the Han and the ascendancy of the Tang were marked by the founding of several of the most important schools of East Asian Buddhism. By the fifth century, a school of popular devotion to *Amida*, the **Buddha of the Pure Land**, was spreading rapidly in China. For Pure Land adherents, no immersion in the texts is necessary for enlightenment: merely invoking Amida's name is sufficient for salvation. Even today, it remains the most popular Buddhist sect in East Asia. Amida is often pictured with the bodhisattva *Guanyin*—Kannon in Japan—the Goddess of Mercy who, like the Virgin Mary in Catholicism, is frequently invoked during times of peril. Another influential Buddhist school, *Tiantai*, centered on contemplation of a scripture called the Lotus Sutra as a vehicle to enlightenment. These schools exercised considerable influence over both the Tang and the Japanese court at Heian during the eighth and ninth centuries, and are widely practiced in Korea and Vietnam as well.

Finally, one rather demanding Buddhist school that later achieved fame, if not widespread popularity, was *Chan*—more widely known by its Japanese name: Zen. Chan departs from both the devotional and scriptural

Amida Buddha. Originally incorporating aspects of both male and female, Guanyin (also spelled Kuan-yin) came to be depicted as female as Buddhism became firmly established in China. For Pure Land adherents, she was the bodhisattva invoked in times of extreme peril, and "the miracles of Guanyin" was a favorite theme of Chinese and Japanese artists.

paths of Pure Land and Tiantai in that enlightenment comes through a tightly supervised program of carefully regulated activities under the guidance of a master. The intense give and take between master and pupil, the discipline involved in performing humble tasks, the contemplation of paradoxical questions, and, in some cases, meditation are all meant to generate an intuitive flash of enlightenment. Although limited in its influence in China, the emphasis on discipline and obedience made Zen the preferred Buddhist school of Japan's warrior aristocracy after the twelfth century. Like the other schools mentioned here, it too was practiced in Vietnam and Korea. The prevalence of all these Buddhist sects, and the classical Chinese texts used to propagate them, thus helped to create a common high culture throughout East Asia and, in the case of popular cults like Pure Land, among ordinary people as well.

The Period of Expansion: Emperor Taizong

Having killed his two brothers and forced his father to abdicate, Li Shimin acceded to the throne as Taizong in 627 and began a reign of more than two decades. He led expeditions into Central Asia, where he defeated both eastern and western branches of the Turks and forced them to recognize him as their *khan* or leader. Tibet had created a powerful kingdom under King Srong-btsan-sgam-po that stretched from modern Kashmir to Qinghai. Taizong led the first Chinese forays into the kingdom and sent his daughter Wencheng to marry the king in 641. During Taizong's reign, Tang China was arguably the world's most powerful and prosperous empire.

Taizong was also central to the development of China's long-standing law code, the *Tanglu*. The code's 502 articles, each with commentaries, subcommentaries, and model questions, tied together the large but less systematic corpus of edicts and customary law accumulated over the years and inherited from the Han and Sui, and became a model for similar codes throughout East Asia.

Although the later Song examination system is often cited as the model for that of the imperial system as a whole, the Tang routinized the process and laid out its basic curriculum and format. The tests was open to all males whose fathers were not artisans or merchants. The curriculum for the first test was based on the Five Confucian Classics, whereas that of the second exam was oriented more toward practical elements of administration as well as such aesthetic skills as essay and poetry writing.

"Emperor" Wu

Following Taizong's death in 649, his son acceded the throne as Gaozong. Historians generally view him as consumed with court intrigues and not terribly effective. However, his wife, Wu Zetian (r. 684–705), was one of the most powerful and intriguing figures of East Asian history. She is the most notable exemplar of both the influence of Buddhism and the surprising degree of agency possible for elite women of the era. The daughter of a public works official, she spent a brief period as an imperial servant before becoming a Buddhist nun, only to return to the palace as a concubine of Taizong. By all accounts, she was beautiful, highly educated, and ruthless in exploiting opportunities for advancement at court.

Having married Taizong's son, Gaozong, who died in December 683, she ruled as Empress Dowager and as regent for her son, the emperor Ruizong. In reality, however, she had effectively held power since Gaozong's later years. In order to maintain it, she kept Ruizong isolated in the palace. Wu's position was precarious as well, but many years at court had made her an adroit political maneuverer. Realizing that the only sure way to keep power was to rule in her own right, she took the risky step of inaugurating a new Zhou Dynasty. No woman before her (and none since) had ever ruled directly as an empress, let alone a claimant to the Mandate of Heaven as a dynastic founder. Partly to deflect such criticism, she insisted on the political title of "emperor" rather than "empress," which implied consort status. A devout Buddhist, she took the bold step of declaring Buddhism the state religion, another precedent-shattering act. The final step came in 693, when she took the Buddhist title "Divine Empress (Emperor) Who Rules the Universe."

Even the most hostile chroniclers of her reign admit that she was a highly capable ruler. She was careful to pick able administrators and widened the pool of examination candidates to classes that had previously been excluded. Though her military record was somewhat spotty, her policy of establishing farmer-soldier colonies added a degree of stability to a number of frontier areas. Her practice of dispensing relief to the common people also ensured her general popularity. On the other hand, she maintained a highly efficient secret police apparatus and encouraged informers from all classes. On several occasions, she launched massacres of real and alleged conspirators. Such enemies multiplied as her reign continued because the act of creating her own dynasty and new titles for herself was considered by many an act of usurpation. It ultimately provoked a rebellion, which she handily suppressed until her death from natural causes in 705.

Empress Wu. The Empress Wu Zetian, one of the most powerful Tang dynasty rulers and perhaps the most colorful. She reigned from 684 to 705 CE and successfully fought off several attempts to unseat her. In her devotion to Buddhism, she declared it the new state religion and took the title of "Divine Empress Who Rules the Universe." In 690, she declared the founding of a new Zhou Dynasty although the new regime died with her in 705.

Cosmopolitan Autumn

The first half of the eighth century is often seen as a golden age both for the Tang and for imperial China itself under the long reign of Xuanzong, whose 43-year rule (712–756) proved to be the dynasty's longest. The prosperity of the Tang Empire expanded, but toward midcentury many of the problems of uneven growth that had plagued the Han Dynasty began to reassert themselves. For example, as the center of population continued to move south, the northern regions languished in relative poverty while the capital grew economically isolated. Moreover, as maritime trade grew and ports increased in size and number, the connecting infrastructure of roads, courier stations, and especially canals required ever more investment and attention. This was a particularly acute problem in the case of communication with the capital. As an administrative center and trade crossroads, Chang'an had ballooned to a size that was now unsustainable without constant grain shipments from the south—and its isolation made it particularly vulnerable to attack.

Xuanzong's efforts to control military outposts along the Silk Road, with its lucrative trade and Buddhist shrines, brought the empire into conflict with Arab expansion as the century wore on. Tang armies suffered a decisive defeat by the Arabs in 751 at Talas in Central Asia. This loss followed a series of setbacks at the hands of the Tibetans and Uyghurs from 745 to 750, and simultaneous uprisings in the border areas of Manchuria, Korea, and the southern province of Yunnan. From 755 to 762, a revolt led by Tang general An Lushan devastated large sections of the empire and resulted in heavy land taxes after its suppression. As with the Later Han, the dynasty was now in a downward spiral from which recovery seemed increasingly unlikely.

For the next century and a half, some economic and political recovery did, in fact, occur, but the problems of rebuilding and revenue loss persisted, accompanied by a questioning of a number of the premises of the regime, particularly by the Confucians. The Confucians questioned the role of the "foreign" faith of Buddhism, which received material and political support from the Tang. At the same time, Buddhist monasteries, which paid no taxes, were tempting targets for an increasingly cash-strapped government. In 845, the Tang forcibly seized all Buddhist holdings, although followers were allowed to continue their religious practice. Sporadic civil war continued for the remainder of the century, leading to the collapse of the dynasty in 907. China again entered a period of disunity as regional states battled for control. None of these states would be victorious until the emergence of the Song in 960.

An Early Modern Period? The Song

The Song era is considered by many to mark the beginning of the "early modern" era of Chinese history. During the Song dynasties, China in many ways achieved its greatest degree of sophistication in terms of material culture, technology, ideas, economics, and the amenities of urban living. Its short-lived incorporation into the huge empire of the Mongols would again open the country to foreign influence and help spread Chinese influence westward, most famously through the accounts of the travelers Marco Polo and Ibn Battuta.

Like the Tang, the Song instituted a strong central government based on merit rather than heredity. They broadened the eligibility of those seeking to take the civil service exams even further, and with increased opportunities to join government service, a huge bureaucracy emerged. This unwieldy system placed an enormous financial strain on the state that, to secure revenue, placed a heavy tax burden on the populace. This constant demand for revenue by the state would ultimately lead to rebellion.

The need for administrative reform spurred the official Wang Anshi (1021–1086) to propose a series of measures designed to increase imperial control over the economy and reduce the power of local interests. Wang proposed state licensing of both agricultural and commercial enterprises, the abolition of forced labor, and the creation of a system of government pawnshops to loan money at reduced rates in order to break the power of usurers and middlemen. He also urged greatly reducing the number of bureaucratic positions in order to lessen the power of local officials. Opposition to his proposed reforms forced Wang from office in 1076.

In addition to such internal problems, the regime faced external challenges as well. Because the Tang had lost much of northern China, including the Silk Road, to nomadic groups, Song lands from the start were substantially smaller than those of their predecessors. Although the new dynasty spent a great deal of treasure and energy to maintain a professional army of more than 1.5 million as well as a formidable navy, this massive force ultimately proved ineffective against the expert and more mobile militaries of invading nomadic groups. The Song also tried careful diplomacy and bribery to maintain its stronghold; such efforts, however, were unable to keep the northern part of the empire from falling to the nomadic Jurchens in 1127. Forced to abandon their capital at Kaifeng on the Grand Canal, the Song created a new capital at Linan, the modern city of Hangzhou.

The Southern Song Remnant

The decreased size of this Southern Song empire resulted in an even more southern-oriented and urbanized economy. The new capital at Linan/Hangzhou, described by Marco Polo as the most beautiful city in the world, may also have been the largest, with a population estimated at 1.5 million. Despite the bureaucracy's disdain for the merchant and artisan classes, the state had always recognized the potential of commerce to generate revenue. Thus, while attempting to bring the largest enterprises under state control, the government pursued measures to facilitate trade, such as printing the world's first paper notes, minting coins, and restraining usury. These practices, combined with an excellent system of roads and canals, fostered the development of a national market. The Song conducted a lively overseas trade, and Chinese merchants established colonies in major ports throughout Southeast Asia and the Indian Ocean.

The Mongol Conquest

Commercial success, however, could not save the Song from further invasion by neighboring nomadic peoples. For centuries, disparate groups of nomadic Altaic-speaking Mongols, known under a variety of names in Chinese chronicles and reports, had lived as loosely organized tribes and clans in eastern Central Asia. There was no real push to unite these groups until the rise to power of the

Song Naval Technology. The Song navy had a wide array of weapons at its disposal, including gunpowder, which undoubtedly gave it a technological edge over its adversaries. The use of "fire arrows"—rockets mounted to arrow shafts—was recorded during a battle with the Mongols in 1232. Song naval vessels were equipped with missiles and even employed ships with detachable sections filled with explosives with which to ram opponents.

Mongol leader, Temujin (1167—1227). As we will see in more detail in Chapter 4, Temujin united the various Mongol groups into one confederation in 1206. He was given the title of *Chinggis* or *Genghis Khan* ("Universal Ruler") of the united Mongol confederation.

While subduing much of the rest of Eurasia, the Mongols launched a half-century of steady encroachment on northern China. Genghis Khan's grandson, Khubilai Khan, resumed the Mongol offensive in southern China after the Southern Song unwisely attempted to enlist Mongol aid against the Jurchens. Linan/Hang-zhou fell to the Mongols in 1276, and the dynasty ended with the death of the young Song emperor in 1279 as he attempted to flee by sea. In 1280, Khubilai proclaimed the Yuan Dynasty, which then placed China in an empire spanning all of Eurasia from Korea to the interior of Poland, and probing as far as Vienna, Java, and Japan.

ECONOMICS, SOCIETY, AND GENDER IN EARLY IMPERIAL CHINA

Throughout Chinese history, the various dynasties actively encouraged and supported agriculture as the basis of the domestic economy, yet from the Han Dynasty on, China exported far more in luxury goods and technology than it imported. The Confucian view of the pursuit of profit as corrupting, however, meant that Chinese governments seldom encouraged merchants, and generally preferred to adopt a passive, but controlling role.

Industry and Commerce

Goods made in and distributed throughout the empire by the time of the Han included some of the best-known items of Chinese production. By the first century CE, Chinese manufacturers were making paper using a suspension of mashed plant fibers filtered through a fine-mesh screen and set aside to dry. By this time, too, artisans were producing a kind of "proto-porcelain" that, with increasing refinement, would be known in the succeeding centuries to the outside world as "china." By the second century CE, the Chinese had perfected silk production techniques developed over millennia and had become world leaders in textile weaving. Both treadle and water-powered looms were in widespread use, and bolts of silk of standardized sizes and designs were produced for export. Supply could barely keep pace with demand, especially in Persia and Rome—both of which ultimately acquired the skills and materials to start their own silk industries.

As noted earlier, the Chinese were also producing cast iron in huge foundries. According to one estimate, by 2 CE, there were no less than 48 major ironworks in north China, while the mining industry as a whole may have employed as many as 100,000 people. The foundries, which produced ingots of standardized sizes and weights, used sophisticated systems of forced-air control, including water-powered bellows. Salt mines employed complex gearing for lifting brine from deep wells, systems of bamboo piping for transferring it, and evaporators fired by natural gas for extracting the salt. Because of the enormous productivity of the ironmaking and salt-mining industries, the government continually sought ways to regulate and control them.

The Silk Road and infrastructural improvements such as the Grand Canal had vastly expanded the internal and external connections of the Chinese economy. The dramatic extension of maritime and caravan trade from the seventh century on under the Tang spread Chinese technology further abroad and brought new products into the empire. For example, tea, imported from Southeast Asia, quickly established itself as the beverage of choice during the Tang and vied with silk for supremacy as a cash crop during the Song. Tea had a profound effect on the overall health of the population in China, Vietnam, Korea, Japan, and Central Asia. The simple act of boiling water renders it potable, and the tea itself contains a number of healthful, even medicinal, properties.

Agricultural Productivity

A number of technical and systemic improvements steadily increased agricultural productivity during this period. In addition to such staples as wheat, millet, and barley in the north, and rice in the south, a wide variety of semi-tropical fruits and vegetables were also cultivated within the empire. New strains of rice introduced during Tang and Song times resulted in larger harvests on more marginal land. Champa rice, a key variety imported from Southeast Asia in the eleventh century, allowed three crops per year in suitable areas. The vastly expanded rice productivity helped prompt a huge increase in the empire's population, per-haps topping 100 million during the Northern Song era. Trade with Central Asia had introduced wine grapes, and fermented grain beverages had also become a substantial industry. New techniques of crop rotation, fertilization, and plowing were gradually introduced, as were the breast-strap harness for draft animals and the wheelbarrow; oxen- and later horse-drawn, iron-tipped plows; treadle hammers; undershot, overshot, and Pelton-type waterwheels; the foot-powered "dragon" chain pump for irrigation; and the *fengche*—a hand-cranked winnow-ing machine with an internal fan to blow the chaff from the grain. With this basic, reliable technology, China led the world in agricultural productivity until the eighteenth century.

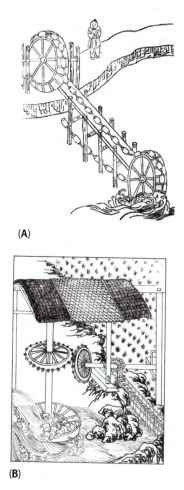

(A)

(B)

Han Era Technology. By the first century CE, Chinese sophistication in crafts and labor-saving devices could be seen in a number of areas. Although the illustrations here are from the famous seventeenth-century compendium of technology *Tiangong kaiwu* (The Works of Nature and Man), both of them illustrate techniques in use during the Han period: undershot water-powered dragon pump (A), and Pelton-type geared dragon pump (B).

By the time of the late Han, China's old aristocracy had largely died out, its place at the top of the social hierarchy taken by the so-called **scholar-gentry**—the educated large landholders from which the bulk of the Confucian bureaucracy was drawn. Despite the elimination of the old aristocracy, however, landlord holdings continued to expand. Since the upper ranks of the landowners and bureaucracy were either exempt from taxes or paid reduced amounts, the tax burden fell increasingly on tenants and owners of small parcels of land. Poor harvests or bad weather, particularly in the arid north and west, made the situation even worse for those already heavily taxed. Because the north, despite its elaborate irrigation works, was far less productive and more prone to crop failure than the south, it was also proportionally more heavily taxed.

Such problems made land reform and redistribution an ongoing concern. The Tang, for example, continued the policy of land redistribution begun during the brief Sui Dynasty by allotting each peasant family a tract of 100 *mou*, only one fifth of which was inheritable, whereas the remainder reverted to the state for redistribution. Although the Tang land redistribution policy resulted in a relatively high level of prosperity, absentee landlordism, tenancy, and usury also rose again, particularly during times of economic stress. Conditions were similar under the Song. The continual cycle of landlordism and tenancy, followed by attempts at land reform and redistribution, marked every dynasty and modern government down to the People's Republic's Four Modernizations of the 1970s and 1980s.

Gender and Family

With the rise of the imperial bureaucracy during the Han, and the increasing emphasis on filial piety within its new Confucian curriculum, a more rigidly hierarchical, patriarchal model of proper women's behavior developed in imperial China. Along the way, the emphasis on sons as carriers of the ancestral line, and their potential to win admission to official state service, led to a devaluing of daughters. In times of severe economic stress when families had difficulty supporting several children, young girls were the first to suffer. Despite the greater flexibility among elites during the Tang period, families, especially in rural areas, would sometimes sell their daughters into prostitution or even kill female infants. By the Song era, problems relating to the treatment of young girls had become so acute that China's first foundling hospitals were opened in 1138.

Other tensions in the patterns of both rural and urban life tended to become intensified in the lives of women and girls as well. Although recent work has shown that the experiences of Chinese women of all classes offered considerably more agency than previously supposed, their lives were generally far more circumscribed than those of men. On the one hand, the education of upper-class women tended increasingly toward those areas aimed at making them more marriageable. Study of proper Confucian etiquette—as outlined in Ban Zhao's *Admonitions for Women*—light verse, and a heavy dose of filial piety occupied a large portion of their curriculum. Among the ideals for women one finds chastity, loyalty, and obedience high on the list. Marriage and property laws were set up to reinforce these qualities—though during the Tang, Empress Wu attempted to equalize them.

In addition to the premium placed on mourning by both sexes, widows were expected to remain single out of duty and loyalty to their departed, and obedient to the eldest son. Indeed, widows who remarried forfeited all inherited property to their husbands' closest male relative—including what remained of the dowry they had originally brought with them. The painful custom of *foot-binding*, originating during the Song, stubbornly continued until its final suppression under the People's Republic after 1949.

Even within these strictures, many women were highly educated, dynamic, and exercised considerable resourcefulness and agency. The noted Han historian Ban Zhao (45–116), for example, came from the most prominent family of historical scholars of her time, including her father Ban Biao and her brother Ban Gu. It was she who, following the death of her brother, was made chief court historian and finished his work, the *Han Shu*. Ban Gu's daughters also became noted historians.

From the fifth century on, the popularity of monastic Buddhism created alternatives for women and men fleeing family pressures. Those engaged in Buddhist schools that required extensive scriptural study became highly educated, and the communities themselves, like Christian monasteries in Europe, often owned large tracts of land and wielded considerable local influence. Especially after the advent of block printing in the eighth century, Buddhism became a powerful force for spreading literacy.

At the same time, the relative strictness of the practices regulating sexual and family life varied, particularly among the high officials and the growing urban commercial classes. Foreign influences and fashions also affected behavior, particularly in Chang'an and places involved in international trade. Tantric Buddhist and Daoist sexual practices, which were used by their followers as means of spiritual liberation, undoubtedly contributed to a more relaxed approach to relations between men and women during the Tang and Song

THOUGHT, SCIENCE, AND TECHNOLOGY

One of the signal developments of the imperial period was the institutionalization of the writing of history. Control of the past was an important preoccupation for Chinese and other East Asian rulers as it spelled out their present relationship to the dynastic cycle and Mandate of Heaven. In terms of intellectual activity, Buddhism played a prominent role, though its centrality would be replaced by the neo-Confucian philosophies developed during the Song era. As we noted above, China was also perhaps the leading technology driver during this time.

The Legacy of the Han Historians

For the men and women charged with writing about the past, much like modern historians, the aim was accurate transmission of information and analysis of events in the service of a larger vision of the direction and purpose of human history. History was cyclical: human events, as manifestations of the great universal cycles of being, are a constant succession of birth, growth, decay, death, and re-birth, in which older ideas of the Mandate of Heaven, dynastic cycles, and *yin* and *yang* theory are imbedded. The moral lessons learned are therefore tied to actions taken at various stages of these cycles.

The basic format of long-term history was laid out by the father and son team of Sima Tan (d. 110 BCE) and Sima Qian (145–86 BCE). Their *Shiji* (The Records of the Grand Historian) attempts the first complete history of the Chinese people from the mythical Yellow Emperor to their own time. One particularly valuable section that became a staple of later histories was a survey of non-Chinese peoples encountered along with their habits, customs, religions, geography, and other significant traits. Hence, the Han records give us our first written accounts of Japan and other places and peoples on the Chinese periphery.

Several generations later, the Ban family comprised another dynasty of Han court historians. Writing after the Wang Mang interval, Ban Biao (3–54 CE) and his son Ban Gu (32–92 CE) pioneered the writing of dynastic history with their *History of the Former Han*, which laid out the format that all subsequent dynastic histories followed. As we noted above, Ban Gu's daughters were also scholars and writers and his sister Ban Zhao (48–116 CE) carried on the family tradition of history writing and contributed her treatise on proper women's behavior, *Admonitions for Women*.

Accounts of the historians' activities themselves may be found in the *Hou Hanshu, The History of the Latter Han*, written after the fall of the dynasty by Fan Ye (398–446 CE). Another epic historical compendium, in this case extending from the Warring States Period to the time of the author (1076), came from the brush of Sima Guang in his *Zizhi Tongjian* of the Song Dynasty. The long period of the intermingling of Confucianism with Buddhist, Daoist, and other systems of thought forced an extensive reformulation of its core concepts. By the twelfth century, this reformulation had matured into **neo-Confucianism**, which combined the moral core of Confucian ethics with a new emphasis on speculative philosophy.

Neo-Confucianism

Neo-Confucianism holds that one cannot sit passively and wait for enlightenment, as the Buddhists were said to do, but must actively "seek truth through facts" in order to understand correctly the relationships of form (*li*) and substance (*qi*), as they govern the constitution of the totality, or Great Ultimate (*taiji*). Concerned with answering the Buddhist doctrine of impermanence, neo-Confucianism taught that just as self-cultivation of Confucian virtues is the means of discovering one's true *li*, so investigation of the physical world is a means of discovering one's place in the larger *li* of the Great Ultimate. Hence, knowledge is a cumulative, unified whole, with the moral dimension of such understanding taking precedence over mere observation. This vision of neo-Confucianism was propounded by the Cheng brothers, Hao (1032–1085) and Yi (1033–1107), and perfected by Zhu Xi (Chu Hsi, 1129–1200), generally recognized as the leading neo-Confucian thinker. Not surprisingly, these ideas came to prominence during the Song period, riding a wave of anti-Buddhist reaction in the wake of the fall of the Tang. The incorporation of Buddhist approaches to cosmology made the philosophy attractive to those who were intrigued by inquiries into the nature of the universe while retaining the Chinese ethical precepts of family relationships and behavior. Variations of these schools dominated Confucian thought in Tokugawa Japan, Korea, and Vietnam as well.

Poetry, Painting, and Calligraphy

To a considerable degree, Chinese concepts of aesthetics, especially those developed during the Tang and Song periods, became the founding principles for the arts throughout East Asia. The most important developments during this period were the maturation of three disciplines: poetry, painting, and calligraphy. These three disciplines are considered closely interrelated and governed by the same overriding principles. Central to each discipline is the idea of spontaneous creation as a reflection of the inner state of the artist.

Tang and Song poetry, especially the compressed "regulated verse" of eight five-character lines, and the terse four-line "cut-off line" poems attempt to do the same thing: suggest powerful emotions or themes in minimalist fashion. For example, the deep Confucian sensibilities of the Tang poet Du Fu (712–770) are often detectable in his emotionally charged poems such as "Mourning Chen Tao." Li Bai (or Li Bo, 701–762), his friend, was in many ways the opposite in both the way he lived his life and in the emotions he sought to stir. Carefree, witty, a lover of wine and women—according to legend, he drowned after a drinking bout attempting to "embrace the moon" reflected in the water—his poetry evokes happier moments, but frequently conveying them as fleeting and thus bittersweet.

A noted exemplar of Song literary art is the woman poet Li Qingzhao (1084–1151; some sources give 1155). She and her husband, the scholar and official Zhao Mingcheng (1081–1129), led a life that seemed to defy convention at almost every turn. Theirs was a passionate, childless, and intellectually engaging union between two accomplished literary figures. Moreover, it was Li's work that was best known and received the most

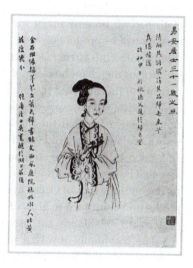

Li Qingzhao. China's most famous woman poet, Li Qingzhao (1084–1151) was a renowned writer and admired calligrapher. Many of her works mourn the loss of her husband, the official Zhao Mingcheng, with whom she shared a passionate interest in art and literary pursuits. According to some accounts, she later remarried a man named Zhang Ruzhou, but his ill-treatment of Li Qingzhao pushed her to divorce him in a few months—both considered transgressive acts for Chinese women. In this portrait, her pseudonym Yi'an Jushi is used and the large character title reads, "A picture of Yi'an Jushi [age] 31 years."

acclaim among her contemporaries and whose intellectual legacy was celebrated long after her death. Even today, she is recognized as China's greatest woman poet. Works of art combining all three disciplines set an artistic and formal standard followed down to the present. Frequently, the master they sought to copy in this regard was Wang Xizhi (303–361), who remains to this day the supreme stylist of calligraphy.

Technological Leadership

As was the case during the period of the Qin and the Han, the Tang through the Southern Song saw an unprecedented number of technological innovations that would have a profound effect inside and outside the empire. The horse collar, moldboard plow, wheelbarrow, advanced iron casting, compass, gunpowder, porcelain, and paper diffused widely throughout Eurasia and the Indian Ocean basin. By the height of the Song period, tea, silk, porcelain, paper, and cotton cloth had all become major industries and China dominated—in some cases, monopolized—production and distribution of all of them. An increasingly sophisticated infrastructure of commercial credit, printed paper money, and insurance for merchant houses and their agents supported and secured China's vast network of industry and trade.

Printing with movable block type had been developed as early as the eighth century, ensuring that the literatures of China, Japan, and Korea would have wide circulation. As it did later in Europe, printing helped the spread of literacy and aided in fostering a common literary and religious culture. The compass, invented by the Chinese and routinely used on their trading vessels, guided ships throughout the Indian Ocean and Southeast Asia. China's early sophistication in production continued to grow: during the Song, the empire's annual production of steel, at 150,000 tons, surpassed that of all of Europe in 1700.

The techniques involved in generating the extremely high temperatures required for steel were also transferable to porcelain production. Although there is debate about when the breakthroughs resulting in true porcelain first occurred, by the Tang period, distinctive brown and green glazed figures, often depicting the colorful parade of peoples and animals of the caravan trade, were widely traded. Following centuries of experimentation with *kaolin* clays, glazing mixes, and extremely high firing temperatures, Song craftsmen hit upon the formula for creating the world's most celebrated pottery. Elegant white and *celadon* (a shade of green) porcelain vessels were manufactured in great numbers and the surviving examples of Song wares today are among the world's most valued art treasures. Later, techniques for using distinctive blue cobalt oxide pigments were introduced from Persia and were soon being utilized by Ming potters to brighten their porcelain ware. Government-sponsored and -run kilns, notably at the Jingdezhen works in Jiangxi Province, allowed for unprecedented volume and quality control.

The most momentous invention to emerge from the era, however, was gunpowder. Perhaps arising from Daoist alchemy as early as the eighth century, its use in rockets, bombs, and primitive types of cannon routinely appear in twelfth-century accounts. It undoubtedly gave the Southern Song a critical, though temporary, technological edge over their northern adversaries, perhaps prolonging the life of the beleaguered dynasty. By the late thirteenth century, its appearance in the writings of the English Franciscan monk Roger Bacon marked its diffusion throughout Eurasia.

CONCLUSION

Despite being the last of the major civilizational areas to emerge, the states and cities of northern China along the Yellow River set the tone in many respects for the cultures that would succeed them. With the Shang came, among other developments, bronze and writing, both of which would be foundational benchmarks in Chinese and East Asian history. The long period of the Zhou created both the models of rulership and the pattern of decentralized rule that ultimately led to China's first great patchwork of states. The political and social turmoil of the late Zhou era also marked an enormously important period in Chinese intellectual and cultural history. During this era, the most important schools of Chinese thought and philosophy developed: Confucianism, Daoism, and Legalism. Although Confucianism ultimately triumphed as the ideology of imperial China, it was the Legalist state of Qin that created the empire itself.

When the Qin Dynasty fell in 206 BCE, much of the infrastructure of the early empire—including the Great Wall—was in place. The Han Dynasty, from 202 BCE to 220 CE, retained the administrative structure of the Qin, but softened the harsh laws and punishments of the Legalists. Eventually, the form of Confucianism practiced by the empire's administrators was taught in the imperial schools, becoming in effect the imperial ideology. By the end of the Han, China had created a solid alliance between the state and this all-encompassing philosophical system.

Perhaps more important than even the structures themselves, however, was that, like the Egyptians and Romans, the Chinese had become accustomed to what has been called the "habit of empire." Four hundred years of unity under the Qin and the Han had conditioned them to believe that empire was the natural state of Chinese political organization and that any interruptions would be but brief interludes in the dynastic cycle. Thus, Chinese history has been marked by rhythms of outside usurpation and inward renewal. Following reunification and an outward posture under the Sui and the Tang came a period of relative inwardness and renewal under the Song. Foreign invasion would shortly place China within the world's largest empire, and with it the imperial era's most "outward" epoch until the nineteenth century.

FURTHER RESOURCES

Chang, Kwang-chih. *The Archaeology of Ancient China*, 4th ed. New Haven, CT: Yale University Press, 1986. Sophisticated treatment of recent archaeology of Shang China. Prime exponent of the view of overlapping periods and territories for the Sandai period. Erudite yet accessible for experienced students.

Ebrey, Patricia B. *The Inner Quarters: Marriage and the Lives of Chinese Women in the Sung Period.* Berkeley: University of California Press, 1993. Pioneering study of women's participation in Song commercial enterprises, urban life, and the institutions of early modern China. Extensive source materials.

Gernet, Jacques. *Daily Life in China on the Eve of the Mongol Invasion 1250–1276.* Stanford: Stanford University Press, 1962, 1970. Pathbreaking popular social history of Southern Song China. A wealth of detail with somewhat dated conclusions.

Huang, Ray. *China: A Macro History.* Armonk, NY: M.E. Sharpe, 1997. Readable, entertaining, and highly useful one-volume history. Particularly good on the complex politics of the post-Han and Song–Yuan periods.

Loewe, Michael, and Edward L. Shaughnessy, eds. *The Cambridge History of Ancient China: From the Origins of Civilization to 221 B.C.* Cambridge, UK: Cambridge University Press, 1999. The opening volume of the Cambridge History of China series, this is the most complete multi-essay volume on all aspects of recent Chinese ancient historical and archaeological work. The place to start for the serious student contemplating in-depth research.

Raphals, Lisa. *Sharing the Light: Representations of Women and Virtue in Early China.* Albany, NY: SUNY Press, 1998. Reexamines the stereotypes of ancient Chinese women as oppressed by patriarchal society and argues the women had considerable influence and agency, particularly in the era before the Han.

Snow, Philip. *The Star Raft: China's Encounter with Africa.* Ithaca, NY: Cornell University Press, 1988. Important, accessible study of the little known area of China's maritime trade with Africa from Han times to the epic fifteenth-century voyages of Zheng He and beyond.

Thorp, Robert L. *China in the Early Bronze Age: Shang Civilization.* Philadelphia: University of Pennsylvania Press, 2006. Comprehensive yet accessible survey of recent archaeological work on the period 2070–1046 BCE, including traditional Xia and Shang periods under the heading of China's "Bronze Age."

Tu Wei-ming. *Way, Learning, and Politics: Essays on the Confucian Intellectual.* Albany, NY: SUNY Press, 1993. Insightful pieces on the history of Confucianism and its current direction and relevance by a leading contemporary Confucian thinker. A number of observations on what it means to be a Confucian in the modern world.

Watson, Burton, trans. *The Tso Chuan: Selections from China's Oldest Narrative History.* New York: Columbia University Press, 1989. Elegant translation by one of the most prolific scholars working today. Excellent introduction to Zhou period and politics. Appropriate for beginning students, although more useful for those with some prior introduction to the period.

Yao Xinzhong. *An Introduction to Confucianism.* Cambridge, UK: Cambridge University Press, 2000. Sound, scholarly overview of the Confucian tradition as it has developed through the centuries in imperial China to its impact today.

WEBSITES

http://lucian.uchicago.edu/blogs/earlychina/ssec/. This is the site of the Society for the Study of Early China. The site is for scholars, and the organization also publishes its own journal, *Early China*, as well as scholarly books.

http://www.ancientchina.co.uk. This site provides access to the British Museum's ancient Chinese collections and is highly useful for students seeking illustrations of assorted artifacts in a user-friendly environment.

CHAPTER 3

✦◯

Interaction and Adaptation on the Sinitic Rim: Korea, Japan, and Vietnam to the Mongol Era

> But I have a theory of my own about what this art of the
> novel is, and how it came into being. To begin with, it does
> not simply consist in the author's telling a story about the
> adventures of some other person. On the contrary, it happens
> because the storyteller's own experience of men and things,
> whether for good or ill . . . has moved him to an emotion so
> passionate that he can no longer keep it shut up in his heart. . . .
>
> Thus anything whatsoever may become the subject of a
> novel, provided only that it happens in this mundane life and
> not in some fairyland beyond our human ken.
>
> —DE BARY, pp. 177–78

In the opinion of many scholars, the words above may well be the world's first reflections on the nature of a newly created art form: the novel. The writer, Murasaki Shikibu, author of the world's first novel, **Genji Monogatori** (The Tale of Genji), put them in the mouth of her main character by way of weaving her own literary theories into the work itself. Like her contemporaries, the writers Sei Shonagon and Izumi Shikibu, she was part of a cloistered world of women at eleventh-century Japan's Heian court. That court marked a pivotal juncture in Japanese and East Asian history. On the one hand, it was the result of more than half a millennium of the clan-based cultures of Japan interacting with Chinese models and adopting many of them wholesale. On the other, it marked a crucial area in which Japan was departing from Chinese forms and striking out in new directions. And this particular direction was marked by women.

The novel itself is a long work dealing with the experiences and loves of a fictional prince, perhaps modeled in part on the influential courtier Fujiwara Michinaga. Its appeal lies largely in what one Japanese scholar called "sensitivity to things": the fragility of beauty, the fleetingness of time, and things powerfully felt that go unexpressed because of the restrictions of station or etiquette.

Murasaki's departure from older and borrowed forms, however, was even more extensive than creating a new literary genre. The literature she and the other women writers at Heian created was also among the first major works to use an entirely new Japanese writing system: **kana**. For hundreds of years, literacy in Japan meant using and understanding Chinese characters. As we have seen, the basis of written Chinese is that meaning is vested in the symbols themselves independently of pronunciation. Murasaki herself understood literary Chinese as it had been used in Japan, but found her métier in the *kana* syllabary of phonetic symbols that much more closely corresponded to spoken Japanese and was far easier to learn and write. At court, *kana* had largely become the language of women, one that afforded them privacy and scope to explore their inner world and secluded circumstances. Over the centuries, it would grow as a tool of literacy alongside basic *kanji* (Chinese characters) to mature into the modern written Japanese of today. Thus, in Japan, we see a pattern of East Asian history developing that will be repeated in Korea and Vietnam: Chinese as a first written language functioning as a lingua franca for largely male elites, but leading to a script more congenial to the spoken language of the common people. It is yet another example of the complexity of the region's cultural interaction and adaptation.

We begin this chapter in Korea, where long-term interaction with, and invasion by, China had implanted the Chinese writing system, Confucian culture and political systems, and Buddhism. Next, we will move to Japan, adjacent to Korea and where Chinese influence came via Korea to be selectively adopted and adapted. Finally, we will examine Vietnam and its long and often painful political and cultural relationship with China.

FROM THREE KINGDOMS TO ONE: KOREA TO 1231

As we have noted, the influence of imperial China became widespread throughout East, Northeast, and Southeast Asia. Chinese writing, literature, law, government, and philosophy, as well as imported systems such as Buddhism, came to overlay local social, cultural, and religious customs and practices. But as these new systems were often imposed from the top down, they met frequent resistance at the village and clan level in all the regions on the Chinese periphery. In the case of Korea, tensions between elites and locals continually played out in the assorted Korean kingdoms against a backdrop of invasion and collaboration. From the beginning, these societies asserted their political independence from the Chinese. Their position on or near the Chinese border, the role of the Korean kingdoms as havens for refugees, and the continual pressures of possible invasion, however, provided a conduit for Chinese cultural diffusion. For the Koreans themselves, shifting relations with China provided both unity and disarray in the struggles of different kingdoms for dominance. This pattern would also hold true during the interval of Mongol rule following the invasion of 1231.

The "Three Kingdoms"

Although developments in northern China have long had a bearing on events on the Korean Peninsula, the first Korean state predated any such influence. Zhou Chinese annals contain apparent references to the kingdom of **Choson** ("the land of the morning calm"). Choson seems to have extended deep into southern

Manchuria, with its capital located on the site of the modern city of Pyongyang. It is believed to have been founded sometime after 1000 BCE. In the absence of a Korean written language, however, no indigenous records exist of its early years.

Evidence of such Chinese cultural influences as the use of the written language appears to have been present in the region even before the first attempt at invasion under the Qin. By 108 BCE, the Han Dynasty briefly succeeded in bringing much of the peninsula under their sway. It is from this period that the first written records of exchanges with such outlying peoples as the Koreans, Japanese, and Vietnamese find their way into Han histories. Long before this, however, Chinese agricultural techniques and implements, methods of bronze casting and iron smelting, and a wide variety of other technologies reached Choson and beyond.

Following the Han conquests, a more systematic Chinese transformation was attempted. The Han incorporated approximately two-thirds of the peninsula into their empire and took over Pyongyang as their regional capital. They also encouraged Chinese settlement in the newly acquired territories to help ensure their loyalty. On the one hand, this ushered in a considerable level of cultural exchange; on the other hand, however, it firmly planted among all Korean kingdoms the idea of combined political and cultural resistance to Chinese influences. One of the indirect effects of the conquest was a steady stream of refugees into the unoccupied regions of the south and to the small tribal societies of Japan. This constant traffic back and forth across the narrow, 100-mile strait separating the islands from the mainland created a floating population of colonists in both places and greatly facilitated cultural exchanges. Koreans became established as important players in early Japanese history and, with the founding of the small Japanese holding of *Kaya* in 42 CE, Japanese territorial claims were established on the peninsula.

At the same time, the foundations had been laid for the so-called Three Kingdoms of Korea: *Koguryo* (37 BCE–668 CE), *Paekche* (18 BCE–660 CE), and *Silla* (57 BCE–935 CE). By the fourth century CE, the dissolution of the Han Empire encouraged the Koreans to push the Chinese from the peninsula. In the wake of this retreat, the three rival kingdoms entered a period of intrigue and intermittent war among themselves for dominance. Koguryo, in the extreme north, created the largest state, moving into southern Manchuria in the absence of any strong rivals. In the south, the areas that had never been under Chinese control had a history of close ties to the developing Japanese clan powers and consequently tended to be more outward-looking (see Map 3.1).

In 372, the Chinese state of Jin began sending Buddhist missionaries to Koguryo. With them came the full package of Chinese writing, literature, and significantly, political philosophy. Within a few decades, as the elites of Koguryo, despite their emotional resistance to Chinese influences, sensed the power of these tools to enhance their statecraft, a Confucian academy was established in the kingdom. In 427, Korguryo remade itself along Chinese lines. At Pyongyang, a central Confucian bureaucracy was established, examinations instituted, and a reconstituted land tax and conscription system installed.

Meanwhile, the two southern kingdoms fought continually to stave off domination by their northern rival. Paekche's maritime contacts with south China aided the spread of Buddhism there, as did, to some degree, its wars with

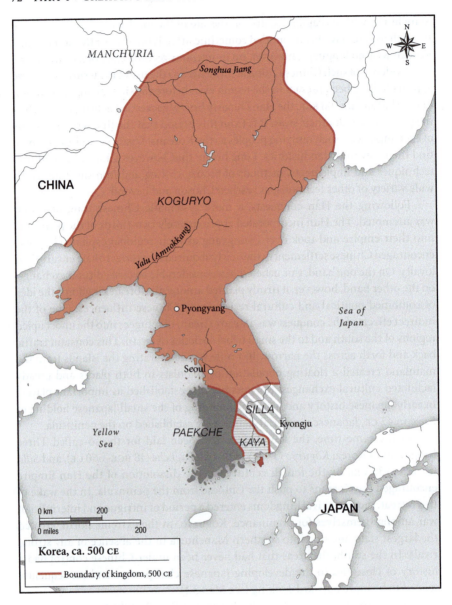

Map 3.1 Korea, ca. 500 CE

Koguryo from 364 to 371. Buddhism had also come to Silla, but Chinese political institutions did not take the same form there as elsewhere. A clan-based, autocratic monarchy, Silla adopted a Chinese-style bureaucracy but retained its system of hereditary ranks, leaving power largely in the hands of warrior aristocrats.

In 550, Silla allied with Paekche against the renewed expansionist aims of Koguryo, in the course of which Kaya was eliminated in 562. The reunification of China under the short-lived Sui Dynasty in 589 soon resulted in another invasion

Pulguksa Temple. Buddhism put down strong roots in Silla after its introduction in the fourth century. The Pulguksa temple was first built in Kyongjiu, the Silla capital, in 535 as part of the state Buddhist school. Its stone pagodas were built in the ninth century under the auspices of the new Son school, better known by its Japanese name, Zen.

of the north. As we saw earlier, the strains of Sui expansion into Koguryo, however, spelled the end of the dynasty, ushering in the Tang in 618. Once again, Tang consolidation in China was followed by renewed attempts to subdue Korguryo. After several Tang campaigns were repulsed, the Chinese decided on a new strategy and concluded an alliance with Silla in 660, spelling the immediate end of Paekche. Threatened along two fronts, Koguryo itself finally submitted in 668. Following decades of resistance against the Tang, Silla was recognized by the Chinese as controlling all of Korea south of Pyongyang in 735. Although politically free of the Chinese, Silla remained a client state of the Tang and shared with them incorporation into an East Asian Buddhist cultural sphere, which now included Japan as well. Meanwhile, remnant forces of K set up a state called *Parhae* in northern Korea and M 926, when it was overrun by the *Qitans*.

The dislocations of the sixth and seventh centuries Northeast Asia. In Silla, the expansion of Mahayana dominance of literary Chinese as a medium of express would be largely supplanted by the creation of a gover system, **han'gul**, in the fifteenth century, even today, kno is still considered an important mark of cultural and ae

Korea to the Mongol Invasion

By the mid-eighth century, Silla was in decline. In 780, the king was assassinated, and revolts led by various pretenders threatened to leave the country unstable for some time to come. Among the most restive members of Silla society were the merchants who, like their counterparts in China, were aware of their growing economic power, although sensitive to the fear and contempt in which they were held by the Confucian-influenced aristocracy and bureaucrats.

One such merchant, Wong Kon (d. 943), subdued the crumbling kingdom and reconstituted it as *Koryo*—from which the name "Korea" derives. The Chinese imperial model proved attractive to Wong, who, following the practice of Chinese emperors, was accorded a posthumous reign name, Taejo. He moved the capital to Kaesong, where he laid out a city in the grid pattern of the Tang capital of Chang'an and adopted Chinese-style bureaucratic and tax systems, as well as military and labor conscription. Koryo even built its own version of the Great Wall along the Yalu River as a barrier to the nomadic peoples of the north (see Map 3.2).

By the mid-thirteenth century, Koryo had begun to feel the pressure of Mongol demands. As we will see in more detail in Chapter 4, the Mongols launched no less than seven invasions of Koryo from 1231 to 1259 before the court finally capitulated. The kingdom was never formally incorporated into the Mongol polity. For the remainder of the Mongol occupation, Koryo remained a tightly supervised client state, beset with high taxes, ruthless corvée labor, and mass deportations.

Economy and Society

Like their counterparts in China, rulers and government officials in the various Korean kingdoms tended to be preoccupied with land reform, problems of landlordism and tenancy, maintaining local infrastructures—especially in wet rice–producing areas—and alleviating want during times of shortage. At various times, therefore, officials proposed schemes of land redistribution based on the Chinese "well-field" model. More ambitious was the *chongjon* system of Silla, begun in 722. Following a combination of Buddhist and Confucian precepts, with an eye to local custom, the *chongjon* system mandated a government-sponsored distribution of land, with taxes paid in kind. Additionally, peasants were instructed to develop specialized cash crops or engage in small craft manufacture. A prime example was the planting of mulberry trees as food for silkworms and the development of sericulture.

The political and social structure of the Three Kingdoms represents a complex blend of monarchy, Confucian, Daoist, and Buddhist influence. Much was written on the proper behavior of rulers, with frequent citations of the Chinese *Shujing* and *Daodejing*. By the sixth century, a highly stratified social hierarchy called "bone ranks" had been promulgated in which the top five ranks (known as "holy bones" and "true bones") were set aside as the pool from which rulers would be drawn. Following them would be ranks six to seventeen encompassing the aristocracy. ʘw them were the commoners, who had no rank. As with the ranks of Chinese s in the Confucian bureaucracy, there were sumptuary laws governing e clothing, accessories, and even utensils for the different ranks.

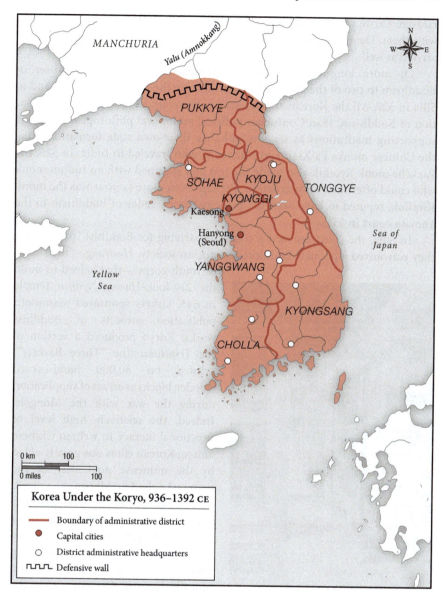

Map 3.2 Korea under the Koryo, 936–1392 CE

Religion, Culture, and Intellectual Life

As with many peoples of north and Central Asia, early Korean religion appears to have been **animistic**—dominated by a spirit world that paralleled the human one. One could appeal to the spirits through shamans or animals believed to have certain powers. Like Shinto in Japan (see below), these beliefs continued at the local level for many hundreds of years after the introduction of more formalized systems. With the invasion of the Han Dynasty came the Chinese concepts of the

Heaven, Earth, and Humankind triad along with the imperial rituals associated with them. Daoism, Confucian ritual, yin and yang, and five-elements theory arrived as well.

Of more long-term importance, however, was the introduction of Buddhism to two of the Three Kingdoms during the fourth century CE and to Silla in 527. All the Korean states seized to varying degrees on the combination of Buddhism, Han Confucian political and moral philosophy, and their supporting institutions as ways to enhance their own state formation. Like the Chinese monks Fa Xian and Xuanzang who traveled to India, in 526, the Paekche monk Kyomik also made the trip and returned with an Indian monk who could offer further instruction. Perhaps even more famous was the monk Kwalluk, reputed to have been the principal ambassador of Buddhism to the Yamato court in 552.

In Silla, the court pursued a course of striving for Buddhist "perfection": they patronized a popular Buddhist–Confucian society, *Hwarang*—"the flower of youth corps"—that helped to build the 210-foot *Hwang Nyonsu* temple in 645. Others sponsored mammoth publication projects of Buddhist works: Koryo produced a version of the **Tripitaka** (the "Three Baskets") printed on 80,000 hand-carved wooden blocks as an act of supplication during the war with the Mongols. Indeed, the relatively high level of functional literacy in written Chinese among Korean elites was greatly aided by the immense popularity of the many schools of Buddhism. As a result, twelfth-century Korea developed into one of the world's handful of centers of printing and publishing. By the 1100s as well, publishers were employing what may have been the world's first movable, cast metallic type. As was the case in China, however, the formidable task of organizing the huge numbers of type necessary for printing the thousands of Chinese characters in use made this breakthrough far less innovative that would be the case in Europe centuries later. Thus, carving individual pages on wood blocks for printing remained the standard practice into the nineteenth century.

The Korean Printing Industry. Because of its position as the northern crossroads of the Buddhist and Chinese literary world, Korea was a major center of printing. Printing with carved wooden blocks had been developed during the eighth century, and large publishers and academies kept great numbers of them on hand. The most famous was this storehouse, which still preserves the 80,000 blocks of the *Tripitaka*, carved between 1237 and 1257.

ISOLATION, INTERACTION, AND ADAPTATION: JAPAN TO 1281

Of all the places we examine in East Asia, Japan raises the most exciting questions about the effects of relative isolation. Japan's geographical position allowed it to selectively interact with and adopt continental innovations, experimenting, refining, and occasionally dropping them as needed. Indeed, having never experienced a successful invasion, Japan's acculturation was almost completely voluntary, a position unique among the societies of Eurasia.

Jomon and Yayoi

As we saw in Chapter 1, the origins of the Japanese are obscure, made more so by millennia of ethnic and linguistic isolation. As of 2018, genetic research points to what has been termed the "hybridization theory." That is, two distinct groups appear to have migrated to the islands from the Asian mainland separated by long intervals. The first group, the ancestors of the people who fashioned the *Jomon culture*, came perhaps 10,000 to 20,000 years ago. As noted in Chapter One, their descendants, the Utari, are today regarded as Japan's aboriginal peoples and referred to by the Japanese as *Ainu*, the "hairy ones," or in early imperial times as *Emishi*.

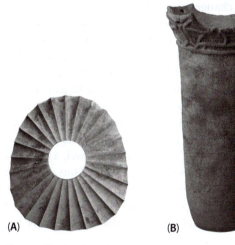

(A)   **(B)**

Yamato Sharinseki Disk and Jomon Jar. This disk, (A) made of finely worked steatite (soapstone), was taken from a third-century CE *kofun* burial mound in central Japan. As a religious object it may be related to similar ornaments found in China. The distinctive herringbone pattern and flared top mark this clay pottery (B) as from the Middle Jomon period, perhaps 5000 to 6000 years old.

The later inhabitants, who share the genetic features of the later *Yayoi* agricultural migrants, arrived perhaps 5,000 to 7,000 years ago, a time that geneticists have tentatively established as the earliest date for which they have evidence of a shared genome. It is believed that they may have originally come from Central Asia and migrated to Korea, from which they crossed the straits to Japan.

Japan's prehistory, which lasted from about 10,000 BCE down to 300 BCE, has been designated by archaeologists as the Jomon period. The most distinctive artifacts from the era are lightly fired clay vessels marked with a unique horizontal herringbone pattern and often fanciful decorations; clay female figurines called *dogu*; and phallic symbols called *bo*. Like Neolithic cultures on the Asian mainland, the Jomon social system appears to have been dominated by matriarchal and matrilineal clans, although here they were mostly clustered near the sea or slightly inland. Because game was increasingly limited on the islands, fishing, catching marine creatures and waterfowl, and harvesting seaweed were the major forms of subsistence.

During the final half-millennium before the Common Era, increased intercommunication among Japanese, Koreans, and some members of the late Zhou Chinese coastal states laid the groundwork for not only the introduction of agriculture and rice cultivation in the Japanese islands, but also the simultaneous Bronze Age and Iron Age. During a 600-year period designated **Yayoi** (300 BCE–ca. 300 CE), imported and domestically manufactured bronze and iron articles made their appearance. The fertile plains of southern Honshu and Kyushu also saw the cultivation of Eurasian vegetables and fruits and, most significantly, rice. The swiftness of these changes came in part because of the dislocations resulting from the creation of China's first empire in 221 BCE, and the influx of Korean refugees in the wake of the initial Chinese invasions of Korea.

As it had in other areas of East Asia, the rice revolution not only allowed the development of larger populations in Japan, it required them for efficient cultivation. The movement away from fishing and gathering combined with the efficiency of metal tools and weapons also fostered the development of larger and more powerful polities among the clans or *uji*. The role of the new technologies in state formation is witnessed by the items included even now in the imperial regalia at the Ise Grand Shrine: a jewel, a bronze mirror, and an iron sword, all of which date from about 260 CE. Thus, sometime after 250 CE, Japan's first real state, *Yamato*, centered on the Kanto Plain near modern Tokyo, emerged, absorbing its weaker rivals on Honshu. Japan's first monumental architecture, enormous burial mounds called **kofun**, date from this period as well.

Early State Building

The earliest written records describing the state, composed by Chinese chroniclers in 297 CE, attest to the increased notice it had achieved—although, characteristically, the writers considered their subjects scarcely civilized. Nearly four centuries

Ishibutai Kofun in Asuka Nara. *Kofun* were tumulus (mound) gravesites characteristic of elite burials in central Japan from roughly the second to seventh century. Some are enormous—up to 400 meters in length—and many are characterized by a distinctive keyhole design visible from the air. Pictured here is the rear of the burial chamber of *Ishibutai Kofun*, a later (seventh-century) site near Nara, the first capital of Japan.

earlier, the first mention of the land of "Wa" appears in Han chronicles, noting that it consisted of more than 100 clan-based settlements. Although there had been steady diplomatic and cultural contact back and forth across the Sea of Japan from the first century CE, a particularly high level was reached during the later sixth century CE. In 552, as noted above, tradition has it that Buddhism was introduced to the islands from Paekche. With it came the Chinese writing system and works of every description. A decade later, in 562, the Korean kingdom of Silla eliminated the Japanese colony of Kaya on the peninsula, precipitating a new flow of refugees to Japan. The years from 589 into the early seventh century saw the rise of the Sui and Tang dynasties in China, resulting in yet more Chinese attempts to dominate the Korean kingdoms, and pushing the level of refugee emigration to new levels.

The growing power of China and Silla helped prompt the Soga *uji*'s Empress Suiko (r. 592–628) and her nephew, Prince Shotoku (573–621), to connect Yamato more firmly to the mainland, adopting Chinese conceptions of politics, philosophy, culture, literature, and, ultimately, the imperial system itself. A few signposts along the way toward Yamato's voluntary Sinicization include the taking of Buddhism as a state religion (594), adoption of the Chinese lunar calendar for state record-keeping (604), and the adoption of Prince Shotoku's 17-Article Constitution modeled on Confucian and Buddhist precepts (604). But the most far-reaching changes came later in the century, with the **Taika**, or Great Reform of 645.

The systematic remaking of the Yamato regime along Chinese lines in the wake of the Taika marks the beginning of the imperial Japanese state. Among other things, Soga clan control of the court was overturned and Fujiwara No-Kamatari, who emerged as advisor to the new emperor Tenchi, ushered in a connection between his family and the imperial court that continued into the twentieth century. In less than a century, the first Chinese-style imperial histories, the *Kojiki* (712) and **Nihongi** (720), were composed; the concept of the Mandate of Heaven was adopted to justify the overthrow of the Sogas; the emperor as the center of a hierarchical system of government run through a rigorously selected bureaucracy was institutionalized; a census, uniform taxation on land and produce, and systems of conscription and labor service were enacted. The edicts mandating these changes were promulgated as the **Taiho Code** of 702, which remained the basis of Japanese law until the late nineteenth century.

Because of the requirements of a far larger and more sophisticated system of government, a permanent capital was built at Nara in 710. Like its counterparts in Korea, it was a close replica of the Tang capital at Chang'an, down to the axial boulevards, grids of streets, and propitious placement of temples and government buildings. In 794, a larger capital was completed nearby along the same lines and was called Heian-kyo, the future city of Kyoto. The era of imperial rule from this capital, which lasted until 1192, is thus often referred to as the *Heian period*.

Imperial Rule

As the imperial order penetrated all the Japanese home islands except Hokkaido, and the widespread adoption of Buddhist culture plugged Japan into an enormous, interconnected economic and culture sphere, Heian Japan became increasingly a land of contrasts, with local rumblings of discontent never far below the surface. For the urban elite, life was not unlike that of their counterparts in Korea, Vietnam, or even China itself. The common currency of Confucianism, Chinese literature, and the various Buddhist schools helped them see themselves as part of a cosmopolitan world, as did frequent travel for trade, diplomacy, study, and pilgrimage. The latest fashions in poetry, literature, fine arts, calligraphy, music, and to a lesser extent, clothing all found their way to court and beyond (see Map 3.3).

For the members of the new classes into which the vast majority of Japan's people had now moved: peasants, artisans, and merchants—with Buddhist monks occupying an increasingly significant position in the hierarchy—many of the changes had been disruptive at best. Perhaps most tellingly, power, and soon military strength, were diffusing from the court and capital out into the countryside. This was particularly true in more remote regions where the most aggressive *uji* had assembled forces in support of their battles with the Ainu. The bureaucracy, a tenuous institution at best, became weaker as local *uji* began to reassert power. This was given a considerable push in the wake of a virulent smallpox epidemic lasting from 735 to 737, during which the population may have been reduced by as much as a third.

Despite court attempts to create a Chinese-style "well-field system," tenancy became a chronic problem. In many cases, the *shoen*, or clan estates, were given tax-exempt status because of their military contributions. The estates of Buddhist monasteries were similarly exempt and in addition provided social services and refuge for outcasts, in effect becoming shadow societies of their own. By the late eleventh century, perhaps half of the land in the empire had become exempt

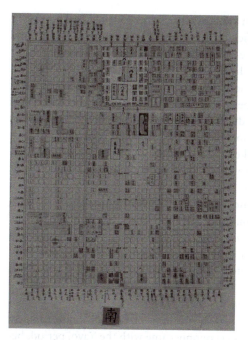

Plan for the Capital Grid at Heian-kyo (Kyoto). Japan's new capital at Heian-kyo was a faithful copy of the plan of the Tang Dynasty capital at Chang'an (present-day Xi'an). The city grid was laid out on a precise north-south axis, with the most important structures like the imperial palace sited in the northern section, and their courtyards and entrances facing south as the most propitious direction. Gardens and outlying structures were also placed according to Chinese conceptions of geomancy called *feng shui*.

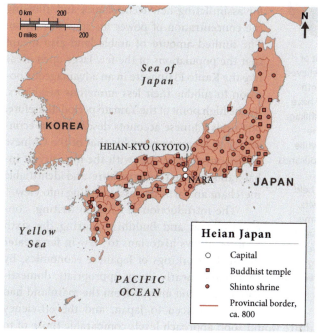

Map 3.3 Heian Japan

Japanese Armor. The suit of armor pictured here is believed to date from the fourteenth century and may indeed have belonged the shogun Ashikaga Takauji (r. 1338–1358). The helmet is bronzed iron, while the cuirass is made of thousands of overlapping iron and lacquered leather scales held together by means of rivets. Unlike European plate armor from this period, the Japanese version provided effective protection while allowing for a remarkable amount of freedom of movement.

from taxes. As the countryside became more self-sufficient, the capital grew more isolated—and more reliant on local military cooperation.

In addition, the court itself was often divided by factional disputes, spurred by the practice of emperors abdicating but staying on as regents or advisors. Three decades of civil war between factions supporting the claims of the Taira, or Heike, clan, and those pledged to the Minamoto, or Genji, finally climaxed in the Gempei War (1180–1185), which resulted in the defeat of the Taira in 1185. Shortly thereafter, in 1192, Minamoto Yoritomo was given the title *Sei-i-tai Shogun* (the Great Barbarian-Suppressing General), and the period of the *shogunates* was inaugurated, lasting until 1867.

Economy and Society

The real beginning of the diversification of Japan's economy came with the Yayoi period, beginning around 300 BCE. As the early Japanese communities adopted wet rice and vegetable agriculture, they gained the ability to sustain a large sedentary population, which would prove crucial for assimilating new technologies and allowing the concentration of power for state formation. The limited amount of arable land also meant that the populations of the few large open areas like the Kanto Plain were in an advantageous position to subdue their less numerous neighbors. By the high point of the Yamato period, therefore, one finds Chinese accounts describing an economy that seems to resemble that of the Chinese or Korean countryside, with the majority of inhabitants engaged in agriculture, and identifiable merchant and artisan classes coming into view.

The introduction of Chinese writing, concepts of law, and Buddhism during the sixth century allows historians to view in far greater detail the workings of Japanese economics. By this point, nearly every appropriate domesticated plant and animal from the mainland had been introduced to Japan, and the efficiency of the island's agriculture would soon approach levels comparable those of to China and Korea. Indeed, according to a Sui Dynasty chronicle from about 630,

Yamato was already being considered a mature state by the Korean kingdoms. Like its counterparts on the mainland, the Yamato court and its successors at Nara and Heian-kyo attempted to regulate economic activity in the form of land and produce taxes, taxes on trade, monopolies on strategic commodities, and requisitions of labor for infrastructural projects.

Almost from the beginning, however, as we noted earlier, these efforts at centralization were only partially effective. The larger *uji*, whose power had theoretically been cut by the creation of a state bureaucracy, got around the problem by supplying many of the officials for the new body. They took advantage of government incentives to reclaim land from the wilderness and the Ainu. By such means, the large *shoen* and monastery estates with their tax exemptions thus tended to acquire regional political and military power.

Family Structure

As in Korea, and perhaps China, the earliest social structures of Japan appear to have been matrilocal and, most likely, matriarchal. *Uji* before the sixth century were organized around female lineages, and the first Chinese accounts mention figures such as "Queen Pimiko." With the coming of Chinese institutions, though, this changed radically at the uppermost levels and more gradually below. During the early importation of Chinese influences during the sixth and seventh centuries, women at the top could still wield considerable political power, as witnessed by Empress Suiko of the Soga clan. By the height of the power of the Heian court, Confucian patriarchal institutions had made a great deal of headway in Japan, but were moderated somewhat by the pervasive influence of Buddhism and Shinto. Thus, aristocratic women controlled property, although they increasingly tended to wield political power through men. They were sequestered at court and forced into a highly refined and regulated ritual life, yet created their own influential cultural world. Women like Murasaki Shikibu and Sei Shonagon (d. ca. 1001) defined the guidelines for literary and aesthetic appreciation for generations to come in the *Tale of Genji* and *The Pillow Book*.

Outside the court, the moderating institution for the commoners, and particularly women, was the Buddhist monastery. As in China and Korea, the monasteries provided havens for women and men who did not marry or had fled bad marriages. They provided enough education for adherents to be able to read the *sutras*, thus helping to increase literacy. They also provided important avenues of political power as large landholders, innkeepers, peacekeepers, and advisors.

As in China and Korea, however, the family life of commoners was mostly governed by a mix of Confucian filial piety, local clan relations, and the desire to improve the family's position through marriage. As in China, girls came to be considered "expendable" because they would move in with their husband's family. Arranged marriages were the norm, and by way of forcing such issues, rape, kidnapping, and family vendettas were all too common. A woman who would not consent to such a marriage, for example, could only evade it if she fled to a monastery before the groom's relatives caught up with her. Failure to escape could result in a beating or even murder.

Religion, Culture, and Intellectual Life

Japan's religious traditions may be said to consist largely of two strains: the indigenous traditions of Shinto and a later arrival, Buddhism. Confucianism as a political philosophy and organizational tool for government also wielded considerable influence, although much less so in the spiritual realm.

The foundations of Japan's original religion, **Shinto**, go far back into remote antiquity. Scholars have used the word "vitalism" to describe its common features: a deep-seated belief in the power of *kami*—spirits of divinities, beings living and departed, nature as a whole, and even inanimate objects like mountains and streams. Reverence for these forces extended early on to fertility and earthly vitality as well. Even today, Shinto priests commonly wear a stiff black hat that has a *bo* phallic figure rising prominently from it. The importance of ritual vitality was reinforced by a tremendous emphasis on ritual purity—as Chinese observers recorded nearly 2,000 years ago, the Japanese seemed to bathe constantly—and waterfalls were enormously popular as places of ritual ablution and even miracle working. On the other hand, death and physical corruption were circumstances to separate from as much as possible—hence, the practice of distancing shrines from burial mounds.

Shinto means "the Way of the Gods," and Japanese mythology recognized a staggering array of deities. Chief among these were Izanagi and Izanami, whose

Shinto Priests, Takayama, Japan. Shinto is Japan's indigenous set of religious practices. Japan's original religion, it was co-opted by Japan's militarist government as state Shinto in the 1930s, but it survives today in harmony with the various schools of Japanese Buddhism. Here, Shinto priests parade with a drum during celebrations marking the Autumn Festival in Takayama, a popular resort and ski area in the "Japanese Alps" in the western part of the main island of Honshu. Note the phallus-shaped ridge (a common fertility symbol) on the hat of the drum bearer.

initial sexual act created the Japanese home islands; and Amaterasu, the Sun Goddess, considered the ancestor of Japan's emperors, purportedly starting with Jimmu in 660 BCE. Until the Emperor Hirohito officially renounced his divinity at the end of World War II, every Japanese emperor had been considered a god in the Shinto pantheon by believers. As is often noted, Shinto has no scriptures or fundamental laws like the Ten Commandments. People are considered to be fundamentally good, although no one is believed to be totally good or totally bad. People do evil because of the influence of evil spirits. Thus, public and private rituals, as well as visits to shrines, are largely aimed at keeping evil spirits at bay.

Buddhism in Japan

Although it had undoubtedly arrived some time beforehand, the customary dating of Buddhism's introduction to Japan is 552 CE, when the king of Paekche sent a collection of Buddhist scriptures as a present to Yamato. Under the missionary Kwalluk of Paekche, the religion soon became well established among Japanese elites. After decades of struggle with the Shinto establishment at court, Buddhism became the state religion of Yamato in 594. Both systems however, were ultimately able to coexist. The ability of Buddhism to adapt the cosmologies of other traditions to its core beliefs, its reverence for nature, emphasis on the transcendental, and lack of a priestly hierarchy made it a relatively easy fit for Shinto. For their part, Shinto believers could add the *bodhisattvas* and other Buddhist entities to the list of *kami*. Coupled with an already great admiration for things Chinese, such accommodations made the spread of the religion relatively easy.

In addition to the Tendai school (Chinese *Tiantai*)—the key revelation of which was that all beings possess a "Buddha nature" and hence have the potential for salvation—there was *Shingon*, or Esoteric Buddhism, which placed more emphasis on deep scriptural study and aesthetics. For both, the degree to which one can grasp the central truth varies according to the capacity of the individual to study and contemplate it, but is in theory open to all at some level. The popular devotional schools of Buddhism also came to Japan during the eighth and ninth centuries. Their simplicity and optimism—simply bowing repeatedly and calling on Amida Buddha with a sincere heart in order to be saved (*nembutsu*)—and the hope for a place in the Pure Land, or Western Paradise, ensured widespread adherence. As in much of East Asia, it remains the most popular of the Buddhist schools in Japan.

Although neither achieved widespread popularity, two other Buddhist schools deserve mention because of their influence. The first is a wholly Japanese development. Nichiren (1222–1282) advocated a Japan-centered, patriotic form of Buddhism. He preached a return to the mysteries of *Tendai*, but with an added emphasis on meditation, personal sacrifice, and direct action. Perhaps more influential was the practice of Zen. Again, the Chinese origins of this movement as *chan*, and the influence of Hui Neng (638–713) and *The Platform of the Sixth Patriarch*, were introduced in Chapter 2. Arriving in Japan in the twelfth century, its popularity spread among the *daimyo* and **samurai,** as well as those who had the discipline to pursue its rigors.

Devotional Buddhist Art: The Miracles of Kannon. Amida Buddhism was East Asia's most popular form of Buddhism, and the most popular bodhisattva was Kannon (Guanyin in China). On this remarkable handscroll dated to 1257, Kannon saves her followers from assorted difficulties. Here she intercedes for two men attacked by soldiers or bandits.

PATTERNS UP-CLOSE

From Periphery to Center: Nichiren, Buddhism, and Japan

As we have seen in a number of instances already—and will see in many more throughout this book—the greater or lesser acceptance of Chinese culture by peoples outside the empire was always accompanied by a powerful streak of independence. This was particularly true in Japan that, alone among the states of the "Sinitic frontier," was never conquered from outside. As far back as the consolidation of Japan's first self-proclaimed imperial state in the sixth and seventh centuries, Chinese diplomats were aghast at what they viewed as the Japanese court's unsurpassed arrogance in addressing a letter to the Tang emperor as from the emperor of the land where the sun rises to the sovereign of the land where the sun sets.

Though the sense of Chinese elites—shared by not a few of Japan's upper classes—that Japan was a cultural backwater conditioned relations between the two states on many levels, the direction of Japanese Buddhism was one area in which a degree of independence was always maintained, sometimes with startling results. Perhaps the most dramatic of these was the career of Nichiren (1222–1282). Like a biblical prophet, he castigated his listeners for abandoning the true path of Tendai Buddhism, but took his preaching one step further by asserting that it was now the role of Japan to lead the world out of its current decadent age by hewing to the sole truth of the central scripture of Tendai, the Lotus Sutra.

Born Zennichimaro to a poor fishing family, he spent time at the famous monastery at Mount Hiei but, discouraged by the monk's adherence to the Shingon Esoteric school, he reached the conclusion that only through Tendai and the Lotus Sutra could the unitary nature of the Buddha be understood and the Buddha nature of all people discovered and cultivated. With this revelation, he changed his name to *Nichiren* ("The Sun and the Lotus") and began a vigorous life-long campaign to propagate his vision of Japan's role in saving the world.

His sense of divine mission was reinforced by the indifference and frequent insults and persecution he actively courted in his preaching. Adamant about the danger Japan faced if invaded from the mainland, he pointedly maintained that it was karmic retribution for Japan's departure from the truths of Tendai. He insisted that Japan's revival must be assisted by "men of superb action" willing to sacrifice themselves in service of the Lotus Sutra's truth. Such action would be called for on a number of occasions in the future when Japan was seen to be in peril—in the 1850s and 1860s, when Japan was "opened" to the West; and in the 1920s and 1930s, as the empire faced the strains of modernity and slid toward war. Arrested by the shogun's men for his preaching and inflammatory rhetoric, he faced his sentence of execution with equanimity. It was said by his followers that as the executioner raised his sword to behead Nichiren, a bolt of lightning struck it and the stunned authorities released him to exile on an offshore island.

A taste of his passion can be had in the following excerpt from "Rectification for the Peace of the Nation":

> If people cast aside doctrines that are all-encompassing and take up those that are incomplete, can the world escape the plots of demons? . . . The Lotus and the Nirvana sutras represent the very heart of the doctrines that Shakyamuni (the Buddha) preached during the five periods of his teaching life. Their warnings must be viewed with the utmost gravity. Who would fail to heed them? And yet those people who forget about the Correct Way and slander the Law . . . grow blinder than ever in their stupidity. (De Bary, et al, Sources of East Asian Tradition, vol. I, Columbia University Press, 2008, p. 778)

(continued)

Significantly, Nichiren reemerged as a national hero in the twentieth century for a rapidly modernizing and expanding Japanese Empire. In 1922, he was given the title of "Great Hero of Rectification" by the Emperor Taisho. He remains a popular figure today and is associated with several prominent Buddhist schools as well as the Soka Gakkai movement. For many Japanese, he will always be a symbol of agency and independence from overweening Chinese influence—particularly now that such influence is so rapidly growing.

Forging a New Japanese Culture

With the importation of Chinese political theory came an understanding of the importance of histories and record-keeping. Thus, the first Chinese-influenced Japanese histories, the *Nihongi* (Chronicles of Japan) and *Kojiki* (Records of Ancient Matters), make their appearance during the early eighth century. At about the same time, the first collection of Japanese poetry published in Chinese, the *Man'yoshu* (The Ten Thousand Leaves' Collection), circulated in 760. This work, however, also illustrates the problems inherent in using Chinese as a method of rendering Japanese sounds.

The *Man'yoshu* uses one-syllable Chinese characters picked for their similarity to Japanese sounds and strings them together into Japanese words. If one can follow the *sounds* of the words, one can grasp the meaning of the poems; if, however, one attempts to read them based on the *meaning* of the characters, they become gibberish. The Chinese literary language, though usable for purposes of conveying meaning, was a singularly poor fit for Japan's spoken language, particularly for such forms as poetry, where sound plays such an important role. Thus by the ninth century, writers were using simplified versions of cursive, simplified Chinese "grass hand" characters as aids in understanding Chinese texts and for informal correspondence. These developed over time into the forty-six sounds of the *hiragana* syllabary used for indigenous Japanese words. A similar syllabary constructed from parts of Chinese characters called *katakana* was developed for foreign loanwords and documents containing it appear around 953. Today, both systems, along with Chinese characters (*kanji*), are still in everyday use. During Murasaki's time, Chinese was still considered to be more refined and the proper written medium for men; *kana* thus became the primary writing system for literate women. Despite its lower prestige, it helped create a degree of autonomy for elite women by ensuring a sense of privacy in their writing that could not be found in any other aspect of court life. Without it, the realism, sensitivity, and intimacy of *Genji* would have scarcely been possible. As in China and Korea, the technology of printing greatly spurred the circulation of these works and over the centuries helped push functional literacy to some of the highest premodern levels in the world.

In addition to the development of the 31-syllable *tanka* poetry form, perhaps the most important literary developments to come from the use of *kana* were the novel and the prose diary. The former, as we have seen, is credited to Murasaki Shikibu. A skilled diarist as well, Murasaki was a tutor to the powerful courtier Fujiwara Michinaga, and she put all her acute observations of the subtleties of court life into *Genji*. Seclusion for court women fostered a considerable amount of self-analysis, and one sees in Murasaki's writing a tension between Buddhist ideas and the requirements of place, name, reputation, and hierarchy at court. Enduring aesthetic guidelines that emerge in the work include *aware*, an intensity of feeling with elements of sadness, melancholy, fragility, and the fleetingness of life, often symbolized by cherry blossoms; *okashi*, an ability to make light of the tragic; *en*, an appreciation for visible beauty; and *miyabi*, courtliness and refinement. Similarly, her older contemporary, Sei Shonagon, in her *Pillow Book*, sets an almost modern tone in her astute, funny, and sometimes spiteful categories of likes and dislikes at court.

Chinese artistic genres also strongly influenced Japanese practitioners of the "three excellences" (painting, poetry, and calligraphy). But Japanese sensibilities often took a slightly different direction from those of their Chinese counterparts. Whereas Chinese artists tended to strive for symmetry in design in their pursuit of the natural, Japanese craftsmen in pottery, interior design, and visual arts frequently sought "purposeful imperfection." Hence, the later *raku* ware of the potter Chojiro, purposely "primitive" in shape, exhibited spontaneously applied and fired glazes; a teahouse might be designed with an asymmetrical placement of its windows and a roughly cut tree trunk placed off-center as a support. Although some designers created interiors with spartan simplicity and almost no ornamentation, those pursuing decorative arts often opted for bold, even garish colors, and washes of gold and silver.

BORDERS OF INFLUENCE AND AGENCY: VIETNAM

In many respects, the position of Vietnam adjacent to China and forming the outer border of Southeast Asia represents a place of enormous cultural interchange. Since the 1960s, the concept of a derivative "Indo-Chinese" history has been challenged by scholars who emphasize the similarities of the lived experience of the common people on both sides of the cultural divide. Of equal importance has been the *agency* of the people in question: their taking of the initiative in deciding matters of acculturation, political systems, and so forth. Our focus on the *patterns* of interactions among peoples, states, and cultures here is intended to explore the agency of people in their acceptance and rejection of certain influences and innovations. As with Korea and Japan, therefore, it is crucial to remember that the history of Vietnam and Southeast Asia is by no means simply an imitation of Chinese or Indian patterns, but the cumulative result of innumerable conscious decisions by millions of people over thousands of years.

Neolithic Cultures

The Neolithic Revolution appears to have taken place in Southeast Asia at about the same time as it did in Southwest Asia. This *Hoabinhian* culture was characterized by the cultivation of root crops, millet, and rice, and by about 6000 BCE, saw the domestication of pigs and chickens. It is believed that yams, bananas, and taro were also domesticated here. By 4500 BCE, the famous *Dongsan* cultures had come onto the scene, marked shortly thereafter by some of humankind's earliest bronze artifacts. The origins of these peoples are still obscure, with contemporary speculation centering on a homeland perhaps in southern China and/or Tibet, like the Thai, Laotians, Burmese, and Cambodians. Out of the fertile, subtropical and tropical regions in which they settled, it is believed that the basics of wet rice agriculture, and the domestication of chickens and pigs, may well have diffused north into China and perhaps west to northern India.

Village Society and Buddhism

The earliest records of the peoples and states in the region are likewise fragmentary. Late Zhou Chinese references frequently mention the state of Yue, but its southern borders appear to have been fluid and probably included parts of the modern provinces of Guangdong and Guangxi and perhaps the northern part of Vietnam. Once more, the social structure suggests a village-based agricultural system in which women enjoyed far more equality than would later be the case. Villages and clans were often bilateral or matrilineal and matrilocal. Men paid a bride price to the families of their wives, and divorce for either spouse appears to have been relatively easy. As in other places in East Asia during the first millennium BCE, women occupied roles as officials, diplomats, merchants, and small business operators. The area also became one of the first outposts of Theravada Buddhism outside India through the efforts of missionaries from Ceylon (Sri Lanka) in the second century BCE. It would come to be the majority religion in the region for the next 2,000 years.

The "Far South"

With the unification of China under the Qin in 221 BCE, Yue, like northern Korea, was incorporated into the First Emperor's new state. This began a prolonged period of Chinese occupation and local resistance in the area, ultimately lasting over a thousand years. Resistance was immediate and would continue to be fierce, if more intermittent, as time went on. As in Korea, the occupation brought with it a cultural invasion, including the full spectrum of Chinese writing, political ideas, and cultural preferences. Like their counterparts in Korea and Japan as well, the new Vietnamese literate elites were later incorporated into the increasingly far-flung world of cosmopolitan China and the Buddhist cultural and religious sphere. Theravada Buddhism in Southeast Asia predated the introduction of Mahayana into China. Now, perhaps as early as the first or second century CE, Mahayana Buddhism moved into Vietnam, over time bringing its various schools as they developed, tying it through pilgrimage, trade, and monastic development to the Tang world by the seventh century. Southeast Asia's geographical position in the center of the maritime portion of this economic and cultural sphere encouraged a considerable openness to outside influences as well (see Map 3.4).

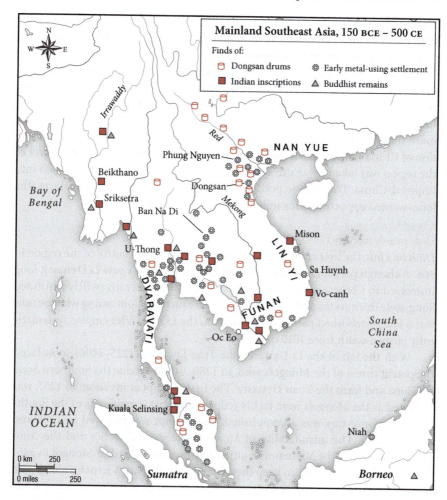

Map 3.4 Mainland Southeast Asia, 150 BCE–500 CE

The invasions from the north also went far to cement an early kind of national identity among the Vietnamese. The collapse of the Qin shortly after the occupation encouraged a rebellion against the local Chinese officials of **Nam Viet** (in Chinese, *Nanyue*), "the far South" as the Chinese had called their new southern province. The Han emperor Wudi reoccupied northern Vietnam in 111 BCE, however, and swiftly reimposed Chinese institutions on the region.

Han attempts at Sinification raised tensions between the new Chinese-influenced elites and those who thus far had managed to retain their cultural independence. The situation was sufficiently volatile that in 39 BCE another rebellion began that to this day is commemorated as helping to form the Vietnamese national identity. Trung Trac, the new widow of a local leader executed by the Chinese, and her sister Trung Nhi led their local militia and defeated the Han garrison, sparking a general revolt. The Chinese shortly regrouped, however, and overpowered the forces of the Trung sisters, who drowned themselves rather than be taken alive. For the next millennium, northern Vietnam would remain firmly within the imperial Chinese orbit.

In the three and a half centuries following the breakup of the Han Empire in 220 CE, the region was able to gain a degree of political autonomy, but the power of Vietnam's Sinified elites continued to ensure their cultural loyalty to China. The growing regional power of the north allowed it to expand into the more Indian-influenced Buddhist kingdoms to the south. With the reunification of China under the Sui and Tang, the drive for Chinese political control of the region was taken up again, and the north was soon fully reincorporated into imperial China. During the political chaos following the fall of the Tang, the long-awaited opportunity for independence finally came.

Independence and State Building

Dinh Bo Linh, the first emperor of Vietnam, solidified his control of the region in 968. Although politically independent of China, Vietnam's new Li Dynasty, long immersed in Chinese notions of Confucianism and statecraft, swiftly instituted Song-style institutions and created its own bureaucracy. Continuing what by now was a long-established pattern of expansion, the Li's Dai Viet empire systematically pushed south from 1010 to 1225.

With the fall of the Li Dynasty, the Tran Dynasty (1225–1400) soon faced the potent threat of the Mongols who, in 1280, would subdue the Southern Song in China and form the Yuan Dynasty. The first attempt at invasion, in 1257, was mounted as the Mongols were busily reducing the last strongholds of the Southern Song. Once this was accomplished, the attempt was renewed in 1285 and again in 1287. The unsuitability of Mongol strategy and tactics and the stubborn resistance of the Vietnamese ultimately prevented further Mongol expansion and allowed the Tran to keep the dynasty intact. Thus, Vietnam, along with Japan, remained one of the few places in East Asia to escape Mongol occupation.

Economy and Society

Since the Neolithic domestication of rice, Vietnam has been one of the world centers of wet rice cultivation. Perhaps 300 strains of rice were cultivated in northern Vietnam by the mid-thirteenth century, with yields running as high as 25 bushels per acre. Roughly 90 percent of the people were engaged in agriculture, a figure consistent with that in other East Asian agrarian-based societies. The area was the first to use the famous Champa strain of rice, and from the twelfth century on, its cultivation yielded two crops per year in the southern areas of the country. The dry season was a time for holiday feasting and mending the dikes, retaining ponds, and other structures and tools involved in farming.

As in southern China and Japan, families could be sustained on relatively small amounts of land and required few complex tools. Along with draft animals like water buffalo, these would often be held communally by clans within the *xa*, or village. Villages commonly consisted of raised, thatch-roofed dwellings, surrounded by a bamboo fence, and centered on the shrine to the ancestral spirits.

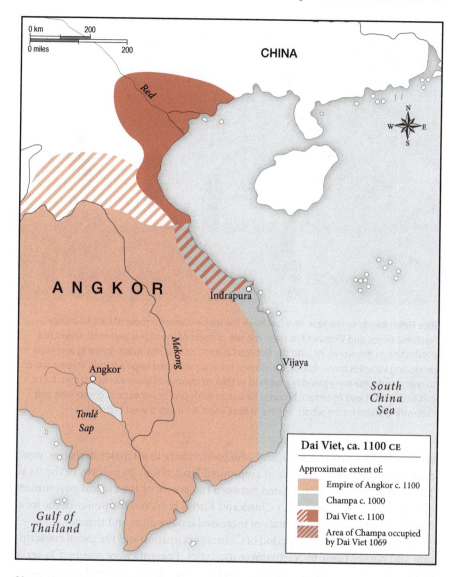

Map 3.5 Dai Viet, ca. 1100 CE

Officials, Peasants, and Merchants

Two key political systems kept order and acted as checks upon each other. The village headman, the *xa troung*, was elected but had to be approved by the imperial court, which, like its Chinese counterpart, ruled through a Confucian bureaucracy of provincial governors, prefects, and magistrates. As in China, the magistrate and his staff were the last official layer above the *xa troung*, so the headman had considerable power and responsibility at the local level. He collected the taxes and dues and sat with a council of notables. His powers, however, were checked by the council itself, which consisted of members of a scholar-gentry

Rice Fields Ready to Harvest. Rice has been the major staple for most of East Asia since Neolithic times, and Vietnam has been the site of some of the oldest and most varied rice production in the world. As with the famous Champa rice strains, quick ripening and high-producing varieties have historically allowed for and mandated large agricultural populations to cultivate it. One long-standing method to take advantage of mountainous terrain for rice cultivation has been to terrace hillsides for use as fields and as a means of conserving and channeling water for irrigation, as here in Mu Cang Chai in northwest Vietnam.

class much like that in China, and who had to share in all major decisions, especially those regarding the use of communal land, about 20 percent of the total. Thus, a balanced tension existed between the power of the central government and local interests. As in both China and Korea, however, the power of the local council often resulted in periods of increased landlordism and tenancy.

One legacy of the long period of Chinese occupation was the use of conscription and corvée labor by Vietnamese dynasties. Peasants were required to serve in the army four months per year—indefinitely during national emergencies. They could also be sentenced to slave labor for various offences. In many cases, they would be sent to open up virgin land for agriculture, which was theirs to keep upon the expiration of their sentences.

The position of Vietnam and Southeast Asia as a whole made it a vital trade crossroads as well as a cultural frontier. This was particularly true as the southern areas were seized from Champa. Nearly all the goods of China, India, and their surrounding trade regions passed through the area. In addition, commercialization for regional and national markets grew rapidly from the fifteenth century on. Competition among villages supplying different commodities or maintaining craft monopolies was fierce. In some areas, women were forbidden to marry outside the village for fear they would take craft secrets with them.

Women and Family

One pattern of history the Vietnamese shared with China and the societies we have examined in this chapter is that of changes in the status of women over time. The nature of the agricultural work undertaken was communal, and men and women tended to work in the fields together. As in Korea and Japan, kinship lines were bilateral—traced through either spouse—or matrilineal. Here again, the long period of Chinese influence and Confucian emphasis on filial piety, hierarchy, and sharply separate roles for men and women eroded this equality somewhat, although much less markedly than in Korea or Japan. In the villages, or in the ports and market cities, women commonly exercised prominent roles as merchants, entrepreneurs, and craftspeople. This was reinforced by the prominence of the different Mahayana schools of Buddhism. Once more, as in China, Korea, and Japan, the role of the monastery for both men and women allowed a place for, and provided an education to, those who for whatever reason lived on society's fringes. Buddhist nuns and abbesses thus wielded considerable power, although their position was often at odds with the Confucian precepts of the elites. Still, women's rights to divorce and property ownership were upheld in the neo-Confucian law code promulgated later on in 1460.

Religion, Culture, and Intellectual Life

Just as the Vietnamese struggled to maintain their own political identity, they continually labored to develop their own cultural distinctiveness. While the porous border region with southern China and geographical and ethnic ties to other Southeast Asian peoples assured a constant flow of influences, not all were readily absorbed and some were played against each other.

Among the most important of these influences was that of religion. Whether the practice of ancestor veneration arrived with the Chinese or whether it was present before the Qin invasion is as yet unsettled. Nearly all villages even into the twentieth century, however, maintained a shrine for a founding ancestor or famous headman, where periodic ceremonies honoring him would take place. As in Korea, the coming of the Han emperor Wudi's armies in the second century BCE brought the imperial system of the Son of Heaven as intermediary between Heaven and Earth. At about the same time, however, Theravada was being established in the Indianized ports of Southeast Asia and became the first division of Buddhism to be established there. Thus, as the Han retreat from the north allowed some political breathing space, the barest beginnings of Mahayana began to come into the area as well. For several hundred years, though, Indian-influenced Theravada dominated the religious and cultural life of much of the region. Buddhist *stupas* were erected and the austere, mendicant, saffron-robed monks held sway in northern Vietnam, as they still do in much of Southeast Asia.

The Tang occupation brought a large infusion of Mahayana influence with its vibrant art motifs, temples, and monasteries as well as the entire spectrum of Confucian and Daoist ideas. Although Mahayana became the dominant division going forward, the Vietnamese at the local level tended to pursue a synthesis of all these systems in their beliefs. As in China, this collection was often referred to as *tam giao*, after the Chinese *san jiao* ("the three religions"). Similarly, the Vietnamese court sought to reconcile the differences among the systems by promulgating edicts on their compatibility. Indeed, some emperors sought to take a leading role in developing a unique strain of Vietnamese Buddhism. Emperor Minh Mang, for example, advocated combining the opposites of "abstention" from the world and "participation" in it. Thus, "an emperor could be a monk, and a monk could be an emperor."

Chu Nom

As in Korea and Japan, Chinese-style histories were compiled and court-sponsored literary projects of various sorts commissioned. Yet again, the literary Chinese favored by the court for such projects continued to be the language of the elites who had the time and means to undertake its study. As in Korea and Japan, an attempt was made to develop a vernacular writing system, in this case sometime during the tenth century. Called **chu nom** ("southern characters."), the new script combined existing Chinese characters picked for the similarity of their sounds to Viet-

White Stupa at Mua Cave Mountain. The influence of the many schools of Chinese Buddhism is readily seen in this stupa located in Ninh Binh, Vietnam. In areas influenced by Chinese Mahayana schools of Buddhism, the dome-shaped stupa characteristic of South Asia as a structure for the keeping of relics and sacred writings emerges as the familiar multistoried pagoda. Often, these structures anchor a monastery and/or temple complex.

namese words with newly invented Chinese-style characters for meaning. It was similar in this respect to the formation of many complex Chinese characters, but would in theory be easier to use as a tool for literacy. The system was used by the thirteenth-century poet Nguyen Thuyen, believed to be the first writer to compose poetry in the new form in 1282. Later, the emperor Ho Quy Ly (1336–1407) ordered the new system to be used in official correspondence. However, it never had the widespread circulation of *han'gul* or *kana* in Korea or Japan.

CONCLUSION

Each of the societies examined in this chapter had its roots in different regions, but all of them emerged deeply infused with a culture either imposed or borrowed from a single place: China. It is therefore impossible to overestimate the importance of China's influence on East Asia. This is particularly important today as the People's Republic of China seeks to extend its influence in many of the same ways and in many of the same places as during its imperial era. For the peoples and states on the receiving end of the exchange, the benefits could be considerable, although their price in terms of political and cultural independence often seemed unacceptably high. In each case, the package of Chinese writing, political theory, cultural, and social assumptions formed the center of the recipient's high culture. Along with Mahayana Buddhism, it plugged them into a larger, more cosmopolitan religious, cultural, and economic sphere, and the myriad interactions of these peoples can be said to have enriched their collective *oecumene*. They enriched those outside of the Buddhist sphere as well, trading via the Indian Ocean with Indian, African, and Islamic states; and along the Silk Route with Central Asia, the Middle East, the Byzantine Empire, and the new states of Europe.

The societal consequences of Chinese influence, however, were not without difficulties. While Japan could remain aloof from the ambitions of expansionist Chinese rulers, Korea and Vietnam were subject to invasion with nearly every Chinese dynastic cycle. While sharing a common elite culture and, to a considerable extent, political structure, the advantages of these institutions were often negated for the common people by the disruption of their traditions. This was particularly the case with women, who in all these societies held more advantageous social positions before the coming of Confucianism than after its arrival.

With the coming of the thirteenth century, all these places would be altered in some way—most in very large ways—by the explosion of the Mongol conquest. As noted in the preface, this brief era of *Pax Mongolica,* in which nearly all of Eurasia was subdued by or forced to confront this unprecedented super-regional empire, marks the true beginning for our purposes of modern East Asia. How the landscape of these societies was so radically altered forms the focus of the remainder of this book.

FURTHER RESOURCES

Holcombe, Charles. *A History of East Asia: From the Origins of Civilization to the Twenty-First Century.* Cambridge, UK: Cambridge University Press, 2011. Well-written and produced comprehensive volume covering China, Korea, and Japan.

Mann, Susan. *East Asia (China, Korea, Japan).* Washington, DC: American Historical Association, 1999. The second volume in the Women's and Gender History in Global Perspective series. Short, informative volume with historiographic overviews and cross-cultural comparisons among the three countries named in the title. Critical annotated bibliographies on the use of standard texts in integrating women and gender into Asian studies.

Murphey, Rhoads. *East Asia: A New History.* New York: Longman, 1997. One of the few one-volume histories that include material on China, Japan, Korea, Vietnam, and Southeast Asia. Written by a leading scholar of modern China and East Asia. Appropriate for beginning students but more useful for those with some background on the area.

Ramusack, Barbara N., and Sharon Sievers. *Women in Asia.* Bloomington: Indiana University Press, 1999. Part of the series Restoring Women to History. Far-ranging book divided into two parts: "Women in South and Southeast Asia" and Women in East Asia." Coverage of individual countries, extensive chronologies, valuable bibliographies. Most useful for advanced undergraduates.

Korea

De Bary, William T., ed. *Sources of Korean Tradition.* Vol. 1: *Introduction to Asian Civiliza-tions.* New York: Columbia University Press, 1997. Part of the renowned Columbia series on the great traditions of East Asia. Perhaps the most complete body of acces-sible sources for undergraduates.

Korean Overseas Information Service. *A Handbook of Korea.* Seoul: KOIS, 1993. Wonder-fully complete history, geography, guidebook, and sociology text. Excellent source, but students should keep in mind its provenance and treat some of its historical claims to uniqueness accordingly.

Vietnam

Steinberg, Joel David, ed. *In Search of Southeast Asia,* rev. ed. Honolulu: University of Hawaii Press, 1987. Extensive coverage of Vietnam within the context of an area study of Southeast Asia. Although weighted toward the modern period, very good coverage of agricultural and religious life in the opening chapters.

Taylor, Keith W. *The Birth of Vietnam.* Berkeley and Los Angeles: University of California Press, 1983. Comprehensive, magisterial volume on early Vietnamese history and his-torical identity amid the long Chinese occupation. Best for students with some back-ground in southeast Asian and Chinese history.

Japan

De Bary, William T., ed. *Sources of Japanese Tradition.* Vol. 1: . New York: Columbia Univer-sity Press, 2002. Like the volume above on Korea and the others in this series on India and China, the sources are well selected, the glossaries are sound, and the overviews of the material are masterful. As with the other East Asia volumes, the complexities of the various Buddhist schools are especially well drawn. As with the others in the series, students with some previous experience will derive the most benefit from this volume.

Reischauer, Edwin O., and Albert Craig. *Japan: Tradition and Transformation.* Boston: Houghton Mifflin, 1989. The companion volume to J. K. Fairbank's *China,* by the lead-ing American scholar on Japan and former U.S. ambassador to Japan. A one-volume history with greater emphasis on the modern than ancient periods.

Totman, Conrad. *A History of Japan.* Oxford: Blackwell, 2000. Part of Blackwell's History of the World series. A larger, more balanced, and comprehensive history than the Reis-chauer and Craig volume. More than half of the material is on the pre-1867 period, with extensive coverage of social history and demographics.

WEBSITES

http://www.britishmuseum.org/the_museum/departments/prints_and_drawings.aspx. Department of Prints and Drawings, British Museum. A comprehensive source for all manner of interests related to Asian studies.

http://www.pbs.org/hiddenkorea/history.htm. Public Broadcasting Service, Hidden Korea. Sound introduction to the geography, people, history and culture of Korea, with links to additional source material.

http://journals.cambridge.org/action/displayJournal?jid=SEA. Cambridge Journals Online, *Journal of Southeast Asian Studies.* Online version of the scholarly publication of the same name, features articles on the history, sociology, cultural studies, and literature of the region. It aims for scholarly but accessible presentations. Recommended for advanced students.

CHAPTER 4

❧

The Mongol Super-Empire

The ceremony continues every day on the hour, although its origins are shrouded in legend, conflicting historical record, and perhaps invented nostalgia resulting from error. In the tower of St. Mary's Church in Krakow, Poland, a lone trumpeter plays a short tune called "Hejnal Mariacki" in each of the four compass directions, stopping abruptly on a high note. It has become a prime tourist attraction in the city, with visitors crowding into the tower to watch the performance. Indeed, it has become a symbol of endurance and defiance for Poles everywhere: when Polish troops fighting with the British and Americans finally captured the famed monastery of Monte Cassino from the Germans during World War II, a Polish trumpeter honored the occasion there with the *Hejnal*. The death of Pope John Paul II in 2005 marked one of the few times the tune was not played in the church.

According to legend, although the documentation is somewhat contradictory on the event, the custom sprang from an incident during the Mongols' 1241 invasion of Eastern Europe. Trumpeters were customarily used to announce the opening and closing of the city gates at dawn and dusk, and to warn of danger. As the Mongol riders approached the city, the trumpeter was said to have sounded the alarm by playing the *Hejnal* in a frantic attempt to alert the gatekeepers to barricade the entrances to the city. They closed the gates in time and the city was saved—but a Mongol archer put an arrow through the trumpeter's throat just as he hit the high note that now marks the end of the song.

The first mention of the *Hejnal* itself is not found until a century and a half later. Other records do indeed refer to the Mongol invasion and trumpeters in the tower, but say nothing of an arrow being the reason for the song's abrupt ending. In the 1920s, a visiting American scholar, Eric Kelley, mentioned the incident in a children's book about the event but admitted later that the translation of the account he used may not have been accurate. The story as he related it, however, took off and was quickly absorbed into the local folklore; the tune was played regularly on Poland's national radio station. In 2000, a Guinness Record was set when the song was played by an international group of nearly 2,000 trumpeters.

For our purposes, the authenticity of the incident is less important than what it represents: the westernmost European reach of the Mongols' Eurasian super-empire. With the inclusion of China forty years later, this formerly scattered, disunited, and numerically miniscule nomadic people created the largest land empire in human history. While the settled peoples they conquered uniformly condemned them as bloodthirsty barbarians, many scholars have come to see their *Pax Mongolica* as the pivotal point marking the beginning of the modern period in Eurasian history. For this history of modern East Asia as well, along with the earlier spread of Chinese cultural influence, it spelled an enormously consequential transition period for all the peoples it touched.

GENGHIS KHAN AND THE MONGOL CONQUEST

The Mongol interval, lasting only from their unification by Genghis Khan in 1206 to the end of their Yuan Dynasty in China in 1368, was one of the great dividing lines in East Asian—and world—history. Students of Mongolian, Central Asian, and world history see it as a defining epoch on a number of levels: It was the largest land empire ever created; it knit together, albeit briefly, most of the Eurasian continent, and those lands that it did not touch were keenly aware of its presence. It swept away or altered political and social institutions over a vast area. It created the biggest trading sphere the world had yet seen, facilitating the circulation of a host of innovations. Finally, the image it fixed in the European consciousness of a source of incalculable wealth ultimately led to the Eurasian encounter with three previously unknown continents and the creation of truly global trading systems and empires (see Map 4.1).

For East Asian history, the impact was even more direct and so we have used it as a convenient starting point for examining the area's modern history. Every region under consideration in this volume was touched by the Mongol's empire: China, Korea, northern Vietnam, and, of course, the vast reaches of Central and Western Asia as well as Mongolia itself. The sole East Asian exception to some form of Mongol occupation was Japan. This is not, however, to say that Japan was insulated from its effects. Two Mongol invasions of Japan in 1274 and 1281 were attempted and aborted, the final one as a result of the typhoon ever after commemorated as the "divine wind"—*kamikaze*. Indeed, the fear of further Mongol invasions animated Japanese commentators for some time afterward. Vietnam faced no less than three Mongol invasions, although the Tran Dynasty managed to survive them all.

As we have noted, the many peoples along the northern Chinese perimeter and extending deep into Central Asia and Siberia have long had a powerful effect on the course of East Asian history. Nomads like the Xiongnu, Toba, Uyghurs, Jurchens, and various other Turkic-speaking groups, , as well as more settled groups like the Tibetans, raided the upper and western tiers of various Chinese states, some occasionally even moving into northern Korea. None of these groups, however, had sufficient military power to mount a large-scale invasion of the Chinese core. Indeed, most of the cultural diffusion traveled in the opposite direction as these

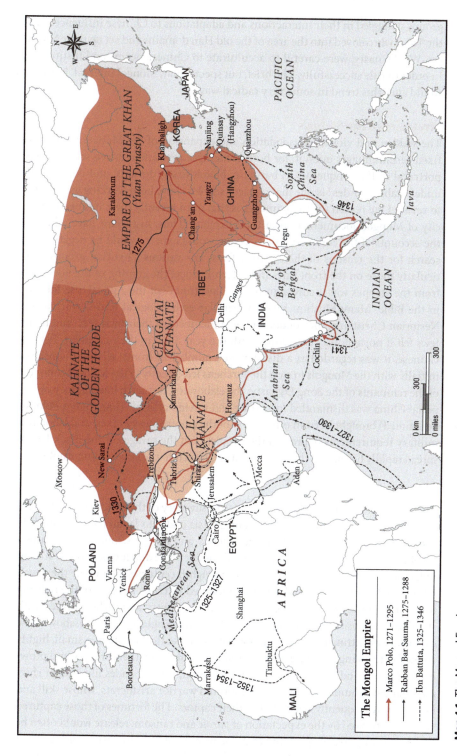

Map 4.1 The Mongol Empire

The Mongol Empire

	Marco Polo, 1271–1295
	Rabban Bar Sauma, 1275–1288
	Ibn Battuta, 1325–1346

groups struggled in their interactions and adaptations to Chinese influence. Even the Toba, who moved into the area of the old Han domains and set up their Northern Wei Dynasty, were careful to acculturate to Chinese norms and institutions in order to rule successfully. The brief, but spectacular, Mongol interval, however, would alter this trend in some very radical ways.

Strategies of the Steppes

The sudden and violent consolidation and expansion of the Mongol world have fixed certain images upon it, for both contemporaries and modern scholars. The portrayal of the conquerors as barbaric, bloodthirsty, devious, and demonically undefeatable "hordes" is one many recent scholars have been working assiduously to revise. One reason for these images is that until recently there has been a paucity of Mongol documentation of their exploits. Thus, historians have relied on the accounts of the conquered that, as one would expect, would be negative and search for the reasons of their own defeats. For various Christian groups, particularly those on the front lines in Eastern Europe, the coming of the horsemen from the steppes was a sure sign of the "end times" of the Apocalypse foretold in the Bible. Many Muslims saw it in similar eschatological terms, whereas for Nestorian Christians, the conquerors held members of their own sect, and many Jews felt it portentously coinciding with the year 5000 in their calendar. For the Chinese, it was regarded as a disaster on a number of fronts: allying themselves initially with the Mongols to stop the Jurchens led directly to the Mongol conquest of the remnants of the Song Dynasty; the elaborate Confucian bureaucracy of imperial China was dismantled for a time and foreign officials (like Marco Polo, so he claimed) brought in from other parts of the empire; heavy taxes, and labor and military requirements oppressed the people; even the ravages of the Black Death spread rapidly because of the integration of China into the larger Mongol holdings.

Clashing Codes of Combat

Their mode of warfare added to the putative savagery of the conquerors. The sedentary societies stretching the length of Eurasia and into Japan had each in their own fashion adopted similar strategies, tactics, and weapons, and in many cases a set of common expectations for battlefield conduct. The development of the stirrup in China, and its spread from the fourth to eighth centuries, had made the development of heavily armed and armored mounted warriors the core of the fighting forces in many areas. These were supported by infantry and archers armed with standard composite bows, longbows (in Wales and England), and crossbows. The expense of outfitting mounted warriors ensured that they would be a small, highly trained elite, vying with each other for honor by showing their bravery and prowess. In Europe and in much of the Muslim world, warrior codes like that of chivalry mandated humane treatment of captured warrior aristocrats, whose skill and bravery were frequently celebrated by their captors. The fortunes of those captured were often buoyed by the expectation of *parole* and ransom: release would often be had by signing a parole pledging that one would not fight in a particular conflict again, often for a specified time; or one's family, colleagues, or lord could pay a

A Persian View of the Mongols. The fury of the Mongols' assaults, and the great gap between their conception of warfare as a hunt and those of the armies of more settled peoples as clashes of champions and auxiliaries, is illustrated nicely in this Persian rendering. Having being lured into an ambush by Mongol horsemen feigning retreat, the vanguard of the erstwhile attackers (top left) now flees in the face of Mongol pursuit (right), with their dead and dying lying on the ground.

ransom for one's release. Although these arrangements were frequently honored more in the breach, and did not apply at all to the commoners who made up the infantry and archers, they had, to some extent, created a system that governed the expectations and conduct of combatants over much of the continent.

For the Mongols, these practices, as for many nomadic warrior peoples, were largely alien, although they had developed their own codes of conduct that were generally observed. Not surprisingly, as peoples of the steppe, they spent most of their lives on horseback, establishing an intimate relationship with the animals and an extraordinary ability to maneuver them, both alone and in formation. Their skill with the powerful composite bows they used was also considerable: nearly every opponent they faced commented on their uncanny ability to continue to shoot at their enemies while riding away from them.

The European and Middle Eastern opponents they faced usually wore heavy coats of chain mail, iron or steel helmets, and some form of plate armor. Theirs was less a war of maneuver than of impact. The stirrup, heeled footware, and a high-back, padded saddle made battlefield tactics highly dependent on charges with long lances to unhorse one's enemy, followed up by individual combat with swords, maces, axes, hammers, morning stars, and other weapons designed for close fighting with an armored opponent. Although the English would famously change this equation with the long bow during the Hundred Years War in the following century, archers and infantry generally played only a supporting role. The archers' job was to try to disrupt the armored charge. The infantry moved in after the opening melee to finish off those unhorsed on the field. Warriors, particularly European knights, saw the field as a place to win renown. They wore elaborate heraldic symbols to identify themselves and their families, and vied for the honor of fighting in the vanguard. For their part, Japanese samurai followed their own code of **bushido** ("the way of the warrior") which, like that of chivalry in Europe, saw combat as an extended set of duels and put a premium on individual daring and prowess.

As the Seljuk Turks, and later the Ottomans, discovered, one way to defeat this kind of army was to put the least proficient troops in the vanguard to be mauled by the mounted warriors, feign retreat, and then surround and charge them with their own elite troops when their opponents were exhausted. It was a variation of this tactic that worked so well for so long for the Mongols.

Although the Mongols certainly valued individual prowess, they viewed battle not so much as a contest of champions than as a hunt. That is, their tactics were similar to those used in pursuing a herd: drive them in such a way as to force them into a small area to limit maneuver, feign retreat to encourage them to charge into a position where they will be surrounded, then close in on them, keeping them from using their own weapons to their advantage. In the rolling grasslands of Central Asia and Eastern Europe, the Mongols proved expert at using the available cover of hills and gullies to hide their forces. They would send a token force out to engage the enemy, pretend to be routed, and draw the charging cavalry into the trap.

Concealment of the main force was always a prime consideration. Time and again, the defending forces of besieged cities would mistake the thinning of the besieging army as discouragement, sally forth to do battle with what they perceived as a remnant, and be utterly routed and slaughtered. This was true as well for those defenders who sought to escape besieged cities or fortresses by night or through tunnels—there was always a deadly force on hand to meet them. At the ancient Iranian city of Nishipur, for example, the sight of the relatively small Mongol vanguard convinced the defenders to fight. When the main force arrived, they invested the walls of the city and lay siege. When the surrender came, the people were led out of the city, all males taller than the wheel of a Mongolian cart were slaughtered, and the women and children were awarded to the conquerors as slaves.

Assimilating Military Technologies

As time went on, the technological know-how of the Mongols increased by way of conquering peoples highly skilled in a variety of military arts. While anxious to accumulate the wealth of the settled peoples, the Mongols valued the practical skills of their craftsmen, doctors, and weapons makers even more. For example, the Southern Song armies the Mongols faced were huge for their time, with some estimates placing them at over 1.5 million, with a formidable navy as well. Moreover, in addition to the various kinds of mechanical siege engines—ballistas, trebouchets, torsion catapults, siege towers—the Chinese had developed a revolutionary array of gunpowder devices by the thirteenth century: bombs as siege engine projectiles and for assaulting walls and gates, rocket arrows, primitive firearms and cannon, even marine and land mines. The Chinese armies, so reliant on infantry, however, could not match the mobility of the Mongol mounted archers and were ultimately worn down.

Mongol Siege Equipment. One of the hallmarks of the Mongol strategy of conquest was the rapid assimilation of military technologies of the conquered. In this, their assaults on fortified cities came to include nearly all the extant techniques of sapping and undermining walls, building siege towers, bridging moats, and, increasingly, using gunpowder charges to blow open gates and rocket arrows to suppress enemy fire on the parapets. This Persian rendering from 1221 features a trebuchet in the lower left corner. A catapult powered by the force of its counterweight, this device was in widespread use throughout Eurasia and remained a primary piece of artillery until replaced by cannon.

Their technical expertise was now utilized by their conquerors. Unlike the armies they faced, the Mongols' emphasis on speed and mobility meant that they did not have their assault forces burdened with heavy siege machinery, a situation that sometimes lulled their opponents into thinking they would be able to withstand a prolonged assault. As often as not, they would build siege engines on the spot of whatever materials were available and bring up whatever they lacked in the slower-moving supply train.

As time went on, Mongols' reputation for invincibility on the battlefield and ruthlessness to those who decided to fight became highly effective propaganda. Cities that surrendered immediately were generally spared and some leading citizens strategically allowed to flee to neighboring cities to warn them of the choices they would soon face. Similarly, after sacking a less fortunate town, some would be allowed to survive the slaughter to warn others of the consequences of not surrendering to the new order. When the Central Asian city of Bukhara's defenders fled the city, the Mongol army lying in wait easily devastated them. On news of this disaster, the fabled city of Samarkand opted for immediate surrender. Perhaps the most dramatic example of this policy occurred in the early 1240s when the Hungarians, led in person by their king Bela, led an army to face the forces of Genghis Khan's grandson, Batu. At one point, the Hungarian army literally "circled the wagons" in hopes of creating a temporary fortress from which to wait things out as the Mongols expended their arrows. For the Mongols, however, their opponents had simply done their herding for them. They brought up fire arrows, fire bombs filled with gunpowder and naphtha, and machines

Mongols Fighting Hungarians. The different fighting styles of the Mongols and Europeans are vividly illustrated in this fourteenth-century illustration from the Hungarian National Library's *Chronicum Pictum*. Dismounted Mongol horsemen in their conical hats on the left fire their powerful composite bows at Hungarian knights wielding swords and shields in a 1285 battle. Captured Hungarian women can be seen on the extreme left, in back of the Mongol front rank.

to hurl them. With the wagons and brush inside the enclosure on fire, the flee-ing knights were picked off piecemeal. A number were driven into a swamp where, burdened with their plate armor, many drowned. Estimates run as high as 100,000 Teutonic, Polish, and Hungarian knights killed and perhaps over a million people of all classes before the campaign ended.

The Mongols' single-minded pursuit of conquest, their skill on the battle-field, and their apparent indifference to considerations of religion (although they often spared the clergy of different faiths), ethnicity, or ideology, not surprisingly made them terrifying to their opponents. Estimates as to the total number of killed in all the Mongol wars of conquest vary but run as high as 30 million. They must have seemed to many contemporaries like a medieval version of the unstop-pable science-fiction collective of cyber-beings called the "Borg" on the television program *Star Trek, the Next Generation*. The unrelenting drive of the Borg was to assimilate all beings they encountered along with their technology; their pro-nouncement to their opponents was always, "Resistance is futile."

The Mongol Conquest: The Initial Phase

How was an unlikely collection of scattered groups of nomads on the periphery of arguably the most technologically advanced, densely populated, well-organized and armed society on Earth able to create the largest land empire on record? Although it is rare in history for a single individual to have such an enormous impact on whole societies, this was one instance in which the interaction of that individual with the social groups of his own society, an understanding of their patterns, habits, and motivations, and a healthy dose of the contingent and the unforeseen conspired to create unprecedented change.

In the mid-twelfth century CE, the Mongols were, in a manner of speak-ing, on the periphery of the periphery: the northern hill regions of what is now central Mongolia. Like the Oirats, whom they would later subdue, their language was part of a subgroup of the large Altaic family, but distinct from the Tungusic and Turkic groups to the south and west. Their lands bordered forested hills and grasslands, and they lived by hunting and herding on the margins of the lands of wealthier peoples. Here, they were separated by the vast Gobi (Govi) Desert from larger nomadic groups like the Uyghurs and from the oasis trading communi-ties on the Silk Road, as well as from more settled peoples further south in what is now the Inner Mongolia Autonomous Region in China. Like many groups in the region, they lived in mobile camps in **gers** (yurts)—family-sized tents made of yak, camel, or sheep fur pounded into felt mats. Their prized possessions were their horses, and they had scant need or desire for things not deemed practical to their life of constant movement (see Map 4.2).

Families, clans, and villages had complex relationships with each other. Intermarriage for economic and political reasons was common, and unlike the sedentary societies they would one day subdue, women had much higher status, more flexible roles, and considerable political power. Thus, into the Borjin clan, a boy called Timujin, a name taken from a man his father killed in a raid, was born in 1167.

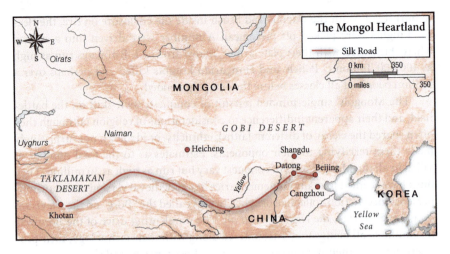

Map 4.2 The Mongol Heartland

As noted above, one difficulty scholars encounter with the Mongols is the relative lack of usable source materials written by them. At this point, they had no written language—it would be decades before Timujin and his subordinates created one based on the Uyghur script. Later accounts, like the early histories of other peoples in the region, would be heavily encrusted with fabrications and mythology. Chronicles of later Mongol governments, such as the history of the Yuan Dynasty in China and those of the Ilkhans in Persia and the Middle East, would prove relatively reliable on the events of their own periods but scanty on earlier times. The most notable accounts of the rise of the Mongol Empire written later by the Persians Ata-Malik Juvaini (1226–1283) and Rashid al-Din (1247–1318) were also penned from an outsider's perspective, although Rashid served as an official in the Ilkhanate.

Thus, one of the great finds of the nineteenth century was a document written in both Chinese and Mongolian that became known to scholars as *The Secret History of the Mongols*. The difficulty with the document, however, was that it was written in a kind of code in which the landmarks and geography seemed impossibly obscure, complicated by the fact that many of the places in question were believed to be in the tabooed area of Genghis Khan's gravesite. Only recently has this source material been sufficiently deciphered to make it usable for historians.

It is frequently claimed in the mythology surrounding famous historical figures that they had some sign or peculiarity about them as children that marked them for greatness. For Timujin, it was said that he was born with a blood clot on his hand that marked him this way, and indeed his rise seemed so unlikely to contemporaries that the signs were difficult to doubt. After the death of his father, Timujin and his mother, Hoelun, spurned as outcasts by their clan, lived a hardscrabble foragers' existence on the steppe. As he grew into manhood, his grit and self-reliance helped him make a mark and reputation in local raids, feuds, and alliances. His hard-won insight into clan politics and intrigue enabled him to gradually knit together the isolated and poor Mongol groups. With each success, wealth in horses and flocks grew. His group expanded northward toward the forested hills of the Oirats and south to the borders of the Gobi, absorbing groups such as the Merkid and Naiman, but, as it turned out, never completely enough to stem any chance of rebellion.

The pivotal moment for expansion came in 1205–1206 when he organized a grand meeting of the tribes. In addition to putting together a written language derived from the Sogdian/Old Uyghur alphabet, Timujin and his allies, in effect, founded the Mongol polity and set up kinship and alliance-based institutions for government. As the premier ruler or **khan,** Timujin acquired the title of *Genghis* (often rendered as *Chinggis*) *Khan,* "The Universal Ruler." His success at creating a Mongol state, and the seemingly miraculous manner in which he managed to avoid death and bounce

Portrait of Genghis Khan. Having never had his portrait painted during his lifetime, Genghis Khan's actual features have remained strictly guesswork for artists in succeeding generations. One early rendering is this one by an anonymous Chinese artist in the Mongol Yuan Dynasty. Here, the conqueror is given the features typical of those used by court painters depicting Chinese emperors, although without the robes and regalia of imperial position.

back from apparent defeat and oblivion, convinced him over time that he was destined by the Mongols' divinities, essentially Heaven and Earth, to be the ruler of a universal empire.

The most attractive places to start building this empire were the steppe lands south of the Gobi and the Silk Road—the main land conduit for the rich trade from China into Central Asia and beyond. The strategic bottleneck of the route was the narrow pass through what is now the Chinese province of Gansu, which became the target for expansion to the west. Those in control of the passage were the Tanguts, a settled Tibetan people who had been used as buffers by the Tang and Song dynasties. By alliances and a few sharp fights, the Mongols brought the Tanguts into their system and married one of Genghis Khan's daughters to the Tangut ruler, who became a subordinate khan. Increasingly, he cemented his alliances by arranging for his daughters to marry allied leaders. His daughters were strong, generally capable rulers, and were enjoined by their father to actually rule as his adjutants and not as subordinates to their husbands, who were now required to serve in the swelling Mongol armies.

With the Gansu corridor safely in their hands, the Mongols moved further out on the Silk Road and concluded a similar arrangement with the Uyghurs. By the time of Genghis Khan's death in 1227, his breadth of control extended along the entire northern tier of China to Manchuria and deep into Central Asia. The wealth of the increasingly Sinified Jurchen conquerors of the Northern Song Chinese Dynasty, who had forced the Song remnant to set up a state to the south a century before in 1127, remained a constant goal although one he was unable to accomplish in his lifetime. The Jurchen Jin Dynasty ultimately fell to Genghis Khan's son Ogodei in 1234.

The Drive to the West

Nonetheless, expansion continued apace. Having tied the Uyghur lands to their empire, the Mongols set their sights one by one on the great cities of the western Silk Road. Valuing the commerce of the oasis towns they subdued, they tended to be generous to merchants and craftsmen in trying to facilitate production and commerce. With the contempt for the settled often shown by nomads, however, they conscripted peasants as laborers. Even more alarming for those of the upper classes, the Mongols saw local aristocrats as potential rebels and tended to exterminate them, while attempting to convince the survivors that their quest was one of universal liberation.

From the eleventh to thirteenth centuries, the conversion of different Turkic peoples to Islam had created a wave of conquests in the lands stretching from Persia into Afghanistan and, through the raids and eventual settlement of the Ghaznavids and Gur, into northern India and western Central Asia. The most powerful of these was Khwarism, which encompassed most of modern Iran and Iraq and extended east past Samarkand and Bukhara. According to Jaivani, Genghis Khan had initially expressed no designs on the empire. Indeed, he sent a trade delegation to the sultan in 1218 with a letter addressing him as an equal. On reaching the town of Otrar in present-day Khazakstan, however, the provincial governor, fearing that the delegation was actually a ruse, had them executed and confiscated their goods. When the Mongols demanded an apology and reparations, the sultan refused and the Mongols mounted an invasion. The predictable result was the fall of Samarkand, Bukhara, and the end of the state altogether by 1231.

The push into the Muslim lands to the west had several profound implications both for the territories conquered and for the long-term health of the Mongol Empire. The first is that these drives under Genghis Khan and, for the remainder of the thirteenth century, his sons and grandsons, would substantially break the power of the old Abbasid Caliphate, the Seljuk domains, and their subordinate states, and replace them with **Ilkhanates**—the domains of subordinate khans like Genghis' grandson, Hulegu. Here, perhaps the most spectacular conquest was the brutal sack of Baghdad in 1258. One of world's largest cities as well as one of the great centers of culture, law, politics, learning, and the home of some of the world's oldest universities and libraries, it never again regained anything like its former prestige.

The Siege of Baghdad. The capture of Baghdad by the Mongols in 1258 spelled the end of the illustrious Abbasid Caliphate and the destruction of one of the world's largest and culturally wealthiest cities. The city itself never regained the prestige and splendor it had enjoyed before its fall, and the destruction of its universities and libraries was a tremendous blow to the intellectual heritage of Islam. In this painting, Mongol armies besiege the city walls, hurl missiles at defenders with portable slings, and invest the city—with its turbaned men and veiled women powerless to stop them.

By the 1240s, the door to Eastern Europe had also been kicked open, and the Mongol conquest of Novgorod and the Kievan Rus was accomplished by Genghis Khan's grandson, Batu (1205–1255). The Golden Horde, as this territory that stretched to Krakow in Poland came to be known (from the word Turkic *ordos*, or *ordu*, meaning "camp" or "territory," but that has come to be associated with great numbers of barbaric warriors, or *hordes*) would extract tribute from the region into the 1400s. The eventual refusal to pay tribute, led by the principality of Muscovy, ultimately led to the development of Russia. Long before this, however, the seemingly unstoppable Mongol drive into Eastern Europe came to an abrupt end in 1242. The reasons for this have long been debated, with one school of thought holding that the death of Ogodei, who had assumed his father's mantle of Great Khan, required choosing a new leader and curtailed the expedition. Another holds that the invaders judged the swampy terrain in which they found themselves operating to be unsuitable for massed cavalry attacks. In 2016, a team of scientists studying tree ring evidence from the period concluded that there had indeed been an interval of extraordinarily wet weather, which might well have discouraged the invaders.

PATTERNS UP-CLOSE

Pax Mongolica

With the coming of the Mongol Empire, nearly all of East Asia, with the exception of Japan and most of Vietnam, would for the first time be under one polity. Unlike previous intruders, however, the conquerors resisted cultural assimilation in all the areas they touched. On the one hand, they tended to retain the distain that nomadic warriors felt toward more settled peoples. On the other hand, as their empire expanded to include Islamic, Buddhist, and Confucian Chinese civilizations, they realized that adopting one of these as their universal system would be unworkable. Once considered to have instituted little in the way of systematic government, the Mongols actually set up a continentwide system flexible enough to incorporate most of the governmental structures of their conquered states—with members of Genghis Khan's family superimposed at the top—and supported by officials from different regions rotated to different posts.

Examples of Paiza. By way of facilitating trade and provisioning official travelers, the Mongols early on began to issue *paiza* (Chinese *paizi*; Mongolian *gerege*): tablets or medallions indicating that the possessor was entitled to ask for and receive goods from the local people. After reports of abuses and counterfeit tablets, their use was restricted to civilian and military officials, although these individuals, in turn, were authorized on occasion to use them on behalf of foreign merchants like Marco Polo, who left a description of their use in his *Travels*. As with many innovations, the Mongols did not invent these passes, which had been in use in northern China, but spread them throughout *Pax Mongolica*. The samples here, bearing Mongolian script, were issued during the last years of the Yuan Dynasty, dated ca. 1361–1370.

Many of the Mongols' innovations strike us as modern today, perhaps a bit misleadingly. Officials were appointed on merit; local aristocracies were dismantled; bridges and infrastructure to facilitate trade and mobility were constructed. Finding the Chinese writing system uncongenial to their needs as a first written language, they developed their own alphabetical script adapted from the Uyghurs. Centuries later, it would replace Khitan as the basis for the written language of the Manchus. While the Mongols of Genghis Khan's time nearly all believed in a shamanistic religion based on the unity of all peoples under the "Eternal Blue Sky," many later converted to Buddhism, Islam, and a small minority to Nestorian Christianity. Religious toleration, however, was practiced throughout their empire, a condition almost entirely unknown in much of western Eurasia. Scholars often refer to the period of Mongol ascendency as the *Pax Mongolica* (Mongolian Peace), because of its parallels to the long domination of the Roman Empire and the relative peace within its borders known as *Pax Romana*.

Although not authors of technological innovation themselves, the Mongols provided the mechanism of technology transfer that allowed such items as gunpowder, the compass, coal, printing, paper, checks and paper money, and a host of other Chinese developments to spread throughout Eurasia and, in some cases (e.g., gunpowder), even further. Moreover, much of the medical knowledge of the Islamic and Mediterranean world now found its way to China through their aegis. In many cases, however, this circulation was accomplished by forced removal of populations and the active rotating of officials and military forces. Nonetheless, the relative openness and ease of travel throughout the empire allowed sojourners like Marco Polo and Ibn Battuta to cement the Mongol interval in East Asia, particularly in China, as the region's norm in the minds of Europeans. When an obscure navigator named Christopher Columbus sailed in 1492, it was Polo's vision—and the now heavily annotated account of his travels—that was his primary guide to the China to which he believed he was heading.

For all these reasons, scholars have recently revised their accounts of the Mongol era, some crediting it with laying the groundwork for the early modern world. Some go so far as to present the Mongol's super-regional empire as "pre-" or "quasi-" globalization. Indeed, taking the term from the concept of the "Columbian Exchange" that spread Eurasian and African knowledge, biota, culture, and technology to the Americas and that of the Americas around the world, one scholar has called the Mongol interval the "Chinggis (Genghis) Exchange."

Subduing China

It was also true, however, that the empire, still vigorous at the front lines of its advance, was now weakening at its core. Although Genghis Khan had named Ogodei as his successor, the transfer of loyalty from person to institution did not take place. Indeed, in the tradition of the nomads of the steppe, for a long time there had not even been an actual capital, a condition abetted by Genghis Khan's dislike of cities. The settlement that functioned as the center of power, Karakoram, was in reality a perimeter of movable camps. Observers were routinely underwhelmed by its amenities, and its essential function was to warehouse accumulated loot.

The power held by Genghis Khan's daughters as subordinate khans, and the power of his grandsons as conquerors, raised potential challenges to Ogodei. Thus, he spent most of his reign attempting to consolidate his position by trying to dismantle the power of his sisters and sons. In doing so, he acquired a reputation for misrule and cruelty that enhanced the Mongols' reputation for both. On his death, the struggle continued. Now the khan in the favored position was Genghis'

Elite Mongol Women. Women held considerable power in Mongol society. Genghis Khan's daughters, for example, functioned as surrogate local rulers relegating the husbands to whom they were married to subordinate status. Pictured here are Chabi, the wife of the first Yuan emperor, Shizu (Khubilai Khan), on the right, and Taji, mother of Renzong (Buyantu Khan), fourth emperor of the Yuan.

Khubilai Khan Khubilai Khan, founder of the Yuan Dynasty of China under the reign name of Shizu. He ruled the Mongol empire overall from 1260 to 1294, and in China from 1280 to 1294. He was a grandson of Genghis Khan.

grandson Khubulai, who attempted to appropriate the title of Universal Khan, and is known through Western chroniclers like Marco Polo as "the Great Khan."

The new Mongol lands wrested from the Jurchens, as mentioned above, were in many respects, like those of their descendants, the Manchus, essentially Chinese with Sinicized nomadic rulers at the top. They were by far the most populous lands in the Mongol Empire, with perhaps 50 million inhabitants, with another 50 million in the lands still controlled by the Southern Song Dynasty. The Jurchen state also extended into Korea, and the Mongols now claimed this territory as well. Having established himself as ruler in his new territories, Khubulai moved the capital from Karakorum to Khanbaligh, called by the Chinese Dadu—the future city of Beijing—in 1267.

The Mongols' hard-won experience in subduing the Jurchen Jin Dynasty was now brought to bear on the Southern Song. The Song military forces, as we mentioned earlier, were enormous for their time and utilized the most advanced military hardware, including a large array of gunpowder weapons. The Mongols, however, had by now extensive experience with these, and a host of weapons acquired from the Jurchens and from the peoples they encountered in other areas. Moreover, the military had never been an honored profession in China, and their armies, although huge, were often ill-provisioned, ill-disciplined, ill-prepared, and financed only fitfully from a shrinking tax base.

With the Chinese armies largely reliant on slow-moving infantry, the Mongols mercilessly hammered at isolated units, stragglers, and supply lines. Walled cities, the most difficult objectives for the Mongols early on, were now much less so because of their decades of experience in attacking and taking them all over Eurasia. In densely populated China, the Mongol tactic of driving refugees before them to add to the burden of a city's defenders was even more effective than it had been along the sparsely populated Silk Road. Their expertise with siege machinery, techniques for undermining walls, and explosives for blowing open gates was now at a peak of efficiency. Although the Song naval forces gave a much more spirited account of themselves than the land armies, theirs was a delaying action at best. Having never needed to reckon with naval power before, the Mongols for a time were held at bay on the Yangzi and its tributaries. By the 1270s, however, the ultimate outcome was clear. The Song capital of Linan (Hangzhou) fell to the Mongols in 1276. The dynasty ended with the death of the young Song emperor in 1279 as he attempted to flee by sea.

From Victory to Disunity

In 1280, Khubilai proclaimed the Yuan Dynasty in his new holdings, taking the reign name of Shizu. In a way, this signaled a significant change in Mongol fortunes. On the one hand, many of the world's richest, most populous, and commercially vibrant areas were now under the control of what was nominally a unified empire. In terms of all the constituent khans encouraging trade, building infrastructure along land routes, and sponsoring and protecting caravans, it did represent a prototype free-trade zone. Politically, however, it became increasingly fragmented. By Khubilai's death in 1294, what had been one super-empire was now essentially four squabbling khanates: the Ilkhans in Persia and the Middle East, whose advance had been halted by the Mamluks of Egypt; the Golden Horde, occupying a vast stretch of territory in what is now Ukraine and Russia; the khanate of Chagatai, centered at Samarkand and occupying a pivotal position astride the trade routes in Central Asia; and the Yuan Dynasty, stretching from Mongolia into Korea, through most of China, and down into Tibet and Vietnam.

This short-lived Yuan Dynasty now faced the familiar problem of those from the periphery settling in to try to rule. Like their predecessors going all the way back to the Zhou, the necessity of adopting and inhabiting the institutions they now commanded required adaptation in order to make them function in an orderly way. This was especially true for the Mongols because their tiny population of about a million now had to govern as many as 100 times that number in their Chinese empire alone. Moreover, the governmental improvisations of Genghis Khan now came up against institutions that in some cases had functioned for over a thousand years, and were based on philosophical and ethical systems even older. Thus, the Mongols, like the Manchus who came after them, found themselves reluctantly adapting to Chinese culture to keep the existing systems in operation while struggling to maintain the culture of the steppes.

In some ways, this was now an easier transition than for those of Genghis Khan's generation. The grandson Khans had come of age when their families were already fabulously wealthy and powerful, and in this respect, it was hardly a leap for Khubilai to take on the trappings and dynastic rituals of a Chinese emperor. Moreover, the rigorous life of the steppe was now a distant memory, its life in the saddle, herding, and hunting replaced with opulent ceremonial commemorations of those days. Even military campaigning was far less rigorous for the khans than in former times, and so the skills so necessary to the Mongols' early successes were already eroding.

To a considerable extent, the fragmentation of the Mongol Empire broke down the idea that the leadership should not adopt a particular religious and cultural tradition because none of them could be satisfactorily stretched to fit the needs of universal empire. Thus, the Ilkhans converted to Islam, married into the local population, and eventually disappeared as a distinct ethnicity. Likewise, the descendants of Chagatai converted to Islam and, although their line did not stay intact, attempted to maintain their genealogy. From this line, the fourteenth-century conqueror Tamerlane claimed Genghis Khan as his ancestor; Tamerlane's putative descendant, Babur, also claiming the legacy of Genghis Khan, became the progenitor of the Timurids (from Tamerlane), the dynasty in India called the Mughals. For their part, some of the Mongols in Yuan territories (as well as Han Chinese and members of other minority groups) also converted to Islam. Others converted to Buddhism, with the Tibetan varieties such as the Yellow Hat sect later headed by the Dalai Lama proving especially attractive.

In the Yuan territories, administrative needs ultimately trumped Mongol practices of governance. Initially, a number of senior Chinese officials were purged and others resigned in protest of the new order. The practice of bringing in officials and advisors from other regions in the empire proved only partially

successful and caused widespread consternation among Chinese officials and aspiring scholar-gentry. Ultimately, the examination system was reinstated in 1315,
continuing until 1905.

Although the four large khanates competed for prestige and resisted
Kubulai's claim to the title of Great Khan, the relative ease of travel and enhanced
commerce continued. As we saw, China was open on an unprecedented scale to
a variety of foreign goods, ideas, and travelers, while Chinese goods circulated in
greater variety and profusion than ever before. A variety of emissaries and missionaries from the developing states of Europe now for the first time traveled east
to the Yuan capital city of Khanbaligh.

Despite the fact that the Mongols had devastated much of Christian Eastern
Europe in the early 1240s, their destruction of the Abbasids in 1258 and reports
of groups of Mongol Christians had fanned hopes that Christianity might be
widely adopted and that the Mongols would assist in crusading efforts. Indeed,
Rabban Sauma, a Turkish Nestorian Christian who had been born in China, traveled from Khanbaligh to Paris and Rome, even celebrating a Mass with the Pope

Caravan across the Steppe. The Mongol dedication to fostering trade is illustrated here in
the Catalan Atlas of 1375. Put together by Cresques Abraham, a Jewish Catalan illustrator,
the Atlas was for Europeans the most complete depiction of the world at the time. The
legend notes that the caravan pictured is traveling from the empire of Sarra (from Sarai, the
bustling capital of the Mongol Kipchak Khanate, or Golden Horde) to "Alcatayo" or China
(from *Catayo*: Cathay), following a well-traveled branch of the Silk Route. Because much of
the information probably came from Marco Polo's *Travels*, this plate is often referred to as
the Polo caravan.

in 1278. The two most famous travel accounts of the era, those of the Venetian Marco Polo (1254–1324) and Ibn Battuta of Tangier (1304–1377), who lived and journeyed throughout the Mongol Empire, are testament to the powerful impact of Mongol rule on facilitating travel over such a vast area.

Overthrow and Retreat

The Yuan period is almost universally regarded by the Chinese as one of imperial China's darkest times. Although the Mongols quickly restored order and allowed a relative tolerance of religious practice and expression, the dynasty was seen as an oppressive time of large standing armies, ineffective administration, forced labor, and heavy taxes. Compounding the intensity of the tensions between Mongols and their subjects was perhaps the single worst disaster of the fourteenth century, the bubonic plague. Although scholars have only recently begun to examine Chinese mortality rates resulting from the plague, accounts suggest that they were in all likelihood similar to those of Europe, with perhaps one-third of the population of about 100 million being eliminated from the 1340s until the end of the century. One thing that seems clear, however, is that by facilitating travel and commerce, the Mongol regimes unknowingly opened the door for the disease to go from being a regional disaster to a continentwide pandemic.

Over the following decades, the power of the Mongols continued to decline, both at the center and in the peripheral states as well. Perhaps the first and most dramatic evidence of this was the overthrow of the Yuan and the restoration of Chinese rule under the Ming Dynasty in 1368. This was accompanied by an exodus of refugee Yuan officials and Mongol civilians, although many Mongols who had settled in China decided to take their chances and stay. Later, under the Qing, Chinese armies would include elite Mongol cavalry units.

As we noted above, the Ilkhanates were quickly melding into the local population and culture, ultimately to yield to the rise of Tamerlane, and by the sixteenth century, the Ottoman Turks. By the late fifteenth century, the Golden Horde was in retreat from local revolts, and Chagatai was fragmented by factional warfare until the coming of Tamerlane. By the early 1400s, the Mongol overlords of most of Eurasia were in headlong retreat, falling back to their original stronghold on the Mongolian steppes. There would, however, be one final attempt to regroup and stem the retreat. In the early 1440's, Esen, a descendant of Genghis Khan's Borijin family, began another attempt to unite the feuding Mongol clans. Unlike recent pretenders to the conqueror's mantle and the strong men who dominated the remaining Mongol realms, Esen was able to alternatively force and persuade the scattered Mongol and Oirat groups. Like Genghis Khan before him, his initial targets were the Gansu corridor of the Silk Road and the northern tier of China.

The Chinese, sensitive to earlier Mongol attempts at reunification, had abandoned their audacious bid for regional maritime supremacy through the voyages of Zhenghe (see Chapter 5), and begun strengthening their defenses north of the Great Wall. In 1449, Esen's forces defeated a Chinese expeditionary force and captured the Emperor Zhengtong. The power of the Ming, which had been enhanced by advances in the number and quality of firearms, was such that the Mongols could not contemplate attempting to make good their claims to China's throne. They could, however, attempt to enrich themselves by ransoming the emperor. Unfortunately, Ming court politics were such that the Chinese were unwilling to pay for the emperor's return and placed his younger brother on the throne. Thus, Zhengtong remained with his captors and developed cordial relations with them until he was finally returned with no ransom to China the following year. After being placed under house arrest for seven years, he regained the throne through a coup and ruled as the Tianshun emperor until 1465. Although the next two and a half centuries saw sporadic attacks on the Chinese borderlands and the Silk Road by the Mongols, they never again were able to seriously challenge the Ming or Qing. By the mid-eighteenth century, punitive expeditions by the powerful Qing emperor Qianlong (r. 1736–1795) broke the scant remaining power of the Mongols forever.

THE MONGOL COMMERCIAL REVOLUTION

As we have seen several times in this chapter, both scholars of Mongolia and many world historians see the *Pax Mongolica* as "a," perhaps "the," Eurasian watershed event. The perceptions of those outside the empire have tended to oscillate over the centuries between seeing Genghis Khan and his successors as representing nomadic barbarism at its most savage and portraying the Mongols as wise, tolerant, and even "modern" innovators. This is especially true of European and Western views: during and immediately after the waves of Mongol invasions, they were the "scourge of God," harbingers of the end times foretold in the Bible, cruel, demonic, and unstoppable. By the time of the first European accounts, the image had begun to change to a more neutral one, as optimism grew that the Mongols might be religiously receptive to Catholicism. It was Marco Polo's *Travels*, however, that reversed the older image and painted the lands of the Mongols, particularly Khubilai Khan's China, as not just the richest, most populous, most fabulous, and best-governed society, but one extending an outstretched hand to merchants of all lands. The Enlightenment and Romantic periods also saw this oscillation with Voltaire painting Genghis Khan in cruel and barbarous strokes as a stand-in for his own monarch, Louis XV, and Coleridge fancifully portraying Khubilai Khan's opulence in "Xanadu."

The switch back to the barbarous image during the age of pseudo-scientific human hierarchies, with the assertion of racial stereotypes such as "Mongoloid" during the nineteenth and early twentieth centuries, began to change for most East Asian peoples after World War II, although the barbarous image of the Mongols—as for many nomadic warrior peoples—remained much longer. From the 1940s through the 1970s, this image only gave ground grudgingly through the dogged efforts of a handful of Central Asian specialists and world historians. Nowhere was this change more evident than in economics.

Rebuilding Agriculture and Infrastructure

As has always been the case in China, the peasants of the Yuan period were caught in the contradiction of being praised as the bedrock of society while bearing the major brunt of taxation and labor conscription. The Mongols initially enacted a system designed to purge taxation of its variability and set consistent rates for peasants. Indeed, earlier, Genghis Khan had reduced taxes in conquered areas: for pastoralists, it was as low as 1 percent. In order to reclaim much of the farmland that had been damaged and neglected during the conquest of the Jin and the Song, the Mongols organized village cooperatives, not unlike the long-standing *baojia* system. Rural areas were organized in groups of fifty families under an approved headman.

The cost of rebuilding, embarking on large infrastructure projects, and construction in Khanbaligh, Kaifeng, Linan, and other cities, however, soon required the raising of taxes and a large leap in conscript labor obligations. Peasants also largely footed the bill and provided the muscle to extend the Grand Canal to the Beihe to serve Khanbaligh, to build new and improve old roads and canals, and to staff the new and highly efficient system of postal stations throughout the empire. By the end of the thirteenth century, the institution of tax farming—awarding the task of tax collection to a contractor who could keep any revenues above the quota he was required to supply—was widespread, as was the corruption it engendered. In many cases, local tax farmers and landlords also served as money lenders, thus enriching themselves further while raising the atmosphere of resentment and oppression among peasants.

Conscription for labor also meant that peasants were increasingly hard-pressed in working their own holdings for produce and cash in remitting taxes. By the 1340s, outbreaks of the plague also had many of the same effects on the peasantry in the Mongol holdings as it did in Europe. With the population radically reduced, labor became scarcer and more expensive, and tax revenues declined, forcing tax increases. The increased need for defense also put pressure on revenues.

Role Reversal: Artisans and Merchants

For the peoples along the Silk Road and in the Muslim Ilkhanates, trade had always been the lifeblood of the economy. Agriculture was spotty at best in the long stretches of desert and arid land in Central Asia. Even at the most flourishing oases, nomadic merchants and middlemen, like their new Mongol overlords, relied on their flocks and herds for sustenance. Farther west in the areas around the Caspian Sea and old Abbasid lands, agriculture was much more dominant. But their position as the central crossroads of the continent, where trade from the Silk Road branched out in dozens of directions toward the Mediterranean and Black Seas, ensured that trade would be a dominant and valued economic factor. For the Mongols, therefore, the status of traders and artisans was already high and much of the region's economy relied on commerce.

The situation in Confucian East Asia was rather more economically and socially complex. Confucian officials tended to view merchants with suspicion as parvenus whose values were inimical to stable society, and whose wealth was mobile and hence without roots. Yet China generated vast amounts of trade, although the government tended to take a passive role toward it. Thus, the social status of merchants was, in theory at least, below that of peasants and artisans—who actually produced useful things—while traders merely trafficked in them for profit. They were seen as vaguely disreputable, though grudgingly necessary, social and economic factors.

Mongol policies now turned these perceptions on their heads. Merchants and artisans became favored classes under the Mongols, who provided generous tax breaks, even exemptions, for craftsmen and merchants. Both classes were also exempt from labor obligations. The extensive system of Buddhist monastery-hostels and region-affiliated guest houses for traveling merchants was vastly expanded by the new system of postal stations throughout Mongol lands. These, in turn, were supported by ambitious programs of road and canal building.

The Mongols drive for trade and growing love of novelty resulted in economic policies designed to enhance and simplify commerce, and make it safer. Passport seals that were recognized in all the Mongol territories were issued to travelers. Paper money, checks, vouchers, merchant banking and credit systems, most of which were developed by the Song, were now extensively employed throughout the empire.

Traditionally, the Silk Road caravans were small-scale operations whereby local traders made relatively short trips between oases towns using Bactrian (two-hump) camels. The goods would then be sold or offloaded to other middlemen, who would take them along the next leg of the journey. This process was slow and quite costly because at each stage someone took a percentage and tolls, taxes, and bribes were exacted at border crossings. Recognizing the potential for expanding trade by easing these obstacles, the Mongols oversaw the kinds of infrastructural improvements mentioned above—garrisons, postal stations, hostels—and the scaling up and extending of the caravans themselves. With accommodations, roads, and safety enhanced, much larger caravans could be assembled. In some cases, they traveled the entire distance from China to the Mediterranean, expanding the supply of goods and lowering the cost. This resulted in an enormous jump in the volume of traffic and made it possible for the first time for Europeans like the Polos to make the journey.

At the same time, shipping by caravan across vast, rugged country with wild extremes of weather, even with a reduced threat of attack and banditry, still entailed considerable risk. Thus, the Mongols set up merchants' associations called **ortogh**, perhaps their most innovative venture, in which traders could pool their investments in a caravan and reduce their personal liability if the caravan met with misfortune along the way. Such associations were taxed at a reduced rate of 3½ percent (as opposed to the usual 5 percent) and functioned much like the limited liability corporations and insurance systems established later on in Europe.

***Caravansarai* in Armenia.** Way stations for long-distance travelers on frequented trade routes had been commonplace for millennia. The Greek historian Herodotus noted such rest stops or *caravanserai* (from the Persian, "a compound with a walled enclosure and open court for travelers") throughout the roads of the Persian Empire. For the Mongols, much concerned with fostering trade, such stops were an absolute necessity, and hundreds were built throughout the empire and within the successor khanates. The rest stops generally included fodder, water, and stalls for pack animals; food and lodging for the travelers themselves; and often bathing facilities and shops for supplies and trade. The structure shown here is typical of the portal for the animals and was built in Armenia in 1332.

FAMILY, GENDER, RELIGION, AND CULTURE

In some respects, the Mongols shared a number of common traits with other nomadic peoples of the steppe. Perhaps most noteworthy among these was a more or less egalitarian division of labor, to some degree even between men and women. But the creation of their super-empire also raised unique challenges in terms of interaction and adaptation in governing and in the social sphere. Although the Mongols fought to keep their own practices and traditions, long exposure to the attractions of the settled life, as well as the difficulties of minority rule, tended to erode their traditions over time.

Egalitarian Patriarchy?

Modern scholars tend to favorably contrast the egalitarian qualities of Mongol family and gender relations with the hierarchical demands of Confucian filial piety and the male-centered practices of Islam. Indeed, Mongol practices do strike us in many ways as seemingly "modern," although they are rooted largely in the demands of a mobile society. That is, the rigid class structures of the sedentary societies the Mongols would conquer did not exist among the scattered clans that all lived by hunting, herding, and foraging, dwelling in felt-covered *gers*. Some clans were wealthier in flocks and herds than others, and men won prestige in raiding and warrior prowess. But there were no hereditary landed aristocracy, peasants, or other hard and fast class designations.

Kyrgyz Family Gathered near a Yurt, Late Nineteenth Century. The rough egalitarianism of Mongol society, while including some aspects that strike us as modern in their sensibility, must also be seen as the product of nomadic life. In this photograph taken around 1865, we see the aspects of a way of life still very much in evidence in the late nineteenth century. Here, a Kyrgyz family of four, encamped on the steppes of old imperial Russian Central Asia in front of their *kibitka*—the Mongol *ger*—more commonly known as a yurt, pose with their pack and food animals: a horse, Bactrian (two-hump) camel, and sheep.

This kind of crude egalitarianism extended to family and gender relations, although by no means completely. Men hunted and herded; women saw to children, took care of domestic matters, sewed, weaved, made felt, and fed the animals. Existing almost entirely on meat and dairy products, constantly on the move, both sexes tended to be robust and healthy, and without the tooth decay common among grain-centered societies. The husband was the head of the family, but women ruled the domestic sphere. A man could have more than one wife, although the first wife was afforded primary status. All children, however, were considered legitimate and entitled to inherit. Moreover, wealth and titles were often passed through a woman's family, a man had to pay a bride price to them, and he was also expected to move into his wife's residence, rather than the bride moving into his household and becoming subservient to both her husband and mother-in-law. There were no sumptuary laws governing the types of clothing one could wear according to rank or class, as in China or Europe, although married and unmarried women were distinguished by the size and type of headdress they wore. Women could inherit, and either party could initiate a divorce. Infidelity by either husband or wife could be punished by death.

The demands of a mobile society also meant that women had to be proficient in many of the same skills, even martial ones, as the men. Accounts by Mongol opponents report with shock, and even grudging admiration, seeing women warriors as skilled with their bows and their mounts as the men. The picture that emerges, then, is one in which, despite the male leadership role in family and clan, women, if not completely independent, were self-reliant and confident in their activities, status, rights, and traditions.

However stable these conditions had been before the unification of the clans, the creation of empire swiftly created cleavages in it. As we saw earlier, Genghis Khan used the abilities of his daughters by positioning them in marriage as shadow rulers over the lands of their spouses, even validating that status by giving them the title of *khatun* ("queen"). Yet this did not negate the fact that his own successors would be men—men who, in fact, did their best to break the power of their aunts and female cousins.

Religion: Toleration and Support

As we saw earlier, the original Mongol religion was a shamanistic set of beliefs involving the spirituality of the natural world, the reading of signs and omens in interpreting the interplay of human beings and the spiritual/natural world, and the overall guidance of the Eternal Blue Sky and Nurturing Earth. In many respects, the relationship between Sky and Earth, with the human world as an intervening layer, is not dissimilar to ancient, enduring Chinese concepts. Shamans, sometimes inhabited by the spirits of animals or other supernatural forces, are called upon to be diviners, interpreters, and at times, healers. Thus, the blood clot on the hand of Timujin at birth was considered a sign of destiny, later reinforced by events.

Although Genghis Khan himself retained this belief system, the Mongols considered religion in a general way to reflect the culture of particular peoples and so saw no need to enforce any kind of orthodoxy. Indeed, they commonly invited representatives of different religious groups to debate each other, sometimes treating these like athletic contests. Thus, in an approach rather rare for such a religious age, the Mongols mandated religious toleration in their lands.

Even by Genghis Khan's time, trade with merchants from China and along the Silk Road had already opened the door for the entrance of Nestorian Christianity, which had established itself among the Naiman and other local nomadic peoples. Nestorianism and Christianity in general remained of interest to the Mongols for much of the period of empire. Khubilai Khan, whose mother, the formidable Sorkhakhtani Beki, was Nestorian, expressed a desire to the Polos that they arrange for a sizable contingent of Catholic clergy to be sent to discuss the merits of Christianity with him. He proved rather disappointed that the two priests who started out with the Polos turned back part way through the journey. There had also been some hope in Rome that the Mongols might be converted and form a united front against Islam, although such hopes were soon dashed.

From the mid-eighth century, Arab armies fresh from conquering Sassanian Persia were advancing along the Silk Road and had defeated Tang Chinese forces at the battle of Talas. Islam was planted firmly among the Uyghurs and other Central Asian peoples from this time, while in China itself, sections of the capital of Chang'an (modern Xi'an) and other cities were set aside for Muslim merchants (as well as Nestorians and Jews). The Ilkhans had converted to Islam, and some Mongol groups in China also converted. Later, during the overthrow of the Yuan and its aftermath, many Muslims would be hunted down because of alleged Mongol loyalties.

Buddhism, which predated Islam and Christianity on the Silk Road and in China, was, after Islam, the most influential missionary religion for the Mongols. Although exposed to a variety of schools and sects within the Mahayana branch

The Golden Stupa at Erdene Zuu Monastery, Mongolia. The religion of Genghis Khan and the early Mongol conquerors was a nature-based belief system centered on Sky and Earth. Open to a number of outside religious influences in the succeeding centuries, such faiths as Nestorian Christianity, Islam, and various schools of Buddhism, the Mongols were famous for the level of religious toleration they practiced. Tibetan contacts ultimately led to popularity and preference given by the Mongols of the heartland to the Yellow Hat sect of the Dalai Lama. The Golden Stupa of the Erdene Zuu monastery, near the old capital of Karakorum, was built by Abtai Sain Khan who, after meeting the third Dalai Lama, declared Tibetan Buddhism the state religion, and ordered construction of this, the oldest surviving Buddhist monastery in Mongolia, in 1585. An enormous walled compound, it survived several wars and revolts, as well as attempts by Communist governments to demolish it in the twentieth century.

of Buddhism, interaction with Tibetans had ultimately led to widespread adoption by Mongols of Tibetan Buddhism, ultimately of the Yellow Hat sect of the Dalai Lama. Like Islam, the mercantile and missionary impulse of Buddhists dovetailed nicely with Mongol trade priorities. Buddhist traders and missionaries had already established networks of shrines, pilgrimage sites, rest-stops, hostels, supply centers, and monasteries that encouraged and supported commerce. More indirectly, Buddhism fostered equality among members, especially among monks and nuns, and the desire to study scriptures pushed the demand for manuscript and printed material, thus encouraging literacy.

CONCLUSION

History seldom flows smoothly from interval to interval with clean, widely agreed upon breaks to serve as convenient transitional markers. For Eurasia as a whole, and East Asia in particular, however, it can be argued that the Mongol era does indeed represent such a pivotal time. None of the countries examined in this volume emerged untouched by the Mongol super-empire, whether politically, institutionally, economically, or culturally—in many cases, all of these. While in most of these places, Mongol cultural influence was minimal and brief, the interval marked the largest circulation of innovation, ideas, and goods throughout the largest area that the world had yet seen. Indeed, it was this era that for the next two centuries fixed the idea of what China and other Asian regions were like in the minds of Europeans, and helped fuel their desire to get to these lands that swam fantastically in their imaginations.

So influential were the effects of the Mongol conquests that historians over the last several decades have seen it as a kind of proto- or quasi-world system because of its reach throughout Eurasia and North and East Africa. The wholesale elimination of landed aristocracies throughout the Mongol lands, and the enhanced trade of the era, have also been said to have prompted the European Renaissance. Certainly, the increasingly idealized semi-egalitarian ethos of the steppe nomads strikes us today as more congenial than the rigidly patriarchal, class-bound, agrarian–urban societies of China, the Muslim Middle East, and Christian Europe. Genghis Khan's edicts against the use of judicial torture strike us as equally progressive, as do economic policies encouraging trade and such "modern" innovations as paper money, commercial credit, and limited liability.

Yet it should also be remembered that the benefits of the Mongol era were balanced by disruption on a colossal scale, often arbitrary rule, internecine warfare, and novel challenges to group identity. In addition to slaughtering and removing whole populations, as in modern genocidal wars and "ethnic cleansing," rape was often used as a weapon. Indeed, so prolific was the family line of Genghis Khan in this regard that it is alleged that one-sixth of the people living today in the old Mongol domains can claim some kind of genealogical connection to him.

The death toll of the conquests is widely debated, since we have few reliable population figures from before the Mongol era, except perhaps in Song China. Thus, like the gargantuan Taiping Rebellion in China from 1851 to 1864, estimates run from a low of 18 to 20 million, to a high of 30 million. With the region's preconquest population estimated at around 150 million, such a casualty rate would be fearfully high among combat troops in a modern war. Factoring in the outbreak of the Black Death in the empire as well, the population was reduced by perhaps a third. China's population alone fell from about 100 million on the eve of the Jurchen conquests in the early 1100s to 60 million by the early Ming. Thus, while many modern historians have come to see the Mongol era as perhaps the key to the transition from the medieval to the early modern world, the cost was for many unacceptably high.

Regardless of the undoubted benefits Mongol rule brought, all the agrarian–urban states they conquered tend to look back on the era as an oppressive time under foreign domination. For East Asian states, it represented rule by "barbarians" from the periphery, although from the Chinese perspective at least, the pattern of the past had been to absorb such conquerors and assimilate them. One could argue, however, that the Mongol era also raised questions among the conquered as to how they defined themselves—their identity as peoples. The requirements of resisting the attempted Mongol invasions of Japan, for example, fostered a brief period of unity, with the Buddhist leader Nichiren asserting Japan as the center of world Buddhism, in part, because of the Mongol defeat. The rise of the Ming has been seen an assertion of "Chinese" identity—particularly when twentieth-century revolutionaries anxious to overthrow another "foreign" dynasty, the Manchu Qing, looked back to the Ming as the last legitimate "Chinese" dynasty. This extended to moving the capital from Beijing, which was now seen as the "Manchu" capital, to Nanjing, the first capital of the Ming. Koreans, Vietnamese, and Tibetans, having spent centuries forging identities in resistance to Chinese incursions and occupations, similarly had their national identities strengthened. From this point on, all these peoples will seek to balance the cultural heritage they share with reconstituting their institutions in ways increasingly suited to their own circumstances and preferences.

FURTHER RESOURCES

Abu-Lughod, Janet. *Before European Hegemony: The World System A.D. 1250–1350.* New York: Oxford University Press, 1989. Path-breaking and controversial work, now considered essential for world historians. Abu-Lughod posits the idea of the *Pax Mongolica* as setting the stage for a global trade system by its influence in creating a super-regional trade network touching three continents.

Biran, Michal. *The Empire of Qara Khitai in Eurasian History.* Cambridge, UK: Cambridge University Press, 2005. Argues that the empire known to Muslims as Qara Khitai (Black Khitans) and to the Chinese as Western Lao, carved out of Central Asia in the 1140s, formed a political bridge and avenue of exchange between the two civilizations little studied by modern scholars.

Bold, Bat-Ochir. *Mongolian Nomadic Society: A Reconstruction of the "Medieval" History of Mongolia.* New York: St. Martin's Press, 2001. One of the first histories of the Mongols to break out of orthodox socialist constructs of "feudal" nomadic society. Best for readers with some grounding in the history of the period.

Carpini, Giovanni DiPlano. *The Story of the Mongols Whom We Call the Tartars.* Translated by Erik Hildinger. Boston: Brandon, 1996. Classic travel narrative by a contemporary Franciscan envoy from the Pope, who spent extensive time with the Mongols at the height of their power.

Juvaini, Ata-Malik. *Genghis Khan: The History of the World-Conqueror.* Translated by J. Boyle. Seattle: University of Washington Press, 1997. Before the *Secret History of the Mongols* was translated and deciphered, Juvaini's account was one of the few near-contemporary extant sources on the rise of Genghis Khan and the creation of the Mongol Empire. It remains a valued source today, although modern scholars advise scrutinizing its biases.

May, Timothy. *The Mongol Art of War.* Yardley, PA: Westholme, 2007. Like several other authors cited here, May seeks to correct the mythology of the Mongols as undisciplined barbarian hordes. He argues instead for their high levels of discipline, shrewd tactical sense, and adroit use of extant technologies in their conquests.

Onon, Urgunege, trans. *The Secret History of the Mongols.* Richmond, UK: Curzon, 2001. Only recently deciphered in terms of understanding the geographical and historical nature of the references it contains, this has become perhaps the chief primary source we have of the formation of the Mongol Empire.

Polo, Marco. *The Travels of Marco Polo: The Complete Yule–Cordier Edition.* Translated by Henry Yule. New York: Dover, 1993. More than any other book, this travel account by Polo, dictated to his cell mate while he was imprisoned, painted the picture of what Asia was like for centuries of European readers. It was a prime source of Columbus's ideas of where he was going and how he would get there.

Waldron, Arthur. *The Great Wall of China: From History to Myth.* Cambridge, UK: Cambridge University Press, 1990. Examines the history of the Great Wall both as reality and myth. Useful on a number of fronts, but particularly in how it was perceived and used by the Chinese and the nomadic peoples on their periphery.

Weatherford, Jack. *Genghis Khan and the Making of the Modern World.* New York: Broadway Books, 2004. Useful to specialists while readable enough for use by beginning students, this is a pioneering work of revisionist research on the Mongol rise of Genghis Khan. Argues that he was far from the bloodthirsty nomad chieftain portrayed by his opponents and that the Mongol era even helped bring on the European Renaissance and early modern era.

Weatherford, Jack. *The Secret History of the Mongol Queens.* New York: Broadway Books, 2010. Companion volume to Weatherford's work on Genghis Khan, this opens up the little studied realm of the rule of his daughters, and the surprising power and agency they wielded in the tough environment of the Mongol Empire after Genghis Khan's death.

WEBSITES

http://afe.easia.columbia.edu/mongols/figures/figu_geng_unity.htm. Asia for Educators/ Columbia University. *Asian Topics in World History: The Mongols in World History.* Excellent starting place for students interested in Mongol history at an intermediate level under the aegis of renowned scholar Morris Rossabi as faculty consultant. Extensive links and world connections.

http://www.historyworld.net/wrldhis/PlainTextHistories.asp?groupid=755&HistoryID=aa
76&gtrack=pthc. History World. *The Mongols.* Sound essays on the history of the rise
and decline of the Mongol empires and states with timelines and quizzes. Extensive
useful links.

https://www.britannica.com/place/China/The-Yuan-or-Mongol-dynasty.   Encyclopaedia
Britannica. *The Yuan, or Mongol, Dynasty.* An excellent introductory resource for
students interested in a comprehensive overview of the Mongol experience in China.
Extensive links to other Mongol and Chinese topics.

"The Vietnamese People Resisting American Aggression." The efforts of North Vietnam
to unite the country under socialism and its portrayal of the United States as engaging in
foreign imperialism in its support of the independence of South Vietnam were frequent
subjects of dramatic Socialist Realist art. In this Chinese poster from 1967, during the Cultural
Revolution, five North Vietnamese soldiers—including one woman—fire their rifles at
marauding American planes.

PART II

Recasting East Asia
to the Present

Timeline

1368–1644	Ming Dynasty, China
1392–1910	Yi Dynasty, Korea
1428–1789	Le Dynasty, Vietnam
1557	Portuguese establish first European colony in Macau
1577	Matteo Ricci, first Jesuit missionary in China
1592	First invasion of Korea by Toyotomi Hideyoshi
1600–1800	England and the Netherlands import 70 million pieces of porcelain from China
1603–1867	Tokugawa Shogunate, Japan
1636	Choson becomes a vassal state of China
1644	Qing Dynasty proclaimed, China
1664–1722	Reign of Kangxi emperor
1689	Treaty of Nerchinsk sets border between China and Russia
1699	Qing permit overseas trade at Canton
1727	China establishes protectorate over Tibet
1733	Yongzheng creates Grand Council
1736–1795	Reign of Qianlong emperor
1771	Tay Son Revolt, Vietnam
1793	Macartney mission to Beijing
1802–1945	Nguyen Dynasty, Vietnam
1839–1842	First Opium War, China
1851–1864	Taiping Rebellion, China

1852–1854	Commodore Matthew Perry's mission to Japan
1863–1885	French colonization of Vietnam
1860–1895	Self-strengthening era, China
1868	Establishment of Meiji Dynasty, Japan
1889	Promulgation of Meiji Constitution, Japan
1894–1895	Sino-Japanese War; Tonghak Rebellion in Korea
1898	Hundred Days of Reform, China
1900	Boxer Rebellion, China
1905	Japan establishes a protectorate over Korea
1910	Japan annexes Korea
1912	Last Qing emperor abdicates; Republic of China founded
1919	May Fourth Movement, China
1921	Founding of Chinese Communist Party
1931	Japan annexes Manchuria
1934–1935	The Long March, China
1937	Rape of Nanking
1949	Founding of People's Republic of China
1945	End of World War II; Japanese Empire dismantled; declaration of Vietnamese independence
1946–1954	French Indochina War
1950–1953	Korean War
1958–1961	Great Leap Forward, China
1963–1973	American War in Vietnam (Second Indochina War)
1964	China detonates its first nuclear device; first "Little Red Book" published

1966–1969	Cultural Revolution, China
1972	Richard M. Nixon travels to China; diplomatic relations between China and U.S. restored
1976	Deaths of Zhou Enlai and Mao Zedong; Vietnam formally unified
1978	Four Modernizations inaugurated, China
1979	China invades Vietnam
1980	Trail of Gang of Four; first Special Economic Zone established in China
1989	Tiananmen Square massacre
1990	Shanghai Stock Exchange opened
1994–1998	Famine in North Korea
1995	Diplomatic relations between Vietnam and United States established
1997	United Kingdom cedes Hong Kong to China
1998	South Korea begins to promote "Sunshine Policy" in its relations with North Korea; Portugal returns Macau to China
2001	China joins World Trade Organization
2006	Completion of Qinghai-Lhasa Railway
2008	Beijing hosts Summer Olympics
2010	China surpasses Japan as second-largest economy
2011	Massive tsunami strikes Japan
2013	China launches its "Belt and Road Initiative"
2018	North Korea in likely possession of a nuclear bomb; summit meeting between Kim Jong-un of North Korea and Donald Trump of the United States; China launches its first domestically built aircraft carrier. United States and China engage in a trade war by raising tariffs on each others' goods.

CHAPTER 5

❧

From Super-Power to Semi-Colony: China from the Ming to 1895

Even today, one can still see the stone markers left by the crews of the enormous "treasure ships." Along the East African and Red Sea coasts, these artifacts mark the furthest extent of Chinese maritime influence until the opening decades of the twenty-first century. The sponsor of the extraordinary expeditions that left the markers was the powerful and dynamic third emperor of the Ming Dynasty, Yongle. Fearful that potential usurpers might have escaped his reach and fled overseas, in 1405, Yongle authorized the launch of what became the largest and most powerful maritime forces the world had ever seen. The ships were the technological wonders of their day. The largest were over 400 feet long—nearly four times the length and many times the bulk of the early European ships of exploration. Powered by easily maneuvered batten-braced sails, steered by sternpost rudders, protected by watertight compartments, guided by gridded maps oriented by magnetic compasses, and defended by shipborne cannon, bombs, and the more than 30,000 soldiers and crew the fleets carried, they were intended to overawe and cow any potential rivals. And they did.

Commanded by the eunuch admiral Zhenghe, a servant and childhood friend of the emperor, the fleets ventured out repeatedly over the next twenty-five years. As the realization set in that there were no pretenders to the throne or maritime powers capable of challenging Chinese naval supremacy, the mission of the expeditions became increasingly commercial and exploratory. Contacts were developed, and Chinese merchants traveled to places throughout Southeast Asia and Indonesia, even to some of the Indian ports. Venturing further west, the fleets set course for the Swahili city-states on the East African coast. In one memorable exchange, the Chinese delegation was gifted with a giraffe from the king of Malindi, which survived the voyage and ended up in the imperial menagerie.

Politics and economics, however, ultimately intervened. To most of China's Confucian officialdom, the fleets gained China little, entailed unsustainable costs, encouraged corruption, and benefited only the merchants. They argued that since there were no enemies overseas who could threaten the empire, efforts

Scroll with Yongle's Giraffe. The nearly thirty years of Zheng He's voyages resulted in, among other things, a constant stream of exotic items flowing into the empire. One of the more striking of these was the gift of a giraffe by the king of the East African trading state of Malindi. The arrival of the animal caused a sensation; it was immediately added to the emperor's menagerie and became the subject of this commemorative scroll.

should be directed instead at shoring up China's land defenses. In 1433, they won the day and the voyages were discontinued.

What had been a prudent decision at the time came to have long-term consequences that would only manifest themselves hundreds of years later. In the period under consideration in this chapter, we will explore the process by which Chinese continental power rose during the Ming and early Qing periods, reaching its peak in the mid-eighteenth century. Naval power, however, would become crucial again as nineteenth-century industrialization in the maritime countries of the West posed increasing threats to China's sovereignty and territorial integrity. Indeed, the age of imperialism cast a long pall over all of Asia, shadows of which remain to this day.

For East Asia, all the countries concerned were at some point affected by imperial powers. China's ports were largely taken over by foreign interests and the country's territorial integrity seriously threatened by the turn of the nineteenth century. Vietnam had become French Indochina by 1887. Japan, following its "opening" by the United States in 1853, had itself become an imperial power and moved to control Korea. But perhaps the most spectacular instance of the era's change of fortune from the days of Zhenghe was the Sino-Japanese War of 1894–1895, where this chapter ends. With this event, an industrializing Japan easily defeated the newly reconstituted Chinese steam war fleet. For the next fifty years, Japan would increasingly encroach on China until defeated at the end of World War II. For the following half century, China would struggle to reestablish its place as the region's leading power. Now, as the twenty-first century moves through its second decade, China's naval power once again is growing. As if to come full circle, Chinese planners invoke the missions of Zhenghe and, tracing the route of his "treasure ships," seek to make commercial allies of the nations along this new "Maritime Silk Road."

REMAKING THE EMPIRE: THE MING

As we have seen, by the mid-fourteenth century, the Mongol Empire spanning Eurasia had begun to dissolve into a series of increasingly combative regional khanates. In 1352, in the process of suppressing a local rebellion, Yuan armies

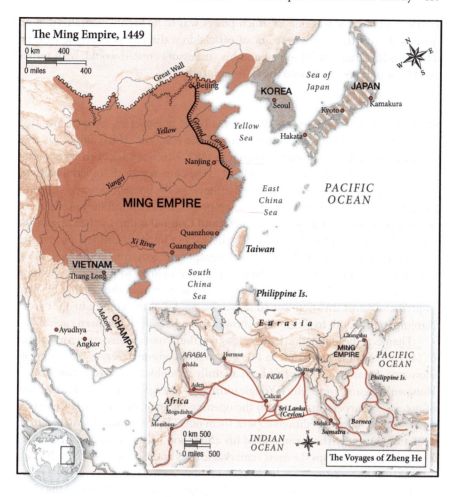

Map 5.1 The Ming Empire and the Voyages of Zheng He

attacked a Buddhist monastery in Anhui Province. One of the monks, Zhu Yuanzhang, who had lost his parents in a famine years before, threw in his lot with the insurgents, who later united with assorted secret societies, most notably the Red Turbans (see Chapter 2). By 1368, the coalition, now led by Zhu, had secured the Yangzi Valley and pushed north, driving the Mongols from the capital at Khanbaligh and proclaiming a new dynastic line, the Ming. The southern province of Yunnan, adjacent to Vietnam, however, remained a Mongol stronghold and was not reduced until 1381 (see Map 5.1).

The new emperor took the reign name of Hongwu ("Vastly/Exceedingly Martial") and spent much of his rule eliminating rivals attempting to set up their own states within the empire, and driving out the remaining Mongols. The new emperor's visage prompted the nickname "Pig Emperor," but his organizational ability was instrumental in establishing the new regime. Fearful of rival claimants, he installed family members in key positions of power. Moreover, his conception of the imperial role was one in which power was to be highly centralized, with all boards and the entire network of officialdom directly responsible to him. This new imperial state Hongwu and his successors created would, with minor modifications, see China into the twentieth century.

Centralizing Government and Projecting Power

Hongwu sought to streamline the reconstituted bureaucracy by concentrating power and governmental functions around the emperor. Thus, one of his first steps was to create the Grand Secretariat in 1382. This was a select group of senior officials who served as an advisory board to the emperor on all imperial matters. The Grand Secretariat became the highest level of the bureaucracy and the most powerful level of government after the emperor. Although military needs eventually moved much of its power to the **Grand Council** set up by the Qing in the mid-1700s, the Secretariat remained at the apex of imperial Chinese power into the twentieth century. With a powerful, centralized government in place, Ming emperors now had a base from which to take measures to protect the empire from incursions by Mongols and other nomadic groups in the north. One step to protect against invasion was to move the capital of the empire in 1421 from Nanjing in the south to Kambaligh, now renamed *Beijing* ("northern capital").

Thanks to the foundation laid by Hongwu, the dynasty's third emperor, Yongle, (r. 1403–1424), inherited a state in 1403 that was already on its way to recovering its economic dynamism. There had been a family scramble for power in the wake of Hongwu's passing, from which Yongle ultimately emerged victorious. Fearful now of potential usurpers, as we saw in the opening vignette, he ordered China's first and last great naval expeditions to seek them out. These voyages, dispatched from 1405 to 1433 under the command of his childhood friend and imperial eunuch, Zheng He, were perhaps the most remarkable feats of their day.

As we saw earlier, the fleets Zheng now commanded were the largest amphibious forces the world would see for centuries to come. Some of the ships were even set up to grow produce on their aft decks while at sea. In addition, they carried all the equipment that the innovations of Eurasia had thus far produced: watertight compartments, which would not be seen on European ships for centuries; sternpost rudders; magnetic compasses; and paper maps marked with navigation grids. Their hulls were built for ruggedness and stability on open seas, while their battened square and partially triangular sails allowed ease of handling and the ability to sail against the wind—innovations that Western shipwrights were only beginning to develop.

Although Zheng He's explorations firmly established Chinese predominance in naval technology and power, Yongle's successors put an end to the expeditions. The beneficiaries of the expeditions, including some court eunuchs and various merchant associations, had done well over the past decades. Indeed, China, with its massive but mostly peaceful show of power, had planted colonies of traders throughout the Indian Ocean basin and especially in Southeast Asia and Indonesia—some of whose descendants are still doing business today. As we saw earlier, however, the primary orientation of the empire, despite its long

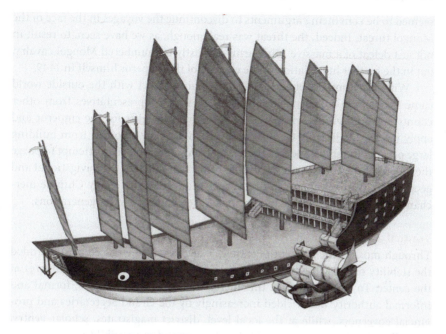

Zheng He's "Treasure Ship" as Contrasted with Christopher Columbus's *Santa Maria*.
The huge fleets and enormous ships of Zheng He's expeditions from 1405 to 1433 were the largest amphibious forces in the world for centuries. With dozens of ships, some over 400 feet long, and up to 30,000 men, they were also technological marvels with their cannon, rockets, sternpost rudders, watertight bulkheads, and gridded maps for navigation. In this image, the relative sizes of Zhong He's largest "Treasure Ships" as they were called and Columbus's flagship *Santa Maria* are shown in dramatic relief. The *Santa Maria* was barely 100 feet long and had a fraction of the capacity of the Chinese ships.

Strong inside, no need to trade

coastline, has been on land, agriculture, and defense of the interior. Moreover, the assumption that traitors and usurpers had fled overseas cast a pall of suspicion over those who chose to emigrate or do business outside the empire—a stigma that endures in some respects to the present.

Within the arenas of power, there were also important rivalries at work. The emperor-centered system now in place allowed considerable informal power to be wielded by the court eunuchs. Those close to the emperor had in some cases acquired considerable wealth and the cachet of access to exotica from all over the maritime sphere. Thus, those in the bureaucracy who lacked such direct influence over the emperor registered repeated charges of corruption. The Confucian suspicion of merchants as a class, resentment toward their occasional attempts to buy their way into the scholar-gentry, and the windfalls that some were accumulating through the new trade further cemented official prejudice.

In addition to reasons of internal politics, there were now new strategic concerns. By the 1430s, the Mongols had regrouped from their defeats, and were again threatening the northern frontiers. The huge expense of the repeated expeditions and the realization that there were no significant naval rivals nearby seemed to be convincing arguments to discontinue the voyages in the face of the Mongol threat. Indeed, the threat was real enough, as we have seen, to result in not just defeat of a massive Ming army by vastly outnumbered Mongol cavalry, but in the further humiliation of the capture of the emperor himself in 1449.

With maritime travel ended, China's main contact with the outside world came through so-called tribute missions in which representatives from other countries would visit the imperial court with native gifts for the emperor and apply for a trade license. Chinese shipyards were now enjoined from building large oceangoing ships. Indeed, there was even something of an attempt to purge the record of the epic voyages, with the result that much of the navigational and geographic history was lost. Moreover, official trade with many Chinese merchant colonies was curtailed and, in some cases, contact lost for generations.

Toward a Regulated Society: Foreign Relations

Through most of the sixteenth century, a succession of weak emperors eroded the stability of the Ming imperial system, so dependent on a strong emperor at the center. To compensate for this increasingly chronic weakness, formal and informal authority was wielded increasingly by the Grand Secretaries and provincial governors, while at the local level, district magistrates, scholar-gentry, and village headmen assumed additional power and responsibility.

Notwithstanding the difficulties presented by weak emperors in the Ming system, China by the late fifteenth century had made considerable progress toward the long-standing goals of peace and stability idealized by Chinese political thinkers. In practical terms, relations with the Mongols had stabilized. Moreover, Ming China was perhaps the leading center of technological expertise in the new types of firearms being developed throughout Eurasia and North Africa (see below). The voyages of Zhenghe, while whetting the appetites of some members of the elite for foreign exotica, had the more immediate influence of demonstrating conclusively that China had no serious rivals overseas. This tended to confirm a view of the empire at the center of a world order defined by Neo-Confucian philosophy and supported by a host of Chinese cultural assumptions.

The Mongol interval and resurgence had also served to at once support the idea of long-term Sinicization of foreigners, and forcefully drive home the danger posed to China's institutions and culture by the presence of influential outsiders. Thus, like the Tokugawa Shogunate in Japan in the seventeenth century, the Ming, and later the Qing, came to view foreign influence as less "civilized" and far too often injurious to the social order. Hence, successive rulers placed severe restrictions on maritime trade, and conceived of diplomatic relations primarily in commercial terms.

The commercial/diplomatic missions sent from Korea, Vietnam, the Ryukyu Islands, and occasionally some of the outer *han* (feudal domains) of Japan worked reasonably well within the long-standing hierarchy of the Confucian cultural sphere. By the late eighteenth century, however, it came into direct conflict with the more egalitarian system of international trade and diplomacy that had evolved among the Europeans and the Islamic states of the Mediterranean and South and Southwest Asia.

Tribute Mission. This illustration, from a popular English travel account first published in 1745, shows the retinue of the Siam (Thailand) ambassador being escorted to an audience with the emperor inside the Forbidden City. For the Qing, these annual tribute missions had as much symbolic importance as anything diplomatic. As the emperor was the "Son of Heaven," his supreme cultural authority over the lands in his "inner" domains was to be acknowledged through elaborate gift-giving and the performing of the kowtow by the ambassador—a deep bow in which one's head touches the ground.

The End of the Ming

Despite the increased attention directed at the Mongol resurgence of the 1440s, periodic rebellions in the north and northwest punctuated the late fifteenth and sixteenth centuries. From a military standpoint, the huge commitment of Chinese troops deployed to Korea against the forces of the Japanese leader Hideoyoshi Toyotomi during his attempted invasion of Northeast Asia (see Chapter 8) from 1592 to 1598 weakened the dynasty further during a crucial period that saw the rise of another regional power: the Manchus. As we will see in the next section, the Manchus soon took advantage of the "disorder within" and became involved in the factional fighting of the late Ming. They had formed their own Qing ("pure") dynasty in the northeastern regions they controlled as early as 1636. Now they would impose it on China as a whole.

THE ERA OF DOMINANCE: THE QING TO 1795

With the Mongol revival during the 1400s, the Ming sought to use the time hon-ored strategy of "using barbarians to check barbarians" and so looked for allies among the ever-shifting nomadic groups beyond the Great Wall. The Jurchens, who ironically had earlier formed the Jin Dynasty (1115–1234) that had eliminated the Northern Song, now seemed a good fit. In the constantly shifting politics of the northern tier, the Ming were anxious to pry them away from both Korean suzerainty and their close relations with the Mongols. At the time, however, they were comparatively weak and disunited. With Ming fortunes on the downturn in the wake of the costly defense of Korea against the Japanese invasions of the 1590s, an opportunity for expansion seemed to present itself. By the turn of the seventeenth century, under the leadership of Nurhachi (1559–1626) and Abahai (1592–1643), the Jurchen groups united and founded a second Jin Dynasty in 1616. They abandoned the old Jurchen script in favor of one based on the Mongol alphabet and began to call themselves "Manchus," a name whose origins are uncertain. By 1636, the newly united Manchus controlled the area including and adjacent to the Liaodong Peninsula and declared the founding of their new Qing dynasty.

They soon found themselves drawn into politics on the other side of the Great Wall. With factional warfare disrupting the Ming, the dynasty's belated attempts to check Manchu power in Liaodong lessened its hold on the western regions around Shaanxi Province, already wracked by famine and a smallpox epidemic. Out of these hardships came two rebel armies by 1642. After a period of confused fighting, the northern army entered the outskirts of Beijing in April 1644. Upon this news, the Ming Chongzhen emperor (r. 1628–1644) committed suicide, allegedly hanging himself from a beam in a pavilion on a hill in the imperial gardens.

On hearing of an impending counterattack by the loyalist general Wu Sangui, the northern army launched a preemptive strike on Wu at the pass in Shanhaiguan, where the Great Wall approaches the sea. In desperation, Wu invited the Manchu leader Dorgon (1612–1650) to cross the Wall and join forces with him. For the Chinese, this event would come to carry the same sense of finality as Caesar's crossing of the Rubicon. Wu Sangui prevailed and pursued the remnants of the northern army. Dorgon's forces, however, occupied Beijing, where, in keeping with the historical pattern of nearly every dynastic change, they announced that they had come to avenge the Ming and correct the mistakes of the past (see Map 5.2).

The Banner System

The **Banner system** (*baqi*, meaning "eight banners") under which the Manchus were organized for military and tax purposes was now expanded under the Qing to provide for segregated Manchu elites and garrisons in major cities and towns. Under this system, the Manchu state had been divided into eight major military and ethnic (Manchu, Han, Mongolian, Tibetan, and Muslim Hui) divisions, each represented by a distinctive banner. By the time of the Chinese conquest, the number of Manchu and Mongol Banners had swelled to twenty-four. Originally organized for a mobile warrior people, the system eventually became the chief administrative tool of the Manchu leadership. The Bannermen themselves were forbidden to engage in manual labor and subject to a separate military legal system. The non-Manchu imperial forces were organized into their own "Armies of the Green Standard," so named for the color of the flags they carried.

Always conscious of their position as a ruling minority in China, with their numbers only comprising about 2 percent of the population, the Manchus, like the Mongols before them, sought to walk a fine line between administrative and cultural adaptation and the kind of thoroughgoing assimilation characteristic of previous invaders. Thus, Chinese and Manchus were scrupulously recruited in equal numbers for high administrative posts; Manchu quotas in the examination system were instituted; edicts and memorials were issued in both Chinese and Manchu; and Qing emperors sought to control the empire's high culture.

In addition, Dorgon instituted the infamous **queue** edict in 1645: all males, regardless of ethnicity, were now required on pain of death to adopt the Manchu hair style of shaved forehead and long pigtail in the back as the outward sign of loyalty to the new order. The edict provoked revolts in several cities, and the attendant casualties in its suppression may have numbered in the hundreds of thousands. For the remainder of the Qing era, rebels and protestors routinely cut their queues as the first order of business.

Manchu Bannerman. The Manchu fighters of the early Qing Dynasty were much feared as expert horsemen and highly competent marksmen with either firearms or bows. This rendering shows a bannerman archer, with the characteristic cap and curved broadsword in a scabbard by his side.

Universal Empire

The Manchus conceived of their empire as a universal state embracing all the ethnicities, religions, and languages under their sway. At the same time, the ongoing pressure of interaction and adaptation resulted in a degree of Sinicization. Although the Qing kept the centralized imperial system of the Ming largely intact, while importing the Banner system as a parallel administrative apparatus, they also made one significant innovation to the uppermost level of the bureaucracy. While retaining the Ming Grand Secretariat, the emperor Yongzheng set up an ad hoc inner advisory body called the Grand Council in 1733. Over the succeeding decades, the Grand Council became the supreme "inner" advisory group to the emperor, while the Grand Secretariat was relegated to handling less crucial "outer" matters of policymaking and implementation.

The Qing had the good fortune to have their three most capable rulers in succession: Kangxi, Yongzheng, and Qianlong. Known as the **Three Emperors**, they reigned collectively from 1664 to 1795, and presided over

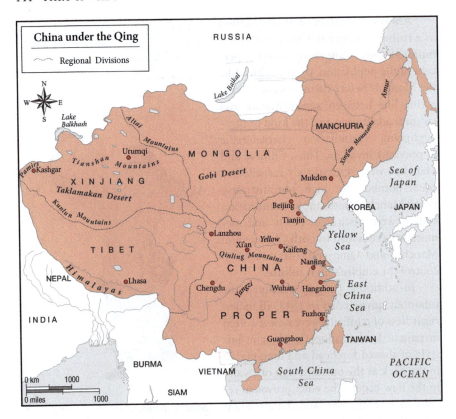

Map 5.2 China under the Qing

what was arguably imperial China's greatest era of global power and influence. During their reigns, China's territory doubled, incorporating Mongolia, Tibet, Taiwan, and most of Xinjiang, as well as exercising suzerainty over Korea and Vietnam. With the new territories and the global trade in new food crops, the population doubled to perhaps 300 million. The empire's enormous internal economy and burgeoning export trade drove that of all of Eurasia, and China's military forces dwarfed those of any potential competitors. Finally, nearly all observers during this period remarked on the peace, prosperity, and excellence of Confucian government, some Europeans even seeing it as a model for their own countries.

Pacification and Expansion

For much of the seventeenth century, however, the internal pacification of the empire remained the primary task. Much of this was accomplished under the able leadership of Nurhachi's great-grandson, the Kangxi emperor, who reigned from 1661 to 1722. Kangxi was a "hands-on" ruler, physically active, often leading military campaigns, and traveling extensively throughout his realm. During the 1640s and 1650s, various remnants of Ming loyalists attempted to create regimes

Emperor Kangxi. The long reign of Kangxi (1661–1722) began a period of unprecedented power, wealth, and influence for both the Qing and imperial China more generally. Here, the emperor, perhaps then in his forties, sits in his study at the peak of his powers.

in the south, although these had been summarily crushed. More serious was the maritime threat posed by the formidable Zheng Chenggong (1624–1662), more popularly known as "Koxinga." In 1659, in an attempt to restore the Ming to Nanjing, his ships sailed up the Yangzi but were soundly defeated by the Banner land forces. Following this setback, Zheng and a number of followers moved to Taiwan. His son now held their island redoubt for another two decades before his defeat by Qing naval forces. From this point on, Taiwan was administered as part of Fujian Province until being ceded to Japan in 1895 as spoils of the Sino-Japanese War. It would remain in Japanese hands until 1945.

Although the threat posed by Zheng's naval power was troublesome, a more serious problem developed for Kangxi in the interior of the empire. Indeed, the most powerful of the three **feudatories** in question was none other than Wu Sangui, who had invited the Manchu forces into China. The commanders of these regions had served the Qing by pacifying the regions but had become regional warlords. When special status for their service was not granted permanently, they rebelled in 1673 in what became known as the "Revolt of the Three Feudatories." The inability of the feudatories to work together allowed the Qing to crush them piecemeal and the threat was subdued by 1683.

In the final decades of the seventeenth century, the danger of the Mongols regrouping seemed particularly acute to the Qing. Under the khan Galban (r. 1671–1697), a group variously called the *Zunghars, Junghars,* or *Dzungars* seemed to be on the verge of just such unification. Kangxi therefore pursued a strategy that reached out to the expansive Russian state in the Treaty of Nerchinsk in 1689 (see below) to blunt any further expansion below Siberia and into the Manchu homeland, and then turned his attention to the Zunghar threat. In 1696 and 1697, Kangxi accompanied his large and well-equipped army on a war of extermination against Galban's forces. He and his successors, Yongzheng

Portrait of Qianlong. Qianlong (1736–1795) was the third in the line of emperors (Kangxi and Yongzheng) who presided over imperial China at its height. As had Kangxi and Yongzheng, he employed European technical advisors in various areas. One of the more intriguing cultural interactions between China and Europe resulted in this portrait by the Italian Jesuit painter and architect Giuseppe Castiglione (1688–1766). Castiglione served Kangxi, Yongzheng, and Qianlong and absorbed Chinese painting styles while influencing his Chinese colleagues in the use of vanishing point perspective. The interaction of these influences can be seen in this portrait of the young Qianlong, portrayed in court dress but gazing confidently, full-on toward the viewer.

and Qianlong, took more than sixty years to finish it. With the help of a simultaneous smallpox epidemic, they accomplished their end. Along the way, they pushed the borders of the empire deep into Xinjiang, where Qianlong's forces defeated the Muslim Khojas in 1758.

The intervention of the Qing in religious disputes regarding Tibetan Buddhism induced the Yongzheng emperor to establish a protectorate over Tibet in 1727. The Dalai Lama was sanctioned to rule as the approved temporal and religious leader. To cement the relationship further, the emperor built a replica of a Tibetan stupa just outside the Manchu quarter in Beijing and a model of the Dalai Lama's Potala Palace at the emperor's summer retreat in Jehol.

With the traditional threats from the borders now quashed, the reign of the Qianlong emperor, from 1736 to 1795, marked both the high point and the beginning of the decline of the Qing Dynasty—and of imperial China itself. The Qing army, although perhaps already eclipsed in terms of drill and weaponry by the leading nations of Europe, was still many times larger than that of any potential competitor. Moreover, Qianlong wielded this power successfully a number of times

Map 5.3 Campaigns of Qianlong

during his reign, with expeditions against pirates and rebels on Taiwan, and in punitive campaigns against Vietnam, Nepal, and Burma between 1766 and 1792. During his long life, he also tried, with limited success, to take up the writing brush of a scholar and connoisseur, creating the collection of art that is today the core of the National Palace Museum's holdings on Taiwan (see Map 5.3).

Encounters with Europeans

Ironically, it was precisely at the time that China abandoned its oceanic expeditions that tiny Portugal on the Atlantic coast began its pursuit of what would become a worldwide maritime trade empire. By the early sixteenth century, the first Portuguese and Spanish traders and missionaries had established themselves at Malacca and within a few decades had involved themselves in the affairs of the contentious Japanese feudal territories. In 1557, the Portuguese acquired a trading post at Macao near Guangzhou on the south China coast, which would remain in their hands until 1999.

Shortly after the arrival of the first European merchants in East Asia came the first Catholic missionaries. Wary of potentially disruptive foreign influences, the Ming at first refused them entry. Once admitted, however, with their limited training in Chinese language and culture, and emphasis on converting the poor, they made little headway. The recently created Jesuit order, however, tried a different tack. Led by Matteo Ricci (1552–1610) and his successors, Adam Schall Von Bell (1591–1666) and Ferdinand Verbiest (1623–1688), they immersed themselves in the classical language and high culture of the empire, and gained recognition through their expertise in mathematics, astronomy, military science, and other new European skills sought by the imperial court. Jesuit advisers served the last Ming emperors as court astronomers and military engineers, and successfully made the transition to the new dynasty. The high point of their influence was reached during the reign of Kangxi, who actively considered conversion to Catholicism.

Observatory in Beijing. Jesuit missionaries in the seventeenth century found an eager reception for their mathematical and scientific skills in the court of the Kangxi emperor. In this observatory designed by Kangxi's Jesuit advisor, Ferdinand Verbiest, one can see calibrated instruments for calculating the position of stars and planets in the rear of the enclosure, with two armillary spheres and a celestial globe in front.

The papacy, however, had long considered Jesuit liturgical and doctrinal adaptations to local sensibilities problematic. Jesuit tolerance of their converts' veneration of Confucius and maintenance of ancestral shrines set off what came to be called the **Rites Controversy.** After several decades of intermittent discussion, Yongzheng banned the order's activities in China in 1724. Christianity and missionary activity were thus driven underground, although the Qing would retain a Jesuit court astronomer into the nineteenth century.

Regulating Maritime Trade

While China's commerce with the maritime Atlantic states grew rapidly in the eighteenth century, the Europeans had not yet been fully incorporated into the Qing commercial/diplomatic "tribute system." Under the terms of the Treaty of Nerchinsk, the Russians had agreed to abandon their last forts along the Amur River and were given rights to continue their lucrative caravan trade in the interior. Formal borders were established in Manchuria, and the first attempts at settling claims to the Central Asian regions of Ili and Kuldjia were made. Significantly, Russian envoys were also permitted to reside in Beijing in a residence like those used by the temporary envoys of tribute missions.

The situation among the European maritime traders, however, was quite different. The British East India Company, having established its base at Calcutta in 1690, shortly sought to expand its operations to China. At the same time, the Qing, fresh from capturing the last Ming bastion on Taiwan and worried about Ming loyalists in other areas, sought to control contact with foreign and overseas Chinese traders as much as possible, while keeping their lucrative export trade at a sustainable level. Their solution, implemented in 1699, was to permit overseas trade only at the southern port of Guangzhou, more widely known as Canton. The local merchant's guild, or **Cohong** (in pinyin, *gonghang*), was granted a monopoly on the trade and supervised by a special official from the imperial Board of Revenue. Much like the Tokugawa Shogunate in Japan more than half a century before, the Qing permitted only a small number of foreigners, mostly traders from the English, French, and Dutch East India Companies, to reside at the port. They were confined to a small compound of foreign **factories**, were not permitted inside the city walls, and could not bring their wives or families along. Even small violations of the regulations could result in a suspension of trading privileges, and all infractions and disputes were judged according to Chinese law. Finally, because foreign affairs under these circumstances were considered a dimension of trade, all diplomatic issues were settled by local officials in Canton.

The period from 1500 to the mid-nineteenth century saw much of China's export trade centered on porcelain. During this time, it was arguably the single most important commodity in the unfolding world commercial revolution. Economic historians have suggested that between a third and a half of all the silver produced in the Americas during this time was spent to pay for porcelain. By the 1770s, however, with Western works now capable of manufacturing porcelain on their own, Europe's enormous thirst for tea had grown to challenge porcelain for supremacy among the Canton traders. The quantity of tea shipped by the British East India Company alone rose five-fold from 1720 to 1730, surpassing a million pounds; between 1760 and 1770, it tripled from 3 million to 9 million pounds.

THE STRUGGLE FOR AGENCY IN
"THE CENTURY OF HUMILIATION"

The century from 1795, when Qianlong stepped down as emperor, to 1895, when China was defeated in a war with an industrializing Japan, marked the structural, cultural, and economic decline of most of the world's great agrarian empires. In the case of the Qing, this decline would not be visible to even the experienced observer until well into the nineteenth century. Even then, such a perception would most likely be associated with the great rebellions, the Taiping and Nian, which tore at the vitals of the empire.

One noteworthy development in this regard was that the reign of the Tongzhi emperor, from 1861 to 1875, was later officially designated as a "restoration" (*zhongxing*), coming as it did in the midst of the anti-Taiping campaigns and in the wake of the return of the imperial family to Beijing after the Anglo-French force had driven it from the **Forbidden City** during the Second Opium War (1856–1860). Moreover, the 1860s marked a period of unprecedented cooperation between the Qing and the Western maritime powers, and the 1870s saw the empire's expansion to its greatest size in history. By the late 1860s and early 1870s, high officials were attaching the raised honorific characters for "restoration" to their memorials to the throne. For many, therefore, it seemed that, far from sliding toward collapse, the empire had been rejuvenated.

Yet by 1900, China's treasury was bankrupt; its export trade was being outstripped by European and Japanese competitors; its domestic markets were turning increasingly to factory-produced foreign commodities; and its land, squeezed by the world's largest population, once again spawned the problems of tenancy and landlordism that had played such a central role in the overthrow of past dynasties.

The Horizon of Decline: The White Lotus Rebellion

In the frontier area stretching across the meeting of Hubei, Shaanxi, and Sichuan provinces, a new version of an older Buddhist cult took root. Many of its adherents were recent arrivals, and the reach of government and administration in the region was minimal. The emigrants had tried rice cultivation in these uplands, but the results were poor. When local officials attempted to collect taxes from them, they rose in rebellion in 1794. Sporadic outbreaks continued for the next decade. The term **White Lotus** given to the uprising dates back at least to the Buddhist school that was home to the founder of the Ming Dynasty, the fighting monk Zhu Yuanzhang. Now the decentralized White Lotus militias routinely frustrated the Banner forces and Green Standard units arrayed against them. Theirs was a classic guerrilla strategy of hit and run, erode the enemy's morale, and force them into bloody reprisals that drive the beleaguered population to your side. Qing commanders routinely complained of their inability to distinguish the guerrillas from ordinary civilians. Finally, after bringing in more troops, they reorganized loyal militia, relocated the populace to fortified villages, and worked to isolate the rebels and reduce their advantage of mobility (see Map 5.4).

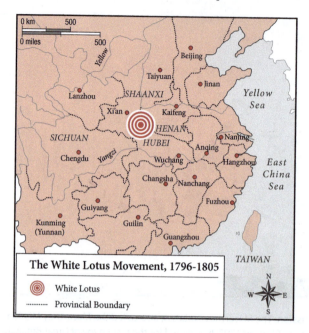

Map 5.4 The White Lotus Movement, 1796–1805

Although the rebellion was effectively suppressed by 1805, it smoldered on for another decade, and there were several results of the conflict that would plague the Qing in later years. One was that the Banner and Green Standard forces, which had proven their fighting ability in earlier campaigns, performed poorly in this struggle. Even more troubling for the long term was that the local militias proved far more effective than their professional counterparts. This would contribute considerably to the power of regional officials at the expense of the government later during the Taiping years of midcentury.

Interactions with Maritime Powers

By the 1790s, with their China trade at record levels and the wars accompanying the French Revolution making European trade increasingly problematic, the British decided to attempt to open diplomatic relations with the Qing. Their hope was to begin the process of placing trade in what the British considered to be more appropriate channels. In the summer of 1793, therefore, they dispatched Lord George Macartney (1737–1806), an experienced diplomat and colonial governor, to Beijing with a large retinue and substantial numbers of presents thought to represent the best of British goods. His mission was to persuade the Qianlong emperor to allow the stationing of diplomatic personnel in the Chinese capital and to sanction the creation of a system for the separate handling of ordinary commercial matters and diplomacy along the lines of European practices.

Macartney Mission. The Macartney Embassy, also called the Macartney Mission, was a British embassy to China in 1793. It is named for the first envoy of Great Britain to China, George Macartney, who led the endeavor. The goal of the embassy was to convince Emperor Qianlong of China to ease restrictions on trade between Great Britain and China by allowing Great Britain to have a permanent embassy in Beijing, and consular representation and reduced tariffs in Canton. Though the mission brought a rich store of presents for the emperor intended to show off Britain's technological skills, all the British requests were summarily rejected.

Despite the precedent of allowing a Russian presence in Beijing, Qianlong rebuffed Macartney's attempts to establish a British embassy there. In addition to observing that China really had "no need of your country's ingenious manufactures," Qianlong stated frankly that permanent foreign embassies were contrary to the current system and would "most definitely not be permitted." A second British mission in 1816 under the direction of Lord William Amherst (1773–1857) met with even more complete rejection.

One compelling reason that Europeans and Americans were pushing to bring the Chinese into their diplomatic and commercial system was the perception that China was benefiting from a huge trade imbalance. Tea imports alone dwarfed what the British earned from all their export goods to China. Thus, the vast percentage of British imports from China had to be paid for in silver. Although recent scholarship has shown that China's economy actually supported much of the interconnected Eurasian commercial system, contemporary merchants were convinced that China's control of trade functioned in the same way as did European mercantilism, draining the West of its stocks of silver. However, Western merchants offered little that the Chinese needed or wanted. As the new century dawned, therefore, European and American commercial interests were becoming increasingly anxious to find trade goods acceptable to the Chinese. By the beginning of the

nineteenth century, a small but growing number of merchants were clandestinely turning to a lucrative new commodity, with tragic consequences.

As a result of the victories of the British East India Company's forces over the French and their allies in India during the Seven Years War (1756–1763), the Company's territory had been extended to include the area around Patna, historically a center of medicinal opium production. While East India Company traders were technically prohibited from carrying opium to China as contraband—and the Qing had prohibited its nonmedicinal use since 1729—an increasing number of non-Company merchants and those Company men trading on the side discovered that they could circumvent Chinese regulations and sell small quantities of the drug for a tidy profit. By the early nineteenth century, an elaborate illicit system of delivery had been set up along the South China coast. The soaring profits from this illegal enterprise fueled piracy and lawlessness along the coast, and the opium trade soon became the most divisive issue in relations between China and the West.

The relationship that the foreign traders and the Cohong had so carefully developed over the previous century was now swiftly eroded by the new commodity. For the British, the mode and profits of the trade collapsed the barriers between legitimate goods and illicit ones. This, in turn, led not only to payoffs to Company officials who connived at this practice, but also to the Cohong and local Chinese officials. The East India Company itself was now fatally compromised, as an estimated one-quarter of its revenues in India were directly tied to opium production by the 1830s.

Moreover, the political climate in England unwittingly opened the doors wider for the opium trade. Free-trade agitation in England put an end to the East India Company's privileged position in China in 1833. With the monopoly lifted, the number of entrepreneurs seeking quick riches in the opium trade exploded. The push for legitimacy among the opium merchants coincided with an aggressive attempt by Westerners to force China to open additional trading ports for legal items. The effects of the trade on the ordinary inhabitants of South China were catastrophic. The accelerating rise of supply and lower prices allowed the drug to permeate all levels of society. Moreover, lax and capricious enforcement of the imperial edicts prohibiting the smoking of the drug coupled with the high levels of corruption further reduced respect for local officials in a region already smoldering with latent anti-Qing sentiment.

The Coming of the Unequal Treaties

The collision that came in the spring of 1839 would shortly grow into the opening event of China's century of *guochi*—"national humiliation"—that would endure until 1949. The Daoguang emperor sent Lin Zexu (1785–1850), a scholarly, uncompromising official with a reputation for courage and honesty, to Canton as an imperial commissioner. Lin's mission was to cut off the opium trade at its source, and he was given wide-ranging powers to deal with Chinese and foreign traffickers. He demanded that all foreign merchants surrender their warehoused opium and sign a bond that they would not, under penalty of death, deal in the

drug anymore. The Canton foreign community, seeing this as perhaps the first unwelcome step toward a major policy shift, stood pat and refused. Lin blockaded the port and withdrew all Chinese personnel from Western firms. His determined stance finally cracked the stalemate, and the dealers eventually surrendered 20,000 chests of opium, with most also signing the pledge. Lin then publicly disposed of the opium by mixing it with slaked lime and flushing the resulting slurry into the sea, accompanied by prayers asking forgiveness of the sea gods. The dealers, however, appealed to the British government for compensation.

The British seized upon the claims to settle the long-standing diplomatic impasse with the Qing over foreign representation and open ports. There were other difficulties, as well, however. Although the precepts of Chinese law and its relationship to personal morality and group responsibility had been an integral part of Confucian culture, the British felt the Chinese judicial system was unreliable and capricious. Moreover, with increasing numbers of British nationals doing business in China, the number of judicial complaints was bound to multiply.

In a show of force, therefore, the British sent a fleet of warships to Canton to demand compensation for the confiscated opium, pressure the Qing to establish diplomatic relations, and open more ports. Four centuries had now passed since China had commanded the seas as the world's premier naval power.

Warfare in the New Industrial Age. The distance in military technology between an industrializing Great Britain and China is on painful display in this rendering of the armored steam gunboat *Nemesis* destroying a Chinese war junk in January, 1841. Specially constructed for fighting on the small rivers of South China, the shallow-draft *Nemesis* featured heavy pivot guns fore and aft and a hull assembled in detachable sections for oceanic transport aboard larger vessels. It this picture it has just fired a Congreve rocket into the Chinese vessel's powder magazine, completely destroying it.

The only vessels available to confront the British were modestly armed with seventeenth-century cannon and used for customs collection. What they now faced were the leading exemplars of the world's foremost navy. When negotiations broke down, the British force promptly sank several Chinese vessels and scattered the rest. The incident inaugurated the use of force by the industrializing maritime powers in their dealings with China and East Asia as a whole. It was a threshold they would cross repeatedly as the century wore on.

The struggle between China and Great Britain would lay bare for the first time in world history the gap between the military capabilities of industrializing countries and those whose armed forces had fallen into disuse. The changes in perception on both sides wrought by this mismatch altered the way Westerners tended to view China for the next century, whereas for the Chinese—and soon all of East Asia—it triggered a long and painful search to capture the fruits of modernity without sacrificing their cultural distinctiveness. The world's largest exporter of technology for so many centuries, China was to now be characterized as hopelessly "backward." Perhaps most painful of all for an empire that had seen itself as the center of world civilization, China was now stigmatized as "barbaric" or "semi-civilized" as its failure to modernize along Western lines became more acute.

Over the next two years of this First Opium War, as it came to be called, the British methodically attacked and occupied ports along the Chinese coast from Canton to Shanghai, for the most part without serious opposition. As the British planned to move north to put pressure on Beijing, Chinese officials opened negotiations in August 1842. The resulting **Treaty of Nanjing** (Nanking) marked the first of the century's "unequal treaties" that would be imposed throughout East Asia by European powers.

Although it did not specifically mention opium—its legalization as an import would come in a later agreement—the Qing ceded to the British the island of Hong Kong, already in use as an important opium transshipment point. The Chinese agreed to open the ports of Shanghai, Ningbo, Fuzhou, and Xiamen (Amoy), in addition to Guangzhou (Canton), and the British imposed an indemnity on the Chinese to pay the costs of the war and repay the value of the opium seized. To crack open Chinese markets for British manufactured goods, the victors imposed *nontariff autonomy* on the Chinese: China could now charge no more than a 5 percent tariff on British goods. As for protecting its subjects from the vagaries of Chinese law, a consular system was set up in the open Chinese ports and a policy of **extraterritoriality** mandated: British subjects who violated Chinese laws would now be tried and punished by British consuls and consular courts. Following the British lead, France and the United States signed similar treaties with the Qing over the next several years.

THE TAIPING AND NIAN ERAS

As China was coming to grips with the effects of the first round of unequal treaties, events were unfolding in South China that would soon lead to the bloodiest civil war in human history, the Taiping conflict. As perhaps the most studied Chinese event of the nineteenth century, scholars have arrived at a number of reasons for its origins and development. As the only port open for maritime trade until 1842, Canton and its adjacent districts in Guangdong Province were arguably the most cosmopolitan region in the Qing Empire. The area's economy was also the linchpin of China's international commerce, the node at which China interacted with the world's global trading networks.

There were political and ethnic tensions as well. The southern regions had a long history of defiance toward dynasties centered in the north. Another factor scholars routinely cite is quasi-ethnic conflict. The founder of the movement, Hong Xiuquan (1813–1864), and most of his early converts were *Hakkas* (in pinyin, *kejia or kejiaren*, "guest families"). Their ancestors had migrated from the north in several waves precipitated by the collapse of the previous three dynasties.

The newcomers were Han Chinese who spoke Mandarin, did not bind the feet of women, and often met ill-treatment at the hands of their neighbors. Their villages, more often than not in poor areas, typically featured protective walls and fortified inner compounds. They also shared in a more general economic downturn that marked the opening of the initial **treaty ports** and Hong Kong after 1842. With the number of open ports increasing from one to five and the British in possession of Hong Kong, centuries-old trade routes abruptly and dramatically shifted. This was particularly true of the silk and tea trades, which now were more oriented toward the Yangzi Basin and Shanghai.

Unlike past peasant revolts that sought to recover existing rights or pass on the Mandate of Heaven to a new candidate, the Taiping movement aimed at a fundamental restructuring of society, prompting some historians to see it as a revolution. All the elements of Confucian society were systematically broken down: the hierarchical relationships of rulers, family, and friends; the veneration of the Classics; and the separation of mental and manual work. Men and women, married and unmarried, lived in separate barracks but were considered equal, even as soldiers on the battlefield. Private property was eliminated: all wealth and materiel captured was to be put into a common treasury.

Like modern revolutions as well, class and religious enemies were to be dealt with ruthlessly, as were Manchus. Scholar-gentry or officials were summarily executed. Confucian, Buddhist, and Daoist temples were looted and destroyed, or turned into houses of Taiping Christian worship. Indeed, Taiping behavior in the scope of their destruction of Confucian society comes close to modern definitions of genocide. As the fighting became more widespread, even peasants were not necessarily exempt. For their part, Qing troops and militia, even from the most disciplined units, looted, burned, and killed on a stupendous scale as well.

The Origins of Taiping Ideology

While preparing to sit for the local Confucian examinations, Taiping founder Hong Xiuquan had come upon some Christian missionary tracts. Not long after this, in 1836, Hong failed the initial Confucian examination for the third time and lapsed into a nervous breakdown. When he recovered, he came to believe that the Christian God had taken him to Heaven and there informed him that he was, in fact, Christ's younger brother. Hong told his startled listeners that it had been revealed to him that he must now work to eliminate the "demons" possessing the country and thus bring about the Heavenly Kingdom of Great Peace (*taiping tianguo*) on Earth.

Hounded from their community, Hong and his converts moved to a mountain stronghold in neighboring Guangxi Province and began to gather followers from the disillusioned and unemployed, anti-Manchu elements, religious dissidents, secret societies, and fellow members of the Hakka minority. Hong had also sought the sanction of Western missionaries and approached the American Baptist preacher Issachar Roberts (1802–1871) for instruction and baptism, although he was refused the latter. By 1851, Hong's group had created a society based on Protestant Christian theology, Chinese pre-Confucian traditions, and a communal vision of social, economic, and gender equality. As a sign that they were no longer loyal to the Qing, the men cut their queues and let the hair grow in on their foreheads, prompting the Qing to refer to them as "the long-haired rebels."

By late 1851, the movement had gathered enough strength to break out of their stronghold and advance to the north. By 1853, they had captured the city of Nanjing and made it their capital. That winter, only a blizzard and determined attacks by the emperor's Mongol cavalry saved the dynasty from being driven from the capital. For the next decade, the rebels would remain in control of the Chinese heartland, and the long struggle to subdue them would leave thousands of towns and villages devastated for decades to come (see Map 5.5).

Defeating the Taipings

Chinese officials were desperate to roll back the threat of encroachment by foreign maritime powers and suppress the Taipings. They were hardly in agreement, however, on how this might be accomplished. As the Taipings were the more immediate threat to both the Qing and, as it had become clear, the treaty ports, both sides attempted a degree of collaboration. Toward this end, a growing number of officials advocated a policy that came to be called *ziqiang*, "self-strengthening." During the 1860s, the two most prominent of these officials were Zeng Guofan (1811–1872) and his protégé, Li Hongzhang (1823–1901). Both men were distinguished by the flexibility of their thinking, willingness to take risks, and, increasingly, by their growing familiarity with the new weapons and techniques brought to China by foreign forces. All these attributes were on display by their use of new Chinese forces armed with foreign weapons and officered by foreign mercenaries. In 1864, Zeng and Li's combined forces finally captured the Taiping capital at Nanjing and forced the suicide of Hong Xiuquan, bringing the movement to an end.

The Nian Rebellion, 1853–1868

As the Taiping movement was gathering momentum in the south, a more diffuse uprising was taking shape in the north. In addition to the mass bloodletting of the Taipings, the period from 1849 through the 1850s saw an extraordinary series of natural disasters in the empire. In 1849 alone, earthquakes, floods, and an outbreak of plague in Zhili (the metropolitan province surrounding Beijing), Hubei, and Zhejiang, and a drought in arid Gansu claimed perhaps 15,000,000 lives. This was followed by two record floods of the Yellow River in 1851 and 1855.

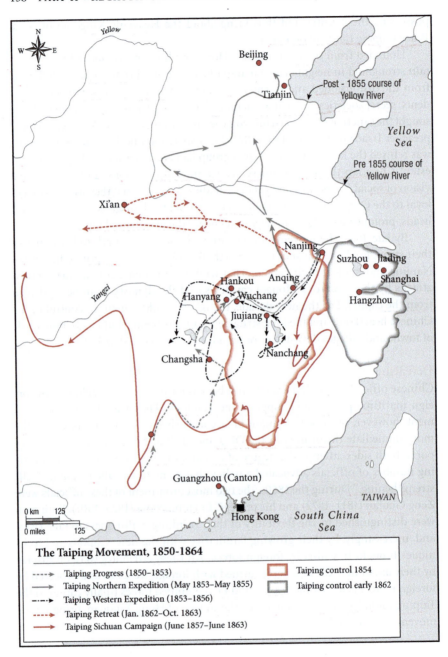

Map 5.5 The Taiping Movement, 1850–1864

Gathering in some remnants of the White Lotus sect, and propelled by the lack of flood and famine relief, the Nian rebels—named for the northern Chinese dialect many spoke—rose up in 1851 largely from frustration at the inability of the Qing to either help them or resist foreign demands for treaty revision. In the end,

Taiping Seal. This seal, probably dating from 1860 or 1861, is a fine example of Taiping religious and political symbolism. The two largest characters, top left and right, indicate an imperial seal, as do the dragon and phoenix motifs around the borders. The four large central characters at the top read "Heavenly Father God (*shangdi*)." Noted historian Jonathan Spence cites Chinese scholar Wang Qingcheng as suggesting that the seal should be read as a kind of acrostic and translates it as:

> *Of God the Father, the Heavenly Elder Brother Christ*
> *The Heavenly King Hong (Xiuquan), the sun, the ruler of the bountiful earth*
> *The savior and young Monarch, the true king Guifu (Honor and Blessedness)*
> *Exalted for myriad years, eternally granting Heaven's favor,*
> *Eternally maintaining Heaven and Earth in gracious harmony and*
> *   convivial peace.*
>
> (Jonathan Spence, *God's Chinese Son: The Taiping Heavenly*
> *Kingdom of Hong Xiuquan*, New York: Norton, 1996, xxviii.)

Qing forces were able to crush them piecemeal until their final collapse and suppression in 1868. The overall death toll for the Taiping, Nian, and smaller conflicts within the empire is estimated to have been between 20 and 30 million people.

REFORM THROUGH SELF-STRENGTHENING, 1860–1895

At the height of the Taiping fighting in 1856, a new dispute arose between the Qing and the British and French. After four years of intermittent fighting, this Second Opium War produced the next round of "unequal treaties" that greatly expanded foreign interests and control in the empire. The catalyst came in late 1856. A Chinese customs patrol in Canton hauled down the British flag on the *Arrow*, a Chinese vessel whose registry had been falsified to take advantage of British trading privileges. The British seized upon this purported insult to their flag as an opportunity to force treaty revision. The French, who considered themselves the protectors of Catholic missionaries and their converts, saw an excellent opening to pressure China on the missionary issue and so joined the British.

The war itself was fought intermittently in a highly localized fashion. The British seized the city of Canton, but as the conflict moved into 1857, the Great Rebellion in India consumed their attention through much of the year, while in China negotiations dragged on intermittently and the Qing remained preoccupied with the Taipings. In 1858, a draft treaty was worked out, but the Qing court refused it. Returning in 1860 with a large expeditionary force, British and French troops fought their way to Beijing, drove the emperor from the city, and burned and looted the Summer Palace. The final treaty stipulated that a dozen ports be opened to foreign trade, opium be recognized as a legal commodity, extraterritoriality be expanded, and foreign embassies be set up in the capital. A newly created Chinese board, the Zongli Yamen, was to handle Qing foreign relations, and the Chinese were invited to send their own ambassadors abroad.

PATTERNS UP-CLOSE

The Cooperative Era and Modernization

As noted above, the end of the Second Opium War began a period of occasional collaboration lasting through the early 1870s, sometimes referred to by historians as the "cooperative era." There were few major disputes between the foreign powers and the Qing; indeed, in several instances, foreigners worked closely with Chinese officials to help them in assessing ways to upgrade their defenses, lay the foundations of modern industrial concerns, and start programs that signaled institutional change.

By the end of the rebellion, therefore, a group of officials had begun to move toward a strategy of what came to be called *zhongxue wei ti; xixue wei yong* (Chinese studies for the essence; Western studies for practical application). It thus enabled the *yangwu* (foreign affairs) proponents to accommodate the need for new foreign technologies within historically and philosophically acceptable terminology. Despite often considerable opposition, the self-strengtheners sponsored an impressive array of projects in the 1860s and early 1870s: as an aid to the new Zongli Yamen (Foreign Office), a foreign language and technical school (*Tongwenguan*) was set up; the Nanjing and Jiangnan (Kiangnan) arsenals and a modern navy yard built at Fuzhou; initiatives to send Chinese students to the United States and Europe were put into motion; a modern shipping concern (The China Merchants' Steam Navigation Company) was established; and the first moves toward sending representatives abroad initiated from 1875 to 1880.

Opposition to such programs also mounted during the period and continued throughout the century. Often highly placed—including, at times, the Empress Dowager Cixi (1835–1908) herself—these opponents believed the kind of change necessary to create an industrial base in China would erode the social, cultural, and economic ties that held that society together. For example, in 1876, while Japan was busily building railroads, the first such line in China—built by foreign merchants in Shanghai—was purchased by the local governor and promptly torn up. The reasons were strategic, socioeconomic, and cultural: railroads would make it easier for foreigners to invade the country; they would put whole classes of people involved in transport out of work; and they would upset the *feng shui* (geomancy) of the land.

Many of the same fears prompted the recall of the Chinese Education Mission that had been maintained in Connecticut for a decade (1872–1881). Inspired by Rong Hong (Yung Wing; 1828–1912), a graduate of Yale, Christian, and naturalized U.S. citizen, and approved by Zeng Guofan and Li Hongzhang, the Mission's intent was to give its 113 boys a thorough understanding of Western science, technology, and military matters, as well as maintaining their Confucian studies. Reports of the boy's "Americanization," the refusal of the military academies to admit them,

Nanjing Arsenal. Among China's self-strengthening programs none seemed more urgent in the 1860's than modernizing armaments. Yung Wing, the driving force behind the Chinese Education Mission, had earlier been sent to the United States to buy the factory machinery that went into China's first Western-style arsenal at Nanjing, set up in 1864. In this 1868 photograph Chinese officials inspect such newly manufactured ordnance as a Congreve rocket, a pyramid of spherical explosive shells, and a Gatling-type gun with multiple revolving barrels.

(continued)

Students Wearing Baseball Uniforms. The transformation of the Chinese students at the Education Mission in Hartford, Connecticut, appeared all too complete to later Chinese commissioners, who feared their Americanization. Here, the Mission's baseball team, "The Orientals," poses on the school's lawn in 1878, stylish in their attire and bats, and relaxed and confident in their appearance. The team compiled winning records during its days at the school and soundly defeated an Oakland, California, team in a pickup game while awaiting their departure home in 1881. (Courtesy of Thomas LaFargue Papers, Manuscripts, Archives, and Special Collections, Washington State University Libraries, Pullman, Washington. In Edward Rhoads, *Stepping Forth into the World*, Hong Kong: Hong Kong University Press, 2011, p. 146.)

and the considerable cost of the project ultimately brought about its recall—despite the lobbying efforts of such American luminaries as former U.S. President Ulysses Grant and the celebrated author Mark Twain.

Thus, the fierce cultural debates, as well as the lack of a clear strategy at the top, worked to frustrate the hopes of the "self-strengtheners" through the turn of the century. Yet the concept of "using foreign things to help China" would again surface in the Four Modernizations of Deng Xiaoping in 1978, and have propelled China's astounding economic growth and technological development ever since. And in the twenty-first century, a high-speed mag-lev train runs along the route of the line once torn up.

Nineteenth-Century Qing Expansion

Despite the Qing Dynasty encompassing China's greatest period of wealth, power, and territory, there was hardly a period within it when a rebellion of some sort was not in progress. Some of them grew from inadequate government responses to natural disasters or famine; some from attempts at tax collection; and some as revolts against foreign minority rule, economic distress, religious conflict, and ethnic rivalries.

Elements of all these struggles could be found within the various Muslim uprisings of the era, especially in the extreme western areas subdued during Qianlong's reign, but ruled by the "loose rein" method of dealing with border peoples. By the late eighteenth, and through nearly all the nineteenth century, Yunnan and Xinjiang marked the sites of protracted conflicts. Despite the stresses of foreign encroachment and the most devastating rebellion in human history, subduing these rebellions marked the high point of Qing agency during the "restoration" period.

In the 1820s, a series of Turkic invaders moved into Kashgaria led or co-led by the Ismaili Khojas from Kokand. Both ethnicity and religion played a role in the sense that Muslim Hui traders resisted the invaders and fought against them alongside Qing forces. A cycle of invasion and resistance then prevailed over the next twenty years until the Qing drove the last of the Khojas, the brutal Wali Khan, back to Kokand in 1857. Upon the Qing withdrawal from the area, however, this region came under the purview of Yakub Beg, who now attempted to establish his own state of "Kashgaria." (See Map 5.6.)

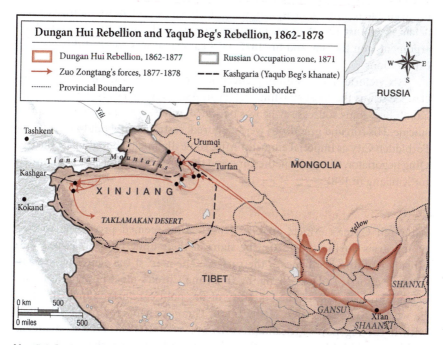

Map 5.6 Dungan Hui Rebellion and Yuqub Beg's Rebellion, 1862–1878

A series of other revolts had brought Zuo Zongtang (1812–1885) to the eastern part of the region in 1867. Although ruthless toward rebels of any sect, he also made infrastructural improvements to the region and launched a successful program to grow grain to help supply his army. But the expeditions were expensive, the land largely uninhabitable and thus difficult to forage on, the people marked by internecine conflicts and shifting loyalties, and the new weapons from foreign countries costly and their operators largely untried. Moreover, the distances were unimaginably vast, and so far beyond the pale of Chinese civilization as to be in another, disturbingly alien, world.

In the midst of this confused situation, Russia, Great Britain, and the Ottoman Empire all claimed a stake. All three empires had been engaged in attempting to exert direct or proxy control over the region of Central Asia north of Afghanistan, in a decades-long series of border intrigues later popularized as The Great Game in a story of that name by Rudyard Kipling. For all three of these empires, Yakub Beg's Kashgaria made a highly useful buffer state against the others. Thus, all three extended tacit recognition to it. For Zuo and his supporters, however, it marked a vital part of China that the Qing could ill afford to lose.

In this matter, he ran into intense opposition from Li Hongzhang. A rapidly strengthening Japan had temporarily occupied Taiwan in 1874, and the various foreign powers had more than doubled their treaty ports in 1860. To Li, Xinjiang was too remote, costly, and unproductive to make it a priority. Moreover, its inhabitants were barely touched by Confucian civilization. A far better use of the available resources, Li argued, would be to employ them to improve coastal defenses against the Western maritime powers and Japan. In the end, Zuo's argument won the day and his 1877–1878 campaign was successful beyond all expectations.

His victories had a stunning effect on the players of the Great Game: one claimed it was the most startling victory in Asia over the last fifty years. As for Yakub Beg, some sources say he was poisoned; some suggest that he committed suicide. His son and grandsons were captured, castrated, and put to work in the Forbidden City as imperial eunuchs. After some diplomatic bungling by the first Qing negotiator, Chong Hou, the Qing and the Russians established new borders for Xinjiang in 1881.

The Limits of Self-Strengthening, 1860–1895

Although China's efforts at self-strengthening seemed promising to contemporaries during the 1870s, the signs of their underlying weakness were already running just beneath the surface. The man at the center of so many of these efforts, Li Hongzhang, by this time China's most powerful official, was painfully aware of the volatility of the political environment in which he worked. The ascension of the infant Guangxu emperor in 1874 brought with it the regency of the Empress Dowager Cixi (1835–1908). Intelligent, ruthless, and highly attuned to the political winds at court, she was desperate to preserve Manchu power, as well as her own. Cixi constantly manipulated factions at court and among the high officials to avoid a concentration of power in any particular area. Such maneuverings, sometimes favoring Li's self-strengthening colleagues and as often opposing them, severely hampered the long-term health of many reform measures. In addition to the vagaries of court politics, the new programs were costly, and often required foreign experts, while China's finances were continually strained by the immense costs of recovery from the rebellions, the artificially low treaty tariffs, and the obligation to pay old indemnities.

Despite the spectacular success of Zuo Zongtang's efforts in Xinjiang, the 1880s saw new foreign tensions elsewhere on China's Confucian periphery. Despite the repeated assertion of Qing suzerainty over the region, France had been steadily encroaching upon Southeast Asia since the late 1850s (see Chapter 12). After a hard-fought conflict with China in 1884–1885, the French emerged with control of the whole of Vietnam, which they promptly combined with Cambodia and Laos into the colony of French Indochina in 1885–1887.

In 1885, as China was still involved with France, tensions with Japan over Korea also threatened to dislodge that kingdom as a Qing client state. As early as 1873, some advisors to Japan's new Meiji emperor had argued for a Japanese expeditionary force to "open" Korea to Japan in much the same way that the United States had pressured the Tokugawa Shogunate to "open" Japan. When this was deemed not feasible, a Japanese force was sent instead to Taiwan to punish the island's aboriginal inhabitants for killing some fisherman from Okinawa. The Japanese soon withdrew their forces, but the expedition was for Li Hongzhang glaring proof of Japan's growing power and presence. In 1879, through negotiations with China and the diplomatic good offices of former American President Grant, Japan purchased the disputed Ryukyu Islands (called Liuqiu by the Chinese).

Now in Korea, Japanese diplomats were exerting influence over the Korean court as it sought to deal with the Tonghak Rebellion, which had been alternately smoldering and flaring up since 1863. China, alarmed again at foreign intrusion into what it considered its own backyard, sent a team of officials to keep watch on Qing interests, and both sides quickly threatened to send troops. In the agreement between Li Hongzhang and Ito Hirobumi (1841–1909) at Tianjin in 1885, both sides agreed to not take any action in the future without informing each other.

By the early 1890s, however, rising tensions surrounding the Korean court and intrigues by Japanese and Chinese agents involving various factions threatened war once again. Japan sent a force that was claimed to be diplomatic; troops of a Chinese counterforce were killed when a Japanese warship sunk their transport. By the fall of 1894, both sides were sending troops and naval forces to Korea and a full-scale war over the fate of Korea and Northeast Asia was under way (see Map5.7).

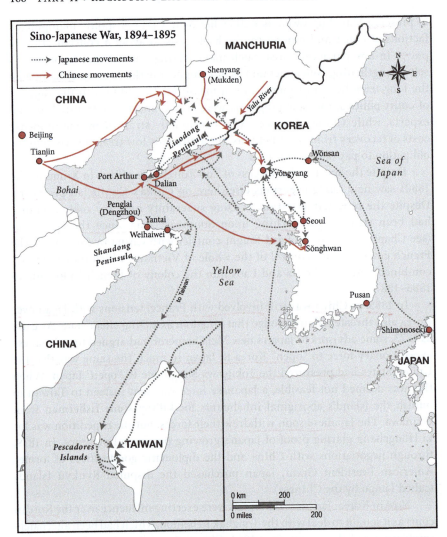

Map 5.7 The Sino-Japanese War, 1894–1895

The Sino–Japanese War of 1894–1895

With stunning swiftness, the war between China and Japan over control of Korea laid bare the flaws of China's self-strengthening programs and of China's position as East Asian's principal power. Because China's programs were generally carried out by individual officials negotiating with foreign firms and advisors, there was little coordination among the forces these men controlled. Different Banner and Green Standard units were armed with a wide variety of non-interchangeable weapons and ammunition, making it difficult for them to support each other. China's newly rebuilt steam fleet of iron-clad and steel-hulled warships, although impressive in size and armament, faced similar problems. Unlike the Japanese ships, in many cases, the components for

China's vessels were separately built at various dockyards in Europe. In one memorable incident during the battle of the Yellow Sea in 1894, the recoil from the mismatched, oversized guns aboard the Chinese flagship destroyed its own captain's bridge. The Chinese fleet was also accompanied by foreign advisors of assorted nationalities, who squabbled among themselves as to tactics and exercised the right of independent withdrawal from the engagement. Worse still, Chinese gunners found to their dismay that many of the shells they were firing were filled with sand rather than explosive—the result, it was said, of the empress dowager's diversion of naval funds to rebuild the Summer Palace destroyed in 1860.

Although many of the land battles were hotly contested, superior Japanese organization and morale enabled them to drive steadily through Korea. A second force landed in southern Manchuria to secure the territory around the approaches to Beijing, while Japanese naval forces reduced the fortress across from it at Weihaiwei. By the spring of 1895, after some preliminary negotiations, Li Hongzhang made a humiliating trip to the Japanese town of Shimonoseki to meet his old Japanese counterpart, Ito Hirobumi, who was now revered as the architect of Japan's Meiji Constitution of 1889. To further add to his humiliation and misery, Li was shot in the face during an assassination attempt, though he recovered shortly thereafter and saw the negotiations through to their conclusion.

Despite the outward cordiality of the two men toward each other, the severity of the treaty provisions served notice that Japan had now moved from the camp of the victims of imperialism to that of the imperial powers themselves. In addition to the annexation of Taiwan, control of Korea, and, temporarily at least, the seizure of the South Manchurian Liaodong Peninsula, China was forced to agree to the largest indemnity yet, around $150,000,000. The only bright spot for China was that France, Germany, and Russia, all of whom had interests in the area, were worried that Japan was growing too powerful and so forced the Japanese to return Liaodong to China in what became known as the Triple Intervention. In 1898, China leased the peninsula to Russia, which soon enhanced it with a fortress at Port Arthur, a move that helped set the stage for the Russo-Japanese War in 1904–1905. (See Chapters 8 and 13.)

The **Treaty of Shimonoseki** signaled to the Western powers in East Asia that China was now weak enough to have massive economic and territorial demands forced on it. Thus, a "race for concessions" shortly began in which all the imperial powers except the United States demanded enhanced spheres of influence in China adjacent to their existing interests. China's total dismemberment was only avoided in 1899 when John Hay, the U.S. secretary of state, circulated a note with British backing suggesting that all powers refrain from securing exclusive concessions and instead maintain an open door for all to trade in China. Through the following decade, after the final imperial humiliation wracked by the Boxer conflict and its aftermath, the Qing would attempt to stave off collapse through reform. October of 1911, however, saw the beginning of the revolution that would bring them down.

Li Hongzhang and Ito Hirobumi at Shimonoseki. (A) In this *ukiyo-e* print of the peace negotiations held in Shimonoseki in early 1895, China's principal representative, Li Hongzhang is seated at the right side of the table in the foreground. His counterpart for Japan, Ito Hirobumi, is sitting across from him wearing a sash. To Ito's left, also wearing a sash, is Japan's foreign minister Mutsu Munemitsu. Former US Secretary of State and advisor to the Chinese for the talks, John W. Foster, stands at the head of the table by Li. The negotiations were conducted in English through interpreters.
Carving Up China. (B) The Race for Concessions in the final years of the nineteenth century came close to dismembering China and was averted by the reluctant adoption by the imperial powers of the Open Door policy proposed by the United States. In this French cartoon the monarchs and national symbols of the powers (Queen Victoria of Britain, Kaiser Wilhelm II of Germany, Tsar Nicholas II of Russia, Marianne, the symbol of republican France, and a samurai of Japan) contemplate the choicest pieces of the flatbread of China—with a frantic Chinese official, perhaps Li Hongzhang himself, entreating them to stop.

SOCIETY AND ECONOMICS IN MING AND QING TIMES

Although China boasted some of the world's largest cities, more than 85 percent of the country remained rural during the period from the Qin through the Ming. As we saw in Chapter 2, at the top of the local structures of power and influence from the development of the Confucian bureaucracy during the Han into the twentieth century were the *scholar-gentry*. As a class, they were by definition the educated and included all ranks of degree holders, whether in or out of office, and their families. By imperial edict and custom, they were expected to exercise leadership over the classes of peasants, artisans, and merchants, and along with the district magistrate, take the initiative during times of trouble in safeguarding the lives and property of the community.

Rural Elites

Scholar-gentry membership was in theory open to most males and their families, although in practice seldom exceeded 1 to 2 percent of the population in most areas of the empire. By Ming and Qing times, the chief qualification was attainment of at least the lowest official degree, which enabled the bearer to attend a government-sponsored academy for further study and draw a small stipend. The demands of memorizing the classical canon and learning to write in the rigid format of the "eight-legged essay" required for the exams, however, were such that the wealthy had a distinct advantage in the leisure time, access to tutors, and connections required to pass the exams. Still, there were enough poor boys who succeeded by hard work and the sacrifices of their families and neighbors to provide a surprising degree of mobility within the system.

Because prestige within the scholar-gentry derived from education even more so than wealth, it was not uncommon for individuals to purchase degrees, although technically they were barred from doing so in the upper three categories. Individuals could also attain honorary ranks for meritorious service in the military, outstanding ability during times of emergency, decades of diligent study unaccompanied by success in the exams, and even for living to a ripe old age: Commoners reaching the ages of 80, 90, and 100 were awarded official ranks of the ninth, eighth, and seventh grades, respectively, and given the honorary title of "Elder."

In keeping with their role as the informal administrative apparatus of the district magistrate, the scholar-gentry enjoyed a number of privileges as well as responsibilities. At the same time, their position as community leaders and their grounding in Confucian ethics frequently placed them in tension with the official bureaucracy, especially when local interests appeared at odds with regional or imperial ones. By a variety of stratagems available only to the wealthy, they were frequently able to conceal the amount of taxable land they possessed and generally paid lower rates than commoners. Along with the district magistrate, they presided over all ceremonies at Confucian temples, and the ones holding the highest ranks led all clan ceremonies. In addition, they mingled with the official authorities more or less as social equals; in the case of those in between appointments to high office, they frequently outranked the local magistrate.

Organizing the Countryside

In the midst of the growth accompanying the Ming economic recovery, the government took steps to simplify the system of land taxation. As in previous regimes, land was assessed and classified according to its use and relative productivity. Land taxes were then combined into a single bill, payable in silver by installments over the course of the year, the so-called single-whip tax system. The installment plan allowed peasants to remain relatively solvent during planting season when their resources were depleted, thus reducing the need to borrow at high rates from moneylenders at crucial times of the yearly cycle. Significantly, the requirement that the payment be in silver also played a crucial role in the increasing monetization of the economy. Corvée labor was effectively abolished as well.

During the sixteenth century, administrative restructuring led to the creation of the *baojia* system. This required families to register all members and be organized into units of 10, with one family in each unit assuming responsibility for the others. Each of these families would then be grouped into 10 and a member selected from them to be responsible for the group of 100 households, and so on up to the *bao*, or 1,000 household level. *Baojia* representatives at each level were to be chosen by the families in the group. They were to report to the magistrate on the doings of their respective groups and were held accountable for the group's behavior. The system was especially important during the Qing, when it allowed the authorities to bypass potential gentry resistance to government directives and guaranteed a network of informers at all levels of rural life.

Population and Sustainability

One of the key problems of modern Chinese economic and social history has been that of the long-term sustainability of Chinese agriculture. From 1700 to 1900, the empire's population tripled, while its land usage only doubled. This increase came despite the enormous death toll of the Taiping, Nian, and Muslim rebellions, which may have eliminated roughly 8 to 9 percent of the population at the time.

Another difficulty in terms of land usage and sustainability revolves around inheritance laws and customs. The average land holding in the fertile areas of central China at this time was slightly less than three acres. The land was held in strips, sometimes in noncontiguous sections, around a central group of village houses, much like the configuration of feudal holdings in medieval Western Europe. China, however, did not practice primogeniture, so each son got a piece of the land. Small holders, often squeezed by their inability to feed themselves on their ever-diminishing tracts, sold them off and joined the labor pool, or migrated to towns and cities to try their luck there. In many cases, they engaged in handicrafts of various sorts and so added to the vibrancy of the empire's commercial sector. The majority, however, rented land as tenants, hoping eventually to make enough to acquire property again. Thus, the rise in tenancy was accompanied by a rise in landlordism, particularly in those areas ravaged by the mid-nineteenth-century rebellions.

The "High-Level Equilibrium Trap" Debate

Given these factors, scholars have long debated the varying trajectories of China and the industrializing countries of the West. In the past, the most common question was that given China's huge population, giant internal economy, abundant resources, and technological leadership, why did it not experience its own industrial revolution? Instead, it is argued that from roughly 1500 on, China's rate of innovation actually slowed considerably, although the population increased. Farming techniques showed little technological advance, but local, regional, and even national commercial networks grew markedly.

Theories growing from these observations have centered on the argument that China had long been caught in a situation called a **high-level equilibrium trap.** That is, comprehensive and sustained innovation like that of an industrial revolution tends to take place when a society is in a state of imbalance or *disequilibrium*. In this view, eighteenth-century England had experienced severe problems of high wages, surplus capital, poor transportation, legal disabilities imposed on religious dissenters, and restrictive laws on imports of cotton goods that prompted investment in technologies and working arrangements to improve efficiency and overcome these problems.

China, however, it was argued, had been able to keep agricultural pace with its population growth but had essentially run out of new lands to cultivate. Having more children in peasant families meant that up to a point their additional labor allowed the farming to be done more intensively. The growing labor supply, however, consumed what commodity surplus there was and did not allow any particular class to acquire a deep pool of capital that could be invested in new enterprises—except to buy more land. Improving labor efficiency seemed unnecessary—even disruptive—because labor was so cheap and abundant. Thus, by the late nineteenth century, these economic factors were in equilibrium but incapable of breaking out of this "trap." At present, there is no strong consensus about definitive circumstances in studying China's agricultural sustainability or possibilities for indigenous industrialism.

TECHNOLOGY AND INTELLECTUAL LIFE

The Ming at their height have been described by some Chinese scholars as a military superpower. Perhaps most important in this regard was that the ascendancy of the Ming in 1368 coincided with the beginning of what one historian has called a "military revolution" in the use of firearms. The first use of metal gun barrels in the late 1200s spurred the rapid development of both cannon and small arms. So much so, that by the mid-fifteenth century, the Ming arsenal at Junqiju was producing thousands of cannon, handguns, and "firelances" every year. By one estimate, in 1450, over half of the Ming frontier military units possessed cannons and one-third of all troops carried firearms. As early as the 1390s, large ship-borne cannon were being installed. Indeed, court historians of the late Ming credited nearly all the military successes of the dynasty to the superiority of their firearms.

By the Qing period, however, following the pacification of the realm, the need for constant improvement of arms was seen as increasingly unnecessary. While marginal improvements were made in the matchlock firing mechanisms of Chinese small arms, such improvements as did occur in larger guns were largely directed by European missionary advisors to the throne.

Philosophy and Literature

As in seventeenth-century France, the centralizing tendency of the government exercised considerable control in the cultural realm through patronage, monopoly, and licensing. The Kangxi, Yongzheng, and Qianlong emperors strove to validate their reigns by being patrons of the arts and aspiring to high levels of connoisseurship and cultivation of the best of the literati. As in the other absolutist realms, they not only set the tone in matters of aesthetics, but also used mammoth cultural projects to direct the energies of scholars and officials into approved areas. At the same time, they sought to quash unorthodox views through lack of support and, more directly, through literary inquisitions. Kangxi, for example, sponsored the compilation of a huge dictionary of approved definitions of Chinese characters—still considered a primary reference work today. Under his direction, the commentaries and interpretations of neo-Confucianism championed by the Song philosopher Zhu Xi became the approved versions. Kangxi's thirteen **Sacred Edicts**, embodying maxims distilled in part from Zhu Xi's thought, became the official Qing creed from 1670 on. Anxious to legitimize themselves as culturally "Chinese," Kangxi and Qianlong sponsored huge encyclopedia projects. Qianlong's effort, at 36,000 volumes, was perhaps the most ambitious undertaking of its kind ever attempted.

Although the urge to orthodoxy pervaded both the Ming and Qing dynasties, considerable intellectual ferment was also brewing beneath the surface of the official world. Two of the most important later figures were Huang Zongxi (1610–1695) and Gu Yenwu (1613–1682). Both men's lives spanned the Qing conquest and, like many of their fellow officials, concluded that the collapse of the old order came, in part, from a retreat from practical politics and too much indulgence in the excesses of the radicals of the Wang Yangming school. With a group of like-minded scholars, they based themselves at the Donglin Academy, founded in 1604. Here, they devoted themselves to reconstituting an activist Confucianism based on rigorous self-cultivation and on remonstrating with officials, and even the court. One outgrowth of this development, which shares interesting parallels with the critical textual scholarship of the European Renaissance, was the so-called **Han Learning Movement**. Convinced that centuries of Buddhism, religious Daoism, and Confucian commentaries of questionable value had diverted Confucianism from the intent of the sages, Han Learning sought to recover the original meaning of the Confucian works through exacting textual scholarship and systematic philology, or historical linguistics. The movement, although always on the fringe of approved official activities, peaked in the eighteenth century and successfully uncovered a number of fraudulent texts, while setting the tone for critical textual analysis during the remainder of the imperial era.

Although China's literati clung to an amateur ideal of poetry, painting, and calligraphy, increasing official patronage ensured that approved schools and genres of art would be maintained at a consistent, if not inspired, level of quality. Here, the Qianlong emperor was perhaps the most influential force. Motivated, in part, by a lifelong quest to master the fine arts, he collected thousands of paintings—to which he added, in the tradition of Chinese connoisseurs, his own colophons—rare manuscripts, jade, porcelain, lacquerware, and other objets d'art.

Although the novel during Ming and Qing times was not considered high literary work by Chinese scholars, the form, as with Europeans in the eighteenth and nineteenth century, proved immensely popular. During the mid-eighteenth century, what many consider to be China's greatest novel, *Hong Lou Meng* (The Dream of the Red Chamber), was written by the shadowy Cao Xueqin (1715?–1764?). Almost nothing is known of Cao, including exactly when he was born and who his actual father was. The novel itself chronicles the decline and fall of a powerful family over 120 chapters. Some scholars see in it a loose autobiography of Cao's own family and a thinly veiled account of events in the early days of the Qing.

Poetry, Travel Accounts, and Newspapers

Although the late Qing period is often seen by scholars as one more concerned with cataloging and preserving older literary works than innovation, there was nevertheless considerable invigoration due to foreign influences toward the end of the dynasty. Reversing the trend of thousands of years, the most significant Chinese developments in science and technology were those arriving from the West as products of the Industrial Revolution and the new kind of society emerging there.

Sometimes confining himself to more traditional fare, Huang Zunxian (1848–1905), for example, wrote many poems based on his experience as a diplomat in Japan and the United States. China's increasing need to understand the nature of the threat confronting it prompted an increasing number of atlases, gazetteers of foreign lands, and by the 1860s, the first eyewitness travel accounts. The most significant of these were written by Wei Yuan (1794–1856), *Illustrated Gazetteer of the Maritime Countries* of 1844, and Xu Jiyu (1795–1873), *Record of the World* of 1848. These accounts, especially Xu's, formed the backbone of what Chinese officials knew about the outside world until the first eyewitness accounts of travelers and diplomats began to arrive in the late 1860s.

Although hundreds of thousands of Chinese had emigrated to various parts of the world by the mid-1860s, it was only in 1866 that the first authorized officials began to visit foreign countries and not until 1876 that diplomats began to take up their posts in foreign capitals and ports. All these men, however, were required to keep journals of their experiences, and by the later part of the century, China began to acquire a far more complete sense of what the outside world was like. The diaries of the diplomats Zhang Deyi and Guo Songtao were particularly significant in this regard.

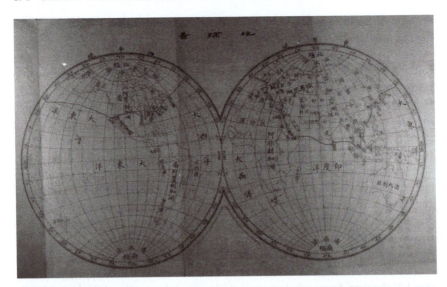

Li Gui's Route around the World. One travel account that was popular among Chinese officials and the interested public was that authored by Li Gui (1842–1903), *A New Account of a Trip Around the Globe*. A clerk in the Imperial Maritime Custom Service, Li was asked to accompany the Chinese exhibitors to the American Centennial Exhibition in Philadelphia in 1876 and write an account of his experiences. He continued on to Europe and passed through the Suez Canal, stopping in Sri Lanka, Singapore, Saigon, and Hong Kong before returning to Shanghai. To enlighten any doubters of the Earth being a globe, he posted daily navigation readings of his shipborne travels and included this map of his route, done in red in the original.

A new popular medium also emerged in the treaty ports and eventually in most Chinese cities as well—the newspaper. For centuries, newsletters tracking official doings at the capital had circulated among the elites. However, the 1860s saw the first popular Chinese-language papers, the most prominent of which was *Shenbao*. By the turn of the century, Liang Qichao (1873–1929) had emerged as China's most influential journalist and scholar, having started and edited five newspapers, each heavily influenced by his views on reform. Such publications and the growing numbers of journals and popular magazines, many started by missionaries anxious to use science and Western material culture as a vehicle for their work, were vitally important in the transfer of ideas between Chinese and foreigners.

CONCLUSION

The cycle of power and increase in imperial China's fortunes waxed, with some interruptions, through the Ming and into the Qianlong period of the Qing. Perhaps the best expression of this power lies in the epic voyages of Zhenghe's enormous fleets, which showed both the technological excellence of the Chinese and their global reach. Echoes of this expansiveness continued into the mid-eighteenth century with Qianlong's expeditions into Central Asia and extending the empire's control over Tibet. The last reverberations could be heard during the Tongzhi Restoration of the mid-nineteenth century with the crushing of major rebellions and the final conquest of Xinjiang.

Yet internal and external changes were already working to undermine the strength of the empire. Although about 80 to 85 percent of China's population remained rural, the old structures of the empire's peasant-based society were slowly beginning to crumble. The White Lotus, Taiping, Nian, and the eras of the Muslim rebellions showed mounting tensions among peasants, village headmen, scholar-gentry, and local officials in regions all over the empire. Landlordism, and especially the growing instance of absentee landlordism, tended to stretch these tensions further. Living on the edge of poverty in many areas, with old trade routes and handicrafts disrupted, many peasants saw in the Taipings, the Nian, and other local rebellions a desperate way to change their situations. But in the end, the radical ideologies and ruthlessness of the rebels disillusioned them, while in many places their poverty increased due to the immense destruction and the flight of many wealthy scholar-gentry to the cities. As some scholars have noted, the land problems of China—and its parallels in India and the Ottoman Empire—were an important impediment to an effective response to the scientific-industrial challenge of Europe and America.

That challenge manifested itself directly in the maritime trading nations' direct confrontation of the Canton system, the demand for more open ports, the mounting pressure placed on the Qing to abandon their customary system of diplomatic and commercial regulation and join that which the Western countries aspired to make the world standard. Beyond this, the increasingly corrosive force of the opium trade and its accompanying corruption and misery worked to dissolve the bonds of local government and society.

China's policies regarding these changes varied immensely in their imaginative approaches and agency. Self-strengthening seemed to hold much initial promise, even as the example of Japanese efforts along similar lines began to outstrip those of China. The fruits of utilizing the new foreign technologies seemed to be apparent as students studied abroad, arsenals and shipyards were built, and especially with Zuo Zongtang's striking successes in Xinjiang. Here, Zuo's Krupp artillery, Remington rifles, and Gatling guns proved their utility. Yet the war with Japan at century's end also demonstrated the long path to modernity that China would need to follow to make itself the equal in power to the industrialized nations—now including Japan.

FURTHER RESOURCES

Crossley, Pamela K. *A Translucent Mirror: History and Identity in Qing Imperial Ideology.* Los Angeles: University of California Press, 1999; paper, 2002. Pioneering study with an emphasis on the transition of the Qing from an ideology of conquest in the seventeenth century to one of universal emperorship under Qianlong.

Desnoyers, Charles. *A Journey to the East: Li Gui's "A New Account of a Trip Around the Globe."* Ann Arbor: University of Michigan Press, 2004. Translation with introduction of Li's extensive visit to Philadelphia and other U.S. cities in 1876, and his voyages to London, Paris, Suez, India, Singapore, and Hong Kong before arriving back in Shanghai.

Elliott, Mark. *The Manchu Way: The Eight Banners and Ethnic Identity in Late Imperial China.* Palo Alto: Stanford University Press, 2001. With access to newly opened Manchu archives, Elliott is a leader in the synthetic, identity-based "new Qing history" that seeks to break out of the standoff between the "Sinicization" and Northeastern" approaches.

Hevia, James. *Cherishing Men from Afar: Qing Guest Ritual and the Macartney Embassy of 1793.* Durham, NC: Duke University Press, 1995. Award-winning examination of the role of symbolic behavior and causes and resolution of conflict within the context of the first British embassy to the Qing.

Ko, Dorothy. *Teachers of the Inner Chambers: Women and Culture in Seventeenth Century China.* Palo Alto: Stanford University Press, 1994. Pioneering work that challenges the stereotype of late Ming and early Qing women as simply hapless victims of Confucian patriarchy.

Miyazaki, Ichisada, and Conrad Schirokauer, trans. *China's Examination Hell.* New Haven, CT: Yale University Press, 1981, Classic study of the workings of the Confucian exam system, of the cramming and aids often available, and the often unbearable pressures brought to bear on aspirants to office.

Mungello, David E. *The Great Encounter of China and the West, 1500–1800.* Lanham, MD: Rowman & Littlefield, 1999. Short, handy volume that serves as a solid introduction to the role of China and Asia more generally in the opening centuries of global empires.

Platt, Stephen R. *Autumn in the Heavenly Kingdom: China, the West, and the Epic Story of the Taiping Civil War.* New York: Knopf, 2012. New perspective on the Taiping era and its interconnections with the global economy and informal Western intervention in the 1860s.

Rhoads, Edward J. M. *Stepping Forth into the World: The Chinese Educational Mission to the United States, 1872–81.* Hong Kong: Hong Kong University Press, 2011. Most complete treatment of Yung Wing's Education Mission and a meticulous tracing of the lives and careers of the students.

Spence, Jonathan. *Emperor of China: Self-Portrait of K'ang Hsi,* New York: Vintage, 1975. Spence is arguably the finest stylist and most interesting writer among twentieth-century China scholars. Here, he attempts to reconstruct the interior world of Kangxi using translations of the emperors' own accounts.

Spence, Jonathan. *God's Chinese Son: The Taiping Heavenly Kingdom of Hong Xiuquan.* New York: Norton, 1996. Using newly discovered documents and exchanges between Hong and missionaries, Spence attempts to recreate the inner world of Hong.

WEBSITES

http://www.cnd.org/fairbank/. Fairbank Chinese History Virtual Library. Material covers a wide range of primary and secondary sources, pictures, and other media. Most material from Qing Dynasty and later.

http://afe.easia.columbia.edu/. Weatherhead East Asian Institute at Columbia University. *Asia for Educators.* The title of the site notwithstanding, the site notes that it is "for students and educators at all levels." Extensive coverage of China, modern and ancient, with links to primary and secondary materials, maps, videos, and other media.

http://besthistorysites.net/ancient-biblical-history/china/. Edtechteacher. *Best of History Websites: China*. Extensive clearinghouse for world history websites, including the two listed above. In addition to the more specific ones on modern Chinese history, it contains sites from all eras and materials and activities for teachers.

CHAPTER 6

✦

Becoming "The Hermit Kingdom": Korea from the Mongol Invasions to 1895

One can only imagine the consternation animating the men of the Japanese invasion fleet. In the late afternoon of May 29, 1592, several large Japanese warships and a host of support craft, having covered their forces going ashore at Sacheon on the southern coast of Korea, spotted what appeared to be Korean vessels milling about, perhaps preparing a counterattack. Having secured the city and invested the overlooking heights nearby, the Japanese commanders decided to give chase. But this would be like no other fight they had ever been in.

The narrative of this early encounter during Korea's Imjin War—the East Asian Seven Years War of Japanese invasion—conjures up visions for American historians of what it must have been like in 1862 when the Confederate ironclad C.S.S. *Virginia*—née, *Merrimack*—methodically attacked the wooden Union fleet at Hampton Roads. In this fight, however, the new type of armored vessel the Japanese encountered did not resemble a crocodile, as one observer said of the Confederate ship, but, as per its namesake, a turtle.

Korean admiral Yi Sun-sin's flag ship, the only one of its kind in the squadron this day, was unlike anything the world outside Korea had seen. Building on design features of earlier warships, this **turtle ship** (*geobukseon*) appeared squat and unwieldy, powered by sails and eighty oarsmen. Its armament, however, was formidable with five different types of cannon firing a variety of projectiles including iron and stone balls, incendiary shells, and a devastating type of harpoon. Its front and rear mounted iron rams. The figurehead on the bow was a large dragon from whose mouth clouds of poisonous smoke issued. Moreover, its U-shaped hull allowed it to turn on its own radius, and it could achieve surprising speed for short distances. The design proved quite stable—and needed to be because the ship's most important feature was an armored shell from which hundreds of spikes stuck out. Naval historians have debated about whether the shell, in fact, made these ships the world's first true ironclads, since the design drawings and accounts of the shipwrights and sailors are unclear on this point. They may have simply been roofed over with heavy timbers with spikes, or the iron shell may have simply been to repel borders, small arms, and flaming arrows. In any case, as the Korean fleet now turned on

178

its pursuers, the Japanese ships, lacking heavy guns and unable to close on and board their opponents, were methodically destroyed. All thirteen Japanese ships were dispatched; Korean casualties numbered five wounded, including Admiral Yi, who suffered a minor wound to his arm. A few days later, on June 2, at Dangpo, the Korean fleet visited similar devastation on the Japanese.

Despite this impressive display of naval innovation and power, the Japanese invasion would last, with a brief interval, until 1598. As with the twentieth-century Korean War, there would also be a massive Chinese involvement, and the war would leave the country devastated and impoverished for years to come. For the Japanese, the new Tokugawa shoguns would attempt to keep their hard-won internal peace through a policy of seclusion and forced stability. Korea would recover its dynamism, but by the nineteenth century, its own policies of seclusion would come under increasing attack by internal critics and by a swiftly changing international order that would once again make Japan an expansive power with designs on Korea. In this new crisis at the end of the nineteenth century, however, naval power would be on the side of Japan, Chinese influence would be pushed from the peninsula; Russia, Germany, and France would intervene; and by 1910, Korea would be reduced to a colony of the expanding Japanese Empire.

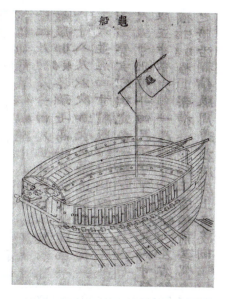

Korean Turtle Ship. The Korean "Turtle Ships" sent to oppose the Japanese invasion fleet were unlike any naval vessels the Japanese—or anyone else outside Korea—had seen before. In this illustration, from a Japanese work of 1795, the dragon bow and rounded super-structure are clearly visible, although the customary spikes studding the upper deck are not shown. The *kanji* (Chinese) characters labeling the illustration read from right to left "Turtle Ship"; the character on the flag reads "Turtle" as well.

TOWARD SEMI-SECLUSION

As we have seen, the arc of the pattern of history on the Korean Peninsula has been profoundly affected by events in China and, to a lesser extent, those in early Japan. The coming centuries would see the pattern of Chinese influence continue through invasion, the "soft power" of cultural influence, and by the assumption of Chinese suzerainty by the Ming and Qing dynasties. This assumption, however, would be challenged by the invasion of the peninsula by a consolidating Japan in the 1590s and more completely by an industrializing Japan in the period from 1873 to 1895. Indeed, by 1910, Korea had been annexed by the expanding Japanese Empire and would remain a colonial possession of Japan until 1945.

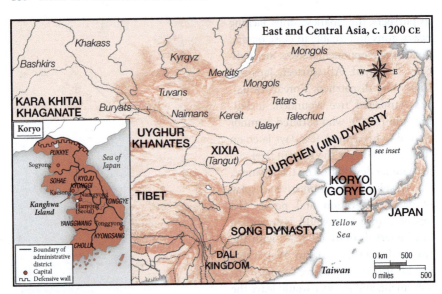

Map 6.1 East and Central Asia, ca. 1200 CE

Yet below the surface of such foreign pressure, the pursuit of political and cultural independence continued. In addition to stubborn resistance to invasion and local adaptations to Chinese-style systems of governance, the Koreans, in an even more thoroughgoing manner than the Japanese or Vietnamese, completely revamped their writing system. In so doing, they created what linguists even today consider perhaps the world's most efficient and easiest to learn syllabary. With the widespread use of printing and a flourishing publishing industry, Korea achieved perhaps the world's highest rate of literacy up to the nineteenth century (see Map 6.1).

The Mongol Era and the Founding of the Yi Dynasty

By the mid-thirteenth century, the Korean state of Koryo (Goryeo), like much of the rest of Asia, had begun to feel the power of Mongol expansion. Armed with a wide array of siege engines and gunpowder weapons acquired from their contests with the Jin in northern China, as well as their seemingly invincible light cavalry, Mongol forces launched invasions in 1231, 1232, from 1235 to 1239, and again in 1251, 1254, 1255, and 1259. Despite early Mongol advances punctuated by several truces, and a number of captured cities in the north, including the capital at Kaesong (Gaesong), Koryo held on. The fall of the capital forced the government to flee ahead of the Mongol advance and began a long struggle to wear down and drive out invaders.

As we saw in Chapter 4, Mongol internal policy frequently mandated the scattering and forced transfer of peoples to other areas of the empire. In the case of Koryo, it resulted in the deportation of perhaps 250,000 Koreans as slave labor to other parts of the empire beginning in 1254. The Koryo court finally capitulated in 1259, following which, as they had in other areas, the Mongols made some largely unsuccessful attempts at intermarriage and cultural assimilation. Koryo continued as a rump vassal state of the Mongols. As in most of the occupied areas of Eurasia, the advantages wrought by Mongol unity in terms of easier travel and transport, the emphasis on trade and commerce, and increased public works were eclipsed in Korea by the length and cruelty of the conquest itself, the widespread perception of misrule, and oppressive taxation.

In what had become almost routine following the inauguration of a new dynasty in China, the Ming Dynasty, having expelled the Mongols and overthrown the Yuan Dynasty, laid plans to invade Korea. In 1388, Yi Song-gye (1335–1408), a military commander engaged in opposing the invaders, made the strategic decision not to resist the Ming but moved against the Korean court instead, founding the Yi Dynasty 1392. He took the reign name of T'aejo and resurrected the name of Choson (Joeson) for the new state. The Yi proved to be Korea's last imperial dynasty, ruling until the peninsula was annexed by Japan in 1910. The Yi concluded an agreement with China that formed the heart of the so-called Ming "tribute system" (see Chapter 5). Diplomacy with the surrounding states was conducted by the Chinese on the basis of their perceived place in a Confucian hierarchy of relationships. Regular ceremonial visits by delegations of Korean, Okinawan, Vietnamese, Japanese, and various Central Asian representatives to the Chinese court were rewarded with smooth diplomatic relations and favorable trade conditions.

Meanwhile, the new dynasty once again set up Chinese-style institutions. The highly centralized governmental structure of the Ming was echoed in Choson, and the adoption of neo-Confucianism slowly began to drive out older local customs and those recently imposed by the Mongols. A new capital was set up on the site of present-day Seoul, and the state was divided into eight provinces. Within each of these, the Chinese model of prefectures and districts was followed. A uniform law code was promulgated in 1485 calling for, among other things, a permanent hereditary class structure—an arrangement later introduced by the Tokugawa Shoguns in Japan from a similar desire for stability. The Confucian exam structure was also broadened to include a two-tiered official class, the *yangban* and *chungin* (see below).

The Yangban. The hereditary official class of Yangban corresponded roughly to their Chinese counterparts in the imperial bureaucracy. As part of their official garb, they were entitled to wear the lacquered horsehair hats pictured in this illustration by the genre painter Kim Hong-do, whose pseudonym was "Danwon" (1745 through 1814–16?). Kim's paintings of everyday events, called "true-view painting," are still admired today. Here, Yangban enjoy food and entertainment behind a walled garden.

Yet for all the advantages created by the new hereditary class structure, old cleavages in many cases remained and new unanticipated ones soon developed. As a means of stabilizing the *yangban* class, and, so it was assumed, society as a whole, the Yi rulers made large land grants to the great officials of the kingdom. These landholders, however, tended to use such grants to amass more and more local power. Unlike the Chinese scholar-gentry bureaucrats, whose official assignments were moved from place to place for just this reason, *yangban* tended to remain in their own territories carrying out their administrative duties, where they could use a host of informal controls to resist attempts from the throne to rein in their excesses. Over time, many became like regional rulers.

The Japanese Invasion

In 1592, at the head of an uncertain coalition of Japan's warring **daimyo**, or regional lords, the Japanese leader Toyotomi Hideyoshi decided that an invasion of China via Korea would be a shrewd outlet for Japan's martial energies. He initially approached the Yi in hopes of an alliance against the Ming. The Koreans, caught between two powerful adversaries, calculated that a Japanese amphibious invasion would be easier to resist than a land assault from China and refused the alliance. As we saw in the opening vignette, although Hideyoshi's forces mounted superior firepower on land, the Korean innovation of the "turtle ship" under Admiral Yi Sun-sin made Hideyoshi's seagoing supply lines quite tenuous. Clad in iron plates roofed over the ships' decking, and armed with rams fore and aft, the Korean craft were impervious to enemy fire and proved more than a match for the Japanese warships.

The heavy losses at sea were now matched by a massive counterattack by combined Ming and Korean land forces. Although not as well drilled in serial firing techniques as Hideyoshi's forces, the Chinese nonetheless fielded considerable firepower. Like the progress of the Korean War of the 1950s, where the weight of China's numbers compensated for the slim technological advantage enjoyed by the United Nations' forces, the war quickly became a bloody stalemate. With neither side able to mount a decisive offensive, and the Japanese supply lines in continual danger because of the harassment of the turtle ships, Hideyoshi felt it wise to avoid a prolonged war of attrition. In 1596, therefore, he abandoned the invasion for the time being and returned to Japan to rethink and regroup. His attempt to renew the war in 1597 was cut short by his death the following year (**see Map 6.2**).

Recovery and the Drive for Stability

The withdrawal of Hideyoshi's Japanese expeditionary forces after his death in 1598 left the Korean Peninsula devastated from Seoul down to the southern coast. The capital had been fought over several times and its public buildings and archives destroyed. The size of the armies—the Japanese force alone numbering 200,000, with the combined Korean-Chinese forces at least twice that—taxed the ability of the areas along their lines of march to support either themselves or the foraging troops for the duration of the war and for some time after it had ended. Finally, the effective but costly exploits of the Korean turtle ships had disrupted

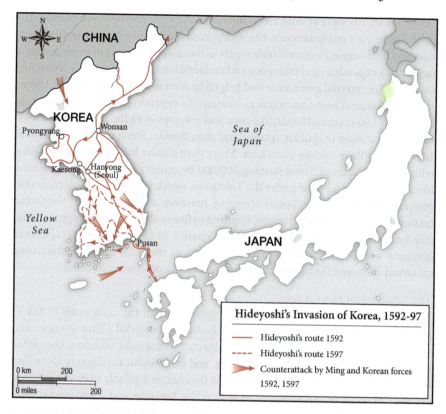

Map 6.2 Hideyoshi's Invasions of Korea, 1592–1597

much of the coastal and oceangoing trade of Korea. Thus, the first, and in many ways most difficult, order of business was the reconstruction of the country.

The court initially feared that the departure of the Japanese was not a permanent condition but one that might be shortly reversed. Although Japan's Tokugawa Shogunate later adopted stringent seclusion policies, the ascendancy of its founder, Tokugawa Ieyasu, in 1603 at first signaled a renewed interest in naval power. Thus, despite the fact that trade missions from Korea were periodically welcomed in Japan, an urgent priority for the Yi Dynasty continued to be coastal defense. A defense council, with members chosen from the various boards of the government, was set up to advise the court, and taxes were imposed on the peasants to pay for the costly elements of maritime defense.

After securing the coast from attack, the most urgent priority was the revival of agriculture and the relief of the increasing misery in the countryside. Although some Yangban had redeemed themselves by organizing militia to resist the Japanese, their overall position continued to decline as their postwar efforts failed to stem the effects of famine and high taxes. Indeed, they made repeated attempts to secure tax relief for themselves by funding tax-exempt "school estates," the number of which multiplied four-fold during the seventeenth century.

Government attempts at land redistribution were only partially successful. Still, by the latter part of the century, the widespread availability of new medical treatises and books on agricultural techniques in the simplified *han'gul* writing system (see below) expanded land clearance and reclamation for food and cash crops, and the revival of internal commerce had helped to reverse the disasters of the 1590s.

As was true in East Asia in general, the rapidly expanding use of new food crops able to grow on marginal lands, like corn and potatoes from the Americas, enabled Korea's population to quickly recover and then double, rising from 2.3 million in 1657 to 5.2 million a dozen years later. There were similar leaps in the size of cities, with the population of Seoul nearing 200,000 by century's end. Moreover, Korea, like Japan at the same time under the Tokugawa, developed a vibrant internal commercial economy. Unlike Japan's economy, however, it did not rely on the forced traffic of the *fudai* (outer) daimyos, required to live in the Tokugawa capital of Edo (the future Tokyo) every other year, for its vitality. In fact, in many ways, Korea's economy was in a more advantageous position as the trade and manufacturing crossroads between the tightly controlled economies of Japan and China.

The Shadow of the Qing

The development of the various Korean states through the early years of the Yi Dynasty had always taken place in the shadow of powerful Chinese states and empires to the north. Even when not subjected to outright invasion, the diffusion of Chinese culture, political systems, and philosophical/religious ideas into Korea had a profound long-term impact on the choices available to its inhabitants. We have noted how the Koreans (as well as the Japanese and Vietnamese) were able to negotiate their adaptation to these influences, while still retaining political independence and a considerable degree of cultural autonomy. In the following 250 years, the Yi's state of Choson once again attempted to rebuild and reform its political and economic systems around the centralized structures of the Chinese model. Qing claims of control over Korean foreign policy and Yi participation in the Chinese "tribute" system of foreign relations, however, led to an intensified Neo-Confucian outlook that saw the Qing as "elder brother" to its "younger brother" of Korea. In this sense, Korean rulers often walked a narrow line between the coercive "guidance" of the Qing and the requirements of peace and stability in their own realms. Within the country, the forces of commercialization were eroding the power of the landed *yangban* class; agricultural advances and new cash crops were increasing social mobility; and a new critical spirit, both within and outside the canons of neo-Confucianism, was creating an intellectual climate that would increasingly demand change as the nineteenth century wore on.

By the 1630s, amidst Korea's recovery from the destruction of the war with Japan, a new set of problems loomed on the northern horizon of the kingdom. Over the previous fifty years, the Manchus (see Chapter 5), a nomadic, Altaic-speaking people believed to be descended from the Jurchens, had moved into the area of the Liaodong Peninsula adjacent to Korea. Under the influence of the Ming, they had adopted neo-Confucianism and, to some extent, Chinese methods of government. The Ming had recognized them as clients, but they were rapidly becoming a critical force in the north as the Ming court became weaker and civil war loomed among potential pretenders to the throne.

Sensing an opportunity for expansion, the Manchus launched a probe into Korea in 1625. The court, divided by partisans of various Confucian reforms, appealed to the Ming for help. By 1636, however, with no help forthcoming from China, the Manchu leader Abahai humiliated the Yi monarch Injo, who surrendered and agreed to allow Choson to become a vassal state of the new Manchu dynasty, the Qing ("pure"). By 1644, the Qing had driven the Ming from power in China and secured the reins of their new relationship with Korea (see Map 6.3).

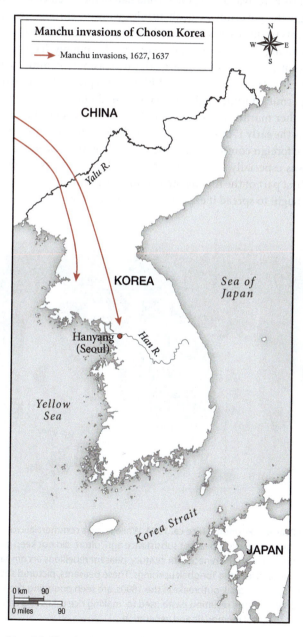

Map 6.3 Manchu Invasions of Choson Korea

The ineffectiveness of the Yi Dynasty, and especially of the Yangban, in defense of the country once again spurred calls for reform. In an attempt to gain the kind of economic efficiency the Ming had earlier achieved with their "single-whip" tax, the Yi court under King Hyojong instituted the "uniform land tax." All males, even monks, were now required pay a single graduated land tax in return for which they were to be exempt from military conscription. Rationalization of the tax structure, relative peace, and the undercutting of Yangban power and prestige all contributed to the agricultural revival during the second half of the seventeenth century.

Although the government dealt fitfully with its chronic agricultural and social problems in rural areas, Korea, like Qing China and Tokugawa Japan, was rapidly developing a robust internal commercial economy. This was, in part, a consequence of Korea's connection to the increasingly commercialized world economy through trade with China. With the exception of a limited number of merchants permitted under tight supervision to do business in Japan, however, trade with other maritime peoples was almost nonexistent. As was the case in Japan and, by the early 1700s in Qing China, the Korean government increasingly tended to see foreign commerce and ideas as potentially disruptive and undesirable. This was especially true of religion. In all three places—and in Vietnam during the first part of the nineteenth century—Christianity was proscribed and those who sought to spread it expelled or driven underground.

Korean Peasants Pounding Rice ca. 1904. While Korea's commercial crops grew in importance and value, peasant subsistence agriculture did not keep pace. Several times during the nineteenth century, peasant rebellions accompanying famines erupted into the Tonghak uprisings. These peasants, pictured shortly after the last of Tonghak outbreaks in the 1890s, are seen pounding rice in a large mortar, with the resulting paste used for making rice cakes and ceremonial dishes for ancestral memorials and veneration.

Strangers at the Gates

The sixteenth and seventeenth centuries had seen the first wave of European traders and missionaries enter the area. In both China and Japan, Portuguese, Spanish, Dutch, and English influence had briefly engaged the warring daimyo, and intrigued the late Ming and early Qing courts. By the early 1700s, however, this influence had largely evaporated. The Tokugawa shoguns had adopted a seclusion policy that mandated the elimination of foreign trade and contact except for select Chinese and Korean merchants and craftsmen. As for the Europeans, only a small Dutch contingent quartered on the tiny artificial islet of Dejima in Nagasaki Harbor was permitted to trade. All Christian missionaries were expelled and Japanese Christians vigorously persecuted. For the Qing, following a series of Jesuit advisors to the court, and a doctrinal and liturgical disagreement with the papacy, the Yongzheng emperor expelled the missionaries in 1722.

The late eighteenth and early nineteenth century, however, saw a marked increase in East Asian maritime traffic, particularly after the Napoleonic Wars. Although Qing regulations kept all legal Chinese trade within the system at Canton (Guangzhou), dealers in contraband cargoes such as opium, and missionaries attempting to penetrate the Chinese interior, increasingly tried their luck farther afield. By the 1820s, they were probing Korean and Japanese ports, though in every case were rebuffed. In the wake of the First Opium War between Britain and China (1839–1842), however, the opening of the first treaty ports and their vastly increased traffic made further attempts to penetrate Korea all but inevitable. (See Chapters 5 and 8.)

As they had in Japan and China, Christianity, improved European firearms, and the new mathematics and sciences had also established themselves in Korea in the seventeenth and early eighteenth centuries. Here, too, they met with varying degrees of approval from reformers and critics of the neo-Confucian order. Not surprisingly, they also came to be seen as subversive by a government that saw itself as the only legitimate source of moral guidance for the populace. As in China, and as with "Dutch Learning" in Japan, the reformers tended to separate what they thought of as "superstitious" aspects of Christianity from the advantages the new knowledge brought to the Korean "Pragmatic Studies" movement. Opponents, on the other hand, tended to see all of it as one package—and therefore culturally and morally dangerous. Thus, Yangban and court opposition resulted in repeated persecutions of Korea's growing Christian population in 1801, 1836, and 1866.

The Hermit Kingdom

Twice during this period, in 1812 and 1862, peasant revolts erupted during times of famine. The most massive and long-lived of these was the **Tonghak**, or "Eastern Learning," movement, combining elements of Confucianism, Buddhism, and a pronounced strain of general anti-foreignism. Although the Tonghaks were suppressed in the 1860s, the forced opening of Korea to trade in the following decade, and the constant intrigues of the Qing and Japanese surrounding the Yi court in succeeding decades, brought about the movement's revival in the 1890s. It would prove to be an important factor in Japan's humiliating defeat of China in 1895 and annexation of Korea in 1910.

In the mid-nineteenth century, however, despite increasing internal problems, Korea's policy of centralization through a revived neo-Confucian bureaucracy and close following of the lead of China in foreign policy seemed, on the surface at least, to have been effective. After rebuffing Western attempts to forcibly open the country to trade, Korea was commonly referred to as the "Hermit Kingdom. And when it was at last forced open, it was Japan that once more took the leading role.

Commercialization and increases in agricultural efficiency had led to greater net prosperity, more social mobility, high rates of literacy, and a number of elements that social scientists have pointed to as key pieces of the process of "modernization." Yet important elements seemed to be missing as well. As in China, there was constant factional fighting at court that often negated government initiatives at reform; the prosperity of commercial agriculture was offset by the lack of Yangban leadership. Perhaps most tellingly, Korea's weak military, its seclusion, and reliance on Chinese leadership in foreign affairs made it brittle and vulnerable when the kingdom was forced open by the very countries that had shortly before forced concessions on the Qing and Japanese.

Korean-American Diplomacy, 1904. Although U.S.–Korean relations got off to a rocky start with the burning of the American ship *General Sherman*, relations with the Yi court in the latter nineteenth century were generally good, as they also tended to be with China and Japan, with the U.S. notably seen as an honest broker during negotiations to end the Sino-Japanese War. Here, crossed Korean and American flags adorn the entrance to the Yongnam governor's compound as Koreans in both traditional and Western garb wait to greet visitors from the United States. The Chinese characters on the ceremonial gate read from right to left in Korean, "Yongnam pojongsa" (Yongnam Provincial Governor).

Korea and the Sino-Japanese War

The story of Korea's opening and its place as the prize in the struggle for hegemony among Japan, China, and Russia is often lost in tracing the course of the conflict. That is to say that the war is usually cast in terms of Sino-Japanese rivalry for control of the peninsula and Korea emerges in this larger struggle as something of a bit player. But despite the Yi Dynasty's growing weakness relative to its neighbors, it occupied the pivotal place around which revolved the evolving new order of East Asian political and military power.

Given events in China and Japan during the 1850s and 1860s, it now seems inevitable that Korea's seclusion would be broken down. China's humiliation at the hands of foreign powers, her opening of treaty ports under foreign pressure, and the Qing's desperate fight to suppress the Taiping, Nian, and assorted Muslim rebellions had come close to creating a new turn of the dynastic cycle there. Complicating matters further, Britain, France, and the United States, fearing that the overthrow of the Qing might endanger their treaty rights, had moved to a position of grudging support of the regime. In Japan, the changes had been even more momentous: following the Tokugawa Shogunate's reluctant opening of treaty ports to the United States and other maritime powers, it was overthrown and the island nation reunified under the modernizing emperor Meiji. Now Japan was engaging in a rapid program of industrialization, the goal of which was to secure the country from further foreign concessions and to roll back existing ones. For many in the Japanese government, this meant expanding Japan's periphery to create a buffer zone. Here, Korea was once again seen by strategists as key to Japan's security and ambition.

From the beginning of the treaty port era in the 1840s, both Japan and Korea had been seen as desirable places to open for Western commerce. With Japan's momentous changes, the pressure on Korea to open mounted. As we will see in more detail in Chapter 8, Japanese planners in the early 1870s proposed creating an incident to use as a pretext for opening Korea, but they launched a punitive expedition on Taiwan instead. In 1866, an armed U.S. merchant steamer, the *General Sherman*, attempted to open up trade with Chinese help in Pyongyang. After negotiations failed and a nervous Korean court ordered the ship to leave, it ran aground, was attacked and burned by Korean fireboats, and the survivors beaten to death by an angry mob. The French sent a small force to investigate and the Americans returned to do so in 1871. In the course of their attempts to investigate the affair, they attacked and took Korean fortifications at Kanghwa (Ganghwa) that had attempted to drive them off. This soured U.S. negotiations with the Yi until a treaty was finally signed in 1882.

Meanwhile, it was Japan that would end Korea's status as the Hermit Kingdom. Knowing that the new Empress Myeongseong (informally known as Queen Min, 1851–1895) favored isolationism, the Japanese sent a fleet to suppress the fire from Korean forts and forced the government into negotiations. In the resulting Treaty of Kanghwa (1876) and a commercial treaty soon thereafter, the three ports of Pusan, Incheon, and Wonson were opened. The Japanese treaties were swiftly followed by similar agreements with other maritime powers.

The end of Korea's seclusion was alarming to the court, particularly the Daewongun (the Regent), although like many in China and Japan (and as we will see, in Vietnam as well), some Korean officials believed that they, too, could now engage in a program of self-strengthening aided by interaction with foreign ideas and technologies. The opening deepened cleavages in the court, however, and Japan's new assertiveness alarmed the Qing in their role as suzerain over

Korea. Meanwhile, Chinese diplomats in Tokyo had met with their new Korean counterparts and encouraged them to seek China's help in their modernization efforts. Seeing the benefits of such a course, the empress pushed for reforms to strengthen the country, balance the influence of China and Japan, and reluctantly engage with the foreign powers as a hedge against both East Asian empires.

In 1874, the new monarch, Gojong (1852–1919), assumed his duties and the Daewongun moved into retirement. Queen Min's new policies, however, had stimulated considerable resistance. In 1882, a mutiny took place among conservative members of the military who objected to what they considered to be Min's tilt toward both China and Japan. They called the Daewongun from retirement to head their movement. Once again in power, his rebels chased the king and queen from the capital, hunted down and executed members of the royal family and Japanese and Chinese advisors in the capital. Alarmed at this turn of events, Korean diplomats requested Chinese aid and Japan sent forces to guard their legation. The Chinese arrested the Daewongun, the king and queen returned to the capital, and both China and Japan received new treaty privileges and compensation.

Queen Min's Funeral. Queen Min, posthumously given the title of "Empress Myeongseong," was ultimately caught up in the Byzantine and deadly politics surrounding the Korean court in attempting to survive amid the intrigues of Japan, China, and Russia. Having seen Japan as the country's chief threat, she had tilted toward China and Russia, earning the enmity of Japan and its Korean supporters. In the wake of the Sino-Japanese War, on October 8, 1895, Japanese assassins hacked the queen and two of her attendants to death, doused their bodies with kerosene and burned them, and scattered their ashes in nearby woods. Two years later, her husband, King Gojong, declared himself emperor and staged a magnificent funeral for Min. In the procession pictured here, huge wooden horses were conveyed along the funeral route for the (now) empress to ride in the afterlife.

As they had in China and Japan, Korean attempts at reform, modernization, and foreign relations created bitter rivalries not just at court but among officials and the Yangban. In China, such rivalries would hamstring efforts at "self-strengthening" for the remainder of the century. In Japan, the opposition was more fragmented and largely dissipated after a revolt by dissident former samurai was crushed in 1878. In Korea, a strong conservative Yangban core saw themselves as guardians of Confucian values (especially against those of Christianity), isolation, and resistance to China and Japan. For those Yangban who favored the reforms, there were two main groups: "Progressives," who favored radical, rapid modernization along Japanese lines—going even further in advocating equal rights and opportunities for women—and wanted to sever ties to China; and *Sadae*, who advocated a more gradual modernization with Chinese help. The queen favored many of the Progressive ideas but believed that Chinese help and support were necessary. An American attempt at negotiations between the two groups failed and prompted a palace coup by the Progressives in December 1884. Issuing edicts in the name of the court and arresting and executing many of their opponents, the insurgents prompted the Chinese under Yuan Shikai (see Chapters 5 and 9) to move in and restore the monarchs. For their part, the Japanese had forced the king to sign a secret indemnity agreement.

The ongoing tension in Korea, and apprehension among Chinese and Japanese leaders that another crisis might lead to war, prompted China's Li Hongzhang and Japan's Ito Hirobumi to sign a protocol (the Tianjin Treaty) in 1885 calling for withdrawal of both their forces, recall of military instructors (to be replaced by Americans), and notification of any further military moves in Korea. The queen, however, convinced the Chinese to leave a small force behind in disguise to watch the Japanese.

While Korea made significant progress in modernizing its urban areas, economy, and military during the next decade, the political situation remained volatile. The Tonghak movement was revived and spreading again by the early 1890s. China was soon poised to send troops to aid in its suppression. Meanwhile, the Japanese were galvanized by the assassination of the pro-Japanese Korean reformer Kim Okgyun in the spring of 1894 while en route to meet with Li Hongzhang. Kim's body was given to the Chinese, who dismembered it and displayed it as a warning to other "treasonous" pro-Japanese activists. When the Chinese troop ship *Gaoxing* on its way to Korea was attacked and sunk by Japanese vessels, the Second East Asia (or Sino-Japanese) War commenced.

Because the course of the war is covered in Chapters 5 and 8, its outlines will not be rehearsed here. Its aftermath, however, went far to steer the country into a long-standing antagonism toward Japan. Japan's victory and its new hegemony set the stage for rural resistance movements, sixty of which would take place in the next fifty years. More immediately, Japanese agents arranged for the assassination of Queen Min, followed soon after by the king fleeing to the Russian legation, from which he ruled a government in exile, now renamed the Empire of Korea. As an empire, Korea claimed equal status with China and Japan, ending centuries of its tributary status with China. The Treaty of Shimonoseki in 1895 stipulated that Korea was a free and independent nation, and to ratify the idea of Korea's status, Gejong moved back to the palace in 1897. After the Russo-Japanese War in 1905, however, he was forced to sign a protectorate agreement with Japan. Following Korean protests of their new status at the Hague Convention in 1907, Gejong was forced to abdicate in favor of his son, Sunjong. Japan formally annexed Korea in 1910 in the wake of the assassination of Japanese statesman Ito Hirobumi the year before. Gejong lived out the final years of his life in the palace. The year of his death, 1919, would prove pivotal for all the nations of East Asia.

ECONOMY, SOCIETY, AND FAMILY

As we have seen, the primary enterprise of the Korean Peninsula—as it was in most of East Asia—from remote antiquity was agriculture. Even with urbanization accelerating up to the time of the Mongol and Japanese invasions, around 90 percent of the population at any given time was engaged in farming and small-scale village industry. As in all agrarian–urban East Asian societies, therefore, control and distribution of the land were prime concerns of government at every level.

Land Reform

As we saw in Chapter 3, the Korean kingdoms, as was the case in China, were preoccupied with land reform, tenancy, water conservancy, and maintaining local infrastructures. Among the various schemes attempted were models based on the well-field system, and the *chongjon* system in Silla during the eighth century. Here, as with many such schemes devised in East Asia, the government redistributed land, received taxes in kind, and encouraged small-scale individual and village cash cropping.

Under the Yi Dynasty of Choson, the implanting of Neo-Confucian values in the countryside as well as among elites became a prime consideration. Like the Ming and Qing in China, model edicts were handed down about proper deportment of family members, inheritance practices, and relations between men and women, as well as land policy. Here, a new system of land tenure was made part of a more general stabilizing of all classes. Peasant rents were fixed at half the crop and a hierarchy of magistrates, subbureaucrats, and village headmen similar to the Chinese system was set up to collect taxes, settle disputes, and dispense justice.

As noted previously, the institution of Chinese systems in Korea tended to attract the elites more than the peasant and artisan classes. Their spotty success in taking root tended in many ways to aggravate societal tensions, despite the governmental efficiencies they created. One factor in this was a repeated attempt on the part of the bureaucracy to enhance its power at the expense of the merchant and artisan classes. In the countryside, power remained in the hands of the landholder aristocracy, which tended to ensure that the peasants would be bound to them in a fashion not unlike the serfdom of their European contemporaries.

On the other hand, particularly in the cities, the high level of Song Chinese–influenced material culture was increasingly evident. Interregional trade was brisk, and luxury items like silk, porcelain, and lacquerware were widely available. Korea's position at the center of the East Asian Buddhist world tended to make it a trade and pilgrimage crossroads, and its artisans became highly proficient in the new technologies of porcelain making and book printing. Many of the oldest Chinese, Korean, and Japanese works extant were printed by Korean publishers.

Social Organization

Under the Yi, the Confucian exams became more open, although the new arrangement called for two official classes: the *yangban*, or scholar-gentry drawn from high civil and military officials; and the *chungin*, or minor officials. Below these were the *sangmin*, commoners of different professions as well as peasants and serfs, whereas the lowest group, the *chonmin*, consisted of bond slaves, laborers, and prostitutes.

Although approximating the class structure in China, the new system was more like the composite one created centuries before in Heian Japan. As in Japan, it proved a troublesome fit, particularly in remote rural areas. Though the Confucian exams theoretically allowed for some degree of social mobility as in China, they tended to be monopolized by the Yangban. The institution of hereditary classes, intended to create a stable and harmonious social structure, instead concentrated wealth in the hands of the rural gentry, who often lacked a proper Confucian sense of the official responsibilities inherent in their positions. In many places, the older patterns of aristocratic local power simply continued with only cosmetic changes. Thus, through the sixteenth and seventeenth centuries, the divide between the wealthy, educated, sophisticated capital and large provincial cities and the tradition-bound countryside steadily increased.

The New Economy

Nonetheless, like their counterparts across the straits, Korea's economy made enormous strides in size and sophistication in the eighteenth and nineteenth centuries. During the mid-eighteenth century, a series of reforms under King Yongjo (r. 1724–1776) were introduced to stimulate the internal economy and bring some relief to the peasantry. Yongjo reduced the military tax while increasing dues on certain profitable commodities, and revamped state accounting practices as a means of fighting corruption. At the same time, he increased coinage while allowing payments in kind for peasants in poorer areas; subsidized the printing and distribution of "how to" books in *han'gul* on medicine, agriculture, and sericulture; and actively championed the idea of more equality of opportunity among commoners.

Although the social effects of some of these measures will be explored in more detail below, it is worth mentioning that they established some long-term trends that run parallel to those under way in places far removed from Korea. As in England during this time, the increase in wealth and land of those

(A)

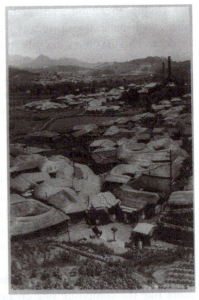

(B)

(C)

(D)

Korean Village Life. Traditional village life in Korea, as depicted in these late-nineteenth- and early-twentieth-century photographs, bears many similarities to rural northern Chinese life, although with local variations. In (A), porters pose with their packs, the frames of which are built to hold extremely heavy and unwieldy loads. In (B), we see thatch roof village houses called *hanok*, with the living spaces built around closed or semi-closed courtyards according to the geomantic principle of "mountain in back, river in front." (C) Throughout East Asia, closed sedan chairs continued to be used into the twentieth century for ceremonial purposes, generally by the wealthy and elite. Pictured here is a children's sedan chair. (D) Rural markets served clusters of villages on different days; pictured here is a shoe market.

who could take advantage of the new farming techniques and new cash crops tended to drive marginal peasants off the land and into other occupations. Urbanization thus kept pace with population expansion, and the expanding labor force was increasingly employed in craft factories and in privately owned mines. The government's constant need for money resulted in institutionalizing the selling of Yangban titles to the newly wealthy. Indeed, the unpopularity of the Yangban did not lessen the attraction of their station for those who sought the titles and privileges of the scholarly class. By 1800, as much as 70 percent of the population had bought their way into Yangban status in some regions. Significantly, the distinctive stovepipe-shaped, horsehair hat once restricted to the Yangban literati was now available to anyone to purchase from a host of retailers. The drive in social mobility perhaps achieved its high point with the emancipation in 1801 of the remnant of the *nobu*, or government-owned bondsmen class.

As noted above, Korean economics shared to some extent in the more general movements in Eurasia toward agricultural efficiency, more diverse food crops, and the development of lucrative cash crops. Unlike China, however, where the scholar-gentry often took the lead in the drive for such innovations, the Yangban showed little interest in exercising such leadership. Indeed, as we have seen, by the nineteenth century, they had become a hereditary class, often living in genteel poverty. Like the **rentiers** of France during the *ancien régime*, they had, as a class, become increasingly home to those who could afford to buy a title and enjoy the safety of steady tenant income.

The economic vibrancy of rural Korea came instead largely from those peasants who were able to take advantage of government incentives to open marginal lands, experimenting with increasingly refined rice strains and techniques of double-cropping (as with rice and barley in the north), and trying the new crops available through expanding world trade networks. Those literate and semiliterate in *han'gul* were also able to take advantage of the increasingly diverse manuals on agronomy and farm management printed by the government.

The eighteenth and nineteenth centuries also saw the maturation of commercial farming, much as it did in China at the same time. In addition to such new food crops as maize, potatoes, and peanuts that could be easily grown on newly reclaimed land, large rural industries were developed around the planting of hemp (for cordage), tobacco, various medicinal herbs, and, especially ginseng root. Even today, ginseng is widely used in a variety of teas, cooking recipes, and medicinal preparations both for specific ailments and as a general tonic, and it was widely believed to enhance male virility. Its importance in Chinese-influenced medicine is unsurpassed; thus, there was a virtually inexhaustible market for it throughout East Asia. Korean ginseng was considered of the highest quality, and it remained Choson's biggest export item throughout the nineteenth century.

The new commodities of the countryside found their way to the cities and to the tightly controlled export markets by means of different guilds of merchants. As in other areas influenced by neo-Confucianism, considerable distrust of merchants existed among the Yangban and government bureaucrats. Yet, perhaps more than in China, there was a tacit recognition of the vital importance of the merchant class to the economic well-being of the country. Thus, with the mid-seventeenth-century reforms of King Hyojong, the government granted charters to various merchant guilds, giving them monopolies for the wholesale distribution of different commodities. They then sold these to market retailers and individual exporters, who in turn formed their own monopoly guilds.

Yet as was also the case in other areas undergoing the commercialization of agriculture, those who could no longer make a living on the land tended to sink into tenancy, move deeper into more remote country, or migrate to the cities. While laborers were always in demand for large-scale projects such as roads, terraces, dikes, and so forth, the migrants ncreasingly found employment in newly privatized mines and, especially, in the growing craft shops, which in some cases—notably porcelain and silk—had grown into full-fledged factories. Indeed, Korean skills in porcelain making had already reached the point by the seventeenth century that a group of potters captured by the Japanese in the 1590s and their descendants were made to labor for generations in Japan, creating the famous *Imari* ware.

The growth in economic mobility helped generate a dramatic increase in social mobility as well. Like their Japanese counterparts, Yi leaders had generally viewed social stability as growing from a frozen set of government-mandated, hereditary classes. Yet they also tended during times of economic crisis to allow the selling of official titles to fund governmental needs. As noted above, during the eighteenth century, this expedient policy was made into a permanent system, allowing anyone with sufficient cash to buy his way into the *yangban* class. This new social mobility for the rich was not lost on a host of social commentators both within and outside the various neo-Confucian schools, and a cry increasingly sounded for greater social equality. As we have seen, two of the most important results of this were the final emancipation of the remaining government bond-slaves in 1801—now allowed the official status of commoners—and the nineteenth-century peasant revolts, which routinely called for general equality of station. The climax of this trend came with the Tonghak movement in which all members were regarded as equals.

Family and Gender Roles

Until the arrival of Confucian institutions in the Korean countryside, local village life, as it also did in Vietnam and Japan, tended toward more egalitarian institutions, especially between men and women, than would later be the case. In Korea, this egalitarianism retained a remarkable vitality even in the face of neo-Confucian precepts in the sixteenth and seventeenth centuries. Even today, there is far less of the traditional emphasis on filial piety and patriarchal customs than in China.

Until the sixteenth and seventeenth centuries, bilateral and **matrilocal** marriage patterns tended to be the norm. As in Japan and Vietnam, the communal nature of rice agriculture, and its emphasis on meticulous, intensive cultivation, helped to lessen the division between "male" and "female" work roles and tended to make women and girls more equal partners in local rural society. Women's property and inheritance rights, far more expansive than in Confucian China, also tended to reflect this. Under the neo-Confucian reforms of the Yi, however, some of this began to change. The idea of strictly delineated gender roles, of males dominating in the "outer" world and women being preeminent in the "inner world" of the home—long a staple among the urban elites and official classes, now became a cornerstone of moral training in rural academies and in the home.

Trends that had begun in the sixteenth and early seventeenth centuries continued in some cases through the nineteenth. Ironically, during the time when social reformers called for more class equality, the neo-Confucian emphasis on filial piety and family hierarchy became increasingly rooted in village life. Here again, however, despite the Confucian insistence on the "three bonds" (minister to state, children to parents, wife to husband), women continued to be allowed to control property—even in widowhood—and divorce could be initiated by either party. On the other

Bride Being Carried to Home of Bridegroom. Traditional Korean wedding ceremonies customarily took place at the house of the bride and were preceded by a four-piece band (large and small gong; large and small drum). Among other parts of the ceremony were the presentation of a pair of "wild geese" (actually Mandarin ducks, which are believed to mate for life), exchange of bows, and offerings of rice wine and side dishes. The party then, as depicted here, moved in procession to the family compound of the groom, where the couple would reside according to Confucian norms.

hand, the long-standing government advocacy of neo-Confucian norms had abetted such social practices as concubinage, child marriage, and the selling of girls to other families for work as servants. These practices would not be outlawed until the final decades of the nineteenth century and would persist long into the twentieth.

CULTURE AND INTELLECTUAL LIFE

As we saw in Chapter 3, the Three Kingdoms had all adopted Buddhism in some form as well as the Chinese writing system, Han-Confucian political and moral theory, and much of China's classical literary corpus. Chinese approaches to history writing and record-keeping, as well as approaches to historiography along Chinese lines, were also adopted, like Kim Pu-sik's 1145 *History of the Three Kingdoms*. These would continue in much the same vein during the Yi Dynasty with the *History of Koryo* in 1451, and the *Complete Mirror of the Eastern Country* in 1484, printed in literary Chinese.

PATTERNS UP-CLOSE

The Development of *Han'Gul*

Perhaps the most momentous cultural achievement of the early Yi was the convening of a body of scholars by the emperor Sejong (1418–1450) to reform the written language. As in Japan and Vietnam, the introduction of written Chinese and the entire panoply of Chinese and Buddhist thought and literature had revolutionized Korean society. As noted earlier, it had brought the wellsprings of Confucian political organization and philosophy and imprinted them indelibly on successive Korean polities. Moreover, the vast literature of the various Buddhist schools and the development of both block printing and early versions of movable type stimulated literacy and created increasing demand for a wide assortment of reading materials. Indeed, Korea was by the fifteenth century in many respects the printing capital of Asia.

As in Japan and Vietnam as well, the demands of learning literary Chinese—especially as adapted to distinctly different spoken languages—made it time-consuming and difficult for ordinary people to achieve even functional literacy. Thus in Vietnam, the *chu nom* system of indigenizing Chinese characters was developed, while in Japan the *kana* syllabary proved highly effective in aiding literacy. Sejong, sensitive to these problems, thus convened his scholars to conceive a writing system that would be easy to learn and have wide utility and appeal.

The system of phonetic writing the board developed was called *han'gul* and was introduced in 1443. King Sejong proclaimed the new system in his 1446 *Hunmin chong-um* (Proper Sounds to Instruct the People). Called the most accurate writing system yet devised, it consisted of a phonetic syllabary of twenty-eight sounds (four have since been dropped), with vowels and consonants each represented by a simple component of a Chinese character. The words that result from these combinations look much like angular complex Chinese characters but have a far more straightforward structure and are much easier to learn and use. Like the *kana* system in Japan, *han'gul* tended to help the spread of literacy in a far more efficient manner than had been the case with literary Chinese.

The effect the system had on knowledge dissemination, literature, and the economics of printing and book culture in Korea cannot be overestimated. Indeed, the country saw a flowering of social commentary, novels, satires, and other forms of popular literature in the following centuries. Unlike in China, however, which saw a similar literary expansion, the wider reach of *han'gul* (as opposed to classical Chinese) enabled its effects to be more pervasive, especially among the increasingly sophisticated

Vowels Consonants	ㅏ [a]	ㅑ [ya]	ㅓ [ŏ]	ㅕ [yŏ]	ㅗ [o]	ㅛ [yo]	ㅜ [u]	ㅠ [yu]	ㅡ [ŭ]	ㅣ [i]
ㄱ [k,g]	가	갸	거	겨	고	교	구	규	그	기
ㄴ [n]	나	냐	너	녀	노	뇨	누	뉴	느	니
ㄷ [t,d]	다	댜	더	뎌	도	됴	두	듀	드	디
ㄹ [r,l]	라	랴	러	려	로	료	루	류	르	리
ㅁ [m]	마	먀	머	며	모	묘	무	뮤	므	미
ㅂ [p,b]	바	뱌	버	벼	보	뵤	부	뷰	브	비
ㅅ¹ [s,sh]	사	샤	서	셔	소	쇼	수	슈	스	시
ㅇ²	아	야	어	여	오	요	우	유	으	이
ㅈ [ch,j]	자	쟈	저	져	조	죠	주	쥬	즈	지
ㅊ [ch']	차	챠	처	쳐	초	쵸	추	츄	츠	치
ㅋ [k']	카	캬	커	켜	코	쿄	쿠	큐	크	키
ㅌ [t']	타	탸	터	텨	토	툐	투	튜	트	티
ㅍ [p']	파	퍄	퍼	펴	포	표	푸	퓨	프	피
ㅎ [h]	하	햐	허	혀	호	효	후	휴	흐	히

The Conventions and Alphabet of Han'gul. As originally given by King Sejong in his 1446 *Hunmin chong-um*, (Proper Sounds to Instruct the People) *han'gul* contained 28 syllables. These were reduced to 24 with five double consonants and the additional vowels shown. The ease of the system has helped Korea achieve one of the highest rates of literacy in the world.

urban middle classes. As early as the late sixteenth century, Ho Kyun (1569–1618) used characters in his popular novels to revolt against the misrule of the Yangban. During the following century, writers like Yun Hyu (1617–1680) and Pak Se-dong (1629–1703) attacked the modern Yangban Neo-Confucianists for neglecting the key concept of "the people's livelihood" that had been so central to the thought of Mencius. Hence, Yun Hyu's *Essays on Social Reform* demanded a more equitable system of land tenure, a fairer system for selecting those in government service, and a complete reform of governmental institutions.

Yet, like *kana* in Japan, and to a certain extent, *chu nom* in Vietnam, *han'gul* also created a two-tiered system of literacy: Chinese tended to remain the written medium of choice among the highly educated and largely male elites, while *han'gul* became the language of the commoners and, increasingly, women. One of the best examples of this is the anonymous, autobiographical *Memoirs of Lady Hyegong* written in the eighteenth century. Such divisions notwithstanding, however, the explosion of vernacular literature—satires, social criticism, fiction, advice manuals for a variety of tasks—all contributed to Korea attaining, with Japan, some of the highest levels of functional literacy in the agrarian–urban, preindustrial world.

Neo-Confucianism and Pragmatic Studies

The challenges of creating stable centralized regimes in the seventeenth century generated parallel approaches throughout East Asia and, in certain broad areas, were reminiscent of those employed at the same time by absolutist regimes in Europe. Central to all was the problem of creating a unified ideology into which individual, family, village, and national behavior could be fit and regulated. In China, Korea, Japan, and Vietnam, the hierarchical, all-encompassing system of neo-Confucianism as developed by the twelfth-century thinker Zhu Xi became the governing orthodoxy (see Chapters 2 and 5). As in Europe, the long period of civil war, invasion, dynastic change, and philosophical disputes among Confucian factions and Buddhist schools pushed governments to impose stability in thought as well as action. The unity of ethics, theories of knowledge, and the *part/whole* construct of the universe—with its parallel relationships down to the level of the individual—made neo-Confucianism an appealing system for stabilization and centralization.

As we have also seen, the ideals of this all-encompassing system often clashed with cherished long-time practices. In Korea, the strict observance of filial piety within a family hierarchy headed by a father or grandfather ran up against traditional notions of women's equality within the home and village. The leading role of the "gentleman" chosen by merit in Confucianism collided from the beginning with the hereditary position of the Yangban aristocracy. Thus, social criticism continually simmered beneath the surface of the cultural canon.

As the calls for institutional reform and practical solutions to rural problems became more pervasive, they gave rise to the *Sirhak* or "Pragmatic Studies" (sometimes rendered as "Practical Learning") movement. Here, such writers as Yi Ik (1681–1763) issued the radical call for the abolition of class distinctions and emancipation of the bondsmen; and Pak Chega (1750–?), Yi Tokmu (1741–1793), and Hang Taeyong (1731–1783) advocated incorporating Western Studies—astronomy, mechanics, mathematics— into the traditional curriculum, and sought the opening of the country to European trade. Christianity, too, as a system of ethics had gained a toehold among some intellectuals, although most tended to dismiss its narratives as irrational—as they did with many Buddhist tales. Thus, despite repeated government bans, some reformers found Christianity's insistence on the equality of believers before God to be a call to action, inspiring them to make similar demands in Korea.

At the same time, there was a rebirth of interest in things distinctively Korean—as opposed to those considered to be overly influenced by China. A number of dynastic histories and novels based on current events, like *The War With Japan* and *General Im Kyongop*, were printed. Paintings depicting scenes of rural and urban life, with the artists purposely distancing themselves from Chinese genres, also emerged during this period. An expanded form of traditional *sijo* poetry was now utilized—often anonymously—to deal realistically with themes of love, class, and family obligations, and the harsher sides of rural and urban life. Efforts were also made to popularize the use of Korean

Korean Scholars. As it had in China and Japan, the adoption of Neo-Confucianism as a means of statecraft and ensuring social stability had also taken place in Korea. As in Japan, however, some of its social conventions were resisted or only partly implemented. For example, the scholarly ideal of the Confucian official was partially offset by the hereditary class structure of the *yangban*. Here, Korean Confucian scholars pose in the early twentieth century in their horsehair hats and *turumagi* overcoats, with tasseled binding appliquéd to their overcoats as a sign of their status.

innovations such as water clocks, pluviometers (rain gauges), and movable metal type for printing. The technology of the latter had been exported to China, where the publication of enormous Qing encyclopedias was undertaken with Korean copper and bronze type.

CONCLUSION

Like that of Vietnam, the history of Korea has been marked by the constant presence, influence, and periodic threat of invasion by China. Just as one of the patterns of Chinese history has been to assimilate and acculturate newcomers and those on what is sometimes called "the Sinitic frontier," so, too, has the pattern of those on that frontier been to grasp as much agency as possible in determining what to adopt and what to reject. The position of Korea, even today as a divided nation, has been one of a struggle to navigate an independent path between the growing influence of China and the often tragic history of its relations with Japan. Thus, the opening vignette and the period of time depicted at the end of this chapter are both emblematic of Korea's difficult position between two powerful states.

Yet as we have also seen, Korea has struggled fiercely for political and cultural independence, and in many ways it has succeeded. Although reduced to a client state for a time by the Mongols, Koryo was never formally absorbed into the Yuan and Mongol domains. Moreover, it took the Mongols decades to subdue Korean resistance, which nonetheless continued throughout the Mongol era.

Much the same could be said of Korean resistance during the Japanese invasion of the 1590s, with the somewhat happier result of the invaders eventually giving up the fight—although a heavy Chinese presence continued to hang over the new dynasty. The coming of the Qing again reduced Korea to client status, but the Yi still managed to hold on to formal political independence. Even as Japan "opened" the "Hermit Kingdom" and steadily increased its influence there, and the Chinese maneuvered to check them, Korea managed to retain its formal independence until 1910. It might be added that resistance to Japanese rule never stopped during Korea's interval of colonization from 1910 to 1945.

Culturally, there was considerable agency as well. Perhaps the most dramatic example of cultural independence was that of the *han'gul* syllabary. Unlike Japanese *kana*, which developed incrementally and slowly filtered down from the court to the feudal lords, samurai, and eventually the common people, the new Korean system was purposefully designed at the behest of the monarch. It was from the beginning "proper sounds to instruct the people"—a tool of mass literacy. Its simplicity and ease of learning, as well as its greater efficiency for printing, raised Korean levels of literacy to among the highest in the pre-industrial world. It also opened up entirely new possibilities for vernacular prose and poetry and lessened dependence on Chinese models.

Viewed from the period at the end of this chapter, however, the drive to create a distinct culture and maintain political independence loomed as increasingly distant goals. The immense presence of China had been supplanted, but it was by the waxing power of Japan. Indeed, in East Asia, *only* Japan was growing in influence: China, humbled by the island empire, was now besieged by foreign powers seeking spheres of influence; and, as we will see in the next chapter, Vietnam had already been absorbed by one of those foreign powers into a new colony called French Indochina. Korea, now a client state of Japan, would shortly be reduced to the same status.

FURTHER RESOURCES

Ch'oe Yong-ho. *The Civil Examinations and the Social Structure in Early Yi Dynasty Korea: 1392–1600.* Seoul: Korean Research Center, 1987. Pioneering but hotly debated work in its arguments about the relative openness of the Yi Dyansty's Confucian bureaucracy. Most useful for students with some grounding in the period.

Eckert, Carter J., et al. *Korea Old and New: A History.* Cambridge, MA: Harvard University Press, 1990. Long-standing foundational work on Korean history with special emphasis on the modern period from the mid-nineteenth century.

Haboush, Ja-Hyun Kim, trans. *Epistolary Korea: Letters in the Communicative Space of the Choson, 1392–1910.* New York: Columbia University Press, 2009. A wide variety of correspondence, official and private, across the Yi period. Useful for students interested in intimate glimpses of great events and everyday Choson life.

Haboush, Ja-Hyun Kim, trans. *The Memoirs of Lady Hyegyong: The Autobiographical Writings of a Crown Princess in Eighteenth Century Korea.* Berkeley: University of California Press, 1996. Revealing personal writings of court life in the latter Yi period. A useful companion to the other translated work listed above by the same author/translator.

Kim, Kichung. *Classical Korean Literature*. Armonk, NY: M.E. Sharpe, 1996. Useful volume of essays on trends in Korean writing up through the nineteenth century. Beginning students will benefit, as well as those students already with a foundation in the history of the period.

Kim, Youngmin, and Michael Pettid, eds. *Woman and Confucianism in Choson Korea*. Albany, NY: SUNY Press, 2011. Essays covering the political, social, and intellectual aspects of the expectations and agency of Korean women under Confucianism. Good up-to-date treatment of what is still an understudied area.

Lee, Peter H., and William Theodore De Bary, eds. *Sources of Korean Tradition*. Vol. 2, *From the Sixteenth to the Twentieth Centuries*. New York: Columbia University Press, 2000. As with other *Sources* in this long-running series from Columbia, these are all high-quality translations with particularly insightful commentary.

Setton, Mark. *Chong Yayong: Korea's Challenge to Orthodox Neo-Confucianism*. Albany, NY: SUNY Press, 1997. Like Columbia, SUNY has published excellent monographs and essay collections in several different East Asian fields. For students with some background in neo-Confucian concepts, this work will prove valuable and revealing.

Turnbull, Stephen. *Samurai Invasion, Japan's Korean War, 1592–98*. London: Cassell & Co., 2002. Although the history of the period is more often covered from the Japanese side, particularly in biographies of Hideyoshi, this provides a more even-handed approach appropriate for those just entering the field.

Yi Sun-shin. *Nanjung Ilgi: The War Diary of Admiral Yi Sun-shin*. Translated by Ha Tae-hung. Edited by Sohn Pow-key. Seoul: Yonsei University Press, 1977. Valuable diary of Korea's most famous admiral, whom we met in the vignette to this chapter, on his experiences fighting the Japanese invasion forces in the 1590s with his famous "turtle ships."

WEBSITES

http://www.history.go.kr/en/main/main.do. National Institute of Korean History. An all-purpose source for texts, primary material, and databases. The site is written in *han'gul* but also offers links to English translations of its contents.

http://www.koreaorbit.com/history-of-korea/history-of-korea-dynasties.html. KoreaOrbit .com. Succinct historical notes on Korean prehistory and dynasties, with a handy time-line for the latter.

http://www.hawaii.edu/korea/biblio/BiblioOpen.html. *Korean History: A Bibliography*. Compiled by Kenneth R. Robinson. Extensive bibliography of history, literature, social sciences, demography, and a host of other subjects. Posted through the aegis of the University of Hawai'i at Manoa.

CHAPTER 7

From "Lesser Dragon" to "Indochina":
Vietnam to 1885

For centuries, tensions among the expansive states in the north and central parts of modern Vietnam and those of the Indian-influenced Chams and Khmers—and between the Chams and Khmers themselves—had kept the region around the delta and southern reaches of Mekong River in turmoil. The Chams had fought the previous Vietnamese dynasties of Dai Viet and the Tran since the inception of both, and the Vietnamese had generally been victorious in these encounters, repeatedly extracting land from the Cham holdings, which were now restricted to a loosely connected set of enclaves in the extreme south.

In keeping with Chinese-influenced theories of expansion during the early stages of dynastic cycles, the Le Dynasty, established in 1428, now set its sights once again on southern expansion. Indeed, there were new scores to settle: the Chams had scored a victory over the previous dynasty in a bitter war from 1400 to 1407 and had fought stubbornly again forty years later. The Vietnamese emperor, Le Thanh Tong, made little secret of his plans and began assembling a huge expeditionary force of over 300,000, nearly half of which were naval forces. Moreover, like other East Asian states impressed by the power of Ming China's armed forces, with their sophisticated firearms and other gunpowder weapons, the emperor made sure his armies carried state-of-the-art arms. The emperor was also gambling on a quick and overwhelming victory, since organizing and equipping his forces were rapidly draining the finances of the realm. Yet the adventure also bore the promise that in eliminating the Cham holdings, the rich lands of the south would be opened up for colonization by Dai Viet farmers and thus pay the endeavor back many times over in revenues and enhanced security.

In the complex evolving state of Ming China's diplomatic relations with its "tributary" states, the entities of the south—Dai Viet, the Chams, and the Khmers—all had equal claim on appealing to China for help against those who would upset the status quo. Vietnam, although the most influenced by China of the three, was also perhaps the most fierce in contesting Chinese control. As time ran short, the Chams appealed to the Ming for help. They also approached the Khmers but, since they had attacked the Khmer capital of Angkor Wat shortly beforehand, they were rebuffed. The Chinese, still preoccupied with the Mongols, threatened Vietnam but took no action.

Thus in December 1470, enjoying a three to one advantage in manpower, the Le defeated the Chams decisively. They burned the Cham capital of Vijaya (Sanskrit for "victory"), slaughtered perhaps 60,000, and enslaved many more. Indeed, there was fear that this was not the end of Le ambitions: an exchange between the Ming and representatives from Malacca enjoined the Malaccans to fight if a Vietnamese attack materialized. It never did. The results, however, of this war with the Chams accomplished many of the Le's goals. Champa was effectively ended as a coherent entity. Many Chams fled west, while others trusted their luck to their new overlords. Total obliteration of the Cham enclaves came incrementally: most of the few remaining outposts were destroyed by the Vietnamese in 1720, with the final one succumbing in 1832.

The story of Vietnam has often been rendered as that of a peripheral state or set of states forcibly Sinicized for a millennium and existing chiefly as a client first of China, then of France, Japan, France again, and, in the South, of the United States. Yet the story of this section begins with an imperial Vietnam, fiercely independent politically, although sharing close cultural ties and Confucian and Buddhist religious and philosophical connections with China. Indeed, imperial Vietnam spread its own traditions of Confucian government—at times forcibly—throughout the territories it controlled. At its height in the seventeenth century, it was recognized as a full diplomatic and trade partner with the emerging maritime powers of Europe. During a period of civil war at the end of the eighteenth century, the ultimate victors, the Nguyen, received recognition and aid from France. It was only later, when the French sought to compete for influence with the English and appointed themselves protectors of East Asia's Catholics that they came into conflict with the dynasty they had once helped come to power. And from that point, the shadow of colonialism grew ever longer for the next century.

THE LESSER DRAGON

From the mythical forming of "Lac Viet" out of the original fifteen tribes, through the third century BCE kingdom of Van Lang, down to the civil wars of the Le Dynasty (1428–1789), the Vietnamese have seen themselves as politically independent and highly selective in their cultural borrowing from the Chinese. In some ways, the experience of occupation by China for a thousand years only solidified this identity, despite the incorporation of Confucianism, Mahayana Buddhism, Chinese writing and literature, and the imperial institution itself. Indeed, Vietnamese distinctiveness was intensified not just by the cross-fertilization of Chinese influences, but by those of the *Indic*, or Indian-influenced, states to the south and west. Once freed of Chinese political occupation, the new Vietnamese polity of Dai Viet (1010–1225) established its own Confucian-based institutions as means of state formation and centralization. Through the Tran Dynasty (1225–1400) and into the Le, it expanded south and westward as it moved toward the Mekong Delta.

Like Korea and Japan, the use of neo-Confucianism as an organizing principle of the state required local compromises with long-standing traditions. More importantly, however, the restrictive policies of China, and the reclusive policies of Korea and Japan, would prove impossible to maintain in Vietnam. The result of this was that its territories would be among the first to have treaties of friendship and assistance with European states as well as the unequal treaties characteristic of nineteenth-century imperialism. It also became the only East Asian state to be subjected to nearly a century of European colonial occupation.

Southward Expansion

Unlike the Yi Dynasty in Korea, whose borders had long been fixed by the sixteenth century, or Tokugawa Japan, where the only movement possible was into Ezo (Hokkaido), the land of the Emeshi, the problems of centralization in Vietnam went hand in hand with those of rapid expansion. The pivotal defeat of the Indianized Hindu and Buddhist, ethnically Malay Chams in 1471 had inaugurated a long period of migration into the south and integration of the new lands into the Confucian systems of the north. Many of the Chams had migrated into what is now Cambodia (Kampuchea). Those who remained, however, were not rapidly accommodated into the new order and became instead a kind of underclass in the region (see Map 7.1).

At the same time, the imperial Vietnam of the north continued its *nam tien* ("southern expansion"). Earlier, Vietnamese pressure on Champa had diverted that state's expansion toward its Indianized rival, Funan. As early as the 600s, the Chams and the Khmers had jointly eliminated Funan. South of the two main divisions of Vietnam, *Tongking* and *Annam*, now lay the revived state of Champa, representing not just a political rival to the Vietnamese territories but within its Indian-influenced Sanskrit, Hindu, and Theravada Buddhist state, a cultural one as well. Hence, in 1471, as related in the vignette that opened this chapter, Vietnamese forces defeated the Chams, who fled to modern Cambodia (Kampuchea.) This state was ultimately absorbed by Vietnam in 1720, except for a small remnant that was finished off just over a century later by the Nguyen emperor Minh Mang.

A new dynasty, the Le, was founded in 1428, following Ming efforts to re-impose Chinese rule on the area, and lasted until 1789. The founder, **Le Loi**, who styled himself ruler of **Dai Viet**, or "Great Viet," like his contemporaries, the Yi in Korea, imposed yet another Chinese-style regime on his new state. In another interesting parallel to the situation in Korea, literary Chinese was adopted for use in a Chinese-style bureaucracy, Confucian exams were held, Confucian law codes, Chinese-style historiography, and sumptuary laws were all adopted.

Perils of Growth

For the Le Dynasty, however, the expanding frontier area became a site of rebellion. Like Japan from the Onin War to the time of Hideyoshi, the expanded Vietnam was split by regional powers: the Mac family, whose leader Mac Dang Dung seized power from the Le and was recognized as the legitimate ruler in

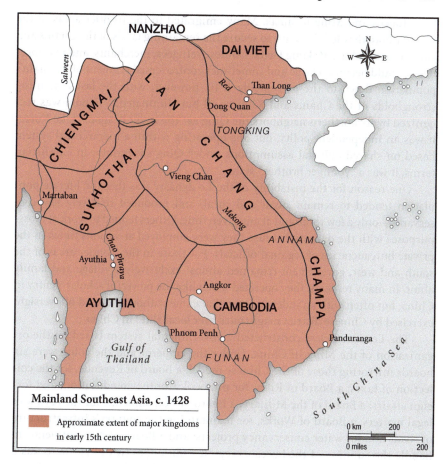

Map 7.1 Mainland Southeast Asia, ca. 1428

the northern capital of Hanoi by the Chinese in 1527; and the Trinh and Nguyen families, who controlled the center and south from their capital at Hue. A civil war over the next fifty years, during which the Trinh turned on the Nguyen at one point, with both sides supporting the reinstatement of the Le house, ultimately resulted in the Le reclaiming the throne in 1592. As in Japan, however, the Trinh acted as the real power behind the throne from 1599, much like the Tokugawa shoguns in Japan. Conflict would erupt once more with the Nguyen family in 1674. Indeed, the Le hold on the country, although lasting until the Tay Son Rebellion of the 1790s, always remained tenuous.

As we have seen a number of times, political disorder in China frequently had a ripple effect within neighboring states. The Manchu subjugation of China though fairly swift in the north, was a more drawn out and bloody affair in the outlying areas. From 1644 to 1690, Ming holdouts on Taiwan, in the south, and in the western areas of the so-called Three Feudatories (see Chapter 5) were systematically crushed, and Vietnam became a prominent destination for refugees and Ming loyalists. Many emigrated to the frontier areas of the south, where they led the drive to secure the remaining lands of the Chams and Khmers around the Mekong Delta. Chinese refugees, merchants, and entrepreneurs would become a large and sometimes controversial segment of Vietnam's population down to the present. By 1740, however, with the last remaining strongholds of the Chams and Khmers all but eliminated, Vietnam was recognized by its northern neighbors the Qing as "the lesser dragon." Like Korea, it was an independent polity, but one operating within a hierarchical system based on shared cultural assumptions under Qing suzerainty; in Confucian terms, it was a "younger brother" state.

One reason for the instability of the Le dynasty was that the literate population tended to remain small and rural, and produced relatively few civil servants—only a few thousand at any given time. Others tended to work at cross-purposes with the dynasty because they were employed at various times in the private bureaucracies of regional officials. For those in the frontier areas of the south and west, government remained almost exclusively a village and family affair. In many respects, they operated much like the powerful scholar-gentry in China, but often with an independence that came without the kind of oversight exercised by Chinese district magistrates over local elites in China.

The Le nonetheless constructed a governmental system based on the organization of the Ming in China. Under the emperor and the court were six boards mirroring those of the Chinese model: a Board of Revenue, for the collection of taxes; a Board of Rites, for protocol, Confucian education, and foreign affairs; a Board of the Military; a Board of Punishments, for the review of legal matters; a Board of Works, for maintaining the country's infrastructure of roads and for water conservancy projects; and a Board of Appointments, to handle the running of the bureaucracy. In addition, as in China, there was a Censorate, to monitor the behavior of officials. Unlike the Yangban in Korea, or the samurai and daimyo officials in Japan, the Le mandated enforcement of the Chinese "law of avoidance" in which officials were rotated every three years and were forbidden to serve in their home districts as a hedge against corruption. Even this, however, was often less than effective among those posted under powerful regional officials.

As everywhere in East Asia, scholars were revered, and as in China, the road to both wealth and prestige for the ambitious invariably led to study for the official exams. During the civil war years, both the Trinh and Nguyen courts held their own triennial examinations in addition to those of the Le. Normally, an aspirant would be tested for his knowledge of the Confucian Classics and certain elements of practical statecraft. If he passed, he would be the equivalent of the Chinese *juren*, or provincial candidate. He would receive a small stipend, perhaps get a position in the provincial academy, and be eligible to compete in the metropolitan exams in the capital. Those who passed these exams would then be selected for government positions, generally starting their careers as district magistrates.

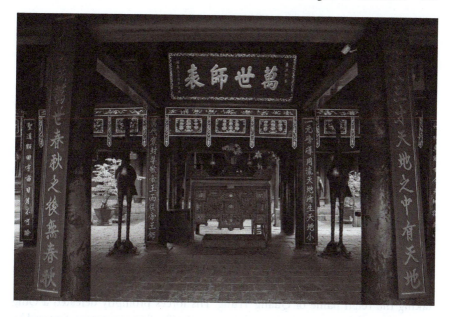

Temple of Literature, Hanoi. The Temple of Literature, founded in 1076, was the first national academy for Confucian training. This building functioned as the examination hall for those taking the equivalent of the Chinese *jinshi*, or metropolitan degree—the highest level of official examinations. The large Chinese characters, read right to left, carry the hall's motto, "A Pattern for Emulation Through the Ages."

Rebellion and Consolidation

Despite the efforts of the regime, the new areas proved increasingly difficult to bring within the ideological and political fold. Once again, it seemed that the forces of expansion had fought those of consolidation to a standstill. The collapse of Le power in 1770 and tensions resulting from increased taxation and slow rural impoverishment sparked three men, also surnamed Nguyen, to lead a revolt. The three, Nhac, Hue, and Lu, are known to history as the "Tay Son brothers," deriving from the name of the district in Binh Dinh Province from which they came. The small number of officials, including both those connected to the remnant Le, and those of the perennially feuding Trinh and Nguyen lords, presided over systems of corruption on an intolerable scale, not unlike those practiced in the early twentieth century by Chinese warlords. Payoffs, kickbacks, irregular tax farming, and the frequent auctioning of official posts to the highest bidders plagued large sections of the kingdom. Thus, like the later Tonghaks in Korea and the Taipings in China in the 1860s, the Tay Son brothers preached a belief system calling for national unification and renewal through social equality and a massive redistribution of land. They also initially claimed to support the restoration of the Le Dynasty to complete power and legitimacy.

As the revolt gained momentum through peasant support, the brothers' ideology grew more sophisticated and their ambitions expanded far beyond the redress of their original grievances and Le restoration. The brothers divided the kingdom, now once again called Dai Viet (Dai Viet Quoc), into three parts: the northern section was ruled by Nhac; the central region by Hue; while the south was still in the hands of the Nguyen lords. In 1776, however, Tay Son forces captured the Nguyen stronghold in the city later called Saigon. In what had become a staple of troubled ethnic relations in the country, they slaughtered the Chinese community there, and the entire Nguyen family was killed except for a nephew, Nguyen Phuc Anh (see the Patterns Up-Close feature below). Anh not only survived but also, following an amazing run of good fortune and French assistance, would emerge as the emperor Gia Long of the new Nguyen Dynasty in 1802.

In 1778, however, Nhac proclaimed himself emperor, and the Tay Son armies continued to consolidate their holdings in the south. There followed several years of fighting remnant Nguyen and Trinh forces, who were now supported by a Siamese invasion in support of Phuc Anh. 1788, Hue declared himself emperor, taking the reign name of Quang Trung. His forces promptly defeated a Qing army sent to help restore the Le and suppress the Tay Son movement. Spurred by his victory and convinced that he had acquired the Mandate of Heaven, Quang Trung now sought to expand Vietnam deep into southern China to recreate the ancient state of Nam Viet. Moreover, he discarded orthodox neo-Confucianism altogether, advocating instead something like the old decentralized state system of Zhou China.

In 1792, Quang Trung died, and by 1802, his successor was unable to hold off the rejuvenated Nguyen forces under Anh that slowly ground him down. After decades of civil war, the Nguyen (1802–1945) formed a new dynasty with its capital at the city of Hue. The new emperor, Gia Long—the former Anh—(r. 1802–1820) swiftly rebuilt the bureaucracy and reinstituted the various structures of the neo-Confucian state. In order to cement the new empire together more effectively, he commissioned the building of the **Mandarin Road** running from Hue to Saigon in the south.

Unlike the process of centralization in Korea and Japan, in which a degree of seclusion for the sake of security was achieved, the rapid increase in European and American trade in the region precluded the Vietnamese from shutting themselves completely off from it. Nonetheless, Minh Mang's policy for Dai Nam ("The Great South"), as he dubbed the empire he inherited, was one of isolation. The French who had worked for Gia Long were increasingly distanced from the court, and attempts by Europeans and the Americans to sign treaties and open diplomatic relations—except for a handful of arms deals—were rejected. The French continued to maintain diplomatic relations, but their consuls were increasingly snubbed. Moreover, despite the relatively large Catholic population, Minh Mang had declared Christianity to be a "perverse" religion and a source of corruption for the people.

Remembering the Nguyen Brothers. In a manner seeming to anticipate revolts in Korea and China in the nineteenth century aimed at national renewal and massive land redistribution, the Nguyen brothers, sometimes called the Tay Son brothers for the district from which they came, sparked a massive rebellion in the late eighteenth century. Pictured here are statues of the three brothers in the Quang Trung Museum in the Tay Son district of Binh Dinh Province. The foremost figure, Nguyen Hue, named himself emperor in 1788, taking the reign name Quang Trung.

PATTERNS UP-CLOSE

The French as Allies of the Imperial Court

Like other East Asian states, Vietnam had seen the arrival of Christian missionaries in the late sixteenth century, the most famous of whom was the French Jesuit, Alexandre de Rhodes (1591–1660). Paralleling their early successes among Japanese daimyo and at the Chinese court, the Jesuits made converts among the powerful in Vietnam during the seventeenth and eighteenth centuries and arranged for exchanges of diplomatic greetings with the court of Louis XIV. The French continued their interest in the area throughout the eighteenth century, but at no point was this on more dramatic display than during the **Tay Son Revolt**. In a very real sense, their

(continued)

role in helping to suppress the revolt and assisting in the creation of the Nguyen Dynasty, Vietnam's last imperial regime, goes against the grain of not only the later imperial adventures of Western powers in Asia, but also those of France itself barely a half century later.

The young prince and future emperor, Nguyen Phuc Anh, who, as we have seen, barely escaped with his life from the Tay Son capture of Saigon in 1776, received protection from Monsignor Pigneau de Behaine, who ran a Catholic mission in the southern district of Ha Tien. Behaine placed the prince out of reach of the Tay Son on the island of Pulo Panjang. With the support of Behaine, Phuc Anh was able to recapture strategic points in the region, climaxing with Saigon in 1778. In the seesaw struggle over the next several years, however, the Nguyen were again driven from Saigon by the Tay Son, and with Behaine, Anh appealed to the Siamese, the Portuguese, and ultimately the French court for help. They signed an alliance with the Portuguese at Macao in 1786, and with the Nguyen boy prince Canh in tow went on to Versailles to argue Phuc Anh's case for French assistance. After difficult negotiations—and considerable charming of the royal family and courtiers by Prince Canh—the Treaty of Versailles was concluded between France and the Nguyen as rulers of Cochinchina in 1787.

Despite the sorry state of France's finances, the Vietnamese were promised four warships and 2,000 soldiers in return for access to Tourane (present-day Da Nang) and the island of Con Son (Pulo Condore). Although French officials at their Indian base in Pondicherry reneged on the promised forces, Behaine, Anh, and an improvised force of French adventurers and Vietnamese supporters strengthened their hold on the south. By the early 1790s, they had built an impressive fleet to battle the Tay Son and constructed a modern European-style fortress in Saigon. Following Father (now Bishop) Behaine's death in 1799, the Nguyen, bolstered by a growing and well-trained force and French support, decisively defeated the Tay Son navy in February 1801. The Nguyen victory opened the door for the capture of Hue later that year and, finally, Hanoi the following July. Nguyen Phuc Anh now took the reign name Gia Long and set up his court at Hue, rewarding his leading French supporters with posts as officials and advisors.

In many respects, this represented the high point of friendly Franco-Vietnamese relations, as well as imperial favor toward missionaries and Catholicism. For many of the same reasons that the regimes in China, Korea, and Japan had turned against the missionaries, however, following the death of Gia Long in 1820, the Nguyen court did so as well. The French missionary efforts, interrupted during the Revolution and Napoleonic interval, were resumed in Southeast Asia with the restoration of the monarchy and Church in France. Confucian gentry and Buddhists, however, renewed their objections to the Christian opposition to ancestor veneration. As had the Rites Controversy in China a century before, Christian attempts to tamper with time-honored filial practices made the government view the missionaries' activities with increasing suspicion. Although Gia Long had employed French advisors, his son Minh Mang (1791–1841) expelled them for ostensibly plotting with a southern regional strongman. He swiftly banned Christianity in 1825 and began the persecution of missionaries in 1830. It would be the position of Catholicism in the region, and France's self-appointed role as protector of the Church in Asia, that would force events in a few decades, leading France to reduce its former ally to a colony.

Father Behaine and Emperor Gia Long. France's long-standing relationship with Vietnam perhaps reached its greatest period of relative equality during the late eighteenth and early nineteenth centuries when the Roman Catholic missionary, Father Georges Behaine (A), rescued the heir to the old Nguyen throne, took him to France, and arranged an alliance that in fits and starts resulted in that heir, Phuc Anh, forming a new Nguyen Dynasty, taking the reign name Gia Long (B). The Chinese characters in the portrait of the emperor bear the title "Gia Long." The Nguyen were destined to be the last Vietnamese imperial dynasty.

The Vietnamese, as we have seen, had long maintained a complex relationship with the minority peoples in the areas coming under their control. For Minh Mang and the renewed neo-Confucian bureaucracy, this raised the need for a program of Sinicizing the peoples under them. The result was that relations with the Khmers and Chams, both Muslim and Hindu, as well as non-Mahayana Buddhists, were often fraught. For the Chams, who had fought for centuries against

Statue of Minh Mang at His Tomb. Although Sino-Vietnamese relations remained close in the early decades of the nineteenth century, the reign of Emperor Minh Mang saw a marked deterioration in their peaceful cooperation. Anxious to combat the influence of Christianity and promulgate a version of Neo-Confucianism, the emperor used the accusation of missionary collusion in a revolt during the 1830s to expel them and sever relations with France. The stylized statue of Minh Mang shown here marks the entrance to his tomb at Huong Tho.

Vietnamese expansion, rebellion was never far below the surface following annexation of their former state. The existing states of Cambodia and Laos were treated as tributary states by the Nguyen, much as Vietnam, Korea, and Japan were by China (see Map 7.2). At times, the government under Minh Mang even attempted to break the food taboos of minorities with forced feedings of pork or beef. Even before this, the Nguyen had routinely referred to themselves as "Han nahn"—"People of Han"—as Chinese had customarily called themselves. Indeed, Gia Long had sometimes used the term *Trung quoc* (in Chinese, *Zhongguo*, "the middle kingdom," i.e., China) to refer to Vietnam. As part of the Sinicizing effort, they had also decreed the wearing of Chinese dress for all.

In the 1830s, these problems came to a head as old Le supporters with Catholic backing began revolting in the north, while a rebellion in the south began over the loss of regional autonomy and the desire to replace Minh Mang with a son of Prince Canh. In this, the leaders of the movement sought support from missionaries and the local Catholic population, as well as ethnic minorities. When the movement was suppressed, all missionaries were ordered to leave the country, with those among the putative leaders of the revolt publicly executed. The remaining years of Minh Mang's rule and those of his successors would be marked by repeated ethnic unrest and local revolts.

CREATING INDOCHINA

For the French, who had taken upon themselves the protection of Catholics in the region, long-standing patronage of the missionary enterprise would repeatedly provide pretexts for pressuring the Nguyen for concessions. These, however, were also coupled with the desire to counterbalance the British in their dealings with China during the treaty port era. Following the Treaty of Nanjing in 1842, the

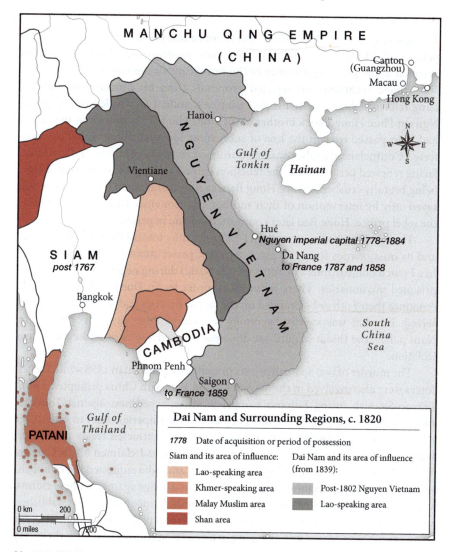

Map 7.2 Dai Nam and Surrounding Regions, ca. 1820

French sought to establish their own opening to China through the south—a goal that would span the remaining years of the century. In 1843, the French sent a naval squadron to seize the southern Philippine island of Basilan to use as a base by way of checking the British, who had acquired Hong Kong the year before. The French, however, abandoned the effort due to Spanish protests. It was believed that such a base would also position them for action in the event of the need to punish Vietnam, the government of which had been condemned by the papacy for its treatment of Catholics. Although the numbers vary, there were perhaps 400,000 Catholics in Vietnam at this time.

First Footholds

The new emperor, Tu Duc (r. 1847–1883), continued the staunch Neo-Confucian policies of Minh Mang and his immediate predecessor, Thieu Tri. Indeed, alarmed at the growing presence of the Europeans in the region, he intensified Vietnamese seclusion and rejected proposals from his officials for modernizing reforms. Shortly after his ascension, a dissident faction led by the prince Nguyen Phuc Hong Bao, a brother of Tu Duc, who felt his branch of the family had been passed over in the line of succession, led a rebellion. Aided by disaffected Confucian officials, peasants burdened by heavy taxation, and Catholics facing renewed persecutions, the rebellion gained a degree of momentum before being brutally crushed. Prince Hong Bao, captured and slated for execution, was saved only by intervention of their mother, who convinced Tu Duc to imprison the rebel prince. Hong Bao later committed suicide in prison.

The rebellion had cemented Tu Duc's antipathy toward the Catholic Church and its missionaries firmly in place. Already, persecutions in 1847 had resulted in a French bombardment of Tourane (Da Nang) during negotiations to free imprisoned missionaries. There followed an order by Tu Duc for all Catholics to renounce their faith or be branded on the face as heretics and have their property seized. In what was swiftly becoming a cycle of European response to Dai Nam policy, the threat of gunboat diplomacy forced Vietnam into even deeper isolation.

The murder of two Spanish priests in southern Vietnam in 1858 while French forces were also involved in the Second Opium War with China prompted a joint Franco-Spanish (using Filipino troops) punitive expedition against Tourane, followed by the capture of Saigon. They forced the imperial court to cede three adjacent provinces and over the next several years extracted treaty port privileges in Annam and Tonkin. By 1864, the French had claimed all of Cochin. While this was transpiring, King Norodom of Cambodia requested the establishment of a French protectorate over his domain as a hedge against Siamese claims, which was duly negotiated. Thus, by the late 1860s, France had firmly established itself as the most powerful entity in the region. Preoccupied with suppressing the Taiping and Nian rebels, and engaging in a grudging cooperation with the treaty powers, the Qing could do little but protest this occupation of land over which they had long claimed suzerainty.

Colonization by Protectorate

As the French consolidated their position, the Nguyen imperial government began to feel increasing pressure on its remaining territories. Nor could they see anything on the horizon that might help them. Burma was in British hands; Siam/Thailand was engaged in an excruciating regional balancing act, trying to maintain its independence while being on friendly terms with both the British and French. For their part, the Qing by the 1870s were undertaking a number of promising "self-strengthening" programs but were not yet strong enough to chance a war with any of the treaty powers. The Chinese traveler Li Gui (see Chapter 5), whom we will meet again in Chapter 8, stopped in Saigon and neighboring Cholon

Storming the Citadel in the Battle of Saigon. Repeated incidents involving missionaries and Vietnamese Christians came to a head in 1858 with the murder of two Spanish priests. France, as the self-appointed guardian of Catholics in East Asia, diverted naval and land forces from the war in China to Vietnam to punish the Nguyen and extract concessions. Following the bombardment of Da Nang and Saigon, an assault force of French, Spanish, and Philippine troops stormed the citadel in Saigon in February 1859, as depicted above. They forced the imperial government to cede the city and three adjacent provinces.

on the final leg of his round-the-world journey in 1876. Although he had enjoyed his earlier stay in France very much, his comments on French colonialism were not encouraging for either the Chinese or Vietnamese communities he visited:

> I found that Saigon was Vietnam's southernmost port . . . the country's fashions, writing, and other things resemble those of China somewhat, and from the Han dynasty on they had been under our tutelage. In the first year of Xian Feng (1851 *sic*), however, an incident involving the killing of Catholic missionaries and merchant seamen prompted the French to move troops in and [attempt to] occupy it completely. When this proved unsuccessful, they negotiated a peace and arranged for three provinces to be ceded to them. . . . As a precaution against any problems in the mountains they have also built forts to defend them, covetously eyeing England's position in India and desiring to put France into a comparable situation. Is Vietnam not in danger from this?

The Chinese in Cholon, as a particularly active entrepreneurial group, were now subject to even higher rates of taxation than their Vietnamese counterparts:

> The French view the increasing numbers of Chinese coming here day by day as an avenue to financial benefit, and have developed new regulations specifically aimed at taking advantage of them. All the Chinese residents here are subject to import taxes, export taxes, a capitation tax, dwelling tax, land tax, and a sign tax, six in all . . . those paying import and personal taxes must have licenses and must carry them on their persons and be prepared to show them

to the police for inspection. Customs are separately assessed and decisions as to taxable items are made quite rigorously. Alas! There is no place in the world so annoyed by this kind of tyrannical treatment! Compared to the English regulations in Singapore they are truly as far apart as heaven and earth. In observing England and France, therefore, we should study them even more minutely on this. (From Charles Desnoyers, *A Journey to the East*: Li Gui's "A New Account of a Trip Around the Globe," (Ann Arbor: University of Michigan Press, 2004) pp. 298–300)

Li Gui's warning about the danger to Vietnam now extended to China as well. The French were interested in finding a trade route via the Red River into Yun'nan and sent expeditions to probe the region in the 1870s and early 1880s. Alarmed at France's progress in moving up into central Vietnam (Annam) and pressuring the Vietnamese court at Hue, Li Hongzhang, China's leading "self-strengthener" and most powerful official, sent aid to local militias, who had given a good account of themselves against the French. Of these, the most powerful were the Black Flags, a largely Chinese group that contained a number of Taiping veterans who fled south when their rebellion was crushed. In 1882, a French force attempted to move on Hanoi without authorization from Paris and push the French government into accepting a fait accompli if they were able to take the territory. They were, however, beaten back and, more disconcerting still, the Qing began to mass troops near the Vietnamese border. Smarting from an earlier Japanese punitive expedition against Taiwan and continuing Japanese pressure on the Qing client Yi Dynasty in Korea, Li Hongzhang resolved to stand firm against the French in Southeast Asia. Thus, Qing troops crossed the border and occupied several towns in the north.

The Sino-French War

As we have seen, China had been pursuing a number of self-strengthening programs following the 1860s, including heavy purchases of English, American, and German arms. In 1877, a Qing expeditionary force bearing Krupp artillery, Remington repeating rifles, and Gatling guns had crushed the rebel Muslim state of Kashgaria and secured the borders of the empire in Xinjiang against the aims of the Russian, the Ottomans, and the British. The Chinese were also actively pursuing a program of coastal defense and building a modern armored steam fleet. Thus, Li was in a position to feel optimistic about his opposition to French adventurism.

The event, however, that came to be called the "Sino-French," or "Tonkin" War, turned into a difficult fight in which both sides attempted to claim victory. In May 1883, a French expeditionary force unwisely attacked a much stronger Black Flag Army and was badly mauled, losing its commander and barely able to retreat to Hanoi. The defeat galvanized the pro-expansionist French government of Jules Ferry, which strengthened its determination to pry Tonkin from Chinese suzerainty. Forcing the issue with the Nguyen court, the French extracted an agreement from the Vietnamese recognizing their protectorate in Tonkin. Chinese and French negotiators then met at Tianjin and concluded an agreement ratifying the new status of Tonkin.

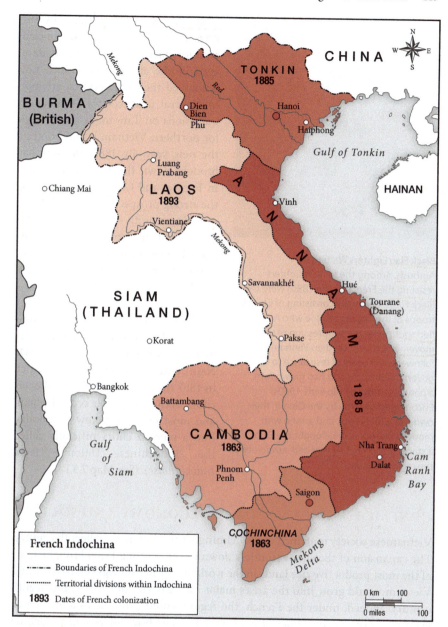

Map 7.3 French Indochina

Unaware of the agreement, however, a Chinese force opened fire on French troops advancing from Hanoi, and the French declared war on China in the fall of 1884. Frustrated at their lack of progress and incensed at what they considered an unwarranted ambush by the Chinese, the French boldly and unexpectedly took the initiative against the Chinese navy in a preemptive strike on the

Black Flag Fighters Waiting in Ambush. Among the fiercest fighters resisting the French in the 1880s were the Black Flags. Originally consisting of Chinese troops of the Taiping regime who had fled south after the suppression of their movement, they picked up Vietnamese followers over years of resistance to government forces and had grown into a powerful army by the early 1880s. Encouraged covertly by the Qing in their own war with France, and armed with modern weapons, they fought the French to a standstill before China ceded suzerainty of the region to France.

Qing base at Fuzhou. Taken by surprise, the bottled up Chinese ironclads and port facilities were severely damaged in the attack. The French now redoubled their land efforts, attempting several unsuccessful diversionary incursions on Taiwan, as the struggle for northern Vietnam ground on into the new year. By 1885, the war had brought down the Ferry government in France, and China was also facing the strong prospect of war with Japan over Korea. Both sides therefore saved face as best they could: Li Hongzhang agreed to the provisions of the earlier Tianjin treaty—implied recognition of the French protectorate in Tonkin—while China would pay no indemnity to France for the war. France now controlled a loose set of protectorates including Cochin China, Annam (Da Nam), and Tonkin in the north, which in 1887 they consolidated with the territory of the Lao people ceded by Siam and most of what is now Cambodia, into a merged entity officially called the "Indochinese Union" (*Union Indochinoise*). (See Map 7.3.)

CONFLICT AND COMPROMISE: ECONOMY AND SOCIETY

Vietnamese society remained overwhelmingly rural into the nineteenth century. The expansion of the state's frontiers down to the Mekong Delta brought some of the most productive rice lands in the world under Le and Nguyen control, and Vietnam would grow into the area's major rice exporter during the nineteenth century. Indeed, under the French, the region would continue as a major rice exporter—even during times of poor harvests. The brief interval of Indochina under Japanese control in 1945 saw a massive famine, even as the Japanese extracted record amounts of export rice in support of their collapsing war effort.

As in China and much of the rest of the region, there had also been a commercialization of agriculture during the eighteenth century, although it had been slowed somewhat by regional tensions and interrupted almost entirely during the Tay Son Revolt. In addition to rice, commercial farmers grew and picked a host of semi- and tropical items, including spices such as pepper and ginger, betel nuts, citrus fruits, cotton, and, as in other areas in eastern Asia, mulberry trees for silkworms.

The New Commercial Development

Accompanying this growth was that of market towns, trade crossroads, and provincial capitals and administrative centers. Like the vital artery that the Tokaido had furnished in Tokugawa Japan, the *Quan Lo*, or "Mandarin Road," in Vietnam bound the country together commercially and politically during the early nineteenth century. Hanoi, Hue, and Saigon grew into considerable cities and, by the nineteenth century, the latter two did brisk business as ports as well. But the major emphasis on urban development came in Hue, the imperial capital. Here, the buildings were not unlike those of Beijing's Forbidden City, but with a lightness of architecture that prompted foreign visitors to call them the most beautiful in Southeast Asia.

Neo-Confucianism in Imperial Vietnam

Like the Tokugawa, the Yi, and the Qing during the seventeenth century, the Le and Nguyen, as we have noted, promulgated a set of neo-Confucian rules to instruct the populace on proper decorum and behavior. These "Forty-Seven Rules for Teaching and Transforming [the People]" placed their central emphasis on filial piety, with extreme reverence for one's parents and the obligation to care for them in their old age. Other familiar Confucian concepts—the Mandate of Heaven, The Five Relationships and Three Bonds—were featured prominently as well. As in the other neo-Confucian societies we have examined, the governing idea was a return to the basics of proper personal and group behavior within the universal system of hierarchical relationships. Society would then revert back to balance, order, and stability on its own through proper leadership and ritual behavior, while the people would have the possibility to be "transformed"; that is, "civilized" in the Confucian sense of automatically wanting what was right according to the natural order.

As the chief exemplars of this proper behavior, the Vietnamese scholar-gentry, like their Chinese counterparts, were expected to devote themselves unstintingly to the study of Confucian ethics and teach the people by example. They were therefore exempted from the labor tax, and bore it as a mark of honor that they labored not with their hands but with their minds. The reverence for learning also extended to the cultivation of talent in promising students. As in Korea and China, villages commonly planted "student fields" to support those studying for the official exams. While the devotion to learning and the firm grip of a self-consciously "Vietnamese" neo-Confucianism continued to hold sway through the nineteenth century, new challenges also emerged within the social fabric. The Tay Son movement, with its calls for equality and land redistribution, had mounted a potent but short-lived threat. More lasting was the spread of Christianity, specifically Catholicism. Under continual pressure from the French to allow freedom of religion, villages that did convert were increasingly torn between traditional modes of ritual, record-keeping, and cultural observances and those of their co-religionists worldwide. Within the structure of the family, too, the greater flexibility that Vietnamese women customarily enjoyed was expanded, thus further antagonizing many of the scholarly class. Periodic persecution intensified these conflicts, which remained long into the twentieth century. Indeed,

Aerial View of Imperial Palace Complex at Hue. The Vietnamese imperial palace grounds are renowned for their beauty and a certain lightness that makes many visitors consider them the most striking in East Asia. The complex's similarity to Beijing's Forbidden City is easily seen in this aerial photo, in which a rectangular wall and moat surround the palace buildings. Unlike the Forbidden City, however, which is built on a north–south axis, the Hue complex is oriented northwest–southeast to take advantage of the geomancy of the Perfume River, which runs by it.

such tensions between Catholics and Buddhists in the early 1960s would be a major factor in the U.S.-backed coup against Catholic President Diem in South Vietnam in November 1963.

Neo-Confucian partisans in Vietnam not only attempted to civilize the "barbarian" peoples within the realm but also frequently argued that Vietnamese Confucianism was, in fact, more authentic than Chinese neo-Confucianism as promulgated by the Qing. As with Nichiren and his interpretation of Japan as the rightful center of the Buddhist world in the thirteenth century, the Nguyen posited themselves as the new rightful inheritors of the neo-Confucian tradition. The Nguyen habit of referring to their realm as "the Middle Kingdom," as the Chinese customarily referred to their own, supported the assertion that the Manchu Qing had strayed from a true understanding of the Song texts of Zhuxi. Incensed that Nguyen representatives were routinely housed in dwellings bearing signs that they were hostels reserved for "Vietnamese barbarians," the Vietnamese argued stridently that they were people of one culture with the Chinese and thus not barbarians at all. In a pattern fairly common in world history, people from the periphery argued that, although politically independent, they were the "true" heirs to the culture they shared with the core, whose followers had fallen away from the True Path. This political self-image was strongly argued by Tu Duc during his long reign lasting up to the eve of the Sino-French or Tonkin War. The attempted coup by his brother was a powerful factor in reinforcing this outlook.

TOWARD "MODERNITY"? CULTURE, SCIENCE, AND INTELLECTUAL LIFE

Like the other societies we have examined in this volume, Vietnam in the late eighteenth and early nineteenth centuries displayed a number of characteristics that scholars formerly assumed were the later result of European contact and thus "modern." As in Korea and Japan, for example, cycles of keen interest and imitation of things Chinese had historically alternated with reassertions of national distinctiveness. By the eighteenth century, Vietnamese scholars' frequent revisiting of their national histories to demonstrate resistance to Chinese occupation has caused some modern scholars to see it as "nationalistic" or "proto-nationalistic."

Asserting Incipient Nationalism

As we observed above, some Vietnamese writers as well as officials and those at court now saw Vietnam as the true repository of Confucian virtues, which at various times had been discarded by the Chinese. Hence, the historian Le Quy Don (1726–1784) wrote his accounts of Vietnam's past within a vision of Confucian humanism constantly threatened by Chinese oppression. Diplomat, encyclopedia compiler, and author of the massive *Dai Viet thong su* history of the Le and Dai Viet as well as the *Frontier Chronicles*, Le Quy Don is considered Vietnam's most prolific and profound chronicler of the tumultuous late eighteenth century. His name today adorns one of Vietnam's premier technical institutions, in addition to several high schools in Vietnam, a number of community centers abroad, and even a Vietnamese naval training ship. As the nineteenth century wore on, the government attempted to cultivate such "nationalist" sentiments by means of patriotic songs, especially as the conflicts with France moved from pressure for religious freedom to territorial concessions in the late 1850s.

The development of the *Chu nom* script as a vehicle for vernacular literature also continued and culminated in the early 1800s with Nguyen Du's epic-length poem "A New Song About Great Heartbreak" (*Doan truong tan thanh*). Known more widely by the names of its chief characters—*Kim, Van, Kieu*—the work crossed class lines and interests as the protagonist leaves her scholar-official lover and, out of filial loyalty, works off her father's debts as a prostitute before rejoining him.

Struggles of Modernization

Late-eighteenth- and early-nineteenth-century contacts with the French had created among some intellectuals an interest in European technical developments and science. As in China and, later, Japan, much of this interest was tied to self-defense. Unlike the leaders of the other East Asian states, the Vietnamese emperor Gia Long took an active interest himself in astronomy and mathematics, and his successors, despite their policies of attempted seclusion, took the lead in ordering the construction of a European-style shipyard in the 1840s. Like early Chinese attempts, however, these first efforts at building steamships were without notable success due to an inadequate understanding of steam engine mechanics.

Nowhere are the tensions of preserving national independence, defending the Confucian order, and the struggle to encourage modernity and religious toleration more evident than in the life of the remarkable Nguyen Truong To (1827 to 1830?–1871). The nineteenth-century collision of the industrializing Western maritime countries with the agrarian–urban states of Asia resulted in a number of extraordinary individuals who sought to reconcile their home cultures with the new forces

The Reformer Nguyen Truong To. Like a number of extraordinary individuals who were exposed to the high cultures of Asia and the West, Truong To sought a way to synthesize the two in a way not unlike Japan's "Western Science and Eastern Ethics" or China's "Chinese Studies for the Base, Western Studies for Practical Application." Through the good offices of Bishop Jean-Denis Gauthier, he visited Hong Kong and Europe; as a patriot, he urged the emperor to modernize Vietnam's military and push back against French imperialism. In his attempts at reconciling Confucianism with Catholicism, he argued that both encouraged the idea of the divine right of rulers and monarchical legitimacy.

increasingly diffused throughout the region. Such examples as Yung Wing (Rong Hong) in China and Manjiro Nakahama in Japan come to mind in this regard. As a contemporary of both men, Nguyen pursued similar goals under similar circumstances but with some important differences unique to Vietnam.

Truong To was born into a Catholic family in central Vietnam during the first wave of Minh Mang's attempts to suppress missionary activity. He proved to be an able student of the Confucian Classics and was soon on the road to what might otherwise be a promising career.

His Catholicism, however, prevented him from being allowed to sit for the official examinations, and he would struggle all his life to convince his emperor and colleagues that the two traditions were not only compatible, but mutually reinforcing of the imperial order. Barred from official posts, he taught the Confucian curriculum in village academies and took religious instruction from the famous missionary Bishop Jean-Denis Gauthier (1810–1877).

With the French and Spanish attack on Tourane or Da Nang in 1858, Emperor Tu Duc redoubled his efforts to suppress the Catholic community as potentially subversive, and Truong and Gauthier fled to the French-controlled area for shelter. From there, Truong traveled to Hong Kong and throughout Southeast Asia, became proficient in French, and studied the newspapers, literature, philosophy, and political systems of the West. Indeed, he is viewed as unique by many modern scholars in the depth of his understanding of both cultural traditions, especially at a time when these subjects were only beginning to be addressed in China and Korea, and known to only a handful of Japanese officials who followed "Dutch Learning."

Returning to Vietnam in 1861, he worked briefly for the French, and although severely criticized by fellow Confucians—some of whom lobbied for his execution—he nonetheless proved his support for the Nguyen by petitioning Tu Duc repeatedly over the coming years to use the interval of peace following the recent treaty with the French for rigorous modernization efforts. Like the self-strengtheners in China and the reformers in Japan, he argued that the goal of Vietnam's efforts should be to modernize its industries and institutions in order to enable the country to roll back the unequal treaties and recover its ceded territories. Like the efforts in China during these decades, however, the fortunes of reform and modernization were contingent on the volatile political environment and the opposition of many of the government's officials.

Convinced of Truong's sincerity, the emperor had several audiences with him and sent him along with Gauthier in 1867 as part of a delegation to purchase machinery in France—much as Yung Wing had been commissioned to do in the United States a few years before. There were also plans to send French instructors to build a polytechnic school in Vietnam. These initiatives, however, collapsed in the face of renewed French pressure on Tu Duc to cede additional territory. Just before his death in 1871, Truong urged the emperor to take advantage of the Franco-Prussian War to seize back the territories taken by the French.

One of the unique aspects of Truong's thought was in the way he sought to reconcile strong faith in Catholicism with his life-long commitment to Confucian values. He urged Tu Duc to see his Catholic subjects not as a hostile population subscribing to a "perverse" religion, but like the Buddhists, one that sincerely believed in the imperial order. As elsewhere in East Asia, despite historical tensions between Buddhism and Neo-Confucianism, the two coexisted in mutual toleration. So, too, Truong argued, could Catholicism and neo-Confucianism. Moreover, he argued that Catholicism offered an opportunity for synthesis with the concept of Confucian filial piety and service to the imperial order because of the European concept of legitimacy based on divine right. In fact, he argued, unlike Mencius's idea that the people were the basis of the state and had the right to overthrow an oppressive ruler, the principle of divine right was a true Mandate of Heaven in that the ruler was the key component of the polity. Hence, to oppose him is to oppose the will of God. Thus, he said, the people can endure a bad ruler until an able one comes along, but to break the line of legitimacy goes against the divine order. In support of this, he cited Japan's putative unbroken line of emperors as an existing Asian model and source of that nation's strength, and saw China's dynastic changes as unfortunate breaches of the true Confucian and divine imperial way.

CONCLUSION

Bishop Jean-Denis Gauthier. As in China, the missionary effort in Vietnam often involved the encouragement of modernization along Western lines. Bishop Gauthier had given religious instruction to Nguyen Truong To early in his career and later accompanied the reformer to France, to purchase industrial machinery and form plans to establish a polytechnic institute in 1867. The scheme collapsed, however, in the face of renewed French pressure for concessions in Vietnam a few years later.

The interval from the end of the threat of Mongol invasions to the late nineteenth century in a way represented something of a departure from previous periods of Vietnamese history. Most of the preceding millennium had been marked by Chinese invasion and occupation accompanied by forced and, at times, voluntary acculturation. The Chinese written language, norms of Confucianism, Mahayana Buddhism, and the routinization of outside pressure and domination had forged a society with many similarities to its East Asian counterparts, although also embodying a number of unique characteristics. Occupied by China for far longer than Korea, Vietnam nevertheless retained the same spirit of political defiance and independence, while maintaining perhaps the closest cultural similarities to China of any East Asian civilization.

With the coming of the Le Dynasty in the early fifteenth century, that sometimes unstable amalgam of "Vietnamized" Chinese culture and fierce independence was strengthened. Despite Ming attempts at invasion, and Qing threats of punitive expeditions, the Le and the feuding Trinh and Nguyen lords nonetheless asserted their independence from their aspirational suzerain to the north. Indeed, in its continuous push to the south, Vietnam in many ways seemed animated by the same imperial drives that had marked China's history. Their traditional opponents, the Indic Khmers and Chams, fought them physically and culturally for control of the Mekong Delta and the surrounding region, but found themselves ultimately defeated and driven west. The final imperial dynasty, the Nguyen, arguably represented the apex of imperial Vietnamese power, triumphing over the stubborn Tay Son partisans and securing during the reigns of its first two emperors Vietnam's greatest extent of territory.

Yet this summer of power contained within it the circumstances that would soon conspire to reduce it to a dependency and colonial territory. Like the Qing during Qianlong's reign, internal weakness would ultimately invite outside incursion. The Nguyen triumphed over their opponents to achieve power, in part, because of the friendly formal and informal hand of France. The first emperor,

Gia Long, had been rescued as a boy by a French priest, and he retained a loyalty to the country and to those who had helped him. Despite his devotion to anchoring neo-Confucianism in the country, he retained a good-natured toleration of Catholic missionaries and converts, and employed them in his administration.

The ethnic strife, local friction between Christians and their neighbors, and the threat of incipient rebellion, however, led to the expulsion of missionaries and persecution of the hundreds of thousands of Catholics in the empire under Gia Long's successor, Minh Mang. The end of the Napoleonic period and France's return to monarchy also spelled the return of Catholic influence in France and the revival of French missionary efforts. Moreover, in addition to enhancing its presence in East Asia as a counterweight to growing British power, France arrogated to itself the role of protector of Catholics in the region. Throughout the 1830s and 1840s, relations between the Nguyen and the French steadily deteriorated until France began active territorial seizures in the name of defending the Vietnamese Church. From 1858 on, they steadily encroached on Vietnam, fought a war with China over suzerainty in the region, and ultimately claimed the state and surrounding lands as part of a new "Indochinese Union."

Despite rebellion, world war, strong nationalist movements, and even occupation by Japan, France would cling to its Indochinese holdings until ousted in 1954. Although nominally free, the newly divided country would find itself a proxy in a cold war between two super-powers until final unification in 1976.

FURTHER RESOURCES

Anderson, James, and John Whitmore, eds. *China's Encounters on the South and Southwest.* Leiden, the Netherlands: Brill, 2015. Part of the Handbook of Oriental Studies series, this volume of essays traces the history and societies of the frontier region between the south and southwest regions of China and Vietnam, Laos and Burma, covering two thousand years of interactions in the region the authors call the "Dong world,"

Cook, Nola, and Li Tana, eds. *Water Frontier. Commerce and the Chinese in the Lower Mekong Region, 1750–1880.* Singapore: Rowman & Littlefield, 2004. Departing from more standard state-based histories of the area encompassing southern Vietnam, eastern Cambodia, and southwestern Thailand, the essays in this book examine the region as an integrated economic sphere with particular attention to the interaction of Chinese traders with local peoples and its role in the larger economies of Southeast Asia and southern China.

Cook, Nola, and James Anderson, eds. *The Tongking Gulf Through History.* Philadelphia: University of Pennsylvania Press, 2011. A volume of essays from a 2008 conference, the authors situate the interdependence of trading factors in the region bordering northern Vietnam and southern China dubbed "the Mini-Mediterranean Sea" as a distinct economic entity from Neolithic times through the nineteenth century.

Dutton, George. *The Tay Son Uprising: Society and Rebellion in Eighteenth Century Vietnam.* Honolulu: University of Hawaii Press, 2006. The first comprehensive English language treatment of this pivotal conflict, which in many respects may be said to be one of the most important milestones marking the opening of the modern history of Vietnam.

Goscha, Christopher. *Vietnam: A New History.* New York: Basic Books, 2016. Excellent one-volume history of Vietnam from ancient times to the present. While the main part of the book deals with the modern period starting immediately before French colonialism, the earlier periods are also authoritatively covered in considerable detail.

Lieberman, Victor, ed. *Beyond Binary Histories. Re-imagining Eurasia to c. 1830.* Ann Arbor: University of Michigan Press, 1999. A volume of essays aimed at examining the integrating and centralizing processes at work in Europe and Asia. Of particular interest are essays on literati culture in Vietnam by John Whitmore and interior perspectives of Southeast Asia by David Wyatt.

Owen, Norman. *The Emergence of Modern Southeast Asia.* Honolulu: University of Hawaii Press, 2005. Traces the period immediately before the arrival of extensive Western colonialism in the region encompassing not only Vietnam but the other states in Southeast Asia plus Indonesia, Malaysia, and Singapore, through their years under imperial control and their emergence after World War II. Attention paid to state-building but perhaps even more to social, economic, cultural, and gender issues.

Reid, Anthony, ed. *Southeast Asia in the Early Modern Era.* Ithaca, NY: Cornell University Press, 1993. A conference volume of essays sponsored by the Joint Committee on Southeast Asia of the Social Science Research Council, the authors cover state-building, society and commerce and religious transitions in the key period from the fifteenth through the seventeenth centuries, with emphasis on the region's development before the period of extensive Western contact and colonialism.

Wade, Geoff and Sun Laichen, eds. *Southeast Asia in the Fifteenth Century: The China Factor.* Singapore: National University Press, 2010. Essays attempting to fill in the understudied period between the "classical" and the "modern" period. The authors argue that the fifteenth century in its state development, growing and diversified commerce, and especially with its cultural and trade relations with Ming China may be seen as undergirding the early modern history of the region.

Werner, Jayne, Whitmore, John, and Dutton, George, eds., *Sources of Vietnamese Tradition (Introduction to Asian Civilizations).* New York: Columbia University Press, 2012. As part of the highly respect Columbia series on the literature of East Asian and Indian civilization, this volume covers the entire realm of Vietnamese history from Neolithic times to the present. Its offerings include expertly selected excerpts of literary works covering chronicles and histories, Chinese accounts, philosophical treatises, colonial accounts, revolutionary documents, and writings on contemporary concerns. Invaluable for students of all levels.

WEBSITES

https://vwam.com//vets/history/vietnam.html. *Vietnam War, A Memoir.* Despite the primary focus on American involvement in Southeast Asia, this site includes substantial material on Vietnam up to the colonial period, illustrations, timelines, and capsule histories of the major dynasties. Appropriate for introductory or intermediate students.

http://academic.depauw.edu/mkfinney_web/teaching/Com227/culturalPortfolios/VIETNAM/VIETNAM/index.html. De Pauw University. *Vietnam.* Although the historical section is succinct, the site also covers "worldview," "traditions," "communication/values," "non-verbal," "family," and "education."

https://www.britannica.com/place/Vietnam. Encyclopaedia Britannica. *Vietnam.* As with other topics in Britannica's online offerings, this covers an extensive range of history with links to related economic, social, political, and legal topics. Most useful for the student gathering basic information for more extensive research.

CHAPTER 8

❦

Becoming Imperial: Japan to 1895

The trepidation was palpable. The penalty for leaving Japan and returning during the Tokugawa Shogunate's long period of seclusion was death, and although Manjiro Nakahama (1827–1898) had already undergone preliminary interrogation about his activities, he had now been summoned to see the daimyo of his native *han*, Tosa. The summons was especially poignant in that he had been reunited for just three days with his family, and his home village of Nakanohama had thrown him a welcome-home party. Having been gone and given up for dead for a dozen years, Manjiro's mother took him to see the grave they had arranged for him in his absence.

The ship he had taken to Okinawa on the first leg of his return to Japan—owned and captained by Manjiro himself—was called *Adventurer*, and it would be hard to imagine a more appropriate name for the vessel. Manjiro's life to this point had indeed been nothing short of extraordinary. As a 14-year-old hand on a fishing boat in January 1841, he and his mates had been caught in a storm and driven hundreds of miles from Japan, only to be shipwrecked on an uninhabited volcanic islet. They survived there until June when an American whaler, the *John Howland*, fortuitously spotted them and picked them up. The captain, William Whitfield, took Manjiro home with him to New Bedford, Massachusetts, where he became perhaps the first Japanese to enter the United States. With the Whitfields as his foster parents in nearby Fairhaven, Manjiro was enrolled in a local school, where he quickly learned English and became highly proficient in mathematics, navigation, and the maritime arts. Known as "John Mung," he became a local celebrity and was recruited to ship out on a whaler, where he was later selected as first mate. Returning to New Bedford in 1849, he turned right around and joined the tens of thousands of gold seekers headed for California. Unlike most of the others, however, he found a large nugget worth $600 and used the windfall to buy the *Adventurer*.

And so despite the risk, his quest brought him home again to Japan. Yet once more, his amazing run of luck and his ability to avail himself of the opportunities accompanying it continued. Satisfied that his return home posed no threat,

Manjiro Nakahama. Manjiro may be said to be one of the nineteenth century's most extraordinary individuals whose life took him from shipwrecked fisherman in his teens to student in New England, to 49er, captain and master of his own ship, and interpreter and liaison between Commodore Perry and the shogun. His legacy is still celebrated today in Japan and the United States. In this 1880 photograph, he is shown in the traditional clothes allowed a samurai—an honor he received for his service.

his daimyo arranged for him to provide intelligence about America and made him a samurai, which entitled him to an honorific surname. He chose "Nakahama" after his home village. With the coming of the American expedition of Matthew Perry to Japan in 1853, Manjiro served as an interpreter and advisor to the shogun, and for the rest of his life remained a vital link between the United States and Japan. In the twentieth century, Presidents Calvin Coolidge and Franklin Roosevelt cited him as an important example of Japanese-American amity—in the latter instance, even as American-Japanese relations were collapsing toward war. Today, in odd-numbered years, the cities of Fairhaven and Nakahanoma celebrate their connection as "sister cities" with a Manjiro festival.

Aside from being a fascinating story, however, Manjiro's adventures raise a number of important points about the course of Japan's and East Asia's historical experience during the preceding seven centuries. For example, how had a government whose origins lay, in part, in the Chinese imperial system come to be ruled by shogun warlords and their local *daimyo* and samurai retainers? What interactions and adaptations led to these shoguns enacting a strict policy of seclusion? How did the intrusion of the industrializing maritime powers of the West help break down not just Japan's restrictions but, as we have seen, those of China and Korea as well? Why was it the young United States that took the initiative in seeking commerce and diplomatic relations with Japan? In short, what were the forces and events that conspired to make it possible for an obscure adolescent fisherman to become a key link between peoples and nations?

THE ERA OF THE SHOGUNS, 1192–1867

As we saw earlier, the Japanese imperial court during the Heian period (794–1185), long dominated by the Fujiwara clan, was split by factional disputes surrounding the retired emperor/regent. The victory of the Minamoto clan in the Gempei War in 1185 resulted in the creation of the office of a chief military officer, the shogun, the first title of which was awarded to Minamoto Yoritomo. The office itself would last until 1867.

Kamakura and Ashikaga Shogunates, and Mongol Attacks

To restore order in the hotbed of Taira opposition, Yoritomo set up his headquarters at Kamakura, several hundred miles from Kyoto, beginning an interval known as the Kamakura Shogunate, from 1192 to 1333. The position also allowed, indeed encouraged, his subordinates to keep up the drive to push Japan's aboriginal inhabitants ever northward and seize their lands for settlement. The court at Kyoto itself remained the center of religious and ceremonial life as well as a forum for intrigue, but the real center of power now resided at the shogun's headquarters. Meanwhile, in 1274, the Mongols launched the first of their two major attempts to invade Japan. Their first armada was defeated handily, while in 1281 a much larger second fleet was smashed by a providential typhoon, known ever after by the Japanese as *kamikaze*, "the divine wind." Although the country was briefly aroused to common action in the face of this threat, the dissipation of imperial power continued for the most part unabated.

Court life became ever more stilted and formalized, obsessed with increasingly arcane rituals. At the same time, emperors very occasionally led unsuccessful attempts to reassert power for themselves—as did Go-Toba in 1221. More ambitious, although also ultimately unsuccessful, was the revolt by Emperor Go-Daigo in 1333. Securing the initial support of the powerful leader Ashikaga Takauji (1305–1358), Go-Daigo's faction was hobbled when the opportunistic Ashikaga switched sides twice during the conflict. He finally placed his own candidate on the throne, drove the aging emperor into exile, and moved his headquarters to the Muromachi district in northern Kyoto. For the first time in nearly 200 years, the seats of political and cultural influence were reunited in the same city. Equally important for the future of Japanese aesthetics and cultural institutions, the refinements of court life were now available to the warrior classes. Thus was born the union of *bu* and *bun*—the "dual way" of the sword and writing brush. The patronage of the daimyo, or regional lords, and their retainers, the samurai, ensured steady development of the Chinese-inspired arts of painting, poetry, and calligraphy, while the introduction of Zen and tea in the twelfth century forged an armature of discipline in both the martial and courtly arts that helped foster the preservation of both for centuries to come (see Map 1).

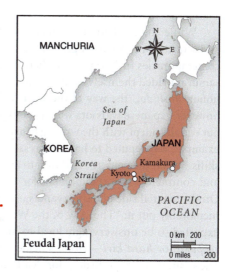

Map 8.1 Feudal Japan

Shogun Ashikaga Mounted in Battle. The position of the shogunate took a decisive turn with the ascendency of Ashikaga Takauji. Taking advantage of factional rivalries and switching from support of, to opposition to, the bid of Emperor Go-Daigo to reassert political control, he moved his headquarters directly into Kyoto. One important result of this was the beginning of the "democratization" of Japanese high culture as it was adopted by the daimyo and samurai attending the capital.

While the aesthetic refinement of the warrior classes proceeded, the size and scope of warfare itself grew larger and ever more deadly. Like their warrior contemporaries in Europe with their developing codes of chivalry, daimyo and samurai prided themselves on acting according to a strict system of loyalty and honor, *bushido*, "the way of the warrior." Unlike their European counterparts, however, Japanese warriors were now expected to be not just expert with sword but equally adept with the writing brush. One warrior of the Hosokawa clan, for example, was reputed to have impressed Go-Daigo immensely with his archery skills. When the emperor told him to approach, he drew a brush from his sleeve and commemorated the moment for all assembled with a spontaneous poem. On the martial side of daimyo and samurai life, however, as the book *Hagakure* memorably put it: "The Way of the Warrior is to seek death." The samurai was expected to be unswervingly loyal to his superiors and indeed, the tradition of *seppuku*, or **hara kiri**— ritual suicide—developed originally as a way to show one's "sincerity" and disdain for death and capture on the battlefield. One was also expected to show honor and respect to one's opponents, and tales from the period tell of warriors perfuming their helmets and decorating themselves so that whoever killed them would have a tolerable aesthetic experience amidst the gore of the battlefield.

Dissolution and Reunification

By the fifteenth century, however, these personal touches were giving way to armies increasingly dominated by massed ranks of infantry, in some cases ballooning into the hundreds of thousands of men. By the middle of the following century, the adoption of European-style firearms and accompanying advances in fortification made Japan perhaps the most heavily armed country on Earth. The fluidity of the military situation had radical social consequences as well, and by the mid-sixteenth century, it was increasingly possible for commoners to rise through the ranks and become commanders and even daimyo.

One important reason for these conditions was the chronic instability of the Ashikaga Shogunate. The position was never intended to be hereditary and was always the subject of daimyo intrigue both in Kyoto—where manipulation of the emperor was vital in order to achieve favor—and in the countryside, where power had become increasingly concentrated. In 1467, factional struggles would finally erupt into all-out war, the effects of which would last more than a century. The opening phase of this struggle, the Onin War, lasted ten years and devastated the city of Kyoto, while leaving the imperial court barely functional and the shogunate in tatters. With no real center of power, a bitter struggle among the daimyos continued into the 1570s.

For the Japanese, the period was called *Gekokujo*: "Those below toppling those above." By the mid-sixteenth century, a handful of daimyo began to painfully consolidate their power and secure allies. One such daimyo was Oda Nobunaga, the son of a small landholder who had risen through the ranks to command. The arrival of the first European traders and missionaries at this time brought improvements in firearms that were quickly imitated by Japanese craftsmen. The tendency of the Japanese to link the religion of the new arrivals with their technology (a common occurrence in early Western–East Asian encounters) convinced Nobunaga that many of his men's conversion to Christianity would aid in their fighting ability, particularly against the Buddhist-dominated armies of his opponents. He thus

Oda Nobunaga in Battle. Along with his protégé, Hideyoshi, Oda, like many Japanese leaders during this era of civil war, had risen through the ranks to become a top commander. In this nineteenth-century, idealized *ukiyo-e* print by the prominent artist Yoshitoshi Taiso (1839–1892), Oda's ferocity takes on an almost demonic quality as he pitches an enemy off a building into a raging fire.

Toyotomi Hideyoshi. Portraits of Japanese daimyo and shoguns tend to position them in similar ways, looking to the front left, with stiff officials robes and facial expressions that reflect their dignity. In this 1601 posthumous portrait, Hideyoshi is shown with the signs of his adopted family and the imperial crests around the canopy to denote his role as imperial guardian.

employed newly converted Christian musketeers to secure the area around Kyoto and reduce the Buddhist fortress monastery at Mount Hiei in 1571. In the process, his forces burned more than 300 buildings and killed upwards of 20,000 people. He had largely succeeded in unifying the country when he was assassinated in 1582. His second in command, Toyotomi Hideyoshi, was another commoner who had risen through the ranks. Now he assumed Nobunaga's mantle and systematically brought the remaining daimyo under his sway over the next nine years.

Hideyoshi viewed a foreign adventure at this point as an excellent way to cement the loyalties of the newly subdued daimyo. Moreover, his well-trained, well-equipped, battle-hardened army might prove dangerous to disband. Hence, as early as 1586, he announced in a letter to his mother that he contemplated nothing less than the conquest of China. So in 1592, he set out with a massive expeditionary force, which at its peak numbered over 200,000 men. As we saw in Chapter 6, although his supply lines were harassed unmercifully by the Koreans' armored "turtle ships," the Japanese for a time made good progress up the peninsula. Hideyoshi's battlefield tactics utilized his musketeers in massed ranks using serial firing techniques—in which one rank fired, while another reloaded. European armies would develop a similar manual of arms in the next century that remained dominant in infantry tactics until the mid-nineteenth century. As if in an eerie foreshadowing of another Korean conflict to come, however, the Japanese soon faced a massive Chinese and Korean counterattack and became mired in a bloody stalemate, their guns and tactics barely enough to compensate for the determination and numbers of their enemies. After four more years of negotiation punctuated by bitter fighting, Hideyoshi finally withdrew to Japan.

His stature as a commander and force of personality kept his coalition of daimyo together until his death during his second Korean campaign in 1598. His coalition then broke in two, and a civil war for Hideyoshi's mantle began between Tokugawa

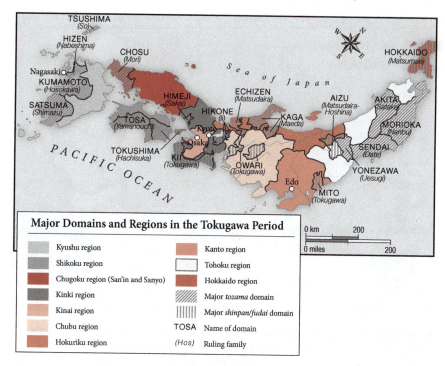

Map 8.2 Major Domains and Regions in the Tokugawa Period

Ieyasu, charismatic leader of the Eastern Coalition of daimyos, and their Western counterparts. In the fall of 1600, the back of the Western Coalition was broken by the Tokugawa victory at the battle of Sekigahara, near Kyoto. Ieyasu, who claimed to be a descendant of the Minamoto clan—the original shoguns—laid claim to the office and was officially invested with it in 1603. His accession marked the beginning of Japan's most peaceful, most secluded, and perhaps most thoroughly regulated period in its long history. Breaking precedent, the Tokugawas would create an avowedly hereditary shogunate that would last until 1867 (see Map 8.2).

THE TOKUGAWA *BAKUFU*

The realm that Tokugawa Ieyasu (1542–1616) had won in the fall of 1600 was one that had been scarred by seemingly endless warfare and social disruption. The daimyo and samurai, their armies swollen to unprecedented size, employed some of the most advanced military technology in the world, but their depredations had broken old loyalties and alliances. The intrusion of European missionaries and merchants, along with their converts and agents, contributed to the social ferment. The brief interlude of unity that had supported Hideyoshi's continental adventures had thoroughly unraveled and indeed been a contributing cause of the civil war that brought Ieyasu to power.

Tokugawa Ieyasu Examines the Head of a Slain Enemy Commander. Although the battle of Sekigahara in 1600 had effectively cemented the Tokugawa family's control over the shogunate, the family of Hideyoshi held out in Osaka Castle, staking their own claim to the title for the next decade and a half. In the fall of 1614, Ieyasu laid siege to the Hideyoshi stronghold and ultimately captured it in June 1615. Here, the celebrated artist Yoshitoshi dramatizes a scene in which the aging Ieyasu inspects the head of the rebel general, Kimura Shigenari, brought to him during the course of the siege.

Ieyasu's assumption of the shogunate in 1603 thus began a process of unparalleled centralization and stabilization. Initially, however, seclusion did not figure among its principles. In fact, under the direction of European advisors, Ieyasu and his son Hidetada (1579–1632) laid plans to build a powerful naval and merchant fleet during their first decade of rule. The most pressing order of business, however, was to erect a system within which to place all the daimyo that would at once reward the loyal and keep a watchful eye on the defeated.

"Tent Government"

The system devised under the Tokugawa *bakufu* ("tent government," referring to the shogun's official status as the emperor's mobile deputy) was called *sankin kotai*, the "rule of alternate attendance." An inner ring of daimyo holdings was annexed by the Tokugawa family and administered by their retainers. All daimyo were then given either *fudai*, or "inner" domains, if they had been allies of the Tokugawa; or *tozama*, "outer" domains, if they had ultimately surrendered to Ieyasu's Eastern Coalition. The shogunate placed its new headquarters in the Tokugawa castle in Edo, the future city of Tokyo. In order to ensure their loyalty, all outer daimyo were required to reside in the capital in alternate years, and return to their domains during the off years. Members of their families were required to stay as permanent hostages in Edo. Daimyo were also required to bring their most important retainers and their households with them during their stays. Almost from the beginning, therefore, the main roads to Edo were the scene of constant daimyo processions. Like the great pilgrimage routes of Islam, Buddhism, and Christianity, they spurred an enormous commerce and array of services to keep the traffic flowing. And like the French nobility a few decades later at Versailles, the daimyo found their power and their purses increasingly depleted by the new order.

Freezing Society

In turning the office of shogun over to his son Hidetada in 1605, Ieyasu made it legally hereditary for the first time. With the possibility of revolt always just under the surface, Ieyasu stayed on as regent and pursued further measures to enhance the stability of the regime. Under his grandson, Iemitsu (1604–1651), most of the characteristic Tokugawa policies in this regard became institutionalized. The shogunate declared that its new officially recognized classes in Japan—daimyo, samurai, peasants, artisans, merchants—would henceforth become hereditary. The Tokugawa adopted Neo-Confucianism (*Shushi gaku*) as the governing social ideology, reworking its long-established precepts of filial piety, models of ethical behavior, social hierarchy, and unswerving loyalty to the government into the new law codes.

Significant differences, however, separated the practice of this system in Japan from others based on it at the same time in China, Korea, and Vietnam. In China and Vietnam, a civil service had long been in place, complete with a graded system of examinations from which the best candidates would be drawn for duty. The situation in Japan was closer to that of Korea, in which the Yangban (see Chapter 6) were already a hereditary aristocracy in the countryside and so monopolized the official classes. The case in Japan, though, differed even further because the samurai and daimyo were now not just a hereditary class of officials, but a military aristocracy as well. Not only was the low position traditionally given the military in Chinese Confucianism totally reversed, but the daimyo and samurai had absolute, unquestioned power of life and death over all commoners. Like their counterparts in China, they were expected to have mastered the Classics and the refined arts of painting, poetry, and calligraphy. But official reports and popular literature are full of accounts of samurai cutting down hapless peasants who failed to bow quickly enough to daimyo processions or commit other infractions, no matter how trivial.

Securing the Place of the Samurai

In order to ensure that the samurai as a class would be free from any serious challenge, the government required them to practice the time-honored skills of swordsmanship, archery, and other forms of individual martial arts. But the rapid development of firearms and their pervasive presence in the realm posed a potent threat to any class whose skills were built entirely around hand-to-hand combat.

Daimyo Procession in Edo. The Tokugawa law of alternate attendance ensured steady traffic on Japan's major thoroughfares leading to and from the capital. In this 1863 depiction, the noted *ukiyo-e* artist Utagawa Hiroshige depicts the passing of a procession at Kasumigaseki in Edo. Note Mount Fuji in the background.

Thus, in a way perhaps unique among the world's nations, the Tokugawa literally "gave up the gun." Tokugawa police conducted searches for forbidden weapons among commoners and destroyed almost the entire stock of the nation's guns. A few museum pieces were kept as curiosities, as were the bronze cannon in some of the Tokugawa seaside forts. Thus, weapons that had been among the most advanced in the world when they were cast in the 1600s were the ones that confronted the foreign ships armed with the first fruits of the Industrial Revolution nearly 250 years later in 1853.

As the shogunate strove to impose peace on the daimyo and bring stability to the populace, it became increasingly anxious to weed out disruptive influences. From the earliest days of European arrivals in Japan, subjects of competing countries and religions had brought their quarrels with them, often involving Japanese as allies or objects of intrigue. The influence of the missionaries on the growing numbers of Japanese Christians—perhaps 200,000 by the 1630s—was especially worrisome to those intent on firmly rooting Neo-Confucian beliefs and ritual among the commoners. Moreover, the bitter duel between Catholic and Protestant missionaries and merchants carried its own set of problems for social stability, especially in the ports where the majority of such activities were carried out.

Tokugawa Seclusion

Ultimately, therefore, missionaries were ordered to leave the country, followed by the merchants. The English and Spanish withdrew in the 1620s, while the Portuguese stayed until 1639. Ultimately, only the Dutch among the Europeans, and Koreans and Chinese in small, controlled numbers were allowed to remain, subject to the pleasure of the shogunate. Furthermore, in 1635, it was ruled that

Dutch Ships in Nagasaki Harbor. This detail from a 1764 Japanese map shows Dutch and Japanese shipping in Nagasaki harbor, the only area permitted the Dutch as the sole Western merchants allowed to trade in Japan. Note the disparity in size between the Dutch and Japanese vessels, a consequence of the Japanese ban on building ocean-going vessels. The fan-shaped area and causeway mark the limits of the Dutch trading zone; they were not permitted in the city itself.

Japanese would be forbidden to leave the islands and no oceangoing ships were to be built. Japanese who left would be considered traitors and executed upon return. Like the Canton system later in Qing China, foreign merchants would be permitted only in designated areas in port cities, and could not bring their families with them. As the only Europeans permitted to stay, the Dutch were chosen because they appeared to be the least affected by the religious bickering that characterized their European counterparts. They were, however, restricted to a tiny island called Dejima (Deshima) built on a landfill in Nagasaki harbor. In return for the privilege, they were required to make yearly reports in person to the shogun's ministers on world events. Over time, the collections of these reports found a small but willing readership among Japanese literati. This "Dutch Learning" and the accounts of Chinese and Korean observers formed the basis of the Japanese view of the outside world as well as insight into the latest scientific developments for over 200 years. Like European learning in Korea and Vietnam, it also provided useful examples for reformers to use in critiquing Tokugawa society.

Much less tolerance was meted out to Japan's Christian community. Dissatisfaction with the new Tokugawa strictures provoked a rebellion at Shimabara just outside Nagasaki in 1637 by converts and disaffected samurai. Many of those trapped in the face of capture and execution by the Tokugawa flung themselves into the volcanic hot springs nearby. Those who were captured were subjected to what their captors understood to be appropriate European-style punishment: instead of being burned at the stake, they were chained together and roasted to death inside a wide ring of fire. Subsequently, remaining missionaries were sometimes crucified upside down, sometimes burned upside down, while suspected converts were given an opportunity to "trample the crucifix" to show they had discarded the new faith. Those who refused to do so were imprisoned or executed. In the end, perhaps 37,000 people were killed. For all their attempts at suppressing the religion, however, tens of thousands continued to practice in secret until Christianity was declared legal again during the reign of Emperor Meiji (r. 1868–1912). Although foreign ships would occasionally attempt to call at Japanese ports, Europeans generally steered clear of the islands. By the middle decade of the nineteenth century, however, the opening of more ports in China for trade, the growth of the whaling industry, and the quest for gold in California would change this situation forever.

What makes them think they need to spread christianity

REUNIFYING RULE

As long as maritime trade with China took ships along a southerly route following the monsoon to Canton, the opportunity or necessity to go to Japan seldom presented itself. By the first decades of the nineteenth century, however, the situation was changing. The vastly expanded legitimate traffic with China and the development of the opium trade increased the volume of shipping closer to Japanese waters. Moreover, the rapid growth of the whaling industry in the northern Pacific increasingly brought European and American ships into waters adjacent to Japan. From their perspective, the need for establishing relations for the disposition of shipwreck survivors, refitting and resupplying whalers, and perhaps trade was therefore becoming ever more urgent.

By the 1840s, the pressure to establish relations with the Tokugawa Shogunate became even more intense for the Western powers with interests in China. The treaty ports created in the wake of the First Opium War included Shanghai, which was rapidly becoming East Asia's chief commercial enclave. Because of its geographical position, major shipping routes to Shanghai now ran directly adjacent to southern Japan. Moreover, the United States' war with Mexico (1846–1848) brought much of the Pacific coast of North America south of the Oregon Territory under the control of the Americans. At the same time, the discovery of gold in California quickly made boomtown San Francisco the premier port for all American trans-Pacific trade. In addition, increasing numbers of Chinese sought passage to the gold fields and the promise of employment in the American West, while the infamous "coolie trade"—recruitment of contract laborers, often by force or fraud-- continually increased human traffic to Cuba and Peru. Plans to open steamship service along the great circle route from San Francisco to Shanghai, and the need for coaling stations to supply it, now threatened to place Japan squarely across the path of this rapidly expanding maritime traffic (see Map 8.3).

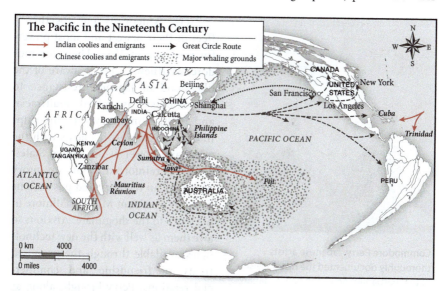

Map 8.3 The Pacific in the Nineteenth Century

The Coming of the "Black Ships"

Scholars have long debated the degree of actual seclusion that Japan experienced between the 1630s and 1850s. It was certainly the case, however, that the Tokugawa were well aware of the humiliation of the Qing at the hands of the British in 1842 and watched nervously as foreign commerce mounted in the Chinese treaty ports. Moreover, by the late 1840s, more than two dozen American whalers and other ships had attempted to put ashore in Japan. Many of these had been damaged or disabled; some sought to repatriate Japanese or Okinawan fishermen who were shipwrecked. As early as 1831, U.S. President Andrew Jackson had directed American vessels to attempt contact with Japan, although this was never accomplished. In 1846, however, an official U.S. naval expedition attempted a landing and contact with Japanese officials at Uraga on Edo Bay. They were gently rebuffed by Japanese guard boats and, under orders not to provoke the Japanese, the vessels left without further incident. A few years later, in 1849, another American warship, the *Preble*, demanded and received the return of some shipwrecked sailors held prisoner in Nagasaki.

As the pressure increased on Japan to open its ports, divided counsels plagued the shogunate. The influential Mito School, long exposed to "Dutch Learning," feared the growing military and technological power of the Europeans and Americans, and advocated a military response to any attempt at opening the country. Others, looking at the situation in China, believed that negotiation was the only possible way for Japan to avoid invasion. The pressure increased markedly as the Americans began preparations to try again, with the Russians also preparing an expedition and the British rumored to be contemplating one as well. Armed with this information, the Dutch informed the shogunate of the Americans' intentions and advised them to sign a treaty if it was offered—but only after signing one with the Netherlands first.

Commodore Perry. Japanese artists thoroughly documented the historic visit of the "barbarian" American fleet to Japan. The ships themselves attracted much attention to their armament, rigging and steam power, while the officers and crew were sometimes depicted as demonic and sometimes, as in this portrait of Perry himself, more or less faithfully.

The Americans put together a fleet of their newest and most powerful warships in 1852. Their commodore, Matthew C. Perry, aware of the likelihood of Japanese resistance to his embassy, assembled multiracial and multi-ethnic crews for his ships in order to impress his hosts with the reach and power of the United States. This was reinforced by the inventory of American territory and possessions listed by President Millard Fillmore in his letter to the shogunate. Anxious to awe them as well with the new technologies available through the proposed treaty of friendship and commercial relations, Perry brought along as presents a telegraph set and a model railroad, both of which proved immediately popular. When negotiations flagged, Perry's men demonstrated the utility of the telegraph by challenging Japanese couriers to beat the speed of the device in delivering messages. The shogun's men also gleefully amused themselves aboard the miniature train, smacking the engine and its operator with their fans to make it go faster. So began a fascination with both technologies in Japan, the legacy of which is Japan's present centrality in telecommunications and the famous "bullet train."

The expedition's interpreter, Manjiro Nakahama—whom we met in the opening vignette of this chapter—worked behind the scenes to convince the shogunate to establish diplomatic and commercial relations. As for the shogunate, spies and sketch artists thoroughly documented the design, rigging, and armament of the ships, although the workings of their steam power were not completely understood. Perry's departing comments about returning with more ships in a year or so while the Japanese contemplated acceptance of the treaty, however, were understood all too well. Thus, on Perry's return trip in 1854 with his enhanced fleet of "black ships," as the Japanese dubbed them, the Treaty of Kanagawa was signed, Japan's first with an outside power. Like China, Japan had now entered the treaty port era.

Restoring the Emperor

The widely differing attitudes toward foreign contact expressed within the shogunate were reflected among the daimyo and samurai as well. The treaty with the Americans, and the rapid conclusion of treaties with other foreign governments, tended to reinforce anti-foreignism among many of the warrior elite, while emphasizing the weakness of the Tokugawa to resist further demands.

Moreover, the new cultural contacts taking place in treaty ports like Yokohama and Nagasaki hardened positions and raised tensions further. Many samurai felt that dramatic gestures were called for to rouse the country to action. Hence, as with the Boxers later in China, they attacked foreigners and even assassinated Tokugawa officials in an effort to precipitate anti-foreign conflict. By 1863, a movement aimed at driving out the Tokugawa and restoring imperial rule had coalesced around the samurai of two southern domains, Satsuma and Choshu. Adopting the slogan *sonno joi* ("Honor the emperor, expel the barbarian!") members of this so-called *Satcho* (*Sat*suma and *Cho*shu) clique challenged the shogunate and fought a smoldering Restoration War, which by the end of 1867 forced the Tokugawa to capitulate. In short order, the new regime moved to the Tokugawa capital of Edo and renamed it *Tokyo* ("Eastern Capital").

Emperor Meiji. In this portrait of the emperor, probably done in the late 1870's or early 1880's, he is depicted as robust and decisive, as well as modern in his European style military uniform, sash, and medals. His carefully trimmed Van Dyke beard also reflects the style of the time among many Western leaders and men of importance.

The new emperor, 15-year-old Mutsuhito, took the reign name of *Meiji* ("Enlightened Rule") and quickly moved to make good on its promise. Supported by a group of able advisors, the **genro**, the throne issued the Charter Oath of April 1868, in which it declared that "all matters [would be] decided by public discussion. . . . [E]vil customs of the past shall be broken off . . . [and] knowledge shall be sought throughout the world so as to strengthen the foundations of imperial rule." An initial constitution was also promulgated that spelled out in more detail how the new government was to be set up.

From Feudalism to Nationalism

Despite Tokugawa measures to create a centralized system run by warrior bureaucrats, Japan was still dominated by regional loyalties and fealty to the daimyo of one's *han*, or feudal domain. Although the samurai held the status and performed the functions of government officials, their direct loyalty was to their daimyo, whose lands were held, in theory at least, in trust for the shogunate. Thus, government centralization was indirect and dependent on the loyalty of the daimyo. The foreign threat and restoration of the emperor provided the opportunity and necessity to forge a more thoroughgoing national unification, particularly since it had been dissident daimyo and samurai who had begun the movement to remove the old order. The new government therefore quickly set about dismantling the feudal *han* and replacing them with a centralized provincial structure; the daimyo were replaced by governors responsible to the central government and the emperor; and the samurai were disbanded, given stipends, and encouraged to form business enterprises or to teach. From 1871 to 1873, a long-term diplomatic mission of high Japanese officials led by Iwakura Tomomi (1825–1883) toured the United States and Europe, carefully studying their governments, society, and culture, and evaluating aspects that might be of practical advantage to the new Japanese state. Thus, in place of the samurai, a new conscript army was organized modeled after that of Germany—acknowledged as Europe's premier land power following its defeat of France in the Franco-Prussian War and final unification into an empire in 1870–1871. A navy modeled on Great Britain's, as the West's leading maritime power, was also established. The new order was to be held together by a national system of compulsory education modeled on the school systems in the United States, although in the Japanese variant, loyalty to the emperor and state was to be carefully nurtured at every level.

Amidst these dizzying changes, some senior advisors advocated an aggressive foreign policy in order to create a buffer zone around Japan. For these men, most prominently former samurai Saigo Takamori (1827–1877), Korea, which so far had resisted Western attempts to end its seclusion, was the obvious place to start. Saigo offered to sacrifice himself in order to create an incident in Korea that would justify Japanese action to "open" the so-called Hermit Kingdom. The Meiji court and inner circle, however, favored restraint. Instead, Japan contented itself with the expedition against Taiwan in 1873–1874 and the purchase of the Ryukyu Islands in 1879 (see Chapter 5).

The social turmoil at home and the tempering of Japan's ambitions abroad stirred discontent among many former samurai. In their view, Japan had abandoned its true character and was rapidly becoming a second-rate copy of the Western countries, fueled by greed for money, lack of honor, and international cowardice. In 1876, such sentiments helped spark a revolt among dissident samurai. Saigo, an imposing giant of a man much admired by the samurai, was persuaded to join them. Their movement, however, was crushed with brutal efficiency by the new modern conscript army of Yamagata Aritomo (1838–1922), and Saigo himself committed suicide in April 1877. Although discontent at the direction of Japanese modernization—by peasant populists as well as elite traditionalists—continued to fester throughout the nineteenth century, it never again reached the level of open rebellion.

The Meiji Constitution and Political Life

Although the Charter Oath and constitution of 1868 were instituted with considerable success, a debate had already begun among the *genro* concerning the liberalization of representative government in Japan. In 1881, the emperor approved a plan whereby Ito Hirobumi (1844–1909) and several senior colleagues would

(A)   (B)

The Old Order and the New. Although both Saigo Takamori and Yamagata Aritomo fought as samurai in the Restoration War of the 1860s, their paths soon radically diverged. Saigo, (A) frustrated at the course of early Meiji policies, was recruited by disaffected samurai who rose in rebellion in 1876. Yamagata became the "Von Moltke of Japan," as photograph (B) proclaims. He played a leading role in creating Japan's modern conscript army, which crushed the Samurai rebellion and led to Saigo's suicide in 1877. Although perhaps on the wrong side of history, Saigo remained an object of admiration for his uncompromising stand and was immortalized in this statue by Takamura Koun.

launch a painstaking study of the constitutional governments of the United States, Great Britain, France, Germany, and other countries, to see what aspects of them might be suitable for Japan's needs. The **Meiji Constitution**, as it came to be called, was promulgated in 1889 and remained in force until supplanted by the constitution created during the Allied occupation of Japan after World War II.

While borrowing elements from the U.S. and British models, Ito's constitution drew most heavily from that of Germany. Much of it was also aimed at preserving the traditions that Ito and the *genro* most valued. Chief among these was the concept of *kokutai,* the "national polity." In this view, Japan was unique among nations because of its unbroken line of emperors and the singular familial and spiritual relationship between the emperor and his people. The sovereignty of the country was placed in the person of the emperor as the embodiment of *kokutai*; the emperor's Privy Council, the Army and Navy, and the Ministers of State were answerable directly to him. There was also a bicameral parliamentary body called the Diet, with an upper House of Peers and a lower House of Representatives. Like the House of Lords in Great Britain, Japan's House of Peers consisted of members of the nobility; the representatives were elected by the people. The primary purpose of the Diet in this arrangement was to vote on matters of financing, deliberate on the everyday issues of governance, and provide advice and consent to the Privy Council, Ministry of State, and Imperial Court.

As for the people themselves, fifteen articles spelled out "The Rights and Duties of Subjects." Duties included liability for taxes and service in the military, while the rights enumerated were similar to those found in European and American constitutions: the right to hold office; guarantees against search and seizure; the right to trial; the right to property; freedom of religion, speech, and petition. All these, however, were qualified by such phrases as "unless provided by law," leaving the door open for the government to invoke extraordinary powers during national emergencies.

As constitutional government began to be enacted in the 1890s, the factional debates among senior advisors naturally began to attract followers among the Diet members and their supporters. In the preceding decades, there had been political parties, but their membership was limited and they were seen by many as illegitimate because of their potential opposition to the government. Now, two major parties came to the fore by the turn of the century. The *Kenseito*, the Progressive or Liberal, Party had its roots in the work of Ito's colleague, Okuma Shigenobu, in 1882. It later was reestablished as the *Minseito*. The more powerful party during this time was the *Seiyukai*, or Constitutional Government Party, founded by Ito and his followers in 1900. Generally associated with the government and *zaibatsu* (cartels), the Seiyukai dominated Japanese politics in the era before World War I; after World War II, its adherents coalesced into Japan's present Liberal Democratic Party.

Becoming an Imperial Power

As we saw in Chapters 5 and 6, rising tensions between Japan and China over the disposition of Korea ultimately led to the Sino-Japanese War of 1894–1895. The issue had been temporarily held in abeyance by the Treaty of Tianjin (signed in 1885), but continuing difficulties arising from the instability of the Korean government, feuding pro-Chinese and pro-Japanese factions within it, and the Tonghak, or "Eastern Learning," movement, kept the region a volatile one. Although the rebellion had been suppressed in the 1860s, the forced opening of Korea to trade in the following decade, and the constant intrigues of the Qing and Japanese surrounding the Yi court in succeeding decades, brought about the movement's revival in the 1890s.

As we observed, Japan's successful showing in the war surprised and alarmed the Western powers in the region. The Triple Intervention of 1895, however, particularly the role of Russia in acquiring the leasehold for Liaodong in 1898, put that empire on a collision course with Japanese aspirations on the Asian mainland. Hence, both Japan and Russia became intensely interested in acquiring concessions in Manchuria. For Russia, it was vital to build rail links from the **Trans-Siberian Railway** to their new outposts of Port Arthur and Dairen or Dalian in Liaodong and to extend the line across Manchuria to Vladivostok on the Pacific. As the twentieth century began, they pressured the Chinese into allowing them the rights to build the Chinese Eastern Railway across Manchuria

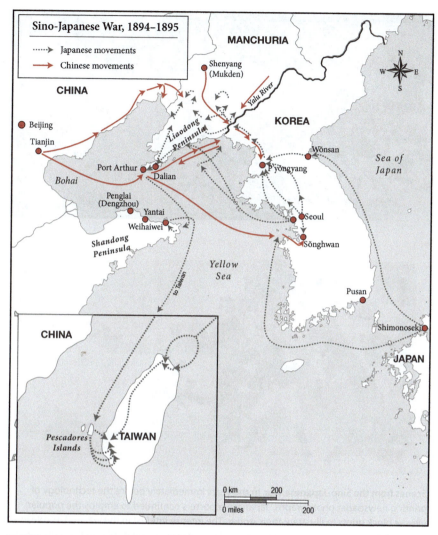

Map 8.4 The Sino-Japanese War

and the South Manchurian Railway to Port Arthur, with a vital junction at Mukden, known today as Shenyang (see Map 8.4).

For the Japanese, the victory over China had reversed centuries of seeing themselves in that empire's cultural shadow. Like their Western counterparts, many Japanese began to refer to the Chinese as "semi-civilized," and to see them in Social Darwinist terms as being increasingly "unfit" in the struggle for international survival. More important for the longer term was that the Japanese began to view themselves as the "natural" leaders of Asia, whose role was to unite the continent to resist further Western penetration and even to roll back previous Western gains. Such ideas would dominate Japan's ideology and strategic thinking until the end of World War II.

Scenes from the Sino-Japanese War. In the years immediately before the technology of printing newspaper photographs, Japanese reporters continued to employ the popular *ukiyo-e* block prints to illustrate their stories. The intense interest in the war and its role in stoking Japanese pride in modernization and nationalism are on display in the print above depicting the assault on Pyongyang. Note the "modern" technology of the searchlight in the upper illustration and the Western-style uniforms of the Japanese troops as they resolutely charge Qing forces in their old-fashioned tunics and turbans.

ECONOMY, SOCIETY, AND FAMILY

The period from 1250 to 1450 saw cycles of expansion in overseas commerce with colonies of Japanese merchants—and often, Japanese pirates—operating in the Philippines, Java, and Malacca as well as Korea and China. Through their wares, the daimyo and samurai became increasingly sophisticated consumers of luxury goods such as silks, jade, porcelain, lacquerware, rare woods, and books and paper. As the early ports, market towns, regional capitals, and, by the sixteenth century, castle towns, grew, Japanese craftsmen became adept at imitating and refining Chinese crafts, in some cases surpassing the quality of the originals. Moreover, a growing and increasingly diverse middle class of merchants, artisans, actors, dancers, *sake* brewers, ship builders, and others organized into trade guilds (*za*) all partook of such luxury items as their prosperity advanced. The increased demand for capital among them spurred a monetization of the economy and the beginnings of banking and credit systems. Indeed, some scholars have cited these developments, especially as they continued during Japan's exclusionary Tokugawa interval, as predisposing Japan toward a relatively easy transition to an export-driven capitalist-cartel economy during the Meiji period and beyond.

Agriculture, Population, and Commerce

Most of this would not have been possible without dramatic increases in food production and its effects on the demographics of the islands. The period from 1250 to 1600 saw a vast increase in both intensive cultivation of Japan's limited arable land and the importation of a host of new crops to multiply its productivity. As it had throughout East Asia, the widespread use of fast-ripening Champa rice strains from Southeast Asia in southern Honshu, Kyushu, and Shokoku vastly enhanced stocks of this staple. In Kyushu, it allowed three crops a year; in other areas, the wet paddy fields it required allowed dry raised beds for vegetables to be made from the soil taken out of the paddies. At the same time, the introduction of the Chinese "dragon chain pump" allowed for easy small-scale irrigation. Finally, a triple-cropping system consisting of buckwheat in winter, wheat in spring, and rice during the monsoon, with vegetables grown on the raised beds in between fields, allowed an average family to sustain itself on only a few acres of land.

If one factors in the use of terracing and dry rice cultivation in more marginal areas, and the introduction of oranges, grapes, and tea—as well as the opening of northern lands acquired from the Ainu— the leaps in population seem almost inevitable. From an estimated population of about 5 million in 1100, a doubling occurred, perhaps as early as 1300; by 1450, it was on its way to doubling again. By various estimates, Japan may have had as many as 33 million people in 1720. Already by the early seventeenth century, families were limiting their size, and there were signs that the land was nearing the limit of what it could support.

Indications of rapid population growth were even more dramatic in the cities. By 1750, Japan had become the most urbanized society on earth. Edo itself reached a million people, making it arguably the world's largest city. Osaka and Kyoto were both approaching 400,000, and perhaps as much as 10 percent of Japan's population lived in cities above 10,000. In a way, such explosive growth is even more remarkable, given that the Tokugawa placed strict curbs on travel within their realms: for example, commoners were not to leave their home districts without permission from the local authorities. On the other hand, as we have seen, the law of alternate attendance ensured an immense and growing t fic in and out of the major cities along the major routes into Edo. The vas of services required to keep the system going aided urban and suburba and also had the effect of spreading the wealth down to the urban merchants, artisans, entertainers, bathhouse proprietors and even refuse collectors.

As we have noted above, the various Tokugawa policies aimed at stabilizing the country politically and socially had the unanticipated effect of spurring the economy. A number of factors contributed to this in addition to the forced movement of the daimyo and their retinues in alternate years. The Tokugawa tax structure set quotas in rice for each village, rather than for individuals, and left the individual daimyos responsible for remitting these to the capital. Thus, an immense traffic in bulk rice further spurred the carrying trade along the roads and in the coastal waters. In addition to guaranteeing provisions for the cities, the need to convert rice to cash for the treasury greatly contributed to building a banking and credit infrastructure. Indeed, the practice of merchant bankers advancing credit to wholesalers against the coming rice crops created what some scholars have called an early kind of futures market. The progress of the famous Mitsui *zaibatsu*, or cartel, of the nineteenth and twentieth centuries followed such a route, starting in 1670 as dry goods merchants and gradually moving into the position of sake brewers, and bankers for the shogunate.

The tastes of the three largest cities—Edo, with its high concentration of the wealthy and well-connected; Kyoto, with the large retinue of the imperial household; and Osaka., the chief port—created a huge demand for ever more sophisticated consumer goods and services. Such enterprises as sake brewing, wholesaling dried and prepared foods, bathhouses, and managing large studios of artisans all became big businesses. Even the import and export trades, slowed to a relative trickle by government regulations, proved quite lucrative for the few engaged in them. Books, porcelains, lacquerware, and objets d'art were exchanged for Japanese specie. Indeed, the vibrancy of Japanese urban life and a burgeoning middle class created what scholars have sometimes called the "democratization of taste." That is, what was once the strict province of the court, daimyo, and samurai was now widely available to anyone who had the money and interest to afford it. Moreover, the new moneyed classes were also creating new directions in the arts and entertainment.

Late Tokugawa and Early Meiji Society and Economics

By the mid-eighteenth century, there were signs of tension among the aims of the government in ensuring peace and stability, the dynamism of the internal economy, and the boom in population. Like the debate on whether China was ~~~ht in a so-called high-level equilibrium trap a century later, some scholars ~~~ approaching the limit of the ability of the land to sup-
~~~n's population remained remarkably steady from the
~~~ the latter nineteenth. Repeated signs of creeping rural
~~~al unrest manifested themselves, however, and were
~~~ors. Inflation in commodity prices ran ahead of efforts
~~~ues, squeezing those like the samurai on fixed incomes
~~~ keep rural families small enough to subsist on their
~~~ frequency of infanticide. Compounding such problems

were large-scale famines in 1782 and 1830. By the early nineteenth century, there was an increasing perception that the government was gradually losing its ability to care for the populace.

The realization of their vulnerability to foreign coercion following Perry's visits quickly induced the shogunate to study the industrially advanced countries of Europe and the U.S. As early as 1860, for example, they sent an embassy to America in which the participants—including the future journalist Fukuzawa Yukichi (1835–1901)—were expected to keep diaries of everything they saw of note. Even during the last days of the Tokugawa regime, Japanese entrepreneurs were already experimenting with building Western-style steamships, arms, and production techniques.

When the Meiji government began its economic reforms, its overall strategy included elements that still mark Japanese policy today. The first was to make sure that ownership, insofar as possible, would remain in Japanese hands. The second was that, taking its cue from the success of the leading commercial nations of the West, Japan would develop its exports to the utmost while attempting to keep imports to a minimum. Thus throughout the latter nineteenth century, Japanese export goods were uniformly stamped with the words "Product of the Industrial Promotion Board." Japanese entrepreneurship also received an enormous boost from the cashing out of the samurai. Although many of the new former warriors found anything to do with commerce distasteful, some took to heart the government's injunction that starting economic enterprises was a patriotic duty.

Japanese Embassy to the U.S. in 1860. Unlike the Chinese, who vacillated for a number of years before sending a mission abroad, the Tokugawa Shogunate moved quickly to send representatives to the United States. The mission precipitated a good deal of interest in the embassy in America, while the delegates themselves noted what they could glean from a nation on the brink of sectional conflict. This official portrait of the delegates was taken by Matthew Brady, whose photographs of the Civil War over the next several years became iconic images of that conflict.

Map 8.5 Industrializing Japan, ca. 1870–1906

By the end of the century, Japan's industrial statistics were impressive by any standards: coal production had increased to six times its 1860 base; iron, copper and other mining industries expanded at a similar rate—but still could not keep pace with Japan's industrial needs. By the turn of the century, Japan already needed to import much of its raw material, a situation that has continued to this day (see Map 8.5).

Not surprisingly, families with long-standing connections to capital swiftly moved to unite their enterprises to gain market share or even monopoly power in some sectors. The Mitsui Company, as we saw, used their extensive brewing, and later banking, profits to fund a host of other enterprises, soon becoming one of Japan's largest industrial concerns. Similarly, the Mitsubishi Company expanded from coastal shipping to dominating the traffic from Chinese ports to Japan, buying up foreign steamers and routes along the way. From a dominant shipping concern, Mitsubishi moved into manufacturing—later creating military vehicles and the most successful Japanese aircraft of World War II, the famous "Zero"—as well as a popular line of cars sold the world over today. The encouragement of the government and the cooperation of social networks among elites in finance and industry led to the creation of a number of cartels called *zaibatsu*. By the end of the nineteenth century, *zaibatsu* would control nearly all major Japanese industries.

PATTERNS UP-CLOSE

Japan's Transformation through East Asian Eyes

The Chinese writer and minor official, Li Gui (1842–1903), achieved some modest fame and considerable influence among Qing self-strengtheners following the publication of his *A New Account of a Trip Around the Globe* in 1878. Li had been sent to report on the American Centennial Exposition and used the opportunity to continue his journey from Philadelphia to London, Paris, Marseilles, the Suez Canal, Aden, Galle (in Sri Lanka), Singapore, Saigon, and Hong Kong, before returning to Shanghai. While at the Centennial, he spent considerable time studying the Japanese exhibit, which was directly across the aisle from that of China. Even before this, however, the initial leg of his journey had taken him to Japan on a Mitsubishi Company steamer. While awaiting the American trans-Pacific liner there, he visited Nagasaki, Kobe, Osaka, Yokohama, and Tokyo and was able to meet with resident Chinese and inspect items of interest to China's reformers. Li took his first train ride in Japan; observed telegraphs and rickshaws; visited museums, customs houses, and Buddhist shrines. In the following excerpt, he talks about what he sees as the great strides and shortcomings of Japan's approach to "civilization and enlightenment" (see below) and comments with a touch of frustration and envy on Japan's greater freedom from foreign control:

> As for the school buildings, post offices, telegraph offices, mines, and steamship companies, all of these are run according to Western methods with Japanese officers in charge of them. They have paid particular attention to officials and posts, with the result that the quality of these is almost comparable to those of Western countries. . . .

> There are also practices [however] that are unsightly and offensive. The boat-men, carters, and rickshaw pullers of the land gener-ally leave their lower bodies naked in plying their trades, and wear only a white strip of cloth . . . wrapped through their buttocks. Words are inadequate to describe it. I hear that no trousers are worn among the gentlemen and merchants, either, but that they wrap themselves instead in folds of cloth. The women and children do so as well. A high degree of clean-liness is part of their char-acter and they must bathe every day. Yet dozens of people, men and women, all bathe together in bathhouses as a matter of course. The al-leyways on the side streets have tubs set up for men and women to take turns using.

The Machine Age Moves into Japanese Domestic Crafts. In Japan's new dedication to "civilization and enlightenment" and "Western Science and Eastern Ethics," the rapid societal changes are plainly evident in this 1890 lithograph of a Japanese seamstress on her sewing machine. The older artistic sensibility of *ukiyo-e* printing emerges even as the woman is dressed in Western style and using up-to-date technology—which is decorated with a formalized demonic figure on its side panel.

(continued)

Fearing that they will be made a laughingstock by foreigners, the government has now ordered the practice discontinued. Their efforts so far, however, have been to no avail since this is a long-standing custom and they must necessarily proceed slowly. . . .

This evening a [Chinese] company manager named Liang Peilin invited us for a drink. Mr. Liang said that Yokohama's merchants and people number about forty thousand, with a Chinese population of about sixteen hundred. . . . The foreign business houses number several dozen families, more or less, and there are goods piled up like mountains. They mostly import foreign commodities and export brass, cloisonné, lacquerware, tea, and antiques. There are, however, no merchants who traffic principally in opium, like the firm of Sassoon in China, a great English trader who specializes in it. This is because the Japanese strictly forbid the smoking of it and users are severely punished, so their nationals do not dare violate the prohibition. Although the punishments are strict and impartial, one can also see that the laws accord with the wishes of the people. What a pity we Chinese do not know when we will be able to extinguish this poisonous flame!

(From Desnoyers, *A Journey to the East*, pp. 253, 256–257)

Railroads and Telegraphs

The rapid development of railroads and telegraphs was one of the most stunning transformations of the Meiji era. The Japanese pursued these devices with an enthusiasm scarcely paralleled anywhere else in the world. Even today, Japan's fabled "bullet train" remains the standard for high-speed ground transportation, while companies such as Sony and Motorola continue to dominate electronic communications markets. By the mid-1870s, Japan had in place a trunk railroad line paralleling the main coastal road and several branches to major cities in the interior. Although Westerners found Japanese trains quaint—along with the custom of leaving one's clogs on the platform before boarding the cars (as one would before entering a room)—they were efficient and marked a trend for railroad building wherever Japanese went. Similarly, telegraph—and by the end of the century, telephone—lines were swiftly strung between the major cities and towns, followed by undersea cables to the Asian mainland and North America. By 1895, Japan was estimated to have over 2,000 miles of private and government railroads in operation and over 4,000 miles of telegraph wires in place.

Family Structure

Outside the court, the moderating institution for commoners, and particularly women, was the Buddhist monastery. As in China and Korea, the monasteries provided havens for women and men who did not marry or had fled bad

The Coming of the Railroad. Japanese enthusiasm for the railroad has been continuous from the shogun's representatives' first ride on the model train Perry brought to the "bullet train" of today. Japan's early railroads provided considerable material for *ukiyo-e* artists of the late nineteenth century as well. In this print, the new Ueno station on the Ueno-Nakasendo-Tokyo Railway is shown with small commuter trains arriving and departing.

marriages. They provided enough education to read the *sutras*, thus helping to increase literacy. They also provided important avenues of political power as large landholders, innkeepers, peacekeepers, and advisors. A famous example was the monastery at Mount Hiei above Kyoto, whose monks provided guidance to the court for centuries.

As in China, Korea, and Vietnam, the family life of commoners was mostly governed by a mix of filial piety, nuclear and extended family and clan relations, and the drive to enhance the position of all these through marriage. Such conditions were eventually regulated further under the Tokugawa Shogunate's strict family codes enforced by the shogun's local officials.

Life in rural areas underwent certain changes as well. As they had with the military houses, the Tokugawa promulgated rules for the comportment of families and their individual members. Like the parish churches in Europe, each local Buddhist temple was to keep the registers of the villagers in its district. Weddings, funerals, travel, rents, taxes, and so forth were subject to official permission either through the village headman or the samurai holding a position equivalent to a magistrate. Within these strictures, however, and subject to the hereditary occupation laws, families, clans, and villages were relatively autonomous.

This was especially true within rural families, where men, women, and children commonly worked together on their plots. Although the "inner domain," so central to Neo-Confucian thought as the strict province of women, retained a good deal of that character, there were also any number of areas that served to mitigate it. Men, for example, routinely helped in the everyday tasks of child rearing.

As late as the 1860s, foreign observers reported watching rural groups of men minding infants while their wives were engaged in some collective task. Women in cities and larger villages routinely ran businesses, especially those involved in entertainment. Indeed, the women of the famous **geisha** houses, owned and run by women, were renowned for their skills, education, wit, and refinement. Even on a more humble level, women ran bathhouses, taverns, restaurants, and retail establishments of all sorts. Interestingly, by the eighteenth century, merchants increasingly utilized the spinning and weaving talents of rural and semi-rural women in parceling out the various steps in textile manufacturing to them—a Japanese version of the English "putting out system" immediately preceding the Industrial Revolution.

"Civilization and Enlightenment"

With the coming of the reunification of the government during the Meiji period came the heyday of government-managed social experimentation. Like the Chinese "self-strengtheners," the *genro* sought to use new foreign technologies and institutions to strengthen the state against further foreign intrusion. Japan's planners, however, proved more unified, systematic, and determined in their efforts and, unlike their Chinese counterparts, had the full backing of the imperial court. Thus, Japan's proclaimed goals of using "Western science and Eastern ethics" in the service of "civilization and enlightenment" were seen as the primary tools in asserting eventual equality with the Western imperial powers and rolling back Japan's unequal treaties.

In addition to creating an industrial base and a constitutional government, Japan's rulers also attempted to curb practices in Japan that were believed to offend foreign sensibilities. Bath houses, for example, were now required to have separate entrances for men and women, and pleasure quarters were restricted in areas near foreign enclaves; meat-eating was even encouraged in largely Buddhist Japan, resulting in the new dish called *sukiyaki*. In the boldest experiment of all, the government mandated the use of Western dress for men and women, accompanied by a propaganda campaign depicting the advantages of this "modern" and "civilized" clothing. Criticism from a variety of quarters, however, including many Westerners, ultimately forced the government to relent and make the new dress optional.

In the same vein, traditional restrictions on women were altered. Although the home remained the primary domain for women, as it does even today, women were far more often seen in public. Concubines were now accorded the same rights as wives. Courtesans and prostitutes were no longer legally considered servants. Among elites, the fad of following all things Western planted to some degree Victorian European standards of family decorum. More far-reaching, however, was the role of the new education system. Even before the Meiji Restoration, Japan had one of the highest levels of pre-industrial literacy in the world—40 percent for males and 15 percent for females. With the coming of compulsory public education, literacy would become nearly universal and the upsurge in specialized women's education created entire new avenues of employment for women.

This same trend toward emancipation was evident among the rural population. The formal class barriers between peasants and samurai were eliminated, although informal deference to elites continued. In addition, some barriers between ordinary Japanese and outcast groups such as the Eta were also reduced. During the latter part of the nineteenth century, aided by better transportation, improved crops, maximum utilization of marginal lands, and the opening up of Hokkaido for development, Japan became the most intensely farmed nation in the world. Japan's already well-developed fishing industry contributed mightily by introducing commercial fish-based fertilizers that boosted yields enormously. The result was that although Japan's population increased to 40 million by 1890, it was a net exporter of food until the turn of the century.

RELIGION, CULTURE, AND INTELLECTUAL LIFE

Although most of the major Buddhist schools had been established in Japan by the time of the Kamakura Shogunate, two more recent arrivals deserve mention here because of their influence. As we saw in Chapter 3, the first was Nichiren (1222–1282), who preached a Japan-centered Buddhism. Japan, he believed, because of its unique history and centrality in the Buddhist world, had become the repository of "true" Buddhism in the present decadent age and must be defended at all cost—a view he believed confirmed by the miraculous Japanese deliverance from the Mongols.

Zen, Tea, and Aesthetics

The other influence was the practice of Zen. Zen seeks to achieve *satori*, a flash of enlightenment signaling the recovery of one's Buddha nature. Everyone's path to this is different, so one must follow the instructions of an experienced master rather than engage in prolonged scriptural study. Zen practitioners seek to open themselves to enlightenment by humble, repetitious tasks, contemplating paradoxes (*koan*), and in some schools, sitting in meditation (*zazen*).

All these practices can be useful to a warrior. Endless drilling with bow and arrow or sword to the point of instinct certainly refines one's martial talents. Such an approach is equally useful in painting, poetry, and calligraphy, where a distinct Zen style of spontaneous, minimalist art suggesting the true inner nature of subject and artist is still a vital area of Japanese aesthetics today. Another area is **Noh** theater, a highly abstract form using little scenery and strictly prescribed movements to depict historical or mythological subjects.

One final area in which Zen permeated the life of the warrior classes was in the use of tea. Introduced from China by the Zen monk Eisai (1141–1215), tea drinking in Japan became widely adopted as an aid to discipline and meditation among monks in the twelfth century. Soon, however, it became quite popular among the upper classes, and its presentation was ultimately refined into the ritual of the tea ceremony. Here, inside the tea house where all were equal regardless of rank, under the movements prescribed by the sixteenth-century tea master Sen-no Rikyu, host and guest were to treat the tiniest details of their encounter as if they were sharing their last moments together on Earth. Since the ceremony was a popular preparation for battle among daimyo and samurai, this was often the case.

The Arts and Literature

As we saw in Chapter 3, Chinese artistic genres strongly influenced the choices of their Japanese counterparts in painting, poetry, and calligraphy.. Here Japanese sensibilities often tended toward the ideal of "purposeful imperfection," in the minimalist design of tea houses and the primitivism of *raku* ware. While the *zen* aesthetic of minimalism appealed to the elite, those pursuing decorative arts often went in the opposite direction, favoring bright colors, often extravagant detail, and uninhibited use of gold and silver washes. Prime examples of such techniques come from the sixteenth and seventeenth century studios of the Kano family, whose screens decorated the castle interiors of Japan's leading daimyos.

(A)

(B)

Landscape Painting and Raku Ware. The fashion for Zen-influenced monochrome, minimalist painting [A] remained a staple throughout the period of the shogunates. Like similar Chinese and Korean types, the artist attempted to suggest the inner essence of the subject at hand, often by means of certain stock elements such as misty mountains, jagged hills, lone pines, and a watercourse. In ceramics, Japanese potters often copied Chinese types, but they also perfected a style of "imperfection" to more closely suggest the way nature works. In raku ware, [B] the chemistry of the clays and glazes was to express itself spontaneously in the kiln in a manner suggesting "primitive" pottery.

As with so many things in Japanese cultural history, major styles of painting, poetry, and calligraphy continued to flourish among the daimyo and samurai, while exerting an increasing pull on the tastes of the new middle classes. Indeed, Zen-influenced monochrome painting, the ideals of tea championed by Rikyu-sen, the austere Noh theater, and the abstract principles of interior design and landscape gardening were carefully preserved and popularized until they became universally recognized as "Japanese."

Bunraku, Noh, Kabuki, and Ukiyo-e

While the "high" arts were becoming increasingly democratized, they coexisted with new forms, some adapting aspects of these earlier forms, others conceived as mass entertainment. Among the former was the development of *bunraku*, the elaborate puppet theater still popular in Japan today. Bunraku puppets, perhaps one third life-size, generally took three puppeteers to manipulate. Their highly facile movements and facial expressions staged against a black backdrop to conceal the actions of their handlers readily allowed the audience to suspend their disbelief and proved a highly effective media with which to popularize the older Noh plays. But renowned playwrights soon wrote special works for these theaters as well. The most revered was Chikamatsu Monzaemon (1653–1724), who skillfully transferred the tragically noble sentiments of the best Noh works into contemporary themes. The fatal tension between love and social obligation, for example, made his *Double Suicide at Sonezaki* wildly popular with Edo audiences. His most famous work, *The Forty-Seven Ronin*, was written in 1706 and based on a 1703 incident in which a daimyo was killed by a political opponent, leaving his samurai as **ronin**, masterless. Out of loyalty to their dead daimyo, the samurai kill his assassin in full knowledge that their lives will then be forfeited to the authorities; they stoically go on to pay the ultimate price.

Originally written as a *bunraku* work, *The Forty-Seven Ronin* was adapted a few decades later as a work for **kabuki**, the other great mass entertainment art of Tokugawa Japan. Originally a satirical and explicitly bawdy form of theater, whose plots often involved satirizing the behavior of foreigners, the government banned women actors from appearing in it, hoping to sever kabuki's association with prostitution. Female impersonators as actors continued its risqué reputation, however, while more serious works also drew immense crowds to the pleasure districts, where the theaters were by law segregated. Kabuki remained by far the most popular Japanese mass entertainment and, interestingly, given the medium's off-color reputation, *The Forty-Seven Ronin* remained the most frequently performed play throughout the Tokugawa period.

The era also marked the golden age of the powerfully brief poetic form of **haiku**, the most famous practitioner of which was the renowned Matsuo Basho (1644–1694). As a poet, he used a dozen pen names; he took "Basho" from the banana plant he especially liked in his yard. In poems like "Old Battlefield," the

The "Floating World." During the late seventeenth century, the new art form of the *ukiyo-e* wood block prints--"pictures of the floating world"--became a popular art staple that lasted through the nineteenth century, and remains iconic of Japanese culture even today. The name comes from the pleasure districts whose people and scenes were perennially favorite subjects in the art form. This work is from a series by the noted artist Kitagawa Utamaro (ca. 1753–1806) on famous courtesans of the "Southern District," part of the Shinagawa section of Edo.

seventeen-syllable couplets compressed unbearable emotion and release in a way that has made them a treasured form in Japan and, more recently, in much of the world:

Old battlefield, fresh with spring flowers again
All that is left of the dream
Of twice ten-thousand warriors slain.

The visual arts found new forms of expression through the widespread use of fine woodblock printing, which allowed popular works to be widely duplicated. The new genre was called **ukiyo-e** ("pictures of the floating world"), a reference to the pleasure quarters on the edge of the cities that furnished many of its subjects. Although largely scorned by the upper classes, it remained the most popular form of advertising, portraiture, and news distribution until the end of the nineteenth century, when it began to be supplanted by photography. During Tokugawa times, one of the most famous practitioners of the art was Kitagawa Utamaro (1753–1806), whose studies of women became forever associated with Japanese perceptions of female beauty. In the works of Katsushika Hokusai (1760–1849) and Ando Hiroshge (1797–1858), such as Hokusai's ***Thirty-Six Views of Mount Fuji***, scenes of landscapes peopled with delicate women holding paper parasols, or gentle snowfalls on temples formed—as in Utamaro's work, many of the first popular images that nineteenth-century Westerners had of Japan.

Intellectual Developments

The eighteenth and nineteenth centuries proved to be a fertile time for critical thought both within and without approved avenues of discussion. Scholars such as Hirata Atsutane (1776–1843) and Honda Toshiaki managed to convey their admiration for **Dutch Learning**, the information about the events in the outside world contained in the reports to the shogun written by the representatives of the Dutch East India Company, while still managing to acknowledge the primacy of Japan. Honda, in particular, advocated Japanese expansion along the lines of what he understood to be the policies of the European countries with regard to mercantilism, colonial possessions, and the pursuit of science in his "Secret Plan for Managing the Country." His late-eighteenth-century colleague Sato Nobuhiro (1769–1850) expressed similar sentiments in his "Confidential Memoir on Social Control."

On the other hand, some writers believed that Japan's problems lay in the stifling of its true national character by the Neo-Confucian institutions of the Tokugawa. Starting as early as the late seventeenth century, this "National Learning" movement, whose most famous exponent was Motoori Norinaga (1730–1801), emphasized Japan's unique governmental tradition of a single imperial line—later an important part of the Meiji era concept of *kokutai*, or "national polity"—and advocated a return to the earliest Japanese histories, the *Kojiki* and *Nihongi*.

Perhaps most influential of all was the outwardly mainstream Mito School. Formed by a branch of the Tokugawa family, and hewing to the Neo-Confucian orthodoxy of the shogunate, writers like Aizawa Seishisai (1782–1863) demanded that the government take a firm stand against any foreign intrusion. Failure to do so would be to surrender the mandate of the shogunate as the emperor's military and political arm. In the turmoil following Perry's visits and the opening of the first treaty ports, the Mito scholars would be at the forefront of advocating the immediate expulsion of foreigners by any means necessary.

Science, Culture, and the Arts in the Meiji Period

As we have seen, although the Tokugawa sought seclusion, they were by no means cut off entirely from developments in other nations. By the time of Commodore Perry's visit, the accumulated amount of "Dutch Learning" was impressive, and much of it consisted of notes on scientific and technical developments. Nevertheless, at the time of their initial contact with the Western powers, the Tokugawa were stunned by the degree to which the accelerating technologies of the Industrial Revolution had armed their adversaries.

The demand for industrial and military technology required large numbers of Japanese to seek technical education. During the initial stages of the Meiji era, thousands of Japanese students studied in Europe and the U.S., and the government and private concerns hired hundreds of foreign advisors to aid in science and technical training. By the 1880s, a university system anchored by Tokyo Imperial University and including Keio, Waseda, and Doshisha was offering courses in medicine, physics, chemistry, engineering, and geology, among other advanced disciplines. By the turn of the century, Japan's Institute for Infectious Diseases had become world famous for its path-breaking work in microbiology. On the whole, however, the bulk of the nation's efforts went into the practical application of science to technology and agriculture in order

Natsume Soseki, 1910. Few authors captured the dizzying changes in Japanese society as poignantly as Natsume Soseki. In his most famous novel, *Kokoro*, he probes the great gap in the perspectives and lives of the generation that went through the Meiji Restoration and came of age toward its end, fully immersed in a modern society. Here, he used the central event of the death of the emperor in 1912 as symbolizing the passing of the old order, while the new one awaited its turn.

to support the government's modernization efforts.

As was the case a decade later in China, Japanese intellectuals eagerly absorbed copies of Western Enlightenment, philosophical, and social science works in translation— including Locke, Hobbes, Spencer, Darwin, and Comte, to name but a few. As was also true in China, journalism played a dominant role as a disseminator of information to the public. Here, Fukuzawa Yukichi, like Liang Qichao in China, held a central place both in fostering the growth of newspapers and in articulating the role of journalists in a modern society. As were nearly all the arts in late-nineteenth-century Japan, the novel was also heavily influenced by Western examples. In some respects, the culmination of this trend was *Kokoro*, by Natsume Soseki, published in 1914. Soseki utilizes the wrenching changes in Meiji Japan set against traditional and generational values to create the tension and ultimate tragic end of the central character in his work.

More traditional arts such as Noh and kabuki, and ukiyo-e printing survived but often in a somewhat altered state. Updated kabuki variations now featured contemporary themes and often included female actors playing female parts. In addition, European plays such as Ibsen's *A Doll's House* enjoyed considerable vogue. As for ukiyo-e, they remained the cheapest and most popular outlet for depictions of contemporary events until the development of newspaper photography. Especially telling in this regard are ukiyo-e artist's interpretations of the Sino-Japanese War.

CONCLUSION

Plagued by the tensions of rival supporters of the Heian throne, the issue was resolved for a time by the institution of the shogun. Following the attempted Mongol invasions of the thirteenth century, and the aborted restoration attempt by Emperor Go-Daigo in the 1330s, the shogunate achieved a degree of stability and cultural refinement during its Ashikaga interval. By the latter 1400s, however, that fragile stability began to unravel. Ravaged by a century of warfare and foreign intrusion, Japan sought to regulate its inner and outer domains and minimize outside influences. As with China, however, the stability perfected by the Tokugawa Shogunate in the seventeenth and eighteenth centuries would be increasingly threatened in the nineteenth by the growing commercial power of the Europeans and Americans. Before the nineteenth century was finished, all of East Asia would be rent by struggle over the direction each of its countries would take in the face of these new challenges. Japan would experience its own restoration conflict and install a unified government under an emperor for the first time since the twelfth century. With the drive for "civilization and enlightenment" to roll back its unequal treaties and make it an accepted member of the great powers, Japan in the final years of the century would once again invade Korea to attack China—this time with very different results. In the process, the more than 2,000-year-old relationship among all three states would be altered forever.

FURTHER RESOURCES

Beasley, William G. *The Meiji Restoration*. Stanford, Calif.: Stanford University Press, 1972. Pioneering study of the context of the late Tokugawa, Restoration War, and the influence of the *genro* on Japan's early industrial, political, economic, social, and cultural modernization.

De Bary, William T., ed. *Sources of Japanese Tradition*, 2 vols. New York: Columbia University Press, 1964. The Tokugawa era spans Volumes 1 and 2, with its inception and political and philosophical foundations thoroughly covered in Volume 1 and the Shinto revival of national learning, the later Mito School, and various partisans of national unity in the face of foreign intrusion covered in the beginning of Volume 2.

Duus, Peter. *Feudalism in Japan*, 3rd ed. New York: McGraw-Hill, 1993. Updated version of a short, handy volume spanning all of Japanese history to 1867, with special emphasis on the shogunates. Good introduction on the uses and limitations of the term "feudalism" with reference to Japan within a comparative framework.

Gordon, Andrew. *A Modern History of Japan from Tokugawa Times to the Present*. Oxford and New York: Oxford University Press, 2009. One of the few treatments of Japanese history that spans both the Tokugawa and modern eras, rather than making the usual break in either 1853 or 1867–1868. Both the continuity of the past and the novelty of the new era are therefore juxtaposed and highlighted. Most useful for students with a background at least equivalent to that supplied by this text.

Reischauer, Edwin O., and Albert M. Craig. *Japan: Tradition and Transformation*. Boston: Houghton Mifflin, 1989. The companion volume to J. K. Fairbank's *China*, by the leading American scholar on Japan and former U.S. ambassador to Japan. A one-volume history with greater emphasis on the modern than ancient periods.

Totman, Conrad. *A History of Japan*. Oxford: Blackwell, 2000. Part of Blackwell's History of the World series. A larger, more balanced, and comprehensive history than the Reischauer and Craig volume. More than half of the material is on the pre-1867 period, with extensive coverage of social history and demographics.

Totman, Conrad. *Japan before Perry*. Berkeley and Los Angeles: University of California Press, 1981. Close study for nonspecialists in the transformations of the later Tokugawa Shogunate. Readers wishing a more comprehensive treatment may prefer Totman's *Politics in the Tokugawa Bakufu, 1600 to 1843*.

WEBSITES

http://www.asian-studies.org/. Association for Asian Studies. This website offers links to sources more suited to advanced term papers and seminar projects.

http://www.asian-studies.org/eaa/. Education about Asia. This site provides the best online sources for modern Chinese and Japanese history.

http://sinojapanesewar.com/. Sino-Japanese War 1894–5. With the website packed with maps, photographs, and movies depicting the conflict between Japan and China at the end of the nineteenth century, students can learn more about the causes and consequences of the Sino-Japanese War.

CHAPTER 9

⚬━⚬

From Reform to Revolution: China from 1895 to the Present, Part I

Even at a time and place as unsettled as China in the mid-1930s, the incident was universally deemed bizarre. For the leader of a tenuously united Nationalist China, Chiang Kai-shek, it came close to being fatal. Yet by virtue of luck, diplomacy, and forced pragmatism, he not only escaped what was widely expected to be certain death, but also emerged in a vastly enhanced position, leading what now seemed to be a genuinely unified state.

For Chiang (1887–1975), the military had been his profession. Although for the most part not outstandingly skilled as a field commander, he had proven adroit at mastering the delicate balancing act of politics in the chaotic quest to build nationalism in the warlord-dominated China of the early 1920s. With the critical pivot of China's revolutionary leader, Sun Yat-sen (1866–1925), away from the Western powers and toward Bolshevik Russia for help in unifying the country, Chiang and a number of his comrades had gone to Moscow for training. Unlike some of the others, however, the experience soured him on the Bolsheviks, particularly their international arm of revolutionaries, **Comintern**. Still, as commander of the Nationalist Party's Whampoa Military Academy, he was well placed to assume the mantle of power upon Sun's death from cancer in 1925.

Commanding the Northern Expedition to unite the country the following year, success followed success. By April 1927, he felt free to purge his party of its left wing, Communists, and Comintern agents, beginning a long civil war that would last with an interruption for World War II until 1949. The Chinese Communist Party leader Mao Zedong fled south to the mountains of Jiangxi to regroup. Chiang then began a long and costly campaign to eliminate Mao's "Jiangxi Soviet." In late 1934, Mao's forces broke out of an attempted encirclement and over the next year completed an epic **Long March** that ultimately led them to remote Yan'an. It was here that Chiang planned to finish them off; and it was here that he would face his most severe trial.

Japan's steady encroachment on northern China following the annexation of Manchuria in 1931 had long since raised alarm bells among many Nationalist commanders. Chiang's single-minded devotion to eliminating the internal enemy first grew less popular with every defeat. Here at last, however, was the opportunity he had been seeking: leading a massive force against an exhausted and depleted enemy with no easy avenue of escape. So in the late fall of 1936, Chiang began to assemble the forces for his final "Bandit Extermination Campaign" and made his headquarters at the famous Huaqing Hot Spring near the ancient capital of Xi'an.

On the night of December 12, however, he was awakened in his villa by a muted commotion. Sensing danger, he leapt from his bedroom window in his nightshirt, even leaving his false teeth in their customary glass, and fled up the stony hillside in his bare feet. Caught on the hill by a detachment of his own men, he was surprised and furious to discover that they were kidnapping him at the behest of one of his abler commanders, "The Young Marshal" Zhang Xueliang, whose father, the Manchurian warlord Zhang Zuolin, had been assassinated by the Japanese less than a decade before. Chiang was certain that a coup attempt was in progress and that he would be killed; what happened next shocked him even more.

His captors instead arranged to meet with Mao's men for negotiations. Indeed, there was discussion of killing the generalissimo. But with the intercession of the Communist's ablest diplomat, Zhou Enlai, they instead pushed Chiang to accept an agreement to end the civil war and form a new united front to oppose Japan. On Christmas Day, 1936, Chiang reemerged and informed the government and media that China was now united and ready to stand against Japan.

The "Xi'an Incident," as it came to be called, proved to be of crucial importance in determining the course of East Asian events for decades to come. China's new stand against Japan prompted that empire to launch an all-out assault on China, opening World War II in Asia and the Pacific. To break the deadlock in China, Japan seized the resource-rich British and Dutch colonies in Southeast Asia, attacking the United States at Pearl Harbor and the Philippines in the process. The war's end and Allied victory saw not only Japan's empire dismantled but also soon thereafter, those of Britain, France, and the Netherlands. Today, however, although not without its political problems, the region enjoys unprecedented wealth and influence. The People's Republic of China and Japan are the world's second and third largest economies; Korea, though divided and politically volatile, is economically vibrant in its southern republic; Vietnam, torn by division and war for decades is gaining economically on its neighbors.

For Chiang, the 1940s saw his fall from leader of "Free China" to loser in the renewed civil war. In 1949, it would be Mao who would lead in the creation of the People's Republic of China; Chiang would resettle Nationalist China on Taiwan, where it remains today. Zhang Xueliang, who viewed his role in the kidnapping as a patriotic duty, paid the price for his action: placed by Chiang under house arrest for forty years, his freedom came only with Chiang's death in 1975. The Young Marshal lived out his remaining years in Hawaii, where he died in 2001 at 101. And the Huaqing spa, the site of the Tang Dynasty palace built by Emperor Xuanzong in 723—and said to be a favorite retreat for his love affair with Yang Guifei—was to be known for decades in the People's Republic as "Capturing Chiang Kai-shek Spring."

THE REPUBLICAN REVOLUTION

Amid the growing foreign tensions brought on by the earlier Sino-Japanese War, its aftermath produced a domestic crisis as well. A group of officials headed by Kang Youwei (1858–1927) petitioned Emperor Guangxu, now ruling in his own right, to implement a list of widespread reforms, many modeled on those recently enacted in Japan. Guangxu issued a flurry of edicts from June through September 1898, attempting to completely revamp China's government and many of its leading institutions. Resistance to this "Hundred Days' Reform" program, however, was extensive, and much of it was centered on the emperor's aunt, the empress dowager Cixi. With support from her inner circle at court, she had the young emperor placed under house arrest and rounded up and executed those of Kang's supporters who could be found. Kang and his junior colleague, the writer and political theorist Liang Qichao, managed to escape to the treaty ports. For the next decade, they traveled to overseas Chinese communities, attempting to gather support for their Constitutional Monarchy (literally, "Preserve the Emperor") Party.

(A)

(B)

Kang Youwei and Liang Qichao. (A) Kang Youwei (1858–1927) was a Chinese scholar noted initially for his role in popularizing the notion of Confucius as reformer. After the Sino-Japanese War, he dedicated himself to institutional reform. Meeting with the young emperor Guangxu to put forth his ideas, the emperor issued a number of edicts based on Kang's suggestions in the summer of 1898 that became known as the Hundred Days' Reform. Following the Empress Dowager Cixi's coup against the emperor, Kang and his colleague Liang Qichao went into exile, where he continued to promote his advocacy of a constitutional monarchy until the revolution of 1911–1912. (B) Liang Qichao (1873–1929), Chinese scholar, journalist, philosopher, and reformer, took part in the Hundred Days' with Kang Youwei, and barely escaped with his life after the empress dowager's coup. Like Kang, he traveled extensively, visiting the many Chinese communities around the world and seeking support for the Constitutional Monarchy Party (*Baohuanghui*; literally, "preserve the emperor party/association"). One of China's most prominent pioneering journalists, he had a hand in founding a number of newspapers and was instrumental in popularizing Western philosophical and scientific works among Chinese intellectuals.

The Last Stand of the Old Order: The Boxer Rebellion and War

The turmoil set off by the "race for concessions" among the imperial powers was particularly intense in north China, where the ambitions of Russia, Japan, and Germany clashed. The privileges of extraterritoriality now extended beyond the foreign community to Chinese Christian converts under the protection of missionaries. Thus, with the stepped-up activity of German missionaries on the Shandong Peninsula came a new wave of anti-foreign sentiment, increasingly emanating from a group called the Society (later "Militia") of the Harmonious Fists. Initially anti-Qing as well as anti-foreign, the members' ritual exercises and name prompted the foreign community to refer to them as the **Boxers**. By late 1899, the Boxers were regularly provoking the foreign and Christian communities with the aim of pushing their governments to pressure the Qing to suppress the movement, by which they hoped to stir up rebellion against them (see Map 9.1).

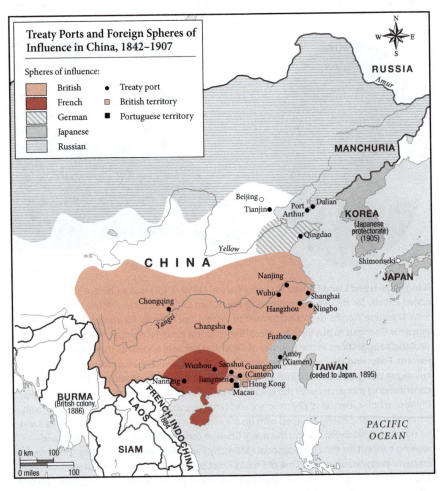

Map 9.1 Treaty Ports and Foreign Spheres of Influence in China, 1842–1907

In the spring of 1900, matters came to a head. An anti-foreign Manchu body-guard assassinated the German ambassador, Baron Klemens Von Ketteler (1853–1900), and the Germans demanded that the Qing crush the Boxer movement once and for all, pay a huge indemnity, and erect a statue to their ambassador as a public apology. In the midst of this crisis, the empress dowager, who had been negotiating in secret with the Boxers, declared war on all the foreign powers in China and openly threw the court's support behind the movement. The result was civil war across northern China as Boxer bands hunted down missionaries and Chinese Christians. Many Chinese army units aided the Boxers in attacking foreigners, and the foreign diplomatic quarter in Beijing was besieged from June until August.

The foreign governments quickly put together a multinational relief force, the Eight Nations Alliance, led by the Germans and British and largely manned by the Japanese. By August, they had fought their way to the capital and nearly chased the imperial court as far as Xi'an. Amid considerable carnage in the mopping up of Boxer sympathizers, Li Hongzhang, in his last official duty before his death, was commissioned to negotiate an end to the conflict for the court. With Qing power utterly routed, the foreign governments were able to impose the most severe "unequal treaty" yet: they extracted the right to post troops in major Chinese cities, they demanded the total suppression of any anti-foreign movements, and they received such a huge indemnity—450,000,000 silver taels, or $335,000,000—that China had to borrow money from foreign banks in order to service the interest on the payments. The only bright point in the Boxer Protocols of 1901 was that the United States agreed to return its share of the indemnity money to China on the condition that it would be used to send Chinese students to study in American institutions. Some of it also supported the founding of Tsinghua University in Beijing.

The Twilight of Reform

With the return of the imperial court to Beijing in 1901 and the presence of substantial numbers of foreign troops stationed in the capital, the Qing finally turned to institutional reform. The Boxer catastrophe showed clearly the need for the kinds of reforms that had made the Eight Nations Alliance so powerful. Now finally in the majority, therefore, the reformers put together a systematic program to attempt the reinvigoration of Qing rule. At the end of January 1901, an imperial edict was issued announcing the new direction. With regard to Western learning, it was argued that it had been limited to superficial study of technology and military matters. An entirely new approach would now need to be undertaken to understand the deeper wellsprings of Western wealth and power.

The old Confucian eight-legged essays were abolished for military, local, and provincial exams. The new examination material was to be oriented more toward technical expertise and practical affairs. The old Zongli Yamen was now reorganized as the Ministry of Foreign Affairs and placed above the existing six boards in terms of protocol status. The old Imperial Academy had been replaced during the **Hundred Days' Reform** in 1898 by a newly created Imperial University. Now other universities on the new model were swiftly set up. In 1904, a complete

Hlo [beheaded criminals tied by queues to stakes, on Street near West Gate—Tientsin, China.   Copyright 1901 by Underwood & Underwood.

The Boxer Conflict and Aftermath. The sudden shifting of sides by the empress dowager in support of the Boxers and the siege of the foreign legations in Beijing prompted a hastily assembled Eight Nations Alliance to suppress the anti-foreign movement and eliminate the threat to diplomats in the capital. In (A), soldiers representing the different nations of the Alliance—including three areas of the British Empire—line up for a group picture. From left to right, they are troops from Great Britain, the United States, Australia, India, Germany, France, Austria-Hungary, Italy, and Japan. Atrocities both real and rumored against foreigners and Chinese Christians by the Boxers resulted in brutal and often indiscriminate reprisals by troops of the Alliance. In (B), two heads of presumed Boxers or sympathizers hang by their queues outside the West Gate of Tianjin, while two foreign soldiers and a young boy look on by the gate.

overhaul of the educational structure of the country was undertaken. The old Confucian academies were closed, and a graded primary and secondary school system based on the Japanese model was introduced.

The former armies of the Green Standard and Manchu Banner units were disbanded and two large armies, Northern and Southern, established. The colorful but anachronistic uniforms of the old armies were abandoned in favor of the modern khaki and olive drab coming into use in foreign forces. Up-to-date weapons and ordnance were phased in. Perhaps most dramatically, the government itself was to be restructured more or less along the lines envisioned by Kang Youwei and Emperor Guangxu—who still languished under house arrest.

As had Japan and Korea in previous decades, China now sent an imperial commission abroad to study the constitutional systems of the great powers, and upon its return a plan to turn the Qing into a constitutional monarchy over the next decade was created. In 1908, the court accepted a draft constitution based on elements of several European models, although most heavily influenced by Japan's. The court announced that these reforms would be phased in over the next nine years, after which the constitution would go into effect. The first element, the creation of provincial assemblies, was begun in 1909. The following year, a National Assembly was convened, with half of its makeup members of the provincial assemblies, and half those who had connections to the court. After repeated petitions from various quarters to convene the new parliament, the court agreed that it would open in 1913, several years ahead of schedule.

While Qing reform efforts were proceeding apace, however, the plans of revolutionaries were moving even more rapidly. In this, the central figure was Dr. Sun Yat-sen (1866–1925), a man in many ways emblematic of the changes in China during the nineteenth century. Born near Canton, Sun received the fundamentals of a classical education but then undertook Western medical training in Hong Kong and developed a thriving practice in Canton. Sun lived for a while with his brother in Hawaii and traveled extensively throughout the worldwide Chinese diaspora, where he gained exposure to a wide spectrum of dissent.

While many, like Kang Youwei and Liang Qichao, saw China's salvation in following the Japanese model of constitutional monarchy, the war with Japan convinced Sun that the feeble and corrupt Manchu government was itself the biggest obstacle to China's regeneration. Thus, during his time in Hawaii in 1895, Sun formed his first revolutionary organization, the *Xing Zhong Hui* ("Revive/Resurrect China Society").

Within a few months of the war's end in 1895, Sun had embarked on a course of insurrection. His initial attempt was nearly his last: convinced that the Qing were on the verge of collapse, he smuggled a few men and guns into Guangdong and attempted to draw the local villagers to his colors. His first revolutionary battle was a disaster, and most of his small band were killed or captured. Sun barely escaped with his life. It did nothing to diminish his determination, however: over the next sixteen years, his groups would make a dozen more attempts before finally succeeding.

Sun Yat-sen and the Ideology of Revolution

From this point on, Sun spent most of his time in the treaty ports and among Chinese expatriates looking for financial support, recruits, and connections to other dissident groups. When he visited London in 1896, however, the Qing legation there took direct action: he was secretly kidnapped and held in the Chinese

Sun Yat-sen and Family in Hawaii. Sun Yat-sen (1866–1925) was in many ways emblematic of the "new" Chinese men and women coming of age in the late nineteenth century in the era of treaty ports, foreign influences, and growing unrest with the apparent shortcomings of Qing rule. By the 1890s, there was an extensive network of overseas Chinese communities throughout Asia and increasingly in Europe and the Americas. Sun's brother, Sun Mei, had emigrated to Hawaii, at the time an independent kingdom, where he became a successful merchant and farmer. Sun Yat-sen spent a total of seven years in Hawaii, living with his brother and family, and founding his first revolutionary organization, the Xingzhonghui ("Revive/Resurrect China Society"), there in 1895. At one point, anxious to emigrate to the United States and even apply for citizenship, he obtained a Hawaiian birth certificate in an attempt to document his residence in what had become American territory.

diplomatic compound pending trial and execution. Sun, however, was able to smuggle a letter out to an old friend, James Cantlie, who alerted British authorities to negotiate his release. From an obscure amateurish revolutionary on the dissident fringe of Chinese politics, Sun was transformed into an international celebrity as newspapers all over the world picked up the story. The prestige gained gave him increasing entrée to like-minded groups, and became an invaluable funding and recruitment tool.

With the collapse of the reform movement in 1898, Sun's efforts faced competition from an unexpected quarter. Now Kang Youwei and Liang Qichao were moving among the same expatriate circles, trying to expand and fund their constitutional monarchy party. The rivalry was bitter between the two groups, with each side trying to undermine the other's efforts. For Sun and his allies, however, coalition building continued apace. In Tokyo on August 20, 1905, the founding of the *Tongmeng hui* ("Revolutionary Alliance" or "Chinese United League") took place with Sun as its first president. In the inaugural issue of its official publication that November, Sun promulgated for the first time his most famous doctrinal statement: **The Three People's Principles** (*San min zhuyi*).

Sun once credited his time in the United States and study of American history—particularly the phrase "of the people, by the people, for the people," in Lincoln's Gettysburg Address—with inspiring the Three Principles. They are:

- *Minzu* (Nationalism): Expulsion of the Manchus and all imperial interests, and complete control of national sovereignty.
- *Minquan* (Democracy): Representative institutions based on a constitution.
- *Minsheng* (The People's Livelihood): Sun believed that nationalization of certain key industries would be necessary and that China's dominant enterprise, agriculture, should revolve around an equitable system of land distribution and usage. Nationalization was seen as a way to spur capital-intensive heavy industrialization, while the government's right to buy back and redistribute land at its assessed value would curb speculation and absentee landlordism.

The steady growth of the influence of the movement, and the pervasive sense that the Qing were on the verge of collapse, allowed Sun's groups to penetrate nearly all levels of society. By the end of the decade, this influence was growing rapidly in the overhauled and newly organized Qing army.

On October 10, 1911, celebrated ever after as "Double Ten," an accidental explosion in the Wuchang army barracks signaled a premature takeover of the base by the revolutionary faction. In the confusion, the revolutionaries, lacking a commander, gave the base commandant, Li Yuanhong (1864–1928), the choice of leading the insurrection or being executed. "I am your leader!" he is reported to have replied. He went on to twice serve as the president of the Chinese Republic. The military revolt quickly spread to other bases, and the Qing collapse so long expected by Sun and his allies appeared to be unfolding.

The **Xinhai Revolution**, so named for the year 1911 in the old Chinese calendar, had spread by November to many provincial capitals, where the New Army factions made common cause with reformist scholar-gentry and other nationalists. There were some pitched battles, notably a victory by Qing forces under Yuan Shikai at Hanyang in November and, more tellingly, a crucial win by the revolutionaries the following month at Nanjing. On the whole, however, it consisted primarily of uprisings in provincial cities whose new governments seceded from Qing rule piecemeal.

It was here that the role of the Qing commander, the durable Yuan Shikai (1859–1916), proved crucial. Yuan had been selected by the Qing to quash the revolution but stalled for time and tried to get a sense of the drift of events before committing himself. He then agreed to command the imperial forces on the condition that he be named premier in the new constitutional monarchy. Meanwhile, he had attempted to open negotiations with the revolutionaries, who initially rebuffed him. Following the Nanjing victory, however, he struck a deal with the insurgents whereby his forces would ally with them in return for his selection as president of the new republic, formed upon the abdication of the Qing on February 12, 1912. Thus, Sun Yat-sen was elbowed aside by the revolution he had done so much to begin.

The New Warring States Era (1916–1926)

The new Republic of China was freighted with difficulties right from the beginning. Pro-Sun factions within the government lobbied for his return. The Revolutionary Alliance became a political party, the **Guomindang** (*Kuomintang*) or Nationalist Party, which won a plurality in the initial elections. Its leader, Song Jiaoren, however, was assassinated before he could form a government. In addition, because so much of the revolution had consisted of provincial revolts, the vast majority of which were not led by Revolutionary Alliance groups, the country was left regionalized and fragmented, and ruled in many places by military strong men. Anxious to quash dissent, Yuan suppressed the Guomindang, which responded with a revolt sometimes called "the second revolution." Yuan crushed the revolt by the summer of 1913 and drove Sun Yat-sen out of the country.

With the coming of World War I, the situation unraveled further. Japan, allied with Britain, quickly acted on this relationship to seize the German concessions in Shandong and colonies in the Pacific (see Chapter 12). Capitalizing on the preoccupation of the imperial powers with the war in Europe, Japanese strategic planners moved swiftly to further their aims of a united East Asia under Japanese aegis. Encouraged by China's difficulties in creating a viable government, the Japanese issued the Chinese a document in January, 1915 that became known as the **Twenty-One Demands**, although because its demands were divided into five groups, the Japanese insisted on calling it the "Five Requests."

Japan's war with Russia had yielded effective hegemony in Manchuria. Japan had also extracted mining and development rights in the region and increasingly saw Manchuria as a destination for Japanese immigration as its home islands grew more crowded. Over the long term, Japan viewed Manchuria as a client territory and buffer zone against Russian expansion into China or Korea. Thus, the Demands addressed a number of issues designed to reinforce this state of affairs. Japanese planners sought to unite a weak China with a strong Japan in order to create an "Asia for the Asiatics" to resist further imperial encroachment by the European powers.

The first group of demands was therefore aimed at confirming and consolidating Japanese control over the former German concessions in Shandong. The second group demanded an extended sphere of influence in Manchuria, including extraterritoriality, rights of settlement, control over the administrative and financial sectors, and access to raw materials in adjacent Inner Mongolia. Group 3 would give Japan control over the heavily indebted Hanyeping mining and manufacturing complex. In Group 4, China was forbidden to grant additional coastal or island concessions to any other power but Japan. The most contested set of conditions came with Group 5. Japan reserved the right to hire or approve all financial and law enforcement officials in China. It would also receive railroad concessions in China and acquire effective control of Fujian Province, directly across the strait from Japanese-annexed Taiwan.

As discontent with his regime swiftly mounted, Yuan felt he could not take on Japan. He managed, however, to leak the contents of the Demands, which Japan had insisted be kept secret, to the Americans and Europeans and stalled for time. In a sharply worded note sent by American Secretary of State William Jennings Bryan, Japan was warned that the Demands constituted a serious breach of the Open Door Policy. Great Britain, for its part, retreated from its alliance with Japan. Realizing the international furor the Demands had generated, the Japanese dropped the last set of provisions and sent an ultimatum to Yuan demanding a quick reply. Yuan agreed to the revised Demands on May 9, and the treaties were signed later that month. For the next thirty-four years, May 9 was commemorated in Republican and Nationalist China as National Humiliation Day.

As anger with the provisions of the appeasement policy grew, and with an anti-Japanese boycott barely suppressed, Yuan decided that the country would be more manageable if the monarchy were restored. In September 1915, he announced plans to inaugurate a new dynasty. Predictably, forcing through the new order encouraged rebellion rather than stabilization. Within a few months, Yunnan, Guizhou, Sichuan, Shandong, and several other provinces had declared their independence of Yuan, vowing to protect the republic. Yuan belatedly backed away from the restoration that, in any case, effectively ceased with his death on June 6, 1916.

With Yuan's death, his successor, the former Wuchang commander and now president, Li Yuanhong, declared China a republic once again. If anything, however, the government's control continued to erode in favor of rival cliques in the north centered on the remnant of the republic in Beijing, and the governors and military leaders of the south based in Canton. By the summer of 1917, both claimants to the Republican mantle in China declared war on Germany. Although China sent no troops to the Western Front, the British and French recruited 140,000 Chinese laborers to free their own soldiers for combat duty.

Disagreements about China's role in the war, factionalism among the emerging class of *dujun*—military governors—and different interpretations of the functions of the republic led to what was, in effect, a civil war. The government in Beijing, dominated by the "Anfu Clique," loosely controlled the north, while a floating coalition of southern *dujun* and civilian provincial governors held sway in much of the rest of the country. In the middle of this highly confused and shifting situation, Sun Yat-sen's Guomindang set up its own Republic of China in Guangdong Province.

For the next decade, a chaotic pattern of fighting, expropriation of land, and exorbitant taxes levied by rival *dujuns* wore down the remnants of civil society, impoverished countless millions, and left the country so disunited that many foreign and Chinese observers despaired of it ever having a functional government. The warlords themselves were, as disordered times often produce, a highly eclectic group. Some warlords made public displays of cruelty to terrorize enemies and suppress dissention; others were simply out to enrich themselves and live lives of gilded debauchery (see Map 9.2).

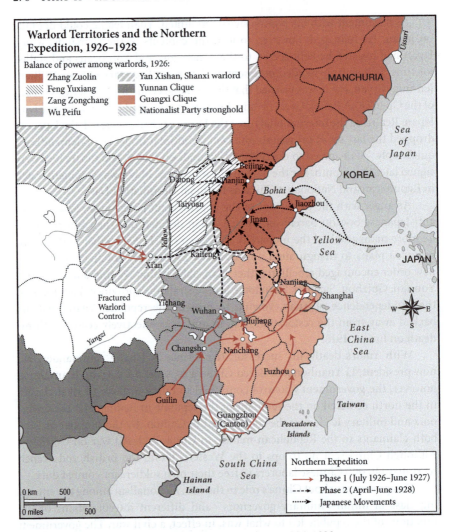

Map 9.2 Warlord Territories and the Northern Expedition, 1926–1928

Creating Nationalism

Although some warlords arguably had the desire to help the country, none of them developed a political program solid or appealing enough to garner widespread support. In addition, none of them commanded sufficient power to subdue the others or their coalitions. Even Sun Yat-sen at this point, though he had a political program, controlled only a small area around Canton. With the republic in shambles and China hijacked by the warlords, Sun remained a profoundly inspirational figure for Chinese Nationalists, mostly through his numerous publications issued from exile in Canton.

For the moment, however, the impetus toward a new Nationalism would come from a different quarter. With the armistice ending the Great War in

November 1918, and the opening of the peace conference at Versailles in 1919, the victorious Allies faced a myriad of daunting issues, a number of which directly affected the political configuration of East Asia. The American president, Woodrow Wilson, in his famous Fourteen Points had advocated "self-determination" for all peoples. Throughout the colonies and territories held by both the Allies and Central Powers, many interpreted this as a hopeful sign of increased colonial autonomy, or even independence. Indeed, in the Covenant of the proposed League of Nations, a **mandate system** was created in which existing Allied colonial powers would act "in trust" for those territories not yet able to govern themselves. Those territories deemed capable of forming states were to be given independence immediately or within an agreed-upon time.

The yawning gap between promise and performance, however, showed itself at the outset. Nationalists in both Vietnam and Korea would face bitter disappointment; in India, the frustration led to the Amritsar Massacre in April 1919. In China, expectations were high that the republic's contributions as an Allied and Associated Power might lead to the revision of the unequal treaties it had acquiesced to. Most observers expected that there would at least be some settlement of the status of the German concessions Japan had seized. For its part, Japan wanted a racial equality clause inserted into the League Covenant. Failing that, the Japanese wanted to retain the German concessions in Shandong.

For Wilson and the British, such a clause would prevent ratification of the treaty. In the U.S., senators from the Jim Crow South would vote it down, as would senators from the Pacific coast, the source of opposition to Asian immigration.

May 4 Demonstrations. The keen sense of betrayal by the victorious Allies at the Versailles Conference felt by Chinese who had believed that China's contribution to the Allied war effort merited rolling back the unequal treaties and restraint on the part of Japan erupted into protests beginning May 4, 1919 at Beijing (Peking) University. Here, protesters demonstrate outside the Gate of Heavenly Peace (Tiananmen) marking the entrance to the old Forbidden City.

The British Empire, too, had placed internal and external immigration restrictions on Asians. In the end, the League decided that it would be better to have Japan sign the Covenant and try to settle the Shandong dispute separately.

The decision announced on May 4, 1919, by the Allies to allow Japan to keep the German concessions in China set off mass demonstrations and a boycott of Japanese, and in short order, other foreign concerns. The decision was especially dispiriting because feelings were already running high in anticipation of National Humiliation Day. This **May Fourth Movement**, as it came to be called, is often cited as the modern beginning of Chinese Nationalism. Combined with the intellectual and cultural ferment of the **New Culture Movement** (see below) a new political assertiveness increasingly made itself felt. Shortly thereafter, inspired by the Bolshevik Revolution in Russia, a **Chinese Communist Party (CCP)** was founded in 1921. Among the few dozen charter members was an obscure assistant librarian at Peking University named Mao Zedong. Two years later, despairing of assistance from the democracies of the West, Sun Yat-sen availed himself of aid offered by the Third Communist International, Comintern, and began to recast the Guomindang along Bolshevik lines. It would be the uncertain union of these two parties in a united front from 1924 to 1927 that would finally effect a degree of unification in China. It would also create the preconditions for a devastating civil war that would not be decided until 1949.

The First United Front

Among the most insistent and influential founders of the Communist Party were Li Dazhao and Chen Duxiu. Li (1888–1927), a professor and librarian at Peking University, was an early contributor to the literary magazine *New Youth*, of which Chen was the editor (see below). They posited imaginary figures of "Mr. Science" and "Mr. Democracy" to take on what they considered the false premises of "Mr. Confucius." In November 1918, Li published an article signaling a new direction. Having dabbled in Marxism, his "The Victory of Bolshevism," celebrated the end of World War I not as an Allied victory over the Central Powers, but rather as a victory for the masses over militarism. In short order, he started a Marxist study group that came to include the young Mao Zedong (1893–1976). In July 1921, thirteen delegates from various provinces representing a little over fifty members—and two Comintern representatives—met in Shanghai to form the Chinese Communist Party (CCP). Chen Duxiu was appointed to its Central Committee, while Mao became secretary of the branch in his home province of Hunan.

Marxist-Leninist theory insisted that the proletariat of industrial wage workers would be the vanguard of a socialist revolution; Lenin's theoretical and practical activities further insisted that the Communist Party should be a vanguard of the vanguard, a select group of professional revolutionaries who would seize political control at its center and then proceed to remake society from the top down. Peasants were considered a problem in this schema because they were essentially conservative and thus lacked the revolutionary spirit that would inspire them to risk all for sweeping societal change.

(A)   **(B)**   **(C)**

Founders of the Chinese Communist Party. (A) Chen Duxiu (1879–1942; wearing the Western suit), played a prominent role in a number of pivotal arenas in early-twentieth-century China. He participated in the Xinhai Revolution, was a proponent of the New Culture Movement and founder of its signature journal *New Youth*, and took an active role in the May Fourth Movement. Along with Li Dazhao, also pictured here (with the mustache), Chen was a cofounder of the Chinese Communist Party in 1921 and its first general secretary. (B) Like Chen, Li Dazhao (1888–1927) had championed the New Culture Movement and the idea of making science and democracy central to the new Chinese society struggling to develop. He was also an early champion of the Russian Revolution, writing "The Victory of Bolshevism" for publication in *New Youth* in 1918. (C) Mao Zedong (1893–1976) would emerge as the best known and most influential of the founders of the CCP, becoming the Party's chief theoretician, military leader, Chairman, and head of state of the People's Republic from 1949, with a brief interruption from 1959 to 1966, until his death in 1976. Even today, the core ideology of the CCP and People's Republic is still described as "Marxism-Leninism-Mao Zedong thought."

Hence, the CCP came to the conclusion that a Communist revolution in China would have to await the country's national unification and its evolution into some form of constitutional capitalist state before the structures would be in place to seize control. In this connection, Sun's Nationalist Party seemed like the best candidate to effect such a transformation. Sun had picked up considerable support in the wake of the May Fourth Movement. Indeed, he became increasingly strident in campaigning for a more unified Chinese national spirit, noting that the Chinese people were currently like "a heap of loose sand" (often rendered as "a sheet of loose sand") in their lack of national cohesion. On December 31, 1923, in a speech to the Canton YMCA, Sun declared, "We no longer look to the Western Powers. Our faces are turned toward Russia."

Help from that quarter was not long in coming. Comintern agents approached Sun with money, weapons, and training in revolutionary organization and tactics. As we saw in the opening vignette, among those who went to Moscow but come away distrustful of his new allies was Chiang Kai-shek (in pinyin, *Jiang Jieshi*). That distrust would play a central role during China's next five decades. For now, however, the new association yielded dividends. The price that Comintern extracted from Sun was the creation in 1924 of the First United Front: CCP members were to be allowed to join the GMD as individuals, and all would work toward eliminating the warlord territories and unifying the country.

Sun's death from cancer in 1925 temporarily halted the plans for the Northern Expedition to reunite the country. Already, however, members of both parties were propagandizing the people in the rural areas. Mao, in particular, proved adept at this and was already beginning to part with the Marxist-Leninist notion that the peasants lacked revolutionary potential. In fact, in his later *Report on the Hunan Peasant Movement,* he waxed rhapsodically about their zeal and organizational acumen. With United Front organizing being carried out in multiple provinces, and GMD leadership assumed by Chiang Kai-shek, the Northern Expedition was launched in July 1926. The GMD organized a National Revolutionary Army in the south and the CCP fomented Communist-inspired strikes in the industrial cities of the Yangzi Delta.

Sun Yat-sen and the Reorganized Guomindang. On the heels of Sun's disappointment with the lack of Western aid for his Nationalist (Guomindang) Party's efforts to create a united China, he turned to the new Soviet Union and its Third International (Comintern) agents for help. In return for agreeing to allow members of the newly formed Chinese Communist Party to join with Sun's party in a united front, Comintern sent organizers, weapons, money and provided training to key personnel. Sun (seated) and the young Chiang Kai-shek in 1924 at the Whampoa Military Academy pose in Canton, the center of Guomindang training and political organization, of which Chiang was president.

From the beginning, support for the movement was overwhelming. By November, the GMD/CCP forces had secured most of the Yangzi Valley and were moving into position to strike north. As 1927 moved through its early months, however, the bonds between the GMD and CCP ruptured. The CCP and the left wing of the GMD had taken the important industrial center of Wuhan, while Shanghai (excluding the foreign concessions) was in the hands of Chiang's wing, setting the stage for a showdown. The growth of the CCP through the campaign and its key role in fomenting strikes in cities yet to be taken made Chiang increasingly mistrustful of their intensions as well as those of Comintern and the left wing of his own party. In April, therefore, he launched a preemptive purge of Communists in Nationalist-held areas. Caught between Comintern's insistence on maintaining the First United Front and the situation on the ground confronting them, the Communists hesitated, then mounted a series of hopelessly ineffective coup attempts in various cities. Much of the old CCP leadership was lost. Li Dazhao was seized from the Soviet embassy and executed. Chen Duxiu was condemned by his own party as a "right-wing opportunist." A remnant under Mao Zedong fled to the remote province of Jiangxi to regroup and create its own socialist Jiangxi Soviet. Here, and later in the caves of Yan'an in the north, Mao would put into practice his ideas of peasant revolution and their power to build socialism.

CIVIL WAR, WORLD WAR, AND PEOPLE'S REPUBLIC

The collapse of the First United Front and the retreat of Mao's forces appeared initially to mark a decisive victory for Chiang and the right-wing GMD. As had so many other groups in China's history, however, the CCP's sojourn into the remote highlands of Jiangxi put them out of reach of the Nationalists and allowed them to regroup and attract new followers.

The Nationalist Interval

Believing the Communist threat to be effectively eliminated, Chiang resumed his Northern Expedition in 1928, submitting Beijing to his control but failing to eliminate the strongest northern warlords. Nevertheless, China was at least nominally unified, with the capital in Nanjing. The GMD Party Congress now functioned as a parliament with Chiang as its president. Chiang made substantial progress with railroad and road construction, as well as cotton and silk textile exports, even during the Great Depression of the 1930s. He made little headway, however, with land reform. Hovering above all after 1931 was the Japanese annexation of Manchuria and creeping encroachment on northern China.

Although never as successful as Sun in attracting favorable international attention, Chiang did at least attempt to act the part of a modern "generalissimo," the title by which he was commonly known in the West. His greatest asset in the international arena, however, was his wife, born Soong (in pinyin, Song) Meiling. The daughter of influential Shanghai banker "Charlie" Soong, Meiling (1898–2003) and her sisters Qingling and Ailing were, with the exception of Mao's wife Jiang Qing, the most powerful women in twentieth-century China. Qingling (1893–1981) was now the widow of Sun Yat-sen and would one day be a member of the CCP Politburo. Ailing (1888–1973) married the Nationalist finance minister, H. H. Kung. Of the three, it was said that one loved power (Meiling), one loved money (Ailing), and one loved China (Qingling). A graduate of American schools, Methodist congregant, and speaker of mellifluous English, Madame Chiang Kai-shek would become the ablest wartime propagandist of a Nationalist China presented as standing alone for democracy against Japan before 1941, and as a valiant ally of the United States and Great Britain for the remainder of World War II.

By the early 1930s, however, despite Nationalist China's apparently promising start, the signs were already there to give its leaders pause. Mao Zedong and the Communists had not been destroyed as previously believed but had begun to build a viable state in the form of their Jiangxi Soviet. Mao's experiences in

The Soong Sisters. China's most powerful women in the first half of the twentieth century, the three Soong (Song) sisters are shown here attending a ceremony in China's wartime capital of Chongqing in 1942. From left to right: Soong Meiling, Madame Chiang Kai-shek; Madame H. H. Kung, Soong Ailing, center; and Madame Sun Yat-sen, Soong Qingling, on the right.

Hunan had led him to a theory and practice of seeing landlords as the equivalent of bourgeois capitalists in the countryside and thus the class enemy of the peasants, who now assumed the role of the proletariat. The promise of land reform by means of overthrowing the landlords as a class stimulated the revolutionary fervor of the peasants to change the governmental and social structure to ensure the new order. Moreover, the peasants would be the leading participants in a "people's war"—a three-stage conflict involving the entire populace and borrowing from sources as diverse as Sun Zi's *Art of War* and American tactics against the British in the War for Independence. In this, the efforts of Zhu De (1886–1976) as army commander proved indispensable. The first stage was guerrilla warfare to wear down a more powerful enemy's strength and morale. The second phase came with the armies in rough parity, allowing more conventional tactics and wider flexibility while retaining momentum. The third phase would be signaled when the insurgents were more powerful than their opponents and could finish them off, mopping up any remnants.

By late 1930, although aware that Japan's maneuvers in Manchuria were becoming increasingly aggressive, Chiang was anxious to completely eliminate his internal enemies. Anticipating that the Manchurian warlord Zhang Zuolin—who had escaped a Japanese assassination attempt in 1917—might throw his loyalty behind Chiang Kai-shek, Japan's Kwantung Army succeeded in blowing up his train in 1928. One effect of this killing was that Zhang's son, "The Young Marshal,"

Zhang Xueliang, now made common cause with the Nationalists. Another, however, was that the Kwantung Army had become the effective rulers of Manchuria.

Thus, on September 18, 1931, the Japanese manufactured an incident near the Manchurian city of Mukden (modern-day Shenyang), which they used as a pretext to occupy the city and annex the entire region. They placed the last emperor of the Qing, Aisingioro Henry Puyi (1906–1967), now a grown man, on the throne of an allegedly independent state called *Manchukuo*, "the country of the Manchus." The Japanese also briefly encroached on territory near Beiping (meaning "northern peace"; the name given to Beijing after the Nationalist capital was moved to Nanjing) and briefly occupied Shanghai. The incident became the first real test of the League of Nations' resolve. The League's Lytton Report the following year condemned Japan for its actions and revealed Manchukuo to be a plain case of annexation. The Japanese response was to resign from the League.

While events were unfolding in Manchuria, Chiang, despite the advice of many of his generals, elected to pursue a more conservative course. Starting in November 1930, therefore, he mounted increasingly massive "Total Encirclement" and "Bandit Extermination" campaigns over the next four years aimed at eliminating Mao's expanding Jiangxi Soviet. Each one, however, was defeated by the superior mobility, local loyalty, and guerrilla tactics of Mao's growing **People's Liberation Army (PLA)**.

The Long March; Mao Zedong. Having broken out of the Nationalist encirclement of the Jiangxi Soviet, Mao's forces embarked on an epic and torturous year-long journey from 1934 to 1935 before the remnant of the army arrived in remote, cave-ridden Yan'an. In this often reproduced photo of Mao and his troops on the March, Mao occupies the center on horseback with his third wife, He Zizhen (1910–1984), riding behind him.

Because the earlier attempts at encirclement did not work, Chiang adapted his strategy with the help of German advisors. Under the new approach marking this Fifth Encirclement campaign, Chiang turned to bordering the CCP areas with a ring of trenches and blockhouses to eliminate the mobility of his opponents. As each ring was secured, the army then advanced further inward and dug in again, slowly robbing Mao's army of its greatest asset. Although urged by his Comintern advisors to fight a positional battle, Mao broke out of the contracting Jiangxi Soviet area with perhaps 100,000 troops in an attempt to find a secure base from which to continue the fight.

The Long March and Xi'an Incident

Once free, the majority of the Red Army embarked on its epic Long March of 6,000 miles, drawing a semi-circle from the south through the far west and then northeast toward Beiping. Along the way, harassment by Nationalist troops, warlords, and local people, as well as hunger, famine, heat, swamps, bridgeless rivers, and desertion, decimated the bedraggled marchers. Some were also left behind to organize peasants in areas that looked promising. About 30,000 eventually straggled into the small enclave of Yan'an in 1935, for the moment out of Chiang's reach. Living in caves cut into the loess soil, they set up communes and concentrated on agricultural production and reconstituting their forces.

Within the Guomindang, Chiang's continuing obsession with eliminating his internal enemies increasingly subjected him to the charge of appeasing Japan. Nonetheless, as we saw in the opening vignette to this chapter, he went ahead with plans to launch a sixth campaign to destroy Mao's forces, and in early December 1936, he arrived in the ancient capital of Xi'an to set up his headquarters. Roused from his sleep on the night of December 12 by troops of the Young Marshal, taken to Yan'an, and agreeing to a Second United Front to resist Japan, unity was proclaimed on Christmas Day (see Map 9.3).

East Asia at War

By early 1937, Japanese and Nationalist encampments faced each other in the Beiping suburbs separated by an uneasy truce. Seeing their chances for additional unchallenged acquisition quickly fading, the Japanese accused the Chinese of capturing a Japanese soldier near the Lugou (Marco Polo) Bridge and on July 7 demanded his return. Although the soldier later came back to his unit, the Japanese seized on the so-called Marco Polo Bridge Incident and launched an all-out assault on China. World War II in Asia was now on.

Japanese troops moved on Beiping and attacked Shanghai, and soon most of the Chinese ports. Chinese resistance was stiff in the opening months, particularly at Shanghai. The Japanese, however, were able to use the big guns of their fleet, and their superior mobility and air power, to flank the Chinese forces and force them to retreat toward the capital at Nanjing. Knowing that the capital required a determined stand, Chinese forces dug in, but also took the precaution of moving the government far west to Chongqing (Chungking), where it would remain for the duration of the war. After a week-long siege, Nanjing surrendered.

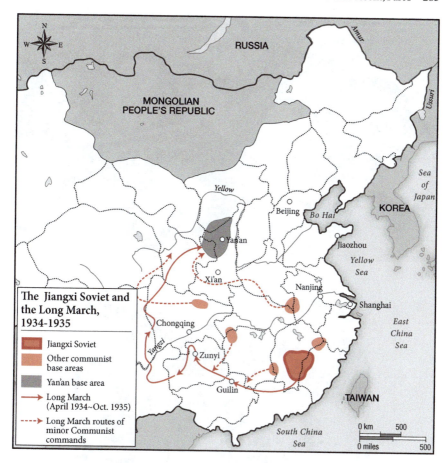

Map 9.3 The Jiangxi Soviet and the Long March, 1934–1935

Realizing the need to defeat China as quickly as possible in order to avoid a war of attrition, the Japanese subjected the capital to the first major atrocity of World War II: the **Rape of Nanking**. Although scholars are still debating the exact number of casualties, it is estimated that between 200,000 and 300,000 people were systematically slaughtered in deliberately gruesome ways: hacked to death, burned alive, buried alive, used for bayonet practice, and beheaded. Rape was used as a strategic weapon to further terrorize and humiliate the populace.

Continually harassed as they retreated from Nanjing the Chinese, like the Soviets a few years later in the face of Nazi invasion, pursued a scorched earth policy of trading space for time to regroup. In an epic mass migration, Chinese soldiers and civilians stripped the land of every usable article—including the invaluable contents of the Palace Museum—and moved them to the remote region around Chongqing. Thereafter, both Nationalists and Communists used the vast interior for hit and run tactics, effectively limiting the Japanese to the northeast and coastal urban centers, but remained incapable of mounting large offensives.

(A)

(B)

The Rape of Nanking. The mass, orchestrated slaughter of hundreds of thousands of men, women, and children following the Nationalist surrender of the capital at Nanking (Nanjing) to the Japanese expeditionary force in December 1937 was the first major atrocity of World War II. Called by some today "the forgotten Holocaust," it was, however, widely reported at the time with extensive photographic and newsreel footage. Japanese commanders urged their men on to brutal torture and execution, using rape in particular as a means of spreading mass terror. In the grisly photo shown here (A), a group of severed heads marks the spot of one such execution. Beheading contests between Japanese officers were routinely organized and even followed in the Japanese press. Bayonet practice (B) was commonly carried out on unarmed civilians, captured soldiers, and in some instances, infants and children.

Japan faced international condemnation for its invasion, particularly in the United States. The U.S., Britain, and France repeatedly demanded that Japan stop the war over the next several years, but by 1939, both sides had settled into a stalemate. With the coming of World War II in Europe and the Rome, Berlin, Tokyo Axis in 1940, Japan acquired powerful allies, and with the defeat of the Netherlands and France that year, the position of those countries' Pacific colonial empires now became imperiled. In carrying out a plan to seize the resources of those colonies, Japan, increasingly squeezed by US sanctions, took the bold step of striking the American naval base at Pearl Harbor.

As one wry observer in Chongqing put it: "Pearl Harbor Day in America was VJ (Victory over Japan) Day in China." In one stroke, China's allies now included two of the world's most powerful military and industrial powers: Britain and the United States. Assured of ultimate victory, and with a small but growing supply of Lend-Lease equipment coming by air into "Free China," Chiang could bide his time, not overly risk his forces, and consolidate his hold to resume the civil war when Japan had been defeated. With the coming of the new B-29 long-range bomber, the first systematic American raids on Japan would fly from Chinese airfields in June 1944. Not long after, American planes would subject Japan to massive incendiary raids from bases in the Mariana Islands.

If the Nationalist strategy against Japan tended to be defensive and conservative, the Communists had no alternative but to be more aggressive. In many important respects, Japanese strategy played remarkably into Mao's hands. The Japanese pursued a "points and lines" occupation strategy of northern China, preferring to take towns and cities along major road and railroad lines. This left vast swaths of territory potentially in the hands of the mobile guerrilla bands of the CCP's Eighth and Fourteenth Route Armies. Moreover, to cow the populace, the Japanese favored the "Three-All Policy": kill all, burn all, loot all. The few survivors of these attacks were purposely left alive to tell their neighbors of the horrors they could expect if they resisted the Japanese. More often than not, this induced local people to join the CCP resistance instead. By the time of Japan's surrender in September 1945, the CCP's control extended over most of northern China and included about 100 million people (see Map 9.4).

From Coalition Government to the Gate of Heavenly Peace

Chiang Kai-shek and Madame Chiang Kai-shek had become international celebrities by 1943 as well as symbols of a free, modernizing, and democratizing China. Moreover, China's position as an ally of equal standing with Britain and the U.S. was validated at the Cairo Conference in November 1943. As part of the understanding that emerged among the three leaders, Nationalist China would get both Manchuria and Taiwan back from Japan, Korea would be made independent, and China would be recognized as the new dominant power of East Asia. Of enormous practical and symbolic importance was that just over a hundred years after the Treaty of Nanjing, the U.S. and Britain finally abrogated all

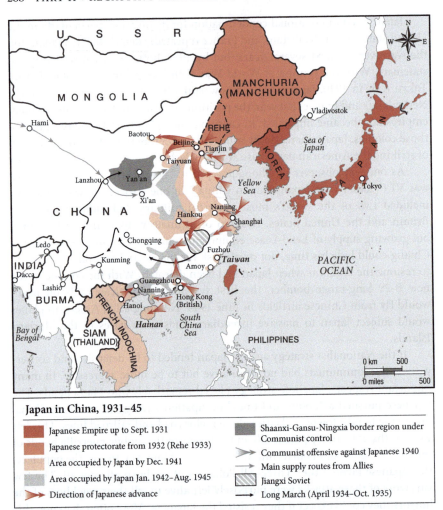

Map 9.4 Japan in China, 1931–1945

unequal treaties—including the Boxer Protocols—and abandoned the principle of extraterritoriality for their citizens in China.

When the end came in August–September 1945, the situation in China was enormously confused. The Soviets had, per the Yalta Agreement in February 1945, come into the war against Japan three months after Germany surrendered, which coincidentally was two days after the first atomic bomb was dropped on Hiroshima. They immediately drove deep into Manchuria. Mao's forces moved swiftly there to take Japan's surrender, and Chiang prevailed on the U.S. to airlift his forces there as well. On arriving, the Chinese found that the Soviets had stripped nearly all the industrial equipment from the region. Both sides adopted a wary truce over the next several months. The Americans, anxious that a united

China dominate the region in the postwar order, sent Secretary of State General George C. Marshall to China in an attempt to work out a compromise between the antagonists. In January 1946, both sides agreed to a set of preliminary steps toward creating a coalition government, and a People's Consultative Conference promulgated plans to recognize all political parties and nationalize all the armed forces. By the end of the year, however, both sides had broken on when to call a National Assembly to put together a new constitution. When the CCP boycotted the proceedings, the Nationalists pushed through their own constitution.

Fighting between the two groups, which had continued sporadically during the negotiations, now began again in earnest. Marshall frantically tried to embargo U.S. aid to either side,

Mao and Chiang toasting coalition government. The Second United Front of Nationalist and Communist forces had remained shaky throughout the war and had already begun to unravel by the final days of the conflict. In a desperate attempt to mediate, American Secretary of State General George C. Marshall attempted to steer both sides toward a coalition government. In this ironic photograph from September 1945, Mao and Chiang toast each other in the euphoria of victory over Japan. They would shortly be at war again for the final time.

but the State Department, despite many of its representatives favoring the CCP's position, ultimately tilted toward Chiang. By 1947, with the tensions of the developing Cold War rapidly increasing, and the U.S. pursuing a policy of "containment" toward the USSR, aid to Chiang was increasingly seen as part of a world strategy to reign in the expansion of the Soviet Union and Communism (see Map 9.5).

When the civil war resumed, the huge gains made by the CCP during the war allowed them to begin the next phase of "people's war": equality of forces. Despite the material superiority of the Nationalists and the still potent but withering American resupply efforts, the PLA had moved into its strongest position yet by mid-1947. Mao's forces increasingly dominated the rural areas, where its land reform efforts stimulated the revolutionary zeal of the peasants. By ceding these areas, however, the Nationalists allowed themselves to be economically strangled. Through 1947 and 1948, the CCP-held areas launched an embargo of goods to urban areas, causing hyperinflation and sowing panic among the populace, now swollen with refugees. The U.S., seeing that there was no hope of salvaging the Nationalist position, cut off aid amid bitter recriminations that would continue through the 1950s over "who lost China."

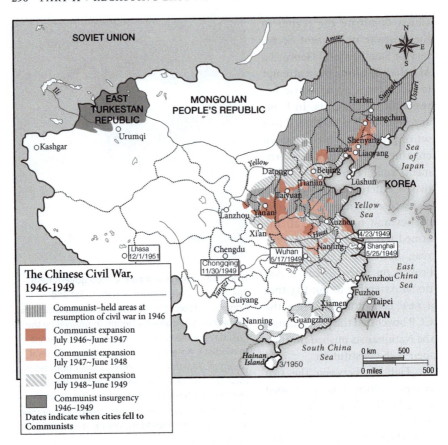

Map 9.5 The Chinese Civil War, 1946–1949

In January 1949, PLA forces occupied Beiping, and Chiang Kai-shek re-signed the Republic of China's presidency. Through the next several months, the large cities fell and the Nationalist forces scattered, some changing sides, some surrendering, others going home. Toward the end of the year, several large units moved down into remote Yunnan and northern Burma and Thailand. Already many were being evacuated to Taiwan, where, with renewed American aid, they would build a Nationalist redoubt and Chiang would spend his final years in the frustrated hope of retaking the mainland. For his part, Mao would mount the enormous Gate of Heavenly Peace, the great portal of the Forbidden City, and announce the founding of the new People's Republic of China on October 1, 1949. The long "century of humiliation" had ended.

A NEW SOCIETY AND CULTURE

To some extent, the modernization of the Chinese intellectual and cultural world in the early twentieth century was paralleled by a pattern of modernization of economic and social conditions. That is, even during the most chaotic years of the Warlord Period, China's industrial indices rose, in some cases dramatically, but always more or less on a par with rates of growth in more economically advanced countries. It must be remembered, however, that the base from which they are measured is quite low. China built thousands of miles of paved road, two major trunk railroads, and even began air service between some cities by the beginning of the war with Japan in 1937. But its overall industrial production was below that of Belgium. Even so, the country's halting steps toward unification and infrastructure building disproportionly affected the cities. There, one had access to electrical service, the cinema, automobiles, and streetcars. The people increasingly dressed in the international standard of suits for men and dresses for women. In the rural areas, however, grinding poverty remained the order of the day, providing fertile ground for Mao's theories of peasants' revolutionary potential.

The New Culture Movement

The last decade of the Qing had been marked by a growing tide of translations of such seminal Western thinkers as Darwin, Spencer, Huxley, Mill, Marx, Malthus, the British political economists, and an ever-expanding group of Enlightenment and Romantic writers. The rise of China's university system, with Peking University as the most vital center of philosophy, politics, and literature, opened up the intellectual scene to a growing number of people who had passed through the new primary school system. Many, as we saw earlier, believed that China's new status as a republic required not just political change but radical social change as well. Literary realism, pragmatism, positivism, and materialism were among the intellectual hallmarks accompanying this trend.

Scholars have perceived a number of phases within what was coalescing into the New Culture Movement. One important part of this movement was the drive to abandon the literary language of the elites in favor of the modern vernacular. Sometimes called "the Chinese Literary Renaissance," this movement saw a surge of not just vernacular literature, but "modern" literary forms as well. Such writers as Chen Duxiu argued that one needed to be scientific, not philosophical; value youth, not age; value democracy, not monarchy—even value women equally with men, not hierarchically. The vitality of China's intellectual scene through the early 1920s and the connections that many of the advanced students and faculty had to Western institutions also attracted high-profile visitors like John Dewey, Bertrand Russell, George Bernard Shaw, and Albert Einstein. Politically, the New Culture Movement meshed effectively with the nationalism to which the May Fourth Movement gave rise.

Other key figures associated with or influenced by the movement include Lu Xun (1881–1936), Lao She (1899–1966), and Ding Ling (1904–1986). Lu Xun, the pen name of Zhou Shuren, is widely regarded as China's greatest twentieth-century writer. His earliest work appeared in *New Youth* toward the end of World War I. He had spent time immersing himself in Russian literature and borrowed Nicolai Gogol's title for his pivotal short story, "Diary of a Madman." In perhaps his most famous piece, *The True Story of Ah Q*, as in all of Lu's work, there is a heavy sense of the social and cultural entropy of a China mired in its most destructive traditions. Indeed, in "Diary," the narrator's madness revolves around a vision of China as a nation of cannibals consuming each other and devouring their young. The final entry penned by the Madman still haunts today: "Save the children!"

Lao She, the pen name of Shu Qingchun, was a writer and playwright of Manchu descent. He studied in London, where he was influenced by the work of Charles Dickens, and much of his writing bears both the bite of social commentary and the sly humor of his model. Later, during the war, he worked as a commentator and propagandist for China and the Allies. Lao She's most important novel was *Luotuo Xiangzi*, literally "Camel Xiangzi" but often translated as "Rickshaw Boy" or simply "Rickshaw." It traces the gradual wearing down and death of a Beijing rickshaw puller. His later three-act play, *Teahouse*, traces the tumultuous history of China from 1898 to 1949 through the lives of those who meet in a Beijing teahouse.

Ding Ling, born Jiang Bingzhi, was China's most widely known woman writer. In many ways epitomizing the trends toward women's emancipation and feminism, she fled the prospect of an arranged marriage for the progressive environment of Shanghai. Her most influential early work was *Miss Sophia's Diary*, in which she traces the trials of a young woman's coming of age in the repressive atmosphere she understood so well. By the early 1930s, she had become an activist and joined the Communist Party following the Nationalist's execution of her husband, the poet He Yepin. Ding Ling herself was put under house arrest and brutally interrogated by the GMD before escaping and joining Mao's forces in Yan'an. There, however, her satirical writings on Party hypocrisy toward women made her unpopular with Mao and the Party leadership, a circumstance that hounded her during the Anti-Rightest campaign of the late 1950s and Cultural Revolution of the 1960s.

City and Country

As we noted above, much had changed in the cities by the early twentieth century. The treaty ports especially were the places that provided not just refuge from China's confused politics, but also the most modern social, political, and cultural trends. Although plenty of traditional practices—concubinage, arranged marriage, informal bond servitude, private vendettas—could still be found there, they were also the hotbeds of radical politics and bohemian lifestyles. Bars, nightclubs, dance halls, cinemas, posh modern and traditional restaurants could all be found as well. Like Ding Ling, many women of the new generation born after 1900, caught between the glimpses of modernity they saw in newspapers, magazines, and even movies, and their extended families' insistence on strict Confucian morality, fled to the new enclaves of modernity seeking the freedom they promised.

The New Culture Movement. (A) Cai Yuanpei (1868–1940) was a Chinese educator and the president of Peking University (Beijing Daxue) at a time when it was the center of China's modern intellectual life. (B) Lu Xun (or Lu Hsun) was the pen name of Zhou Shuren (1881–1936), one of the major Chinese writers of the twentieth century. Considered by many to be the founder of modern Chinese literature, he wrote in the vernacular as well as Classical Chinese. Lu Xun was a short story writer, editor, translator, critic, essayist, and poet. His best-known works, such as *The True Story of Ah Q* and "Diary of a Madman," savagely depict the entropy and collapse of the old social order during the warlord period. In the 1930s, he became the titular head of the Chinese League of Left-Wing Writers in Shanghai. (C) Lao She (1899–1966) was another highly versatile writer, noted particularly for his novel *Luotuo Xiangzi* or *Camel Xiangzi* (or "Rickshaw Boy"), tracing the gradual descent and death of a rickshaw puller. His play *Teahouse* traces the history of the first half of the twentieth century through a group of friends who gather regularly at a Beijing teahouse. Here, he tends his home garden in 1964, two years before his death during the Cultural Revolution. (D) Perhaps China's most famous woman writer of the mid-twentieth century, Ding Ling (1904–1986). With her writing about women's lives at a time when feminism was increasingly rooted in progressive Chinese intellectual circles, her most influential early work, *Miss Sophia's Diary*, traces the coming of age of a young woman in a brutally repressive family environment. Joining the Communist Party, she periodically ran afoul of its leadership for her outspoken critique of Party actions toward women.

Fashion tended to reflect this as well. The political act of cutting off one's queue after 1911 completely changed men's hairstyles for the remainder of the century. Men increasingly abandoned their traditional gowns and adopted Western-style shirts and trousers, suits, and leather shoes. Even more striking were women's fashions. Stylish urban women were bobbing their hair in the 1920s; some adopted the short dress of "flappers." Others adapted more traditional full-length dresses by shortening them and creating a slit on the side to reveal the leg, creating the famous *qipao*. Many also began to wear foreign-style high heels—especially as bound feet were rapidly going out of fashion. Women and men both avidly took up smoking cigarettes, and it was considered the height of chic behavior to enjoy the latest cocktail with a cigarette in a nightclub and to dance—even with strangers.

For China's vast majority of rural peasants, however, relatively little changed. Despite the verbal support consistently given to the idea of land reform and a number of promising ventures involving model farms and cooperatives, the GMD government remained constrained by lack of finances and the pressures of civil war, encroachment by Japan, and suppressing or winning over the surviving warlords. Chiang's primary base of support, moreover, was the urban bourgeoisie, whom he continually squeezed for revenue. Thus, the land reforms of Mao's Jiangxi Soviet stood in marked contrast to the bootless efforts of the Nationalists. Nonetheless, the period saw a number of demographic and sociological studies of rural life, most notably by Fei Xiaotong and the one-time husband of novelist Pearl S. Buck, John Lossing Buck. What the studies revealed, however, was the utter destitution of large areas of the country punctuated by small isolated regions of relative prosperity.

CONCLUSION

The period from 1895 to 1949 was among the most politically convulsive and culturally diverse eras of modern China and, arguably, East Asia as a whole. It began with the (First) Sino-Japanese War, and each passing decade of the first half of the twentieth century saw a major conflict: the Boxer War, the Xinhai Revolution, the Warlord Era, the Northern Expedition, the Nationalist/Communist civil war, the war with Japan, and the reprise of the civil war. The pattern of incomplete revolution begun with the founding of the republic in 1912 continued throughout the period against a backdrop of continuous warfare. The Guomindang unification was never stable enough to ensure uniform development of all sectors of the polity and economy.

World War II, though, put Chiang's China, however flawed, into the position of a major power and, with the end of the war and beginning of the Cold War, a key recipient of American support. Even after Chiang's defeat and flight to Taiwan, that support continued, although in progressively reduced form. With both Chiang and Mao Zedong claiming the mantle of Sun Yat-sen, it would be Mao's People's Republic of China that would ultimately emerge as the major power. What that polity would look like, however, would be contested for decades to come.

(A)

(B)

The Modern City: Scenes of Shanghai Life. Shanghai in the 1920s and 1930s had grown into the booming "Paris of the Orient," and its modern conveniences and amenities set the pace for urban development for all of China's large cities. In the two photographs here, we see (A) the mixed traffic of street cars, automobiles, and pedestrians on a typical street; and (B) the contemporary fashions of young urban women with unbound feet wearing heels, some sporting the Chinese contribution to modern elegant dress, the *qipao*.

FURTHER RESOURCES

Buck, John Lossing. *Land Utilization in China.* Chicago: University of Chicago Press, 1938. A classic of sociology and demography, Buck's study encompassing tens of thousands of rural farms in twenty-two Chinese provinces gives us the most complete snapshot of China's rural conditions before land reform under the People's Republic.

Esherick, Joseph. *Reform and Revolution in China: The 1911 Revolution in Hunan and Hubei.* Berkeley: University of California Press, 1976. The 1911 Revolution has been comparatively underexamined, and this volume represents a pioneering effort.

Esherick, Joseph. *The Origins of the Boxer Uprising.* Berkeley and Los Angeles: University of California Press, 1987. Award-winning, if somewhat dated, treatment of the Boxer Movement and its effects on the end of the Qing and China's course in the first decades of the twentieth century.

Levine, Marilyn A. *The Found Generation: Chinese Communists in Europe During the Twenties.* Seattle: University of Washington Press, 1993. Interesting account of the little known experiences of young Chinese radicals studying in Europe, many of whom had served in the Labor Corps during World War I.

McCord, Edward A. *The Power of the Gun: The Emergence of Modern Chinese Warlordism.* Berkeley: University of California Press, 1993. The most thorough monographic treatment of the individuals and the period. Examines military and political motivations of the major actors. Sees the pattern of warlordism as a symptom and failed attempt at a solution of federalism to the collapse of the republic.

Salisbury, Harrison E. *The Long March: The Untold Story.* New York: Macmillan, 1985. Solid, well-written account of the Long March by veteran *New York Times* reporter, who retraced the route and interviewed veterans and locals along the way. Reflective of interactions between Western reporters and Party members during the early days of the Four Modernizations as well.

Shoppa, R. Keith. *Chinese Elites and Political Change.* Cambridge, MA: Harvard University Press, 1982. An early work in which the author uses a micro-regional approach in a study of Zhejiang Province. The regional zone and analysis of identity is used as well in his text *Revolution and Its Past.*

Taylor, Jay. *The Generalissimo: Chiang Kai-shek and the Struggle for Modern China.* Cambridge, MA: Harvard University Press, 2009. Magisterial biography of Chiang by a former State Department official and author of a biography of Chiang Kai-shek's son, Chiang Ching-kuo. Sees Chiang as a far more complex and important figure than he is generally portrayed.

Tuchman, Barbara. *Stillwell and the American Experience in China, 1911–45.* New York: Macmillan, 1971; Grove Press, 2001. Pulitzer Prize–winning work of popular history. Traces Stillwell's career as a military "China hand" in the years before World War II and his especially stormy relationship with Chiang Kai-shek.

Waldron, Arthur. *From War to Nationalism: China's Turning Point.* Cambridge, UK: Cambridge University Press, 1995. Looks at the critical events of 1924–1925, especially the May Thirtieth Movement, the death of Sun, and the introduction of increasingly radical nationalism as precipitating factors.

Xu Guoqi. *Chinese and Americans: A Shared History.* Cambridge, MA: Harvard University Press, 2014. Examines a number of case studies of Chinese in America and Americans in China. Particularly good in looking at the influence of Frank Goodnow on Yuan Shikai's efforts to revive the monarchy and the influence of John Dewey on the New Culture Movement.

WEBSITES

https://www.extension.harvard.edu/open-learning-initiative/china-history. Harvard University Extension School. *China: Traditions and Transformations Open Learning Course.* Part of Harvard's online series of extension courses, site includes course information, free video lectures, and links to other courses in Chinese history.

https://www.loc.gov/today/cyberlc/feature_wdesc.php?rec=4043. Library of Congress webcasts. *China Rediscovers Its Own History.* A 109-minute lecture with biographical notes by a leading scholar of Chinese intellectual history, Yu Ying-shih. A talk on "the current debate within the Chinese Communist Party on the roles that democracy, tradition, Confucianism, and Maoism play in reinterpreting China's history...."

https://www.pbs.org/kqed/chinainside/. Public Broadcasting System. *China From the Inside: An Exploration of China, Her People, Her Past, and Her Present.* Informative and entertaining overview of Chinese history and society, with an emphasis on recent developments.

CHAPTER 10

↜◌

From Continuous Revolution to Authoritarian Modernity: China from 1895 to the Present, Part II

The task of rebuilding the country that now fell to the new government was a formidable one. The civil war had further exhausted the national resources from their already minimal levels at the end of World War II. China was still fundamentally a peasant-based country, with perhaps 80 percent of the population involved in agriculture. What industry existed was concentrated in or near the major cities, especially Shanghai. Hong Kong and Macau remained European colonies. Much of the industry developed by the Japanese in Manchuria had been stripped and carried away by the Soviets in the last days of World War II. Mao's theories of revolution had adapted Marxist principles to put peasants instead of industrial workers at the forefront of the movement toward socialism. Although this appeared to work as a strategy for revolution in a peasant-based society, it was still an open question as to whether such an approach would work in rebuilding the infrastructure and economy of the country as a whole. Therefore, as had Lenin with his New Economic Policy of the early 1920s, Mao decided that now the government would encourage a degree of capitalist flexibility among the "patriotic bourgeoisie."

THE MAOIST YEARS, 1949 TO 1976

A central aspect of Mao's theories was the idea that the Chinese people were really the only reliable resource the country possessed. Lacking a workable industrial and transportation base, China's early Maoist years were thus marked by a pattern of repeated mass mobilization campaigns. These were organized under the rubric of the "mass line": The Party was to solicit ideas "from the masses" and formulate policies based on these suggestions that went out "to the masses."

Early Mass Mobilization Campaigns
With the outbreak of the Korean War, support from the new Chinese regime was largely moral and propagandistic. As UN forces in Korea drove on the Yalu River border with China in October, 1950, however, a massive force of "people's

298

volunteers" crossed the river and attacked them. By November they were pushing the UN forces back into South Korea. As part of the seesaw fighting over the next three years, UN troops pushed the Sino-Korean army out of Seoul in March 1951, and the fighting stalemated around the 38th Parallel dividing north from south (see Map 10.1).

In support of the Chinese effort in Korea, the People's Republic mounted the **Resist America-Aid Korea** mobilization campaign. Its aims were to break down latent friendly feelings toward the U.S. as well as expose any remaining pro-Guomindang sentiment. Party workers carried out propaganda initiatives insisting on solidarity with Korea and all socialist states, called for volunteers for the army, and encouraged citizens to ferret out those with American ties, or suspicious activities or ideas. Several alleged spy rings were broken up and their members executed, and the program merged with a more general effort to eliminate "counter-revolutionaries."

At the same time, the **Three-Anti and Five-Anti Campaigns** were aimed at consolidating Party supremacy in government and the economic sector. As we have seen, the Party had briefly encouraged "patriotic bourgeoisie" to re-open factories and industrial enterprises, and was willing to tolerate a certain degree of capitalism in order to stimulate the economy, restore a degree

Map 10.1 The People's Republic of China and the Republic of China, 1950

of urban normality, and reassure overseas Chinese and foreign investors as to the new regime's intentions. The war in Korea and the hardening of Cold War positions, however, cut this short. Thus, toward the end of 1951, the Party announced the "Three-Anti" (*san fan*) campaign: anti-corruption; anti-waste; anti-"bureaucratism." This campaign aimed to purge non-Party members, test the loyalty and reliability of Party officials, and eliminate real and potential Guomindang sympathizers.

Within months, in January 1952, the Party launched the Five-Anti (*wu fan*) campaign. In a pattern that Maoist-era Chinese painfully learned to anticipate, the Five-Anti movement targeted the capitalists and "patriotic bourgeoisie" that it had previously encouraged. The practicesto be opposed in this campaign were: bribery, theft of state property, tax evasion, cheating on government contracts, and stealing state economic information. By 1953, the government had effectively reined in the business community and had begun the process of nationalizing most of its assets.

Land Reform

The largest campaign, however, was land reform. As we have seen in all the chapters pertaining to China, how best to divide and utilize farmland had been a problem faced by every Chinese regime. Mao's idea, which had been pursued previously in the areas controlled by the Party, was expropriation of landlord holdings and distribution of that land directly to tenants and the landless. In June 1950, the new government enacted the **Agrarian Reform Law**, under which

Land Reform with a Vengeance. In this photograph from 1952, a farmer kneels at gunpoint before a Communist court enforcing land redistribution policies. Like thousands of others, the landowner was convicted of being a "class enemy" and was executed.

the land of landlords was to be confiscated, along with that of monasteries and religious institutions, and distributed to the poor and landless. "Patriotic landlords" who voluntarily submitted to the process were for the moment accorded relatively lenient treatment. Those who resisted, or were disliked by their tenants, were "struggled." They were commonly trussed up and made to kneel while Party cadres urged their tenants to verbally and physically abuse them. They were then often summarily executed by the cadres or lynched by their former tenants. By some estimates, land reform took as many as 2 million lives.

Peasant land ownership, however, caused agricultural productivity to increase markedly. By 1952, the government announced that land reform had been completed and that the national budget was balanced and commodity prices stabilized. Since so much of the livelihood of the country and the revenues to fund industrialization hinged on agriculture, land reform was seen as the first step toward collectivization, which, it was believed, would result in far greater efficiency and yields. With land reform accomplished, China's first five-year plan went into effect in 1953. As with the Soviet model in the 1930s, the immediate goal was the ratcheting up of heavy industry, with a secondary emphasis on light industry and consumer goods. China received a loan from the Soviet Union for the construction of power stations, and began operations at its first open pit coal mine.

The Great Leap Forward

Mao desperately wanted to avoid the mass chaos and bloodletting that accompanied Soviet collectivization in the late 1920s. The Party leadership believed that by going slowly and consolidating their gains at each step, they could greatly ease the transition. Thus, in 1953, peasants were encouraged to form "agricultural producers' cooperatives" (APCs) in which villages formed units to share scarce tools and machinery. By 1956, agricultural production had recovered to pre–World War II levels and was registering impressive gains.

Mao and his inner circle, however, were growing impatient with the pace of collectivization. If production could be ramped up sufficiently, the surplus agricultural funds from taxes and exports could then be used to fund a more ambitious Second Five-Year Plan. Moreover, the Chinese had been borrowing heavily from the USSR through the 1950s and had availed themselves of Soviet technicians and engineers. All the progress of the decade might be radically slowed or halted if agricultural revenues could not keep pace. Mao therefore prodded the Party into its most colossal mass mobilization project yet: **The Great Leap Forward**, slated to start January 1, 1958. The entire population of the country was to be pushed into a campaign to communalize agriculture into self-sustaining units that would function like factories in the fields. Men and women would work in shifts and live in barracks on enormous collective farms. In Mao's view, the campaign would not only vault China into socialism but would also go far toward eliminating "contradictions among the people" that were key impediments to such a transition: contradictions between urban and rural, between the industrial and agricultural, and between mental and manual labor.

Modern Communist

Eliminating Contradictions: The Great Leap Forward. The Great Leap Forward was an economic and social campaign of the Communist Party, reflected in planning decisions from 1958 to 1961, which aimed to use China's vast population to rapidly transform the country from an agrarian economy into a modern Communist society through the process of rapid industrialization and collectivization. Here, workers in Beijing attempt to make steel in a small, rudimentary smelting furnace in October 1958. The Great Leap Forward created a massive upheaval in Chinese society and by effectively disabling the agricultural and small manufacturing centers contributed greatly to a record famine that by 1962 cost China some 30 million lives.

By way of bringing industry to agricultural areas, peasants were to surrender all their iron and steel tools and utensils to be melted down and recycled into steel to build the new infrastructure of the communes. A stated goal of the campaign, in fact, was to surpass the steel production of Great Britain within fifteen years. The most recognizable symbol of the campaign became the backyard steel furnace, which commune members were to build and run for their own needs. Technical problems were to be solved by the "wisdom of the masses." The entire country would therefore modernize its rural areas and infrastructure in one grand campaign.

In reality, the Great Leap was the most catastrophic policy failure in the history of the People's Republic. The initial wave of enthusiasm that greeted the mobilization swiftly ground to a halt as peasants began to actively resist the seizure of their land and implements. The quality of almost all the steel produced was virtually worthless, while the effort used a considerable amount of precious energy resources. Moreover, in sacrificing scarce tools and utensils, millions of peasants now had few or none to use in sustaining themselves. So many were forced into building the communal structures and making useless steel that by 1959 agricultural production in China had plummeted, and the country experienced its worst famine in modern times over the next several years. By 1962, an estimated 30 million people may have died in its wake.

The Hundred Flowers and Anti-Rightist Campaigns

In May 1956, long before the disaster of the Great Leap and with the progress of land reform and the APCs' cause for optimism, Mao felt the time was opportune to take the temperature of the nation's intellectuals. Many had initially been enthusiastic about the general direction of the Party, but Mao was not sure whether they actually supported the programs or were simply being circumspect. The Party therefore proceeded to apply the "mass line" technique to intellectuals: teachers, professors, writers, editors—opinion makers of any kind.

Adopting a slogan from China's philosophically rich Late Zhou period, "Let a hundred flowers bloom, let a hundred schools of thought contend," they threw open the door to public criticism of the Party's record, assuring the intellectuals that offering their critique was patriotic.

By mid-1957, the trickle of criticism had become a torrent. When some critics questioned the basic foundations of socialism and suggested forming an opposition party, Mao acted swiftly. In early June, the **Hundred FlowersCampaign** was terminated and the **Anti-Rightist Campaign** launched. Calls for an opposition party were denounced as the worst kind of right-wing thinking—as opposed to the correct left-wing thinking of the Party. Those accused of "rightism" were rounded up and subjected to "re-education"; in addition to being imprisoned and made to endure endless "self-criticism" sessions, many were also sentenced to long stretches of "reform through labor" in remote peasant villages.

Taking a Breath in the Revolution

The miscalculation of intellectual sentiment during the Hundred Flowers program and the hasty capping of it by the Anti-Rightist Campaign marked the first large misstep for Mao's road to socialism. The Great Leap Forward debacle of the following year convinced even many of Mao's closest supporters that the Party needed to change its path. Thus, 1959 saw a major shakeup in Party and national leadership. Mao had already announced that he would not seek another term as chairman. Liu Shaoqi, whom Mao in a few years would denounce as the "number one person taking the capitalist road," now assumed leadership. His new State Council included Madame Sun Yat-sen (Song Qingling)—whose sister, as we have seen, was Madame Chiang Kai-shek—and a new army chief, Lin Biao, who would play a central role in Mao's comeback and the Cultural Revolution that followed.

The new regime represented a tilt toward the "expert" camp (as represented by Liu and China's later leader Deng Xiaoping), as opposed to those like Mao who insisted on the primacy of ideology—"redness"—as the key to solving all problems. In many respects, the history of the People's Republic has been the history of the struggles of such "reds" and "experts." Thus, Mao's brand of Communism—with its pattern of mass mobilization and proper political attitude over technical expertise—was dialed back considerably.

The decade began unpromisingly, however, with the "Sino-Soviet Split," in which apprehensiveness in the USSR about China's radical programs and Mao's distrust of Soviet policy under Khrushchev led to a complete withdrawal of Soviet aid and advisors in 1960. The Chinese had earlier been taken aback by Khrushchev's denunciation of Stalin's excesses, and as Khrushchev appeared to be softening his stance toward the United States, the Chinese believed that the USSR had departed from Lenin's "correct" views on capitalism and imperialism. For their part, the Soviets, faced with the possibility of nuclear war with the United States, felt that Mao had been irresponsibly cavalier in his attitude toward such a possibility.

Nonetheless, China made several important technological advances. Chief among these was the detonation of China's first nuclear device in October 1964.

China Joins the Nuclear Club. Ever since the People's Republic faced the threat of American use of nuclear weapons during the Korean War, Chinese scientists had been working to develop a weapon of their own. With the Sino-Soviet Split in 1960, Soviet technical and financial assistance evaporated, but the nod to "experts" over "reds" during the early 1960s allowed Chinese scientists to move forward and conduct their first successful test in October 1964. A great deal of propaganda footage was taken, including this (unauthenticated) shot of the sinister "mushroom cloud" characteristic of nuclear blasts.

This was quickly followed by the testing of a thermonuclear (hydrogen) device in 1966. Chinese scientists also synthesized insulin and made advances in missile technology that would yield the first Chinese satellites in the following decade. Extensive studies of China's natural resources also disclosed large coal deposits and led to the discovery of oil fields at Daqing and in the extreme west.

Liu's regime also engaged in an assertive policy of border rectification. Chinese forces had entered Tibet in 1959 to suppress an independence movement, resulting in the flight of the Dalai Lama to India. In securing Tibet, however, disputes arose regarding the actual border with India. In 1962, Chinese forces moved into the disputed regions and fought a brief undeclared war until withdrawing and submitting the issue to negotiation. This kind of display of force in order to make a point would be seen again in Vietnam in 1979, although with far less effectiveness (see Map 10.2).

As China's Communist Party and government assumed a more Soviet-style approach to running the People's Republic, Mao Zedong grew increasingly uneasy about the direction of policy. For Mao, the Party was reverting to bureaucratic behavior and increasingly unresponsive to the needs of advancing the revolution toward pure Communism. Though out of power, Mao was still revered in Party circles as the great revolutionary leader. In plotting his political comeback, therefore, he played to his seemingly unassailable strengths as an exponent of selfless Communist virtues. Thus, Mao spent the early 1960s writing widely circulated essays extolling the virtues of devoted Communists and creating a new base for himself, especially among younger Party members. Perhaps the most important step in this regard was the publication of his famous **little red book**, *Quotations from Chairman Mao Zedong*, in 1964. His ideological ally, Lin Biao (1907–1971), as head of the People's Liberation Army, made it required reading for the troops and helped Mao establish a vitally important power base there.

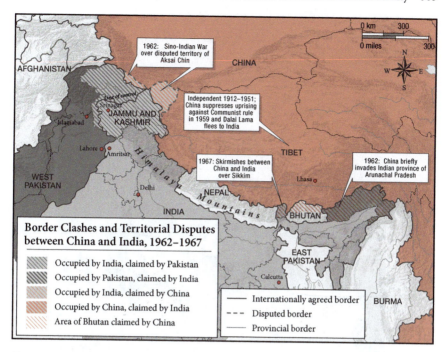

Map 10.2 Border Clashes and Territorial Disputes between China and India, 1962–1967

Becoming Proletarian: The Cultural Revolution

By the spring of 1966, Mao was ready to make his move. His guiding precept was that of "continuous revolution": that the class struggle must go on until true socialism—as opposed to the bureaucratic Soviet model—had been achieved. In order to do this, the people must be inculcated with "proletarian consciousness" and purged of the last vestiges of "feudal," "bourgeois," and "revisionist" thinking. Only with such an all-pervasive revolutionary proletarian consciousness could China make the final leap to complete socialism. The country's youth were encouraged to criticize their elders and form their own pure ideological path to socialism. Students formed themselves into squads of Red Guards and attacked their teachers and elders. Those with any foreign connections, or who had supported the former regime, or were perceived to be tainted by bourgeois or feudal thinking, or simply lukewarm in their support for the present campaign were singled out for public interrogation and humiliation.

Teachers were trussed up, made to wear dunce caps with their "crimes" emblazoned on placards around their necks, and splashed with ink as they were paraded through the streets. Hundreds of thousands of people from all walks of life were "struggled" before jeering crowds and made to confess their alleged crimes over and over. Millions were required to write constant self-confessions of their ideological misdeeds. Vast numbers of young people responded with enthusiasm to Mao's injunction to "learn from the peasants" and embarked for

Red Guards in the Cultural Revolution. Mao Zedong's urging of students to question the authority of their elders and even the Communist Party bureaucrats created enormous chaos in the country, set different elements of society against each other, and by 1968 brought the PRC close to open civil war. Emblematic of the Cultural Revolution were the Red Guards, young people who created a cult of personality around Mao, carrying the "Little Red Book" of the Chairman's quotations and shouting slogans from it as they challenged the existing order. Here, a Red Guard detachment, Little Red Books in hand, parade with red banners and portraits of Mao.

rural areas to work on farms. As in past campaigns, millions more of the less fortunate were sentenced to be "sent down" to work on farms or subjected to "reform through labor."

From 1966 until 1969, when the Cultural Revolution was declared successfully completed, millions of people were hounded, tortured, killed, or driven to suicide by Red Guards and their allies. Incalculable damage was done to the country's cultural heritage in the name of eliminating the traces of China's "feudal" heritage. The "little red book" became the talisman of the movement, with people struggling to interpret it correctly to prove their ideological fitness. Study groups sprang up throughout the country as constant and correct reference to the work was mandatory in any discussion. Score settling among rivals and neighbors became endemic to the Revolution. Guilt by association or, especially, class background, became a special concern. Those coming from peasant and proletarian backgrounds were among the most favored.

The End of the Maoist Era

By 1968, the country was in complete chaos as pro– and anti–Cultural Revolution factions battled each other in several regions, most notably around the cities comprising Wuhan. It was chiefly to end this endemic civil war that the Cultural Revolution was declared over. The next two years, however, saw a vastly enhanced political position for the People's Liberation Army (PLA) and Lin Biao. Despite its own factionalism, the army had played a vital role in suppressing the worst fighting and in restoring a semblance of order in the country. Thus, Lin Biao was named Mao's "official" successor.

Despite their outward show of unity, Mao periodically had his doubts about Lin's ultimate loyalty to him and his programs. The politicization of the army, moreover, had placed the most powerful force in the land at Lin's disposal, and a split was developing between the civilian and military members of the **Politburo.** Although debate still continues about what happened next, it appears that members of Lin's family and an inside group of supporters planned a coup in which Mao and many of the Politburo would be killed and Lin installed as chairman. Whether Lin was actively involved in the conspiracy or played a passive role is unknown. In any event, on September 13, 1971, Lin and his wife and staff were killed in a plane crash in Mongolia while on their way to seek asylum in the Soviet Union. Fleeing at treetop level to avoid Chinese radar, the plane may have been flying too low, although there is also some evidence to suggest it was shot down.

The final years of Mao's life witnessed a number of contradictory trends, though each in its own way would deeply shape the future of China after the Chairman's passing on September 9, 1976. Mao was shaken by the Lin Biao incident, the economy had been severely disrupted by the Cultural Revolution, and much of the Party leadership now consisted of radicals who had replaced older members purged during the last few years. Mao's wife, Jiang Qing, along with Zhang Chunqiao, Yao Wenyuan, and Wang Hongwen—reviled shortly after as the **Gang of Four**—were at the center of the radicals, although it was never clear how much their activities took place at Mao's behest or how much was on their own initiative.

In the midst of these maneuverings, the Nixon administration in the United States launched an epoch-changing initiative to restore relations with the People's Republic. The U.S. and many of its allies still recognized Chiang Kai-shek's Nationalist regime on Taiwan as the legitimate Chinese government, and Nixon himself had been seen as an arch-anti-Communist Cold Warrior. Yet as he and his National Security Advisor Henry Kissinger realized, reaching out to the PRC might give the Americans leverage (the so-called China Card) in their dealings with the Soviets. Moreover, a better relationship with China would also be advantageous in the ongoing negotiations to end U.S. involvement in Vietnam. In 1971, therefore, Kissinger met secretly in Beijing with Zhou Enlai, paving the way for a visit by Nixon the following year.

The 1972 Nixon trip to China and meeting with Mao saw most of the major diplomatic issues resolved, and agreement on talks to resolve the remaining ones. In the resulting **Shanghai Communique**, both sides agreed to mutual diplomatic

Nixon Plays the "China Card." As the United States pushed ahead in winding down its commitment in Vietnam, the Nixon administration hoped to obtain a degree of assistance from China in pressuring North Vietnam to accept American peace proposals. Following a secret trip to the PRC by Secretary of State Henry Kissinger, Nixon, famous for his staunch anti-Communism and antagonism toward the People's Republic, traveled to Beijing to meet Chinese dignitaries and, as in this photo, confer and banquet with Chairman Mao himself. Shortly after, the U.S. announced it would re-open diplomatic relations with the PRC and sanction its representatives, displacing Taiwan on the UN Security Council.

recognition. The issue of Taiwan was finessed by allowing the Nationalists to have a "special interests office" in place of their embassy in the U.S. The U.S. agreed to recognize the PRC as the official government of China, although it would still provide Taiwan with weapons and defense, a provision that has remained a sticking point ever since.

A U-TURN ON THE SOCIALIST ROAD

The death of Mao Zedong in September 1976 opened the way for a new generation of Communist Party leaders in China. The end result was a repudiation of the Cultural Revolution and those who promoted it, and an entirely different direction in strategy for building a New China. The chairmanship passed within a month to the moderate Hua Guofeng (1921–2008). Although Hua claimed he had been Mao's choice to succeed him, he was less than dynamic as a leader. His initial policies were described as the "Two Whatevers": whatever policies originated with Mao were to be supported, and whatever directions Mao had given to the Party were to be followed.

The Gang of Four. The arrest and subsequent trial of the so-called Gang of Four, at the center of which was Mao's widow Jiang Qing along with several other individuals, signaled a marked shift in China's policies. The members had been among the most avid proponents of the Cultural Revolution and sought to continue its most radical policies after most of the other high Party officials had backed away from them. They were charged with conspiracy and counter-revolution. Jiang Qing and Zhang Chunqiao received death sentences in 1981, although these were commuted to life in prison; the rest of the Gang received long prison terms. Jiang Qing committed suicide in 1991 while undergoing treatment for throat cancer.

One policy that would change almost immediately, however, involved the Gang of Four. In November 1976, they were arrested and put on trial in 1980 for counter-revolution, plotting to overthrow the state and assorted other offenses. In 1981, Jiang Qing and Zhang Chunqiao were sentenced to death, with a two-year reprieve, later commuted to life imprisonment. Jiang Qing ultimately committed suicide in 1991 while undergoing treatment for throat cancer.

China's Four Modernizations

Hua continued to pay lip service to the legacy of Mao, but looked more and more to the hardy Deng Xiaoping (1904–1997) and other "experts," who at this point seemed to favor a return to Soviet economic models. Deng emerged on the scene in 1978 with the title of vice premier, but in fact held the real power in the regime as Hua was increasingly criticized for his "Two Whatevers" policy. The ascendancy of the pragmatic Deng to "paramount leader" (although he kept his official title of vice premier), whose motto was "It doesn't matter whether the cat is black or white, as long as it catches mice," swiftly led to the unveiling of the fundamental policies that remain in force in China to the present: the **Four Modernizations**.

As a repeated victim of the shifting political winds in the Party, Deng recognized the immense damage that radical mass mobilizations could bring about. Having long been involved in economic and technical matters, he was also aware that China's communal agriculture system was rife with inefficiency, and that the Cultural Revolution had, in effect, stalled the country for a decade. Moreover, the Chinese military and industrial sectors had long been outmoded and were falling further behind at an alarming rate. China's isolation had prevented it from benefiting from most international trade, while consumer goods in general and the burgeoning market in electronics in particular were practically nonexistent in the PRC.

Thus, Deng's strategy was bent on upgrading the quantity and quality of agriculture, industry, science and technology, and the military as quickly as possible. In a move reminiscent of that urged by the "self-strengtheners" of the nineteenth century, China would pursue a new policy under an old slogan, "Use foreign things to help China." A key part of this endeavor was a "new Open Door" policy with regard to foreign expertise from the West. Having just restored its higher education system and reinstituted college entrance exams, China would now also allow its students to study abroad and welcomed foreign students to its universities.

Most tellingly, the plan would allow the market forces of capitalism to create incentives for innovation in all sectors of the economy. The introduction of such wholesale changes would take place in stages, then adopted by the nation as a whole where appropriate. A popular motto, soon emblazoned on a new kind of garment import from the West—the t-shirt—thus became "To get rich is glorious!" The most pressing need was to raise agricultural productivity. The communes there were experimentally disbanded, land was doled out to village families, and peasants were allowed to sell surplus produce and livestock at local markets after the rent and taxes were paid. The "responsibility system" in agriculture worked so well that by the early 1980s it was adopted countrywide. By the mid-1980s, China was rapidly approaching self-sufficiency in food production. By the 1990s, it would register surpluses and export a variety of food products.

In much the same way, the responsibility system was introduced into industry. A **Special Economic Zone (SEZ)** was set up in South China at Shenzhen to take advantage of capital and expertise from nearby Hong Kong. Again, the Shenzhen model proved so successful that the town itself grew into a large municipality with considerable domestic and foreign investment. Over the next several years, other SEZs were set up around the country and, cautiously at first, then with increasing rapidity, the older state-run enterprises were turned over to private ownership. Despite problems with corruption—deals were often made by means of *guanxi* ("connections") through "the back door" (*houmen*) with local Party officials—the experiments in capitalism were enormously successful. Through the 1980s and 1990s, China's gross domestic product (GDP) grew at an astonishing double-digit rate.

An important element of the program was the "new Open Door" policy. As they had in the nineteenth and early twentieth centuries, large multinational firms turned hungry eyes toward the virtually untapped market encompassing nearly a fifth of the world's population. The government and Party, however,

Modeling the "New Open Door" Policy. As part of Deng Xiaoping's sweeping Four Modernizations, China was to open itself to "using foreign things to help China," as well as foreign expertise. Shortly after diplomatic relations were restored between the U.S. and PRC in January 1979, Deng embarked on a trip to the United States. In this photo, he shakes hands with President Jimmy Carter behind a podium at the White House on January 29, 1979.

wanted to be extremely circumspect in setting up agreements and enterprises with foreign concerns. Hence, such joint ventures were limited initially to the SEZs and the foreign firms saddled with complex restrictions. By the 1990s, however, as such enterprises became more common, the government steadily made doing business in China less burdensome to foreign firms, a trend that has continued to the present.

As China's middle class grew, so did the sophistication of consumers, and the demand for everything from cars to fast food to electronics skyrocketed. By 2010, China had by far the world's largest middle class in absolute terms, over 500 million. As the new century began, China had, as had Japan a few decades before, a large and growing export-driven manufacturing center built on low-cost infrastructure and low wages. Many multinational companies as well as European and U.S. giants like Walmart became increasingly reliant on low-cost Chinese goods to keep their own prices competitive.

Modernizing National Defense

With Sino-Soviet relations still frosty, the PRC began to court eager Western countries for help in modernizing their military capabilities. From the American and NATO viewpoints, a strong China would be an effective card to play against the Soviets. This was especially true after China invaded Soviet ally Vietnam in 1979 to punish them for their incursion into Pol Pot's Kampuchea to drive out the genocidal Khmer Rouge (see Chapter 11). Although much of the world openly or covertly supported Vietnam's action to end Pol Pot's reign of terror, their initial enthusiasm waned as the Vietnamese attempted to place their own strongman in power and dominate the region. As a demonstration of China's military prowess, however, the incursion was a disaster. The PLA's weapons were obsolescent, the Chinese attacks were uncoordinated, leadership was wanting, and units even mounted the kind of human wave attacks that had proved so casualty-ridden in the Korean War.

The military thus demonstrated conclusively that it was in dire need of modernization. The official inauguration of full diplomatic relations between the PRC and the U.S. on January 1, 1979, was followed in a few weeks with Deng's visit to America. The following year, the Carter administration arranged for U.S. Defense Secretary Harold Brown to meet in China with officials there about establishing American listening posts to monitor Soviet activities in return for American cooperation on modern weapons.

Another, more controversial innovation aimed at modernization was the **One-Child Policy**. Population pressures were a powerful brake on China's development. Thus, a policy was inaugurated in 1979 mandating that families (excluding those of most minorities) were to have only one child. A second child would result in loss of subsidies for childrearing; a third pregnancy required a mandatory abortion. Despite the many problems in enforcing such a policy, and its severe cultural impact on the male-centered traditional Chinese family structure, China's population has remained remarkably stable since the 1980s, at around 1.3 to 1.5 billion. It has, however, abetted problems of selective female abortion, giving up girl babies for adoption, and in extreme cases female infanticide. With the population stabilized and fears of a generational bulge of seniors with too few people of working age to support them, the policy was effectively abandoned in November 2015.

The "Fifth Modernization"

The heady atmosphere of the early days of these sweeping reforms brought political reformers temporarily out of hiding. Encouraged by the air of experimentation and the perception of openness surrounding the programs of the Four Modernizations, demonstrators began to call for a wide array of democratic reforms by hanging big-character posters on the walls near Tiananmen Square. The most famous was also one of the first to be put up: On December 5, 1978, Wei Jingsheng's poster called for "the fifth modernization: democracy." The outpouring that followed in Beijing and other Chinese cities over the next several months was dubbed the "Peking Spring." Although Beijing municipal authorities granted the growing number of protestors considerable leeway, the demonstrations were ultimately suppressed. Political agitation, however, continued in muted form throughout the decade. Wei himself has continued his agitation down to the present: imprisoned from 1979 to 1993, he was released briefly before being re-arrested for talking with foreign journalists. Imprisoned again in 1994 he was deported to the United States in 1997.

Peking Spring. From the end of 1978 through the "Peking Spring" of 1979, prominent walls became "Democracy Walls, (A) covered with posters criticizing the government and advocating a variety of reforms, as at this bus company near Xidan in Beijing. The poster in the middle is, ironically, of Premier Hua Gufeng with children. (B) The most notorious critic was Wei Jingsheng (shown reading from a statement during his trial), who wrote an important essay titled "Democracy: The Fifth Modernization." Wei was branded a counter-revolutionary and sentenced to 15 years' imprisonment for supposedly supplying a foreign newsman with Chinese military intelligence and carrying out "counter-revolutionary agitation." Freed briefly in 1993, he was re-arrested and held until being deported to the United States in 1997.

TIANANMEN SQUARE AND THE NEW AUTHORITARIANISM

For Deng and the Party leadership in the 1980s, the familiar problem of achieving "modernity" without becoming culturally "Western" was growing more complex. China's old Confucian culture had been conclusively altered. The governing ideology, Marxism-Leninism-**Mao Zedong Thought**, however, was a relatively thin veneer superimposed on deep civilizational roots that even the Cultural Revolution could not eradicate. Now with China opening itself again to foreign influences, and with the country increasingly hungry for the new technologies being developed, the cultural baggage accompanying the material imports threatened the socialist mores fostered by the Party. The problem grew steadily more acute as the PRC's citizens became increasingly consumer conscious and avidly followed foreign fashions in clothes and entertainment.

In 1983, therefore, the Party launched a program to fight what it called **spiritual pollution**. Characteristically, computers were welcome, pornography and videos by performers such as Madonna were not. Literature was routinely screened for politically sensitive subjects like dissent or China's position in Tibet. Such was the public hunger for all things foreign, however, that guidelines proved difficult to enforce. The programs were, in a way, harbingers of the ways in which the government would attempt to control electronic communication by phone, fax, and in the following decades, the Internet.

Ending the Colonial Era

As part of the PRC's new market liberalism and its efforts to develop a way to play the "Western card" against the Soviets, Deng and the Party leaders decided the time was opportune to address the remaining legacy of imperialism in the area. China still confronted colonies on her south coast in the form of Hong Kong and Macau (Macao), and so entered negotiations with Great Britain and Portugal about the eventual return of these territories. Negotiations for the return of Macau began in June 1986 and resulted in an agreement to return Macau to Chinese sovereignty in 1999. Hong Kong had become one of the larger cities in East Asia and a crucial financial hub. Moreover, its position less than an hour from Shenzhen, and its connections with that SEZ, made it crucial to the success of the experiment there. Its acquisition by the PRC would vastly enhance China's modernization efforts. Liberal treatment of the colony's citizens would also help prevent human and capital flight on the eve of the transition. The result of the negotiations, therefore, was the Basic Law, which would govern Hong Kong's status for 50 years after the return of the colony, set for 1997, the year in which the 99-year lease on Hong Kong's New Territories would expire. Both would become Special Administrative Regions (SAR) overseen by Beijing, but their local governments would remain intact. Freedoms currently enjoyed in both places were guaranteed and municipal ordinances were to be honored.

In Hong Kong, however, constant friction among pro-Beijing factions and those in various degrees of opposition have made its politics volatile despite the region's economic vitality. One bone of contention has been over what degree of approval Beijing requires in vetting candidates for political office. In the fall of 2014, opposition to Beijing's insistence on approving the candidates for the 2017 municipal elections resulted in massive demonstrations that paralyzed the city and developed ties to the more loosely organized "Occupy" movements that had sprung up in the U.S. and Europe over the preceding years.

Tiananmen Square

The speed and progress of the economic reforms, coupled with the waves of Western cultural influence breaking out throughout the country, led to cleavages within the Party. Deng sought to balance these by including in the Politburo hardliners, like Li Peng, along with those associated with more liberal policies, like Zhao Ziyang and Hu Yaobang. In 1986, after criticism of his handling of Party members suspected of "bourgeois-liberal" leanings, Hu resigned his post as Party secretary. After a certain period of shuffling among the Politburo members, Zhao took over Hu's old post and Li Peng emerged as premier in 1988.

The chief catalyst of what was to follow, however, came with the death and funeral of Hu Yaobang in April 1989. An official memorial service was held on April 22 in Tiananmen Square, and an outpouring of grief and emotion filled the Square with tens of thousands of students. Over the next several days, the crowds grew, especially after Zhao's positive comments and suggestions for dialog with the students. As May 4 came, the parallels between this student movement and the one that took place seventy years before were unavoidable. At one point, students even constructed a large statue they called "the Goddess of Democracy" that dominated the center of the square near the Monument to the People's Revolutionary Martyrs. Meanwhile they had mounted a hunger strike as pressure increased for comprehensive talks. The

(A)   (B)

Tiananmen Square Demonstrations and Aftermath. At their peak in May, 1989, students demonstrating for greater government accountability and a more open political system were joined by workers and people from all walks of life. In photo (A), a large statue created by the protesters dubbed the "Goddess of Democracy" confronts the iconic portrait of Mao that hangs on the Gate of Heavenly Peace (Tiananmen) across from Tiananmen Square. The violent suppression of the protesters beginning on June 4 produced one of the world's most famous photographs (B): A man to this day known only as "Tank Man" confronts an armored column sent to help quell the demonstrations. The man refused to move, would not let the tanks maneuver around him, and even climbed up on the lead tank to try to entreat the startled driver to leave the square.

demonstrations now included people from all walks of life, and there was talk of organizing a general strike. Even as negotiations were proceeding, however, the decision to declare martial law and clear the Square had already been made, and troops were being moved into position outside of Beijing and other major cities. On June 4, they began to violently clear the demonstrators from the places they had occupied.

The shock of the attack was perhaps even more devastating to the national psyche than the material and human destruction. The People's Liberation Army from its earliest days had worked ceaselessly to cultivate its image as, quite literally, the "people's" army. It was unthinkable that the people's army would ever fire on "the people." Thus, even as the troops bivouacked around the square, demonstrators and locals mixed freely with them, seeking assurance that they were there as a show of force rather than to mount an attack. Even amidst the lingering shock in the aftermath of the assault, many undoubtedly saw the lone figure who came to be called **Tank Man** confidently remonstrating with an entire armored column's lead driver as the stubborn residue of the people's faith in the people's soldiers. To this day, the casualty figures remain in dispute: the government put the numbers at 241 dead, whereas observers on the scene and later placed the number of dead in the thousands. Many of the demonstrators themselves used video cameras to capture the confusion and carnage, and transmitted reports and photos abroad by fax in attempts to foil government censors.

"Confucian Capitalism"

Even as the after-effects of Tiananmen Square unfolded, Deng worked to accelerate the pace of economic reform. The momentum it generated in the 1990s also led to a new ideological emphasis for the Party. The Communist Party's legitimacy to rule had been historically tied to its revolutionary legacy, its championing of peasants and proletarians, and more recently, the unleashing of the people's entrepreneurial energies. To help ensure that the reforms would stay in place, President Jiang Zemin announced a new set of principles in 2000 that became known as **The Three Represents**. As the centerpiece of Jiang Zemin Theory, they have become the nexus of the CCP's claim to ongoing legitimacy. They are as follows:

> Our Party must always represent the requirements for developing China's advanced productive forces, the orientation of China's advanced culture, and the fundamental interests of the overwhelming majority of the Chinese people.

By the late 1990s, China was experiencing an astonishing double-digit growth in its GDP, but officials were increasingly worried that if the old state-owned industries were not swiftly privatized, the pace might slacken, perhaps even resulting in a recession. The Chinese economy hovered in a kind of transitional hybrid state. New enterprises appeared all the time, government controls on foreign ownership and investment were being loosened, and the rural economy was more than keeping up with food production. The state enterprises, however, which guaranteed at least a degree of universal employment and government benefits during earlier years, were now hopelessly inefficient and an increasing drain on the economy with their lifetime pensions and interconnection with the welfare system.

Thus, in 1998, the new premier, Zhu Rongji, initiated a program to shut down the state-run enterprises, sell them off, and encourage more complete privatization. Although over the next several years this caused considerable disruption and created a degree of unemployment, it did provide yet another boost for the economy that would last even through the worldwide recessions of the early twenty-first century. It did, however, require vast changes in the country's social safety net and an effective end to the "iron rice bowl."

With the economy half-privatized by the late 1990s, the cost of social welfare programs was becoming prohibitive. Thus, one by one, state benefits were rolled back and fee-for-service systems put in place. Doctor and hospital visits now required fees for various procedures and medications according to a sliding scale tagged to a percentage of an average worker's income. Primary and secondary education is still free, but there has been an explosion in tutoring institutions and charter schools. As in Japan, extra tutoring is considered absolutely essential by those who can afford it because of the rigor of the three-day *gaokao*, the grueling college entrance exams. Scholarships are still available to outstanding students for university and graduate studies, but tuition fees and room and board are charged to the rest. Foreign study, which used to be subsidized by the government, must now be paid for out of pocket. One result of this has been that foreign universities have opened branch campuses in China so that students can get the "experience" of overseas study more cheaply and closer to home.

Growth and Its Discontents

As the new millennium dawned, China's role as the up-and-coming economic powerhouse continued to build. It became the largest holder of U.S. Treasury Bills and enjoys to this day lopsided balance-of-trade surpluses with the U.S. and other economic leaders. On the one hand, with giant companies such as Walmart and Target acquiring more and more of their inventories from Chinese factories, prices could be held to a bare minimum, helping to keep inflation at bay in the consumer economies of China's customers. On the other hand, China itself began to mature as a consumer market, luring more and more foreign investment and stimulating the creation of such huge Chinese companies as Haier and Lenovo. In many ways, China was following a similar economic pattern to Japan, and more recently, Taiwan and South Korea (see Chapters 11, 12, and 13). One by-product of this pattern was that wages increased as these countries increased their prosperity. By 2015, China was well on the way to following the Japanese pattern of rising wages and a growing middle class, and farming out low-cost manufacturing to Vietnam, Indonesia, India, and most recently, African countries.

By the end of the first decade of the new century, China had the world's largest middle class, over 300 million—about the size of the entire population of the United States. It is estimated that this number will more than double to 630 million by 2022. However, the expectation of achieving middle-class status and sharing the urban amenities and consumer bounty of China and the world is increasing even faster. One milestone in this regard is that in January 2012, China's National Bureau of Statistics reported that for the first time in history, more Chinese were living in urban areas than rural ones.

With China's rush into economic growth have come rising expectation on the part of many for greater political liberalization. The Party's position on this, as we have seen, has been to steadfastly oppose any notion that its "socialism with Chinese characteristics" will lead away from authoritarian one-party rule. Many have suggested, however, that as the culture becomes more materialistic, and the legal system increasingly deals with matters of property rights, these developments will necessarily lead to redefinitions of individual human rights and a drive toward more open and representative government. The renewed authoritarian rule of Xi Jinping, however, seems for the moment to be stemming that drive.

Tibet and Minorities

Nowhere have these rising expectations been on more dramatic display—and led to more bitter disappointment— than in the case of minority rights. As in the case of religion, China recognizes more than fifty minority groups and tends to use such official recognition to accord them certain group rights and privileges. In the cases of Tibet and Xinjiang, the minorities are largely located within specially designated Autonomous Regions. As we saw with the Qing, Chinese suzerainty over Tibet and Central Asia was fairly loose in imperial times and sometimes utilized political-religious interests in cementing the loyalty of different groups. As a nation-state, however, the People's Republic not only attempted to quell any attempts at additional autonomy or independence, it also crushed incipient rebellion on several occasions, most dramatically in Tibet in 1959. One result of this was that the Dalai Lama fled to a life of exile in India. From there, he has been a catalyst for activist movements within Tibet, agitating across the political spectrum for everything from complete independence to more autonomy within the present system (see Map 10.3).

Tibetans have long charged that China has been attempting a kind of "cultural genocide" in the country by encouraging Han Chinese emigration and settlement. This accelerated considerably after 2006 with the completion of the impressive engineering feat of the Qinghai-Lhasa Railway, the world's highest-altitude railroad. Anti-Chinese riots broke out in Lhasa and other Tibetan cities in March 2008. Anxious to quell the violence well in advance of the 2008 Olympics, PLA soldiers and police put the disturbances down with brutal efficiency and considerable loss of life. Over the last several years, Tibetan Buddhist monks have resorted to self-immolation to bring their cause before the world media.

Even before this, however, the attacks on New York City's World Trade Center of September 11, 2001, and the subsequent "war on terror" afforded Party leaders an opportunity to reinforce their military position in Muslim areas of Central Asia, ostensibly in solidarity with the U.S. in its wars in Afghanistan and Iraq. Taking the diplomatic initiative in a way that has become increasingly common as China's power expands, the PRC signed the Shanghai Cooperation Organization Regional Anti-Terrorism Structure (SCO-RATS) with Russia, Tajikistan, Uzbekistan, Kazakstan, and Kyrgystan. Any chance that the Muslim Uyghurs in Xinjiang thought they had to bargain for more autonomy quickly evaporated as PRC authorities began a crackdown aimed at al-Qaeda and putative Turkic separatists. This has continued markedly with Xinjiang being used as a pilot program of intense cell phone monitoring and the use in many cases of mandatory security apps.

Map 10.3 Open Cities, Special Economic Zones, Autonomous Regions, and Special Administrative Regions in China, 1980–2000

The Party's insistence on clamping down on unapproved religious or ideological activity was dramatically illustrated in April 1999, with the suppression of **Falun Gong**. Founded in 1992 by Li Hongzhi, a low-level civil servant, Falun Gong draws from several traditional Chinese sources, although mostly from Buddhism and the theories of *qi* (energy) that animate traditional Chinese medicine and the practice of *taiji zhuan*. Followers engage in exercises meant to strengthen the internal "wheel of law," or *falun*, which draws "cultivation energy" (*gong*) to the practitioner. By the end of the decade, Li claimed millions of followers worldwide, and the group had organized itself into a kind of alternative society within China, with its own insurance and financial structure. To the Party, it looked suspiciously like a dissident movement. From 1999 to 2003 therefore, it drove Falun Gong underground, breaking up public gatherings, arresting numerous

Tibetan Protests. The exile of the Dalai Lama and Tibetan refugees since the PRC's suppression of Tibet in 1959 has resulted in a worldwide movement embracing a variety of goals ranging from greater autonomy for Tibet within the People's Republic to complete independence. Here, protesters on a march to Tibet are stopped by Indian police in Himachal Pradesh in March 2008 during the run-up to the Beijing Olympics.

members, and launching a propaganda campaign to discredit the group. They remain active worldwide, however, and even have their own television network, "Tang Dynasty TV."

Toward Harmony and Stability?

The cleavages appearing in Chinese society as a by-product of the frenetic pace of China's unequaled economic growth had become all too evident by 2006. The country was riven by growing separations on multiple levels: between rich and poor; between rural and urban; between low-wage workers in factories and mines, and those comfortably in the middle class; between migrants and legal residents in the cities; between those within the tattered social safety net and those outside of it; between those with Party connections and those without them; between dissident groups and minorities, and the mainstream; and between those with separatist ambitions and the government security apparatus. Moreover, seven of the world's ten most polluted urban areas were in China, crime and divorce were on the rise, and the country appeared so caught up in making money that its moral center seemed to have vanished with nothing to replace it.

Hu Jintao, who had replaced Jiang Zemin as party chief in the PRC's first orderly and peaceful transfer of power, called on the Party's Central Committee in a plenary session in October 2006 to step back from breakneck economic development for a moment to concentrate on addressing these social tensions. The result was an endorsement of Hu's concept of the **Harmonious Society**. Hu's vision was that economic development and reducing societal tensions must go hand in hand. Particular attention needed to be paid to reducing the gap between rich and poor. Thus, he called for a model reflecting what economists call *sustainable development*—growing the GDP at a rate that will fully satisfy consumer demand, without creating excessive surpluses that need to be exported. Increasing the use of technology in the service of efficiency is another aspect of the overall goal.

A third part of the approach is to increase openness and honesty in government in order to ensure political and public harmony. Anti-corruption campaigns, of course, had been a staple of Communist Party policy since the early 1950s. One of the patterns of China's political economy since the inception of the Four Modernizations, however, has been the disproportionate power of the single legal political party within the developing market economy. The almost universal practices of *guanxi* (connections) and *houmen* (the back door), which benefit immensely those with an entrée to the Party, became further entrenched not only in the business world, but also in society more broadly. Finally, there was an ongoing emphasis on pursuing harmony among minorities and safeguarding their rights—although separatism, "splittism," and terrorism would not be tolerated. Hu expanded this vision somewhat before he stepped down in 2011 to include reducing tensions between nations in order to work toward a "harmonious world."

The Olympic Moment

Against this backdrop, China staged arguably the most spectacular Olympic Games since their modern reincarnation in 1896. Past Olympics, most notably the Berlin Games of 1936 in Nazi Germany, had often been used to showcase the wealth and modernity of the host country. Similarly, the Beijing Olympics, nineteen years after the disaster at Tiananmen Square, were to be a symbol of China's breakneck economic progress and modernity. The capital underwent a massive building program, including a complete updating of the subway system, highways, and surface transportation. The venue itself was studded with spectacular

The Beijing Olympics. Not having obtained the 2000 Olympic Games, Beijing's award of the 2008 games stimulated unprecedented construction in the city as well as a considerable upwelling of national pride. Many of the city's older buildings and a large number of its famous residential hutongs were razed to obtain the space for the assorted spectacular venues. Two of the iconic structures were the Aqua Cube swimming and diving arena (A) and the Bird's Nest outdoor stadium (B) shown here lit up at night.

architecture, including a high-rise building meant to suggest the Olympic torch, the "Bird's Nest" stadium, and the unique "Aquacube" natatorium.

The Olympics also showcased a high degree of grassroots nationalism, far beyond the usual attempts by the government to orchestrate it for its own purposes. Millions of PRC fans followed the daily medal count in hopes that China would surpass the United States. Red t-shirts emblazoned with the slogan "Go China!" appeared everywhere. All this engendered a popular feeling that China was no longer a "developing nation" but one rapidly rising to economic superpower status—and accruing the prestige that rightly belongs to it. The Games showed that China had an unsurpassed capacity to stage spectacles, and Chinese athletes were likewise out to make their mark as "warriors for the nation."

Thus in most respects, the Olympics had the desired effect of placing China prominently back onto the world stage, as did China's first world's fair of the Communist era, the Shanghai Expo of 2010. Less successful was the aftermath of the disastrous Sichuan earthquake in May 2008, which destroyed large sections of the huge municipalities of Chengdu and Chongqing, killing upwards of 70,000, injuring 37,000, and leaving 20,000 missing. The defects of the slipshod construction of so many of the new buildings were put on painful display under the extensive international media coverage. Much attention centered on the tragic collapse of an elementary school and a high school; in total, 5,335 schoolchildren are believed to have perished. The government mounted a massive rescue and relief effort, but the damage was so extensive and the infrastructure so damaged that many rural areas saw no relief for weeks. One of the notable innovations of the event, however, was that for the first time Chinese reporters and TV crews had a largely free hand in reporting the unfolding tragedy in real time. While the government attempted to rein news organizations in afterward, many reporters and viewers insisted more strongly than ever on their rights to uncensored coverage.

Xi Jinping and "The Four Comprehensives"

The ascendency of Xi Jinping (b. 1953) from 2013, renewed in 2017, as president and general secretary of the Party has resulted in a redoubled drive for Hu Jintao's vision, with an economically and militarily powerful China leading the way toward this harmonious world. Xi's program, The Four Comprehensives, builds on the Three Represents:

> Comprehensively build a moderately prosperous society; deepen reform; govern according to law; and strictly govern the Party.

Bound up in this vision is Xi's conception of the "Chinese Dream." Like the American Dream, it seeks "prosperity for all." Other aspects include "revival of the nation" and a strong military. An oft-cited goal is for China to achieve a level of world preeminence currently enjoyed by the United States by the centennial of the People's Republic in 2049.

Under Xi's leadership, the Party has engaged in numerous crackdowns on national and local corruption in its own ranks, as well as on individuals outside its circle. Factionalism among Party technocrats and so-called princelings—descendants of Party officials—has been endemic as well. Using the anti-corruption campaigns as leverage, Xi has exerted a control not seen since the heyday of Mao. This has been bolstered by a massive government program aimed at hacking information abroad and developing ever more intrusive tools with which to monitor the compliance of the PRC's citizens.

PATTERNS UP-CLOSE

Confucius Institutes and China's Soft Power

As China's economic, political, and diplomatic power has increased, so has its informal influence that social scientists call "soft power." The United States, for example, wields enormous soft power through its movies, television, music, and fashion. China, too, seeks to extend its soft power in a number of areas. One of the most remarkable aspects of this effort has been the reclaiming and reshaping of China's "feudal" Confucian past. In this respect, nothing has been more remarkable than the rehabilitation of the Sage himself. As we have seen, a central goal of the Maoist years, and particularly the Cultural Revolution, had been to "eliminate the **four olds**" (old customs, old culture, old habits, and old ideas) and even more explicitly, "smash Confucius." How then can we account for such an abrupt ideological turnabout?

One factor may be Deng Xiaoping's admiration for the model of "Confucian capitalism" practiced by the former prime minister of Singapore, Lee Kuan Yew (1923–2015). Lee's government created one of the most vibrant market economies and financial hubs in the world, while retaining a powerful one-party authoritarian government. It was argued that the reverence for authority and hierarchy that marked Confucianism had a vital place in creating a well-ordered state built upon "Asian values"—as opposed to the individual rights-based systems of the West. Evidence was also adduced for this in how even the representative governments in Japan, Taiwan, and more recently, South Korea were run. Moreover, such an approach would allow the PRC to reclaim traditional Chinese culture and thus contest the claims of Taiwan since 1949 to be the authentic heir to China's cultural legacy. The Sage has therefore not only been rehabilitated but also is increasingly presented to the world as part of the "branding" of the PRC.

The most visible and, arguably, influential evidence of this phenomenon has been the proliferation of PRC-sponsored Confucius Institutes throughout the world as outposts of their civilization and values, a kind of cultural missionary enterprise. Founded in 2004 by Hanban, a non-profit organization affiliated with the Ministry of Education, almost

(continued)

Confucius Institutes. One of the most effective marketing—and critics would say propaganda—tools of the PRC in recent years has been Confucius Institutes set up around the globe to introduce students and other interested parties to China's Communist Party's interpretation of the Chinese past. Although this is a marked turn from the condemnation of Confucius and "feudal" China during the Maoist years, it also represents a distinct interpretation of the Sage, his writings, and traditional Chinese culture in general. In this photograph, the entrance to a reading room at the Confucius Institute at Seneca College in Toronto, Canada, holds an attractive display of traditional scholars' furniture and bookshelves of Chinese literature.

500 Confucius Institutes may now be found in countries on six continents, with over 70 in the United States alone. They offer a wide spectrum of Chinese cultural activities such as painting, poetry, calligraphy, literature, and philosophy as well as language instruction. They additionally offer courses and sponsor outreach programs to local schools and colleges.

Their programs, however, are not without controversy. In reading, writing, and language instruction, they follow the PRC's approved system of simplified Chinese characters and the pinyin romanization system as part of the drive to make these the world standard. Here, they are in direct competition with Taiwan and a number of overseas Chinese communities who use other romanization systems and the old-style unsimplified characters. Indeed, Taiwan bans the use of simplified characters, sponsors a holiday devoted to writing and celebrating traditional characters, and has applied for UNESCO World Heritage status for the old script.

More unsettling for many observers, particularly in the United States, has been the relationship the Institutes have cultivated with American universities and public school districts. At a time when many educational institutions face increased difficulties obtaining funds for the humanities, Confucius Institutes have offered substantial amounts of funding in return for a campus presence. In some cases, Chinese language training and cultural studies have been essentially farmed out to the Institutes. One of the catches in their contracts, however, is that those associated with the Institutes must not contravene Chinese law—itself a powerful disincentive toward exploring controversial issues. Perhaps more disconcerting is that officials in the PRC's Ministry of Education have said directly that the Institutes are to be utilized as outlets for propaganda. Thus, while some academics see the trade-off as worth the politics in terms of financial aid and cultural exchange, others see it as a serious challenge to free critical discourse. Some universities in Europe, Canada, and Australia have severed their ties with the Institutes, as have the University of Chicago and Penn State in the U.S., because of these issues. Whatever the outcome, this new element of soft power puts the struggle for control of China's heritage more than ever on a global stage.

SOCIETY, SCIENCE, AND CULTURE

With the exception of more land going into production, and the majority of the landless now having a parcel to work, daily life for peasants changed relatively little in the first years of the People's Republic. While the *danwei* (work unit) system was being set up in cities and towns, rural villages retained their former character as discrete organizational units. The nuclear and extended family in the village—with many villages made up of interconnected families—continued to be the norm. Over time, and with certain periods of interruption, village primary schools became common, as did the famous "barefoot doctors" providing itinerant basic hygiene instruction and health care. As we have seen, the real changes came with the Great Leap Forward. The creation of the giant communes, however, with their factorylike schedules, requisitioning of materials and land, and disruption of village and family life soon made them highly unpopular. Even after the Leap was discontinued, the skeleton of the commune system continued and the practice of paying peasants in work-units for labor and produce would continue until the early 1980s.

Following the catastrophic famine of the early 1960s, rural life settled into a more normal routine as the Party under Liu Shaoqi refrained from introducing new mass programs into the countryside. With the Cultural Revolution, however, came large-scale disruption once again. The same struggles between pro- and anti-Maoist factions in the cities played themselves out in rural villages accessible to Party cadres. Adding to the confusion were the campaigns encouraging students to "learn from the peasants" and the punitive exodus of those who were "sent down" to the countryside. Villagers often found themselves bewildered when faced with trying to use city dwellers and intellectuals to do farm chores. Many saw it as yet one more unwanted disruption in their hardscrabble existence.

Recasting Urban Life

Many of the first mass mobilization efforts were directed at purging the cities of potential resistance and creating a pattern of setting one group against another in order to prevent the building of alliances. By the end of the 1950s, private ownership of property or businesses had been effectively eliminated and the state became the source and controller of employment. Although life in the cities and large towns offered basic services and tended to be better than in the rural areas, the infrastructure grew only in fits and starts. Rail service and urban public transport remained at low a level, while the bicycle became the favored mode of urban transport. Heat, even in large buildings, was rationed, being turned off in April and turned back on in October. Perforated cakes of pressed coal dust remained the primary fuel for heating and cooking stoves into the early twenty-first century.

Family life in urban areas, although often lacking the deep roots of village China, was still built around the nuclear and extended family. Living space in apartment blocks often made familial closeness problematic. The changes in traditional marriage practices begun at the beginning of the twentieth century continued: a new marriage code in 1953, amended in 1980, made divorce much easier, especially for women. The PRC was formally pledged in its constitutions to female emancipation and gender equality. In addition to having equal political rights, such debilitating practices as concubinage, foot-binding, gambling, and opium smoking had been banned from the beginning. However, it was also the case that the old practices of Confucian patriarchy and of the inner and outer domains remaining separate for men and women lingered on.

Along the way, a new conception of the Chinese socialist ideal of marriage and family began to take shape and reached its highest point during the Cultural Revolution. For urban women, new personal freedoms in dress and behavior, and emancipation from home seclusion and arranged marriage meant an increased degree of agency, even if full equality was not yet a reality. But the new ideal for the socialist couple went much further. Romance was now derided as a bour-geois affectation, which those involved in building the country and serving the people must discard. Indeed, the ideal mate for a man or woman was an ideologi-cally compatible "comrade" (*tongzhi*). Physical attractiveness, family ties, wealth, personality—all of these were now considered unimportant. Moreover, one should not choose someone from a "bad" class background, but select instead a person your comrades approve of as ideologically sound, politically correct, and imbued with the proper "red" attitude. Children, for their part, should be brought up to embody these attributes as well. This was reinforced in the schools, especially when mass mobilization campaigns were under way, by encouraging students to report any of their parents' ideological lapses.

Modernization and Society

After the trauma of the Maoist years and the advent of the Four Modernizations, one significant departure from former CCP doctrine was the dramatic effort to slow the rate of population growth. By the early 2000s, the One-Child Policy (rescinded in 2015) had been operating for more than a generation and its results were as pre-dicted in some respects, although totally unanticipated in others. The primary goal of slowing down the rate of growth of China's population had largely been achieved, with the number of people standing at slightly less than 1.4 billion in 2014.

interpreting his works also left him open to criticism in official circles. Likewise, Ding Ling remained a troubling figure, and her feminist criticism of the Party on women's issues resulted in her censure during the Anti-Rightist Campaign and Cultural Revolution. Not surprisingly, both of these campaigns cut deeply into China's literary life. In the case of Lao She, the maximum penalty appears to have been enforced: it is believed that he was beaten to death by Red Guards in 1966. Those whose work was critical of the regime found themselves censored and often imprisoned. Wei Jingsheng was a notable case in point. Perhaps most poignant of all, however, was the case of Liu Xiaobo, writer, critic, political activist, and winner of the Nobel Peace Prize. Imprisoned for his views and dying of liver cancer, he was denied care despite international pleas and offers to get him treatment in exile. The government relented during Li's final days and he was granted hospitalization for his remaining hours, passing away in July 2017.

The most dominant cultural figure of the last decade of Mao's rule was his fourth wife, the former actress Jiang Qing (1914–1991). Named Mao's Cultural Revolution deputy in 1966, she ruthlessly suppressed all artistic forms that were critical of the new political direction, too traditional, or insufficiently proletarian. She was most famous for championing one of the Eight Model Plays that comprised the only theater permitted during the Cultural Revolution: a ballet, *The Red Detachment of Women*. Perhaps the most famous performance of the work occurred during American President Richard Nixon's 1972 visit to Beijing.

The 1980s were regarded by many artists as a kind of golden age for experimentation. One play, for example, was called *Jesus, Confucius, and John Lennon*

Hong Kong Crowds Gather for Memorial Service to Honor Liu Xiaobo. The treatment meted out to Nobel Laureate and Chinese dissident Liu Xiaobo resulted in worldwide demonstrations demanding his release for cancer treatment abroad, and numerous memorial services upon his death. Here, hundreds gather for a global memorial service in Hong Kong on July 20, 2017. Hong Kong had also been the site of a candlelight march and vigil a few days before on July 15.

of the Beatles. The conservative era that set in after Tiananmen Square pushed artists into disguising political statements or socially controversial ideas with additional layers of subtlety. It was, however, a time when the world's focus on China allowed Chinese filmmakers like Zhang Yimou to achieve international stardom with movies like *Raise the Red Lantern, Ju Dou,* and *To Live.*

The 1990s and early 2000s saw an explosion of worldwide interest in Chinese art of all types. The association of modern art with protest made the work of the new generation of Chinese artists increasingly desirable. By the early 2000s, there was a growing fear on the part of many successful artists that the pressure to produce and sell was undercutting the originality and creativity of contemporary Chinese art. Since the commercialization of art is something the government can steer into acceptable channels, it also tends to be that which is most frequently exhibited in galleries and sold in shows. Still, art and dissent remain linked in both the popular mind and that of the authorities.

The Media

China has within it all the modern media to be found elsewhere, but the hand of the government and Party are everywhere to be found, sometimes openly, sometimes all but invisibly. In keeping with the goal of the Harmonious Society, and to avoid the cardinal sin of embarrassing China—and with an increasing degree of grassroots nationalism—the media often willingly engage in self-censorship, although increasingly, as in the aftermath of the 2008 earthquake, they are also taking bold stands. Those sanctioned for their efforts are said only half-humorously to have been "harmonized." In the years of Xi Jinping's presidency, a closer scrutiny of the media, and particularly social media references to such sensitive subjects as Tibet, Islam, and China's endeavors to claim effective control over resources and islands in the South China Sea, has become the norm. It is expected that the policing of cell phone traffic and apps as currently practiced in restive areas like Xinjiang will soon be extended to the country at large.

The government exercises control over content through official outlets like *Renmin Ribao,* the organ of the Party; the *China Daily*; China Central Television (CCT); and a host of regional and local outlets. Hong Kong's press is more free, although under constant pressure to report government stories favorably. Coastal China can pick up programs from Taiwan and South Korea. Larger cities also have access to CNN, ESPN, MTV, and other foreign networks. Foreign programming remains immensely popular, with American comedies such as *The Big Bang Theory* and *Friends*—more than a decade after the last episode was made—being staples for many. In early 2015, the most popular series was the wildly successful PBS production *Downton Abbey.*

CONCLUSION

The pattern of Chinese history that had been followed during the Maoist years bears certain parallels with the brief interlude of the First Emperor from 221 to 208 BCE. Interestingly, it is one that despite drastic reforms attempted in other East Asian countries—for example, during Japan's Meiji restoration—has been replicated in the region only by Pol Pot and to a lesser extent by the Kim Dynasty in North Korea. That is, older institutions were torn up by the roots and discarded, and a radical philosophy forcibly imposed on the state and society. In the first instance, the justification had been the creation of an empire. In the case of Mao, it had been starting from scratch to end the last vestiges of imperialism, and to take advantage of China's "poor and blank" condition to create an authentically Chinese socialism. In both cases, the will of the leader was absolute and his sway nearly complete. In both cases as well, many were sacrificed to the cause at hand.

Without pushing the parallels too far, the post-Mao period resembles the post-Qin period as well. There was no revolution ending Maoist rule, only the quiet departure created with his death. But like the long-lived Han Dynasty that followed the First Emperor, China since 1976 has left the former administrative structures largely in place, but liberalized much else, especially the economy. The Four Modernizations and the drive to achieve the Harmonious Society have vaulted the People's Republic into the upper ranks of world power. The question, however, remains as open as before: Will this unprecedented economic success bring with it political changes?

FURTHER RESOURCES

Chang, Jung. *Wild Swans: Three Daughters of China.* New York: Simon & Schuster, 2008. Most current edition of the widely popular 1991 story of three generations of women in Jung Chang's family and their trials and endurance in revolutionary and Maoist China.

Chau, Adam Yuet, ed. *Religion in Contemporary China.* New York: Routledge, 2011. Sound, current material on Daoist, Confucian, and Buddhist revival and adaptation to contemporary life in China. Also explores the "gray" (unrecognized) religious movements.

De Bary, William Theodore. *Asian Values and Human Rights: A Confucian Communitarian Perspective.* Cambridge, MA: Harvard University Press, 1998. Stimulating discussions of the debate between those who see Confucianism as countenancing authoritarianism, and those who view Confucian notions of the individual as not incompatible with world norms of human rights.

DeWoskin, Rachel. *Foreign Babes in Beijing: Behind the Scenes of a New China.* New York: Norton, 2005. A highly entertaining, accessible account of the author's intercultural adventures as a soap opera star in China during the 1990s.

Li Zhisui. *The Private Life of Chairman Mao.* New York: Random House, 1994. Raw, often disturbing insight into Mao's personal habits and health over the years by his personal physician.

Liang Heng, and Judith Shapiro. *After the Nightmare.* New York: Macmillan; Collier Edition, 1987. Husband and wife team who went back to China to interview victims of the Cultural Revolution to try to get a sense of not only what they endured, but also how they coped with the continuing trauma of the aftermath of the era.

Meisner, Maurice. *Mao's China and After.* 3rd ed. New York: Free Press, 1999. Masterful overview of Chinese history from the May Fourth and New Culture period to the Deng Xiaoping era. Particularly good at explaining the intellectual nuances of CCP debates, economic policy, and Mao Zedong Thought.

Perry, Elizabeth J., and Mark Selden. *Chinese Society: Change, Conflict, and Resistance.* 2nd ed. London: Routledge, 2003. Essay collection that explores the cleavages of modern China, especially those resulting from the rapid changes of the 1980s and 1990s. Although some barriers have been lifted, the writers argue, the government still retains its authoritarian character.

Pillsbury, Michael. *The Hundred Year Marathon: China's Secret Strategy to Replace America as the Global Superpower.* New York: Henry Holt, 2015. Highly controversial warning that China is subtly following strategies from the Warring States Period to expand its influence throughout Asia and in Africa, and plans to supplant the U.S. as global hegemon by 2049.

Pin Ho, and Wenguang Huang. *A Death in the Lucky Holiday Hotel,* New York: Public Affairs, 2013. Fascinating narrative and investigation into the death of British businessman Neil Heywood, and the convoluted and corrupt path to the controversial convictions of the Communist Party chief of Chongqing, Bo Xilai, and his wife, Gu Kailai. Highly revealing about the current state of internal Party politics.

Ruan Ming. *Deng Xiaoping: Chronicle of an Empire.* Translated by Nancy Liu, Peter Rand, and Lawrence Sullivan. Boulder, CO: Westview, 1994. Account of the early years of the Four Modernizations and Deng's rise to power. Ruan Ming was a Party insider and supporter of the reforms, but was purged and moved to the U.S.

Schoppa, Keith. *Revolution and Its Past: Identities in Modern Chinese History.* 3rd ed. New York: Prentice Hall, 2011. Information-rich text for introductory and intermediate students, although even advanced students can read it and still profit. Approaches Chinese history from the Qianlong era to the present from the perspective of the multiple and shifting identities of China and its people—as individuals; family and clan members; inhabitants of villages and cities, regions, empires, and nations.

Spence, Jonathan D. *In Search of Modern China.* 3rd ed. New York: Norton, 2012. Comprehensive history of China from the Ming Dynasty to the twenty-first century by one of the most respected China scholars working today.

WEBSITES

https://beijingtoday.com.cn/. Beijing Youth Daily Publishing Company. *Beijing Today.* English-language site catering to expatriates; comprehensive coverage of contemporary culture, news, social issues, and history.

http://en.people.cn/. *Renmin Ribao* (People's Daily). The official organ of the Chinese Communist Party. Indispensable source of official views on all aspects of life in the PRC. Available in English and many other languages.

https://www.princeton.edu/~lynn/chinabib.pdf. Princeton University, Woodrow Wilson School. *Contemporary China: A Book List.* For intermediate and advanced students. A comprehensive bibliography of sources on all aspects of contemporary China.

CHAPTER 11

✐

A House Divided:
Korea to the Present

The atmosphere in Seoul's Pagoda Park that first day of March 1919 was undeniably electric. It would, however, soon turn tragic. As it had in so many place around the world, and pointedly so in China, India, French Indochina, and now Korea, the convening of the Paris Peace Conference in January 1919, to settle matters at the end of World War I, raised immense hopes—and dashed them almost as quickly. The preceding quarter-century in Korea had been similarly mottled with occasional promise only to see it abruptly aborted. Japanese influence on the peninsula had replaced Chinese claims of suzerainty with a vengeance following the war between those two powers in 1894–1895. Korea's claims to territorial integrity and its short-lived, modernizing "empire" of the late 1890s were quickly ended with Japan's impressive victory over Russia and the establishment of a protectorate over Korea in 1905. The assassination of Japan's revered statesmen, Ito Hirobumi, in 1909 led to the final annexation of Korea by Japan in 1910. For the next decade, Japan exercised tight colonial control over a restive populace who, like so many other inhabitants of so many other colonies, felt their second-class status all too keenly.

Like the dramatic impact they would have in India and China, the American President Woodrow Wilson's "Fourteen Points" presented to the conference delegates in January galvanized the colonial world. Central to the points were Wilson's insistence on "self-determination for all peoples," a concept that resonated deeply with the colonized in the empires of the victorious Allies and the defeated Central Powers alike. In Korea, in addition to this sense of a new beginning, the suspicious death of the former Emperor Gojong on January 21 pushed resentment toward Japanese control that much further. In the months leading up to the gathering in Seoul, Korean students studying in Tokyo had drawn up a list of grievances at Japanese rule and sent them to the Japanese press to publicize them. Shortly after, the historian Choe Nam-seon had taken the fateful step of writing a Korean Declaration of Independence.

It was the reading of this document that had drawn and so energized the crowd. The organizers had hoped to keep the event peaceful and contained, but it soon became neither. As the crowds grew, Japanese military police attempted to quell the demonstration but were soon overwhelmed. Even more dramatically, however, the organizers had arranged for a simultaneous reading of the Declaration at sites all over Korea at 2:00 p.m. As the excitement escalated throughout the peninsula, perhaps as many as a million people ended up taking part. Desperate Japanese police and military took strong measures and finally suppressed the demonstrations, which continued for days. Estimates of the casualties vary widely, with Japanese authorities claiming only a few hundred dead while Korean estimates ran as high as 7,500. The groundswell for independence that grew from these incidents became known as the *Samil* or March 1 Movement. Like its counterparts in India, Vietnam, and as we have seen, China's May Fourth Movement, it is often cited as the birth of modern Korean nationalism. Indeed, refugees in Shanghai established a Provisional Government of the Republic of Korea the following month, and a Korean Liberation Army was organized in China. The struggle would not cease, however, until the defeat of Japan in 1945. With the peninsula then divided by Soviet and American occupiers, the new Republic of Korea (South Korea) declared March 1 a national holiday.

Korean Independence Demonstration, March 1, 1919. As they had in so many other places under colonial rule, the ideals of self-determination expressed as U.S. war aims in World War I and at the Versailles Peace Conference fired Korean patriotism. Here, demonstrators rally in Seoul for a reading of the Korean Declaration of Independence, an event also held at a number of other sites all over Korea. March 1 was later celebrated as a national holiday in South Korea.

In many respects, the history of Korea in the twentieth and early twenty-first centuries follows a pattern of East Asian history similar to that of its neighbors. Like China, it was confronted with an expansionist Japan; unlike China but similarly to Taiwan and Manchuria, it was formally incorporated into the Japanese Empire. Like Vietnam, which was ruled by the French, and like China as well, there was a quickening of nationalism during that eventful spring of 1919; for Korea and Vietnam, it would be coupled with a movement for independence.

Yet the Korean pattern also involves important differences. The post–World War II era and Cold War saw the emergence of two Koreas and a devastating war from 1950 to 1953, which is still without a peace treaty and with both sides actively hostile and occasionally provocative toward each other. Although Vietnam went through a similar division and devastating war, it ultimately was reunited and has been steadily pursuing Chinese-style market reforms within its socialist political and economic system. The divisions between the Koreas have become increasingly stark in terms of economics, politics, and international standing and the threat of war—now with a nuclear-armed Democratic People's Republic of Korea (North Korea) ruled by a secretive regime headed by the frighteningly unstable scion of a modern political dynasty. Indeed, North Korea has tested an intercontinental ballistic missile (ICBM) capable of hitting the United States, and the Americans have resolved that this will not be allowed to happen. South Korea, on the other hand, has created one of the world's most dynamic economies and is Asia's most democratic government.

Thus, the future of the peninsula remains an open question and international flashpoint, surrounded as it is by China, Russia, and Japan, and with a substantial American military presence still in the south. In this chapter, we will explore the modern patterns of Korean history as a small nation frequently beset by larger ones, yet, like Vietnam, also one of remarkable resilience animated by considerable agency.

THE EBB AND FLOW OF COLONIALISM

The historical arcs of Japan and Korea toward each other from 1895 to 1945 are in many respects so divergent as to seem not only incongruent but also incommensurate. As we will see in Chapter 13, much of East Asia sees Japan as having a "history problem." Japan's view of itself as one of the "victim nations" of World War II has allowed its officially approved histories to avoid or downplay many incidents, policies, and institutions of its colonial and wartime era that loom as traumatic for the colonized. Even today, China and Korea routinely register protests at what they consider the yawning gaps in coverage of the period by approved Japanese textbooks.

Here, the colonial era in general is viewed as Japan's attempt to create a united East Asia to stand firm against Western encroachment. The colonies are seen as junior partners in a corporate autarkic structure whose independence would be granted by a victorious Japan at war's end. Indeed, Japan is portrayed as the chief modernizing and industrializing influence not only in Korea, but also in Manchuria and Taiwan. The war with the United States and the Allies (seen as the separate "Pacific War") is sometimes characterized as a "reckless" but necessary and desperate attempt at survival; the final years of American bombing then cemented Japan's victimhood.

For Koreans, however, whether in the north or south, Japanese rule is seen as an interval of unrelieved oppression, of the stifling of national identity, of economic hardship, and of conscription to serve Japan as labor, military personnel, and even as **comfort women** for Japanese to employ in brothels for their armed forces. The industrialization and modernization that did take place is seen as not for the benefit of Koreans, but to service the Japanese metropole. And whereas Japanese see their actions in Korea as benign and unifying compared to the picture they paint of Western colonialism, Koreans emphasize a narrative of almost continual resistance to Japanese rule until 1945.

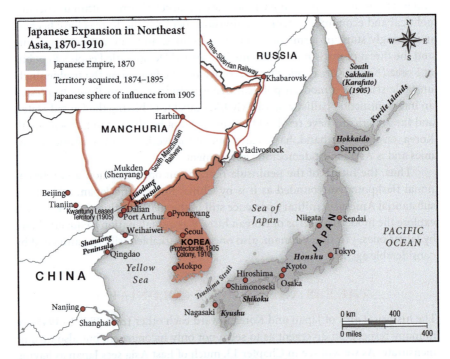

Map 11.1 Japanese Expansion in Northeast Asia, 1870–1910

Military Rule

The assassination of Prince Ito Hirobumi in October 1909 by Korean nationalist An Chung-gun while on a visit to Harbin in Manchuria to meet with Russian delegates for talks on Japan's plans for annexation had been preceded by considerable resistance. Korean mobs had burned the residence of the prime minister who had signed the Protectorate Agreement with Japan in 1905. One Japanese advisor to Korea had already been shot by Korean students while visiting San Francisco. From 1907, large guerrilla bands, by some estimates numbering up to 50,000, had challenged Japan's claims and presence on the peninsula. Thus, when the last Korean government was forced to sign the annexation treaty on August 29, 1910, Japanese forces were immediately put in place to smother further resistance (see Map 11.1).

The Japanese set up a Government-General responsible to the Japanese prime minister, and in a highly symbolic move established its headquarters in front of the Yi Dynasty's major royal residence, Kyongbak Palace. As has often been noted, every governor-general until 1945 was a military man, as were many of the officials under them. As has been frequently pointed out as well, the colonial governmental structure was far more rigid and intrusive than had been the case under the Yi, with colonial officials appointing all personnel down to the county level—with these same officials appointing or approving all district and village headmen.

It was the military presence, however, that proved most jarring. Anxious to prevent further disturbances in the newly created colony, a system of military police was established and repeatedly increased over the years. The mixed Korean-Japanese force grew from 6,200 in 1910 to 60,000 by 1941. Similarly, colonial officials, administrators, and military personnel numbered in the vicinity of 300,000 by the late 1930s, with perhaps 700,000 Japanese living in the colony. In the era leading up to the March 1 demonstrations, the government clamped down heavily on political activity, and estimates routinely cite the detention of tens of thousands on various pretexts. One result of these measures was that, like China in the early twentieth century, much of the political activity moved to overseas Korean communities in Manchuria, Russia, the foreign-controlled treaty ports in China, and Hawaii and California. Japan's role in World War I and further involvement in Manchuria and China also prompted crackdowns in Korea.

Relative Restraint: The Cultural Policy

As noted in the opening vignette to this chapter, the March 1 demonstrations had a profound effect on the next decade of Japanese rule in Korea. The reasons for this were not dissimilar to events that took place in other areas of the colonial world. Korean students in the United States had petitioned President Woodrow Wilson to support a bid for Korean independence. Their Vietnamese counterparts engaged in similar lobbying efforts at Versailles. The May Fourth Movement in China had spawned anti-Japanese boycotts. And the Amritsar massacre in India in April 1919 had shocked the world and made the British rethink their position there as well as propelling Gandhi's movement forward.

The scale and intensity of the March 1 demonstrations had shocked Japan as well. In the period following the death of Japanese emperor Meiji in 1912, the old oligarchs were fading from the scene and power was increasingly wielded by political party leaders and politicians. The new Japanese emperor, Taisho, was weak and infirm much of the time, and as we will see in Chapter 13, the period of his reign from 1912 to 1926 is often characterized as the era of **Taisho Democracy**. The post–World War I period was one in which Japan was increasingly accepted as a great power—indeed, the leading power in Asia. With the signing of the Washington Naval Agreement and the Nine-Power Treaty on China in 1921–1922, Japan's claims on the Asian mainland appeared to be secure, and the remainder of the 1920s was seen by Japanese officials as one in which diplomacy rather than force would mark its international endeavors. The political liberalization of "Taisho Democracy"—including universal manhood suffrage in Japan—also lent itself to somewhat of a restructuring of Japan's colonial policy in Korea.

Thus in August 1919, the political boss and now prime minister, Hara Takashi (Kei), issued a new set of directives for the Government-General of Korea. The new approach was marked by the slogan "Harmony between Japan and Korea," and the new governor-general, Admiral Saito Makoto, moved swiftly to eliminate or reduce some of the more oppressive policies pursued by his Army predecessors. Most notable of these were the abolition of the military police force and its replacement with a civilian arm. The practice of Japanese civilian administrators wearing military uniforms and carrying swords was discontinued, as were forms of corporal punishment for minor offenses and a general lifting of formerly suppressed cultural practices. Symbolic of the new order was the marriage of the Korean Crown Prince Euimin (of the vestigial Yi Dynasty) and Japanese Princess Nashimoto Masako in April 1920. Taken together, the putative unity of the two royal houses and the loosening up of the most repressive policies in Korea were all part of what became known as the "Cultural Policy."

"Harmony between Japan and Korea." During Japan's period of relative liberalization in the 1920s, colonial policies in Korea were loosened under what came to be called the "Cultural Policy." A central symbol of this new approach was the marriage of Korean Crown Prince Euimin, whose Korean title was Yi Un, to Japan's Princess Nashimoto no miya Masako, whose Korean title now became Yi Bangja. The couple appears in this 1923 official photograph with the prince dressed in Japanese-style uniform, while the princess is fashionably attired in a Western-style dress and coif.

The first half of the 1920s, as it was in both China and Japan, marked an unprecedented period of cultural blossoming and press and political freedom in Korea. At least in part, this was to control and direct any movements toward cultural and political nationalism into channels that could be supervised by the colonial authorities. It was still forbidden to openly advocate independence but the influence of radical politics—especially emanating from pro-Western and Bolshevik sources—was in marked evidence.

The period was distinguished by a proliferation of exile and domestic groups, most of which were arrayed across a continuum from conservative and cultural nationalism to extreme varieties and, by the mid-1920s, several iterations of what became the Korean Communist Party. In some ways, they resembled the directions taken in the previous decade by the New Culture Movement and Literary Renaissance in China. Some groups advocated looking to Western examples, believing as their Chinese counterparts did, that the Neo-Confucian recent past and even slavish imitation of Japanese examples had left Korea a backwater. Among the more conservative writers in this group were those who felt that Korea would not be viable as a modern, independent nation without developing a "modern" literary and political culture. Thus, some were reluctant to advocate independence and counselled their colleagues to work within the colonial structure and adopt a gradualist approach toward proving worthy of independence. Their view in some respects echoes the despair of Sun Yat-sen during the same time when he saw the Chinese as a "sheet of loose sand" in terms of their national cohesion. Among these gradualists were a significant percentage of Christians and those who had prospered to a certain extent under the new order and/or had acquired their championing of modernity at foreign or Japanese schools.

As in other colonial areas—and echoing earlier debates in East Asia about adaptation (e.g., self-strengthening in China) versus fundamentalism (those seeing solutions in a purer Neo-Confucianism), or even the famous "Westernizers versus Slavophiles" arguments in Russia—there were those who sought salvation in a rediscovery of the national heritage. For many, the unique cultural heritage of the peninsula was a touchstone, representing a "third" great tradition after that of China and Japan. In response to the assertions of Japanese scholars that as the "Hermit Kingdom," Korea had been a roadblock to East Asian modernity, they championed the innovative and even "modern" features of han'gul as a tool for mass literacy and an important step toward national regeneration. A movement in support of national education and advocating the founding of a national university also gathered momentum but fell apart with the establishment of the Japanese-sponsored Keijo University in 1926.

Yet another development in aid of national unity was the creation of the Society for the Promotion of Korean Production in the early 1920s. In a rough foreshadowing of North Korea's juche self-supporting policies decades later, and like Gandhi's efforts to develop self-sufficiency in India and repeated anti-Japanese boycotts in China, the movement encouraged Korean industrial and economic self-sufficiency as a weapon against colonial economic exploitation. The government did not shut down the movement but eventually obviated it with subsidies to Korean merchants and bans on public demonstrations in support of the effort. During the more restrictive 1930s, it was banned altogether.

On the extreme left were those advocating direct action, most prominently various Marxist-, Bolshevik-, and Comintern-related groups. Here, the urge toward modernity, nationalism, and independence, and against imperialism as the "highest stage of capitalism" merged with the concrete example of the Bolsheviks and offers of aid and training through their creation of the Third International (Comintern). Although all these forces were at work in creating the Chinese Communist Party and in bolstering the Guomindang in the early 1920s, Japanese authorities were quick to move against the various attempts at creating a Korean Communist Party—as they had been with the Communist and Socialist parties in Japan. In Japan, the promulgation of the Peace Preservation Law in 1925 coupled with the various cabinets' staunch anti-Bolshevik orientation effectively outlawed Marxist parties. In Korea, the carryover from the new law and a growing vigilance by officials and police resulted in the founding and dismantling of no less than four Korean Communist parties before Comintern decided the time was not ripe to support any more. Indeed, most of the Communist influence that arrived in the north at the end of World War II came from Korean Communist exiles already in the Soviet Union.

Militarism, Colonialism, and War

The later 1920s marked a turn away from the diplomatic approach to international affairs and toward a more direct and confrontational one in Asia. The success of the Chinese Nationalists in consolidating their rule up to the Japanese-held areas in Manchuria suggested that Japan's free hand in the northeast might be jeopardized. The assassination of Manchurian warlord Zhang Zuolin and the tilt of his son, Zhang Xueliang, toward Chiang Kai-shek pushed this process even further. The onset of the Great Depression, the retreat of international trade upon which Japan was so reliant, and the move toward autarky spurred by the Mukden Incident and annexation of Manchuria all lent themselves toward a more militaristic approach both in Japan and in the empire outside of the home islands.

In Korea, the process had already begun as early as 1926. Police and security forces had been on the alert in expectation of demonstrations marking the death of the last Yi in the royal line. With the annexation of Manchuria and the creation of the puppet state of Manchukuo by 1932—soon followed by Japan's withdrawal from the League of Nations—Korea now became an important staging area for further advances into North China and Inner Mongolia. Moreover, the policies involved in creating in Manchukuo the model for the organization of the empire and the Greater East Asia Co-Prosperity Sphere a decade later also spilled over into Korea. As a movement toward "harmony among the races" in the region and to facilitate industrial and agricultural cooperation, attempts were made to strike bargains between labor and management and tenants and landlords, and to diversify Korean agriculture. This was especially important with regard to strategic cash crops such as cotton and sheep for wool.

PATTERNS UP-CLOSE

Nationalism, Empire, and Athletics

As Japan sought to ameliorate the effects of the Depression, draw increasingly on the economic resources of its empire, and redress the stigma of its rebuke by the Lytton Commission and defiant withdrawal from the League of Nations, it turned increasingly to militarism at home and within the territories it controlled. Thus, it was vitally important to organize the ideological unity of the empire for the widely anticipated coming struggle. An early taste of this would come during the 1936 Berlin Olympics. Organized by Nazi Germany to be the most spectacular Olympic show to date, its purpose for Hitler was in large part to show the world how thoroughly Germany had recovered from the war and to showcase the prosperity and accomplishments of the first three years of the Third Reich.

Japan was equally anxious to show its mettle to a world that it believed viewed Japan as an established power, but as an Asian people, racially inferior. If the Germans were eager to use athletic accomplishment to validate their claims to being a "master race," the Japanese were equally adamant about using sports as a vehicle to demonstrate their fitness to rule. Thus, the empire had to be seen as a seamless whole, with Japan playing the commanding role. In practical terms, this meant that whoever qualified for the Games from the empire would be presented as Japanese, regardless of their place of origin. This policy would have a profound effect on the Korean participants, bolster the cause of Korean nationalism, and lead to a crackdown on the Korean press. It would also create new Korean national heroes.

The most famous of these was Son Gi-jeong (sometimes referred to as Sohn Kee-chung). Born in 1912 in Sinuju in what is now North Korea, Son's early coaches made him run carrying rocks and bags of sand to strengthen his legs and increase his endurance. A successful middle distance runner, he began competing in longer races after 1933. Before the Olympics, he had completed twelve marathons, finishing all of them in the top three and winning nine. In 1935, he set a world record for the distance in Tokyo that remained in place until 1947. It was broken then by another Korean runner, Su Yun-bok, who had been coached by Son. Son's closest competitor was another Korean, Nam Seong-yong, and with a third Korean, they comprised what was now the "Japanese" Olympic marathon team.

The Koreans tried several times in interviews with the press to let it be known that they were representing Korea rather than Japan, but their Japanese chaperones and interpreters kept them from driving the point home. In the event, Son won the gold and Nam the bronze, with an English runner, Ernie Harper, claiming silver. The world press praised the "Japanese" runners, since

(continued)

the Koreans were forced to compete under Japanese transliterations of their names, but the photograph of the winners contained Son's subtle refutation of that status: the victor held the oak leaf cluster he received across his uniform to conceal the Japanese flag on it. At home, the Korean newspapers published the photo with both men looking down in shame at their feet while the Japanese anthem played, and blurred or scratched out the Japanese insignias on their uniforms. The Japanese authorities, incensed at this demonstration of Korean defiance, promptly shut down the leading Korean daily, *Dong-A Ilbo*, for nine months and arrested and tortured several of its reporters.

After the war, Son was seen as a national hero and coached South Korea's Olympic teams. His protégées Su Yun-bok and Ham Kee-yong won the Boston Marathon in 1947 and 1950, respectively. Perhaps his greatest triumph as a coach, however, came at the 1992 Olympics in Barcelona, where another runner he trained, Hwang Young-cho, won the gold. Even before this, he had the honor of carrying the Olympic torch into the stadium for the 1988 Seoul Games. Son died in 2002, but his legacy lives on in South Korea in

Korean Olympians. Hwang Young-cho won the marathon gold at the 1992 Barcelona Olympics. Korea's proud tradition of athletic achievement, particularly long-distance running, began in the 1930s. Although Korean athletes were forced to compete as Japanese in those days, they won gold and bronze at the Berlin Olympics and attempted to convey their true nationality to the international press. The winner, So Gi-jeong, tried to conceal the Japanese emblem on his jersey and became a national hero because of his victory and defiance. His legacy includes international gold medalists he trained over the years, culminating here in the victory of his protégé, Hwang Young-cho, at Barcelona.

> myriad ways. His autobiography is still a top seller, he has been portrayed on stage and screen, and a park was named in his honor in Seoul. In the modern history of Korea and its place in modern East Asian history, he is a reminder of the fiercely independent spirit and struggle for self-determination that marked so much of the nation's past and continues to this day.

In November 1936, Japan signed the Anti-Comintern Pact with Germany and Italy and soon after was fully at war with China. As it did in Japan, this prompted much more stringent security measures and a progressively tighter organization of the populace. Most Korean-organized associations were shut down and replaced with a bewildering array of Japanese-sponsored patriotic mobilization schemes. These ran the gamut from pushing those of all religions to visit Shinto shrines, to devoting the first day of every month to working for Greater East Asia, to forcing Koreans to change their names to the Japanese form under the motto, "Japan and Korea as one body."

Even more demanding was the militarization of education. In Japan, all elements of the school system were run as military organizations, with strict discipline, military subjects, and even weapons and self-defense training. Similar mobilization for national defense was undertaken in Korea. At first, school-age boys were recruited as volunteers for the armed forces. By 1943, all were required to register for service. Those not in the armed forces were required to work for labor mobilization teams at home, in fields, mines, and factories in Japan, and in various places throughout the empire. Most notorious of all was the systematic recruitment, kidnapping, and forced conscription of "comfort women" to service Japanese personnel in military brothels. Perhaps as many as 200,000 women from Korea (as well as tens of thousands from Manchuria, China, Taiwan, and other areas of the empire) were used in this fashion.

COLD WAR, HOT WAR, AND COLD WAR

As we have seen, one of the ironies of World War II outside of the European Theater is that although by far the largest concentration of Japanese troops was on the mainland of East and Southeast Asia, the main dynamic thrusts—indeed, where the war was lost for Japan—were in the Pacific. As we will see in more detail in Chapter 13, this has been one of the key elements of Japan's "history problem." Having adopted the term "Pacific War" from what the Americans called their own struggle against Japan, Japanese apologists for colonialism and the war years have found it a handy tool to separate the two struggles.

In terms of the unfolding strategies of the combatants, however, what was called the "China-Burma-India Theater" was initially seen as central in the struggle against Japan. Here, the plan called for Nationalist China under Chiang Kai-shek to be built up as the main bulwark against further Japanese expansion, and as the stepping stone to roll back the Japanese Empire and the initial site for

Comfort Women. Japanese colonialism included forced labor from all sectors of the "Greater East Asia Co-Prosperity Sphere." This category included "comfort women" from Korea, forced to serve in brothels at Japanese military posts. In the decades since the war, survivors and the South Korean government have sought recognition of their plight and compensation from Japan. Compensation came periodically over several decades, whereas recognition by Japan only occurred in 2007. In the photograph here, U.S. Marines interview women freed from a Japanese brothel on Okinawa while fighting raged nearby at the end of April 1945.

bombing missions against Japan. Although all these early expectations were ultimately undone, there was still much discussion throughout the war of what was to happen to Japan's empire in Asia after its expected defeat. For the British, French, and Dutch, it was anticipated that their colonies in the region would be restored or, like the League of Nations mandates at the end of World War I, arranged into some kind of graded system of trusteeship on the road to eventual independence. The United States under Franklin Roosevelt was on record as saying that it expected immediate or early independence after the war for India, the Dutch East Indies, Burma, French Indochina, and Korea. In the case of these last three, however, the picture was complicated by the presence of China as a contiguous neighbor, which could be expected to demand a share in the Occupation duties and perhaps even a say in how the new borders would be drawn. In the case of Korea, there was also the looming presence of the Soviet Union, which, although neutral in the war against Japan until the final weeks of the war, could nonetheless be expected to demand a say in any final settlement in Northeast Asia.

Thus, although the disposition of the islands won back from Japan would be rather straightforward, that of the lands of Japan's empire on the Asian mainland was potentially a thicket of complexity and competing interests. For Koreans, a steady, if not always locally powerful backer was Chiang Kai-shek's Nationalist China. The Nationalists saw the best chance for a friendly, non-Communist Korea in the exiled Korean Provisional Government operating in China. By 1943, with American backing, Chiang was accepted (rather reluctantly by the British) as a full Allied partner alongside Roosevelt, Churchill, and Stalin and thus attended the Cairo Conference and engaged in discussions on a final strategy to finish the war and arrange liberated territory in its aftermath. Unlike Chiang, Roosevelt, though favoring ultimate independence for Korea, believed that it should be held in trusteeship immediately after the war by the occupying Allied powers. Thus, the idea of Korean independence "in due course" was incorporated into the Cairo Declaration.

As we shall also see in the case of Indochina, however, a smooth transition of power and occupation was not to be had. Japan's sudden collapse in the face of the atomic bombs and Soviet declaration of war in August 1945 left only the Soviet forces swiftly moving through Manchuria and into northern Korea in a position to accept a Japanese surrender there. Frantic that the Soviets might unify a Korea under the influence of their own occupation, the Americans proposed an arbitrary division of the peninsula along the 38th Parallel as the dividing line for their Occupation forces to meet those from the USSR. Seventy-three years later, with the **Demilitarized Zone (DMZ)** that has marked the armistice line of the Korean War since 1953 crossing it, the parallel still essentially delineates the border between what became two Koreas (see Map 11.2).

A Korean Civil War?

By September 1945, a wide political spectrum of delegates was meeting in Seoul and declared the Korean People's Republic. Long-time activist Syngman Rhee (1875–1965), Ivy League–educated and residing in the U.S. during the war, had now returned home and emerged as chairman. A welter of other parties and claimants to power came forward in the ensuing months as well. In the Soviet zone, a number of groups, including those with strong Christian connections, also vied for legitimacy. The Soviets, however, soon moved their tacit support to Kim Il-sung (1912–1994), raised in a Protestant family and a convert to Marxism, who had fought with Soviet-supported Korean Communist guerrillas. The hurried plans to divide the country into four Occupation zones like Germany (with American, British, Soviet, and Chinese sectors) and establish a brief trusteeship in late 1945 was already falling apart by the spring of 1946. Korean groups in the American Occupation zone bitterly opposed the move, and although many in the Soviet zone did as well, the increasingly powerful Communists under Kim supported Soviet trusteeship. Within a few months, travel between the sectors became restricted, and both sides of the 38th Parallel were settling into what would soon become two rival regimes.

As we have seen, wartime cooperation between the U.S. and the Soviet Union was already breaking down by 1946, and tensions between the two allies continued to mount. The resumption of the Chinese civil war and momentum of Mao Zedong's Chinese Communist Party, Soviet repression of opposition parties in its European-occupied areas, and the developing American strategy of "containment"

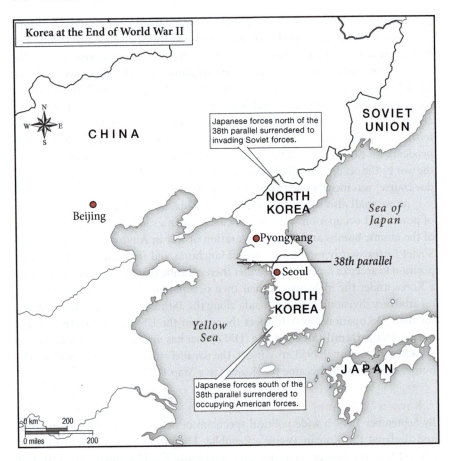

Map 11.2 Korea at the End of World War II

of Soviet expansion and influence—all lent themselves to creating what came to be called the Cold War. As we will see in Chapter 13, this also resulted in a reevaluation of Occupation policies in Japan and Korea. American efforts to create new institutions, often with scant regard for differentiating among collaborationists and nationalists, increased the fear of Communist influence. Korean resistance to the trusteeship, and American desire to withdraw from the region, both pushed events toward the hasty creation of a National Assembly in the south, swiftly recognized as the legitimate government of Korea by the UN, and the formation on August 15, 1948, of the Republic of Korea (ROK) with Syngman Rhee as its first president. In the Soviet zone, stung by UN recognition of the ROK as Korea's "legitimate" government, the Occupation authorities completed the process of entrenching the North Korean Workers Party and Kim Il-sung as the leader of the new Democratic People's Republic of Korea (DPRK) shortly thereafter.

Despite the intensification of the Cold War during the following years, Korea was seen in very different ways by the U.S. and the Soviet Union. The attempts to cut off Berlin in Europe and subsequent airlift (1948), the victory of Mao's forces in China (1949), and the detonation of a nuclear weapon by the Soviets (1949) all raised tensions and increasingly committed the United States to the policy of containment. In this schema, however, Japan was increasingly seen as the chief bulwark against Communist expansion. Korea was in the anomalous position of being on the front line but subject to dwindling American commitment as the ROK became more firmly established. Thus, American forces were largely withdrawn, military and economic aid was reduced, and the confusing impression created that Korea was outside of "America's defense perimeter."

A Divided Korea's First Leaders. With the onset of the Cold War in the early years after World War II, the occupation zones of the Soviets and the United States became the Democratic People's Republic of Korea (North Korea) and the Republic of Korea (South Korea), respectively. With the North's attempt to reunify the peninsula under its own aegis, sparking the Korean War in 1950, Kim Il-sung and Syngman Rhee became bitter opponents, a situation still marking the two states today, sixty-five years after the armistice agreement. Syngman Rhee was succeeded by military men, but by the turn of the century, South Korea had begun to create democratic institutions. Kim Il-sung, on the other hand, has created a highly authoritarian family dynasty through his son Kim Jung-il and (presently) his grandson Kim Jung-un. Here, a 1000-won note (B) bears a portrait of the founding Kim; next to him is an early photo of Syngman Rhee from 1939 (A).

For their part, however, the Soviets saw opportunity in Korea, as did Kim Il-sung. The overwhelming majority of Koreans North and South wanted to see the peninsula reunited and nearly all expected that the division would be short-lived. The Soviets made increasingly heavy commitments to bolster North Korea's economy and military forces and increasingly saw Kim's desire to be the agent of unification as both doable and desirable. Planners in the North also calculated that there was a strong undercurrent of support for unification and growing dissatisfaction with the Rhee government. Proof for this was adduced from intelligence gleaned from occasional raids conducted by both sides. Coupled with the facts of a small, underequipped South Korean army, a minimal American presence, and inconsistent U.S. policy toward the South, by the spring of 1950, Kim, Stalin, and Mao were in basic agreement that an attempt at unification by force would be a gamble worth risking.

From Seesaw to Stalemate

In what was termed the "June 25th Incident," in the ROK, the DPRK launched a massive invasion across the 38th Parallel with a view to crush the far weaker Southern forces and swiftly capture Seoul, which both sides considered the "true" capital of Korea. Caught completely by surprise, South Korean forces were soon forced to give up the city and fled south, fighting increasingly desperate rear-guard actions. With little artillery, and almost no armor or air cover, the rout was accompanied by hundreds of thousands of vulnerable refugees, many of whom were killed in the confused retreat. American President Harry Truman ordered General Douglas MacArthur, commanding the Occupation of Japan, to render such military aid as he could. The U.S. appealed to the UN Security Council for a judgment on North Korea as an aggressor, which would then authorize UN forces to resist the incursion. The Soviet Union, which could have vetoed such a ruling, instead boycotted the proceedings, making the effort to oppose the invasion a sanctioned multinational effort, although with American and ROK forces constituting the vast majority of the armed forces.

The United States did not have large numbers of troops in the region, but it did have powerful land- and carrier-based air forces on the scene. Almost immediately, North Korean forces were pounded by American planes, which provided cover for the retreat of the South Korean army and the few U.S. ground troops available as they established a defensive perimeter around the southern port of Pusan. Throughout the summer, American forces were built up in Pusan, the perimeter was held, and plans for a counterattack were laid. As commander of the UN forces, MacArthur decided on a bold and extremely risky move: using their overwhelming naval and air power to maximum advantage, U.S. forces would undertake an amphibious invasion of Seoul's port of Inchon while simultaneously breaking out of Pusan. The Northern forces would then be trapped in a great pincer movement and driven back across the border. The plan was extremely risky, particularly because tidal conditions made close timing of the landings absolutely critical.

Nonetheless, on September 15, landings began and almost immediately the combined UN forces began to push back the North Koreans. Now the DPRK forces were routed, and by the end of the month, UN forces had retaken Seoul and were moving into the North. Although they had no official sanction to move beyond the original border, MacArthur and the Rhee government believed that they now had the long-sought opportunity to unite the peninsula and roll back Communist advances in spectacular fashion.

The situation in the North thus began to resemble that which beset the South only two months before. UN forces captured Pyongyang and were moving swiftly northward toward the border with China. In the meantime, the U.S. had sent a fleet to the remnant of the Chinese Nationalists who had re-formed the Republic of China on Taiwan, to protect it from a threatened invasion by a newly Communist China. Thwarted in the south at Taiwan, Mao Zedong took the incautious pronouncements of MacArthur about raiding Chinese supply bases on the North Korean border seriously. Stalin, on the other hand, opposed an escalation and gave Mao only token support (see Map 11.3).

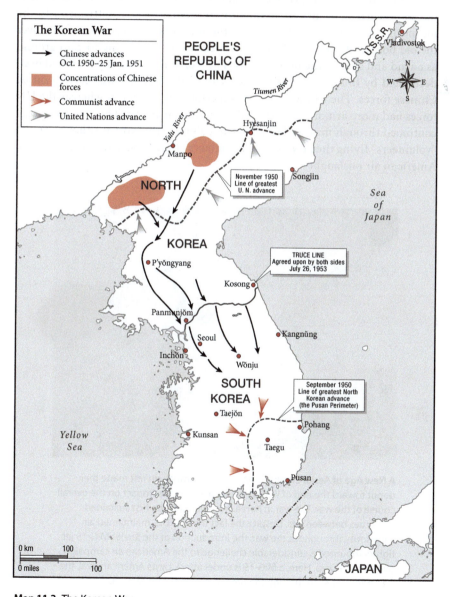

Map 11.3 The Korean War

Secretly marching to the border in October 1950, Communist Chinese "People's Volunteer Army" troops launched a massive surprise offensive into the peninsula, pushing the U.N. forces back through North Korea and deep into South Korea. By April 1951, MacArthur's talk about bombing China—even suggesting the possibility of using nuclear weapons—had escalated tensions with President Truman. Amid accusations of insubordination, Truman relieved MacArthur of command and replaced him with Matthew Ridgeway. By the summer, both sides had agreed to peace talks, but arguments over a host of details ranging from prisoner exchanges to the shape and arrangement of the conference tables tended to undermine any permanent settlement. In the meantime, over the next three years, the war seesawed back and forth over the old border of the 38th Parallel, with each side attempting to gain ground as an aid and spur to the negotiations. The North Korean army itself had been decimated by this point, and the majority of the fighting was carried on by Chinese forces. The Chinese enjoyed superiority in numbers, whereas the UN forces had more armor, artillery, and especially air power. This last advantage continued through massive bombing campaigns of the North, although Soviet "volunteers" flying the new MiG-15 jet fighters offered spirited resistance to the American air onslaught.

A New Age of Aerial Combat. Although jet combat aircraft made their debut toward the end of World War II, they had little impact on the overall course of the war. The war in Korea, however, saw the first sustained air battles between jets. Despite the fact that the U.S. maintained air superiority throughout the war, the introduction of the Soviet MiG-15 jet fighter mounted a considerable challenge to the American air campaign over North Korea. Here, a MiG-15 is under attack by its American rival, the F-86 Sabre, as seen through the American plane's gun camera.

By 1953, both sides were anxious to come to an agreement. For the Americans, the prospect of a large, endless ground campaign on the Asian mainland was unthinkable—as it would be in the following decade during the American war in Vietnam. For the Chinese, the war was a serious drain on the scant resources with which they were attempting to build their new state. The new American president, Dwight D. Eisenhower, had campaigned on a platform of bringing the war to a close, and his prestige as commander-in-chief of Allied forces in the European Theater during World War II lent itself to his efforts. In the summer of 1953, therefore, both sides signed an armistice agreement, which established a DMZ encompassing some of the old 38th Parallel border, a truce village for further negotiations at Panmunjom, and protocols for prisoner exchanges, repatriation, and the handling of refugees. As noted above, despite a number of subsequent provocations on both sides, the truce is still in force today.

As scholars and commentators from both sides have noted, the war devastated the peninsula as thoroughly as any place on Earth during the twentieth century. American and UN dead numbered about 41,000. ROK and DPRK dead may have exceeded 250,000 and 300,000, with Chinese forces accounting for another 200,000 dead. Civilian dead estimates range from about a million in South Korea to perhaps 1.5 million in the North. Given the relatively small population of the North, about 15 million, such losses were that much more crippling. Nearly every major city in both the North and South suffered damage, with most of the larger ones seeing it on a catastrophic scale. Both Seoul and Pyongyang, fought over multiple times, were laid waste. American reliance on air power as a strategic and tactical weapon made damage to the infrastructure of the North particularly widespread. Nearly every factory, airfield, bridge, railyard, shipyard—practically every productive enterprise—had suffered heavy damage or destruction. Finally, untold numbers of people were injured, made homeless, uprooted, and stranded far from home, unable to return.

As some economists have noted, the completeness of the destruction on both sides allowed them to start almost from scratch in rebuilding. As was the case with Germany and Japan, it provided an opportunity to replace old or outmoded industrial and transportation complexes with the most modern items available. For the North, the relatively small contribution made by the Soviet Union, accompanied by Stalin's death in 1953, allowed Kim Il-sung to operate more independently. At the same time, the massive Chinese participation to some degree reestablished ties that have continued to this day. Both socialist powers contributed aid in the North's reconstruction[...] 1950s, North Korea's economic indicators tended to surp[...] By the early 1960s, it appeared the gap was actually wid[...] spite American military and economic aid, the South[...] sluggish. By way of comparison, on the eve of its inde[...] rule, Ghana's economic indicators were substantially hi[...] ROK. In the next decade, however, these conditions wer[...]

Destruction in Korea. With the shifting of the fortunes of war a number of times on the Korean Peninsula before becoming locked in a stalemate around the present border at the 38th Parallel, destruction was widespread throughout the region. The heavy use of air power by the UN forces to compensate for North Korean and Chinese numbers made the devastation even more complete. Here, an American tank controls an intersection in Seoul as captured North Korean troops are marched to the rear. This fighting took place during the UN counteroffensive in September 1950, following the amphibious landing at Inchon.

POLITICAL AND ECONOMIC DEVELOPMENTS SOUTH AND NORTH

The last half-century has seen the North and the South grow farther apart culturally, economically, and politically than at any other time in the peninsula's history. The DPRK, locked into a Stalinist form of government, reliant on a multigenerational cult of personality toward the Kim family of rulers, committed to extreme economic self-reliance, isolated from its neighbors (with even China distancing itself from the North's most extreme positions and behaviors), and constantly seeking to develop weapons of mass destruction, remains one of the world's most repressive and economically stagnant states. The ROK, on the other hand, is perhaps the most economically vibrant, modern, globally oriented, democratic, and most recently, avowedly multicultural state in East Asia. One might add that it is the only state in Northeast Asia to have been governed by a woman, Park Geun-hye, until her impeachment and removal from office in 2017. Given the fact that these two states existed in such different circumstances in the early years, how did this dramatic role reversal take place?

Economic and political theorists have long debated the relationship between market economics and representative government. The demands raised by capitalist/market-driven economies for stability, laws respecting property rights, consent to the structure of taxation, a well-regulated banking and monetary system, business environments favorable to entrepreneurship and capital accumulation, and other related conditions, it is argued, tend to force governments to become more responsive and, hence, over time more representative. East and Southeast Asia in the late twentieth and early twenty-first centuries provide interesting test cases of this idea. One the one hand, there is the example of Singapore, which appears to hold the line against this condition by maintaining a free-wheeling market economy but an authoritarian regime. This early example of "Confucian capitalism" was emulated by Deng Xiaoping in China, in recent years by Vietnam, and for much of the last fifty years by South Korea, Taiwan, and, some would argue, because of the close relationship among government, finance, and industry, Japan. Yet Japan's democratic institutions are nonetheless effective. Taiwan and South Korea, moreover, have moved solidly in democratic directions, thus adding support to this idea. For South Korea, prosperity brought increasing pressure for democracy which, by the 1990s with the elections of Kim Young-sam and Kim Dae-jong, was solidly established.

Republics and Coups

During its first forty-four years, the ROK oscillated between direct military rule and governments that were constitutional in the legal sense but authoritarian in practice. These were punctuated by short-lived regimes that were

North and South Korea in Satellite Imagery. The larger population, prosperity, and relatively massive power consumption of South Korea are on stark display in this photograph of the Korean Peninsula taken from the International Space Station in January 2014. North Korea appears as a ghostly blank space in the area between the brilliantly lit South and China. The huge light spread in the right center is metropolitan Seoul, whereas the only obvious light in the dark space of the North is Pyongyang.

more openly democratic but quickly shut down because of political turmoil and the putative need to restore "order." Thus, the history of the ROK is often, like France, divided into numbered "republics," each with a new or heavily amended constitution. The First Republic was that of Syngman Rhee, from 1948 to 1960.

Syngman Rhee's record of anti-colonialism and anti-Communism had provided him with much support during the Korean War and in the years immediately thereafter. He also made himself popular with many by periodically resisting American demands while maintaining a fairly close relationship with the U.S. as the ROK's main backer. Rhee's dominance in ROK politics was such that he was able to engineer a constitutional amendment allowing him to run for a third term, which he won handily in 1956. As we noted above, however, despite the massive infusion of American defense funds and other aid, the South's economy was only gradually improving. The North, by way of contrast, was benefiting from aid from Communist bloc countries and rebuilding the heavy industry that had earlier been set up, in part, by the Japanese. Under Japanese colonialism, the North, because of its proximity to resource-rich Manchuria and its own resources, had been the preferred area for industrial development. The South had remained largely agricultural. The war, despite the destruction in many of the South's cities, had also made them refugee centers and desirable places for impoverished rural people to try their luck. Thus, by the late 1950s, there were developing two South Koreas: one conservative, rural, and only now in the process of recovery; the other, more cosmopolitan, politically active, and anxious for change and economic growth. Moreover, Korea historically had one of the highest literacy rates in Asia, and this continued despite the disruptions of the war. For the chief opposition to Rhee's Liberal Party, the Democratic Party, the increased urbanization and growing opposition spelled opportunity for a more open and less corrupt government.

Although Rhee ran for a fourth term and won in 1960, his age (85) left voters in all parties concerned about his successor. When his vice-presidential candidate also won, widespread allegations of voter fraud sparked massive demonstrations in Seoul. Police killed 139 of the demonstrators and the day of the event, April 19, is commemorated as "Student Revolution Day." As the ROK's defender and benefactor, and worried that instability in the political system would tempt another reunification effort by the DPRK, the U.S. convinced Rhee to retire to Hawaii. After additional political turmoil in which Rhee's vice-presidential candidate committed suicide, a new and short-lived democratic Second Republic with a replacement constitution was sworn in. Hampered by lack of a genuine mandate, racked by strikes and demonstrations, and demands for new talks at Panmunjom, the military stepped in and launched a successful coup in May 1961. The man who emerged as the new head of the South Korean government was General Park Chung-hee (Pak Chong-hui). After two years of direct military rule, he would establish authoritarian but formally constitutional rule in the South for nearly two decades. He would also, however, lay the foundation on which the South would build its new economy.

President Park and President Kennedy. The relationship between the United States and South Korea was strained at times despite their joint efforts to avert conquest by the North and unwavering anti-Communism. South Korea's devastation was still evident by the end of the 1950s, and student demonstrations and a military coup resulted in the two-decade rule of Park Chung-hee. While maintaining authoritarian military rule, Park also launched a successful economic recovery plan for the South, laying the foundations for its present prosperity. Here, President Park (on the left, wearing glasses) and U.S. President John F. Kennedy (on the right) confer at the White House a few months after Park's coup in 1961.

Land Reform and the Export Economy

Even before the coup and the military government's establishment of a Supreme Council for National Reconstruction, changes were under way in the countryside of the South that were to have far-reaching consequences. From 1949 through the mid-1950s, a series of land reform measures were put into place limiting the acreage of private holdings, redistributing the overage, and setting easy terms and interest rates for purchases. As one study shows, in the dozen years from 1944 to 1956, ownership of land shifted from 3 percent of the population owning 64 percent of the land, to the top 6 percent only owning 18 percent. Thus, tenancy had largely been replaced by small farmers, rural poverty had steeply declined, and the last vestiges of the *yangban* class had almost entirely vanished.

Even though South Korea's economic recovery was frustratingly sluggish in the 1950s and, critics charged, more than half of the government's budget was funded by the United States, two important pillars of a strong economy, widespread literacy and education, and a healthy agricultural sector were already falling into place. For the Park government, anxious to make South Korea economically independent of the U.S., even if dependent on America for its nuclear umbrella and military support, the next step was the first Five-Year Plan. Anxious to be economically self-reliant, the Rhee government had pursued a rigorously nationalistic policy of import substitution: Koreans should rely as little as possible on imports and make the products required for its consumers. It should guard its recovering industries from foreign competition—and especially have as little to do as possible with former colonial master Japan. This policy, however, was slow going and hampered to some extent by the distortions produced by funneling so much American aid into the military and simply running the government.

The SCNR's new direction was to make the country export-driven. This was the strategy that had early on been adopted by Japan—and would be again with the end of the American Occupation. In fact, some form of this approach has over the last half-century been adopted by nearly every successful Asian economy. The idea of protecting the nation's home industries from foreign competition by tariff barriers and other means is retained. But much of one's manufacturing sector is directed toward goods for export in order to accumulate capital for further development. By identifying demand for certain items in different countries and developing these "niche markets," one can then diversify and expand them. In the early 1960s, therefore, following the earlier lead of Japan, South Korea began exporting inexpensive consumer goods.

A first step was to get the business community in line and willing to follow a central scheme of manufacturing prioritization. At the same time, the banks were nationalized to regulate the flow of scarce capital and direct it toward the goals of the Five-Year Plan. It was expected that as the ROK's economy improved, foreign companies would express interest in investing in Korea. Given sensitivity to the huge American presence and recent Japanese colonial era, there was understandable reluctance to open the investment doors too widely. Nonetheless, by the mid-1960s, Japan's booming economy and rising manufacturing wages made South Korea attractive as a site for low-wage factory production. Thus, the Park government signed a treaty with Japan and, with the ROK's economy surpassing expectations, offered tax abatements and other incentives to foreign companies willing to invest in Korea. Over the coming decade, Japan's investments in Korea would come to ten times its opening 1965 total and contribute an estimated 60 percent of technology transfers to Korea.

The results of the first phase of the export strategy were impressive. Overall, they showed a GDP growth rate of almost 9 percent per year. Exports, the centerpiece of the strategy, grew at nearly 30 percent per year; manufacturing grew at 15 percent per year. Subsequent plans called for developing infrastructural items and transportation. In the early 1970s, as Park's rule turned increasingly authoritarian, the emphasis moved more toward heavy industry, shipping, and automobiles. An additional significant development was one that in some respects followed the earlier Japanese model of the *zaibatsu* and post-Occupation *keiretsu* conglomerates. These were **chaebols**, companies engaged in strategically important economic sectors that received favorable credits, tax breaks, and other incentives to fulfill their assignments quickly and efficiently. Like their

Japanese counterparts, a number of these have become household names with worldwide recognition: Samsung, Hyundai, Daewoo, and LG among dozens of lesser-known enterprises.

From Authoritarian Rule to Democracy

Park and the military leaders who had engineered the coup of 1961 had promised to restore the state to civilian control. By 1963, with the first Five-Year Plan in place and showing promise, the military government put together a new constitution, Park had resigned from the army to run for president, and the government—under pressure from the U.S. to make good on its promises—went ahead with elections. Park had cobbled together various supporting groups into a new Democratic Republican Party, which won a narrow presidential victory and, because of a "winner take all" election rule regarding at-large seats in the National Assembly, gained a solid majority in the legislature. Thus, with this Third Republic, the mechanisms were falling into place for a more open representative government, but Park as president still controlled the military, executive apparatus, and the increasingly formidable Korean Central Intelligence Agency (KCIA).

Nonetheless, South Korea's economic progress accompanied by a loosening of free speech and press restrictions seemed to augur well for the future. Korea's quasi-client relationship with the United States continued to prove an annoyance for most Korean leaders, who resented the huge role that the U.S. still played in the ROK's economy and defense—and especially the leverage it gave the Americans to pressure Korean governments on issues related to democratic reform, corruption, and foreign policy. From the mid-1960s through the early 1970s, Park was able to counter this somewhat by contributing ROK combat and support troops to the American effort in Vietnam. The troops soon acquired a reputation as tough, fierce, and durable fighters, the ROK was seen as doing its part in the Cold War struggle against Communism abroad as well as in its own backyard, and the program kept aid, training, and state-of-the-art equipment flowing to the South Korean military. It also enabled the KCIA to extend its reach throughout the region and even into the U.S.

The early 1970s brought both political and economic crises to the ROK. Like his predecessor, Park now sought a constitutional change to run for a third term in 1971. His young opponent was the future president Kim Dae-jung (Kim Tae-jung, 1925–2009). Park won the election, but the results showed that there was now a strong and viable opposition coalition to Park's DRP, particularly in the increasingly cosmopolitan and affluent urban areas. Nevertheless, a new constitution was drawn up (the *Yushin Constitution*), and the Fourth Republic was inaugurated.

Despite the overall strengthening of the export economy and heavy industry initiatives of the early 1970s, there were also disruptions on the economic and foreign relations fronts. The American commitment in Vietnam was being rapidly reduced, slowing down the military and financial aid the U.S. had supplied in support of Korea's participation in the war. The U.S. was also moving into a recession in the wake of the wind-down in Southeast Asia and into a more protectionist economic policy with regard to textiles, the ROK's largest export to the U.S.

Most startling for nearly all of East Asia was the abrupt American tilt toward the People's Republic of China. In 1972, the U.S. and PRC unveiled the Shanghai Communique, in which travel restrictions were dropped between the two countries, plans were laid for mutual diplomatic recognition, the diplomatic status of Taiwan/Republic of China was reduced, and the U.S. dropped its opposition to the PRC joining the UN. For Japan and Taiwan as well as the ROK, the news was particularly jarring as all three (as was South Vietnam) had been part of the overall containment policy aimed at China. Moreover, these American allies felt a keen sense of betrayal because they were not informed in advance of this dramatic move. Finally, relations with the DPRK had recently heated up. On January 21, 1968, a commando squad of North Koreans attempted to assault the ROK presidential mansion (the Blue House). Two days later, the North Koreans seized a U.S. Navy research vessel, the *Pueblo*, and held the crew for eleven months, while using them for a variety of propaganda purposes. By the early 1970s, there had been repeated provocations by the North in which infiltrators had attacked ROK military personnel, conducted kidnappings and assassinations, and even constructed a tunnel under the DMZ. Later, in 1974, Park's own wife would be assassinated.

The Blue House. Since the armistice in 1953, there has been a shadow war going on between the two Koreas, which includes spycraft, infiltration, and even tunnels under the DMZ and occasional forays into the Zone itself. In January 1968, two spectacular incidents took place within days of each other as North Korean infiltrators attempted to attack the South Korean executive mansion, the Blue House, pictured above. Note its classic Korean geomantic orientation of "mountains behind." Two days later, North Korean vessels seized the U.S. Navy research and surveillance ship *Pueblo*, precipitating a long and acrimonious showdown with the United States.

In the midst of these developments, Park declared a state of emergency in October 1972, dissolved the legislature and suspended the constitution, and in short order declared martial law. Soon thereafter, a new constitution granting the executive sweeping powers was instituted. Dogged by the growing power of opposition groups, Park employed the KCIA widely at home and abroad, particularly to deal with dissidents. In 1975, shortly after the Watergate scandal had forced the resignation of U.S. President Nixon, KCIA activities in the United States were brought to light in the "Koreagate" investigations, delivering another blow to the ROK's international status. The recession in the U.S., worsened by the OPEC moves and Arab oil boycott, also stalled Korean economic development. Human rights pressure from the Carter administration also played a role in a now growing drive to force Park from office. The outbreak of student demonstrations through 1979 and Park's refusal to compromise with his opponents in the end alienated even his closest supporters: on October 26, he was assassinated by the head of the KCIA.

In the confusion that followed, Park's prime minister assumed the role of president but was swiftly overthrown on December 12 by General Chun Doo-hwan. The government now marked the Fifth Republic, although its early days were particularly chaotic. Most noteworthy, and tragic, of these events was the nine-day protest mounted by the Gwangju (Kwang-ju) Democratization Movement and their violent suppression at the hands of the military. The **Gwangju Massacre**, as it became known, produced an official death toll of 200, with another 850 injured. Despite this tragedy, Chun was elected president under the new constitution that instituted, among other changes, a single seven-year presidential term (by indirect election), but also devolving more power on the National Assembly and placing greater barriers between the executive and judiciary. Chun's rule was economically quite successful. Exports rose; Korean companies made rapid headway in shipping, electronics, and automobiles in domestic and international markets; and foreign investments continued to multiply.

Perhaps even more hopeful from an emotional perspective was an apparent loosening of tensions with the North. Despite ongoing border provocations, the DPRK had proposed talks toward a "one-nation, two-system" unification scheme, not dissimilar to what the PRC was proposing to Hong Kong and Taiwan at the time. In 1985, for the first time since the truce, families were allowed to visit relatives across the DMZ on a limited basis.

Despite these progressive steps, opposition to the heavy hand of the military and the indirect election process continued to mount. Chun's picked nominee Roh Tae-woo, under heavy pressure by opposition groups, now announced his support for constitutional changes that would allow direct presidential elections. This, and the lack of unity of his opponents Kim Young-sam and Kim Dae-jung—who would, in fact, become the next two presidents—allowed Roh to win the election and thus commenced the Sixth (and present-day) Republic. Faced with mounting pressure to initiate democratic reforms, Roh allowed increased press freedom and eased travel restrictions. He also won considerable international praise for the success of the 1988 Olympic Games in Seoul. As had been the case with Tokyo in 1964, and would be with Beijing in 2008, the Seoul Games put the dramatic rebuilding and modernization of the ROK on global display and did much to reinforce Korea's status as one of the **Four Tigers** (or "Little Dragons")—South Korea, Taiwan, Singapore, and Hong Kong—that had moved into economic prominence in recent years. Finally, the momentum of talks toward eventual reunification continued, cultural and athletic exchanges were undertaken, and in 1991 the ROK and DPRK issued a joint announcement in support of nuclear nonproliferation on the peninsula.

The Democratic Era, 1993 to the Present

The election of Kim Young-sam to the presidency in 1992 marked a milestone on the path to genuine representative government in the ROK. As has often been noted, he was the first nonmilitary man since Syngman Rhee to hold that office, and his election signaled important changes in Korean politics. Widespread elections from the National Assembly down to the local level were held over the next several years, with old opposition parties now assuming positions of power. Both Chun and Roh were called to account for the considerable bribery, corruption, and abuse of government powers in which they engaged while in office and both were given severe sentences: Chun was sentenced to death, although this sentence was commuted, and Rho to life imprisonment.

Ironically, as South Korea has become an increasingly mature democracy and economic power over the last two decades, relations with the North have deteriorated to the point where even the DPRK's old ally, China, has come to see its present regime under Kim Il-sung's grandson, Kim Jung-un, as an ongoing threat to the stability of the region. Kim Il-sung's death in 1993 cancelled plans for a North–South summit. Kim Jung-il and Kim Jung-un have since launched numerous raids on the South and provocations in the DMZ. More ominously, they worked toward constructing a nuclear weapon and missile delivery system, which despite several rounds of talks and even food shipments to spur Northern cooperation on nonproliferation, have now been completed.

The election of Kim Dae-jung in 1998 celebrated another significant event in the progress of democracy in Korea: the orderly transfer of power to a president-elect of the opposition. Although South Korea has wrestled with an economic crisis in the region since 1997, its economic strength and the willingness of the government to pursue austerity measures and solidify the cooperation of the *chaebols* helped guide the economy to a soft landing. Perhaps Kim's signal accomplishment was a renewal of peace talks with the North. Under his "Sunshine Policy," efforts were resumed to reunite families with relatives in the North and, in recognition of his efforts, Kim was awarded the Nobel Peace Prize in 2000.

The ROK's latest presidents, Roh Moo-hyun (in office from 2003 to 2008), Lee Myung-bak (2008–2013) and the republic's first woman president, Park Geun-hye (2013–2017), like their immediate predecessors, dealt with periods of economic slowdown while trying to increase democratic participation and thus solidify South Korea's status as the region's, and one of the world's, most wide open democratic

(A)

(B)

The Kim Dynasty. Unlike the numerous presidents arriving by coup, appointment, and election in South Korea, North Korea has only had three successive leaders, all members of the Kim family. On the postage stamp (A), father and son Kim Il-sung (left) and Kim Jung-il (right). (B) The grandson and present-day North Korean leader, Kim Jung-un.

states. Korea's industrial might continues to grow as its *chaebols* like Samsung and Hyundai view for dominance in world markets. For Roh, the political fight became one of survival. Impeached on charges of election fraud, he was reinstated in 2005. Following a corruption investigation, however, he took his own life in 2009.

Lee's administration fared rather better. Although hit hard by the great recession of 2008, his government concluded trade agreements with the U.S. over food imports—a perennial sticking point—and passed on a recovering economy to his successor, President Park. The daughter of Park Chung-hee (b. 1952), and a long-time presence in the National Assembly, she had routinely been listed as one of the most powerful women in Asia even before her election. Leading her Grand National Party and its restructured "New Frontier Party" to victory in 2012, on a platform of "hope and happiness," her politics tended toward conservative, market-oriented policies, including a close relationship with the United States. Seeing the alliance with the U.S. as key to regional stability, her policies

(A)

(B)

South Korean Presidents Park and Moon. The election of Park Geun-hye in 2012 marked the coming of the first woman to the Korean presidency and, as the daughter of Park Chung-hee, the arrival of a dynasty of sorts. Unfortunately, her time in office was marred by charges of bribery and corruption, for which she was impeached in December 2016 and sentenced to prison in 2018. In (A), she is shown visiting NASA's Goddard Space Flight Center in the U.S. Her successor and the current president Moon Jae-in (B) campaigning in 2017.

toward the DPRK were resolute but hopeful that a strategy of small trust-building endeavors might lay the groundwork for eventual unification, although this does not seem to be in the offing in the immediate future.

On December 9, 2016, Park was impeached by the National Assembly because of the bribery and extortion committed by her major supporters; her presidency was consequently suspended. Many members of her Seinuri Party, believing that she had departed from traditional conservative aims, withdrew to form a new party. In October, 2018 she was convicted and sentenced to twenty-four years in prison. The new president, Moon Jae-in, took office in May 2017.

THE NEW HERMIT KINGDOM OF THE NORTH

As scholars have frequently noted, the differences between the evolving DPRK and ROK far surpassed those separating the two Germanys, Chinas, or Vietnams. United as a people through the era of Japanese colonialism, their paths have so radically diverged in the interim that sometimes the only connection between them seems to be their geographical position. The South, despite its slow recovery in the early postwar period, has built arguably the most dynamic economy in Asia. The North resolutely, many would say "stubbornly," hews to Kim Il-sung's policy of *juche* self-reliance, building heavy industry and the military, with the result that it has virtually no consumer goods and little trade, and since the 1990s has danced on a razor's edge of food shortages and famine. All through its cycles of authoritarianism and democracy, South Korea moved by fits and starts toward a working democracy, which is arguably the most open in Asia. The North has moved little from its Stalin-like Communist cult of personality around the three generations of Kim family rulers, each of which has proven more erratic and destabilizing than the last. As noted earlier, the present regime of Kim Jung-un, with several successful nuclear tests and, it appears, an intercontinental delivery system, poses an ongoing local, regional, and global threat.

War by Other Means

The nearly complete destruction of the North Korean army during the UN counterattack of 1950 and the North's heavy reliance on Chinese forces to contest the Americans and their allies quickly faded in the years after the truce was signed. The regime received massive aid, although less than that supplied to the South from the U.S., and from both the Soviet Union and PRC. Much of this money went into rebuilding the military as a hedge against the feared Southern resumption of the drive to unite the peninsula. The industrial infrastructure of the North similarly was boosted and modernized with Soviet and Chinese help, so much so that, as we have seen, the North outstripped the South in economic growth and industrial production until the mid-1960s. The North had been the industrial heartland of Korea, with nearly all its heavy industry, nine-tenths of its electrical capacity, and most of its mines being a valuable resource for capital and expertise exchange.

Kim's overall strategy for development was remarkably similar to Mao Zedong's at roughly the same time. North Korea conducted a land reform and producer's cooperative program much the like Chinese model in 1956, and in 1957 announced its first Five-Year Plan. Collectivization and elimination of private businesses were both part of the process. Like their Chinese counterparts, the North Koreans organized peasants into large collectivized farms, although for the most part without the mass chaos and economic paralysis that resulted in the PRC. A mass education program ensuring schooling at least through the elementary level was enacted. Thus, by the time of Park Chung-hee's coup in the South, North Korea could point to impressive economic and social gains at comparatively little cost with regard to China or the Soviet Union.

The ideology of the DPRK, however, changed little during this time. Less populous than the South, with less agricultural potential, the country was kept more or less continuously on a war-footing. This was abetted by the events of the Cold War and the ongoing possibility that Korea could quickly become a new flashpoint. The American policy of "massive retaliation" in the event of Communist aggression anywhere, continual tensions between the PRC and ROC, especially during the Quemoy/Matsu crisis of the late 1950s, the building of the Berlin Wall, and the Cuban Missile Crisis had all raised tensions. In Korea, the expectation continued that support for the ROK was rather weak, and Northern probes and provocations across the DMZ thus continued and provided propaganda value to the Kim regime.

In addition, Kim increasingly concentrated Party leadership around an inner circle consisting of those who had undergone the experience of guerrilla warfare with him in Manchuria. Throughout the 1950s, he purged those who had not shared this same experience and treated those who had with a special reverence reminiscent of that reserved for survivors of the Long March in China. Kim grew increasingly suspicious of Party members who had spent time abroad and made loyalty to his family and its inner circle the criterion for positions of responsibility—sometimes even survival. Thus, even by the standards of Communist bloc countries, North Korea grew increasingly insular and unwelcoming for foreigners, Koreans with foreign experience, and Koreans wishing to return home from the South or abroad. Students were recalled from foreign schools in Communist countries, and Koreans with foreign spouses were required to divorce them.

Juche *and the Cult of Personality*

The most significant program, however, was the creation of the policy of *juche*. Within months of Mao Zedong embarking on the Cultural Revolution in the summer of 1966, Kim began a similar movement in North Korea. Here, however, the emphasis on eradicating remnants of bourgeois or feudal behaviors was coupled with a concept of the special circumstances of Marxism-Leninism in Korea. Central to this movement was the idea of self-reliance in all things, *juche*. This was now placed in the context of the Monolithic Ideological System, which Kim intended to supplant what he considered the historically imported systems of Confucianism, Buddhism, and Christianity, among others. As with Marxism-Leninism-Mao Zedong Thought in China, this new ideology was also intended to elevate Kim as a revolutionary thinker whose programs would make a complete break with the past. As in China as well, a cult of personality quickly grew up around Kim. His works and utterances were scrutinized and studied, and knowledge of and adherence to his ideas became the basis for orthodox behavior.

Meanwhile, the *juche* concept reinforced the insularity of the regime and to some degree its aggressiveness. The injunction against borrowed ideology extended to matters military, political, and economic. North Korea conducted little in the way of foreign exchanges, limiting visitors to closely supervised groups shepherded around Pyongyang and a handful of model farms and factories. Those few allowed to come to Pyongyang uniformly remarked on its spaciousness and cleanliness, but also on its stark Socialist-Realist architecture, complete lack of motor vehicles, and the apparent absence of economic dynamism. It was, in a sense, a kind of large Potemkin village designed to impress not only the few outsiders allowed in, but also to reassure the populace that they were indeed living in a socialist paradise. The continuous propaganda and rigorous efforts to keep foreign media from penetrating the borders aided in this effort immensely. So static were the living conditions for nearly all residents except for the Workers Party elites that escapees from the North were flummoxed and astonished when confronted with the wealth of the South as reflected in the modern appliances and conveniences available there. Programs were even established to help them through their culture- and techno-shocks.

Pyongyang Skyline. Like Seoul, Pyongyang was largely destroyed during the Korean War. Much of its rebuilding was done along lines that were in fashion in Communist bloc countries during the 1950s and 1960s. Under Kim Jung-un, however, efforts have been under way to modernize areas of the city as showplaces for Party elites and foreign guests. In the photo here, we see the characteristic mix of Socialist architecture and newer high-rise buildings dominated by the city's tallest structure, an unfinished pyramidal skyscraper planned to be 105 stories high when completed.

The 1970s and 1980s saw some abortive attempts to revitalize the DPRK's stalled economy. These, however, were continually undermined by lack of modern technology, energy resources, and most of all the complete domination of the *juche* ideology. Like China in the Maoist years, North Koreans were continually marshalled into mass-mobilization campaigns to increase agricultural production, boost factory output, combat "bureaucratism," and especially ferret out and punish dissenters. At one point, Kim visited the Soviet Union, and projects were undertaken to modernize aging equipment and upgrade manufacturing technologies. These, however, were continually undercut by shortages of electrical power, petrochemical resources, and an urge to undertake huge, spectacular projects that simply could not be supported to completion. Similarly, the success of China's Four Modernizations during the 1980s created some interest among North Korea's elite for increased regional trade, but were undercut by the lack of available currency resources.

The Kim Dynasty

As we have seen, Kim Il-sung's resolute provincialism and determination to control his domain by walling out competing ideas—punctuated by provocative moves and attacks on the South—occasionally developed cracks. Pushed, in part, by the collapse of the Soviet Union and removal of its military support, Kim participated in several initiatives in the early 1990's to reunite families separated by the DMZ, and there was momentum toward resuming talks on possible steps toward reunification. His death, however, in July 1994 brought the process to a halt and elevated his son, Kim Jung-il (1941–2011), to supreme, uncontested power.

In many respects, Jung-il continued and extended the veneration of his family. He stepped into his father's exalted role as center of the national cult of personality, passing from "Dear Leader" to "Great Leader," and acquiring as many as 1,200 other honorific titles including "Guardian Deity of the Planet." In 1997, to honor his elevation to supreme leadership on completion of the mourning period for his father, the regime took out a full-page ad in the *New York Times*, hailing Jung-il as "The Lodestar of the Twenty-First Century." Thousands of memorials and statues of his father were erected, and any failure to show appropriate respect for the Kims was subject to swift and sure punishment.

Ideologically, however, the North Korean system of socialism began to move toward a much more militarist cast during his watch. Cementing the loyalty of his generals, he promulgated the slogan of "military first," and the resources of the country were increasingly used to enlarge and upgrade the armed forces. Despite previous nonproliferation agreements under his father, he also began a concerted effort to develop nuclear power stations and build nuclear weapons. Indeed, so central was the military in these developments that the term "supremacist-nationalist" seems a more appropriate description of the present regime than "socialist." His repeated pronouncements on the ethno-linguistic and historical unity of all Koreans also support the "nationalist" tendencies of the regime.

Through it all, however, North Korea's economy and food situation are still powerful brakes on the regime's viability. Less than a fifth of North Korea's land is suitable for agriculture, and the inefficiencies of collectivization coupled with the continuing push for *juche* keep the regime in increasing need of foreign food aid. Floods, poor land conservancy practices, and mismanagement conspired in the early 1990s to unleash a famine lasting from 1994 to 1998. A deal had previously been struck with the United States in which American nuclear fuel for power generation would be sent to North Korea in exchange for the DPRK's discontinuing its nuclear weapons programs. However, the U.S., South Korea, China, and the UN stepped in to send massive food relief to the North. Ironically, the U.S. in 1999 was the biggest contributor to North Korean food aid. Estimates of famine casualties vary widely from several hundred thousand to several million dead. For his part, Kim experimented with opening markets along the lines of the early programs of China's Four Modernizations, but their contribution to food security has been sparse. Trade exchanges planned in response to South Korea's "Sunshine Policy" and proposals for a large industrial park at Kaesong in the North featuring a number of South Korean firms similarly fizzled during the early 2000s.

One of the sources of this collapse of cooperation came from American and South Korean responses to the announcement that the DPRK had secretly continued to work on its nuclear program, had acquired nuclear weapons, and tested a device in October 2006. This came soon after the U.S. had drastically cut back on food shipments to the North because of the resumption of its nuclear program. Here, the U.S. was accused of "using food as a weapon," which Kim pointed to as further proof of the need for a nuclear deterrent against the U.S. presence in the South.

Jong-il's death from a heart attack on December 17, 2011, brought his son Kim Jung-un (b. 1984) to the fore. His background was largely unknown due to the intense secrecy surrounding the activities of the Kim family. It is believed, for example, that he attended school in Switzerland under a pseudonym and is said to enjoy American professional basketball. He has met and briefly entertained former Chicago Bull basketball star Dennis Rodman and is said to be a fan of legendary rock guitarist Eric Clapton. By the end of 2011, he had acquired the titles of leadership and has since pursued his family's practices of sole leadership and cult of personality. Under his leadership, both proven and alleged human rights violations have been routinely condemned by the UN that, along with the U.S., has imposed economic sanctions on the DPRK.

In terms of economics, Kim Jung-un has expanded the concept of selective autonomy for business although it is expected to distribute products according to "socialist principles." In a move reminiscent of Lenin's NEP policies of the early 1920s, he has also emphasized the practice of private vegetable gardens as a way to boost agricultural productivity. Both policies appear to have achieved modest success, but enough perhaps to encourage more market experimentation.

It is the erratic nature of his behavior, however, especially with regard to the DPRK's military and growing nuclear capability, that has become the largest threat to the region's stability. Despite condemnation and real and threatened sanctions by South Korea, Japan, Russia, the U.S., and even long-time ally China,

Jung-un has engaged in repeated threats and provocations toward his neighbors and the United States. He has on several occasions threatened to launch preemptive nuclear strikes against the U.S. and, as of 2018, may have already developed the capacity to launch a nuclear weapon at the U.S. mainland. What gives these threats considerable immediacy is that the DPRK now possesses not only nuclear devices, but also has been testing missiles with increasing range and accuracy. Unknown as well is whether his claim to possess a thermonuclear device (a hydrogen bomb) is valid. Despite U.S. and UN condemnation and multiple rounds of sanctions, Jung-un has vowed to develop North Korea's economic and nuclear power simultaneously. In June, 2018, in a surprise move, US President Trump agreed to meet with Kim in Singapore, where the two leaders agreed to move toward an agreement on the nuclear issue and regional security. (See Chapter 14)

CONCLUSION

Since 1895, Korea has experienced as varied a history as any place on Earth. Traditionally fighting to maintain its political and cultural sovereignty throughout its long past, it found the one forcibly taken from it and the other under severe challenge for much of the period under consideration here. A prize whose suzerainty was being contested by Russia, China, and Japan in 1895, it was firmly in Japan's orbit within a decade and annexed within a decade and a half. It endured a difficult position as the closest part of Japan's overseas empire, during which it saw always intrusive and often oppressive government, considerable Japanese colonial emigration, and repeated attempts at economic and cultural integration into what eventually became the Greater East Asia Co-Prosperity Sphere. Through it all, Korean resistance continued across the political spectrum, providing the seedbed from which its post–World War II governments would ultimately spring.

Freed from Japanese colonialism in 1945, the peninsula immediately became captive to Cold War considerations. From the Soviet zone of occupation arose the Democratic People's Republic of Korea—North Korea—and from the American zone, the Republic of Korea—South Korea. The attempted unification by the North in 1950 spawned an enormously destructive war involving the United States, the United Nations, both Koreas, the People's Republic of China, and even pilots and aircraft from the Soviet Union. Three years of war left not only the issue unresolved to this day, but also the entire peninsula devastated.

It was from these events that differences grew between the two Koreas that make them perhaps the most radically different states in history to share a homeland and ethnicity. North Korea followed an increasingly Stalinist line while borrowing a number of ideas from the PRC, creating an unbreakable cult of personality around the Kim family. Its economics have sharply deteriorated since the 1960s, markedly so after the collapse of the Soviet Union. Despite being wedded to enhancing its military and developing nuclear weapons, its ideology of *juche* or self-reliance has forced it to rely on food aid from other countries. Following a slow start, South Korea, on the other hand, became hailed as an economic miracle, one of the world's leading economies by the turn of the twenty-first century. Its politics, although including an impetus toward representative government, oscillated through authoritarian rule and constitutional "republics" until the 1990s, when the final pieces of a workable democracy were finally in place.

Korean commentators have often expressed the idea that their history and culture should be seen as the third of the "great traditions" (after China and Japan) that had guided the history of East Asia. As we move toward the end of the second decade of the twenty-first century, resolving the immense contradictions between the two Koreas might indeed represent an attractive new "great tradition" in the region.

FURTHER RESOURCES

Clark, Donald N. *Korea in World History*. Ann Arbor: Association for Asian Studies, 2012. Slim, highly useful volume, particularly for the beginning student, with an emphasis on Korea within the larger sweep of global change. Part of the AAS series " Key Issues in Asian Studies."

Cummings, Bruce. *Korea's Place in the Sun*. New York: Norton, 2005. Accessible, yet sophisticated volume by one of America's leading historians of the region. Suitable for beginning students or those with some familiarity of the region.

Fulton, Bruce, and Kwon Young-min. *Modern Korean Fiction: An Anthology*. New York: Columbia University Press, 2005. Highly eclectic collection of fiction over the last hundred years, including entries across the political spectrum and from the colonial period, with women writers and other neglected groups faithfully represented.

Hassig, Ralph, and Kongdam Oh. *The Hidden People of North Korea: Life in the Hermit Kingdom*. Lanham, MD: Rowman & Littlefield, 2009. Like Lankov's work below, this volume examines in surprising and disturbing detail what the lives of ordinary people are like under the "Kim Dynasty." The isolation, government surveillance and intrusiveness, and hardships of the guiding policy of *juche* forcefully emerge in the telling.

Lankov, Andrei. *North of the DMZ: Essays on Daily Life in North Korea*. Jefferson, NC: McFarland, 2007. Few Western scholars have had any substantive access to the DPRK, and this work remains among the handful of authoritative glimpses of the contemporary North.

Millett, Allan R. *The War for Korea*. Vol. I, *1945–1950: A House Burning*. Lawrence: University of Kansas, 2005. Part of a comprehensive, exhaustively researched series on the Korean conflict. This first volume traces the beginnings of the war to the clashes of various factors in the post–World War II years, particularly as the Cold War entered its initial and increasingly intense phase in the late 1940s.

Millet, Allan R. *The War for Korea*. Vol. 2, *1950–1951: They Came from the North*. Lawrence: University of Kansas Press, 2010. The second volume in the trilogy. Highly detailed military history from the invasion by North Korea in June 1950 to June 1951, the period of the most intense fighting and changes in fortune for the two sides.

Myers, Brian R. *The Cleanest Race: How North Koreans See Themselves and Why It Matters*. Brooklyn, NY: Melvin House, 2010. Fascinating and disturbing look at the worldview and self-view of North Korea through the limited literature available in the DPRK. Important read for anyone concerned about the area and its volatility.

Oberdorfer, Don. *The Two Koreas*. New York: Basic Books, 2002; ev. ed., 2013. Highly readable and important journalistic survey of the recent histories and contemporary issues in the divided peninsula. A must for anyone struggling to understand the issues underneath the continuing tensions in the region.

Peterson Mark, and Philip Margulies. *A Brief History of Korea*. New York: Facts on File, 2010. Comprehensive history of the peninsula from Neolithic times to the present. Evenhanded survey of political, social, economic, cultural, and religious histories of the various Korean kingdoms and solid treatment of the current conditions and challenges given the present state of both regimes.

WEBSITES

http://koreanhistory.info/japan.htm. Koreanhistory.info. *The Japanese Colonial Period, 1910–1945*. Factual summary histories of the period with photographs and video. Download available. Covers all Korean history, strong on Tonghaks as well. Comes with audio pronunciation guide.

https://www.shmoop.com/korean-war/websites.html. The Korean War Websites. Compendium of sources from the Library of Congress, Truman Library, National Archives, and National Public Radio. Focused primarily on the American experience in the war.

https://piie.com/blogs/north-korea-witness-transformation/northkorean-websites-complete-list.

North Korean Websites: The Complete List. Peterson Institute for International Economics. All twenty-eight sites available to outsiders in North Korea. Wide-ranging listings including official news, culinary notes, charity activities, education, youth, and children.

CHAPTER 12

❧

Colonized, Divided, and Reunited: Vietnam to the Present

The news footage that April day in 1975 was as heart-rending as it was spectacular. On the last day of that month, a Bell UH-1 "Huey" helicopter—perhaps the most emblematic aircraft of the American effort in Southeast Asia—teetered precariously on the roof of an apartment building adjacent to the U.S. embassy in Saigon, the capital of the Republic of Vietnam—South Vietnam. A remarkably versatile machine that had seen nearly every type of service in the U.S. military from gunship to medivac duty, it was now concluding its final mission. On the steps leading up to the emergency helipad, hundreds of people stood anxiously in line hoping against hope to be airlifted out of the capital to waiting American ships offshore. On the ground, soldiers of the remnant Army of the Republic of Vietnam (ARVN) remaining in the capital struggled in vain to stem the tide of refugees fighting their way toward the stairs and sort out those approved for this last rescue flight. With North Vietnamese armor already securing the northern sectors of the city, the helicopter, dangerously overloaded and with people desperately attempting to cling to its skids, finally took off. With it went the final members of a United States' presence in Vietnam that a few years before had numbered over half a million. The helicopter itself, along with the others involved in this last airlift, would shortly be unceremoniously dumped overboard from the aircraft carrier on which it landed, as if to suggest that what had been America's longest war must now be banished from memory.

For the Vietnamese, however, regardless of which side they supported, it was the day of the final unification of the country, although one that had been extraordinarily painful and would continue to be so for those on the losing side. Yet for all the wounds marking unification and festering afterward, it would also be the first time since 1858 that the country would not be under foreign control or influence.

That control and influence had waxed and waned a great deal over the years with the fortunes of the countries wielding it. France, which had begun taking Vietnamese territory in the 1850s, had fought a war with China for domination over the country and swiftly incorporated it into a Southeast Asian colony called "French Indochina" by 1887. With the fall of France to the Nazis in 1940, Germany's Japanese allies assumed indirect control of the colony, content to let the French Vichy bureaucracy continue with administrative tasks. In March 1945, however, with Japan's empire in desperate trouble, the Japanese launched a coup against the French in Indochina. With the Japanese surrender a few months later came a declaration of Vietnamese independence, swiftly followed by the return of French colonialism until defeated by the Vietnamese in 1954. The country's independent status soon changed again as it was split, like Korea, into Northern and Southern states, with the Southern part increasingly supported by the United States. After eight years of bitter war that left both North and South devastated— and the United States riven by dissent—a peace accord between North and South Vietnam was reached in 1973 and American forces withdrew. Within two years, however, the fragile Republic of Vietnam in the South succumbed to a final offensive from the North.

In a sense, events in the country had come full circle twice over: an all-too-brief interval of independence after World War II that ended over eighty years of French and Japanese colonialism was followed by more French colonialism and American domination. That April day in Saigon, however, saw the final circle complete: independence *and* unification. Yet the long struggle for unity and self-determination did not immediately yield the benefits so many had expected. The new socialist state purged those who had served the old regime and the Americans.

Saigon Airlift. Operation Frequent Wind, the evacuation of refugees from Saigon as it fell to North Vietnamese forces, called up many poignant images. Original estimates called for evacuating only around 100 people; by the time it was over, an astonishing 1,373 Americans and 5,595 Vietnamese and foreign refugees had been evacuated. Here, one man and his two children are helped off the rescue helicopter by its crew chief.

In the following years, thousands of "boat people" attempted to escape the new order, many of them journeying to the United States. Confronted with the wanton slaughter conducted by the Khmer Rouge in the increasingly unstable neighboring "Democratic Kampuchea," Vietnam invaded that state, which prompted a brief invasion of Vietnam by Kampuchea's ally and Vietnam's ancient occupier, China. By the 1980s, Vietnam's economy was stagnant at a time when its neighboring East Asian states were forging ahead on the Japanese export-driven model.

Somewhat belatedly, the socialist government, like China under Deng Xiaoping, passed a series of reform measures to move the country into a market economy and slowly opened it to foreign investment. Ironically, yet perhaps fittingly given the intense American presence in the 1960s and 1970s, the country once again developed strong economic ties to the United States. Today, Vietnam's economy is one of increasing vitality and a hotbed of investment and entre-preneurship, foreign and domestic. Ho Chi Minh City, as Saigon was renamed, assumed a renewed place as a fashionable international destination. And in a relationship that gives some closure to the memory of the war years for both sides, one of Vietnam's fastest-growing sectors is tourism, especially among the conflict's veterans.

THE FIRST COLONIAL ERA, 1885–1945

As we saw in Chapter 7, France's interest in Southeast Asia long antedated its impe-rial moves in the mid-nineteenth century. French trade and Roman Catholic pros-elytization in the region went all the way back to the reign of Louis XIV. At the end of the eighteenth century, a French missionary, Monsignor (later Bishop) Behaine, helped lead the organization and arming of militia to fight on behalf of the Nguyen claimant to the imperial throne, which was accomplished in 1802. Although its provisions were honored more in the breach than in the observance, the ancien régime had even signed a treaty of support for the Nguyen cause. France continued to enjoy good relations with Vietnam during the Revolutionary and Napoleonic eras, the latter of which coincided with the reign of the first Nguyen emperor Gia Long. Indeed, despite Gia Long's ardent Neo-Confucianism, he employed French advisors and displayed a generally tolerant attitude toward Vietnam's Christians.

The reign of his son, Minh Mang (1820–1841), saw the revival of France's missionary efforts soon after the restoration of the monarchy. For Minh Mang, the French increasingly represented an unwanted foreign presence, and the mis-sionaries a threat to the social order. By 1830, he had banned Christianity and executed or driven out the remaining missionaries. The dawn of the treaty port era and diplomatic and trade agreements with China in the 1840s and 1850s re-doubled France's interest in the region. France's self-appointed role as protector of Catholic missionaries and their converts in Asia involved it in a cooperative move with Great Britain to strong-arm the Qing into a treaty revision in the Second Opium War in 1856. Accompanying this was the incremental extract-ing of concessions and territory from the Nguyen emperors over the next two decades. Finally, the capping of the process came with the war with China in the mid-1880s, and the seizure of the whole of Vietnam and its incorporation with Laos and Cambodia into the Indochinese Union from 1885 to 1887. The Nguyen would retain nominal dynastic rule until 1945, with the last emperor, Bao Dai, presiding under France's reoccupation of Indochina until 1954 (see Map 12.1).

"The Civilizing Mission" and Rebellion

France in the latter nineteenth century was still seen as one of the "Great Powers," but one riven by considerable self-doubt and goaded by humiliation. Continen-tal Europe's leading military power through the 1860s, France's Second Empire of Louis Napoleon was maneuvered into a war with expansive Prussia that climaxed with brutal suddenness and surety in a series of desperate charges at Sedan in 1870. Napoleon himself was taken on the battlefield, and France was forced to sign a

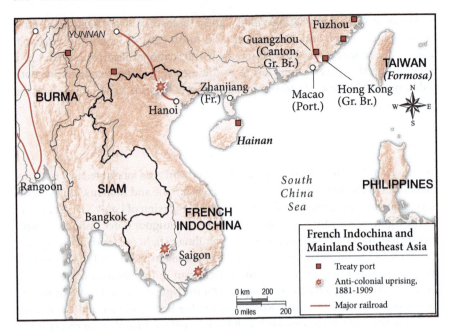

Map 12.1 French Indochina and Mainland Southeast Asia

humiliating peace at Versailles, which saw the newly created empire of Germany seize the territories of Alsace and Lorraine. A brief and bitter uprising against the occupation in Paris during the days of the Commune ended in the creation of the Third French Republic, destined to last until another German invasion in 1940.

The architect of the new Germany, the "Iron Chancellor" Otto Von Bismarck, sought to keep France isolated and to direct French desire for *revanche* into colonialism. Through the last decades of the nineteenth century, with rage at Germany always just beneath the surface, but in the rueful knowledge that France simply could not stand alone in a war with the new empire, successive French governments sought to keep the peace in Europe and search for ways to recover France's former glory through imperial adventures abroad. Already in possession of great swaths of territory in Africa, the addition of Indochina was thus welcomed as another step in recovering France's proper place among the Great Powers.

As was true of the era's other imperial powers, France sought to exploit the resources of its new possessions and use the people there as a captive market for French goods. In addition, opposition to colonialism within the ruling nations often centered on the expenses of maintenance and defense of empire, and so right from the beginning—as we saw in Li Gui's description—the colonies were prodded to pay for themselves. Unlike the British in India, however, where the great revolt of the 1850s had extracted Queen Victoria's pledge that India's culture and customs would not be Anglicized, the French sought to push forward their vision of the **mission civilistrice**, the "civilizing mission." As time went on, the policy engendered a degree of debate in France and among French administrators in the colonies. Nonetheless, the peoples of France's possessions were to be educated and assimilated into the greater entity of "Overseas France." For the most fervent champions of this policy, the goal would be for the empire's inhabitants to be cognizant of their own cultural roots but be cosmopolitan French men and women.

Divided counsels plagued the French as to exactly how all this could be accomplished in Southeast Asia, where, despite regional differences and local resentment toward Nguyen expansion earlier in the century, a well-organized Confucian bureaucracy had taken root. Moreover, throughout the colonial period, relatively few French settled in Indochina, compared with the extensive emigration of **pieds noirs** ("black feet"; European settlers in the French colonies of North Africa) to Algeria, who numbered over a million and elevated the colony to *department* (an administrative region immediately below the national "territorial collectivity") status. Thus, as with the British in India, French administration would rely heavily on divide and rule tactics, intimidation of potential resistors, and indigenous cooperation.

At first, however, resistance to the new order resulted in outright rebellion, abetted in many places by the local Confucian officials and Black Flag remnants. The French suppressed several uprisings through the 1890s, while painfully attempting to organize their own bureaucratic institutions and co-opt as many members of the court and Confucian officialdom as possible. The fighting, which also had elements of civil war about it, was often furious, with little or no quarter given. Indeed, one startling memento of this era was the fashion of photos and postcards of French soldiers, officials, and Vietnamese scouts posing with the severed heads of rebels.

17. TONKIN – Hanoï — Têtes des artilleurs indigènes, empoisonneurs exécutés le 8 Juillet 1908, selon la loi Annamite

"Kisses from Saigon." The brutal retribution meted out to rebels in the 1890s and early 1900s in Indochina is no better illustrated than in this postcard with its photo of three severed rebel heads. Postcards depicted executions and punishments as both exotica and in service of the "civilizing mission," and proved to be popular items for troops to send home to wives and sweethearts.

With the initial wave of rebellion suppressed by the turn of the century, however, the inhabitants of Indochina and their new rulers faced a constellation of problems resembling those of the other East Asian countries subjected to Western imperialism, but with some key differences. As we have seen, China and Japan faced by imperialism responded at various times with reaction, reform, and revolution. In the case of China, these were spread over more than a century; for Japan, they happened within a decade and a half. Significantly, neither country completely lost its sovereignty, although China seemed to teeter on that edge in the late 1890s. Moreover, Japan itself became an imperial power, invading, occupying, and colonizing the other three countries within the Confucian cultural sphere at various times.

A key difference in the cases of Korea and Vietnam, of course, is that both countries did, in fact, lose their sovereignty and become part of outside empires. Thus, unlike China or Japan, which had at least a degree of choice in acculturation from outside, the colonial status of Korea and Indochina resulted in forced interaction and adaptation.

Reform and Republicanism

The success of Japan's reforms and modernization and the intellectual ferment in China during the last years of the nineteenth century and the first decades of the twentieth had, as we have noted, a profound impact on their neighbors. Whereas idealistic French reformers were anxious to plant the seeds of the Western intellectual tradition in their possessions, literate Vietnamese were getting most of their introduction to these ideas through Chinese translations of them, sometimes in the form of Chinese translations of Japanese versions. The large Chinese community played an important role in this regard, especially as exiled Chinese reformers and revolutionaries increasingly circulated among them, fundraising and recruiting. As it did for so many Chinese exiles—and even for many from Korea—Japan proved to be the most exciting model for a core group of Indochinese modernizers. This was particularly true after 1905, when Japan's defeat of Russia dissolved forever the mystique of Western military invincibility.

As it had throughout the colonial world, a wide spectrum of political views emerged in Indochina with regard to how to recapture agency in the face of French control. As we have noted above, like the British in India, the French, without the aid of large numbers of settlers, were heavily reliant on the cooperation of their new subjects. To that end, they sought to co-opt the imperial family, Confucian bureaucracy, and families of the wealthy and influential. Thus, they struggled to find a balance of Indochinese who would buy into the new order, oscillating between severity and engagement with local traditions and institutions.

For the Indochinese, this meant proposals for expanding autonomy ranging from royalism to outright revolution. There was also a substantial movement for reform within the system. Perhaps the most notable exponents of this approach were Prince Cuong De (1882–1951) and Phan Boi Chau (1867–1940).

Influenced, as were many, by the Constitutionalist movement of Kang Youwei and Liang Qichao, and the impressive success of constitutional government in Japan, Cuong traveled extensively in Europe, and lived for much of his adult life in exile in Japan. Through much of this time, he sought to negotiate an autonomous arrangement with the relatively liberal French colonial government of Albert Sarraut. The French, however, increasingly tied economically to the colony, and recruiting Indochinese as soldiers for their depleting ranks during the Great War, proved unwilling to grant significant concessions. For the prince, a further disappointment was the French selection of the adolescent and more pliable Bao Dai (1913–1997) as emperor in 1926. Frustrated in his hopes for a top-down, Meiji-style reform, he placed his hopes on Japanese assistance. As they had with other would-be nationalists in Japanese-controlled areas during World War II, however, Japanese promises of independence within the Greater East Asia Co-Prosperity Sphere were never fulfilled and Cuong De died in Tokyo in 1951, while the French fought Vietnamese nationalists to retain their fading empire.

The case of Phan Boi Chau was perhaps in the end more substantive, but hardly more successful. Inspired by Chinese reformists like Liang Qichao, whom he looked to as a mentor, Chau (although Phan is the family name, it is customary to refer to individuals by their given name) traveled throughout Indochina and East Asia, forming study groups and networking with like-minded individuals. He supported Cuong De, who for a time was honorary president of Chau's Vietnam Modernization Society. Like the prince as well, he looked to Japan as a model and also as a powerful ally in the struggle against Western colonialism. At the time, there was considerable sentiment for **pan-Asianism**, with Japan as the "natural" leader of a unified East Asia to challenge Western regional hegemony. In this capacity, Phan even met with Okuma Shigenobu, one of the architects of Japan's rise to power. Indeed, during the opening years

Memorial Card for Phan Boi Chau. As in China and Korea during the early twentieth century, reformers in Indochina could be found across the political spectrum. Among the most famous, although ultimately unsuccessful, was Pham Boi Chau (1867–1940), whose Vietnam Modernization Society initially took its ideas from Chinese reformers like Liang Qizhao and those who had made Japan a powerful entity. Following Japan's annexation of Korea, however, and encroachment on Manchuria and China, he began to lose hope of any Japanese assistance in helping to overthrow the French in Southeast Asia.

of the twentieth century, a "Go East" movement to study in Japan was widespread among Vietnamese intellectuals. As scholars have noted, such terms as "revolution," and "nation" began to appear in the lexicon of East Asian anti-imperial writers.

There were, however, also suspicions of Japan's motives in this regard, and these increased substantially after Japan and France signed an agreement of mutual recognition of each other's colonial territories in 1907. The annexation of Korea in 1910 and the empire's encroachment on Manchuria effectively quashed any hopes Chau had of enlisting Japanese military assistance to oust the French. His colleague Phan Chu Trinh (1872–1926) rejected the idea of violent revolution in favor of using France as a model with which to build a republican government. With French socialists, republicans, and reformers of assorted political stripes as his intimates, he sought to create a republican, civic consciousness among the people, wean them off of their traditional Confucianism, and break the power of the imperial bureaucracy. With these new institutions in place, he believed he could make a successful argument with the French that the implanting of republican consciousness in Indochina entitled the people to self-government: they would have fulfilled France's "civilizing mission." In seeing the old imperial order of the Nguyens and their mandarinate as the chief obstacle to Vietnamese modernization, Trinh felt that the French had unknowingly helped Vietnam by breaking down its outdated institutions.

As it did in so many other areas, World War I had a profound effect on the colonial empires of the Great Powers. France recruited over a million men from its colonies, nearly a hundred thousand from Indochina alone. Moreover, the movement of vast numbers of people within the empire and to other parts of the world engendered increased knowledge and cosmopolitanism among even ordinary workers, sailors, cooks, and other members of various support professions. As we have seen with China, Japan, and Korea, support for the war in the colonies, Allied war aims and promises, and the considerable contributions in money, materiel, and men raised hopes that the Allied imperial powers would pay their debts to the colonies with increased autonomy—perhaps even independence. In Asia and Africa, these hopes were almost universally dashed.

Ho Chi Minh and Revolution

One who had pinned considerable hope on some latitude from the victors in this regard was Ho Chi Minh (1890–1969), born Nguyen That Than to a scholarly family. His father had been part of Confucian scholars' resistance to Paul Doumer's attempts to co-opt the imperial bureaucracy. Young Ho worked as a teacher and itinerant scholar and, like Phan Boi Chau and other reformists, assembled study groups concerned with modernizing the country and expanding Vietnamese agency. Like other East Asians who had first looked to Japan as a model and for material aid in the cause, he was bitterly disappointed in Japan's agreement with France and in the empire's annexation of Korea.

With the coming of World War I and the mobilization of "Overseas France," Ho shipped out as a cook on a freighter, seeing it as an opportunity to broaden his practical education, network with overseas Vietnamese, and further his language study. He visited a number of places in Asia, spent a period in New York and Boston, and ended up in Paris at the war's end. Now styling himself as "Nguyen Ai Quoc" (Nguyen the Patriot), he lobbied with his colleagues at Versailles for Vietnamese independence—even sending a letter to American President Woodrow Wilson.

As with many colonial anti-imperialists, particularly in East Asia, he was excited by the Bolshevik success in Russia and impressed by the new government's renunciation of Tsarist territorial claims. As with Li Dazhao and Chen Duxiu in China, he began an intense study of Marxism with particular reference to Lenin's ideas of the relationship between imperialism and capitalism. During the course of his activities in France, he met like-minded French socialists and communists and became a founding member of the French Communist Party in 1920.

The formation of Comintern and its encouragement of revolutionaries attracted Ho to Moscow, where

The Young Nguyen That Than (Ho Chi Minh) at the Marseille Communist Conference, 1921. The man who would come to be known as Ho Chi Minh had a colorful career as a young reformer and revolutionary, working as a deckhand and cook, residing in a number of foreign ports, and attending the Versailles Peace Conference. Always advancing the cause of Vietnamese autonomy and independence, he changed his name early on to "Nguyen Ai Quoc" (Nguyen the Patriot) and during the period pictured here was one of the founders of the French Communist Party in 1920 and soon a member of Comintern.

he received further training, and he was soon sent to Canton, where he assisted in helping to organize, fund, and arm the Guomindang. In between Comintern work, he helped to found the Vietnamese Revolutionary Youth League in 1925. In the heady days of revolutionary ferment in East Asia during the 1920s, Ho's group found itself in competition with a panoply of reform, nationalist, and revolutionary groups with little cooperation or coordination. His relations with groups in China were severely strained by the Nationalist–Communist civil war, the isolation of Mao's group in Jiangxi, and the hesitation of Comintern to formulate a coherent policy in Asia. Finally, at least in part at the urging of his

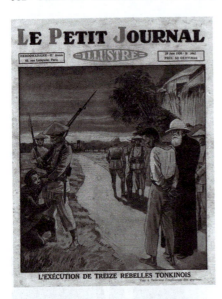

French Depiction of Scenes from Yen Bay Uprising. The suppression of the abortive Yen Bay uprising was seen by the French as a strong blow to Indochinese nationalism at a time when the economic consequences of the Great Depression were beginning to be felt in the colonies. On the cover of this June 30, 1930, issue of *Le Petit Journal*, a popular French illustrated newspaper, retribution is being meted out to thirteen Yen Bay rebels.

Comintern contacts, Ho formed a coalition of left-leaning nationalist groups and his Vietnamese Communist Party that, in 1930, became the Indochinese Communist Party. During the late 1930s, he spent time with Mao Zedong and the Chinese Communists in Yan'an, a practicum that proved particularly useful in the coming years.

The relatively tolerant policies of the French colonial government during the 1920s abruptly changed in the wake of the attempted uprising by nationalists at Yen Bay in February 1930. The authorities rounded up and imprisoned a number of leaders including Pham Van Dong (1906–2000), clamped down on the radical press, and dealt swiftly and forcefully with demonstrations. The worldwide Great Depression and its effects on the markets for rice, tin, oil, and rubber caused a dramatic economic downturn. The Michelin rubber plantations in Indochina produced more than a quarter of France's latex, and they pushed their workers to keep production high as wages declined. Worse still, the drive to keep rice exports up contributed to famines in several areas, further isolating rural regions from the urban-centered French officials.

Worrisome as well was the international situation, although many revolutionaries saw potential promise in it. Japan's assault on China starting in July 1937 had served to unite the country for the sake of survival, but Japan's occupation of Canton and southern China caused anxiety among the French. Following France's surrender to Nazi Germany in June 1940, the question of the disposition of its overseas empire remained unresolved. With no clear instructions from Vichy, and with Japan now part of the Rome-Berlin-Tokyo Axis, the Japanese felt free to strong-arm the French colonial government in Indochina into allowing them free use of naval and air bases in return for allowing the existing colonial government to remain in charge. In light of this situation, the Indochinese Communist Party merged with several nationalist groups to form the League for the Independence of Vietnam (Viet Minh) in 1941.

PATTERNS UP-CLOSE

Parsing the Language of Independence

As it had in many formerly independent polities, the brief but dramatic interval of European and American imperial control and interaction in Vietnam implanted language and ideas that not only appealed to the desire for "modernity" on the part of many revolutionary leaders, but was also seen as turning the conquerors' own values back against them in an argument that could not be refuted. This was particularly true in the nationalist movements that multiplied rapidly in the wake of the League of Nations Covenant and a mandate system that stipulated criteria and time tables for independence for many colonial possessions. World War II, in exhausting the power of the two leading prewar colonial empires, Britain and France, as well as the Netherlands, while bringing to prominence the United States, on record as opposing the reimposition of colonial status on those territories newly liberated from Japanese control, greatly accelerated the process.

Thus, Ho Chi Minh and his Viet Minh fighters felt relatively secure in declaring themselves now independent from both France and Japan. American OSS (Office of Strategic Services, the predecessor of the Central Intelligence Agency) agents had dropped supplies to the Vietnamese and gave them weapons training during the war with Japan; for their part, Vietnamese had helped downed Allied airmen during the war. It was with high expectations of success, therefore, that Ho wrote a "Declaration of Independence of the Democratic Republic of Vietnam," carefully crafted to echo the strains of both the American document and the French Declaration of the Rights of Man and the Citizen. Notice, too, how closely it follows the format of the U.S. model in establishing its principles in the preamble and then launching into a catalog of colonial tyranny—using terminology virtually identical to its American counterpart— before concluding that the signers:

> solemnly declare to the world that Vietnam has the right to be a free and independent country—and in fact is so already. The entire Vietnamese people are determined to mobilize all their physical and mental strength, to sacrifice their lives and property in order to safeguard their independence and liberty.

THE DECLARATION

1. "All men are created equal. They are endowed by their Creator with certain inalienable rights; among these are Life, Liberty, and the pursuit of Happiness."

(continued)

2.   This immortal statement was made in the Declaration of Independence of the United States of America in 1776. In a broader sense, this means: All the peoples on the earth are equal from birth, all the peoples have a right to live, to be happy and free.

3.   The Declaration of the French Revolution made in 1791 on the Rights of Man and the Citizen also states: "All men are born free and with equal rights, and must always remain free and have equal rights."

4.   Those are undeniable truths.

5.   Nevertheless, for more than eighty years, the French imperialists, abusing the standard of Liberty, Equality, and Fraternity, have violated our Fatherland and oppressed our fellow citizens. They have acted contrary to the ideals of humanity and justice.

6.   In the field of politics, they have deprived our people of every democratic liberty.

7.   They have enforced inhuman laws; they have set up three distinct political regimes in the North, the Center, and the South of Vietnam in order to wreck our national unity and prevent our people from being united.

8.   They have built more prisons than schools. They have mercilessly slain our patriots; they have drowned our uprisings in rivers of blood.

9.   They have fettered public opinion; they have practiced obscurantism against our people.

10. To weaken our race they have forced us to use opium and alcohol.

11. In the field of economics, they have fleeced us to the backbone, impoverished our people, and devastated our land.

12. They have robbed us of our rice fields, our mines, our forests, and our raw materials. They have monopolized the issuing of banknotes and the export trade.

13. They have invented numerous unjustifiable taxes and reduced our people, especially our peasantry, to a state of extreme poverty.

14. They have hampered the prospering of our national bourgeoisie; they have mercilessly exploited our workers.

15. In the autumn of 1940, when the Japanese Fascists violated Indochina's territory to establish new bases in their fight against the Allies, the French imperialists went down on their bended knees and handed over our country to them.

16. Thus, from that date, our people were subjected to the double yoke of the French and the Japanese. Their sufferings and miseries increased. The result was that from the end of last year to the beginning of this year, from Quang Tri province to the North of Vietnam, more than two million of our fellow citizens died from starvation. On March 9, the French troops were disarmed by the Japanese. The French colonialists either fled or surrendered showing that not only were they incapable of "protecting" us, but that, in the span of five years, they had twice sold our country to the Japanese.

17. On several occasions before March 9, the Vietminh League urged the French to ally themselves with it against the Japanese. Instead of agreeing to this proposal, the French colonialists so intensified their terrorist activities against the Vietminh members that before fleeing they massacred a great number of our political prisoners detained at Yen Bay and Caobang.

18. Notwithstanding all this, our fellow citizens have always manifested toward the French a tolerant and humane attitude. Even after the Japanese putsch of March 1945, the Vietminh League helped many Frenchmen to cross the frontier, rescued some of them from Japanese jails, and protected French lives and property.

19. From the autumn of 1940, our country had in fact ceased to be a French colony and had become a Japanese possession.

20. After the Japanese had surrendered to the Allies, our whole people rose to regain our national sovereignty and to found the Democratic Republic of Vietnam.

21. The truth is that we have wrested our independence from the Japanese and not from the French.

22. The French have fled, the Japanese have capitulated, Emperor Bao Dai has abdicated. Our people have broken the chains which for nearly a century have fettered them and have won independence for the Fatherland. Our people at the same time have overthrown the monarchic regime that has reigned supreme for dozens of centuries. In its place has been established the present Democratic Republic.

23. For these reasons, we, members of the Provisional Government, representing the whole Vietnamese people, declare that from now on we break off all relations of a colonial character with France; we repeal all the international obligation that France has so far subscribed to on behalf of Vietnam and we abolish all the special rights the French have unlawfully acquired in our Fatherland.

24. The whole Vietnamese people, animated by a common purpose, are determined to fight to the bitter end against any attempt by the French colonialists to reconquer their country.

25. We are convinced that the Allied nations, which at Tehran and San Francisco have acknowledged the principles of self-determination and equality of nations, will not refuse to acknowledge the independence of Vietnam.

26. A people who have courageously opposed French domination for more than eight years, a people who have fought side by side with the Allies against the Fascists during these last years, such a people must be free and independent.

27. For these reasons, we, members of the Provisional Government of the Democratic Republic of Vietnam, solemnly declare to the world that

(continued)

> Vietnam has the right to be a free and independent country—and in fact is so already. The entire Vietnamese people are determined to mobilize all their physical and mental strength, to sacrifice their lives and property in order to safeguard their independence and liberty.
>
> Ho Chi Minh, "Declaration of Independence of the Democratic Republic of Vietnam," in *Selected Writings* (Hanoi: Foreign Languages Publishing House, 1977), pp. 53–56.

Despite the appeal to world sentiment in general, and American sensibilities in particular, the French, citing the Cold War needs of containing Communism, ultimately received American backing for their campaign to re-impose their rule on Indochina. Although the Asian section of the U.S. State Department supported Ho's efforts, their European colleagues won the argument in support of America's old ally, France. And, in a crowning irony, the United States provided the bulk of the financial and materiel support for France's effort at recolonization

Reading the Vietnamese Declaration of Independence, 1945. In one of history's more interesting coincidences, on the date of Japan's formal surrender to the Allies, September 2, 1945, Ho Chi Minh read the Vietnamese Declaration of Independence to a cheering crowd of half a million people in Hanoi. Here, on the crowded dais, surrounded by fellow Viet Minh dignitaries, Ho (fourth from the right, behind the microphone) delivers his historic address.

The Japanese had committed themselves to using local nationalists to further the dismantling of the East Asian colonial empires of the Europeans and Americans. This was the rationale for the Greater East Asia Co-Prosperity Sphere, in which each country within the growing Japanese empire would be given nominal independence, dependent on the course of the war. In the meantime they were to function, voluntarily in theory—by force if necessary—as an organic part of the new Japanese corporate polity. This was formalized at the Tokyo Conference in early 1943, in which constitutions were proposed and a certain degree of nervous bonhomie prevailed among the participants from China, the Dutch East Indies, Burma, Malaya, the Philippines, India, Korea, and Manchuria.

American advances in the Pacific had already put Japan on the defensive by this time, however, and the most important result was perhaps the Indian National Army under

Subhas Chandra Bose, whose attempted invasion of British India from Burma in 1944 with Japanese support was ultimately halted and reversed. In Indochina, the Viet Minh and other anti-Japanese groups worked covertly with the Allies, established and expanded their base areas, and awaited the end of the war. Seeing their war effort collapsing by early 1945, the Japanese launched a coup against the Vichy colonial government, disarmed and rounded up as many French officials as they could, and attempted to establish an allegedly independent government under Emperor Bao Dai. Japan's policies of keeping Indochinese rice exports high to feed her empire caused widespread famine, however. The French, helpless to stem it, looked on as the Viet Minh and other groups attempted to capture and distribute grain stores. Thus, when Ho Chi Minh read his declaration of independence in Hanoi as the formal Japanese surrender was taking place in Tokyo Bay, the government he was attempting to create had considerable support.

Emperor Bao Dai. The last Vietnamese emperor, Bao Dai (1913–1997), spent his entire reign under the control of first the French, then the Japanese, then the French again. In this photo, he is portrayed as a mature man on a Vietnamese colonial postage stamp issued in 1951, while the French were battling Vietnamese nationalists to retain control of the colony.

Conditions, however, soon collapsed into conflict. In the north, Nationalist Chinese troops were to supervise the surrender of the Japanese; in the south, the British were to do so. Both were enjoined from recognizing Ho's government and were not allowed to turn Indochina back to the French. In a bizarre twist, the British re-armed the Japanese to use as police, while negotiations were taking place to edge the Chinese out of northern Vietnam.

The War for Independence

In contrast to India, where postwar Britain gave in to the inevitable, the French under Charles de Gaulle (1890–1970) in 1944–1946 were determined to reconstitute their empire. Widespread collaboration with the German occupation led to widespread retribution against those who had cooperated, and for a time France seemed to be a country teetering on the brink of civil war. In the end, it required the founding of the Fourth Republic for democracy to be reestablished. De Gaulle and a majority of French politicians found it inconceivable that this new republic would be anything less than the imperially glorious Third Republic. Hence, his relations with the Allies, particularly the Americans, who were on record as being opposed to the re-imposition of colonialism in East Asia, were often strained. Already to de Gaulle's chagrin, French military efforts to hold onto Lebanon and Syria failed against discreet British support for independence and the unilateral establishment of national governments by the Lebanese and

Syrians in 1943–1944. After these losses, the politicians of the Fourth Republic were determined not to allow any repetitions.

Unfortunately for the French, however, when they returned to Indochina in the fall of 1945, the prewar Communist movement for independence had already taken over. As we have seen, with covert American assistance, the Viet Minh had fought the Japanese occupiers in a guerrilla war and on September 2, 1945, the day of Japan's surrender to the U.S., Ho Chi Minh had read his Vietnamese Declaration of Independence to half a million enthusiastic people in Hanoi. (See Patterns Up-Close: Parsing the Language of Independence.)

Following a number of armed clashes, including the French naval bombardment of Haiphong, as well as protracted negotiations, by early 1946 Ho and the French were locked in a stalemate. Ho did not budge from the demand for independence, while the French insisted on returning to their "colony." The war thus resumed. Because of the rapid escalation of the Cold War, particularly the Communist victory in China, the Soviet atomic bomb, and the Korean War, the French were successful in persuading the American administration that a victory of the Viet Minh was tantamount to an expansion of Communism in the world. By the early 1950s, the United States was providing the bulk of the funding, and the French and allied Vietnamese troops of Bao Dai's regime did the actual fighting.

In May 1954, nevertheless, the Viet Minh forces under their most able general, Vo Nguyen Giap (1911–2013), defeated the French decisively. Having created an isolated base at Dien Bien Phu in the northwest, and believing it to

Dien Bien Phu. Hoping to draw the Vietnamese forces into a fight in the valley of Dien Bien Phu, where their superior firepower and air supremacy could win the day, the French found themselves instead surrounded by Viet Minh forces in the surrounding hills and pounded by artillery—which French strategists had declared could not be hauled up to the high ground in such rugged territory. Here, beleaguered French forces hunker down in their slit trenches, cut off from resupply except by air transport, until they surrendered while the Geneva talks were ongoing in 1954.

be protected by the surrounding rugged mountains, the French allowed Viet Minh forces to encircle them and pound them with heavy artillery from surrounding hills—from which they had assumed it to be impossible to mount heavy guns. As their perimeter was squeezed ever tighter, resupply through air drops eventually became impossible. During the Geneva negotiations carried out later that year, the French surrender of the base and abandonment of their efforts in Indochina resulted in a division of Vietnam into North and South along the 17th Parallel, pending national elections, and the creation of the new nations of Laos and Cambodia. The United States, although refusing to sign the accords, now assumed the role of guarantor of the process of territorial integrity and ultimate unification.

THE AMERICAN WAR

In 1956, however, fearful that Ho Chi Minh would win the agreed-upon elections, the government in the South, with American backing, refused to participate. The U.S. now began to funnel military support to a series of pro-Western governments in South Vietnam, functioning as a separate Republic of Vietnam in counterpoint to Ho's Democratic Republic of Vietnam in the North. In the early 1960s, the Kennedy administration sent advisors to combat Communist insurgencies in both Laos and South Vietnam. Ho Chi Minh's Democratic Republic of Vietnam was aiding the Vietcong, or National Liberation Front (NLF), which from 1960 was the Communist guerrilla force in South Vietnam. To further the resolve of South Vietnam, in November 1963, the U.S. stood by in passive support of a coup by South Vietnamese generals that overthrew President Ngo Dinh Diem and put in place a military government. Thus, South Vietnam had narrowly survived a regime change and a growing insurgency but would continue to do so only through increasingly massive American military engagement (See Map 12.2).

Tearing Two Nations Apart

As recently declassified material (including audio tapes) from the successive Kennedy (1961–1963), Johnson (November 1963–1968), and Nixon (1969–1974) administrations clearly shows, American leadership saw little worth in the defense of Vietnam in and of itself but was adamant in its reluctance to yield further ground to what was perceived to be the threat of world Communism. The larger the commitment, however, the higher the stakes and the more psychologically and strategically abhorrent the thought of failure became. Moreover, all three administrations insisted on an incremental application of American military force in the hope of convincing their opponents that their cause was unwinnable. At the same time, this reluctance to resort to a more conventional strategy of massive force and territorial conquest was strongly conditioned by the recent experience of the bloody stalemate in Korea. The nightmare scenario of all three presidents was another large protracted war on the Asian mainland.

Thus, the Kennedy administration decided to negotiate an agreement for Laos to remain neutral, and confined its military presence in Vietnam to

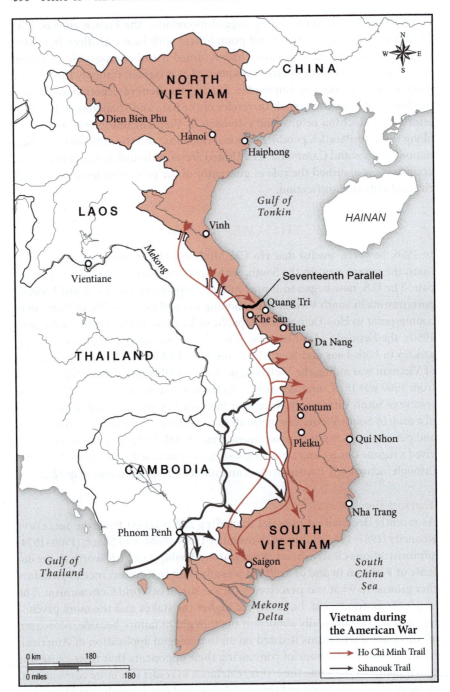

Map 12.2 Vietnam during the American War

An Unfolding Tragedy for All. Above, 1966, U.S. forces of the Army's First Infantry Division are pinned down by Vietcong, while urging a local woman and her child to take cover behind the raised pathway (A). Below, a Vietcong (NLF) fighter crouches low inside his bunker. NLF guerrillas were remarkably skilled at building and utilizing camouflaged bunkers and tunnels, as one can see from the circular opening to the lower right of the fighter that led to deeper shelter underground (B).

sending "advisors" and CIA personnel to the South Vietnamese government. In 1965, however, in the wake of the shadowy "Gulf of Tonkin" incident—in which American ships were allegedly attacked by North Vietnamese patrol boats—the U.S. began to send combat forces to South Vietnam in rapidly increasing numbers. These were to work in coordination with ARVN (Army of the Republic of Vietnam; South Vietnam) troops in attempting to isolate and eliminate NLF forces, while an air campaign against the North was implemented to discourage Ho's support of the Southern guerrillas.

Despite the vast superiority of American firepower and technology, the war became a textbook example of what is now called "asymmetrical warfare." Like Mao Zedong's forces in the 1930s and 1940s, the Vietcong, supported by Giap's North Vietnamese Army (NVA) units, remained stubbornly elusive and were continually able to paint the Americans as foreign invaders and ARVN as collaborators. The Americans attempted a number of seemingly promising tactical directions: widespread use of helicopters to attack remote enemy strongholds; "search and destroy" missions; fortified "strategic hamlets" as safe areas for friendly villagers; "winning hearts and minds" with projects meant to help needy regions. Despite the additional fact that the military seemed to be winning most of its battles and killing large numbers of the enemy, American leadership became increasingly pessimistic about the chances of ultimate victory.

By 1967, the United States had committed more than half a million personnel to the war in Vietnam. As the conflict dragged on, growing numbers of Americans became increasingly disturbed by its apparent open-endedness, and the rising weekly "body counts" of dead American soldiers and airmen. Moreover, the ongoing military draft and the sense that the war was aimless and endless triggered massive demonstrations against the conflict, particularly among the young.

What is often considered to be a key turning point of the war began on January 30, 1968. With the onset of the Vietnamese lunar new year—Tet—the Vietcong mounted an all-out offensive in several key South Vietnamese cities, including Saigon and Hue. Caught by surprise, U.S. and South Vietnamese forces quickly regrouped and, in some of the most bitter fighting of the war, ultimately blunted the **Tet Offensive** and resecured the cities. For the Vietcong, the defeat spelled their end as the principal fighting force; the fighting would now be increasingly assumed by North Vietnamese Army regulars. Indeed, in the early days following the battle, there was a deep sense of discouragement in Hanoi at the extent of the defeat. Much to their astonishment, however, what might otherwise have been regarded as a decisive victory in the U.S.—perhaps along the lines of the Battle of the Bulge in World War II—was now widely viewed as a profound strategic failure of overall American policy. The revelations of the **My Lai Massacre** and heart-rending photos and film footage of children burned by napalm, as well as a South Vietnamese officer executing a Vietcong suspect, intensified public revulsion at the horrors of the conflict and fueled the opposition.

(A)

(B)

Turning the Tide in the "American War." The year 1968 would prove pivotal in the U.S. war in Vietnam, and one in which the tide of American opinion began to shift toward opposition to the conflict. During the Vietnamese lunar New Year, or Tet, in January, the Vietcong launched their great push to capture Saigon, Hue, and other important cities. The result was a bloody battle with U.S. and South Vietnamese ARVN forces as they slowly retook the cities at great cost. What was a devastating defeat for the NLF, however, was seen by increasing numbers of Americans as a sign that the war was not winnable. In (A), ARVN troops hold their ground in the battle for Saigon.

In March of that same year, reports surfaced of U.S.-led massacres of villagers alleged to be concealing NLF fighters in My Lai and several other locations. Although the immediate commanders on the ground were court-martialed, when news of these killings became public, it reinforced the outcry against the conduct of the war. (B) Vietnamese villagers as they await their execution, an image later used by Army prosecutors as evidence of the crime.

"Peace with Honor" and National Unification

So widespread was disillusionment with the war that President Lyndon Johnson announced he would not run for a second term. By spring, Democratic hopefuls Eugene McCarthy and Robert Kennedy were campaigning on anti-war platforms. The sense of crisis in the U.S. increased further with the assassinations of revered civil rights leader Martin Luther King in April and Robert Kennedy himself in June. The ultimate winner in the presidential election, Republican Richard Nixon, had campaigned in large part on a "secret plan" to end the war.

Nixon's plan revolved largely around trying to force the North Vietnamese to the conference table and negotiate a U.S. withdrawal while ensuring the integrity of South Vietnam—what Nixon called "peace with honor." Despite a stepped up bombing campaign, Ho's death in 1969, and the spread of the conflict into Laos and Cambodia in an attempt to interdict the flow of supplies to North Vietnamese forces in the South along the Ho Chi Minh Trail, the DRV clung tenaciously to its position of unification and withdrawal of U.S. forces. In the United States, opposition grew ever more intense with the revelations of the Pentagon Papers and the 1970 killing of four students at Kent State University by Ohio National Guard troops. Finally, the Paris Peace Talks in 1972 produced a

Kent State. The mounting protests against the Vietnam War in the U.S. turned deadly in the spring of 1970. On May 4, about 600 protesters at Kent State University in Ohio faced off against National Guard troops. As the protests became more aggressive, the troops panicked and fired into the crowd, killing four students. In perhaps the most famous image of the protest era, and one that further galvanized opposition to the war, student Mary Ann Vecchio screams in horror and anguish over the body of fellow student Jeffrey Miller. This photo later won a Pulitzer Prize.

plan whereby a truce would be enacted in 1973, U.S. forces would be withdrawn, and South Vietnam's integrity would be recognized until such time as unification could be effected peacefully by both sides.

The optimism surrounding the agreement, however, was tempered by the realization that it would at best provide a flimsy cover for the withdrawal of the U.S. Within two years, South Vietnam had collapsed, and the scenes unfolding in the spring of 1975 as described in the opening vignette of this chapter were in progress. Southeast Asia was plunged once again into conflict; this time, however, in Cambodia, accompanied by arguably the most thorough and horrific genocide since World War II.

FROM REUNIFICATION TO REGIONAL POWER

The newly unified Vietnam was dominated by Communist Party leader Le Duan (1907–1986). As Party secretary during the 1960s, he progressively replaced Ho Chi Minh, who was increasingly in ill health until his death in 1969. Le Duan quelled opposition to his vision of a Soviet-style command economy for the new polity, and on July 2, 1976, the new Socialist Republic of Vietnam (SRV) was created.

Building the New Socialist State

As part of the new unified state, the Communist Party changed its name to the Vietnamese Communist Party. This was followed in 1980 by a new constitution proclaiming the polity to be a "Marxist-Leninist state led by the dictatorship of the proletariat, the peasants, and the workers." Meanwhile, the Party had worked assiduously to create a populace unified in ideological loyalty to the new order. Toward that end, Buddhism and Catholicism were co-opted and/or suppressed. The Party attempted to create a kind cult of deceased personality around Ho Chi Minh—even to the point of requiring his picture to be present on the altars of houses of worship. As they moved into the South, they created Party organizations echoing those long in operation in the North. In the larger cities of the South, such as Saigon—renamed Ho Chi Minh City—and Hue, these moves were greeted with worldly skepticism, fear, and weary acceptance. Some expected that such "purifying" efforts would soon be neutralized by "corrupt" Saigon. Instead, however, Vietnam descended into a state of poverty and failed institutions that surpassed those of any other Communist bloc country. Making matters even worse was the new state's involvement in over a decade of warfare in Cambodia (see Map 12.3).

One immediate difficulty was the withdrawal of subsidies from the USSR, the PRC, and for the South, the U.S. at war's end. An American aid package promised after the peace accords was withdrawn, as was China's financial aid following its tilt toward the United States and Vietnam's involvement in Cambodia. The Soviet Union renewed military aid in hopes of retaining a presence in Southeast Asia and in opposing Chinese influence. Meanwhile, Le Duan and his faction insisted that a stringent Marxist program similar to that

Map 12.3 Reunified Vietnam

of the North be extended to the South. The South, however, long plugged into the global economy because of its American ties, found its economy stifled by this new isolation, while those in the North grew increasingly impatient with the government's rosy pronouncements on building abundance in the postwar socialist paradise.

Although in many respects the new state's efforts were modeled more on Soviet examples than those of the Chinese in the early 1950s, there were some parallels to the latter. Unlike China, where land reform resulted in the killing of over a million landlords and rich peasants, redistribution in the South, though often forced, went much more smoothly. In part, this was because much of it had already been undertaken by the Thieu government in Saigon and in NLF-controlled areas. Organized into collectives and assigned stringent quotas for rice production, however, the 75 percent of the population involved in agriculture found themselves ground down by arbitrary government price controls. A program to allow open market sales of rice when a collective's quota had been fulfilled boosted production, but also stimulated an already thriving black market economy.

All citizens were now required to register their class backgrounds, and those with "bad" class affiliations were subjected to employment and educational barriers. As in China, the Party confiscated religious property for redistribution. Needless to say, tens of thousands of former ARVN personnel, government officials, and others perceived as "bad elements" or collaborators were ferreted out, executed, or sentenced to various terms of "re-education."

The Party also nationalized the financial, industrial, and commercial sectors of the economy. It was in these areas that the Chinese and other minorities took the biggest hits. The Party abetted popular perceptions of Chinese merchants and bankers as capitalist exploiters and over 800,000 were sent to re-education facilities or left the country. Several waves of such pressures created the famous images of **boat people** fleeing the country in makeshift vessels. Ironically, those involved in this emigration after 1978 were welcomed in a People's Republic of China seeking exactly the kind of expertise the commercial classes brought with them to power Deng Xiaoping's new direction of the Four Modernizations. Many fled to other places in Southeast Asia, especially those with large Chinese communities, as well as Australia, Canada, and the United States.

Politics and Genocide: Fighting the Khmer Rouge

Against the backdrop of Vietnam's trials in creating a new socialist state, the dire situation of Pol Pot's (b. Saloth Sar; 1925–1998) wholesale slaughter of urban Cambodia (or Democratic Kampuchea, as it was now called) unfolded with daily increased ferocity. Determined to completely ruralize the new state along what they perceived to be Maoist lines, the Khmer Rouge ("Red Khmer"; the Cambodian Communist Party) systematically uprooted and executed perhaps as many as a third (an estimated 1.5 million) of all Cambodians and rendered the former capital of Phnom Penh a spectral ossuary of chilling silence. In ad-

Boat People. The political, social, and economic turmoil in the years following Vietnam's unification under socialist rule left many, especially those who had prospered in South Vietnam, dissatisfied with life under the new order. In addition, the invasion of Kampuchea to combat the Khmer Rouge, the incursion by China, and the mounting discrimination toward ethnic Chinese in Vietnam spurred many to take their chances in escape. By the early 1980s, thousands of "boat people" were attempting to escape the country, many in flimsy, improvised, unseaworthy craft. A U.S. rescue effort was mounted to save as many as possible, including the fortunate refugees in this photo, picked up by the American ship USS *Blue Ridge* in 1984.

dition to attacking ideological enemies, the Khmer Rouge engaged in "ethnic cleansing" of minority groups on a massive scale. Their hunts for Vietnamese even extended into attacks on Vietnamese border villages, and they had an ongoing fear of Vietnamese expansionism.

Alarmed at the rampant genocide—and the potential for disrupting Vietnam's fragile socialist state building—the SRV took the initiative and intervened. On December 25, 1978, they launched an invasion of Cambodia with the intent of backing an opposition leader, Heng Samrin (b. 1934), who had fled to

Vietnam. The invasion precipitated the Third Indochinese War (resistance to the French and Americans marked the first two conflicts.) Although Vietnam was suffering economically, its military was well armed and trained, and self-confident after its victories in the struggle for unification. Within three weeks, it drove Pol Pot from power and established Heng as the leader of a new state called the "People's Republic of Kampuchea."

Although the invasion effectively ended the genocide, resistance to the new regime remained in pockets of the country, and Pol Pot had fled to Thailand. Because of Soviet support of Vietnam's invasion, the U.S. and China refused to recognize the new state and, as we saw earlier, China mounted a brief and rather unsuccessful invasion of northern Vietnam in early 1979. Thanks to American and Chinese pressure, the UN continued to recognize the Khmer Rouge regime in exile for the next decade, while factional fighting persisted in Cambodia. After protracted negotiations, Vietnamese forces finally withdrew in 1990. In a somewhat surprising historical twist, after a short-lived coalition government, Cambodia became a constitutional monarchy with Prince Noradom Sihanouk—ousted in the early 1970s—now brought back as head of state (see Map 12.4).

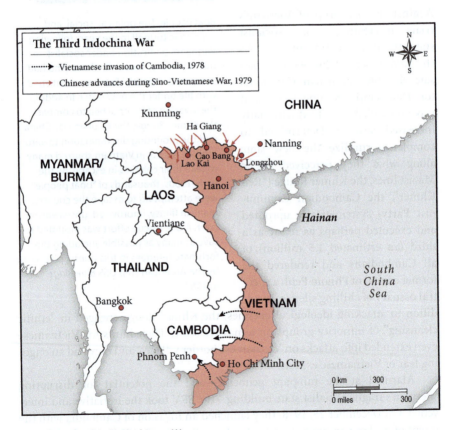

Map 12.4 The Third Indochinese War

Recovery and Prosperity

Vietnam's economic struggles and international isolation became the Party's priorities after the death of Le Duan in 1986. Seeking to ease tensions with China, it sponsored visits by dignitaries, including General Giap, and became increasingly interested in China's rapid economic progress. Vietnam's isolation on the global front reversed considerably with its withdrawal from Cambodia in 1990, and also when it exchanged formal diplomatic recognition with the United States in 1995. On the economic front, Vietnam achieved spectacular progress with its reform policy of *doi moi* ("renovation"). Like China's Four Modernizations, the new policy called for dismantling of agricultural collectives and state-run enterprises typical of the command economy, and the introduction of market incentives. Moreover, restrictions on foreign investment were lifted even more rapidly than in China with the result that, by 1993, Vietnam's economy was, next to China's, the region's most vibrant.

As in China, the opening of the country and the transition to market-driven economics posed serious challenges to the SRV's authoritarian government. The south, with its long exposure to the freewheeling market forces of the U.S. during the 1950s and 1960s and surviving expatriate connections, was soon assuming its familiar cosmopolitan face. Ho Chi Minh City has rapidly regained considerable stature as a commercial hub. As such, it is also a gateway for forces tending to disrupt the hold of the socialist leadership seeking to hang on to the vestiges of its ideological purity. This has been abetted by Vietnam's increasing popularity as a vacation destination. The September 2017 airing of the Ken Burns PBS documentary on the Vietnam War undoubtedly helped to engender renewed interest in the country as a tourist destination among Americans.

Present-Day Ho Chi Minh City. Vietnam's remarkable economic recovery and development impress nearly all who visit the nation. An attractive investment site, the country has quite successfully followed in the pattern of Japan, South Korea, and China. Like present-day China, the streets of Ho Chi Minh City, formerly Saigon, now teem with the latest vehicles of all makes and sizes, with motorcycles and scooters still retaining the popularity they had acquired as far back as the 1960s.

In Vietnam, Internet and social media usage have skyrocketed in recent years: as of 2017, there were over 124 million mobile phone subscriptions out of a population of slightly less than 95 million. Active Internet users number more than half the population (50.05 million), whereas active social media accounts number slightly less than half of it (46 million). Facebook, still prohibited in China, saw an increase in its users within Vietnam from 1.4 million in 2011 to 31.3 million in 2015. That same year, Vietnamese averaged 3.1 hours per day on social media, surpassing time spent in the U.S. (2.7 hours; all data from http://chabrol.net/2017/01/10/internet-statistics-in-vietnam-compared).

All this connectivity has made it virtually impossible for the Party to impose the kind of "Bamboo Firewall" that continues in China. It has also fed grassroots demands for a loosening of the authoritarian grip of the Party. As Christopher Goscha has pointed out, the government has not only grudgingly allowed an increasingly vigorous civil society of independent organizations and NGOs for a wide variety of purposes to develop, it has also attempted to work with and on occasion co-opt them as useful ways to market its policies (Goscha, Christopher. *Vietnam: A New History.* New York: Basic Books, 2016, p. 456). On the political front, the struggle for increased government responsiveness, a wider spectrum of political views, and the suppression of corruption have come increasingly to the fore. Prominent among these has been BLOC 8406 (named for the date of the group's founding on April 8, 2006), a coalition of dissidents building on a 2006 "Declaration of Freedom and Democracy," which demanded a representative government, basic freedoms of religion, press, and individual rights, and in a move that would have brought down severe repression in China— regime change.

CONCLUSION

The history of Vietnam during the last century and a half may be said to encapsulate nearly every trend that has affected East Asia and, more generally, the world. Colonialism, world war, revolution, a second interval of colonialism and outside influence, nationalism, Soviet-style Communism, and now renewed political ferment have all left their mark on the country. As of this writing, Vietnam may be on the verge of change yet again. Part of this is due to the constant pressure for a more liberal government, but a large part has been precipitated by, as has so often been the case in the past, the growing colossus to the north.

Although Sino-Vietnamese relations improved significantly during the 1990s, the historic tensions of expanding Chinese influence and its new, seemingly insatiable hunger for resources have ratcheted up feelings considerably and stimulated a growing agency among Vietnam's grassroots. Since the turn of the twenty-first century, China has been increasingly aggressive and confident in pushing claims to offshore islands near Vietnam, the Philippines, and even Japan—as well as attempting to build offshore islands out of unoccupied reefs and atolls (see Chapter 10). Tensions over the Spratly Islands and their potential oil and gas reserves have lent themselves to this situation. More recently, however, the controversy over Chinese strip mining of bauxite in Vietnam's Central Highlands has boxed Vietnam's Communist Party into a corner from which it may not emerge unchallenged and unchanged.

Vietnam is home to the world's third richest bauxite deposits, and in 2012 theSRV agreed to permit a joint business venture that gave Chinese companies unfettered access to them. The goal was to have an investment of 15 billion dollars in the extraction project by 2025. Aside from the outcry against China's draining of Vietnamese resources, numerous studies have concluded that strip mining in the Central Highlands will be disastrous for the environment there. Despite a mounting protest movement against this venture, the government has allowed the mining to proceed (. In 2017, bauxite production in Vietnam nearly doubled from its 2016 totals moving from 1200 to 2000 metric tons. Within the Party itself, however, growing resentment over this Chinese operation that employs a largely Chinese workforce—with the national icon General Giap figuring prominently among the protestors—has led to the charge that the Party can no longer adequately protect the country from this new form of colonialism. The call is thus growing for Vietnam to transition to a European model of socialism or risk being left behind in global development. As recently as January 2017, though, the official line remains that, despite the failures of Soviet bloc countries, Vietnam would follow "correct" Marxist policies adapted to its own circumstances, study the experiences of other socialist countries, and struggle against the inroads of exploitative capitalist and democratic forces.

FURTHER RESOURCES

Aung-Thwin, Maitrii, M. C. Rickleffs, Bruce Lockhart, Albert Lau, and Portia Reyes. *A New History of Southeast Asia*. New York: Palgrave, 2010. Handy, comprehensive work by a group of scholars at the National University of Singapore. Especially good on recent and global connections.

Chapuis, Oscar. *A History of Vietnam from Hong Bang to Tu Duc*. Westport, CT: Greenwood Press, 1995. A one-volume history of Vietnam that concentrates on the development of a cultural and national identity up to the period of French colonialism.

Duiker, William J. *Ho Chi Minh*. New York: Hyperion, 2000. Pioneering one-volume biography of Ho by noted scholar William Duiker. Accessible, scholarly but readable by non-experts.

Fforde, Adam, and Stefan De Vylder. *From Plan to Market: The Economic Transition in Vietnam*. Boulder, CO: Westview Press, 1996. Early look at Vietnam's movement away from earlier Soviet-style top-down economics toward a market-driven economy. Accessible and carrying a wealth of economic data.

Hayslip, Le Ly, and Jay Wurts. *When Heaven and Earth Changed Places: A Vietnamese Woman's Journey from War to Peace*. New York: Doubleday, 1989. Harrowing memoir of Hayslip's adolescence and young womanhood in war-torn Vietnam, through torture, rape, emigrating to America, and returning to find family in Vietnam.

Herring, George. *America's Longest War: The United States in Vietnam, 1950–1975*. Boston: McGraw-Hill, 2002. Best-selling popular history of American involvement in Vietnam, with an emphasis as well on Vietnamese conflicts and aims.

Luong, Hy V. *Postwar Vietnam: Dynamics of a Transforming Society.* Lanham, MD: Institute of Southeast Asian Studies and Rowman & Littlefield, 2003. In-depth study of Vietnamese economics and society, with a view toward tracing the growing disparities in wealth and the rural–urban divide.

Ngo, Vinh Long. *Before the Revolution: The Vietnamese Peasants under the French.* Cambridge, MA: MIT Press, 1973; New York: Columbia University Press, 1991; Washington, DC: Council for Research in Values and Philosophy, Institute of Philosophy, Vietnamese Academy of Social Sciences, 2008. Updated reissue of a classic pioneering study on the role and position of the peasantry of Indochina under French colonialism. Especially detailed with regard to the hardships faced under colonial goals of making the colony profitable.

Pham, Andrew X. *The Eaves of Heaven: A Life in Three Wars.* New York: Harmony Books, 2008. Memoir of the author's father, recounting his adventurous and often dangerous life throughout the final days of French colonialism, during U.S. involvement in Southeast Asia, and under the new socialist Vietnam.

Tran-Nam, Binh, and Chi Do Pham. *The Vietnamese Economy: Awakening the Dormant Dragon.* New York: Routledge, 2003. Detailed economic study by two Vietnamese scholars of the programs and policies of Vietnam's economic modernization and its trends in the early 2000s.

WEBSITES

https://vietnam.vassar.edu/overview/. Vassar College. *The Wars for Vietnam.* Excellent site with sections offering an overview of the modern history of Southeast Asia, key documents, and biographies of prominent individuals.

http://www.ibiblio.org/vietnam/vnpic.html. Ibiblio.org. *The Vietnam Pictures Archives.* Extensive and wide-reaching archive of images on a wide variety of subjects related to Vietnam, including useful links to other sites on culture, language, religion, and society, although some of these are no longer available.

https://www.bbc.com/news/world-asia-pacific-16568035. BBC News. *Vietnam Profile Timeline.* Highly useful and detailed timeline on Vietnamese history from 1868 to 2017 (updated April 2018).

CHAPTER 13

◆○

Becoming the Model of Modernity: Japan to the Present

It was the most momentous radio broadcast in the history of Japan. Even so, the weight of its message and the bearer of that message shocked those sitting anxiously by their radios at noon on August 15, 1945. The Jewel-Voice Broadcast (*Gyokuon-hoso*), as it was called, was to be the first time the Japanese people— or anyone else within the range of Japanese transmitters—would hear the high-toned, affectless, elaborate ceremonial language of the Showa emperor, Hirohito. The message had been pre-recorded the evening before and was so extraordinary and controversial that a secret cabal of Japanese military officers attempted to steal the recording and destroy it. Little wonder as this most famous announcement in Japanese history has been known ever since as the Imperial Rescript on Surrender.

As we learned in previous chapters, Japan's expansion into a far-flung empire from the late nineteenth century through the early 1940s had itself led to momentous changes throughout East Asia. Taiwan, Korea, Manchuria, naval and air bases in French Indochina, and much of China itself had fallen under Japanese control by 1941. Indeed, during the first six months of Japan's gamble to acquire the resources it so desperately needed by attacking the American base at Pearl Harbor and launching a general offensive in Southeast Asia and the South-west Pacific Ocean, the victories had been swift and stunning. The plans to build an unbreakable barrier of fortress islands, exploit the resources of the empire, and secure the surrender of China, however, began to unravel by June 1942. The unexpected and complete victory of the United States at Midway Island early that month marked the beginning of an accelerating build-up by Allied forces in the Pacific. American industrial power soon began to reveal itself as U.S. forces bypassed Japanese island strongholds and created their own bases from which to advance toward Japan. By late 1944, Japan itself was under air attack from bases in China and the Mariana Islands. Through the spring and summer of 1945, re-lentless incendiary attacks had reduced nearly every Japanese city and industrial area to smoking ruins.

Then came the final blow. As the emperor put it: "The enemy has begun to employ a new and most cruel bomb, the power of which to do damage is, indeed, incalculable, taking the toll of many innocent lives." Moreover, the Soviet Union had now declared war on Japan (as arranged at the Yalta Conference in February), three months after the surrender of Germany. Hence, as Hirohito obliquely put it, "The war situation has developed not necessarily to Japan's advantage. . . ." These factors now being in play, the emperor said, to fight on "would not only result in an ultimate collapse and obliteration of the Japanese nation, but also it would lead to the total extinction of human civilization" (William Theodore De Bary, et al, *Sources of East Asian Tradition*, Vol. II, New York: Columbia University Press, 2008, p. 625).

Thus, Japan, one of the world's most powerful nations a few years before, was now among its most impoverished and devastated. The impact of defeat and Occupation by American forces for the next seven years would, along with the founding of the People's Republic of China, the Cold War with the Soviet Union, and the dismantling of colonialism, play a pivotal role in the history of East Asia down to the present. The American Occupation led to a massive restructuring of the Japanese polity and society—including a new constitution and radical demilitarization. In a sense, the Occupation continues today, with American forces still stationed on Okinawa. As the base from which United Nations forces fought in Korea in the 1950s, Japan was the recipient of massive American aid. From the time the Occupation ended in 1952, Japan's economic picture became astoundingly robust until stagnation began to set in during the early 1990s. Even with decades of slow or flat growth, however, Japan remained the second largest economy in the world until surpassed by China in August 2010.

In a way, however, Japan's growth after the interruption of the war years continued much as it had from the time of the Meiji Restoration. Moreover, the export-driven manufacturing model resumed after the war provided a powerful blueprint for the economic strategies of all of East Asia. Japan's progress in gaining initial momentum through cheap labor and low-cost products had moved by the late 1960s to high-quality goods, shipping, construction equipment, electronics, and automobiles. This, in turn, raised wages and created a large and active segment of middle-class consumers. Japanese manufacturers were at the forefront of the computer and cell phone revolutions and remain so today. Their model of economic development has been so successful that it has been copied by Taiwan, South Korea, China (PRC), Vietnam, and most recently India and some African countries. Indeed, so pervasive was the Japanese economic model, as well as Japanese capital and managerial expertise in the region, that it was sometimes said that in economic terms Japan had emerged as the real victor of the Pacific War.

In this chapter, we first trace the arc of Japanese expansion to Great Power status from 1895 to the World War II years. Along the way, we will examine the attempts at liberalization during the move toward "Taisho Democracy," from 1912 to 1926, as well as the quashing of this trend during the militarist decade of the 1930s and the war years from 1937 to 1945. We will then examine the impact of the American Occupation and the protection of the U.S. nuclear umbrella on Japan's reemergence, Japan's postwar relationship with the nations of East Asia,

Casualties of the Nuclear Age. The US bombing campaign of Japan, starting in late 1944 with long-range B-29 bombers caused perhaps the most complete destruction of any country during World War II. Frustrated by the jet stream during high altitude conventional attacks, the US Army Air Force turned to low-level incendiary attacks with deadly effectiveness on combustible Japanese cities. The culmination of the air campaign was the dropping of the two atomic bombs on Hiroshima and Nagasaki on August 6 and 9, 1945. Here, a mother and child who survived the Hiroshima attack sit amid the complete devastation of their city in December, 1945.

the shifting patterns of politics in the region, and the struggle to maintain the elements of an ancient cultural tradition in what many consider to be the world's most "modern" nation.

"A WONDERFULLY CLEVER AND PROGRESSIVE PEOPLE"

As we have noted in previous chapters, Japan's stunning victory over Qing China in 1895 had far-reaching implications not only for East Asia but also among the Western powers. The Triple Intervention by Russia, Germany, and France showed the foreign powers' fear of Qing weakness in the face of Japan's newly demonstrated prowess. Korea became a Japanese client state. China saw patriotic demonstrations and ever more strident calls for reform, with many proposing programs along Japanese lines. Qing weakness further spurred attempts by Western powers—and now Japan—to carve up China into spheres of influence. Even the United States, in calling for an "open door" in China, did so in part because of Japan's new status as an up-and-coming regional power. This enhanced position could be seen vividly in a turn-of-the-century American world atlas. The section on Japan was headed, "A Nation of Wonderfully Clever and Progressive People." In contrast, the chapter on China was subtitled, "Her Great Problems a Menace to the World." Japan's cleverness and progress notwithstanding, those Americans arguing in favor of acquiring the Philippines after the Spanish-American War couched their arguments partly out of fear of further Japanese expansion in the region. On the other hand, many of those resisting Western colonialism saw hope in the rise of the first modern Asian Great Power.

The Russo-Japanese War

As we noted previously, the desperate tilt of the Qing toward Russia in the wake of the Sino-Japanese War and Triple Intervention was seen as an act of treachery by Japan. Japanese soldiers abandoning their encampments in Liaodong scooped up handfuls of soil and tearfully vowed to return. Russia's lease of Port Arthur and Dalian or Dairen, and development of the former into a powerful naval base adjacent to Korea and dominating the approach to Beijing, were seen as ominous as well. The presence of both Japanese and Russian troops in north China as part of the multinational force during the Boxer War did little to ease tensions. Both Russia and Japan had plans to acquire concessions in Manchuria, and Japanese patriotic expansionist groups such as the famous Black Dragon Society or *Kokuryukai* (so-named for the Amur River border of Manchuria and Siberia; *heilong jiang,* "Black Dragon River," in Chinese) and their Russian counterparts were deeply involved with intrigue among local leaders. Chinese acquiescence to Russian proposals to build a spur of the Trans-Siberian Railway through Manchuria to the port of Vladivostok (the Chinese Eastern Railway)—a considerable shortcut—alarmed the Japanese, as did Russian plans to build another spur from the new headquarters of the Chinese Eastern Railway at Harbin through Mukden (today, Shenyang) to Port Arthur (the South Manchurian Railway.)

The Japanese saw these actions as Russian attempts to box in Korea and box out Japanese influence in the region. For Japan, Manchuria represented a much-needed buffer against possible Russian designs on Korea, as well as a potential resource-rich and spacious frontier for emigrants from the increasingly crowded home islands. As a hedge against Russian hegemony, in 1902, Japan concluded an alliance with a provision of "benign neutrality" with Great Britain in which both signatories pledged noncombat aid to each other in the event of a war of one against a third party. Both Russia and Japan entered into negotiations aimed at resolving their disputes in 1903. Debate has continued among historians ever since about the intentions of both sides, in particular whether Tsar Nicholas II of Russia was attempting to buy time to build up his forces or was negotiating in sincerity. The Russians and Germans saw Japan as the "yellow peril" but had

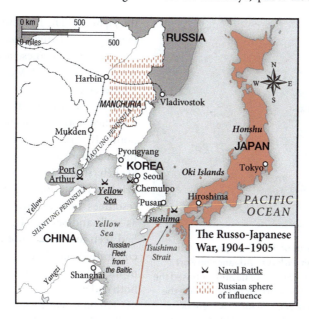

Map 13.1 The Russo-Japanese War, 1904–1905

scant respect for its growing military power. Hence, the Russians believed that they would be the arbiters of whether or not a war occurred.

With the collapse of the final offers by both sides, however, the Japanese struck. On February 8, 1904, three hours before the official declaration of war was issued, the Japanese fleet launched a devastating torpedo boat attack on the Russian squadron anchored at Port Arthur. For the coming months, the surviving Russian warships were kept bottled up at the base, while Japanese forces landed in Korea and advanced to the Manchurian border. Realizing the need to take the base before another Russian fleet could raise the blockade of Port Arthur, the Japanese landed troops in Liaodong and began a siege of the fortifications that was to last for months. In many respects, the fight was a bloody foreshadowing of the carnage that was to mark World War I. Japanese troops repeatedly stormed Russian positions defended by trenches, barbed wire, heavy artillery, and machine guns, only to be thrown back with appalling losses. The Japanese commander Nogi Maresuke saw both his sons killed in the campaign (see Map 13.1).

Japanese forces made more rapid progress engaging the Russians in the Manchurian interior, driving them back toward Port Arthur. In desperation, the Russians decided to send their Baltic Sea Fleet on a desperately long attempt to relieve the siege. Here, however, the Anglo–Japanese Alliance came into play: the British denied the Russians access to port facilities or coaling stations within their empire and, most crucially, refused to let them pass through the Suez Canal, adding thousands of miles to the Russian voyage. Meanwhile, the Russian commander at Port Arthur, in the face of the Japanese advances in Manchuria and capture of the hills surrounding the fort, surrendered, much to the surprise of

Japanese Troops of the 9th Regiment, 4th Division, Await Orders to Advance on Port Arthur. With the Japanese having surprised the Russian fleet at Port Arthur to commence the Russo-Japanese War, the fortress there became the object of a prolonged and bloody siege by Japanese forces lasting for almost the entire war. In a foreshadowing of the carnage to come during World War I, both sides employed heavy artillery, machine guns, mines, barbed wire entanglements, and trenches, with the result that the assaulting Japanese forces suffered heavy losses. The 4th Division pictured here suffered catastrophic casualties at Port Arthur in repeated assaults on the fort, losing all its regimental commanders.

the Japanese. The Russian fleet, now making for Vladivostok, was intercepted by the Japanese at Tsushima Strait at the end of May 1905 and annihilated.

The strains of the war had stretched both sides to the breaking point. In January 1905, following the massacre of demonstrators in St. Petersburg, Russia stood on the brink of revolution. Japan's military resources were pushed to the limit as well, and several Japanese cities had seen food riots. Both sides had committed hundreds of thousands of men, and the total casualties for both sides may have run as high as 170,000, with perhaps 20,000 civilian lives lost. It was with considerable relief that both empires agreed to peace talks proposed by the American President Theodore Roosevelt. On September 5, 1905, they signed a peace treaty at Portsmouth, New Hampshire. For Japan, the cost was high but the territorial gains considerable. It was agreed that Korea was now in Japan's sphere of influence; Russia agreed to leave Manchuria, allowing Japan a free hand there—despite it formally remaining part of the Qing Empire— and in possession of the vital railroads. Japan received leaseholds on Port Arthur and Dairen, and acquired the southern half of Sakhalin Island. For their part, the Russians were relieved of any obligations to pay indemnities or reparations.

The Limits of Power Politics

If the Sino-Japanese War had established Japan as a rising East Asian state, the Russo-Japanese War, in marking the first decisive defeat of a European country by an Asian one in modern history, had confirmed the empire's Great Power status. The initial limits of what that status might mean for an East Asian country in a world dominated by Western imperial powers was, however, soon evident. As we have seen, the United States had passed Chinese exclusion legislation in the last decades of the nineteenth century. While Japanese emigration was negligible during this time, it began to accelerate by the turn of the century. Many of the same arguments leveled against Chinese immigrants were now also raised about the Japanese. The founding of the Asiatic Exclusion League (AEL) in 1904 pressured the legislatures of West Coast states to limit or ban Japanese immigration and refuse naturalization to those already there. In 1906, the AEL pushed the San Francisco School Board to place Japanese students in segregated classes with Chinese children, prompting protests from Japan and pushing the Roosevelt administration into negotiations with the Japanese government. The result was the Gentlemen's Agreement of 1907, which barred the future immigration of Japanese laborers but allowed family members of those already here to emigrate. For the Japanese, this signaled that, regardless of their political and military clout, they would still be considered racially inferior by the West. It also marked an important turning point in the empire's relations with the United States. From this point forward, despite the often cordial diplomatic exchanges between the two countries, tensions would continue to rise over several decades. Strategists in both countries increasingly considered war a distinct possibility at some point. Even the architect of Japan's conscript army in the 1870s, Yamagata Aritomo, prophesied a kind of racial Armageddon between a resurgent Japanese-led Asia and the Anglo-Saxon world.

In Asia, however, while the Qing were pursuing their last attempts at reform along lines pioneered in Japan's Meiji Constitution, the developer of that basic law was assassinated in Korea in 1909. The death of Ito Hirobumi, who had done so much to create the institutions of the Meiji Restoration and to advance Japanese interests in East Asia, now prompted the final act in the complete Japanese takeover of Korea, which was formally annexed in 1910. Japan's position in Manchuria was thus considerably strengthened. It would grow rapidly over the coming years with the abdication of the Manchu Qing, the feeble control of the new Chinese Republic, and the Warlord Era after 1916. A large amount of momentum, however, was generated by the opening of World War I.

Two years before, however, another momentous shift occurred with the death of the Meiji emperor. For the Japanese, it marked the end of an era of dizzying change, strong centralized nation-building, and an unprecedented rise from isolation and social stasis to dynamic world power. In three decades, Japan had gone from being forced to conclude unequal treaties and yielding treaty ports to Western powers, to not only reversing those treaties but also imposing them on other nations and besting a European power in modern warfare. Victorious wars, industrial development, and a standardized education system inculcating patriotic values all lent themselves to a burgeoning national self-confidence. This was abetted by reformers and revolutionaries in other Asian countries now looking to Japan as a model of wealth and power worthy of emulation—even in China and Korea, both victimized by Japan's imperial ambitions.

With the death of Meiji, however, pride in achievement was also tinged with a sense that the old order was passing and that the future of the new Japan was uncertain. One spectacular sign of unease, related memorably in Natsume Soseki's 1914 novel *Kororo*, was the suicide of General Nogi. As a young commander, Nogi had lost his flag during the Samurai Rebellion and had participated in suicidal charges attempting to redeem his honor. The emperor, considering him too valuable to

Funeral of Meiji Emperor, September 1912. It is difficult to overestimate the importance of the Meiji emperor in transforming Japan into a modern military and industrial power, and his death generated an enormous outpouring of public grief. The sense of Japan caught at this moment in the profound transition from the old order to the new—captured so vividly in Natsume Soseki's novel *Kokoro*—is on display here as officers and men of Japan's modern army line the sides of the procession, while Shinto mourners accompany the emperor's cortege.

lose, forbade him to do so, but Nogi believed that honor compelled him to not outlive his master. Moreover, he was also haunted by the frightful losses at Port Arthur—including his sons—and felt the need to atone for them. Thus, with the cannon booming a final salute to the deceased emperor, Nogi and his wife took their own lives—he by *seppuku*—ritual disembowelment. The act was presented in the samurai tradition as *junshi*—following one's master to the grave.

It was widely believed, however, that such ritual noblesse was out of step with the times. The new Japan was one increasingly dominated by political parties and Diet battles over appropriations—particularly for the military. The new emperor, Yoshihito (1879–1926), ascended the throne in July 1912, taking the reign name Taisho ("Great Righteousness"). He was, however, rather sickly, erratic in his conduct, and less than dynamic—especially compared with his father. He favored an extravagant moustache like that of Germany's Kaiser Wilhelm II, and opened the 1913 session of the Diet by rolling up the draft of his remarks and looking through it, as one would gaze through a small telescope, at the astonished legislators. Increasingly, matters of state were handled by the remaining *genro*, cabinet ministers, privy council, and political bosses. For many, this ushered in a period of drift; for many others, however, it signaled an opportunity to expand representative government in Japan. Hence, the reign is sometimes characterized as the period of **Taisho Democracy**.

The Great War and The Five Requests

With the opening of World War I on July 28, 1914, the disaster engulfing the European imperial powers represented an unprecedented opening for Japan to increase its growing hegemony in East Asia. As the war demanded increasing amounts of men and materiel, the powers drew on their own colonial armies and on recruits from the colonial populations they controlled. By the end of the war, the colonial powers on both sides had drawn perhaps as many as 4 million men for use in combat and noncombat roles from their Asian and African possessions. Moreover, as we have seen, the entry of China into the war in 1917 produced a substantial additional labor contribution. In every case, expectations were high that the contributions of these areas would achieve concrete recognition by way of increased autonomy, independence, or in the case of China, abrogation of unequal treaties and settlement of territorial claims.

A significant portion of those territorial claims were a direct consequence of Japan's entry into the war.

Yoshihito, the Taisho Emperor, as Crown Prince, 1909. The short reign of Taisho (1912–1926) was marked by a considerable liberalization of Japanese politics and, to some extent, society. The emperor's ill-health and erratic behavior increasingly left practical power in the hands of his ministers and the popular political parties. His reign saw universal manhood suffrage and the use of diplomacy to consolidate Japan's gains from World War I. However, it also witnessed the introduction of the Peace Preservation Law, widely used later on to suppress dissent.

With the 1902 treaty still in effect with Great Britain, Japan dispatched its navy and land forces to aid the Allied cause. Declaring war on Germany and Austria-Hungary in August 1914, Japanese forces secured the German concessions and naval base at Qingdao and Jiaozhou Bay by October. Along the way, the Japanese navy displayed its technological prowess by mounting what is widely considered to be the first shipborne aerial bombing mission in world history, attacking an Austro-Hungarian warship with planes launched from a seaplane tender. Within a few months, the Japanese navy had cleared the Pacific of German shipping and captured German possessions in the Marshall, Caroline, and Mariana Islands—all destined to be battle sites in World War II. In the ensuing years, Japanese vessels helped the British patrol the Mediterranean, ferried hundreds of thousands of Allied troops, and conducted anti-submarine patrols. Ironically, Japan's presence in the region as a Russian ally in the war now allowed large numbers of Russian troops to join the fight against the Central Powers on the eastern front.

Japanese Sailors Coming Ashore to Occupy Qingdao, 1914. Entering the Great War on the Allied side through its 1902 treaty with Great Britain, Japan moved swiftly to secure the German possessions in China and in the Central Pacific. Here, Japanese bluejackets—armed sailors—move ashore to join the British in a siege of the German fortress in their leasehold at Qingdao. In a battle lasting from October 31 to November 7, both sides pounded each other with heavy artillery until the Germans ran out of ammunition and surrendered. The battle marked the first use of aircraft in air–sea engagements, with planes used by the Japanese, British, and Germans.

Japanese cooperation with the Allies also allowed them the means and opportunity to advance their position in Manchuria and China largely unrestrained by foreign opposition. Thus in January 1915, the government of the aging *genro*, Okuma Shigenobu, presented the Chinese Republic of Yuan Shikai with a document most commonly known as the Twenty-One Demands, although in Japan it was called **The Five Requests**. These are explored in detail in Chapter 9. In summary, however, they demanded Japan's right of first refusal on any international financial or development schemes contemplated by China; proprietary rights to several Chinese mining operations; confirmation of Japan's place in Manchuria and control of the seized German concessions in Shandong; control of police; and effective control of Fujian Province across from Japanese-held Taiwan. The final provision was that the contents of the agreement be kept secret.

As we have seen, Yuan notified the British and American governments, prompting the British to withdraw somewhat from their close relationship with Japan. For the United States, already positioned as a supporter of republican China, the tensions with Japan increased markedly, particularly after U.S. Secretary of State William Jennings Bryan sent several frank notes to the Japanese about this violation of the Open Door policy. For their part, the Japanese dropped the harshest demands for the moment, Yuan accepted, and the Chinese mounted one of many boycotts of Japanese goods during the era.

For the Americans, however, the situation cooled down to a degree with their own entry into the war in 1917, now as an ally of Japan. In order to smooth tensions, the new U.S. secretary of state, Robert Lansing, and a Japanese special envoy, Ishii Kikujiro, signed an agreement whereby both sides pledged to uphold the Open Door policy but the United States recognized that Japan had "special interests" in China as a result of the "territorial propinquity" of its possessions. Both sides pledged in a secret protocol to not take advantage of other friendly states for the duration of the war.

Intervention and Versailles

The year 1917 marked a turning point in the war on a number of levels. Both the United States and China entered the conflict, thus making it a true world war. Russia, fielding the largest but most technologically and industrially hampered force of the major powers, collapsed in March and by November its provisional government, put in place after the tsar's abdication, fell to Bolshevik insurgents. Now a civil war among the Bolsheviks (Reds) and various "White" forces for control of the world's largest state was on, while the world war was reaching its climax. The Bolsheviks had concluded a separate peace with the Germans at Brest-Litovsk in March 1918, ceding about a third of the former Russian Empire to the Central Powers. The Allies, anxious that the caches of war supplies they had sent to Russia would fall into German hands—and with a view to aiding friendly "White" forces against the new regime—mounted an intervention to seize the materiel. France, Britain, the United States, and Japan all played a role in this Allied Intervention. For Japan, it was a welcome opportunity to move from Manchuria deep into Siberia.

Although Japanese forces did not establish any permanent bases in Siberia, they remained for nearly four years and amassed a large amount of intelligence about conditions there. Two decades later, they would attempt a more determined expansion—only to be soundly defeated by the reconstituted Red Army of the Soviet Union. With the war's end, the settling of territorial issues raised by the breakup of so many old empires occupied the attention of the victorious Allies. Buoyed by American rhetoric about "self-determination for all peoples," citizens of the colonies on both sides held out hope that this would apply to them. China, too, for its contributions expected favorable consideration of its claims on the former German concessions within its territory.

So did Japan, however. Moreover, the Japanese still smarted from British and American racism, especially as it pertained to immigration. As we noted in Chapter 9, therefore, they insisted that a racial equality clause be inserted into the covenant of the League of Nations that was being formulated as part of the peace accords. The incentive for the signatories would be Japan's relinquishing claims on the captured German concessions in Shandong. Knowing, though, that little chance existed of either Britain or the U.S. agreeing to such a provision,

ラヨヱヲエチスンクロ占領皇軍の武威全西伯利を壓す

The Japanese Army Occupies Vragaeschensk (Blagoveschchensk), 1919. The fortified border town just across the Amur River from Manchuria was a key entry point for Japanese forces during the Allied Intervention at the end of World War I. The intervention in Siberia, allegedly to protect Allied arms caches and assist the "White" or anti-Bolshevik forces, fixed the region as a goal of Japanese expansion up to World War II. Here, Japanese troops, backed by naval vessels and aircraft, secure the town as the surrendered garrison stacks arms on the right. Although the caption labels them as Bolshevik troops, some accounts insist they were members of the legendary Czech Legion stranded in Siberia.

Japan kept the territory, which precipitated the May Fourth Movement in China. Japan would ultimately sell the territory back to China as part of the Nine-Power Agreement on China in 1922 (see Map 13.2).

The enormous hope, soon to be gutted, placed on the peace and the League spurred a number of efforts at disarmament during the 1920s. The first of these, the Washington Naval Conference, took place during the winter of 1921–1922. Its chief goal was naval disarmament and limits to capital ship construction in order to prevent the kind of intense naval race that had preceded World War I. The Five-Power Treaty resulting from these talks stipulated that the United States and Britain, with their two-ocean navies, would be allowed the greatest tonnage of warships (500,000), whereas Japan would be allowed the next largest (300,000), and the smallest tonnages (175,000) would be allotted to France and Italy. Thus, Japan would be positioned to have the largest fleet in the Pacific. The agreement also allowed the island possessions held by the signatories to remain in their respective hands, but they were not to be expanded or fortified any further. A Four-Power Treaty, abrogating the 1902 Anglo-Japanese Alliance, and calling for consultation among the U.S., Britain, France, and Japan before

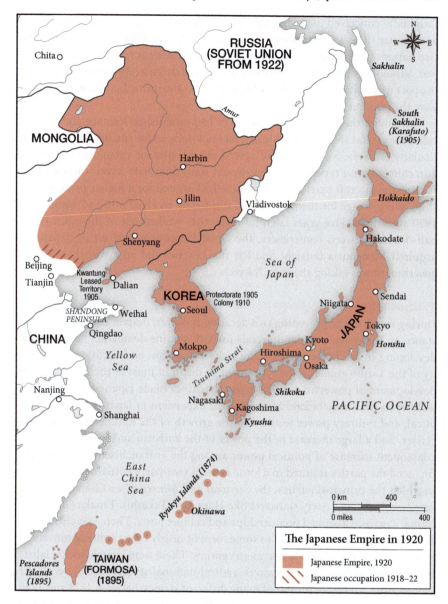

Map 13.2 The Japanese Empire in 1920

any action would be taken in East Asia, was also signed. Finally, the Nine-Power Treaty (U.S., Britain, France, Japan, Italy, Belgium, the Netherlands, Portugal, and China) guaranteed the territorial integrity of China, recognized Japan's position in Manchuria, returned the German possessions seized by Japan to China, and upheld the spirit of the Open Door.

Perhaps the high point of the peace and disarmament movement came in 1928 with the signing of the Pact of Paris or Kellogg–Briand Peace Pact.

Originally conceived as a bilateral agreement outlawing war between the U.S. and France, it was soon thrown open to include the world. In the end, sixty-two nations, including Japan, signed on to an agreement renouncing aggressive war, although permitting war in cases of national defense. As a symbolic gesture, the pact was quite dramatic. More important for the immediate future, however, were the London Naval Conferences.

Although the Washington agreement had established tonnage and number ratios for capital ships (battleships), it had not done so for smaller warships, particularly cruisers. Nor were there agreed-upon limits for submarines, maximal gun calibers, or a type of ship that would soon dominate naval warfare in the Pacific: the aircraft carrier. The Japanese had argued for a higher percentage of ships and tonnage for themselves, and ultimately received a 10 to 7 ratio in the 1930 agreement. Five years later, however, they walked out of the talks. In the half-decade between conferences, the Great Depression had set in, Japan had acquired Manchuria outright and left the League, and an avowedly militarist government was taking shape in Tokyo.

Taisho Democracy

During much of the preceding two decades, however, despite Japan's aggressive stance on the Asian mainland, trends toward genuine democracy seemed to be developing in the home islands. The lack of direction and occasional incapacity of the Taisho emperor, the retirement or death of most of the *genro*, and the development of powerful political party machines made Japanese politics more wide open than ever before. Moreover, the expansion of Japan's economic, political, and military power resulted in the growth of the middle and propertied classes, and a large increase in the power of the *zaibatsu* and their owners. The consequent increase of political power among the enfranchised and those who financed the parties resulted in a loose form of two-party parliamentary politics in which the principal parties, the *Seiyukai* and *Minseito* (see Chapter 8), alternated cabinets, and party stalwarts like Hara Kei (Takashi), Tanaka Giichi, and Inukai Tsuyoshi assumed premierships and cabinet posts. There was also a lively tier of political parties devoted to some form of nearly every political movement found elsewhere in the early twentieth century. There were anarchists, socialists, communists, populists, progressives, radical nationalists (see below), feminists, monarchists, and labor unions of many different stripes: between 1874 and 1940, there were at least twenty recognized political parties, not counting military groups and ultra-nationalist organizations like the Black Dragon Society.

Perhaps the high point of this process took place in 1925. That year, the Diet passed a bill mandating universal manhood suffrage for everyone over the age of 25. This move opened the door to political activity on an unprecedented scale and brought a brief period of mass politics to Japan before the war. The signs, however, were also present that there would be limits on this rollicking political picture. Japan's experiences on the Asian mainland and in Siberia during the Allied Intervention convinced many leaders that Japan's greatest enemy was Bolshevism. The development of the Soviet Union, Comintern, and Communist parties in the region—including in Japan itself—was considered proof that the *kokutai* needed protection from dangerous, and/or alien, ideas. Thus, the same year, 1925, saw the Peace Preservation Law enacted, which specifically barred dissent from official interpretations of the *kokutai* and the emperor's role as the center of national sovereignty, and effectively criminalized communist or socialist beliefs and activity. A branch of the secret services, the *Tokko*, made widespread use of this law, with some 70,000 mostly arbitrary arrests between 1925 and 1945. The law marked a turning point along the way of Western-inspired liberalism swinging toward militarism.

The Road to Women's Suffrage in Japan. The political scene in Japan during the era of Taisho Democracy opened up considerably and spawned a plethora of political movements, parties, and advocacy groups. Although women had campaigned for the right to vote and hold office from the Meiji period onward, only manhood suffrage was approved in the 1920s. Women were, however, given the right to assemble and form political action groups in 1921 and, as depicted above, vote in their own organizations, the most prominent of which was the Women's Suffrage League, founded in 1924. Women won the right to vote in 1946 during the initial year of the Allied Occupation.

MILITARISM AND CO-PROSPERITY: THE WAR YEARS

The death of Taisho in 1926 marked the ascension of his son Hirohito (1901–1989), whose reign would be named Showa ("Enlightened Harmony"/alternatively, "Radiant Japan"). The new emperor, born in the twentieth century, in many ways seemed to represent a new generation, one that would build on the development of Japan as a modern nation-state and empire. As crown prince, he had traveled and socialized with royal peers in Europe, golfed in Britain, and to the outside world seemed a model constitutional monarch. In many ways, however, his long reign would be the most tumultuous in Japanese history: presiding over Japan's bid for Asian and Pacific domination; weathering defeat, Occupation, and the renunciation of his unique role as a living *kami* divinity; and living to see Japan become, after the United States, the world's premier economic power.

Creating Manchukuo

The second half of the 1920s witnessed the high point of Japan's diplomatic success in establishing its place as East Asian hegemon. Already, however, there were signs of increasing assertiveness by more direct means. As we saw in Chapter 9, Japan's activities in China had lent powerful momentum to the development of Chinese Nationalism through the May Fourth Movement, the subsequent First United Front, and the Northern Expedition that had eliminated much of the warlord stranglehold and placed most of China under the control of the Guomindang. The possibility of a strong Chinese republic was met with some apprehension among the treaty powers, especially Japan, whose interests in Manchuria might well become undone if the new China decided to move in force into the region.

Crown Prince Hirohito and Princess Nagako, 1924. The long reign of the Showa Emperor Hirohito saw Japan's ultimate rise as a military power, utter defeat and Occupation, and the nation's revival to become the world's second-largest economy before his death in 1989. Princess Nagako (1903–2000), Empress Kojun, became the longest-reigning empress-consort in Japanese history. On the passing of Hirohito, she became empress dowager, a title she held until her death at the age of 97.

Although Japan's hold on the area increased considerably in the years immediately after the war and Allied Intervention, and her claims given a degree of international sanction through the Ishii–Lansing and Nine Power agreements, China's legitimate claims on the region might well supersede these. In addition, the chaotic political situation in Manchuria, in which the warlord Zhang Zuolin was a pivotal player, might take a decidedly Chinese direction if Nationalist courting of Zhang were to bear fruit. The Japanese had moved against Zhang once before, in 1917, and were not able to eliminate him. In 1928, the Japanese Kwantung Army—the forces guarding Japanese interests in Manchuria and active participants in the region's intrigue— succeeded in blowing his train up near Mukden (Shenyang). The incident resulted in international condemnation and forced the Japanese Prime Minister Tanaka Giichi to step down.

As we saw in Chapter 9, it also induced Zhang's son, "the Young Marshall," Zhang Xueliang, to quietly move into Chiang Kai-shek's Nationalist orbit.

Japan's Kwantung Army had long acted as a force unto itself in the region, propping up local warlords, eliminating others, and pursuing Japan's interests as it suited them. As with this "certain important incident in Manchuria," as it was officially termed, they were often roundly criticized by liberal politicians seeking to maintain Japan's interests in more peaceful ways. Even Hirohito was upset at Zhang's assassination and blamed Tanaka for not bringing the perpetrators to justice. For the Kwantung Army, a pliable new Manchurian warlord whom they might support was found, and for the moment, the aftermath of the incident faded into the background.

With the stock market crash in the United States in October 1929, and the onset of the Great Depression, however, matters began to heat up again. As the Depression took hold, international trade fell off dramatically as countries raised tariff barriers to protect their domestic industries. Japan, which relied heavily on its export trade for revenue and on imports of raw materials and fuels for its industries, was hit particularly hard. Like many other countries struggling to cope with the shrinking volume of world trade, it now sought to create a self-sufficient economy within its empire. Manchuria, with its vast spaces, large agricultural potential, and coal reserves, was seen as a vital economic link in this system. Politically, however, there was division in the Japanese government about what the status of Manchuria should be.

Sensing opportunity in the uncertainty following Zhang Zuolin's assassination and the Nationalists' movements in northern China, the Kwantung Army's adventurous General Ishiwara Kanji (1889–1949) and his subordinate, Colonel Itagaki Seishiro (1885–1948), plotted to seize control for Japan. As we saw in Chapter 9, without permission from either Tokyo or the Kwantung Army leadership, Ishiwara and his men created an incident near Mukden on September 18, 1931, which they used as a pretext to seize the region. His move was supported by ultra-nationalist junior officers and, presented with a successful fait accompli, the Japanese government acquiesced. To thinly legitimize the coup, they placed the last emperor of the Qing, Aisingioro Henry Puyi (1906–1967), on the throne of their newly created state of "Manchukuo."

Ishiwara in many ways is an enigmatic figure, in some respects recalling the samurai of the 1860s who styled themselves *shishi*—men of high purpose—who engaged in spectacular, violent deeds to induce action on the part of a reluctant government. Indeed, contemporary radical nationalists of the 1930s assassinated politicians on a number of occasions that they considered craven tools of the plutocrats who headed Japan's cartels or political hacks in the Western mold. These men, however, often saw themselves as fundamentally concerned with destruction as the first step toward reform. As one of the assassins of Japan's premier, Inukai Tsuyoshi, put it: "We never considered taking on the duty of construction. We foresaw, however, that once the destruction was accomplished, somebody would take charge of the construction" (De Bary, Sources of East Asian Tradition, 2008, p. 599).

Emperor Aisin Gioro Henry Puyi, ca. 1915–1920.
Certainly, few rulers were the captives of fortune to the degree of the last emperor of the Qing, Puyi (1906–1967). Enthroned as the Emperor Xuantong while a toddler, he chose the name "Henry" after his favorite English king while under the care of a Scots tutor. Under the Republic, he was allowed to live on a pension in the Forbidden City, had a second brief stint (in 1917) as emperor of an abortive Qing revival, and was expelled from Beijing as a private citizen in 1924. Living in the Japanese Concession in Tianjin, he became something of a socialite among the cosmopolitan elite, and following the Japanese takeover of Manchuria in 1931, was made chief executive of the new entity of Manchukuo, and restored again as the Kangde Emperor from 1934 until the war's end in 1945. Held by the Soviets and then repatriated to the People's Republic in 1950, he endured variations of "reform through labor." Harassed unmercifully during the Cultural Revolution, he died of kidney failure in 1967.

For Ishiwara, however, the actions in Manchuria were tinged with a kind of idealism. He shared the apocalyptic vision of an ultimate war between Asia and the West and believed Manchuria and Inner Mongolia would be vital in Japan's bid to lead a united Asia in that conflict. His plan for the new state was that it would be a model of harmony among the ethnicities inhabiting it. Japan would provide capital and leadership; Chinese, Koreans, Mongols, and Manchurians, and any Russians who had settled there would all provide labor and expertise according to their abilities. The whole would function as a kind of corporate state. Versions of this vision would be proposed later as the idealized model of the empire as **Greater East Asia Co-Prosperity Sphere**. Unfortunately for the architects of this new model state, it would never function quite as advertised. Its independence was the flimsiest of fictions, made evident to the world community in the Lytton Report on the situation for the League of Nations in 1932. Japan's response was to walk out of the League. Aside from the momentary displeasure of the League members, however, no action was taken. The premise of the League had been collective security—aggression was to be met with united action by the member states. With the most powerful members struggling to cope with the Depression, however, and the United States never joining the organization, the new order in Manchukuo stood unscathed. This did not go unnoticed in Germany and Italy, both of which would soon treat the League in similar fashion.

State Shinto and Militarism

In *Patterns of World History*, (Von Sivers, Desnoyers, and Stow) we outlined three visions of modernity that grew to dominate the approaches to government in much of the world from the 1920s to 1945. The first of these, capitalist-democracy, included the United States, France, and constitutional monarchies with universal or broad suffrage, such as Great Britain. The second was the enormous experiment under way with Marxism-Leninism in the Soviet Union. The third category we called "supremacist nationalism," and by the early 1930s, it included Nazi Germany, Fascist Italy, and Japan. In contrast to Communism, which has a relatively consistent and coherent ideology, the systems of Fascism, Nazism, and Japanese militarism were far more diffuse, cobbled together from a wide variety of sources. Each of these was forged from dissatisfaction with the directions their countries had taken after World War I. Whereas Fascism had become entrenched in Italy in the 1920s, Nazism and militarism in Japan became dominant only once the Depression hit and appeared to discredit capitalist democracy as being incapable of weathering the crisis.

Japan's swift rise to power had exacerbated cleavages in society that became increasingly evident during the period of Taisho Democracy. Rural regions had long lagged behind urban areas and remained, despite occasional populist outbursts, bastions of traditional values. These were supported by the nationalist values of the education system and the military. Military training had an air of brutality about it, particularly among junior and noncommissioned officers, who saw their duty as inculcating unswerving and unquestioned loyalty to the emperor and the military hierarchy. The military, despite the dissolution of the samurai as a class, had included a number of ex-samurai in its early leadership. Japan's armed forces thus continued the ethos of the samurai in many respects, and by the 1930s, they had informally revived some old traditions and practices.

The ascendency of political parties and the power of the moneyed classes rankled many who viewed them as representing rampant corruption and collusion at the top. At the time of change and unease about Japan's future during the interwar period, many also saw these as signs that Japan had drifted away from the uniqueness of the *kokutai*. Indeed, many regarded Japan as rapidly becoming an imitation of Western states—and a second-rate one at that. Among the most vocal and influential critics of Japan's new course was the radical nationalist Kita Ikki (1883–1937). Kita was widely read in Western socialist and other radical literature. He had been a strong supporter of the Chinese revolution in 1911 but became increasingly disillusioned by the collapse of the Chinese Republic and what he considered the weakness of Sun Yat-sen's leadership. Like many, he came to see Japan as the only hope for a resurgent Asia, and Japan in his view could only do this by successfully merging the best of Asian and Western ideas and practices. First, however, Japan had to be completely reorganized around a clear understanding of its unique *kokutai*.

In 1919, while living in Shanghai, Kita put forth his proposals in "An Outline Plan for the Reorganization of Japan" (*Nihon Kaizo Hoan Taiko*). Among other things, Kita called on the emperor to suspend the constitution for three

Radical Nationalist Kita Ikki. The great changes taking place in Japan during and after World War I proved unsettling for a number of people concerned with corruption, politicking, and a sense of social malaise. Among the most prominent was Kita Ikki (1883–1937) whose "Outline Plan for the Reorganization of Japan" called for the country to be placed under martial law while the position of Japan's unique *kokutai* was to be "clarified." By the 1930s, given the Depression and Japan's more aggressive foreign policy, Kita had attracted a following of young nationalists and officers calling themselves the Imperial Way Faction. Following an attempted coup in February 1936, the Imperial Way leaders including Kita were arrested, tried, and executed.

years and place the country under martial law so that his position in the national polity could be "clarified." All cabinet ministers, privy counselors, and other high government officials should be fired and the nation combed for talent to advise the emperor during the transition. He called for universal manhood suffrage, but not women's suffrage. He advocated a general election for a new House of Representatives in a "Reorganization Diet"; the selling off of imperial land holdings; an eight-hour workday; nationalization of industry; and radical land reform. Kita's "Outline Plan" was quietly circulated among like-minded nationalists, although it was only published after a number of editorial cuts to make it more acceptable to the censors. He later emerged at the center of a group of nationalists and military men known as the Imperial Way Faction (IWF). As with many ultra-nationalists during the 1930s, the IWF advocated direct action, a key ingredient of which was the assassination of politicians in hopes of setting events in motion to effect the hoped-for revolution. On February 26, 1936, the IWF attempted a coup and succeeded in seizing control of parts of Tokyo before the revolt was suppressed. Kita was among those tried and executed for his actions.

As the government wrestled with the Depression and rising popular discontent on the left and right, the military became increasingly central as the institution most reliably dependable in its loyalty to the imperial order. Japan's autarkic policies, consolidation of its hold on Manchukuo, and a degree of romance attached to the Kwantung Army's activities solidified the military's place in the national consciousness. This tendency was abetted further by what is sometimes called "State Shinto." It is often said that Shinto itself is not really a religion as commonly understood in the West, but rather a "super-religious" framework of understanding the world and the cosmos and the place of human beings in it. With the Meiji Restoration, a renewed emphasis on the special status of the emperor in this vision was promulgated in the education system, reinforced by the ideology of Japan's unique *kokutai* and unbroken line of divine rulers. State subsidies were given to Shinto shrines, which were required to promote this official vision; others subsisted on private donations. The late 1920s and 1930s, with their upsurge of nationalism, placed renewed emphasis on this system to the point where shrines not supported by the government were banned and those using them subject to persecution. Thus, state and religious ideology reinforced each other in the service of strengthening nationalism.

The change in ideological atmosphere of the 1930s was put on dramatic display by the experience of Minobe Tatsukichi (1873–1948). For thirty years, he had been Japan's leading jurist and constitutional theorist, whose decades of work at Tokyo Imperial University were celebrated not just in Japan but among scholars throughout the world. Such was his prestige that he had received a noble rank and occupied a seat in the Diet's upper body, the House of Peers. In February 1934, his fellow peer, Baron Kikuchi Takeo, publicly denounced Minobe's famous "organ theory." Decades earlier, Minobe had posited that the relationship of the emperor to the constitution was one in which the emperor was an "organ" of the state. More than a generation of Japanese lawyers and scholars had internalized and practiced law according to what had been this almost universally accepted precept. Now, however, Minobe stood accused of belittling the emperor's role in the *kokutai*.Minobe defended his position, saying that the emperor as an organ of the state simply means that he rules for the state and not for himself. Following more attacks in the Diet, Minobe resigned from his position, narrowly escaped being tried for his views, and was nearly assassinated in 1936. For their part, the cabinet banned his works from study or circulation.

By 1940, the stalemate in China had reached the point that the government of Prince Konoe Fumimaro (1891–1945) announced sweeping changes designed to streamline government control and introduce a new national structure (*shin taisei*). In August, the political parties in the Diet dissolved themselves in a bid to demonstrate the end of politics as usual. In a manner reminiscent of Fascist and Nazi pronouncements, the new order expressly rejected "the old party politics predicated upon liberalism," in favor of "concentration of all the forces and resources of the nation." It was to be a national movement standing above parties and all rival factions "uniting all in public service" (De Bary, 2008, p. 621). In a radio address one month later, Prince Konoe explained the formation and rationale of a new national political organization, the Imperial Rule Assistance Association, which would, in effect, create one-party rule in Japan. The new structure was meant to quell factionalism and dissent, replacing it with "the perfection of a political system founded on the principle of unity of subject and sovereign" (De Bary, 2008, p. 621).

The "China Incident"

As we saw in Chapter 9, Japan faced a government in China in the 1930s attempting to complete national unification, but locked in a continual civil war between Chiang Kai-shek's Nationalists and Mao Zedong's Communists. For the Japanese, this interval was one in which they consolidated their hold on Manchuria/Manchukuo, made inroads into Inner Mongolia, and extended their influence steadily toward Beiping (the new name for Beijing after Nanjing became the Nationalist capital). By the time of the Xi'an Incident in December 1936, Japanese forces operating under the rubric of keeping order among the remaining independent warlords on the periphery of their occupied territory had moved into the suburbs of Beiping. There, they were confronted by Nationalist units and both sides fitfully observed a shaky truce.

The new United Front of 1937 brought renewed speculation and anxiety for Japanese military and civilian leadership. Most Japanese strategic planners had long given up the idea that a strong China would be a good partner in building a united Asia. Japan's expansion had largely been premised on creating a powerful Japanese-led bloc of states to stand against Western encroachment and perhaps even general war. Moreover, the Depression had reinforced the economics of autarky and provided a model in Manchuria for handling the organization of a united Asia. Thus, a China united under the Nationalists would be an enormous obstacle to Japanese hegemony and leadership in its bid for an "Asia for the Asiatics."

Thus, as we have seen, the Marco Polo Bridge affair in July 1937 was a kind of preemptive general offensive to force Chiang to terms before he could fully bring his armies to bear on the Japanese in North China. The experience of Japan's armies in 1894–1895, Chiang's lack of success against Mao's forces, the perception of Nationalist weakness at the core, and widespread discontent with the regime convinced Japanese planners that they could win a quick war with a determined all-out effort. A long war, however, would soon bleed Japan's manpower and resources. Thus, a centerpiece of Japanese strategy was to cow the civilian population in order to induce a quick surrender. Although the miniscule and obsolescent Chinese air force was largely destroyed in the opening days of the war, they actually managed the first raid on Japanese territory, hitting bases on Taiwan. The far larger and more technologically advanced Japanese army and naval air arms, however, attacked Chinese cities virtually unopposed. Their monopoly on the skies would last until late 1941 when Chiang hired the American Volunteer Group—better known as the Flying Tigers—to provide a degree of air defense. The Japanese navy, with its large capital ship force, provided powerful cover for Japanese coastal landings, while superior Japanese mobility on the ground managed to repeatedly flank Nationalist defensive lines and fixed positions. The climax of this offensive as the first step in what the Japanese officially called the China Incident, as we saw, was the enormous carnage of the Rape of Nanking in December 1937 (see Map 13.3).

While the city was being conquered and occupied, the chaos within its walls and in the surrounding area generated two widely reported incidents that considerably ratcheted up tensions between the United States and Japan. American and British gunboats had been stationed in the Yangzi near Nanjing to evacuate foreign nationals and aid refugees as best as they could. On December 12, Japanese planes attacked and sank the U.S. gunboat *Panay*. They also sank several Standard Oil Company tankers that had taken refugees aboard. The Japanese swiftly apologized for the attack, saying that it had been a case of mistaken identity; the presence of large, easily visible American flags painted on the *Panay's* deck, however, makes this explanation unlikely. Recent revelations about American decryption of coded Japanese radio messages confirmed that the attacks had been deliberate,

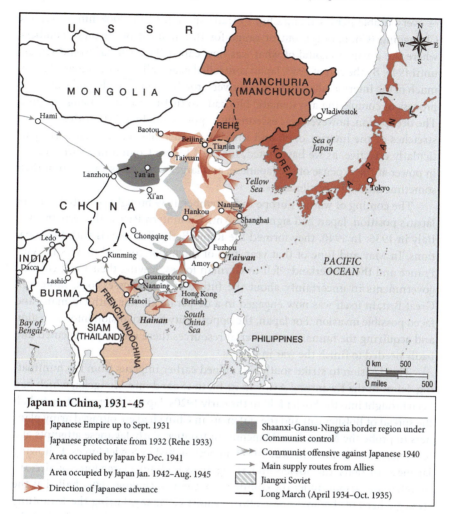

Map 13.3 Japan in China, 1931–1945

possibly authorized by junior commanders who were most active in the massacre in the city. A detachment of Japanese soldiers also attacked and looted the U.S. consulate, hitting the consul himself in the face, and raising tensions even further.

For the Roosevelt administration, Chiang's regime had increasingly been seen as a democratizing force in Asia, and the American connections and Christianity of Madam Chiang and her sisters adduced as proof that a modernizing China was now fighting democracy's battle against the brutal forces of totalitarian militarism. Japan's strategy played directly into this perspective: in one famous newsreel sequence, the camera pans around the widespread destruction in Shanghai, and zooms in on a naked infant crying by a bombed out railyard, while Madam Chiang intones in mellifluous English, "Death comes from the clear blue skies. . . ."

Japanese forces made further landings over the next year, while the remnants of Chiang's army and millions of refugees fled west, stripping the country of every usable item. Chiang's bid to trade space for time took him to remote Chongqing (Chungking), out of range for the moment of Japanese bombers, where the wartime capital of what was now called "Free China" would remain until 1945. By the end of 1938, Japan controlled nearly all of China's coastal cities, much of the interior adjacent to major rivers, roads, and railroads, and was in the process of completing a systematic blockade to further isolate Chiang's regime. The occupation, however, was essentially a "points and lines" affair that left vast stretches of the interior open and inviting to guerrilla activity. This was particularly effective, as we have noted, for the Chinese Communists, who waxed in power at the expense of the Japanese, and largely enjoyed isolation from their sometime allies, the Nationalists.

The coming of war in Europe in September 1939 brought potential help for Japan's position. Japan had signed the Anti-Comintern Pact with Germany and Italy in 1936. In 1940, they formed the Rome-Berlin-Tokyo axis with those nations. In May and June of that year, two of the major colonial powers in Asia, France and the Netherlands, fell to German forces, leaving their weak colonial governments in uncertainty about the future of these possessions. Moreover, Great Britain itself was now engaged in a desperate air war with Germany and faced possible invasion. For Japan, the opportunity for expansion into the region and acquiring the human and material resources there was unprecedented and badly needed to finish the war in China.

The decision to strike south had gained earlier impetus from the humiliating defeat of the Kwantung Army in its bit to expand into Mongolia, which had been brought into the Soviet fold in the early 1920s. Japan's determination to halt the spread of Bolshevism and the stalemate in China had encouraged army planners to probe the Mongolian/Manchurian frontier. Early Japanese attempts at a reconnaissance in force in May 1939 had been halted by Soviet forces. Following Japanese air raids, the Soviets and Mongolians built up a large force of aircraft, infantry, and armor under the command of Georgy Zhukov—later hailed as the strategic hero of the Soviet war effort against Germany. Luring the Kwantung Army into a trap at Khalkin Gol in late summer, Soviet tanks outflanked the Japanese and utterly crushed them. Estimates of Japanese losses run as high as 75 percent in a battle involving over 100,000 men and more than 1,000 tanks and planes. For Stalin, the results helped in his efforts to secure the nonaggression pact with Germany; the vast reserves he built up in Siberia were later used to crucial advantage in the desperate battles against the German invasion after 1941.

The move south began with strong-arming the Vichy-controlled French colonial regime in Indochina to allow Japan to use air and naval bases there. They would soon be in de facto control of the colony, leaving the French to run it until March 1945. In addition to providing Japan with much needed oil, rubber, tin, and rice, control of the region helped seal off South China from resupply— a strategy that would be complete with the occupation of Burma the following year. The move south, however, was also risky in several respects. It raised tensions with Britain, which, although at war with Germany and Italy, was not yet at war with Japan. It put the Dutch East Indies, technically now controlled by the German-occupied Netherlands, in an anomalous position. Perhaps most crucially, the strategy moved Japan closer to a confrontation with the United States because of American control of the Philippines. For its part, the U.S. had begun to introduce sanctions on strategic exports to Japan. The American position was that Japan should immediately withdraw from China and abandon its expansionist policies, a position that, obviously, Japan was not willing or able to fulfill.

As the war in Europe now moved to the east with the German offensive against the Soviet Union in June 1941, and nearly all of Western Europe secure under Nazi and Fascist control, the time seemed opportune to make the move to secure the resources of all of Southeast Asia. With the signing of a treaty with Vichy France granting Japan essential control of Vietnam, the United States applied additional pressure by freezing Japanese assets and banning oil exports to Japan. With limited reserves and growing American resolve to oppose further Japanese expansion, the plan to launch a surprise offensive in the Pacific, cripple the power of the United States to retaliate, and seize the Philippines to push American influence from the region was thus conceived.

The Japanese position was one of mounting frustration with what they perceived as American intransigence on pivotal issues and provocation through sanctions. Through the spring of 1941, talks continued with the United States, but American insistence on Japanese withdrawal from their gains since 1937 and nonrecognition of the Japanese-supported Wang Jingwei government in Nanjing proved to be essential stumbling blocks. Further difficulties arose from the U.S.'s close ties with Britain, and the perception that they were engineering a cordon of "ABCD countries"—America, Britain, China, the Dutch—designed to thwart further Japanese expansion in the area. By November, the plans for war with the U.S. were being pursued simultaneously with a desperate final attempt at talks by two Japanese special envoys in Washington. With the U.S. holding firm to its position, the decision was reached on December 1, 1941, to launch the attack, barring any eleventh-hour breakthroughs.

As U.S. President Franklin Roosevelt put it to Congress in his war message of December 8, "Japan has therefore undertaken a surprise offensive throughout the Pacific area." Indeed, through a variety of ignored and misinterpreted warnings, disregarding of years of war gaming and strategic planning, and of what in retrospect seemed a tragically negligent failure of imagination, American forces were caught utterly unprepared at Pearl Harbor and in air raids on Philippine bases. Attacks were carried out against British possessions in Malaya, against the Dutch East Indies, and against the American outposts in the Central Pacific at Guam and Wake Island. Although many Japanese leaders were flushed with victory in these opening days of the war, others took a more measured approach to the situation. Perhaps the most sober analysis came from the architect of the Pearl Harbor attack, Admiral Isoroku Yamamoto (1884–1943) himself. As one who had spent time in the United States, studying at Harvard and the Naval War College, and as a naval attaché in Washington, D.C., Yamamoto had seen firsthand the vast material strength of the United States and realized that Japan's prospects in taking on the United States and Britain while heavily committed

The Sinking of the Battleship *Arizona* during the Attack on Pearl Harbor, December 7, 1941.
Japan's desperate gamble to "strike south" to obtain resources for its war effort began
with the drive to cripple the U.S. Pacific Fleet based at Pearl Harbor, Hawaii. The attack was
accompanied by strikes on the Philippines, Malaya, Wake Island, and several other points
in the Southwest Pacific. Although conquering the Philippines, Singapore, Malaya, and the
Dutch East Indies, the gamble did not induce the Allies to come to terms with Japan in the
region, but instead drove the United States into a commitment to total war. Although many
of the ships sunk or crippled in the Pearl Harbor attack were raised and repaired, the *Arizona*
was fatally damaged and to this day remains a memorial to the attack in its final resting
place in the harbor.

in China were not bright. As he bluntly told Prince Konoe, "In the first six to
twelve months of war with the United States and Great Britain I will run wild
and gain victory after victory. But then, if the war continues after that, I have no
expectation of success." As it happened, he was right on both counts; he paid for
his gamble with his own life. Having decrypted his inspection itinerary in April
1943, the Americans sent long-range P-38 "Lightning" fighter planes to ambush
his bomber transport and shot it down.

World War II in the Pacific

From January to June 1942, however, Japanese forces did indeed run wild. In
turn, they overcame American resistance on Guam and, after a sharp fight, Wake
Island. They swiftly landed troops at several points on the Malayan Peninsula
and sunk Britain's two capital ships in the region, *Prince of Wales* and *Repulse*.

Through the use of highly mobile bicycle troops, they repeatedly outflanked the British and Indian troops' fixed defensive lines in Malaya and, in February 1942, forced the surrender of the great naval base at Singapore, Britain's "Gibraltar of the East." Having secured Hong Kong and forced the cooperation of Thailand, Japanese forces then drove British, Indian, American, and Chinese forces from Burma—closing the Burma Road, the last overland supply route to China. For most of the remainder of the war, China was to be dangerously and inadequately resupplied by air over the Himalayas. The shocked, poorly supplied, and under-manned "ABCD" forces in the Dutch East Indies offered only token resistance before retreating to Australia and India to recover and regroup.

The Philippines defenders gave a rather better account of themselves. Despite having lost the bulk of their air cover in the opening days of the war, the "Filamer-ican" troops fought a stubborn rear-guard action on Luzon against a Japanese force several times their size. Their commander, Douglas MacArthur, declared Manila an open city and retreated to prepared defenses on the Bataan Peninsula backed up by the island fortress of Corregidor. Unfortunately, American strate-gic planners decided to give up the Philippines and left the defenders to fight on as best they could; for his part, MacArthur was ordered to Australia. Haunted by leaving his men to their fate, MacArthur famously proclaimed, "I shall return." Two and a half years later, he did. In the meantime, the defenders of Bataan sur-rendered in April and Corregidor surrendered soon after in May. The defenders were then subjected to the infamous "Bataan Death March" to a prison camp 70 miles distant. Along the way, the weak, thirsty, starving, and infirm were ruthlessly beaten, bayonetted, shot, and beheaded. As in other parts of their new possessions, the conquerors were anxious to show the people that their former colonial masters had been thoroughly bested by fellow Asians. Japan's new south-ern empire now extended from the Indian border through the Dutch East Indies, to the South Pacific Islands girding Australia, and as far east as Wake Island in the Central Pacific. In the coming months, they would even establish a toehold in North America in the Aleutian Islands (see Map 13.4).

Allied Counterattack

Japan's astonishing advances in the Pacific and in Southeast Asia swiftly de-bunked prewar caricatures of their armed forces as being imitative and techno-logically deficient. Indeed, Japan's innovations in jungle warfare, the manifest superiority of their naval air forces—particularly the maneuverability and dog-fighting abilities of their frontline fighter, the Mitsubishi A6-M1, known to the world as the "Zero," and the coordination of their offensives—now created a ste-reotype of the Japanese as supermen imbued with samurai invincibility. This stereotype, too, would now be sorely tested in the second half of 1942.

In the opening months of the war, Allied planners had made the momentous decision to place their maximum efforts toward the defeat of Germany and Italy, and fight holding actions in the Pacific until sufficient forces could be marshalled to go on the offensive. Thus, the few American aircraft carrier task forces avail-able mounted largely inconsequential raids on Japanese-held islands to put them

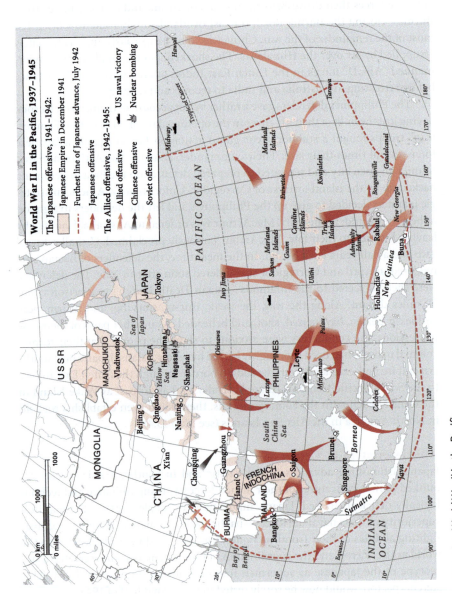

Map 13.4 World War II in the Pacific

on notice that the U.S. would not seek terms, intending instead to prosecute the war. More daring, and disconcerting for the Tojo government, was the famous **Doolittle Raid** in April 1942. Casting about for a way to aim a blow quickly at Japan, the U.S. army and navy improvised a carrier force that launched Army Air Force medium bombers that raided Tokyo, Kobe, Osaka, and several other Japanese cities. The raid did little damage and the planes, launched prematurely owing to fear of discovery, all failed to land in their assigned fields in China. The psychological impact, however, was considerable. It drove home to officials of the Japanese government the message that their citizens were potentially vulnerable even in the empire's heartland, and they swiftly took steps to enhance the air defenses of the home islands. They also moved against the areas in China where the raiders were supposed to have landed.

Despite the unmistakable response from the United States that it would fight on, plans for continued offensives went ahead. In early May, a Japanese task force was sent to take the Allied base at Port Moresby on the side of Papua New Guinea facing Australia. In response, the Americans sent a carrier task force in an attempt to disrupt the invasion. The resulting **Battle of the Coral Sea** in many ways set the tone for much of the subsequent naval warfare in the Pacific Theater. For the first time in history, a sea battle was fought in which the ships never came in contact with each other. In fact, they remained about 200 miles apart. The entire engagement was fought from the air. In material terms, the result was a draw, with both sides losing one aircraft carrier and having a second carrier sustain heavy damage. Strategically, however, it was a considerable setback for Japan in that the invasion had to be cancelled.

Even earlier, it had become apparent to Japanese planners that the remnants of the American Pacific Fleet, especially the aircraft carriers, had to be destroyed if they were to have any hope of bringing Washington to the bargaining table. Thus, an elaborate plan was laid to invade the American base at Midway Island, which, as the forward post for U.S. naval and air operations, the Americans would be obligated to defend. By bringing overwhelming strength to bear on the island while luring part of the American force north to contest a simultaneous Japanese landing in the Aleutians, the dual objectives of taking the island and eliminating American resistance in the Pacific would be accomplished. The U.S., it was believed, concentrating with Britain on Germany, would then deem it too costly to contest Japan's Asian and Pacific hegemony.

Unknown to the Japanese, however, American cryptographers had broken not only Japanese diplomatic codes, but also their principal naval operations code. By sending bogus messages and hearing them referenced in Japanese naval radio traffic, the Americans were able to determine that Midway was the immediate target. They thus beefed up the island's air and ground defenses and sent nearly all their remaining carrier strength to attempt to ambush the Japanese task force. The ensuing battle, it may be fairly said, was where Admiral Yamamoto's prediction proved prescient. Having found the Japanese fleet, the Americans launched attacks from land-based planes to little effect, while Japanese raids on the island did considerable damage. The U.S. carrier-based aircraft, however, had an incredible stroke of luck and took full advantage of it. A bootless, uncoordinated attack by American torpedo bombers alerted the Japanese that the American carrier force was on the scene. As they fueled and armed their planes on the carrier flight decks, American dive bombers, previously lost trying to locate the Japanese fleet, suddenly showed up and attacked to devastating effect. Three of the four Japanese carriers were sunk immediately and the remaining one was heavily damaged and later sunk. Japan lost a crippling 322 planes and about 5000 crewmen. The Japanese managed to sink an American carrier, but the invasion once again had to be cancelled. In one climactic battle in the first week of June 1942, Japan lost its initiative and the bulk of its naval air power. From this point on, American forces would move from defensive measures to a rapidly intensifying offensive strategy. As for production, Japan would build seven more aircraft carriers; the United States would build eleven times that number.

U.S. Dive Bombers in Action during the Battle of Midway, June 1942. The epic Battle of Midway, June 4–6, 1942, is generally seen as a key turning point in the Pacific War. The Japanese task force was sent to invade the island and force the depleted U.S. Navy into a decisive battle. During the battle, squadrons of American torpedo bombers without fighter support were shot to pieces in a fruitless attack on the Japanese fleet. In an incredible stroke of luck, the American dive bombers (pictured above), at first unable to find the Japanese fleet, appeared just in time to catch the Japanese aircraft carriers re-arming and fueling their planes on deck. Within minutes, the dive bomber attack fatally crippled three of the four carriers and destroyed the majority of Japanese planes and pilots. From this point on, Japan was never able to mount an effective offensive in the Pacific, and the momentum permanently shifted to the United States and its Allies.

The extent of the defeat at Midway was withheld from the Japanese public for the moment. Meanwhile, plans moved forward to complete occupation of the Solomon Islands, anchored by the large forward base at Rabaul, that would continue the encirclement of Australia. It was here, however, that U.S. planners decided to launch their first offensive to counter the Japanese drive. The island chosen became the site of some of the most bitterly contested combat of the Pacific War: Guadalcanal.

The Japanese strategy of occupying numerous island strongholds to create an impenetrable defensive perimeter for the empire presented their opponents with a number of problems, not least of which was how to get close enough to the home islands to put them within bombing range. Moreover, with Japan's control of the region's airspace and still considerable naval power, how could the Allies disrupt the empire's supply routes? American naval planners wanted to bypass the most powerful bases and move as quickly as possible to possess islands within bombing range of Japan. The army, under MacArthur, however, believed that it was vital for the U.S. to return to the Philippines along the way. A compromise solution of "island hopping" was therefore worked out: the strongest Japanese bases would be bypassed and neutralized by occupying nearby islands and using them as airbases from which to harass Japanese supply routes, as U.S. forces leapfrogged toward Japan through the various island chains guarding it. MacArthur's forces would then wind their way through New Guinea and up into the Philippines in an inner prong of the Pacific offensive. The China-Burma-India Theater would be supplied as much as possible, and Chinese units would undergo American training. The first test of the island-hopping strategy was Guadalcanal.

Japanese engineers were in the process of building an airfield on the island when U.S. Marines landed there in August 1942. They drove off the Japanese, finished the airfield, and soon began establishing their own base in earnest. Japanese commanders, however, recognized that if they could defeat the Americans here, it might upset their entire strategy for the area. Thus, they committed sizable forces to driving the Americans from the island. Continual nighttime naval engagements took place, as well as daytime air raids, and larger and larger troop commitments were made to push out the U.S. forces. It was only in early 1943 that the Americans declared the island secure. By that time, the drive continued into the Caroline and Marshall Islands, and Japanese forces were in retreat on New Guinea.

Co-Prosperity and Conditional Independence

As the Japanese Empire expanded to include much of East Asia, Southeast Asia, and most of the islands in the Southwest Pacific, the government of General Hideki Tojo (1941–1944), who now presided over the prime minister's office as well as the military ministries, began to pursue its plans for decoupling the peoples within its domains from Western colonialism. As we have seen, the model for this vision of a Japanese-led "Asia for the Asiatics" was Manchukuo. Thus, in January 1942, Japan's Total War Research Institute released its "Draft Plan for the

Establishment of the Greater East Asia Co-Prosperity Sphere (GEACPS)," which reads in part:

> The states, their citizens, and resources, comprised in those areas pertaining to the Pacific, Central Asia, and the Indian Ocean formed into one general union are to be established as an autonomous zone of peaceful living and common prosperity on behalf of the peoples of the nations of East Asia. The area including Japan, Manchuria, North China, the lower Yangtze River, and the Russian Maritime Provinces, forms the nucleus of the East Asiatic Union. The Japanese Empire possesses a duty as the leader of the East Asiatic Union. The above purpose presupposes the inevitable emancipation or independence of Eastern Siberian, China, Indo-China, the South Seas, Australia, and India.

> [From Ryusaku Tsunoda, Donald Keene, and William Theodore De Bary, *Sources of Japanese Tradition*, Vol. 2 (New York: Columbia University Press, 1964) p. 294.]

The Draft Plan also presupposed that Japan would win the war. Until such time, those within the GEACPS were to strain all human and material efforts toward victory. Among other programs in this vein were the wholesale drafting of Koreans and Taiwanese to serve in Japan's armed forces, with many women, especially from Korea, held in military brothels as "comfort women"; forced labor brigades of prisoners of war and local people; and requisition of food and natural resources for the war effort. In the spirit of Western decolonization, volunteers and conscripts were also sought among Indians, Chinese, Vietnamese, Burmese, Malayans, and Filipinos to form units to fight for Japan. The largest and most noteworthy of these was the Indian National Army led by the revolutionary, Subhas Chandra Bose, which spearheaded the Imphal invasion of the Indian province of Assam in 1944.

To convince the empire's peoples of the sincerity of Japan in organizing the GEACPS, a conference was held in Tokyo in November 1943, at which the leaders of occupied territories and collaborationist governments were offered nominal independence and constitutions carefully crafted to reflect their place within the larger cooperative entity. Most remained politely noncommittal, especially since America's putative war aims included moving to end colonialism—although this enthusiasm was not shared by the British, Dutch, or Free French. As events unfolded, however, the Japanese in many cases offered material aid to local independence fighters at the end of the war as a last-ditch effort to frustrate the Allied victors.

Endgame

As we saw earlier, the war in China against the Nationalists, despite continual American efforts to prod Chiang Kai-shek into action, remained largely stalemated. There were periodic overtures from Wang Jingwei's collaborationist government and even from the Japanese, but these were, for the most part, not seriously entertained. The Communists in the north, however, took full advantage of the yawning gaps in Japan's "points and lines" approach and extended their reach throughout the war. Although the Allies saw little gain in the

Kamikaze Attacks on the USS *Bunker Hill*, May 11, 1945. By early 1945, American B-29 bombers were within range of targets in Japan itself and had begun a campaign of systematically fire-bombing Japanese cities. As part of the effort to close the island ring around Japan's home islands, American forces had taken Iwo Jima and were fighting a bloody battle to secure Okinawa. Japan's air forces had been devastated to the point where many remaining planes and pilots were organized into "Special Attack Units," more popularly known to the world as *kamikaze*, named for the "divine wind" that had saved Japan from Mongol invasion in the thirteenth century. Despite formidable fighter and anti-aircraft defenses, enough bomb-laden suicide planes made it through to take a heavy toll on American ships. Here, the aircraft carrier USS *Bunker Hill* receives the second of two near-simultaneous kamikaze hits. The ship remained afloat and was eventually repaired, but more than 500 men were killed or wounded in the attacks.

China-Burma-India Theater, it had the effect of holding down about 2 million Japanese troops, and China would also be the initial staging ground for the first air campaign against the Japanese home islands. In the summer of 1944, Japanese forces launched their last major campaigns in China, moving toward Guilin and driving American air units from bases in unoccupied eastern China. Although these raised considerable Allied concern about the viability of Chiang's forces, they did relatively little to alter the course of the war.

Throughout 1943 and 1944, the immense material might and technological skill of the American forces in the Pacific increasingly pressed the Japanese Empire. The bypassed island strongholds Japan had relied on were left to "die on the vine" as their supply lines were squeezed by Allied submarines and aircraft. The impressive performance of the Japanese "Zero" was soon matched and surpassed by new generations of American land and carrier-based fighters.

American forces overwhelmed Japanese garrisons in the Aleutians, and in the Marshall, Caroline, and Mariana islands, while the dwindling power of the Japanese naval and air forces was reduced with each passing month. In October 1944, MacArthur returned to the Philippines. In an all-out effort to stop the invasion, Japanese forces attempted to draw the supporting American fleet away from the invasion beaches, while sending in most of their remaining battle fleet to attack the landing zone. The resulting Battle of Leyte Gulf was the largest naval engagement in world history—and included one of the two largest battleships the world had ever seen, Japan's *Yamato*. In the end, however, Japan's surface fleet was essentially destroyed.

The following month saw the first sustained air raids on Japan. The new American long-range B-29 bombers now flew from airfields on the freshly captured Mariana Islands, which would provide the principal bases for the remainder of the American bombing campaign. As the campaign proceeded, damaged American planes soon required emergency landing fields as well as bases from which fighter escorts could be flown. Thus, in what many scholars view as the climax of the Pacific War, the island strongholds of Iwo Jima (February 1945) and Okinawa (April 1945) were invaded. Iwo Jima was a sulfurous rock, honeycombed with caves, and heavily fortified. It was taken but at enormous cost. Okinawa, much larger and with a considerable civilian population, was the site of an even bloodier conflict, with over 77,000 Japanese and 14,000 Allied soldiers killed. Estimates of civilian deaths run from 40,000 to as many as 150,000—about half of the pre-invasion population of the island.

As American naval forces closed in on Japan, the dwindling supply of Japanese planes and pilots were increasingly used as kamikaze: loaded with as many explosives as possible, their mission was to crash into American vessels and create carnage reminiscent of the "divine wind" that had devastated the Mongol fleets in 1281. Despite dense American anti-aircraft fire and fighter cover, many kamikaze pilots found their marks and took a considerable toll on U.S. warships. The devastation now rocking Japan's cities, however, was infinitely worse.

Frustrated by fierce jet streams in their initial high-altitude raids and the fact that, unlike the large factory complexes that provided high-value targets in Europe, much of Japanese industry was widely dispersed as a defensive measure, the Americans adopted a devastating new tactic. Instead of high-explosive ordnance, the B-29s would now fly at low altitude at night and drop thousands of small napalm canisters on Japanese cities. The resulting firestorms—thermal tornadoes whose intense heat and powerful drafts make firefighting all but impossible—reduced Japan's cities to rubble over the spring and summer of 1945. In the opening raid on Tokyo in March 1945 alone, 15 to 16 square miles of the city were destroyed and more than 100,000 people killed; countless more were made homeless. By August, the Americans were running out of viable targets and debate over how to force surrender—which the Allies had resolved must be "unconditional"—was vigorously waged. The battles on Iwo and especially Okinawa convinced many among the American leadership that an invasion of Japan would be unbearably costly. As we saw in the opening vignette, the development of the atomic bomb—as well as the Soviet declaration of war on Japan—ultimately cut that debate short. In both Japan and the U.S., however, its use continues to be a matter of fraught debate and at the center of a pervasive attitude among generations of Japanese that they were also victims of the war. As interesting signs of movement toward a more conciliatory perspective on both sides, U.S. President Barack Obama visited Hiroshima in May 2016 and embraced survivors of the attack, although he pointedly refused to apologize for it. As for the Japanese, Prime Minister Yoshida quietly visited the site as early as 1951; Emperor Akihito had planned to visit it in 1994 but decided not to because of protests from nationalist groups in Japan. Japanese Prime Minister Shinso Abe visited Pearl Harbor in 2016 but, like the U.S. president, offered no apology for the attack.

With no recourse but agreement to Allied terms as outlined in the Potsdam Declaration, uncertain about the status of the emperor or *kokutai*, and the prospect of Occupation for the first time in its history, Japanese military and civilian representa-

Supreme Commander of Allied Powers, General Douglas MacArthur, Opens the Surrender Ceremony aboard the battleship *Missouri*, September 2, 1945. Following the atomic bombings of Hiroshima and Nagasaki, and the Soviet Union's declaration of war on Japan in early August, Emperor Hirohito delivered his historic surrender address that officially ended the fighting. The surrender ceremony depicted here was conducted by MacArthur in the name of all United Nations (Allied Forces) at war with Japan, of whom representatives from the U.S., Great Britain, France, the Soviet Union, Canada, Australia, New Zealand, the Netherlands, and China may be seen surrounding him. The Japanese representatives stood to the right (not shown in this photo). Significantly, the American flag in the background was that carried by Commodore Perry in 1853 on his mission to establish relations with Japan.

tives signed the "instrument of surrender," with General MacArthur presiding aboard the American battleship *Missouri* in Tokyo Bay on September 2, 1945. What happened next would be the wholesale reinvention of the Japanese polity during an Occupation that would last seven years. In the ensuing decades, Japan would swiftly re-emerge into a stunningly powerful economic entity, for years second only to the United States. And, uniquely among the world's nations, it would do it with a constitutional provision banning armed forces as generally understood.

THE MODEL OF MODERNITY:
FROM OCCUPATION TO THE PRESENT

As has often been noted, the Japan that presented itself to the General MacArthur as Supreme Commander Allied Forces (SCAP) and the first waves of Occupation forces was that of a nation reduced to the barest essentials. A barely functional government had been set up to oversee the initial stage of the Occupation, and the people were enjoined to "endure the unendurable." There was virtually no resistance to the Occupation forces, who themselves were remarkably restrained in their behavior compared to the expectations of the Japanese—and the experiences of surrendering Japanese troops in other areas of the empire. The caretaker government sought to drive home the poverty and extent of the destruction by providing the SCAP with a charcoal-powered car—as testimony to the lack of gasoline in the country. Thus, one of the first orders of business was simply providing enough food for the populace to get through the fall and winter of 1945–1946.

The New Order: Reform and Constitution

The personnel supervising the Occupation included many who had been active in reform and New Deal programs in the United States and were therefore anxious to implement similar reforms in Japan. Despite an immense Allied intelligence effort during the war and the influence of such works as anthropologist Ruth Benedict's study of Japan, **The Chrysanthemum and the Sword**, there were relatively few among the Occupiers with deep expertise in Japanese language, history, or politics. This coupled with the essential *carte blanche* enjoyed by SCAP encouraged wholesale experimentation in what is today called "nation-building" on a scale never before seen—even at the same time in Occupied Germany. By the fall of 1945, directives were flowing down from SCAP freeing political prisoners—including socialists and communists—breaking up the *zaibatsu* cartels and encouraging market competition; mandating the founding of unions, women's rights, and female suffrage; and democratizing the education system.

The issue of the status of the emperor, which had been a major reason for Japan's refusal to come to terms to end the war, was now also a point of contention among the Allies. Many in the United States wanted and expected Hirohito to be indicted as a war criminal; the governments of China, Australia, and the Philippines also expected him to face a similar fate. MacArthur, however, believed that retaining the emperor as a figurehead constitutional monarch and shielding him from the upcoming war crimes tribunals would be useful in his efforts to remake Japan along democratic and peaceful lines. For his part, Hirohito adapted himself to his new role with alacrity, renouncing his divinity, dressing in business suits, touring the country, and allowing himself to be photographed with MacArthur physically towering over him. As a subtle symbolic gesture, he also replaced his bust of Napoleon with one of Abraham Lincoln.

At the same time, reforming the emperor-centered Meiji Constitution was a top priority. The caretaker government of Shidehara Kijuro (1872–1951) was therefore tasked with putting together a new document, but because this document was little different than the existing constitution, the Americans secretly drafted their own version of what SCAP expected in a remarkable six days. In February 1946, SCAP presented the American version to the Japanese representatives, who were aghast at how thoroughly it had been changed. As one remarked, "We have been basking in the atomic sunshine. . . ." Ultimately, the newly formed Diet—which now included a substantial number of women representatives—approved the replacement constitution with minor changes; it has remained the fundamental law of Japan to the present. The document contains a number of provisions considered progressive by contemporary standards, in some cases exceeding those contained in the U.S. Constitution: equality of the sexes in all institutions, the right to an education—and the obligation to educate boys and girls— the right to "minimum standards of wholesome and cultured living"; the right to work and of workers to organize; the right of academic freedom. More controversial was the most well-known provision, Article 9:

First Meeting of MacArthur and Emperor Hirohito, September 27, 1945. One of the key debates among both the Allies and Japanese during the war revolved around the issue of exactly what "unconditional surrender" would mean and how it would affect the position of the emperor. Despite widespread belief that the emperor should be indicted as a war criminal, MacArthur as supreme commander of the Allied forces decided that the emperor would be of great use in effecting an orderly and peaceful Occupation. In this photo of the two men, the symbolism of the new order is unmistakable: the diminutive emperor standing stiffly in morning dress next to the hulking MacArthur in his work uniform, with his hands nonchalantly in his pockets.

> Aspiring sincerely to an international peace based on justice and order, the Japanese people forever renounce war as a sovereign right of the nation and the threat or use of force as means of settling international disputes.
>
> In order to accomplish the aim of the preceding paragraph, land, sea, and air forces, as well as other war potential, will never be maintained. The right of belligerency of the state will not be recognized.

This provision remains popular even today, although many in recent years have come to argue that Japan's enhanced position as an economic superpower demands an appropriate expansion of the nation's Self Defense Forces (SDF).

Tojo Hideki Receives His Death Sentence at the Tokyo War Crimes Trials. With the beginning of the Occupation came a mass round-up of those allegedly responsible for war crimes, and the International Military Tribunal Far East (IMTFE) began to screen suspects and witnesses in Shanghai, Manila, and Tokyo. At the top of the list was General Tojo, seen as the architect of Japan's wars of aggression and of Japanese atrocities during the war. Tojo had attempted suicide in September 1945 as American military police came to his house to arrest him. The pistol shot he aimed for his heart, however, had missed and he soon recovered. He was hanged on December 23, 1948.

Another controversial element of the Occupation years was the International Military Tribunal Far East, more commonly known as the Tokyo War Crimes trials, convened on April 29, 1946, and continuing into 1948. Like their counterparts in Europe pursuing "de-Nazification" and prosecuting those who led Germany into aggressive war and committed atrocities of various kinds and degrees, the IMTFE, held in Manila and Shanghai as well as Tokyo, aimed to ferret out and purge those whom it believed had deliberately and egregiously committed political and military war crimes, classed as A, B, or C depending on the seriousness of the offense. Right from the beginning, SCAP's shielding of the emperor aroused resentment, as did the exempting of members of the imperial family (including those who had served in the military) from prosecution. Of the Class A war criminals convicted, six were sentenced to death, including General/Prime Minister Tojo; sixteen received life sentences; and the rest were given sentences of from five to twenty years. By 1958, all those who remained in prison had been released. For many, even some involved in conducting the trial, the charges seemed unworkably vague. For many Japanese, it was simply "victor's justice." In the end, five of the twelve judges filed independent or dissenting opinions.

The Reverse Course: Japan and the Cold War

For many ordinary Japanese, the initial years of the Occupation, ironically, held immense promise. Political parties rebounded with a vengeance, labor quickly found a powerful voice, women took immediate advantage of their new rights, and the stunned war-weariness of the first postwar months seemed to be fading into a new political and cultural vibrancy. Even the rural sectors of the country, so long depressed by absentee landlordism and tenancy, and plagued by artificially low wartime price controls, were radically transformed. The Shidehara government had made some initial moves in this direction, and by the time of the election of the Yoshida Shigeru (1878–1967) government in the spring of 1946, Japanese initiatives and SCAP directives had mandated all holdings over 3 *cho* (a *cho* is about 2.45 acres) were to be given or sold on easy terms to tenants or the landless. By 1952, when the last of these sweeping measures was enacted, the rural landscape had been transformed and farmers were also benefiting from subsidized prices and heavy tariffs on food imports, policies that have remained in force for decades.

With the immediacy of the developing Cold War in 1947 and 1948, however, the pace of experimentation and reform would be markedly curtailed, and emphasis shifted away from further democratizing Japan to making it a bulwark against Soviet and Communist influence. In Europe, the era was characterized by the Marshall Plan, the Berlin Airlift, the first Soviet nuclear test, and the evolving U.S. policy of "containment." In East Asia, the perception of a Soviet threat was coupled with the development of two Koreas—one occupied by the USSR, the other by the U.S.; with decolonization in Indonesia, Malaya, Burma, India, and a war of independence in Indochina; and the increasing prospect of Mao Zedong's Communist forces winning the resumed civil war in China. Thus, Japan became the front line in the American strategy of containment, requiring a massive economic effort there to counter the threat of Communism. The old unity of government, finance, and industry was thus informally revived, strikes discouraged, and socialist and communist parties and politics increasingly seen as suspect.

All these trends increased with the victory of the Chinese Communists (1949) and the opening of the Korean War (1950). Japan now became the principal staging area for the United Nations forces operating in Korea and an important base for the U.S. Navy in responding to potential threats to the remnant Nationalist Chinese forces who had fled to Taiwan, and for supporting the French effort to defeat Ho Chi Minh's forces in Indochina. Such circumstances resulted in a massive infusion of capital into Japan, rapid rebuilding of Japanese heavy industry, and the beginning of a long-running boom in shipping and consumer exports.

The rapid, if somewhat uneven, recovery of Japan by the time of the Korean War, and Japan's vital part in the defense perimeter of what was now frequently referred to as the "Free World" (the U.S. and its allies), pushed forward the process of concluding a formal peace between Japan and its former enemies. With the war still raging in Korea, a final peace treaty returning national sovereignty to Japan was signed in San Francisco on September 8, 1951, between Japan and her former enemies among the Allies, with the People's Republic of China, Soviet Union, and India abstaining. In the treaty, Japan renounced all claims on the Asian mainland and Taiwan, the Kuriles, and South Sakhalin. They also agreed to "any proposal of the United States to the United Nations" to place under American trusteeship the former Japanese-controlled islands, including the Bonins, Okinawa, and the Ryukyus. The U.S. would retain possession of Okinawa until 1972 and, as of the early twenty-first century, still maintains a military presence on the island. In recognition of Japan's new strategic position—but without a powerful military—the U.S. and Japan also concluded a bilateral security

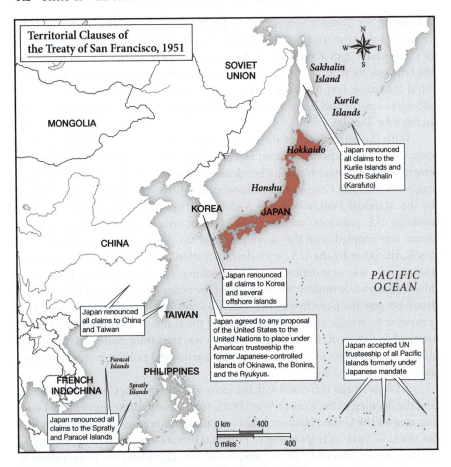

Map 13.5 Territorial Clauses of the Treaty of San Francisco, 1951

treaty, effectively putting Japan under the American nuclear umbrella, but giving American personnel in Japan extraterritorial protection—a point of contention between the two nations ever since. As a final ratification of Japan's readmission to full nationhood, it was admitted to the United Nations in 1956. An important cultural affirmation of Japan's recovered status was the Tokyo Olympic Games of 1964. As had London in 1948, Japan's Olympic moment was meant, in part, to demonstrate its remarkable recovery from the war. Like the games in Beijing in 2008, it was also meant as a showcase of modernity and athletic achievement (see Map 13.5).

Moving Toward the Twenty-First Century

As Japan moved into its recovered status as a sovereign nation, its political system with a more responsible Diet—with the weight of power now shifted to the lower house—and executive roles vested in cabinet ministers chosen from that house, and the emperor in his new status as constitutional monarch, its politics in many respects still retained the character of an extended family, rather than that of highly contentious competing political parties. One illustration of this is the forty-year dominance of the Liberal Democratic Party (LDP), in office until 1993. At that point, attempts were made to splinter off factions from the LDP in order to form other parties to supplement marginalized parties, such as the Japan Socialist Party. The economic recession since the early 1990s has encouraged a degree of political experimentation, with some advocating a two-party system like that of the United States. The LDP remains a dominant force, however.

As we have seen in earlier chapters, Japan's postwar relations with other East Asian countries have generally been cordial, although for many of them, the legacy of the war years is difficult to erase. This was especially true of Korea and Taiwan. Both places were part of Japan's empire for decades and the subject of considerable investment and infrastructural development. Thus, despite much destruction during the war in Korea, a good deal of groundwork had been laid for their industrial rise in the 1960s and 1970s. The legacy of colonialism, however, retained its sting, and Japan's economic dominance of the region into the 1980s continued to rub feelings raw.

This, of course, is particularly true in China. The legacy of Japanese intervention and atrocities in China has become a useful tool for the government there to use when it feels the need to whip up nationalism. Increasingly, however, Chinese nationalism is coming from the grassroots, and resentment of Japan's wartime role plays a central part in it. A continual mark of this antagonism, as we have seen, comes with each new edition of history texts approved for use by the Japanese Ministry of Education. Japan's general unwillingness to fully come to grips with the legacy of the war years was most recently in evidence in Prime Minister Shinzo Abe's visit to the USS *Arizona* memorial at Pearl Harbor, with no formal apology issued. Visits to the Yasukuni Shrine to honor the spirits of Japan's war dead—including the Class A war criminals who were executed—tend to abet this trend as well.

PATTERNS UP-CLOSE

Japan's History Problem

Several times in this chapter, we have referred to Japan's overall unwillingness to examine the darker side of its history from 1895 to 1945. This is particularly true of the years 1937 to 1945, from the invasion of China to Japan's surrender. Critics of this reticence outside Japan, particularly in the United States, South Korea, Taiwan, and the PRC, generally find the official approach of Japan's approved texts and the view of a large and influential group of Japanese historians toward Japan's wartime behavior

(continued)

disingenuous or, in some cases, willfully distorted. They often contrast this perspective with that of all but a few German historians and the official view of the governments of the former East and West—and now united Germany—toward Nazism and the Third Reich's behavior during the war. There, the full horrors of the Nazi interval have been explored; formal and deeply emotional apologies have been offered to victim nations and to Israel; and the laws even forbid the display of Nazi memorabilia and any advocacy of neo-Nazism. To be sure, there is active debate about the complicity of Germans during the war. The program of "de-Nazification" in the early postwar years engendered the assumption that Hitler and his supporters had, in effect, hijacked a nation struggling to democratize. More recently, highly contentious revisionist views have suggested that, especially in the realm of the Nazi's eliminationist policies toward Jews and the Holocaust itself, the Germans were, as Daniel Goldhagen's book title puts it, *Hitler's Willing Executioners*.

Although Emperor Hirohito himself and his son Emperor Akihito expressed regret for Japan's role in World War II, as have several prime ministers in the more recent past, their apologies have been viewed by most outsiders as forced and formulaic. Government leaders also regularly visit the Yasukuni Shrine to Japan's war dead, which includes Japan's executed war criminals, who are regarded in this context as sacrificial victims to "victor's justice." Moreover, the rising sun ensign of the war years is not restricted from display, as is the swastika in Germany, although for many of Japan's neighbors, it bears the same kind of sinister resonance. Not surprisingly then, the Japanese perspective on Japan's wartime activities has tended to downplay or ignore Japan's wartime atrocities and instead sees Japan as a "victim nation."

One reason for this perspective is that the leaders of imperial Japan generally saw themselves as acting in self-defense against Western colonialism and the creation of their empire as the only realistic way to unite East Asia against the predatory Western powers increasingly arrayed against it. Moreover, unlike Hitler's Germany, Japan had no specific policy of genocide—indeed, Japanese policy was avowedly *inclusive* insofar as it sought to organize and harmonize peoples in the empire's task of creating an "Asia for the Asiatics." The attack on Pearl Harbor was viewed as the desperate but justifiable (the still controversial term "reckless" is often used) response to America's unacceptable attempt to roll back Japan's efforts at unifying Asia, the squeezing of Japan's access to resources through sanctions, and the encirclement of Japanese interests by the "ABCD" countries. Thus, any act, no matter how cruel, could be understood in the context of the necessity of victory by any means. Finally, the trauma of the American incendiary air campaign and atomic bombings, it is felt, was expiatory and ushered in Japan's new role as the world's leading advocate for peace.

One of the more contentious issues in this regard has been the 1937 massacre at Nanking. Despite the IMTFE's pronouncement that Japan's forces had systematically and purposefully slaughtered perhaps 200,000 to 300,000 people during this brutal episode, and the massive documentary and film footage of the atrocities, it remains a favorite target of Japanese critics. Organizations such as the "Society for the Dissemination of Historical Fact" bombard historians with arguments ranging from flat statements that it did not take place, to saying that it was much smaller than reported (a death toll of 40,000 is frequently cited), to asserting that any killing that took place was the spontaneous reaction of overwrought soldiers.

There has, however, been a vocal though marginalized set of historians and writers who have fought this perception and struggled to provide a fuller picture of Japan's colonial and wartime policies and activities. Most prominent among them was Ienaga Saburo (1913–2002), who spent most of his career attempting, among other things, to debunk the postwar decoupling of what had come to be officially called "the Pacific War" (also the title of his breakthrough 1968 book). What had been adopted as the official name for this conflict, he asserted, was that which the Americans called the war they fought against Japan from 1941 to 1945. Seeing this as entirely separate from Japan's war in China and previous colonialism in Asia, he argued, allowed Japanese to conveniently forget Japan's record of oppression there and adopt their postwar stance of victimization. One small victory in Ienaga's campaign was the increasing use in Japan of the more expansive term "Asia-Pacific War" by the 1990s.

Ienaga became an intellectual celebrity and hero among the growing number of Japanese historians questioning the official stance taken by Japan's Ministry of Education in vetting textbooks for use in schools. From 1965 to 1997, he mounted a series of lawsuits arguing that the changes demanded of his own books constituted a violation of the postwar constitution's conceptions of academic freedom. In the end, he lost the constitutional argument, but in part because of his efforts, historians increasingly included more material critical of Japan's wartime activities.

Yet conservative groups continued to pressure the Education Ministry to re-sanitize coverage of such facts as Nanking, "comfort women," and the chemical and biological experiments undertaken at the infamous Unit 731 in Manchuria. Several times since the late 1990s, the textbook controversy has stirred up international tensions. The latest of these occurred in April 2015. Prime Minister Abe expressed the view that Japanese should not engage in "self-torturing history" by stressing the severity of Japan's wartime activities. The relegating of the Nanking massacre to a textbook footnote and the dropping of coverage of the conscription of Korean comfort women prompted condemnation in Beijing and a tense meeting between the South Korean foreign minister and the Japanese ambassador.

(continued)

Given the increasing tone of nationalism in East Asia as a whole, it seems likely that what is referred to in the region as Japan's "history problem" will not be resolved in the immediate future.

Hiroshima Memorial Genbaku Dome. Testament to the vast destructive power of the "Little Boy" uranium bomb dropped on Hiroshima on August 6, 1945, is this lone surviving building of the "ground zero" blast zone. The ruggedly constructed "Hiroshima Prefectural Industrial Promotion Hall," today surrounded by modern buildings at the site, bears mute testimony to the horror of that morning when more than 80,000 people were instantly killed. Known today as the Genbaku Dome (the "Atomic Bomb Dome"), it attracts tourists from all over the world and remains a touchstone for a persistent strain of Japanese sentiment that they, too, were victims of the war.

Japan's relations with the United States have at once been marked by its inability to come to grips with this history—indeed, positing itself as a victim of American economic sanctions and, of course, atomic bombing—and dependence on the U.S. for security. In the 1950s, critics among socialists and communists and members of the ultra-nationalist remnant roundly criticized elements of the peace treaty, and especially the bilateral security treaty. Those on the left believed that Japan should be closer to China and the Soviet Union; many of those on the right resented Japan's demilitarized status. Criticism of Japan's relationship with the United States boiled over in 1960 when anti-American demonstrations turned into a riot during the visit of American Vice President Richard Nixon.

America's insistence on Japan's anti-Communist position during the Cold War provoked ongoing resentment among many, as did increasing U.S. involvement in Vietnam. Perhaps more resented, however, were the "Nixon shocks" of the early 1970s. Although Nixon's overtures to the PRC were hailed by many in the international community, Japan's leaders were deeply hurt that this unexpected and abrupt change of course was conducted without any prior notice to them. For many, there was fear that the "China card" America was playing against the Soviet Union might also work against Japan. The fact that the shocks came at a time when the U.S. was winding down its commitment in Southeast Asia—with the accompanying decline of American economic infusion into Okinawa and Japan—and putting pressure on Japan to open itself to more American exports, particularly food, was not welcome either.

ECONOMY, SOCIETY, AND CULTURE

The 1980s and early 1990s saw a role reversal of sorts. Japan's economic power appeared to be soaring without limit. It had long since become the world's second-largest economy when it surpassed West Germany in 1968. In the 1980s, especially from 1986 to 1990, Japan was experiencing its hugely expanding "bubble economy" at a time when the U.S. economy was moving haltingly under "Reaganomics" and recovering from record high interest rates. Moreover, Japanese investors were buying up American companies and investing in American real estate at a furious pace. This spawned a number of studies in both countries attempting to analyze Japan's "economic miracle" and to propose ways that the U.S. could improve its economic standing by following Japanese leads in education, industrial organization, and financial organization. Perhaps the climate between both economic super-powers was best expressed by the famous 1989 essay "The Japan That Can Say No: Why Japan Will Be First Among Equals," written by Japan's Minister of Transport Shintaro Ishihara and Sony founder Akio Morita. In it, both men argued for the superiority of Japan's approach to business, government, and economics, and insisted that Japan move from being a "yes man" to American policies and adopt a far more independent stance.

As the recession of the early 1990s continued through the decade and the "Confucian capitalist" states of East Asia—now led by China and South Korea—waxed in power, American fear of being surpassed by Japan dissipated. Moreover, the U.S. economy, enjoying its own "tech boom," was expanding at very healthy rates. For the Japanese of the new century, however, the 1990s were referred to as "the lost decade." Despite repeated economic stimulus packages, Japan's economy remained in the doldrums far longer and more severely than that of the U.S. after the financial crisis of 2008. With a slow recovery from the long recession now gaining momentum, however, Japan's unemployment rate for 2018 is currently 2.3 percent.

Further evidence of stagnation was adduced in the wake of the Tohoku earthquake in March 11, 2011. At magnitude 9.0, it was the strongest quake ever recorded in Japan, surpassing that of the famous Tokyo quake of 1923. With the hypocenter of the earthquake about 50 miles off the coast of Sendai, the initial wave and aftershocks were swiftly accompanied by a devastating tsunami that traveled more than 6 miles inland. Estimates of the damage included nearly 16,000 dead, over 8,000 injured or missing, and about a million structures destroyed or damaged.

Government spokespeople claimed it was Japan's biggest crisis since World War II. Making the situation worse was the fact that the quake and tsunami had severely damaged the nuclear reactors at Fukushima, causing a meltdown at one and gas explosions at three others. Millions were without electricity, and hundreds of thousands of people had to be evacuated. The emperor addressed the nation in an unprecedented telecast. Dozens of governments offered help and humanitarian aid. Widespread accusations of government incompetence and cover-ups soon followed, however. The media, it was said, simply parroted official reports in a cooperative effort to avoid panic. This was particularly true in the case of the reactors, which international media almost from the beginning had characterized as experiencing a meltdown. It was months before the government admitted that this was the case. According to the World Bank's estimates, it was the costliest natural disaster in world history, with an estimated cost of $235 billion.

Aerial View of Earthquake and Tsunami Damage near Fukushima.
On March 11, 2011, the strongest earthquake ever recorded in Japan—magnitude 9 on the Richter Scale—took place off the coast of Sendai. In addition to devastation from the quake and numerous aftershocks, the worst damage occurred with the resulting tsunami, as shown here in this view, taken a week later, of the town of Kirikiri in Owate Prefecture. In addition to causing the deaths of nearly 16,000 and leaving countless people homeless, the event severely damaged the nuclear power station at Fukushima, causing a meltdown and gas explosion, and leaving millions without power. Officials termed it the worst disaster in Japan since World War II.

From "Made in Japan" to Total Quality Management

One of the most dramatic success stories of Japan's rise to economic superpower in the years after the Occupation has been the transformation of its industrial production techniques toward what came to be called "Total Quality

Management." Although the basis of the concept may be traced to the "scientific management" practices of American industries starting before World War I with the time–motion studies of Frederick Taylor, Japanese producers refined a constellation of techniques and attitudes that allowed their products to become world leaders in quality and consistency. They then began to introduce these practices to American and European companies.

During the years of the Occupation and, in decreasing fashion through the 1950s, Japan's export of inexpensive consumer goods had stereotyped these commodities as cheap, derivative, disposable items. As such, the term "made in Japan" became a euphemism in the U.S. for the shoddiest toys, transistor radios, clothes, and so forth. At the same time, however, Japanese manufacturers anxious to shed this reputation increasingly began adopting the methods championed by the American engineer and business consultant W. Edwards Deming (1900–1993). Deming's philosophy of efficient quality manufacturing was deceptively simple: think of the manufacturing process as a unified, coherent system, and constantly look for ways to make it more efficient. By making it increasingly efficient, costs related to waste, downtime, litigation, and so forth go down over time and quality goes up, thus ensuring customer loyalty and enhancing product and company reputation. Moreover, all personnel at every stage of the process should have a hand in supervising the highest standards in quality. Instead of distinct, specialized departments working independently on different parts of design and manufacture, borders should be broken down and advice sought and used from all those involved in the system.

One of the pioneers of this concept in Japan was Ishikawa Kaoru (1915–1989), who translated Deming's works and added his own concept of the "quality circle": small groups of workers who meet periodically to assess and critique the processes in which they participate. The supervisor facilitating the group then shares the findings with managers, thus constituting a continual feedback loop of information from those actually performing the most basic manufacturing tasks. The entire management philosophy became known internationally as Total Quality Management (TQM). Ishikawa's 1988 book *What Is Total Quality Management: The Japanese Way* laid out in detail how Japanese companies had implemented these ideas after 1960, and how they were now practiced by tens of millions of Japanese workers. Its implementation on a large scale in Japanese industries also suited the cooperative cultural aspects that had long been a hallmark of Japanese life.

The transformation of Japanese business and industry was aided greatly by close cooperation among finance, government, and industry. The creation of the Ministry of International Trade and Industry (MITI; replaced in 2001 by the Ministry of Economy, Trade and Industry or METI) immensely facilitated this process. Created in 1949 to guide and aid Japan's export trade, it wielded immense power in the 1960s and 1970s, although its influence gradually diminished during the 1980s. Though not a central planning agency, MITI arranged for financing and coordination among Japan's export—and some domestic—corporations and **keiretsu**, the informal successors of the *zaibatsu*, and identified potential markets. Unlike most public corporations in the U.S. funded by stocks and responsible to shareholders for quarterly profits, most Japanese companies were funded by long-term loans on friendly terms that allowed companies to weather years of losses overseas in order to establish markets and gradually expand them. Such arrangements allowed Japanese automobile manufacturers to penetrate and even dominate overseas markets in the later twentieth and early twenty-first centuries. Over the last few decades, however, many Japanese corporations have begun financing through stock issues, and Japan's financial markets have been in recession since the early 1990s.

Aside from international dominance in shipping and automobiles in the 1970s and 1980s, nowhere was Japanese corporate excellence more in evidence than in consumer electronics. Although in recent years, its companies have been challenged by Korean, Taiwanese, and PRC manufacturers, Japan still boasts the largest consumer electronics industry in the world. As in motor vehicles, the concepts of TQM and cooperative quality control at all levels of the manufacturing process have resulted in some of the highest-quality radios, stereos, televisions, VCRs, cameras, and other video equipment, CD/DVD systems, computers—and computer games—in the world. Global leaders such as Sony, Hitachi, Casio, Panasonic, JVC, Toshiba, Atari, Nintendo, Canon, and Nikon long dominated the industry and propelled such innovations as transistor radios, color televisions,

Child Playing with a Sony Aibo Robot Dog. Japan's postwar devotion to the concepts of Total Quality Management (TQM) and movement into the key industries of automobiles and, especially, electronics helped to vault the nation into a commanding position in these and numerous other consumer items. Japan's predominance in computer technology and robotics has also led to a fad for more whimsical items, such as the toy pictured in this photo. Such items represent the cutting edge of technologies built around Artificial Intelligence (AI) that are revolutionizing our lives on a daily basis.

VCRs, laptop computers, printers, and cell phones. Indeed, many of the competitors of these companies in other East Asian countries originated because the rise of wages in Japan pushed many of their manufacturing sectors into what at the time were lower-wage countries like South Korea and Taiwan—themselves now prosperous enough to farm out lower-wage manufacturing to the PRC, Vietnam, Indonesia, India, and Africa.

The Dominance of the Middle Class

Indeed, the rise of Japanese corporate giants not surprisingly coincided with rapid individual growth to the point where the vast majority of people consider themselves to be part of the middle class, and that unemployment—even in the recession years of the 1990s—hovers around 4 percent, considered "full employment" by economists. On the other hand, prices, particularly for certain foodstuffs like rice, had long been relatively high because of subsidies to rice farmers and protective tariffs on foreign food products. Not surprisingly, too, real estate in this island nation is also extraordinarily expensive: a number of farmers in the 1980s and early 1990s discovered much to their amazement that even the small parcels of farmland they owned made them, on paper at least, millionaires.

There are a number of reasons often cited for this middle-class dominance. One is that Japanese companies generally hire personnel for the long term. In this respect, the stereotype of the white-collar "salaryman" working long hours but enjoying considerable job security has a strong basis in fact. The vast expansion of Japanese industry in the postwar decades coupled with stable population growth and little immigration also helped ensure employment for most people. Moreover, the export of the lowest-wage jobs has tended to keep even the lesser-paid workers in Japan in higher income brackets than workers with comparable positions in other countries. The salaries of CEOs and other top corporate personnel are, on the other hand, much lower than those of comparable positions in the U.S. and Europe. Thus, Japan's income distribution is among the most equitable in the world. Finally, Japanese have continued to maintain savings rates that are among the highest in the world, averaging about 15 to 20 percent per annum. Part of the reason for this is that less of a social safety net exists than in other wealthy countries. Still, Japanese families enjoy considerable disposable funds because of these savings, which has also fed a consumer culture.

Women and Family: "A Half-Step Behind"?

Although Japan may be said to be among the most—some would argue *the* most—modern nations in the world, it is also, like other East Asian nations, a palimpsest of continual cultural overlays. A prime example of this is the evolving institution of the family. The centuries of Neo-Confucian gender hierarchy have left their ongoing traces. Despite the fact that the majority of Japanese women now have a college education, and that a higher percentage of them work (65 percent) than in the United States, the "glass ceiling" for management is still very much present, and Japanese women make roughly 60 percent of what Japanese men earn. In terms of health, however, their life expectancy is the highest in the world: age 87.

Despite the pervasiveness of the "office lady" in corporate culture, the expectation is that the vast majority of women will marry and make home and family the focus of their adult lives. The old Confucian divide between "inner" (female) and "outer" (male) domains is still very much present. The expectation is still strong that a woman's primary vocation is to make the home a refuge for her husband, and to be nurturer and academic coach to her children. The fierce competition and famously rigorous tests to which students are subjected for acceptance at Tokyo University and other top schools make academic preparation a continual job for every mother as well as student. "Pass with four; fail with five" has become a popular slogan, referring to the hours of sleep the ambitious student should get at night. When the normal school day ends, students routinely go to a private tutoring school, following which it is the mother's duty to supervise a student's homework. With the stakes so high, and a significant rate of failure associated with the initial shot at the exams, it is not surprising that despondent students have frequently taken their own lives or retreated from the world to their rooms for months at a time. By the 1990s, millions of so-called parasite singles were still living at their parents' homes into their thirties, though many were employed. They have been cited as one reason for Japan's falling fertility rate (see below).

Although Japanese women legally enjoy the same rights as women in most developed countries—divorce, with remarriage restricted in some instances for 100 days after the decree; access to abortion, with some restrictions—the cultural legacy of the Confucian past still weighs heaviest on women. As in China, there is now apprehension about the falling birthrate and the resulting stasis and decline in population. Like women in many wealthy countries, Japanese women often wait until their late twenties or early thirties to have children. The fertility rate is among the lowest in the world, 1.4 per woman; the replacement rate (the rate needed to maintain population stability) is 2.1. In some respects, this should be welcome news: not only is a low birthrate a marker of a wealthy and advanced society, but the Japanese home islands have always been squeezed demographically. Thus, a dwindling population should be less of a strain on political, economic, and social institutions. Like China, however, the fear is also present that with fewer people to pay taxes, even the minimal social safety net of Japan might prove inadequate for the present generation as it ages.

While Japan's women have made important advances in the postwar period—legal emancipation, suffrage, easier divorce, and reproductive rights—the cultural hindrances persist. In past centuries, it was said that a woman should walk three steps behind a man. In the early 1990s, a popular work on the status of Japanese women included a variation on this theme in its title: *A Half Step Behind*. Perhaps we can now say that women in Japan have picked up the pace a bit further.

Godzilla *and* Sailor Moon: *Postwar Culture*

The trauma of war and defeat had a profound effect on Japanese culture in the 1940s and 1950s. Initially, as part of the culture of *amae* or extreme dependence on authority figures, many Japanese had replaced complete loyalty to the wartime government to total submission to the Occupation. American influence permeated

Japanese popular culture in the form of magazines, radio programs, cinema, and other outlets. For their part, Japanese authorities hoped to soften the behavior of Occupation forces by enjoining full cooperation among the people, even to the point of setting up officially sanctioned brothels as a preventive measure against rape. As we noted earlier, the political culture, freed from wartime restraints, re-emerged vigorously, although the Occupation authorities maintained censors to guard against what SCAP considered to be inflammatory or obscene materials.

With the end of the Occupation came a flurry of artistic experimentation in a variety of media. Perhaps most influential were Nobel Laureate in Literature (1968) Yasunari Kawabata (1899–1972) and avant-garde writer, poet, actor, and playwright Yukio Mishima (1925–1970) in such novels as *Confessions of a Mask*. Despite his original genre-defying work, Mishima remained a committed nationalist. Like General Nogi, he chose to take his own life in spectacular fashion by *seppuku* following an abortive coup attempt by his militia group.

It has been in the realm of popular culture, however, that Japan has arguably seen its most startling innovation in the decades since the war. The nuclear age ushered in by the devastation of two Japanese cities hung heavily over Japan, as did the incipient threat of a third world war in the 1950s and early 1960s. Not surprisingly, the apocalyptic visions this conjured up resulted in the phenomenon of Japanese "monster movies." This trend was by no means limited to Japan. It was the huge popularity worldwide of the pioneering hit *Godzilla* (1954) and its sequels, however, that established the genre as a cultural symbol of postwar Japan. Spawned by radiation from atomic explosions, Godzilla, a huge dinosaurlike creature, devastates Tokyo until a way is finally found to defeat it. Its offspring return periodically, however, and the franchise later included other nuclear-induced creatures such as "Mothra."

By the 1960s, Japanese animated fantasy characters were also finding worldwide audiences. Two of the most popular were the android *Astro Boy*—which started as a **manga**, or magazine cartoon, in 1952, and was introduced as an animated television series in 1963—and *Speed Racer*—introduced in 1967 and a forerunner of the famous **anime** fantasies of later decades. The astonishing popularity of both manga and anime had become a global phenomenon by the turn of the century and spanned nearly every type of genre and literary form from realistic, even historically accurate, adventure to stunningly frank pornography. The stories and characters were further circulated by their use in video games and fashion accessories, like those associated with Hello Kitty.

Perhaps the most popular cross-over from manga to anime (and beyond to movies, television series, specials, and video games) in recent years has been the *Sailor Moon* franchise. Originally run as a manga by Naoko Takeuchi from 1991 to 1997, under its various names like *Pretty Soldier Sailor Moon* and *Pretty Guardian Sailor Moon*, the series popularized the character of the "girl hero" who as a middle school student takes on magical powers and unites with similarly endowed pre-adolescent "sailor guardians" to fight the powers of the "Dark Kingdom" of evil that threaten the world. The complex plots, interwoven story arcs, and growth of the characters over time have made the series wildly popular—even classic—among the millions of anime and manga fans throughout the world.

Japanese Pop Culture. Postwar Japanese popular culture has had not only a profound effect on Japanese tastes, particularly among young people, but also a worldwide impact over the decades. The earliest of these is also perhaps the best known: *Godzilla*. Awakened by the radiation of nuclear explosions from its prehistoric sleep, the creature Godzilla (A) has appeared in dozens of movies, cartoons, comics, and video games since the original film in 1954. Indeed, the original film was responsible in many respects for the international "monster movie" fad of the 1950s and 1960s, with the majority incorporating nuclear fears into their storylines. More benign has been the global popularity of manga and anime characters, usually depicted as large-eyed innocent creatures, although some are associated with sinister and even pornographic tales. In (B), two young women engage in "cosplay"—costume play—dressing as their favorite characters. The productions of anime and manga images also ballooned into an entire genre of fashion, with perhaps the most well-recognized worldwide being Hello Kitty (C).

CONCLUSION

In many respects, Japan underwent a complete historical cycle in little more than a century from 1895 to the present. Politically, economically, and militarily on the ascendant at the beginning of the period, it continued to wax in all these areas for nearly fifty years. Yet the end of that upswing came with even more stunning speed than its beginning. Enmeshed in a stalemated war in China, Japan's leadership took a fateful—and as it turned out, fatal—chance on striking south to acquire the resources it calculated could win the war for them. Taking on the United States and Britain (among other adversaries) along the way, with the Soviet Union joining in at the end, Japan was defeated as thoroughly as any nation in history.

Yet its recovery, if not quite as swift, was certainly spectacular. Occupied principally by the United States for seven years, Japan rejoined the international community as a nation now dedicated to peace, formally renouncing war as an instrument of national policy in its new constitution. The Japan of the following decades also remade its industries into world leaders in such cutting-edge sectors as motor vehicle manufacturing and consumer electronics. As early as 1968, it had become the second-largest economy in the world. By 1990, there was considerable speculation that it would surpass the U.S. to become number one—only to fall into recession before being surpassed by China in 2010.

Through all events, Japan has managed to keep a firm hand on its traditional culture while moving ahead in the most advanced industrial sectors—even post-industrial sectors—in the world. It remains Asia's most mature economy and provides the most enduring model for nations seeking to become modern without becoming entirely "Western." Challenges, however, also abound. The recession persists; the economy, so long priding itself on its egalitarianism, is becoming more divided between rich and poor; the population is now demographically far below the replacement rate; and the Abe government is moving in a more nationalistic direction. As China becomes more assertive in the region, will Japan feel the need to revamp Article 9 of its constitution? Will it maintain its close relationship with the United States? Will the center of gravity of East Asia now move even more rapidly toward Beijing?

FURTHER RESOURCES

Bix, Herbert. *Hirohito and the Making of Modern Japan.* New York: HarperCollins, 2000. Pulitzer Prize–winning biography of the more than six-decade rule of this Japanese emperor. Based on previously unavailable records, Bix makes a strong case that, far from being the passive, removed head of state, Hirohito was an active agent in Japan's expansion and worked in partnership with MacArthur to downplay his activities in order to retain the imperial throne.

Borg, Dorothy, and Shumpei Okamoto, eds. *Pearl Harbor as History: Japanese-American Relations, 1931–1941.* New York: Columbia University Press, 1973. This work of essays is part of the series Studies of the East Asia Institute at Columbia. Although dated in some respects, the essays are written by top scholars, such Warren I. Cohen, Earnest May, Norman Graebner, and the editors themselves.

Buruma, Ian. *Inventing Japan, 1853–1964.* New York: Modern Library, 2003. Bookended by the arrival of Perry and the Tokyo Olympics, Buruma's interpretive history is also a critique of the militarism of the war years and the left and right political battles of the postwar period.

Dower, John. *War Without Mercy: Race and Power in the Pacific War.* New York: Pantheon, 1986. Path-breaking study of the images of race, militarism, bravery, and culture as revealed in wartime propaganda toward the Japanese in the U.S. and toward the U.S. in Japan. Particularly useful in what it reveals in terms of Japan's self-image and that which it projected to the world.

Dower, John. *Embracing Defeat: Japan in the Wake of World War II.* New York: Norton, 1999. One of the premier historians of wartime Japan examines the complex interactions of the defeated Japanese with their American Occupiers. Particularly vivid in describing the destitution of the country in the opening months of the Occupation and the reaction to the Reverse Course of the late 1940s.

Duus, Peter, ed. *Cambridge History of Japan.* Vol. 6, *The Twentieth Century.* Cambridge, UK: Cambridge University Press, 1988. Like its counterparts for other countries and regions, this series on Japan is among the most authoritative and useful resources, especially for those beginning research in any area of Japanese history.

Ienaga, Saburo. *The Pacific War 1931–1945.* New York: Pantheon, 1978. One of the few postwar Japanese historians to critique the Japanese policy of expansion and ultimate war with the Allies. While not sparing in his coverage of American actions, his scathing indictment of Japan's wartime leaders makes for an important work of historical revision.

International Military Tribunal for the Far East (IMTFE). *Proceedings*, 19 vols. New York: Garland, 1981. This reprint offers the official records of the war crimes trials of Japanese military leaders and civilian officials. Vitally important primary source for serious researchers.

Shirokauer, Conrad, and Suzanne Gay. *A Brief History of Japanese Civilization.* Belmont, CA: Wadsworth, 2012. Handy one-volume treatment by prominent scholars with an emphasis on culture and religion as well as more standard topics such as politics and economics. Recommended for introductory students.

Walthall, Anne, ed. *The Human Tradition in Modern Japan.* Lanham, MD: Rowman & Littlefield, 2002. Biography-based social history of ordinary Japanese men and women from Tokugawa times to the postwar period. A useful corrective to more standard histories emphasizing political and economic topics.

WEBSITES

http://www.oxfordbibliographies.com/view/document/obo-9780199791279/obo-9780199791279-0027.xml. Oxford Bibliographies. *Sino-Japanese Wars, 1895–1945.* Partial list available directly; subscription necessary for complete entries. Complete and current.

https://www.pbs.org/thewar/resources.htm. PBS. *Learn More About World War II.* Useful bibliography of the overall war as well as Japan's role. Covers websites, books, and other materials.

http://aboutjapan.japansociety.org/content.cfm/japan_in_the_world_since_1945#sthash.NJMpDSPV.dpbs. The Japan Society. *About Japan: A Teacher's Resource. Japan in the World Since 1945.*
Although geared for secondary school teachers, the site contains a wealth of background information and links to important documents, articles, and photographs. Students may also get insight into the structure of history exercises that can prove useful in exploring the material.

Epilogue
Breakneck Change and the Challenge of Tradition

In November 2017, an event took place that may well be remembered as initiating the reordering of the political, economic, and perhaps even the social and cultural spheres of East Asia. The occasion was the visit of the new American president, Donald J. Trump, to the region. In whirlwind stops in Japan, South Korea, the People's Republic of China (PRC), the Philippines, which was hosting the ASEAN (Association of Southeast Asian Nations) summit, and Vietnam, which was hosting the APEC (Asia Pacific Economic Cooperation) conference, the president made clear that the United States intended to radically recast its relationship with the region as a whole and with each of the countries he visited.

His predecessor, Barack Obama, while conscious of the limits of American influence in the region, was also well aware of the growing power and influence of China and the somewhat nervous position in which the PRC's neighbors found themselves as a consequence of it. China's growing ability to project power had already emboldened its military to claim wide expanses of open sea as territorial waters, contest existing claims to islands with the Philippines, Vietnam, and Japan, and even to build its own islands as sites of resource extraction and military outposts. Thus, the Obama administration's relations with the PRC were at times strained over these issues as well as computer hacking, copyright infringements, the US's longstanding trade deficit with the PRC, and perennial criticism of China's human rights record.

Far more serious was the situation in Korea. As we saw in Chapter 11, Kim Jung-un had, in defiance of warnings from the United States and pressure from China, Russia, and Japan, accelerated its nuclear weapons program. Despite ever more strident statements from both Obama and the new Trump administration, Kim had built and tested missiles capable of delivering a nuclear warhead to North America. In a startling speech to the United Nations General Assembly, the President Trump derided Kim as "little rocket man" and promised to destroy North Korea if it threatened the United States.

The previous administration had made a well-publicized "rebalance" toward making Pacific issues a priority. It had negotiated a multilateral treaty dubbed

A New Order in East Asia? Then U.S. Secretary of State Rex Tillerson, Deputy Prime Minister and Minister of Foreign Affairs Pham Binh Minh, and President Donald J. Trump chat during a state dinner hosted by President Tran Dai Quang of Vietnam in Hanoi on November 11, 2017, at the APEC Conference.

the Trans-Pacific Partnership (TPP) as a way toward containing China's expanding influence and establishing common labor standards and free-trade compacts with its signatories. In the 2016 American presidential campaign, however, both candidates, Trump and Hillary Clinton, had promised to dismantle the TPP as it had come to be viewed as endangering American jobs. Trump had complained repeatedly that China was a "currency manipulator" and that the Chinese were "raping us" on trade, leveling similar charges against Japan, South Korea, and Vietnam as well.

Perhaps more unsettling for long-term allies in the region, however, was the new attitude of the administration's "America First" policy. Whether consciously or unconsciously hearkening back to the isolationist movement of the same name on the eve of World War II, the new president made it clear early on that not only were all of America's allies now expected to pay their own way for defense, but also the U.S. would in the future be much more circumspect about risking its forces in their support. Regarding the looming crisis in Korea, for example, it was suggested to South Korea and Japan that they should consider developing their own nuclear weapons systems—something the Japanese, as history's only victims of a nuclear attack, viewed as particularly repellent.

Thus, the future course of American–East Asian relations, and by extension relations among the East Asian countries themselves, already seemed to be in flux on the eve of the president's trip. The TPP, which its proponents had promised would bring the countries within it closer, as well act as a counterpoise to China, had seen the United States withdraw on President Trump's first day in office (it was ratified by the other signatories in early 2018). In June, the administration withdrew from the Paris Agreement on climate change. With his record of suspicion toward even multilateral defense pacts, his trip, dubbed by the press as "a charm offensive," was intended in part to reassure allies of U.S. support and use his putative negotiation skills in crafting new agreements.

This strategy appeared surprisingly effective in China. On his first day in office, Trump had spoken with the president of the Republic of China (ROC, Taiwan), an act that had initially rankled leaders in the PRC. Now, the president's apparent bonhomie with Xi Jinping, his status as a blunt-spoken billionaire politician, his emphasis on business rather than human rights, his daughter Ivanka's personification of the role of successful woman entrepreneur, and even his granddaughter's singing in Chinese all found praise in the Party media and at the grassroots level. As one interviewee put it to the *New York Times* on November 9, 2017, "If he's doing good for China, I like him. If not, I don't like him."

In the end, however, parties on both sides of the Pacific were not sure of how to view the results of the trip and its meetings. In every country he visited, the American president raised the issue of scrapping present agreements and crafting new ones. Exactly what the substance of these would be, however, was far from clear. The president claimed to get on fabulously with the leaders who met him. Indeed, his reputation as a negotiator was built on his facility in such face-to-face meetings. In this, his preference tended to be toward leaders who wield power largely unencumbered by checks and balances. Thus, his famous admiration for Russian President Vladimir Putin, whom he encountered briefly at the APEC conference, was now shared with the PRC's Xi Jinping, Vietnam's Tran Dai Quang, and the Philippines' Rodrigo Dutarte—who made no secret of his contempt for President Obama and had been widely condemned for his programmatic sanctioned killings of drug traffickers. Indeed, Trump had previously even expressed his admiration for the power of leadership wielded by Kim Jung-un, before he had to deal with Kim's nuclear ambitions.

For the Asian leaders who had received the American president, it seemed clear that something fundamental in their relationship with the U.S. was changing. At every stop on his trip, Trump complained about the host country's policies as being unfair because of the trade surpluses it ran with the U.S. He railed against the World Trade Organization's policies, which he claimed were detrimental to American interests. As he stressed to the APEC members, he would "not let the United States be taken advantage of anymore" and would no longer take part in "large agreements that tie our hands, surrender our sovereignty and make meaningful enforcement practically impossible." At the same time, however, the administration had embarked on a broader "Indo-Pacific" strategy, more in line with previous long-standing, rules-based, free-trade practices overseen by the U.S.—and also seen as a counter to China's initiatives in the region.

Thus, the contrast with Xi Jinping's speech to the assembly could not have been a more stark and confusing reversal of recent roles. APEC members (including the U.S.) make up more than 60 percent of the world's GDP, and there is no doubt Xi captured the mood of the majority of members. In words reminiscent of the previous American view of world trade, Xi encouraged more globalization, more multilateral agreements, and more technology exchanges. Free trade and globalization, he noted, were "irreversible historical trend[s]." In a nod to American complaints, he also asserted that trade needs to be "more open, more balanced, more equitable, and more beneficial to all." There seemed little indication, however, that any of the East Asian states running large trade surpluses with the U.S. would be open to rescinding their own protectionist policies. Indeed, as we have seen, starting with Japan, this has been the fundamental model of their economic rise to power. Thus, those favoring a more aggressive American protectionist policy applauded the president's blunt statements. Summing up the new situation, one BBC commentator framed the struggle as one between the "Chinese Dream" and "America First."

But is the United States really moving away from commitments in the region, or is it simply recasting its emphasis to a more assertive policy on trade? With the exception of the immediate threat of destabilizing the region presented by North Korea, the U.S. in some respects seemed to be moving away from its long-time direct involvement in the region, and implicitly ceding much of its influence to China, while also articulating an even broader vision than before. In the case of North Korea, the threat of massive retaliation for any perceived threat to the U.S., and the president's mercurial statements, may well have pushed Kim Jung-un into talks with South Korea in advance of the 2018 Winter Olympics. Such, at least, was the sentiment of the South Korean president.

In one of the most startling moves of his young administration, President Trump then agreed to meet with Kim in Singapore in June, 2018, in hopes of beginning talks to resolve the more volatile issues between the two countries. The results of that meeting were not dissimilar to those of previous negotiations: general agreement on the need to de-nuclearize the Korean peninsula, with the US agreeing to provide "security guarantees," and implicit acknowledgment of the eventual need for a peace treaty officially ending the Korean War. Trump also agreed to cancel upcoming US-South Korean joint military exercises, and Kim pledged to destroy ballistic missile sites. Soon after, footage emerged from North Korea of underground missile test sites having their entrances demolished, though how many and how thoroughly is still an open question. While the US did scale back its joint military exercises with South Korea, the International Atomic Energy Agency (IAEA) reports that as of late November, 2018, satellite imagery indicates the North Korean nuclear facilities are still in operation.

In the case of China, while President Xi had noted that nations could not evade the "historical trend" of globalism, PRC media also expressed approval of America's apparent retreat from from the region as a whole, seeing it as tacit recognition of China as an equal power as well as an equal partner in stabilizing the region. This sense of approval began to change markedly, however, as the US began to impose tariffs on Chinese goods, starting with solar panels in January, 2018. Soon, a growing list of Chinese goods was added to the tariff lists and by April, China was retaliating with tariffs on American goods—in many cases deliberately targeting products from regions in the US that had supported the president in the 2016 election. What was now being called a "trade war" continues as of this writing with the next round of US tariffs schedule to go into effect in January, 2019. With China retaliating in kind this will mean essentially all goods traded between the US and the PRC will have duties of up to 25% imposed on them. Presidents Trump and Xi were scheduled to meet at the G-20 summit at the end of November, 2018, and despite encouraging pronouncements from both sides, a resolution to the tariff question does not seem immanent as of this writing. Given these developments, what might the new relationships among the states of East Asia look like?

ONE REGION, THREE SYSTEMS?

As we have seen throughout this book, two major trends have dominated the modern history of the region: the quest for autonomy and independence among those states dominated by China, and the more recent challenge posed by imperialism and its postcolonial legacy of "facing up to modernity" without becoming "Western." Ironically, it was this second trend that had proved most traumatic for China itself. In some respects, this is not surprising. The "Sinitic Rim" had millennia of experience in acculturation to the overwhelming influence of China. Indeed, in some cases (as in Yamato Japan), cultural and political borrowing was actively pursued. This, of course, was always tempered by spirited resistance to political absorption and constant negotiation of physical and civilizational boundaries. Thus, there was in some sense a long-standing cultural and psychological template for interpreting and reacting to powerful influences arriving from the outside. This is not to restate the substance of the old, conceptually limited, "impact-response" approach to the region's history, but rather to note that the historical experience of occupation, and forced and voluntary acculturation, contributed to different modes of encountering the "other" than had been the rule in China.

Colonialism and Imperialism

In the case of Korea and Taiwan, moreover, imperialism and cultural onslaught came most forcefully from a newly industrialized East Asian state, Japan. Japan, of course, had been a model of walking the line between modernization and Westernization for these states as well as for early Vietnamese and Chinese reformers. It was a model, however, that was not without critics of its early "Enlightenment and civilization" approach. As Japan added Taiwan, Korea, Manchuria, and later substantial parts of China, and briefly, the whole of Indochina, to its empire such protests exploded into determined resistance. Yet the history of such colonialism—as in the case with the French in Indochina—was also marked by efforts at industrialization and resource extraction that gave these places a push toward twentieth-century modes of modernization. Moreover, the example of a postwar Japan rising from the near complete destruction of its cities and industries to becoming the second-largest economy in the world within four decades after the war's end provided the most attractive model of export-driven "Confucian capitalism" for the entire region.

Here, the contrast with the experience of China is instructive. In a sense, modernization and the attendant struggle for cultural balance saw China lagging behind in overall economic growth until the Four Modernizations. Among scholars writing into the 1980s, the long-standing debate as to why Japan was "successful" as opposed to China, when not occupied with parsing the relative levels of imperialism suffered by both states or how they could be seen through the lens of world systems theory, revolved around culture. Confucianism was antithetical to science, it was said. Its emphasis on family made it a bad match for capitalist industrialization. Having never had to acculturate to the civilization of a powerful invader until the late nineteenth and twentieth centuries, it stubbornly held on to its tradition of being the "middle kingdom" from which culture and innovation flowed out to others. It was thus ill-prepared and unwilling to adapt. Such adaptation as did occur, it was said, was uneven at best, abortive at worst. Even in its adaptation to the most radical Western political theories of Marxism-Leninism, critics noted, it retained in its Maoist core key elements of the old imperial order.

Yet China's recent development seems to have put to rest many of these assumptions. China has surpassed Japan as the world's second-largest economy. It has become a world leader in science, technology, and industry. Its power, prestige, and influence grow by the day. In this respect, its historical arc has curved back to its norm. Seizing on and bettering the models of the earlier Confucian capitalist states, it has been the most assertive in bringing the Sage back to the center of its efforts. Indeed, where only a short time ago, the goal of the Maoist years was to "smash Confucius" and the "feudal" order for which he stood, the People's Republic now vies with the Republic of China or Taiwan to be the true claimant of China's cultural heritage. China's path to modernity without Weternization is thus a curious hybrid of one-party authoritarian rule and a vibrant, yet protectionist, capitalism whose excesses the Communist Party seeks to soften in its quest for "the Harmonious Society" and global economic supremacy.

Twentieth-Century Conflict and Political Configuration

Obviously, the world wars and Cold War have also had a marked impact on the region and, in effect, have been the catalysts for creating what might be called "one region, three systems." This, of course, is a play on the PRC's "one country, two systems" policy toward Hong Kong and Macao. However, it might also be seen as a broad approach to the relative positions of the states of East Asia in the coming decades. The world wars effectively broke the back of Western and Japanese colonialism in the region, with the final French adventure in Indochina a doomed rearguard action. The Cold War, by involving the U.S. and Soviet Union, in part set the stage for the political systems in play today.

I. China and Vietnam: Authoritarian Capitalism

China. The first, and most influential, is of course the PRC. Its political system, officially described as "socialism with Chinese characteristics," aptly describes its syncretism. Although Singapore under Li Kwan Yew provided a model for

China's seemingly incongruous blend of authoritarian rule and market-driven economics, the sheer size and complexity of the PRC daily challenge its viability. Social scientists have long held that market economies will tend to pressure repressive governments to become more open and representative. Indeed, decades of American policy built around "constructive engagement"—bitterly opposed by successive CCP leaders—aimed at inducing just such changes in Communist bloc regimes. Yet despite the apparent fulfillment of this theory in South Korea and Taiwan—or perhaps because of it—the CCP under Xi Jinping has doubled down on its control in China. Dissent is now ferreted out more efficiently than ever via the frighteningly intrusive tools of government-implemented social media apps and a good citizenship rating system to reward and punish the populace

China's enormous economic accomplishments and growing power have prompted some observers to see parallels in its position vis-à-vis the United States to those of a fast-rising German Empire and Great Britain before World War I. With possible flashpoints including the status of Taiwan, the danger of war on the Korean Peninsula, increasingly assertive claims on islands and territorial waters, and cyber-spying and sabotage, chances of a military confrontation may indeed be increasing. The recent trade war with the US might also affect the economy sufficiently to de-stabilize the Communist Party's rule.

Nonetheless, as economic competition continues to grow, China's influence is steadily expanding beyond East Asia. The proposed American "Indo-Pacific" strategy is motivated in large part by China's ambitious Belt and Road Initiatives (BRI). In speeches in Kazakhstan and Indonesia in 2013, Xi Jinping outlined two plans for cooperative regional development—with the active participation of China's answer to the World Bank, the Asian Infrastructure Investment Bank (AIIB). "The Silk Road Economic Belt" aims at cooperative and coordinated resource and infrastructural development for China and the countries along the old Silk Road. The other plan, the "Twenty-First Century Maritime Silk Road," retraces the course of the 15th-century voyages of Zheng He and seeks to involve the countries running from South China through Southeast Asia and on to India, Africa, and the Arabian Peninsula. Perhaps even more ambitious is a "Polar Silk Road" initiative, announced in January 2018. Anxious to take advantage of new passages opening in the Arctic Ocean ice, the Chinese proposal is aimed at spurring development and transport of resources across the region, radically shortening the sea routes to and from Asia, Europe, and North America (see Map 14.1).

The impact of these giant projects has already been felt throughout the region. In addition to American concerns about security and its own economic position, countries in Central Asia, while enthusiastic about the prospect of economic development, are also nervous about the degree of power China will wield among them. Pakistan's enthusiasm for the BRI, for example, has rankled India because the Belt will pass through contested Kashmir. The same concerns grip those along the Maritime Silk Road: Indonesia, a majority-Muslim state, also has a substantial Chinese population; Vietnam, of course, has a long history of opposing Chinese hegemony; India is busy with its own rapid development and in maintaining its influence in the Indian Ocean region.

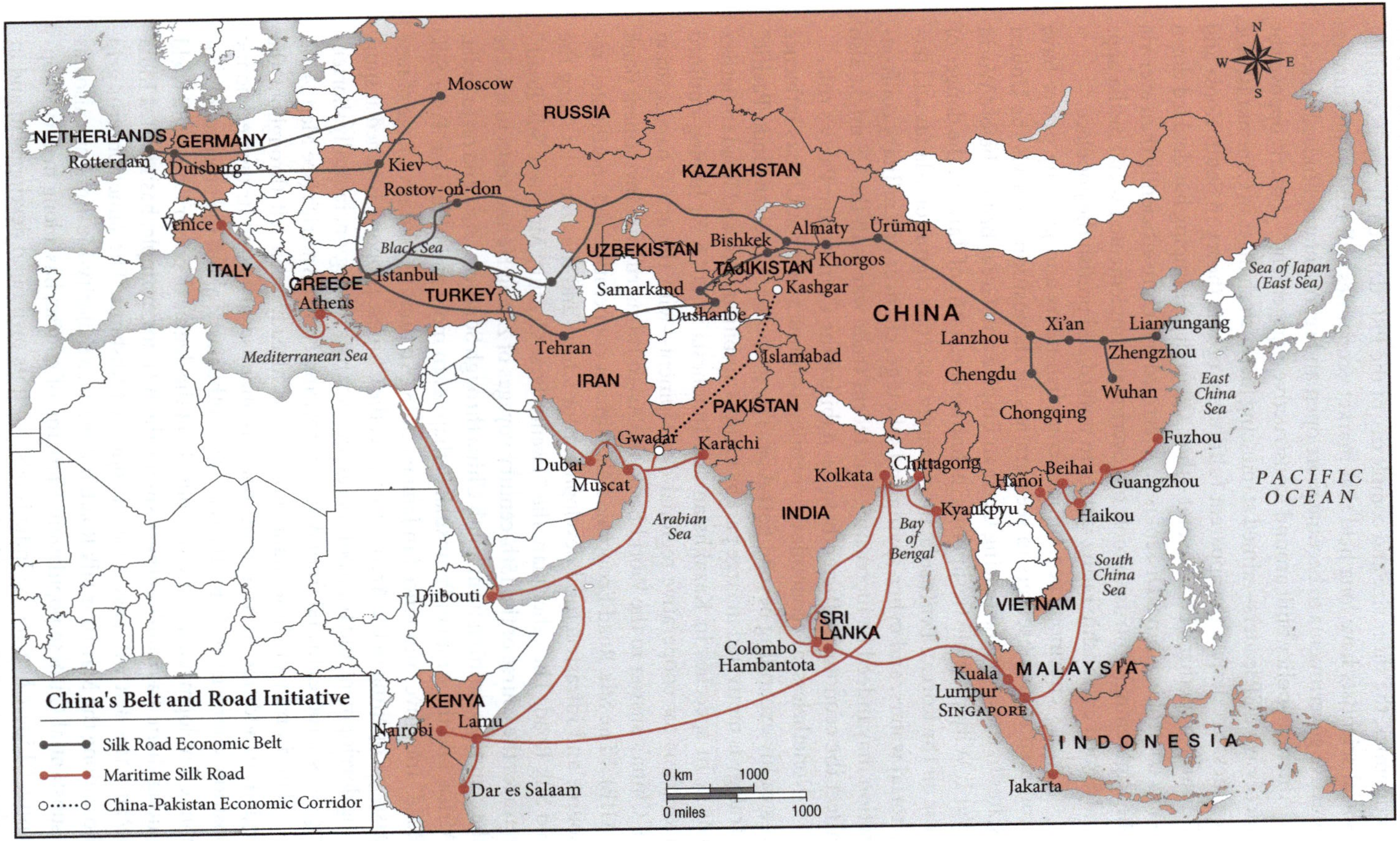

Map 14.1 China's Belt and Road Initiative

China's Belt and Road Initiative

— Silk Road Economic Belt
— Maritime Silk Road
○┈┈○ China-Pakistan Economic Corridor

Moscow
Kiev
Rostov-on-don
Istanbul
Athens
Venice
Rotterdam
Duisburg
NETHERLANDS / GERMANY
ITALY
GREECE
TURKEY
RUSSIA
KAZAKHSTAN
UZBEKISTAN
TAJIKISTAN
Samarkand
Dushanbe
Bishkek
Almaty
Khorgos
Kashgar
Ürümqi
Islamabad
PAKISTAN
IRAN
Tehran
Gwadar
Muscat
Dubai
Karachi
INDIA
Kolkata
SRI LANKA
Colombo
Hambantota
Chittagong
Kyaukpyu
Hanoi
VIETNAM
Haikou
Beihai
Guangzhou
Fuzhou
Chongqing
Chengdu
Lanzhou
Xi'an
Wuhan
Zhengzhou
Lianyungang
CHINA
Kuala Lumpur
SINGAPORE
MALAYSIA
INDONESIA
Jakarta
Djibouti
KENYA
Lamu
Nairobi
Dar es Salaam

Sea of Japan (East Sea)
East China Sea
PACIFIC OCEAN
South China Sea
Bay of Bengal
Arabian Sea
Black Sea
Mediterranean Sea

0 km   1000
0 miles   1000

464

Vietnam. Vietnam's long struggle for independence and unity, coupled with its conflicts of the 1970s and 1980s with China and the Khmer Rouge, has left it on the one hand a regional power eyed by its neighbors with a certain degree of circumspection, and on the other, as a growing economic power based on the Chinese model. Indeed, it is the only state outside of China that has successfully combined its brand of market economics with its avowedly socialist one-party system. As in the past, however, the broader influence of China hovers over Vietnam. Despite opposition, China and Vietnam had worked out plans to build highways from Yun'nan into Vietnam's northern provinces. The recent scandal involving China's development of bauxite mines in Vietnam has underscored the conflict felt by the Party and ordinary citizens about the growing Chinese presence, while Vietnam's growing prosperity and openness, its participation in regional organizations like ASEAN and APEC, and its normalized relations with the U.S. provide it with some leverage in dealing with its neighbor to the north. Internally, pressure to allow opposition parties continues to grow, while government control on the Chinese model—especially via technology—proves increasingly problematic. Yet historical difficulties remain. China's claims on the Spratly Islands resulted in a military clash that killed seventy Vietnamese troops. Although ongoing talks have resulted in both sides pledging cooperation, tensions remain high, as they do with China and the Philippines, Indonesia, and Brunei. Japan, South Korea, Taiwan: Representative Government and Capitalism

Japan. Here, Japan represents the oldest model of syncretizing modernity and indigenous culture, and the most mature in its institutions. In its postwar resurrection, Japan has managed to maintain peaceful relations with its neighbors, and its American-written constitution renounces war as an instrument of national policy and puts stringent limits on its military spending for self-defense. Economically, it seemingly achieved its maximum influence in East and Southeast Asia from the 1970s to the 1990s, when it was the financial and managerial engine that drove the economies of the Confucian capitalist "Little Dragons." During the latter part of the twentieth century, it became the world's second-largest economy and the model for developing export-driven economies throughout the region and the world.

What will happen next in this regard is wide open to speculation. China's exports to the U.S. alone are three times those of Japan. Japan is only now beginning to emerge from a recession that had commenced in the early 1990s. Moreover, its demographics are increasingly skewed toward seniors, and the islands' population levels hover at or below the replacement rate. More alarming for many are the possibilities of radical changes in its defense needs. Long secure, along with Taiwan and South Korea, under the U.S. nuclear and conventional umbrella, China's rising power, the ongoing alarming nuclear threat from North Korea, and the America First policy of the U.S. seem very likely to alter what had been a secure environment in which Japan could thrive.

Flawed as they are, Japan's democratic institutions continue to provide the model for the region's other democracies. Japan had been the only successful constitutional monarchy in the region until falling under militarist influence and defeat in World War II. With its new constitution, it continues in a more democratic fashion, although older Confucian values of deference, group identity, family, and national loyalty endure. As has often been noted, nothing ever disappears in Japan; it always remains covered by layers of the new, only to reassert itself in different forms.

South Korea. The evolution of democratic institutions in South Korea and Taiwan, although not a product of Japanese colonialism, had at least a rudimentary agricultural and economic base from which to start after World War II. As we have seen in Korea, independence and movement toward representative institutions had repeatedly asserted themselves under Japan's occupation, only to be put down. Similar dissent, though less dramatic, took place on Taiwan during the same period. The Cold War in large measure transformed both places, but transformed them for a time into something more reminiscent of China's present authoritarian capitalism than the institutions developing in Japan under American tutelage. Yet the inclination had been there throughout the period. In South Korea, strongman rule was seen as necessary due to the threat from the North and the need for order. As South Korea's economy grew, that need receded and the drive toward freer institutions intensified.

Taiwan. A similar phenomenon occurred on Taiwan. With the imposition of Nationalist rule following the Guomindang defeat on the mainland, the rule of Chiang's one-party system was justified in part by Sun Yat-sen's dictum that "tutelage" in democratic institutions was required before the system could be opened up. By the 1990s, the system was indeed opened up, and both Taiwan and South Korea now possess some of the most vibrant democratic systems in the region.

North Korea: Stalinist Self-Sufficiency

The regional outlier in this paradigm is the Democratic People's Republic of Korea, North Korea. Like Vietnam and the PRC, it sees itself as a Communist regime, but one much closer to the vision of Stalin and, in terms of its economic policies, Mao Zedong, than either of those regimes. The Kims have made North Korea unique among the world's nations: obsessively opaque to outside observers, brutally repressive to its people, erratically aggressive to its neighbors, and wedded to its *juche* theory of self-reliant development that has sacrificed even agricultural subsistence to its oversized military and nuclear programs. Kim Jung-un has remained bellicose toward his near neighbors Japan and South Korea, while continuing a degree of sub rosa trade with the PRC and Russia. The regime's special ire, however, is directed toward the U.S. Despite diplomatic overtures and threats, direct and veiled, by its neighbors, it seems bent on extending *juche* to countering, as it sees it, the nuclear power of the United States. While the recent exchanges between the US and North Korea have prompted cautious optimism about the future of their relations among some observers, the overall volatility of the region has scarcely abated.

The "Chinese Dream" as the East Asian Dream?

What then might the immediate future hold for the region? Uncertainty about American policy at the moment, aggravated by the present trade war, tends to work to the advantage of Xi Jinping's vision of the "Chinese Dream" extending its influence outward. Buoyed by the confidence he enjoys for the moment in the Communist Party, which just elected him to a second five-year term as president, his influence seems likely to expand in the region—particularly if China is perceived not to have lost the tariff struggle. China's ongoing Belt and Road Initiatives, aimed at opening up markets and developing resources in Central Asia, Southeast Asia, and the Indian Ocean, continue to proceed, although not without disquiet about Chinese intentions. The Chinese-sponsored Asian Infrastructure Investment Bank is busily working to supplant the role of the U.S.-backed World Bank and International Monetary Fund in Asian and African projects. The

U.S. withdrawal from the Paris Agreement on climate change places China in a world-leadership position in terms of its "green" projects and other efforts to reduce carbon emissions. China's recent championing of the basic outlines of globalism long supported by the U.S. now places it, in the perception of many, in the vanguard of the fight to reduce poverty and support world development. In short, many see a tectonic shift in global and regional leadership as the U.S. retreats from its position as, in the words of one Chinese citizen, "boss of the world."

Satirical Image of Xi Jinping. "Pax Sinica": Xi Jinping with champagne flute and noisemaker celebrating China's resurgence dressed as an emperor. Note the stylized images on his robes of very modern items: Skyscrapers, warships, fighter planes, and civilian aircraft surrounding a caricature of the old imperial dragon.

Given this vast and growing economic influence, and its soft power through such endeavors as the Confucius Institutes, how will all these circumstances play out for China's

East Asian neighbors? Certainly, all of them will increasingly trade with China, but one might also expect that with the economic ties will also come more intense assertions of political and cultural independence. When a burgeoning Japanese economy challenged that of the U.S. for influence, the following slogan arose from the title of a popular book: "the Japan that can say no!" One sees signs of just this dynamic in both China's relations with the U.S. and in China's neighbors asserting themselves in a similar fashion toward the People's Republic.

Perhaps the most important debate that takes place in the near future, however, may revolve around self-determination and human rights. All of the East Asian nations except North Korea can claim a host of NGOs, political parties, and/or individuals speaking up for human rights and pressuring their governments to improve their policies on this issue. Vietnam, despite its efforts at repression of dissent, has faced ever-more determined assertions of openness. Even China, with its comprehensive efforts to monitor the activities of citizens, still has advocates for increased openness beyond the alleged transparency of the Party's efforts, and is rife with grassroots movements to gain more individual and local agency. Thus, it seems safe to say that, in addition to the economic vitality of the region, its history of resistance to domination by hegemons and the drive for agency in its political institutions will increasingly loom large in the constellation of vital issues facing East Asians.

Glossary

Agrarian Reform Law June 1950 law marking the formal opening of nationwide land reform. Landlords were encouraged, more often forced, to turn land over to their tenants; large nongovernment institutions such as monasteries saw their lands confiscated and distributed. Rough justice was meted out to those who refused to cooperate or those widely disliked by their former tenants. (Ch. 10)

Ainu The descendants of the people believed to have emigrated from the Asian mainland who founded the *Jomon* culture. Called in Japan's imperial times *Emishi*, and today, *Utari*, they are largely confined to the northern island of Hokkaido and are ethnically and culturally distinct from the modern Japanese, as indicated by the word *Ainu*, meaning "the hairy ones." (Ch. 1)

anime Animated cartoon series. On the heels of the popularity of manga, many were turned into animated movie and television series. By the 1960s, these had achieved a substantial following in Japanese pop culture and many, such as the *Sailor Moon* series, became cult favorites all over the world, inspiring clubs and spawning an entire fashion subculture. (Ch. 13)

animistic A religion or belief system that sees spiritual qualities within natural phenomena, animals, or even objects, such as rock formations, waterfalls, rivers, etc. In Japan, it is characteristic of Shinto and its beliefs in *kami*, or spirits animating the natural and supernatural worlds. (Ch. 3)

Anti-Rightist Campaign Movement to shut down the Hundred Flowers Campaign and round up the Party's critics guilty of "rightist" thinking and submit them to "re-education." (Ch. 10)

Art of War Classic treatise attributed to Sun Zi (Sun Tzu) (544–496 BCE) that outlines both strategy and tactics in warfare, as well as examining the reasons for going to war. A staple of Chinese philosophy regarding conflict and a work studied at military academies around the world. (Ch. 2)

bakufu "Tent government." A term denoting the mobile nature of the shogun in acting on behalf of the emperor as his generalissimo. Often used to refer to the shogunate of the Tokugawa. (Ch. 8)

Bamboo Firewall The nickname for the restrictions and impediments the PRC imposes on Internet use in China. The government attempts to force large providers to block pornographic or politically sensitive sites, and some services, like Facebook, are unavailable altogether. (Ch. 10)

Banner system Mode of tax and military organization among the Manchus and during Manchu Qing Dynasty rule in China. Under the Qing, there were eight banners representing military and ethnic divisions in the empire: Manchu, Han, Mongolian, Tibetan, and Muslim Hui. Families within each Banner furnished men who were organized into companies of 300. (Ch. 5)

baojia Systems of rural social organization that appeared in various forms from at least the Song period through the Nationalist period (to 1949). Each group of ten families would choose a headman, the families of each ten headmen would choose a captain, and the leaders at the district level would be responsible to an informal official who acted as intermediary between the people and the district magistrate. (Ch. 5)

Battle of the Coral Sea Fresh from their impressive string of victories in early 1942, the Japanese launched an invasion force to attempt a landing at Port Moresby in Papua New Guinea. Aware of the need to stop the invasion, which posed grave danger to Allied forces in New Guinea, a U.S. task force including two aircraft carriers attempted to intervene. In what came to be called the Battle of the Coral Sea, May 4–8, 1942, Japanese and American aircraft fought the first naval battle in history in which the warring fleets never saw each other. In the end, each side lost one carrier, but the Japanese invasion could not be mounted. And although in terms of losses, the battle was essentially a draw, it is usually seen as a strategic victory for the U.S. (Ch. 13)

boat people In the early years of the newly unified Vietnam during the late 1970s, pressures on ethnic minorities, especially Chinese, pushed them to flee the country, often in flimsy boats. Many ended up in the PRC; others made it to different parts of Southeast Asia, and Australia and North America. (Ch. 12)

Boxers The secret society known as *Yihetuan* ("Militia of the Harmonious Fists"). Anti-Christian, anti-foreign, and at first, anti-Qing until Empress Dowager Cixi allied herself with them in 1900, their name and exercises caused foreign observers to nickname them "boxers." (Ch. 9)

Buddha of the Pure Land Amida Buddha, the center of the devotional Pure Land school. No immersion in esoteric scriptures or ascetic practices was necessary for salvation, which was available to all: simply chanting the name of Amida with sincerity was enough. The bodhisattva *Guanyin* was popularly associated with Pure Land Buddhism, and often depicted as intervening to save those in peril. (Ch. 2)

bushido "The way of the warrior." The code by which Japanese feudal lords (daimyo) and their retainers (samurai) conducted their lives. In addition to rigorous training and ferocity in battle, they were expected to prefer death to captivity or dishonor. (Ch. 4)

chaebols Korean business combines engaged in strategic industries, especially with regard to exports. These business interests were given favorable loans and tax breaks and some, like Samsung, Hyundai, and Daewoo, have become world famous. (Ch. 11)

Chinese Communist Party (CCP) Inspired by the success of the Bolsheviks in Russia and intrigued by the power of Marx's economic and revolutionary arguments, a small group that included Chen Duxiu, Li Dazhao, and Mao Zedong founded the Chinese Communist Party (CCP) in 1921. Although at first, they hewed closely to the Bolshevik example and party line as communicated to them through Comintern, the CCP, after its purge by the Nationalists in 1927, moved to Mao's concept of using peasants as the prime revolutionary force instead of industrial workers. (Ch. 9)

chungin The upper classes in Korea were divided into two classes: *yangban* and *chongin*. The *chongin* comprised the minor officials in the Korean neo-Confucian system. (Ch. 6)

Choson An ancient Korean kingdom, founded perhaps as early as ca. 1000 BCE, whose first recorded mention is in later Chinese records. The name, meaning "the land of the morning calm," was used by the Yi Dynasty (1392–1894). (Ch. 3)

chu nom The attempt by the Vietnamese in the tenth century to make literary Chinese more useful as a written language. Chinese characters were used for its basis, and newly developed Vietnamese characters also added to clarify meaning. (Ch. 3)

The Chrysanthemum and the Sword A 1946 anthropological study of Japanese culture by the American, Ruth Benedict, at the invitation of the U.S. government in 1944 to try to better understand the forces that motivated Japanese behavior in anticipation of the defeat and Occupation of Japan. (Ch. 13)

Cohong In pinyin, *Gonghang*. The licensed monopoly of Chinese merchants in the Canton (*Guangzhou*) trade permitted to deal directly with foreign maritime merchants who had journeyed to China. (Ch. 5)

comfort women Women drawn from areas within the Japanese Empire, particularly Korea and Taiwan, and forced to work in brothels set up to service Japanese military, and in some places, civilian personnel. The role of Japan in this regard has remained a troubled one in postwar relations with the countries from which these women were taken. Over the years, some attempts at compensation have been enacted by successive Japanese governments. (Ch. 11)

Comintern Short for "Communist International." With the creation of the Bolshevik regime in Russia came the Third International—the third iteration of an international communist support organization. Known as Comintern, its mission was to advance the cause of Marxism throughout the world by instruction, training, arms, money, propaganda, and revolutionary struggle. (Ch. 9)

daimyo Japanese feudal lords during the period of the shogunates, from the 1180s until the end of the Tokugawa era in 1867. (Ch. 6)

Dai Viet The name of the state in modern Vietnam founded by Le Loi in 1428. (Ch. 7)

Dao Literally, "the Way," or "the Road." A fundamental Chinese philosophical concept. The Dao (Wade–Giles, Tao) is the animating principle of the cosmos. It is unlimited and indefinable, though its attributes can be hinted at by human beings attempting to grasp its underlying principles and put themselves in tune with it. (Ch. 2)

Daode Jing Variously translated as "The Classic of The Way and Its Power" or "The Way and Its Virtue," it is the central Daoist (Taoist) text. It is noted for its use of short, paradoxical verses meant to suggest the nature of the Dao (the Way) of the universe and the proper relationship of human beings to it. (Ch. 2)

Demilitarized Zone (DMZ) The "neutral" zone marking the border between North and South Korea roughly along the 38th Parallel. Both sides of the Zone are heavily fortified, and clashes resulting from violations of it have occurred periodically since the armistice of 1953. (Ch. 11)

Doolittle Raid Anxious to find a way to strike at Japan following the attack on Pearl Harbor and Japan's impressive gains in Southeast Asia and the Pacific, the U.S. developed a daring plan to launch twin-engine bombers from an aircraft carrier to raid Tokyo and nearby Japanese cities in April 1942. Led by Colonel James Doolittle, the planes had to take off prematurely because of the fear of Japanese discovery of the convoy, and although they caused little damage in Japan, and none of them reached the Chinese airfields where they had planned to land, it was a propaganda victory for the U.S. and sent the message that the Americans intended to pursue the war rather than negotiate. (Ch. 13)

dujun: Chinese military governors; during the period from 1916 to 1926, the term was usually rendered as "warlord." (Ch. 9)

Dutch Learning By the 1630s, the Tokugawa Shogunate had expelled all Western foreigners except the Dutch, who were required to make reports to the Shogun on events in the outside world. The accumulated information was shared among a select group of Japanese and became known as "Dutch Learning." (Ch. 8)

dynastic cycle An idea related to the Mandate of Heaven and formalized in Chinese historiography. In this view, dynasties tend to start with ethical, energetic rulers who have received the Mandate, expand and consolidate their territory, enrich the country, and serve as proper models for the populace. Over time, however, dynasties lose their momentum, coast on past accomplishments, and usually end up with a succession of weak and/or oppressive rulers. At this point, Heaven often manifests its displeasure with weird omens, natural disasters, and ultimately rebellion. With a successful rebellion, a new ruler assumes the Mandate and the next cycle begins. (Ch. 2)

extraterritoriality Sometimes shortened to "extrality." In diplomacy, the practice of exempting resident citizens or subjects of a country from the laws of the host country; diplomatic immunity is a form of extraterritoriality. In China until 1943 and Japan until 1899, the practice was a centerpiece of "unequal treaties" and "treaty ports." In China, the exemptions were extended to include territorial concessions and ultimately the Chinese converts of Christian missionaries. (Ch. 5)

factories In this case, not machine-driven manufacturing centers, but the places where merchant "factors" met to do business. In Canton/Guangzhou, these were the locations in which merchants from European and American companies were allowed to live and work under strict regulations overseen by Chinese authorities. The intent was to restrict their business contacts to the Cohong merchant guild, keep them as isolated as possible from the locals, and forbid them from going into the interior of the country or even the city of Canton itself. (Ch. 5)

Falun Gong Founded in 1992 by Li Hongzhi, Falun Gong draws from traditional Chinese sources, although mostly from Buddhism and the theories of *qi* (energy). Followers engage in exercises meant to strengthen the internal "wheel of law," or *falun*, which draws "cultivation energy" (*gong*) to the practitioner. By the end of the decade, Li claimed millions of followers, but the Chinese government views the movement as subversive and has attempted to suppress it. (Ch. 10)

fengjian Often translated and interpreted as a kind of feudalism, *fengjian* was a decentralized form of government devised by the Zhou in which individuals were granted lands and titles in return for remitting taxes, local governance, and military service. (Ch. 2)

feudatories Chiefs of military districts awarded to those deemed loyal to the Qing in their early years of power. Their strongholds were crushed in the Revolt of the Three Feudatories (1673–1681). (Ch. 5)

The Five Requests The Japanese term for the Twenty-One Demands. So-called because the demands were divided into five groups. (Ch. 13)

Forbidden City The enormous walled compound within the capital of Beijing that contained the quarters and working areas of the emperor, imperial family, imperial eunuchs, and the chief officers of the empire. The main entrance was through the Gate of Heavenly Peace, *Tiananmen*; the famous square of the same name is across the street. Today, the Forbidden City is a museum and tourist destination. (Ch. 5)

Four Modernizations Deng Xiaoping's policy reforms of 1978 mandating modernization of agriculture, defense, industry, and science and technology. Among other things, the new policy advocated international exchanges, a new "open door" for trade, a responsibility system for a transition to market economics, and sending students abroad to study. (Ch. 10)

Four Noble Truths The four fundamental insights attributed by Buddhists to the Buddha: (1) All life is marked by suffering. (2) Suffering is caused by craving. (3) If one can eliminate the craving, one can eliminate the suffering. (4) One eliminates craving by following the Eightfold Path. (Ch. 2)

Four Olds One of the goals of the Cultural Revolution was the elimination of the vestiges of older ideas and the creation of "proletarian consciousness." Hence, a campaign was launched calling for the exposure and eradication of the "Four Olds: old customs, old culture, old habits, and old ideas. In addition to the human cost of the campaign, a vast amount of China's irreplaceable cultural heritage was destroyed in the course of pursuing its goals. (Ch. 10)

Four Tigers Sometimes called the "Little Dragons" because of their booming economies in the 1980s: South Korea, Taiwan, Singapore, and Hong Kong (Hong Kong is now once again part of China) (Ch. 11)

Gang of Four After the death of Mao in 1976, more moderate leadership came to the fore with Hua Guofeng and, shortly afterward, Deng Xiaoping. Condemning the excesses of the Cultural Revolution, the new leaders brought the so-called Gang of Four—Mao's widow Jiang Qing, Zhang Chunqiao, Yao Wenyuan, and Wang Hongwen—who had been instrumental in pursuing the Revolution's goals of "proletarianization," to trial in 1980. Jiang Qing and Zhang Chunqiao were sentenced to death, later commuted to life imprisonment; Wang received life and Yao, twenty years. Jiang Qing committed suicide in 1991 while stricken with throat cancer. (Ch. 10)

geisha Professional female entertainers. Highly skilled in conversation, traditional music, dance, and other arts, they provided chaste, ritualized female companionship for formal social occasions among elite men. Their costumes and elaborate makeup were also along traditional lines. (Ch. 8)

Genji Monogatori The Tale of Genji, attributed to Lady Murasaki (Murasaki Shikibu). Its subject matter concerns the life and loves of a loosely fictional Prince Genji during the tenth- and eleventh-century Heian Japanese court; it is considered to be the world's first novel. (Ch. 3)

genro The Emperor Meiji's group of senior advisors during Japan's swift transformation into a modern nation-state and empire. Among the most prominent was Ito Hirobumi, the architect of Japan's constitution in 1889. (Ch. 8)

ger Felt tent carried by the Mongols and other nomadic steppe peoples; often called a "yurt." (Ch. 4)

Grand Canal Still the world's longest artificial waterway at 1,104 miles, running from Hangzhou to Beijing. Like the Great Wall, it was initially composed of a number of smaller canals knit together, in this case by the Sui, and expanded by subsequent dynasties. Provided vital north–south transport, particularly for commercial products, food, and tribute grain for the imperial capitals of the north. (Ch. 2)

Grand Council Advisory body set up by the Yongzheng emperor in 1733 to discuss matters of state. It soon supplanted the Grand Secretariat as the most important deliberative body during the Qing Dynasty. (Ch. 5)

Greater East Asia Co-Prosperity Sphere In keeping with its wartime propaganda as the leader of an "Asia for the Asiatics" and liberator of peoples from Western colonialism, Japan attempted to organize the peoples within its empire as an entity called the Greater East Asia Co-Prosperity Sphere. Countries were promised autonomy and even independence and were called upon to support Japan's war effort. The alleged benefits of the organization, however, would only be realized when Japan won the war; in effect, they remained void. (Ch. 13)

The Great Game The strategic struggle, ultimately lasting through the nineteenth century and continuing in modified form until World War II, for control and hegemony in Central Asia among Russia, Great Britain, the Ottoman Empire, Russia, and the Qing. After World War I, although the Qing and Ottoman empires were gone, the struggle continued among Britain, the former Soviet Union, and Nationalist China. (Ch. 5)

The Great Leap Forward The drive to communize China in one massive mobilization campaign in 1958. Peasant lands were consolidated into huge communal farms, each commune was supposed to make its own implements from iron and steel tools, and household goods were requisitioned to be melted down into ingots in backyard furnaces. The Leap was such a catastrophic failure that Mao stepped down from Party leadership and the famine shortly thereafter may have taken upwards of 30 million lives. (Ch. 10)

Guomindang In Wade–Giles, *Kuomintang*. The Nationalist Party. Usually abbreviated as *GMD* (in pinyin), or in older works and on Taiwan, *KMT*. (Ch. 9)

Gwangju Massacre Following the December 12, 1979, coup staged by General Chun Doo-hwan, which had been accompanied by student demonstrations, a nine-day protest by the Gwangju Democratization Movement was violently suppressed by the military. The Gwangju Massacre, as it became known, produced an official death toll of 200, with another 850 injured. (Ch. 11)

Hagakure "Hidden Leaves" or "Hidden by the Leaves." A guide to the spirit and practice of *bushido* compiled from commentaries by Yamamoto Tsunetomo, a retainer in the feudal domain now encompassed by Saga Prefecture from 1709 to 1716. (Ch. 8)

haiku Short (seventeen-syllable), emotionally charged poems that are today among the most recognizable—and widely imitated—forms of Japanese literary craft throughout the world. Among its masters was Basho, active in the latter seventeenth century. (Ch. 8)

Hakkas In Mandarin, *kejia* or *kejiaren*. Not an ethnic group but a minority composed of Mandarin-speaking Han Chinese who migrated south from the north during earlier dynastic changes and maintained customs separate from their neighbors, who discriminated against them and sometimes attacked them. One of the core groups of the Taiping movement. (Ch. 1)

han The old feudal domains of Japan during its various shogunates. The *han* were dismantled in the 1870s and a modern provincial and prefectural system instituted under Emperor Meiji. (Ch. 8)

han'gul A syllabary (a writing system based on the sound of syllables) introduced by King Sejong of the Yi Dynasty in 1443 as a simple and effective way of writing the Korean language. Called *Hunmin chong-um* ("proper sounds to instruct the people"), it was an immense aid to encouraging literacy—as opposed to literary Chinese—and is still used today. (Ch. 3)

Han Learning Movement A literary movement by a group of Chinese scholars in the seventeenth and eighteenth centuries dedicated to close textual examination for the purpose of pursuing original texts and intent within the Confucian canon. (Ch. 5)

hara kiri seppuku; ritual suicide of the warrior meant to show his sincerity in being willing to seek death. The ritual involves ablutions, following which the warrior opens his kimono, takes his short sword, and then stabs himself in the belly, cuts horizontally, and then upward. A companion stands behind him with a long sword, to behead him to prevent his crying out in pain and thus dishonoring himself. (Ch. 8)

Harmonious Society A conceptual approach to policy articulated by Hu Jintao in 2006 and endorsed by the Chinese Communist Party, in which rapid economic growth should be accompanied by efforts to reduce social tensions among classes, regions, and minorities. Economically, it calls for "sustainable development." Politically, it seeks to reduce corruption and collusion between Party members and those in the private sector. At the same time, it also strongly opposes any attempts at regional and/or ethnic minority "splitism." (Ch. 10)

high-level equilibrium trap Still controversial theory first proposed by Mark Elvin in his *The Pattern of the Chinese Past* (1973). The theory suggests that despite having the necessary preconditions for an industrial revolution, China did not experience one because its economy, although near the limits of its pre-industrial capacity, was still in equilibrium. For an industrial revolution to begin, the theory goes, the economy—like Britain's in the eighteenth century—must be in disequilibrium and require innovation to correct the deficit. Thus, China was caught in a "high-level equilibrium trap." (Ch. 5)

Hundred Days' Reform The accession of the young Guangxu emperor in 1898 spurred hope for genuine reform among many Chinese officials and scholars, among them Kang Youwei and Liang Qizhao. In the summer of 1898, Kang sent a series of proposals to the emperor, who attempted to enact them, thus prompting what became known as the Hundred Days' Reform. Alarmed at the wholesale changes promised by the reforms, however, Empress Dowager Cixi launched a coup against the emperor, had him placed under house arrest, and drove Kang and Liang out of the country. (Ch. 9)

Hundred Flowers Campaign The 1956–1957 drive in which the Chinese Communist Party encouraged intellectuals to critique the government's performance. At first hesitant, the intellectuals were assured that criticism was their patriotic duty. When the criticism mounted and suggestions were made to allow an opposition party, the CCP shut down the campaign and launched the Anti-Rightist Campaign. (Ch. 10)

Ilkhanates The Mongol-controlled Islamic states in Persia and the Middle East during the thirteenth and fourteenth centuries following the sack of Baghdad in 1258. (Ch. 4)

Jomon The long Neolithic period in Japanese history from ca. 10,000 to 300 BCE, marked by distinctive clay pottery with herringbone designs, and clay female figurines and male phallic pieces. (Ch. 1)

juche The policy in North Korea of strict self-reliance begun by Kim Il-sung as a kind of Korean counterpart to the Chinese Cultural Revolution; it was meant to eliminate vestiges of bourgeois thinking and create a cult of personality around Kim and his successors. The policy continues today. (Ch. 11)

junshi The practice of accompanying one's master in death. Originally carried out by favored samurai with the departure of their lords, it was also practiced in sensational fashion by General Nogi Maresuke and his wife in 1912 when he followed Emperor Meiji in death. (Ch. 13)

junzi In Confucianism, the "gentleman" or "superior man" who has progressed through his understanding of *li* to *ren*. (Ch. 2)

kabuki The most popular form of theater in Tokugawa times, noteworthy for its often bawdy behavior and raucous performances, with female parts played by male actors. (Ch. 8)

kamikaze The "divine wind" of the typhoon that, providentially for Japan, scattered the second Mongol attempt at invasion in 1281 and allowed the Japanese to defeat the surviving forces. It was later used as a term for the desperate attempt by Japan's air forces to disrupt the American invasions of Japanese-held islands in the Pacific by crashing bomb-laden planes into American ships during the final months of World War II. (Ch. 4)

kana Japanese syllabary consisting of fifty characters developed from simplified Chinese characters and character fragments. The two main types are *hiragana*—meant to depict sounds and compose words from indigenous Japanese sources; and *katakana*—a more angular script used for foreign loanwords. In addition to both of these scripts, modern Japanese also includes full Chinese characters called *kanji*. (Ch. 3)

keiretsu Japanese conglomerates formed during the 1950s and 1960s in the wake of the dismantling of the *zaibatsu* cartels during the Allied occupation of Japan. (Ch. 13)

khan From the Mongol term for "ruler." Used initially to simply describe clan leaders or local rulers, the term came into widespread use with the conquests of Genghis Khan ("The Universal Ruler"). The rulers of individual Mongol states and substates were also referred to as *khan*, the most famous of whom was Kubulai Khan during the Mongol-ruled Yuan Dynasty in China. (Ch. 4)

khatun "Queen." Title ascribed to each of Genghis Khan's daughters when given in marriage to subordinate local rulers to cement their loyalty. Because of their bloodlines and the Mongols more egalitarian view of the role of women, the *khatun* were often, in fact, the real rulers of the realms into which they married. (Ch. 4)

koan From the Chinese *gongan* ("public case"). In Zen training, masters pose paradoxical questions and statements for contemplation to their students. Called *koan*, they are meant to raise doubts, shake up the certainties of the novices, and open them to a state of mindfulness—along with the performance of humbling tasks—that aid in the achievement of enlightenment (*satori*). (Ch. 8)

kofun Large burial mounds found on the Kanto Plain dating from the third century CE, the beginnings of the Yamato state. (Ch. 3)

kokutai "The national essence." A difficult-to-define spiritual and cultural quality that was said to embody Japan's unique place among the world's nations. At its center stood the imperial institution that was said to have existed in an unbroken line from the Sun Goddess, Amaterasu, and had begun with the first emperor, Jimmu, in 660 BCE. (Ch. 8)

Kong fuzi Literally, "the Master Kong." The name by which Confucius is often called in the Confucian canon. Jesuit missionaries in the late sixteenth century transliterated the title into Latin as "Confucius." (Ch. 2)

Legalism The system of government established in the state of Qin and in the first Chinese empire created by the Qin. Championed by Han Fei and Li Si and put into practice by the first emperor, it called for all subjects to devote themselves to the power and welfare of the state, for the emperor to be the ultimate arbiter of what is good for the state, for the suppression of all knowledge not approved by the state, and for a comprehensive and strict code of laws and punishments enforced equally on all classes. (Ch. 2)

Le Loi Founder (1384–1433) of the Le Dynasty of Dai Viet (1428–1789), which adopted neo-Confucianism as its governing ideology. (Ch. 7)

li Variously interpreted as "ritual" or "rules of decorum," *li* is the framework of action by which one may come to "humaneness" (*ren*). The proper rules of behavior based on the best moral examples, rites and rituals designed to reinforce proper behavior, just laws that not only restrict the bad but also encourage the good are all part of *li*. Immersion in *li* in one's personal life, family, and society leads to internalizing its principles and in its full actualization allows one to know how to act morally in any situation. One's desires and *ren* then become one. (Ch. 2)

little red book The nickname of the pocket-sized volume, *Quotations from Chairman Mao Zedong*, that became the icon of the Cultural Revolution. For a time, it was the source of all wisdom for Chinese people desperate to grasp the direction of the political winds and place themselves on the "correct" side of any political discussion or campaign. (Ch. 10)

loess A light, dry, mineral-rich soil, reddish-yellow in color blown into North China and built up by centuries of prevailing winds. It provides the fertile silt so important to agriculture in ancient China and gives the Yellow River its name. (Ch. 1)

Long March The year-long trek of Mao's troops from Jiangxi to Yan'an from 1934 to 1935. Desperate to break out of the tightening circle of Chiang Kai-shek's forces, Mao forced a breach and retreated with his army into the back-country, where his troops endured starvation, rugged topography, often hostile locals, and constant harassment by Chiang's forces and local warlords. (Ch. 9)

Longshan culture Neolithic communities to the east of the Yangshao settlements that flourished from about 4500 to 1500 BCE, marked by finely crafted black pottery made on a potter's wheel and fired at high temperatures. (Ch. 2)

Mandarin Road The Quan Lo, or "Mandarin Road," in Vietnam running from Hanoi and eventually to Saigon bound the country together commercially and politically during the early nineteenth century. (Ch. 7)

Mandate of Heaven A guiding concept of the Chinese view of history in which Heaven gives its approval to rule (the Mandate) only to leaders who are ethically fit to rule. If they prove oppressive, dissolute, or inept, the people are authorized to rebel and replace the ruler. If such a rebellion is successful, the new ruler receives Heaven's Mandate, founds a new dynasty, and the "dynastic cycle" begins anew. (Ch. 2)

mandate system The Treaty of Versailles ending World War I provided for the founding of an international body called the League of Nations. The League's Covenant called for trusteeship of the colonies of the defeated Central Powers under a system of "mandates." Some were deemed ready for independence; some were slated to be governed by one of the victorious Allied countries temporarily and then granted independence; the third group would need long-term supervision before they could stand on their own. Although idealistic in conception, in practice, the system retained the basic qualities of colonialism. (Ch. 9)

manga Magazine cartoon series, beginning in the 1950s, that became hugely popular and emblematic of Japanese pop culture throughout the world. Two of the most famous, both of which also became animated features, were *Astro Boy* and *Speed Racer.* (Ch. 13)

Mao Zedong Thought The collective term for Mao's writings, particularly his theories on Marxism and peasant revolution. China's official philosophy includes Mao Zedong Thought along with Marxism-Leninism, and the ideas of recent leaders such as Deng Xiaoping, Hu Jintao, and Jiang Zemin. (Ch. 10)

matrilocal Located or centered on the family or residence of the wife. (Ch. 6)

May Fourth Movement The movement that is usually cited as galvanizing modern Chinese Nationalism. Dates from May 4, 1919, when the representatives at the Versailles Peace Conference decided to award Japan the former German concession in Shandong. The move sparked national demonstrations and a boycott against Japan and the foreign powers. (Ch. 9)

Meiji Constitution Starting with the Meiji Restoration in 1868, Japan's efforts at modernization had included studying the political systems of the Western powers. In 1889, under the direction of Ito Hirobumi, Japan's first constitution—often referred to as the Meiji Constitution—was promulgated. Remaining in force until 1945, it provided for a Diet, a group of ministers responsible to the emperor, and limited voting rights for subjects, expanded to universal manhood suffrage in 1925. (Ch. 8)

mission civilistrice The French "civilizing mission" whereby French colonialists and their supporters championed the idea that France's imperial endeavors were meant, at least in part, to be altruistic by helping "backward" peoples reach the "higher" level of civilization of the West in general and France in particular. This was often coupled with the idea that the colonies were being developed into a larger entity called "Overseas France." (Ch. 12)

monsoon system A regular weather pattern governing activity in the Indian Ocean and Western Pacific. It is most notable for its reliable winds and large, consistent rainfall in summer, flowing from the East African coast northeast to the Indian subcontinent, Southeast Asia, Southern China, and much of Japan and Korea. (Ch. 1)

My Lai Massacre In March 1968, American soldiers searching for guerrillas killed between 340 and 500 unarmed men, women, and children in the village of My Lai, South Vietnam. The event pushed opposition to the war to a new height in the U.S. (Ch. 12)

Nam Viet The "far South" region encompassing modern South China and northern Vietnam during the Qin and Han Chinese dynasties. (Ch. 3)

Neolithic Revolution The period beginning with the retreat of the last Ice Age approximately 12,000 years ago, when human groups began to domesticate plants and animals and to live in settled societies. (Ch. 2)

Neo-Confucianism The philosophy developed over several centuries during the Confucian revival of the Song, and subsequently refined during the Ming and Qing periods, when it became China's official ideology. Taking the ethical ideas of older Confucian self-cultivation and synthesizing them with Buddhist and Daoist speculative thought, the brothers Cheng Hao and Cheng Yi, and especially Zhu Xi during the eleventh and twelfth centuries, added a cosmological strain of thought and distinctive epistemology (approaches to acquiring knowledge) to Confucianism. (Ch. 2)

New Culture Movement The movement among intellectuals in the early years of the Chinese republic and warlord period to discard Confucianism, the old literary language, and old customs in general in favor of the latest trends in Europe and the U.S., science and democracy, and vernacular language. (Ch. 9)

New Youth The emblematic literary journal of the New Culture Movement. Its title was popularized as the French *La Jeunesse*, and its early contributors included some of China's greatest writers of the twentieth century: LuXun, Hu Shi, Li Dazhao, and Chen Duxiu. (Ch. 9)

Nihongi Along with the *Kojiki* (712), the *Nihongi* (720) was the earliest history of Japan. It was written according to Chinese models using literary Chinese, which had become Japan's first written language. (Ch. 3)

Noh A highly abstract form of traditional theater that became popular among the warrior elites during the Ashikaga and Tokugawa periods, often featuring romanticized historical themes. It is today regarded as being among Japan's great cultural traditions, and some of its most celebrated performers have been awarded the honor of being named as "living national treasures." (Ch. 8)

One-Child Policy As part of the overall trends springing from the Four Modernizations, in 1980, China put into place a policy restricting families to one child in an effort to curb population growth. Although a number of exemptions were introduced over the years—a second child was permitted if the first one was a girl; second children were also permitted if one of the parents was an only child; most minorities were exempt as well—the rate of population growth dropped. Loss of benefits and fines were imposed for violators and abortion mandatory for a third pregnancy. With China's demographics skewed increasingly toward the elderly because of the program, however, the policy was discontinued in 2015. (Ch. 10)

Open Door The "race for concessions" following China's defeat by Japan in 1895, and the abortive attempt at reform in 1898, spurred foreign powers to stake out spheres of influence for themselves in advance of the possible collapse of the Qing Dynasty. To head this off, the American Secretary of State John Hay advocated a policy of equal trading rights in China, which came to be called the "Open Door policy." With British backing, the other powers agreed to the policy. (Ch. 5)

oracle bones The shoulder blades of oxen or plastrons (bottom shells) of tortoises used in Shang divination. Questions are asked of the heavenly ancestors, the bones are heated and tapped with a rod to induce cracks, which are then interpreted as answers. The questions and answers are then inscribed on the bones.

The caches of thousands of such bones near Anyang are the closest thing archaeologists have to a Shang historical archive. (Ch. 2)

ortogh Pioneering effort by the Mongols in setting up merchant associations in which capital could be pooled to finance long-distance caravans to reduce risk and personal liability. Such associations received tax benefits and are seen by some scholars as foreshadowing the later development of limited liability corporations centuries later. (Ch. 4)

Outline Plan for the Reorganization of Japan The 1919 treatise by Japanese nationalist Kita Ikki calling for a suspension of the constitution, clarification of the *kokutai* and emperor's role, an eight-hour workday, and nationalization of key industries. The plan inspired nationalists to attempt a coup in February 1937, during which Kita himself was captured and executed. (Ch. 13)

Pan-Asianism A political concept developed in the early twentieth century advocating a united East Asia or, in some variants, all of Asia as a bloc to resist Western colonialism. Japan had taken the most active role in this regard and posited its imperial expansion as leading the way to such a united Asia—an "Asia for the Asiatics." (Ch. 12)

Pax Mongolica A term often used to denote the period of the height of the Mongol Empire, from the late 1200s to the later 1300s, when, like the *Pax Romana* of ancient Rome at its furthest extent, a period of relative peace and order prevailed, and trade within the Mongol sphere was fostered. (Ch. 4)

People's Liberation Army The military of the CCP and, since 1949, the People's Republic of China. The philosophy behind this force was that it was initially a guerrilla army made up of ordinary citizens, who also did civilian work when they were not fighting. They cultivated the image of being at one with the ordinary people, treating them fairly and refraining from harassing them. (Ch. 9)

pieds noirs Literally, "black feet." These were colonists from France who settled in North Africa, especially Algeria. Their relatively large numbers resulted in Algeria achieving an elite governmental status in France's empire and also encouraged the French to fight a bloody war to keep the colony until its independence in 1962. (Ch. 12)

Politburo The central policymaking body of the Chinese Communist Party. (Ch. 10)

qing Minister or chief functionary of the Zhou rulers or the various feudal lords (*hou*). (Ch. 2)

Qin Shi Huangdi The founding emperor of the Qin Dynasty and imperial China itself (literally, "First Emperor of the Qin"). (Ch. 2)

queue The Manchu hair style for men, which became a mandatory sign of loyalty to the Qing Dynasty from 1645 to 1912. The forehead was shaved, with the remaining hair long and plaited into a braid. (Ch. 5)

Rape of Nanking The capture of the Nationalist Chinese capital of Nanjing by the Japanese in late 1937 set off a period of horrendous rape, massacre, and other atrocities by Japanese troops. It later came to light that this had been a purposeful policy aimed at breaking Chinese morale and encouraging them to negotiate a settlement. Instead, it encouraged the Chinese to fight on and resulted in worldwide outrage at Japan. Estimates of the dead vary from 100,000 to 300,000. (Ch. 9)

Records of the Grand Historian (Shiji) The first attempt at a complete history of China from the mythical period to the Han Dynasty, authored by the father and son Sima Tan (d. 110 BCE) and Sima Qian (145–86 BCE). Its format and subject matter became the standard for nearly all subsequent Chinese dynastic histories. (Ch. 2)

ren "Humaneness" or "humanity" (as behavior). A fundamental Confucian concept in which the study of moral examples and principles, and rigorous self-cultivation, all lead one to instinctively act in a moral way and thus move toward being in tune with the *dao*. (Ch. 2)

rentiers From the French. People—and often their extended families—who live off of fixed incomes like rents or securities. (Ch. 6)

Resist America-Aid Korea One of the first mass mobilization campaigns of the Maoist era. It was aimed at showing solidarity with North Korea, supporting the Chinese counterattack on UN forces in Korea, and identifying potentially disloyal elements in the new state. (Ch. 10)

Rites Controversy During the period of Jesuit influence at the court of Emperor Kangxi, the papacy objected to Jesuits allowing such practices as ancestor veneration to continue among Chinese converts. The controversy continued into the reign of the Yongzheng emperor who finally expelled the order in 1724. (Ch. 5)

ronin Masterless samurai. Often associated with the play by Chikamatsu Monzaemon called *The Forty-Seven Ronin*. (Ch. 8)

Sacred Edicts A set of sixteen maxims on leading a proper neo-Confucian life issued by Emperor Kangxi which became part of student curricula. (Ch. 5)

samurai The warrior retainers of Japanese feudal lords (daimyo), who pledged to give their lives for him and lived according to the code of *bushido*, "the way of the warrior." (Ch. 3)

sankin kotai "The law of alternate attendance." Under the regulations established by the Tokugawa, the "outer" (*tozama*) daimyo (those who surrendered last to the Tokugawa) were required to spend every other year in the capital of Edo and leave their families as hostages in the interim years to safeguard against rebellion. (Ch. 8)

satori In Zen Buddhism, the flash of insight that leads to enlightenment among practitioners. (Ch. 8)

scholar-gentry The elite class in rural imperial China. Entry into the scholar-gentry required passing at least the first round of Confucian examinations or, in some cases, purchasing a degree. Since the surest route to both wealth and power was the exams to secure a government post, these men and their families generally acquired land and wealth along with their positions. Their wealth, prestige, and the fact that many of them were retired or awaiting official appointments gave them leading status in their communities. (Ch. 2)

Shanghai Communique The announcement resulting from U.S. President Richard M. Nixon's trip to China in 1972 stating that both sides would extend official diplomatic recognition to each other, that the U.S. would no longer oppose the PRC's entry into the United Nations, and that the U.S. would downgrade its diplomatic relationship with the Republic of China on Taiwan. (Ch. 10)

shi The lower officials, some of noble families, some of commoner households. Confucius was a member of this class. (Ch. 2)

Shinto The indigenous religion of Japan marked by the intersection of the spirit world of *kami* with that of the material one, and notable for frequent purification rites and its emphasis on fertility and reverence for nature. (Ch. 3)

Shujing Known variously as "the Book of History" or "the Classic of Documents," it is a detailed compilation of historical materials allegedly from 2357 to 631 BCE, much of it of questionable accuracy. It remains, however, along with oracle bones, the primary literary source of the history of northern China in remote antiquity. (Ch. 2)

Sinification The process by which non-Chinese peoples become acculturated to Chinese norms and society. (Ch. 2)

Socialist Realism Artistic, architectural, and literary style imported from the Soviet Union and popularized throughout the People's Republic in the 1950s and early 1960s. It was intended to elevate ordinary people to heroic proportions, depicting them marching bravely against capitalist imperialism, singing on their way to the fields, and so forth. The most widely recognized painting of this genre is the giant portrait of Mao that still hangs over the Gate of Heavenly Peace in Beijing. During the Cultural Revolution, the style was pushed out in favor of the more severe and restricted Socialist Idealism, or Revolutionary Romanticism. (Ch. 10)

Special Economic Zone (SEZ) As part of Deng Xiaoping's Four Modernizations, older collectivist forms of agriculture and industry were to be dismantled in favor of more privatization, market economics, and the "responsibility system." Special Economic Zones were set up in various places in order to experiment with different ideas, the most effective of which would then be adopted by the country as a whole. One of the earliest and most famous of these was Shenzhen, near Guangzhou, now one of China's larger cities. (Ch. 10)

spiritual pollution With China's increased openness to foreign trade and technology came the increasing flow of foreign culture, much of it considered by the Party to be injurious to public morals and to Party ideology. In 1983, a campaign was launched against such popular expressions as as risqué music videos, pornography, revealing fashions, and cultural exports—literature, art, film—containing potentially subversive material. Such items were lumped under the heading of "spiritual pollution." (Ch. 10)

Taiho Code: As part of the changes following the adoption of Chinese models of government, philosophy, writing, architecture, and culture more generally, the Taiho Code of 702 outlined the basic laws of Japan for over a millennium until the promulgation of new codes under Japan's emperor Meiji in the latter part of the nineteenth century. (Ch. 3)

Taika The Great Reform of 645 that spelled the thoroughgoing transformation of the Yamato government and culture according to the model of Tang-era China. (Ch. 3)

Taiping The movement founded by Hong Xiuquan (1813–1864) based on a radical interpretation of Protestant Christianity in which Hong believed himself to be Christ's younger brother. The movement sought the creation of the "Heavenly Kingdom of Great Peace" (*taiping tianguo*), mandating the equality of all believers—including men and women—abolition of private property, elimination of gambling and opium smoking, and the overthrow of the Manchus and the Confucian system. The struggle they initiated lasted from 1851 to 1864 and took some 20 to 30 million lives. (Ch. 5)

Taisho Democracy The period in Japan from the accession of Emperor Taisho in 1912 until his death in 1926. Because Taisho was an infirm and comparatively weak ruler, power during his reign shifted to cabinet ministers, political parties, and popular politicians. The government's most noteworthy development in this regard was the granting of universal manhood suffrage in 1925. (Ch. 11)

Tanglu The code of laws developed under Tang Emperor Taizong that tied together previous law codes and the large corpus of customary law into a body of statutes of 502 articles and commentaries and explanations. It remained the basis for imperial Chinese law and became a model code for states modeled on the Chinese system. (Ch. 2)

Tank Man During the watershed suppression of the demonstrators in Tiananmen Square on June 4, 1989, and in the days following, a lone man—whose identity is still unknown—stood in front of a line of tanks and for a time forced the column to halt. He even climbed up on the lead tank to intercede with the driver. The video and still pictures of the incident became the symbols to the world of the political cleavages in China under the Four Modernizations. (Ch. 10)

taotie Artistic motifs characteristic of Shang and early Zhou bronze vessels, with stylized shapes and faces, sometimes incorporating elements of real and mythical animals within them. (Ch. 2)

Tay Son Revolt The Nguyen brothers, sometimes called the Tay Son brothers for the district from which they came, sparked a massive rebellion in the late eighteenth century. Nguyen Hue named himself emperor in 1788, taking the reign name Quang Trung. (Ch. 7)

Tet Offensive The mass offensive organized by the Vietcong during the Vietnamese New Year (Tet) in early 1968. Although the attack ultimately failed, it had the effect of convincing the Johnson administration in the U.S. that its Vietnam War was unwinnable. (Ch. 12)

Three-Anti and Five-Anti Campaigns (in pinyin, *sanfan* and *wufan*). Like the Resist America-Aid Korea movement of the early 1950s, these campaigns, launched in 1951 and 1952, were targeted at eliminating certain practices (corruption, waste, "bureaucratism," bribery, theft of state property, tax evasion, cheating on government contracts, stealing state economic information) and more broadly purging the disloyal, routinizing people to report on each other, and preparing to nationalize business and industry. (Ch. 10)

Three Emperors The three most dynamic and powerful Qing emperors, Kangxi, Yongzheng, and Qianlong, who served sequentially from 1664 to 1795. (Ch. 5)

The Three People's Principles *San min zhuyi.* The statement of Sun Yat-sen's Revolutionary Alliance, and later the Nationalist Party, of the goals for a Chinese state. Sovereignty—expulsion of the Manchus and abrogation of the unequal treaties; democracy—a constitution-based democratic republic as the basic governmental structure; and "the people's livelihood"—sometimes translated as "socialism" but based on government-sponsored division of the land and elimination of absentee landlordism. (Ch. 9)

The Three Represents Jiang Zemin's set of principles laid out in 2000 that anchors the reforms of the previous two decades firmly in place as Party policy. According to Jiang, the Party must always represent the "requirements for developing China's advanced productive forces," "orientation of China's advanced culture," and "fundamental interests of the overwhelming majority of the Chinese people." (Ch. 10)

Thirty-Six Views of Mount Fuji A famous series of ukiyo-e of various subjects, all of which include some rendering of Japan's most famous peak, by the artist Katsushika Hokusai (1760–1849). (Ch. 8)

Tonghak "Eastern Learning." A movement combining elements of Confucianism and Buddhism with the desire to resist foreign incursion and cultural influences. The movement led to several peasant rebellions during the nineteenth century, the most momentous of which in the 1890s contributed to Japan's intervention and subsequent invasion of the peninsula during the Sino-Japanese War of 1894–1895. (Ch. 6)

Trans-Siberian Railway Rail system connecting Moscow and other western Russian cities with Vladivostok, with branches extending into Manchuria to Harbin, Mukden, and Port Arthur. Japan acquired control of two branches, the South Manchurian line and the Chinese Eastern Railway, after the Russo-Japanese War. (Ch. 8)

Treaty of Nanjing The treaty between Great Britain and the Qing ending the First Opium War (1839–1842). The first of the so-called unequal treaties, it mandated the opening of five ports, the cession of Hong Kong to Britain, Chinese indemnities, extraterritoriality, and nontariff autonomy for China. (Ch. 5)

Treaty of Nerchinsk An agreement, in 1689, between the Qing and Russia whereby Russia gave up its forts on the Amur River, retained its rights to the caravan trade to Beijing, settled claims in Central Asia, and set up formal borders in Manchuria. The Russians also gained the right to have trade officials reside in Beijing because of its role as the caravan terminus. (Ch. 5)

Treaty of Shimonoseki The agreement ending the Sino-Japanese War of 1894–1895. It marked n historic role reversal of the two empires in that Japan, which had been regarded as a cultural satellite by China, had now soundly defeated the Qing and imposed its own version of Western-style "unequal treaties" on the empire. Japan established a protectorate over Korea, forced China to cede Taiwan, initially acquired Manchuria's Liaodong Peninsula (until forced to return the territory through the Triple Intervention of France, Germany, and Russia), and imposed a record $150,000,000 indemnity on the Qing. It marked the beginning of Japanese expansion on the Asian mainland. (Ch. 5)

treaty ports Ports in East Asian countries forced open for foreign trade by treaty. Most of these included some kind of extraterritoriality for the treaty powers in the form of consular privileges, and some, like Shanghai, included territorial concessions given outright to foreigners. Although a modernizing and increasingly powerful Japan was able to roll back such arrangements by the beginning of the twentieth century, China remained hobbled with them until the end of World War II. (Ch. 5)

Tripitaka The "Three Baskets," considered to be the earliest Buddhist canonical writings. The first group is the "Discipline Basket" outlining the rules for monastic communities; the second is the sutras or "Discourses" relating elements of meditation and behavior; the third is "The Higher Knowledge" containing miscellaneous elements of philosophy and psychology. (Ch. 3)

turtle ship Sixteenth-century Korean warships, the topsides of which were fortified with heavy timbers or iron plating with implanted spikes, and mounting a variety of cannon. (Ch. 6)

Twenty-One Demands With the Western treaty powers fighting on the Western Front in 1915, Japan took the opportunity to attempt to force severe concessions from the weak Chinese Republic of Yuan Shikai. Known as the "Twenty-One Demands," they included de facto Japanese control over much of China's economy and internal security, recognition of Japan's position in Manchuria, and keeping the Demands a secret. The Chinese alerted U.S. diplomats who sent a strong letter of protest to Japan; in turn, the Japanese rescinded the most extreme of the Demands. Yuan was then left with no alternative but to accept the new proposals. (Ch. 9)

ukiyo-e Woodblock prints that even today remain among Japan's most recognizable and popular mass art forms. (Ch. 8)

well-field system A system of rural organization in which each square *li* of land is divided into a grid of nine fields of 100 *mou*. Eight families receive parcels, and the ninth is farmed in common to cover rents and taxes. The term "well-field" comes from the character *jing*, meaning "water well," which is shaped like the grid in the system. (Ch. 2)

White Lotus Rebellion Long, persistent uprising in the border region of Hubei, Shaanxi, and Sichuan, originally precipitated by attempts to collect taxes from poor peasants. Starting in 1794, the fighting continued sporadically through the early 1800s. It took its name from an older Buddhist sect that the Qing derisively ascribed to the rebels. (Ch. 5)

Xinhai Revolution China's Republican Revolution that began on October 10, 1911 (*xuangshi*, meaning "double ten"). *Xinhai* is the year 1911 in the old Chinese calendar. (Ch. 9)

Xiongnu One of many Altaic-speaking nomadic groups along China's northern tier beyond the Great Wall. Some see them as related to the Huns; others see them as the ancestors of the Turks. The Xiongnu dominated Central Asia from the third century BCE until their state was destroyed by the Han Dynasty in 89 CE. (Ch. 2)

yang In Chinese philosophy, the complementary opposite of *yin*. It is the male principle, associated with the sun, light, Heaven, etc. (Ch. 2)

yangban The upper tier of the Korean ruling class. Although corresponding in many ways to the Confucian officials in China, theirs was also a hereditary position. (Ch. 6)

Yangshao culture Sometimes called "painted pottery culture" that flourished from about 5000 to 3500 BCE. Characterized by Neolithic villages like Banpo, near Xi'an. Noted for colorful pottery with geometric designs that some have suggested might be an early form of writing. (Ch. 2)

yangwu Literally "foreign affairs." Generally used in connection with the term *ziqiang* ("self-strengthening") to refer to the idea of using foreign technologies or institutions to help strengthen imperial China. (Ch. 5)

Yayoi Period from roughly 300 BCE to 300 CE, during which the techniques of bronze making, ironmaking, and rice agriculture arrived from the Asian mainland. (Ch. 3)

yin In Daoism, and Chinese philosophy more generally, the complementary female principle. It is usually associated with the moon, darkness, Earth, etc. (Ch. 2)

zaibatsu Japanese cartels. Large commercial and industrial enterprises that were essentially monopolistic and often horizontally and/or vertically integrated. Prominent examples included Mitsui and Mitsubishi. (Ch. 8)

zazen A school of Zen that emphasizes sitting for long periods in meditation. (Ch. 8)

zhongxue wei ti; xixue wei yong The philosophical formula of the self-strengtheners. Usually translated as "Chinese studies for the base/essentials; Western studies for practical application." (Ch. 5)

Credits

Part 1

National Museum of China Collection/ChinaStock, p. 2

Chapter 1

Xinhua/Wang Peng, p. 10; (A) Rawpixel.com/Shutterstock.com, p. 20; (B) Gregory Johnston/Shutterstock.com, p. 20; (C) May_Chanikran/Shutterstock.com, p. 20; (D) MAHATHIR MOHD YASIN/Shutterstock.com, p. 20

Chapter 2

(A) Liu Liqun/ChinaStock, p. 25; (B) Li Liqun/ChinaStock, p. 25; Collection of the Lowe Art Museum, University of Miami/Bridgeman Images, p. 26; Pictures from History/Bridgeman Images, 29; Xiaolei Wu/Alamy Stock Photo, p. 34; © RMN-Grand Palais/Art Resource, NY, p. 36; HIP/Art Resource, NY, p. 38; Glow Asia RF/Alamy Stock Photo, p. 39; (A) DennisCox/ChinaStock, p. 45; (B) Juan Muñoz/age footstock, p. 49; Collection of the Lowe Art Museum, University of Miami/Gift of George and Julianne Alderman/Bridgeman Images, p. 48; Museum of Fine Arts, Boston, Francis Bartlett Donation of 1912, p. 54; © British Library Board/Robana/Art Resource, NY, p. 56; Liu Liqun Collection/ChinaStock, p. 59; Liu Liqun Collection/ChinaStock, p. 65

Chapter 3

Atlantide Phototravel/Getty Images, p. 76; (A) © The Metropolitan Museum of Art. Image source: Art Resource, NY, p. 77; (B) © The Metropolitan Museum of Art/Art Resource, NY, p. 77; CAPTAINHOOK/Shutterstock.com, p. 79; © The Metropolitan Museum of Art/Art Resource, NY, p. 82; Amehime/Shutterstock.com, p. 84; © The Metropolitan Museum of Art/Art Resource, NY, p. 86; Sirisak_baokaew/Shutterstock.com, p. 94; Pavel Szabo/Shutterstock.com, p. 96

Chapter 4

ART Collection/Alamy Stock Photo, p. 105; History and Art Collection/Alamy Stock Photo, p. 106; IanDagnall Computing/Alamy Stock Photo, p. 109; The History Collection/Alamy Stock Photo, p. 112; Pictures from History/Bridgeman Images, p. 114; The Picture Art Collection/Alamy Stock Photo, p. 117; franek2/Wikimedia Commons, p. 122; Marcin Konsek/Wikimedia Commons/CC BY-SA 4.0, p. 125

Chapter 5

The Philadelphia Museum of Art/Art Resource, NY, p. 126; Gregory Harlin/National Geographic, p. 139; Pictures from

History/Bridgeman Images, p. 143; Pictures from History/Bridgeman Images, p. 145; RMN Grand Palais/Art Resource NY, p. 146; Pictures from History/Bridgeman Images, p. 148; Pictures from History/ Bridgeman Images, p. 159; Peter Newark Pictures/Bridgeman Images, p. 161; "The 'Orientals' Baseball Team, 1878," Thomas La Fargue collection, Washington State University Libraries' MASC, Pullman, WA, p. 162

Chapter 6

Courtesy of the Division of Rare and Manuscript Collections, Cornell University Library, p. 186; Courtesy of the Division of Rare and Manuscript Collections, Cornell University Library , p. 188; Courtesy of the Division of Rare and Manuscript Collections, Cornell University Library, p. 201

Chapter 7

John S Lander/LightRocket via Getty Images, p. 209; Tonbi ko/Wikimedia Commons, p. 211; Chronicle/Alamy Stock Photo, p. 213; Vietnam: Gia Long (8 February 1762 - 3 February 1820), founder and first emperor of the Nguyen Dynasty./Pictures from History/Bridgeman Images, p. 213; Photo by CEphoto, Uwe Aranas/CC-BY-SA-3.0, p. 214; Tonkinphotography/Shutterstock.com, p. 222; Art Collection 3/Alamy Stock Photo, p. 224

Chapter 8

History and Art Collection/Alamy Stock Photo, p. 230; University of British Columbia Library, Rare Books and Special Collection, p. 239; jpatokal/Wikimedia Commons, p. 245; Peter Newark Pictures/ Bridgeman Images, p. 253; V&A Images, London/Art Resource, NY, p. 260

Chapter 9

Pictures from History/Bridgeman Images, p. 267; Pictures from History/Bridgeman Images, p. 267; Reproduced from Sun Yat-sen (Shanghai: Shanghai Museum of Sun

Yat-sen's Former Residence, 1996), p. 272; Pictures from History/Bridgeman Images, p. 277; Pictures from History/Bridgeman Images, p. 279; Tallandier/Bridgeman Images, p. 279; Bridgeman Images, p. 279; AFP/Getty Images, p. 280; AP Photo, p. 282; © Collection J.A. Fox/Magnum Photos, p. 283; Pictures from History/ Bridgeman Images, p. 286; Bettmann/ Getty Images, p. 286; Jack Wilkes/The LIFE Picture Collection/Getty Images, p. 289; Pictures from History/Bridgeman Images, p. 293; Pictures from History/Bridgeman Images, p. 293; Kingendai Photo Library/ AFLO/NipponNews.net, p. 295; Pictures from History/Bridgeman Images, p. 295

Chapter 10

JACQUET-FRANCILLON/AFP/Getty Images, p. 300; Bettmann/Getty Images p. 304; Bettmann/Getty Images, p. 306; AP Photo, p. 309; Dennis Cox/Alamy Stock Photo, p. 313; AP Photo/Hout-xinhua, p. 313; Jacques Langevin/Sygma/Sygma via Getty Images, p. 315; Bettmann/Getty Images, p. 315; STR/AFP/Getty Images, p. 320; parkisland/Shutterstock.com, p. 321; Eastimages/Shutterstock.com, p. 321; testing/Shutterstock.com, p. 329; Dennis Cox/Alamy Stock Photo, p. 330; LO Kin-hei/Shutterstock.com, p. 331

Chapter 11

PA Images/Alamy Stock Photo, p. 344; vkilikov/Shutterstock.com, p. 349; National Museum of the US Air Force/Wikimedia Commons, p. 352; JFK Library/Wikimedia Commons, p. 357; TK Kurikawa/ Shutterstock.com, p. 360; artistVMG/ Shutterstock.com, p. 363; ITAR-TASS News Agency/Alamy Stock Photo, p. 363; NASA/ Goddard/Bill Hrybyk, p. 364; Sagase48/ Shutterstock.com, p. 364; Chintung Lee/ Shutterstock.com, p. 367

Chapter 12

Rykoff Collection/Getty Images, p. 377; Leemage/Getty Images, p. 382; Keystone-France/Gamma-Keystone via

Index

Printed in the USA/Agawam, MA
June 1, 2021

775610.004